1996

From Carnac to Callanish

THE PREHISTORIC STONE ROWS AND AVENUES OF BRITAIN, IRELAND AND BRITTANY

AUBREY BURL

YALE UNIVERSITY PRESS
NEW HAVEN AND LONDON
1993

Dedicated to the memory of

GLYN DANIEL (1914–86)

Archaeologist, author, editor, lover of megaliths,
and bon viveur

whose book, *Lascaux and Carnac*, later enticingly revised as
The Hungry Archaeologist in France,
first lured me to Brittany

Designed by Sally Salvesen
Set in Linotron Ehrhardt by Best-set Typesetter Ltd., Hong Kong
Printed in Singapore by CS Graphics

Half-title page: Farranahineeny, Co. Cork (Con Brogan)
Title page: Callanish, Isle of Lewis, from the South (D.D.A. Simpson)

Library of Congress Cataloging-in-Publication Data
Burl, Aubrey.
From Carnac to Callanish : the prehistoric stone rows and avenues
of Britain, Ireland, and Brittany / Aubrey Burl.
p. cm.
Includes bibliographical references and index.
ISBN 0-300-05575-7
1. Leys – Great Britain. 2. Leys – Ireland. 3. Leys – France –
Brittany. 4. Stone circles – Great Britain. 5. Stone circles –
Ireland. 6. Stone circles – France – Brittany. 7. Great Britain –
Antiquities. 8. Ireland – Antiquities. 9. Brittany (France) –
Antiquities. I. Title.
GN805.B866 1993
936.1 – dc20
93-19539
CIP

CONTENTS

PART THREE FROM LONG TO SHORT

PLATES

PHOTOGRAPHIC ACKNOWLEDGEMENTS

The photographs are by the author with the exceptions of nos: 25, Bristol University; 78, 79, 82, 83, 98, Con Brogan, Office of Public Works, Dublin; 43, Crown Copyright, Belfast; 9, 36, Devizes Museum; 6, 41, D. Heggie; 85, Limerick Archaeological Survey; 81, Ann Lynch; 84, M.J. O'Kelly; 1, 56, 86, 87, 91, 102, 106, RCHM-Scotland; 23, D.D.A. Simpson; 77, A. Watkins.

TEXT FIGURES

TABLES

ACKNOWLEDGEMENTS

During the writing of this book many of my colleagues helped me with information. I am most grateful to Professor Richard Bradley, Dr Alex Gibson, Mr Leslie Myatt, Dr Sean O'Nuallain, Dr Clive Ruggles and Professor Derek Simpson for reading some sections and making constructive suggestions. It is more than mere convention to state that any surviving errors and omissions are mine alone.

I should also like to express my appreciation of the assistance given by Dr Gabriel Cooney; Mr C. Dunn; Mr I. Durham; Mr Martin Green, Ms Frances Griffith; Dr Douglas Heggie; Dr Jean l'Helgouac'h; Mr M.A.M. van Hoek; Mrs J. Hurst; Mr Séan Kirwan; Dr Ann Lynch; Miss Rosemary McConkey; Mr Michael Moore; Mrs Claire O'Kelly; Dr Mike Parker Pearson; Mr Norman Quinnell; Dr Graham Ritchie; Mrs Rosemary Robinson; Mr Ian Shepherd; Mr Ron Shoesmith; Ms Cheryl Straffon; the late Professor Alexander Thom and his son, Dr Archie Thom; Dr Julian Thomas; and Dr John Waddell. Julie McManus developed, and often improved, the black-and-white prints.

My wife, Judith, who accompanied me on many surveys, merits my especial gratitude for her fortitude.

I must also offer my thanks for the assistance of those archivists and librarians whose response to requests for photo-copied references was always courteously efficient: the *Exmoor Review*; the Musée Miln-le Rouzic, Carnac-Ville; the Museum of London; the National Monuments Record of Scotland; the North Yorkshire Archives; the Royal Society; the Society of Antiquaries of London; the Society of Antiquaries of Scotland; the University of Birmingham; the Wiltshire Archaeological Society; and the Yorkshire Archaeological Society.

I must also state my gratitude to John Nicoll, my editor, for the patience and encouragement during the long time of writing; and to Sally Salvesen whose ability to design the format has so enhanced the appearance of the book. I very much appreciate the care with which this work has been treated.

A NOTE ON DATES

The radio-carbon or C-14 method of obtaining dates from organic material is misleading. Comparison of C-14 assays from objects which can be historically dated, such as wooden articles from ancient Egypt, has shown that the C-14 results are too young.

Through the counting of annual growth-rings in long-lived trees, a process which gives the true age of any ring, and then subjecting the wood to radio-carbon analysis it is possible to estimate the amount of error in the radiocarbon 'date' and to construct calibration tables to convert C-14 determinations into real years. Debate remains as to how accurate such conversions are. In this book the calibration table by Pearson *et al*, 1986, based on radiocarbon assays from Irish oaks, has been used. It is the archaeological convention to follow converted dates by BC, and unconverted C-14 assays by bc.

C-14 assays are quoted with the laboratory reference in brackets after them followed by the approximate converted BC date e.g. 1770±70 bc (HAR-2013) c. 2150 BC. Laboratory references are cited as HAR, BM or GU etc, standing for Harwell, British Museum, Glasgow University and the like. A list of abbreviations can be found in *Radiocarbon*, a periodical of the *American Journal of Science* in which the majority of radiocarbon dating laboratories publish their results.

Astronomical dates, based on the regular cycles of heavenly bodies, are chronologically correct and therefore followed by BC.

Radio-carbon assays are always followed by ± indicating that there is a 2:1 chance that the object analysed 'died' between those years. Hence a 'date' of 1315±55 bc for pine charcoal in the row at Maughanasilly, Co. Cork, means that the chances are 2:1 in favour of the tree having died between 1370 and 1260 bc. This would be approximately 1625 to 1515 BC with a midpoint near 1570 BC.

Suggestions have been made that the rows were intended for gymnastic performances, that they were used for solemn Arkite ceremonials, that they are parts of serpent temples, that they formed the processional roads of the Druids, that they were race-courses, that they were once roofed in and formed shelters, that they represented armies drawn up in battle array, that they were intended to guide people over the moor in misty weather, that they have an astronomical signification, and that they are a representation of the passages that led to the chamber in a tumulus ...

From these hypotheses it certainly should be possible for the visitor to select one to his mind.

Crossing, 1912, 36

PREFACE

There is another kind of megalithic monument which has to do, most probably, with bronze-age religion. This is the alignment.

R.A.S. Macalister, *Ireland in Pre-Celtic Times*, 1921, 303

Despite the attraction of the Kennet Avenue at Avebury or the astonishing multitude of lines at Carnac in Brittany stone rows remain the neglected relics of prehistoric Europe. Whereas Stonehenge with its spurious druids has created widespread interest in stone circles little attention has been given to the splendid ranks of standing stones that lead to many of those rings. Worse, what has been written about these marvellous settings has frequently been mistaken.

As recently as 1986 a guidebook provided a whole paragraph of misinformation about the avenue of tall stones attached to the Scottish circle of Callanish (Pl. 1).

Standing in the great stone circle at Callanish, under the windswept skies of the Isle of Lewis, you are aware of a shadowy past. Four thousand years ago the megalith builders raised these silent sentinels. Their priests must have approached, through a long avenue of monolithic standing stones, the central cairn. What rites and sacrifices they celebrated we do not know. Was this a celestial calendar? The north-south axis of the avenue (experts tell us) would have been perfectly aligned with the rising point of Capella in 1800 BC. Other standing stones mark astronomical alignments: to the west the setting point of the equinoctial sun; eastwards, the rising point of Altair in 1800 BC; southwards, the meridian of the sun.[1]

Despite the 'experts' almost everything is wrong. The circle is not great but small. Its suggested age is centuries too young. The priests and their sacrifices are questionable. The central cairn is an off-centre miniature tomb with short passage and burial-chamber. The avenue does not run north-south. The star-lines to Capella and Altair, whose dates were misquoted, never existed.

Pl. 1   Callanish, Isle of Lewis. An aerial view from the NNW showing the avenue and three short rows surrounding the stone circle.

The errors were unnecessary. The circle and avenue have been written about for over three centuries since John Morison around 1680 first reported that 'it is left by Traditione that these were a sort of Men converted into Stones by ane Inchanter'. Others thought they were petrefied giants. The site has been planned in Imperial Feet and Druid cubits, excavated, analysed astronomically, re-excavated, replanned in metres and Megalithic Yards, inhabited by wizards, druids, midsummer cuckoos, astronomer-priests, even by travellers from outer space who erected the stones as a landing beacon.

Imagination about the past, however, is commendable only when it is moderated by information. Lack of knowledge like that of the hero of William Black's novel, *A Princess of Thule* (1878), is not a justification for scepticism. The story contains a summary of conflicting theories about Callanish but its hero, Frank Lavender, 'who knew absolutely nothing at all about the matter, was probably as well qualified as anybody else to answer those questions'. He was not.

Over the past hundred years much has been learned about megalithic avenues, rows and pairs of stones and this book contains the results of research both personal and by colleagues. Enough is now known concerning the age of the rows, their architectural types and the societies that raised them for sensible ideas to be put forward for their purpose.

A word should be written about the manner in which data are presented in this book. As one who walks miles and drinks pints it is Imperial units that I have preferred. Body measurements such as the foot and the yard are more relevant to prehistoric structures than the artificially contrived metre. As a compromise, however, metric equivalents are cited in brackets after the real measurements. I have resisted the temptation to quote the French 'pied' of 32.48 cm (12.79 inches).

To avoid adding confusing detail to the chapters all bibliographical sources for excavation reports and astronomical surveys are to be found in the Gazetteers at the end of this book.

Finally, there is an acknowledgement to be made. My own interest in the great rows and avenues of western Europe owes much to the inspiration of that lover of megaliths, the archaeologist and writer, Glyn Daniel. He had the gift of affecting his students, readers and audiences by his own enthusiasm, an enthusiasm tempered with calm, good sense and a readiness to accept new ideas. Without such teachers, their scholarship tinged with a sense of romance, the archaeological world would be only for the dreary.

And I remember after dinner walking down to the great Carnac alignments and in the moonlight wandering along those miles of serried, large stones, their dark shadows a reminder of their darker past and our ignorance of their makers and builders. For me that was a great and personal moment, and I knew then what I know even better now: that these megalithic monuments of western Europe would exercise an irresistible fascination for me for ever.

G. Daniel, *Lascaux and Carnac*, 1963, 20

PART ONE

Stone Circles and Avenues

CHAPTER ONE

STONE ROWS AND THEIR PROBLEMS

There are also numerous avenues consisting of double rows of not very large stones ...
These avenues have been described by various writers but there is no comprehensive
study ... It seems best to ignore them all until they can be studied as a whole.
A. Thom, *Megalithic Sites in Britain*, 1967, 135

A SHORT STONE ROW IN BRITTANY

The lines of great stones at Carnac are the most famous megalithic rows in the world. Extending for miles across the countryside they have astonished and mystified onlookers for centuries. Every year they receive thousands of visitors, so many that the ground is being worn away and parts of the rows have been closed.

What is rarely appreciated is that these vast settings have smaller counterparts no less important and no less perplexing. Not two miles (3 km) west of Carnac are the six stones of Le Vieux-Moulin at Plouharnel (Pl. 2). The short line stands unnoticed by the motorists hurtling along the dangerously straight road just to the west. Yet the granite pillars are enormous, up to 11 ft (3.4 m) high, the biggest weighing over ten tons. Not far from them are passage-tombs at Rondossec, longer rows and a devastated cromlech, or stone circle, at Ste-Barbe, a megalithic rectangle at Crucuno. But of all these ancient monuments the least understood is the stone row. Its age is uncertain, its purpose unclear. Of the people who raised the stones, and of their dwellings, there is no sign.

The row had no defensive value. Nor was it part of any domestic or industrial structure. Built of rough boulders, unshaped, without decoration or carvings,

arranged in a single line, it is thought to have been the ritual centre of a family, perhaps ten to twenty adults and children. Yet, unlike stone circles and henges, it enclosed no sacred area. Similar short rows were erected by communities in Britain, Ireland and Brittany in the centuries of the Bronze Age between 1800 and 1000 BC.

For over three thousand years before its construction people in the Neolithic or New Stone Age had been farming in western Europe, grazing cattle, growing crops, living a mainly self-sufficient existence that only slowly over many generations established contacts with other communities. Families supported themselves. They built their own homes, made their own tools of stone, flint, antler, bone and wood, hand-shaped their own pots, made their own clothes of softened, smoothed skins, constructed their own burial-places, long earthen mounds in the lowlands, stone-chambered tombs on the rock-strewn hillsides and mountains.

The people were short-lived, dying appallingly early by modern standards, but they were vigorous and enterprising, steadily converting forest wildernesses into open countryside. Slowly, as the population increased and the rich soils of the chalks and gravels were claimed and occupied, descendants of the pioneering farmers were compelled to move on to less productive land.

Pl. 2 The short row of Le Vieux-Moulin, Plouharnel near Carnac. The two central stones are hidden by the others. From the ssw.

It was a society of families. Even at the end of the Neolithic when communal tombs were abandoned and the open-air centres of stone circles, cromlechs and earthen henges replaced them, at a time when the skills of metal-working in copper and bronze became known in western Europe, even then large settlements were uncommon, and where they did exist they had populations of only a few hundred. Even in the Bronze Age society was dispersed and rural.

It was the family that tilled the ground, moved to unexploited parts, to moors and uplands, crossing seas to islands that had remained uninhabited three millennia after farming communities first entered Brittany and the west. Living in isolated farmsteads, separated from their neighbours, each family had its own land-holding and its own standing stone or stone row. Casual inspection suggests that these featureless ritual monuments are so uncomplicated that they justify the neglect of antiquarians who pessimistically ignored such uninteresting stones. The pessimism and the neglect were unjustified.

In spite of its unhelpful appearance the row of Le Vieux-Moulin is subtly informative. The ten tons of the heaviest stone could never have been hauled erect by a single family. At least fifty or more able-bodied labourers were necessary to pull it upright and it must be assumed that families co-operated when such projects were undertaken. There is more. At a time when there was no Pole Star to guide them the builders of the row intentionally aligned its stones north-south. How they achieved this is puzzling, why they did it may be beyond explanation. If such an unpromisingly simple site contains evidence of the

needs and beliefs of early people it is all the more surprising that stone rows have been ignored for so long.

THE UNREMEMBERED ROWS OF WESTERN EUROPE

Despite the amazement of visitors amongst the bewilderment of stones at Carnac in Brittany, or their delight at the elegance of the avenue at Callanish in Scotland the subject of megalithic rows is still an almost unstudied aspect of European prehistory. Although there are hundreds of lines little has been written about them and what accounts do exist are local studies. Until recently there was not even the most provisional catalogue.[1]

No one has asked why the crowded Carnac alignments should be similar to others in northern Scotland 750 miles (1200 km) away with only some sites on Dartmoor like the Breton or Caithness settings between them; nor why northeast Ireland, dense with stone circles, should have scores of rows, short, long, parallel, splayed, while southern England with Stonehenge and Avebury at its heart should contain almost none.

Such archaeological silence is inexplicable. Prehistoric people raised the stones, often with such effort and time that the lines must been vital to their lives. Men and women at Le Vieux-Moulin did not erect enormous stones up to ten tons in weight as an idle winter occupation. Yet since those distant times the row and its more complicated counterparts have been almost forgotten as though they offered no information about the reasons for their construction.

Pl. 3 Harold's Stones, Trellech, Gwent. From the east. A
good example of a short Three-Stone row.

Some, it is true, are well-known: the Kennet Avenue at Avebury; the huddled lines in Brittany; the Dartmoor rows; perhaps even the three stones at Ballochroy on the Kintyre peninsula made famous by claims that the row was aligned on the midwinter sunset.

But for every row that is known there are scores that are never mentioned even in scholarly literature. Only the most dedicated of researchers has heard of the Cordon des Druides, a stuttering line of quartz blocks near Fougères in Brittany, or the serpentine avenue linking cairns and stone circles on Moor Divock in the English Lake District, or the pair of standing stones at Crew Lower in Co. Tyrone, the east pillar tall and pointed, the west low and squat as though they were meant to be symbols of male and female fertility. The very diversity of design amongst stone rows helps towards an understanding of their purpose.

THE TYPES OF STONE ROW

Within sixty miles (97 km) of Minehead, the popular resort on the north Somerset coast, seven varieties of stone row can be found. There is the most basic of forms, two standing stones paired together like an unfinished gateway. There is an example of one of the short rows, lines containing anything from three to six stones but in length seldom longer than 50 ft (15 m). There is a long single row of many stones, and, miles away, a long double row by a river's side. Similar to that is another that approaches a stone circle but passes to its side. There is a proper avenue attached to a circle. And there is one of the rare multiple rows

with several lines standing alongside each other, sometimes parallel, sometimes splayed, narrowing together as they climb a slope towards a cist or a burial cairn.

(a) *A Pair of Standing Stones*
The concentration of types around Minehead is an interesting one because it shows very clearly how stone rows differ. Twenty-seven miles (44 km) east of Minehead, between the villages of Compton Bishop and Cross below the southern slopes of the Mendips, there is a pair of tiny stones in a field, one standing, the other fallen against it. A legend claims that the Devil threw the two from Shute Shelve Hill a high mile away to the east.[2] Little is known about the stones which are far from any other pair. A gold bracelet of twisted wire was dug up near the stones in 1898,[3] but this lovely Middle Bronze Age object of the 'Ornament Horizon' may have been lost around 1400 BC, several centuries before the erection of the stones.

(b) *A Short Row*
Quite unlike the Compton Bishop pair is a Three-Stone row at Trellech in Gwent fifty miles (81 km) north-east of Minehead across the Bristol Channel. Known as Harold's Stones because the Saxon king was supposed to have won a battle there, the three high pillars lean askew, this way and that, like yachts on a choppy sea (Pl. 3). Of local coarse puddingstone they stand on a slope, unshaped and rough except for the one in the middle on which there has been an attempt to smooth its scraping sides. Two manmade hollows of cupmarks have been ground out on its

south-west face. Standing in a 36 ft (11 m) long line orientated from the north-east towards the south-west and the tallest stone, the row is in line with the midwinter sunset, an alignment characteristic of many of these short settings.

(c) *A Long Single Row*

Astronomically this is not true of the long single rows that occupy regions separate from those of the short settings. These elongated lines are seldom straight enough to provide sightlines for mythical astronomer-priests, and instead of the sun or moon they are linked to more mundane targets, a round cairn of stones heaped over a little cremation cist or a stone circle surrounding a similar burial-place. Often the other end of the row culminates in a tall terminal-pillar set at right-angles to the line.

Such rows can be almost twenty times longer than the short lines, the average length for those on Dartmoor being about 600 ft (c. 180 m). Representative of them is Down Tor fifty-four miles (87 km) ssw of Minehead. Its 174 stones increase in height from a blocking-stone and they lead the eye up the hillside towards a fine stone circle 1145 ft (349 m) away with Sheep's Tor jutting on the horizon beyond it. There can be no connection with the sun, moon or any celestial object in this curving line whose people may have built the hut-circles and cattle-pound at the far end of the row.

(d) *A Double Row of Many Stones*

Despite the length of the Down Tor row, however, its heaviest stone weighs no more than five tons and twenty-four workers could easily have set it in place. Even smaller are the midgets at Yelland near Barnstaple in north-west Somerset and thirty-four miles (55 km) wsw of Minehead. This is a double line, two rows placed alongside each other, the fourth variation in the categories of stone rows. Unlike many double rows Yelland was erected on such low-lying land by the Taw estuary that it is completely submerged at high tide, and unlike most of the others it leads from nothing to nothing unless it was the river itself that was the reason for laying out the rows. The quite short (113 ft, 34 m) parallel lines, are six wavering feet (1.8 m) apart, wide enough for people to walk between.

(e) *A Tangential Avenue*

Somewhat similar to Yelland but associated with a stone circle is the tangential avenue of Cerrig Duon high in the Black Mountains of Wales forty-seven miles (76 km) north of Minehead. Its stones are even smaller than those of Yelland, mere spikelets of local sandstone hidden in the reedy grass of the hillside above the River Tawe. The fundamental difference between it and many other double rows is its proximity to an open stone circle rather than to a burial-place.

The association is not a strong one but it is sufficient to distinguish Cerrig Duon, 'the black stone', as an avenue.

At the head of the slope is a terrace and on it is an ellipse of stones, none high but enclosing an area large enough to have accommodated fifty or more people comfortably.

The avenue, narrowing as it climbs from the river, approaches the ring almost timidly, not leading directly to it but at a tangent some 25 ft (8 m) to its east and stopping a full 20 ft (6 m) before drawing level with the ring. It is as though an earth tremor had dislodged the avenue causing it slip several yards downhill.

To its west, on an axis aligned on the ring's centre, is the strange Three-Stone row of Maen Mawr, a gigantic block that must weigh at least eight tons, with two little stones lurking in line some distance behind it.

(f) *A True Avenue*

'Classical' avenues are double rows that are unequivocally attached to a henge such as Stonehenge or a stone circle like that at Callanish. They were popular in north-west and southern England. It is the conjunction of the row with a ritual enclosure that determines its status as an avenue.

Fifty miles (81 km) south-east of Cerrig Duon and forty (64 km) ENE of Minehead are the three stone circles of Stanton Drew near Bath. Standing on a buckled NE – SSW line, the north-east and SSW rings are large but visually diminished when contrasted with the enormous circle between them, the biggest in Britain Ireland and Brittany. Leading to its north-east arc is the wreckage of a short avenue. A second avenue, similar in length and similarly ruinous, stretches from the ESE up to the north-east ring.

If extended from the circles these avenues would have joined, and would have led down towards the River Chew 400 ft (120 m) away. This association with water is one that has been thought significant for other avenues like that at Broomend of Crichie in Aberdeenshire.

(g) *A Setting of Multiple Rows*

Strangest of all the types of stone row and the most difficult to explain in terms of distribution and purpose are the complexes of several lines set alongside each other, sometimes parallel, sometimes splayed, sometimes erratically laid out like the broken ribs of a fan. There is one about sixty miles (97 km) south of Minehead at Corringdon Ball on Dartmoor.

It is a confusion of lines on the far side of a brook from the remains of a long chambered mound, one of three Neolithic megalithic tombs within two miles of each other at the south-eastern edge of Dartmoor.[4] Nothing is known of the long mound's contents. What may have been the massive capstone over its chamber now lies half-buried in the grass.

The rows at Corringdon Ball are likely to have been a thousand years younger than the tomb. They are inconspicuous, the stones so small that a five-year old child could have put them up. Were it not for the surviving quadrant of a despoiled stone circle and a nearby cairn that has been robbed for an adjacent wall it would be easy to overlook the rows altogether.

Although they have been ravaged it is still possible, with care, to make out the original layout. Six rows, perhaps two sets of three with a pair of uprights between them, meander over a distance of about 260 ft (80 m) towards the circle, some so close together that it would be difficult for a nimble lamb to wriggle between them. Just to the north-west, roughly parallel to the others, is a single line 430 ft (130 m) long pointing towards the cairn.

In the present condition of Corringdon Ball it is little more than a matter of conjecture whether the complex is of one, two or more phases. Without excavation the question might seem impossible of resolution. Fortunately, other multiple rows on Dartmoor and in Brittany and northern Scotland provide clues about their purpose.

PROBLEMS OF IDENTIFICATION

Over the centuries interpretations of the rows have been neither numerous, profound nor plausible. Unaware of the diversity of megalithic lines in western Europe early investigators made only the briefest references to them. This is no longer acceptable. Whether at the simplest of rows, the pair at Compton Bishop, or the most complicated at Corringdon Ball, the architectural variations are so great, the regions of each type so rarely overlapping with others, that it could be argued that each category had a different origin and a different function.

A stone row is a prehistoric linear setting of regularly spaced standing stones, closely set, uninterrupted by any other structure. It may lead to a cairn or stone circle but the standing stones alone are the essential components of the row. Lines of round barrows or composite monuments of stones, cists and cairns cannot be accepted as stone rows.

(a) *Other Linear Settings*

A very remarkable alignment of cairns and standing-stones extends from Kilmartin through the whole course of the valley . . . the line passes a standing-stone, having close to the east a remarkable group of standing-stones . . . This remarkable line is 4½ miles in length . . . Another line of standing-stones and burial sites extends from the modern cemetery north of Lochgilphead to Dunadd, a distance of about 2¾ miles.[5]

Also known as Temple Wood and Slockavullin the Kilmartin line of stones in Argyll has sometimes been termed a stone row. It is not. The stones stand on a NNE–SSW alignment 237 ft (72 m) long, one of several monuments in a ritual area which includes a chambered tomb, cairns with decorated cist-slabs, a stone circle, standing stones and cupmarked rocks.

At the NNE end of the line are two close-set stones arranged south-east – north-west. There are cupmarks on the north-west stone. To the SSW, 117 ft (36 m) away, is a high stone with four small stones set edge-on in an open rectangle around it. The stone has cupmarks and cup-and-ring markings on its west face. A little farther SSW is a small cist, and 120 ft (36.6 m) from the tall stone is a second pair of stones of which the south-east has three cupmarks on its south-east face. This unusual arrangement of widely separated pairs of stones with a tall pillar between them is paralleled only at the truncated Barbreck line a few miles to the north.[6]

The long Kilmartin line and that at Barbreck must be excluded from a corpus of stone rows because of the cists and rectangles and because of the wide and irregular spacing of the stones. Kilmartin is best interpreted as two pairs, both arranged south-east–north-west, with a solitary standing stone between them. Barbreck was probably the same before its disruption.

These idiosyncratic settings are somewhat analogous to the genuine rows at Ballymeanoch a mile south of the Kilmartin line where a Four-Stone row stands to the north-west of a pair which in turn stands north-west of a single standing stone. Some of these stones also are cupmarked.

(b) *Non-Prehistoric Lines and Trackway Markers*

It is dismayingly easy to be misled into thinking that a row of stones is a prehistoric stone row (Pl. 4). South-east of Morebattle in Roxburgh a ragged line of twenty-six low stones, known with untutored mediaeval innumeracy as the Eleven Shearers, stretches almost east-west below the Late Bronze Age earthwork of Hownam Rings. Because of its bearing the row has been claimed as an astronomical alignment on the equinoctial sunrises.[7]

The line may or may not be prehistoric. What it is not is a stone row. Almost certainly it is the basal course of an old and decayed field-wall. And as its ends are not inter-visible any claim that it acted as a sightline can be discounted.[8]

There are delusions elsewhere. Stones put up in mediaeval times to guide travellers across moorlands can be mistaken for prehistoric rows. On the Hebridean island of Mull a series of high stones stand intervisibly though widely spaced along the south-west coast by Loch Scridain. The line was once as much as seven miles long but some stones have been thrown down by treasure-hunters, and others removed for walls and buildings. They are not prehistoric but Christian, 'intended as guide-posts to strangers visiting Iona on pilgrimage'.[9] As the final stone stands by the coast at Aridhglas near the ferry-crossing to the holy island of

Iona where St Columba landed in AD 563, this is the most likely explanation for the wandering line.

Marker stones can often be recognised because they have been split from living rock and dressed into a regular shape. They are also set far apart.

Prehistoric people only rarely quarried stones or smoothed them. They preferred to use boulders and glacial erratics lying conveniently to hand, setting them up in their natural state with no attempt to improve their appearance. The outstanding exception to this practice, the neatly shaped sarsens of Stonehenge, was the handiwork of woodworking natives on Salisbury Plain where there was no good building stone.[10] There is nothing comparable to their carpentry techniques amongst all the megalithic monuments in Britain, Ireland or Brittany.

This difference between historic markers and prehistoric standing stones can be seen on Dartmoor where in 1803 guidestones were actually added to a prehistoric row along the Ugborough-Harford Moor boundary. 'These added stones can at once be detected, since they bear the drill marks incidental to their cleavage'.[11]

Stones with a 'T' and 'A' carved on opposite faces were set up between Tavistock and Ashburton.[12] On Bodmin Moor in Cornwall the stone circle at Altarnun

was chosen as the focus for two lines to its south-west and north-east, their small stones marking a parish boundary. The idea that the north-east line was orientated on the minor northern moonrise[13] is ill-founded.

Rather less conclusive is the problem of a short Dartmoor row. Three stones stand near Hexworthy, half a mile south-west of a farm just west of the River Swincombe. Farther west are cists and eastwards, across the steep river valley, are enclosures and at least twenty Bronze Age hut circles.

There has been a cautious suggestion that the stones are a prehistoric Three-Stone row containing an alignment on the Lammas sunrise in early August,[14] the time of the important Celtic festival of Lughnasa.

There are several reasons for suspecting that the Swincombe stones are not prehistoric. They have been tooled. Moreover, there is only one other possible Three-Stone row, the dubious site at Stannon, amongst the scores of known rows on Dartmoor.

It is significant that the stones are nowhere mentioned as noteworthy by writers about prehistoric antiquities on Dartmoor: by Crossing although he frequently referred to Swincombe; by Worth who did not include them among the many stone rows he described; and there was a similar silence from Baring-Gould and Pettit.

Pl. 4 Bryn-y-Chain, Gwynedd. From the south-west. Not a Three-Stone row. The two stones on the left are probably prehistoric but re-used as gateposts. The stone on the right is modern.

The stones may be remnants of a line of guide-stones that once led across the moor from Merrivale Bridge to Ashburton. Many of the markers along this twelve-mile-long (19 km) trackway have been removed but a few isolated stones survive and the three at Swincombe could be amongst them.

If so, they probably date not from around 1700 BC but from AD 1699–1700 when there is a record 'towards defraying the charges of putting upp Moore-stones on Dartmoor . . . for the guidence of Travellers passing that way the sume of £2.0.0.'[15] The Lammas Day alignment would therefore be an astronomical illusion.

A site, however, that does create uncertainty is the line of coarse schist boulders a few miles south-west of Crieff in Perthshire. Starting at the north at a stone by Craigneish farm the row crosses the Machany Water on to Dunruchan Moor, a wasteland of hills, hollows and emptiness. From the first stone on the moor, a leaning rough block of conglomerate, two others can be seen to the south with a single, very tall pillar away to the east. The southern pair are within ninety yards (80 m) of each other.

It is a temptation to regard this line, two-thirds of a mile long, as a series of prehistoric guidestones although the stones are not all intervisible and the line does not appear to lead anywhere except to the slopes of Dunruchan Hill.

Suggestions that the row was erected by Romans whose forts at Ardoch and Kaims are not far to the east are not convincing. Fred Coles, who surveyed the row in 1910, disbelieved it.

> The Romans did not erect huge, unchiselled, somewhat amorphous and totally unlettered Standing Stones in commemoration of any event. And, as similar monoliths are to be found in other districts not traditionally associated with Roman sites, it is a fair inference that these at Dunruchan may be as justly entitled to the term prehistoric as any others.[16]

Unshaped but not intervisible, in line but without apparent purpose as a trackway, the Dunruchan Stones emphasise how difficult it can be to establish the status of a stone row.

(c) Misinformation about Stone Rows

There is another pitfall. Reliance upon written sources unconfirmed by fieldwork can result in the acceptance of wrongly-identified sites. John Aubrey, the seventeenth-century antiquarian, was a victim of this.

In 1692 an Oxfordshire gentleman, James Tyrell, sent a letter to Aubrey about a row of three stones near Uttoxeter in Staffordshire. He likened them to others he had seen in Ireland twenty years earlier. Visiting his grandfather, James Ussher, the Archbishop of Armagh who is still remembered for his calculation that the world had been created in 4004 BC, Tyrell

Pl. 5 Checkley, Staffordshire, from the south-east. The three carved stones in the churchyard. They are Late Saxon, not prehistoric.

noticed standing stones in the counties of Armagh, Monaghan and Meath, stones that were almost certainly prehistoric. Knowing Aubrey's interest in such ancient matters he wrote describing them, stating that there were others akin to them in England. His information was misleading and incomplete. Having mentioned the Irish stones he wrote, 'At the Church yard of a Towne about three miles from Uttoxeter in Staffordshire; there are three such upright Stones in a row together; what the tradition of them is together with the name of the place you may see in Dr Plots history of Staffordshire. p-'.[17] He omitted to quote the page number.

Tyrell's description excited even this writer. Reference to a prehistoric Three-Stone row, perhaps destroyed since the seventeenth century, so far to the east in England would widen the known distribution of these short lines. None is known in the Peak District or anywhere else in the Midlands. An editorial comment in the 1982 edition of Aubrey's *Monumenta Britannica, II* remarked that the churchyard was 'not otherwise located though Rocester is three miles from Uttoxeter'. Reference to Plot's *Staffordshire*, however, did give the precise location and showed that Tyrell's stones were not prehistoric.[18]

Pl. 6   Blanefield, Stirling. The stones are more likely to be the remains of the façade of a chambered tomb than a ruined short row.

His 'Towne' was not Rocester but Checkley, a small village with a lovely church described by Pevsner as 'very curious'. To its south, in the churchyard, is an 8 ft (2.4 m) long row of three stones, arranged north-south (Pl. 5), respectively being 4 ft 8, 4 ft 3, and 5 ft 3 (1.4, 1.3, 1.6 m) high. These measurements of length and height conform to the dimensions of many Three-Stone rows but inspection of the stones shows them to belong to the tenth or eleventh centuries AD.

Of sandstone from Hollington twelve miles (19 km) east of Checkley, they are Saxon Christian shafts from which the crosses are missing. All have been dressed rectangularly and smoothed to receive decoration. The one nearest the church is plain but the others are intricately carved with interlace patterns and human figures, reputedly of three bishops slain in a battle nearby at Deadman's or Naked Green. 'A more likely explanation is that it [the churchyard] was a preaching area, where possibly, St Bertelin, the hermit of Stafford, gave religious instruction'.[19] No one seeing these stones, rather than just reading about them, would consider them prehistoric.

(d) *The Remains of Megalithic Tombs*
Further words of warning are necessary about this problem of deciding whether stones, even those known to be prehistoric, ever formed a stone row. In some cases they could be the denuded remains of a chambered tomb. In other instances the reverse has been true.

At Kames, a hamlet by Loch Fyne in Argyll, there are three standing stones. Two, separated by a road from the third, have been considered the entrance

pillars of a megalithic tomb whose cairn, passage and chamber have been demolished.[20] This is unlikely and it 'does not account for the third stone' twenty yards (18 m) away.[21] The site is more probably a Three-Stone row or a pair with a detached single stone like East Cult in Perthshire.

Conversely there are settings claimed as rows which are more likely to be the survivors of a forecourt or façade of a Neolithic tomb. At Blanefield near Strathblane in Stirling a big stone, its longer sides aligned east-west, stands at an angle amongst a south-west–north-east line of four others, fallen, of which one just off the line seems to have been added this century (Pl. 6). The setting has been presumed a collapsed Four-Stone row. Known also as Duntreath and Dumgoyach the setting is slightly concave.

'This ruinous alignment indicates notches to the North East and these show approximately the midsummer rising sun'.[22] 'The standing stone has a flat face exactly aligned on a hill notch to the east', quite neatly in line with the equinoctial sunrises.[23] These astronomical analyses would seem to confirm that Blanefield was undoubtedly a row set up by prehistoric observers to record two important solar events.

Excavation in 1972 discovered signs of burning, flints and charcoal that yielded a C-14 assay of 2860±270 bc (GX-2781) c. 3650 BC, a time in the Middle Neolithic when chambered tombs were still in vogue but an extremely early date for any stone row. This, coupled with Blanefield's isolated position for a row in central Scotland, raises doubts about its origins.

It is a lonely megalithic line, those nearest to it being over forty miles (64 km) to the west in Argyll. Straddling a ridge overlooking the Blane Water it is arguable that the stones are relics of the crescentic façade of a Clyde chambered long cairn with an entrance facing the south-east. There are least four other Clyde tombs in the vicinity.[24] One, Auckeneck, stands on a spur only three and a half miles (5.6 km) to the west, and Craigmaddie Muir is no more than four miles (6.4 km) to the south-east. 'Might not the five stones be the remains of the horned façade of a long cairn . . . fires are often found under long cairns while the radio-carbon date of 2860 [bc] would fit very nicely as a long cairn?'.[25] Only excavation of the area where the passage of the possible tomb once stood could resolve the question. For the present its anomalous date must leave Blanefield very questionable as a stone row.

This is rather less true of Eightercua, one of the most famous and impressive sites in the far south-west of Ireland. It is a line of four stones graded in height from the north-east up to the south-west. The situation is spectacular, the stones silhouetted on a ridge overlooking Lough Currane to the east and to 'Ballinskelligs Bay, resounding with the monotonous roll of the ocean' to the west.[26]

With its grading and south-westerly orientation the setting would be accepted as an indisputable row except for an untypical low slab, set at right-angles to its south side. A second stone lay by it.

The site 'looks like part of a grave chamber, set in a somewhat oval cairn'.[27] The stones 'stand on the perimeter of a demolished stone fort and since stones of megalithic proportions are sometimes found marking the entrances to ancient enclosures their status must remain in doubt'.[28]

Yet despite the gentle arc formed by the line it is feasible that the stones were erected as a short row that was later incorporated into a defensive structure. There is a good sightline to the south-west where the tallest stone stands, aligned on the midwinter sunset,[29] an astronomical characteristic of many short rows in Ireland and Scotland. Like those of Blanefield the stones of Eightercua remain enigmatic, further admonition against hasty statements about their origins.

(e) *Rows from which Stones are Missing*
A further dilemma confronting anyone studying stone rows is to know how many stones a line once contained. Standing stones have been convenient sources of material for gateposts, lintels and walls and many have been toppled and hauled away over the centuries. Others, like the pillars of the Parc y Meirw long row in south-west Wales, have been used to demarcate a field, some incorporated in a wall, two forming a gateway, others perhaps taken away for buildings.

Near a small pool on Dartmoor the double row of Sharpitor North-West was helplessly exposed to road-builders working within yards of it and many of its stones were torn up leaving only a few heavier or more distant stretches intact. So little remains that even to people in the adjacent lay-by it lingers unnoticed.

With stone circles the problem is less. It is usually possible to make out where a stone once stood because of an unusually wide gap in the ring. A row is not so amenable. A stone removed from its end may leave no evidence of its former existence, its hole half-filled with collapsed packing-stones, choked with earth and overgrown. Only excavation could establish where the stone once stood.

On occasion history helps. The Devil's Arrows in western Yorkshire are three towering needles of millstone grit spaced irregularly 198 ft (60 m) and 360 ft (110 m) apart. The uneven distances are explicable because it is known that in the early seventeenth century a fourth stone, pushed over in the hope of finding treasure, was later dragged into Boroughbridge for the foundations of a bridge over the River Tutt.[30] Folklore speaks of a fifth stone but there is no documentation to confirm this.

Excavations sometimes reveal the holes of missing stones. Investigations between 1978 and 1980 at the Alignements du Moulin, twin rows at St-Just in central Brittany, showed that some stones had been thrown down and cut up when the nearby windmill was built and that in between the pillars of the south row there had been at least four wooden posts.[31] Similarly, it was discovered that many sarsens of Avebury's Kennet Avenue had been carefully buried in the fourteenth century, presumably at the urging of the village priest anxious to get rid of those symbols of paganism.[32]

The absence of stones from a row is not necessarily a catastrophe for the fieldworker if the row is a long one. It might affect the estimated length but probably not the direction or the grading in heights or the general layout. For long rows and avenues the remaining stones may be adequate.

With short rows and pairs the matter is different. Lacking external evidence one cannot be sure that today's Three-Stone row was not yesterday's Four-Stone line, or even whether a single standing stone is not the relic of a prehistoric setting of several great pillars.

For individual sites it is a disadvantage that can seldom be overcome by observation. Overall, however, it is not a calamity. There are so many of these short rows, almost 600 of them, nearly 300 pairs, more than 180 Three-Stone and over 110 Four- to Six-Stone rows, that the misinterpretation of a few is not statistically critical.

CHAPTER TWO

HISTORY OF RESEARCH

All this does not shed any very clear light on the function of the menhirs. Whether isolated or in groups, they remain shrouded in mystery. This is no doubt why their study has, unjustifiably, been comparatively neglected.

P.-R. Giot, *Brittany*, 1960, 127

INTRODUCTION

Today there is no reason for neglect. During the last hundred years over a thousand rows have been recorded in Britain, Ireland and Brittany: pairs of standing stones, short and long lines, avenues, multiple complexes.[1] Much information about the societies that raised them is contained in their architecture, their alignments, their art, the finds of pottery, artefacts and bone, the dates from a few, and, most obviously, in their distribution and associations.

EARLY BELIEFS ABOUT STONE ROWS

(a) *Mediaeval Times*

Classical writers such as Pliny and Strabo were ignorant of the rows and even in early Christian times the pagan standing stones were mentioned only as places at which worship was forbidden.[2]

A reference, however, that seemed specific about Avebury occurred in a charter of AD 939. The document defined the boundaries of some land in Wiltshire given by King Athelstan to the nun, Wulfswyth. Part of it, translated, read, 'These are the bounds of Overton. From Kennet to the elder tree . . . Thence northward up along the stone row, thence to the burial-places . . .'. In the nineteenth century it was believed that the 'stone row' referred to Avebury's Kennet Avenue, a view that has been repeated recently.[3] It is mistaken.

A better rendering of *stan raethe* would be 'stony way or ride'. This is the track, once sarsen-scattered, that leads from the hamlet of Huish towards Pumphrey Wood almost three miles (5 km) south-east of the nearest stretch of the Kennet Avenue.[4] It still forms part of the boundary between the parishes of West Overton and Marlborough but it was never a prehistoric avenue or line of standing stones.

The idea, however, that a row had been built to mark the division between pieces of land was not unreasonable. The eighteenth-century Cornish antiquarian, William Borlase, wrote, 'It may, from the ex-

tent of the Monuments, be presumed, that they were boundaries . . . On the Downs, leading from Wadebridge to St Columb . . . is such a line of Stones'.[5] This was the long row of the Nine Maidens in Cornwall a few miles east of Newquay. The name came from a legend that this was a file of girls turned into stone for dancing on the Sabbath. To the north a single standing stone, The Fiddler, was the musician also transformed for encouraging them. But the row was not a boundary.

To mediaeval countryfolk, unaccustomed to working with heavy boulders, stones so big and cumbersome as those in many lines could never have been set up by human beings and they were variously explained as the handiwork of giants or the Devil, or sinners petrified for acts of sacrilege.

The three enormous Devil's Arrows in Yorkshire were supposed to have been thrown by Satan at Aldborough. With his usual incompetence they fell a mile short near the town of Boroughbridge. Harold's Stones, a Three-Stone row near Trellech in Gwent, were pillars flung by the Devil in a contest against Jack o'Kent, a local hero. The Devil lost.

Giants were as capable as the Arch-Fiend at moving ponderous stones. The three blocks of Tri-Men at St-Goazec in Brittany were hurled by an ogre who lived in the megalithic tomb of Castel-Ruffel. Learning that his daughter had been seduced by a servant and was eloping with him the angry father shied stone after stone at the fleeing couple but missed them completely.[6] Three other stones by Tweedmuir church in Peebles were claimed to be the burial-place of Jack the Giantkiller who died shortly after his last fight.[7]

The well-known Carnac rows of Brittany were sometimes thought to have been raised by giants but a more popular belief was that they were lines of Roman legionaries turned into stones for pursuing the local saint, St-Cornèly.[8] If so, the unmilitary disorder of the ranks must have enraged their centurions.

Impiety caused the transmogrification of a Breton

Pl. 7 An Eured Ven, Finistère. A straying line of quartz blocks, supposedly merrymakers petrified for offending a priest.

wedding-party. Chancing upon a priest carrying the Eucharist the merrymakers repeatedly refused to let him pass and were duly punished. He passed. They stayed. Their long and drunkenly staggering row, *An Eured Ven*, 'the stone marriage', survives near St-Michel Brasparts in the Arrée Mountains of Finistère (Pl. 7).[9]

Clach an Tursa, three stones north of Loch Carloway on the island of Lewis, were similarly transmuted. 'Some of the ignorant Vulgar say, they were Men by Inchantment turn'd into Stones'.[10] Martin added that not far away was the stone circle of Callanish but failed to say anything about its origin. An earlier observer, John Morison, recorded that 'It is left by Traditione these were a sort of Men converted into Stones by ane Inchanter', and this folk-story was gradually elaborated to combine both giants and petrification.

'The Gaelic name *Fir Bhreige* (false men) was applied to the stones of Callanish because, from a distance, they looked like human figures. There was also a legend that they were giants turned to stone by St Kieran for failing to embrace Christianity when he came and preached to them',[11] a perplexing disaster as St Ciaran of Clonmacnois, a proselytising monk of the sixth century, never left Ireland.

(b) *The Seventeenth Century*
By Tudor times scholars were more sceptical about supernatural origins for megaliths. Instead, human beings, particularly the Romans, were favoured as the builders, the rows being trophies of war or cenotaphs.

'Some authors think that erected Stones, placed in a straight line, are memorials of Battles or Druids',[12] a view shared by the great Elizabethan antiquarian, William Camden, who thought that the avenue at Shap in Westmorland was 'design'd to preserve the memory of some Action or other; but the injury of Time has put it beyond all possibility of pointing out the particular occasion'.[13]

In the first English edition of his *Britain* (1610) there was an entry about the Devil's Arrows at Boroughbridge. 'I am of opinion with some, that they were monuments of victorie erected by the Romans'. Significantly, this was later changed in the enlarged 1695 edition, *Britannia*, to 'they were British Deities . . . before the arrival of the Romans'.[14]

This novel suggestion that megalithic monuments were prehistoric came from John Aubrey, a Fellow of the Royal Society best known for his wittily scandalous and bawdy *Brief Lives*, but the first great British fieldworker and, archaeologically, the first person to consider sites as members of regional groups. Through his persistent correspondence with colleagues in Britain and Ireland he compiled a disorganised but invaluable collection of data about standing stones, circles, rows, hillforts and burial-places. His *Monumenta Britannica* has never been published in its entirety but the first three of its four parts appeared in 1980 and 1982 and, despite the shortcomings of the edition, the two volumes are essential to anyone interested in the history of archaeology.

Until Aubrey no one had been concerned to collect a body of material about particular types of monument. Aubrey thought differently, realising that it was only by relating one with another that any pattern could be seen. 'But all these Monuments are of the same fashion and antique rudenesse: wherfore I Conclude, that they were Works erected by the Britons: and were Temples of the Druids . . . 'Twas in that Deluge of Historie, the account of these British Monuments utterly perished: the Discovery whereof I doe here endeavour (for want of written Record) to work out . . . by comparing those that I have seen with another . . . to make the Stones give Evidence for themselves'.[15]

To this end he gathered information from all over the country. His papers included notes about previously undescribed stone rows such as those at Stanton Drew in Somerset where there seemed 'to be the remainder of the Avenue as at Kynet'; the Devil's Arrows which he thought might be the survivors of a gigantic stone circle; 'stones pitched in order, some trianglewise' on Exmoor; 'stones of Dartmoor'; Avebury's Kennet Avenue where 'a showre of raine hindred us me from measuring it'.[16]

There had never been such a collection of megalithic data and it was to be many years before anything similar was attempted. It is a pity, therefore, that Aubrey was never informed of the avenue and rows at Callanish or of the great rows in Brittany. Even in

France those astonishing lines were never mentioned until 1721 and, even then, only inaccurately.[17]

As Professor Stuart Piggott remarked, Aubrey was 'at pains to bring together a corpus of archaeological evidence ... and to present it as source material with the minimum of comment or theory'.[18] Quite unlike many of his successors he could be sensibly matter-of-fact, offering the simplest explanation for stone rows. Of the avenues of the Stanton Drew stone circles he wrote, 'the stones ... might be a leading to another Temple, as for W. Kynet to the Monument on the top of the hill'. For the Kennet Avenue itself he added 'and very probable this Walke was made for Processions', believing that similar approaches had once existed at Stonehenge and the Rollright Stones in Oxfordshire 'though now decayed by Time'.[19]

Such a down-to-earth interpretation was not that of his contemporaries nor of later antiquaries.

(c) Callanish and Carnac: AD 1700 to 1900

So far from Hanoverian and Victorian times being periods of advance in ideas about megalithic monuments they were ages of retreat. Country fables of giants and devils gave way to druids but these Iron Age law-givers were portrayed as gentle philosophers and proto-Christians rather than as the blood-spattered priests of Roman historians.

Stone rows suffered. 'These happened to be a focus upon which their [the druids] claims could be centred ... circles and alignments of massive uprights ... Nothing was known as to the use of these or their origin, and when the druids were paraded as their probable builders the attraction of priests without temples to temples without priests proved irresistible'.[20]

Given the eighteenth-century ignorance of prehistory this was understandable but it was wilful of antiquarians such as William Stukeley to transform the druid into 'a scholar and a gentleman'[21] rather than accepting him as an inhabitant of the savage world of the Celts recorded by Greek and Roman contemporaries of druids: Strabo, Diodorus Siculus and Pliny the Elder. The historian, Tacitus, was unequivocal about British druids, their altars clotted with the blood of prisoners, divining the future through the writhings of human entrails.

Such men, moreover, were of almost historic times, living two or three thousand years after the raising of stone rows and circles. It is just possible that they were descended from a remote priesthood many centuries before them. References to sacrifice by bows and arrows, weapons almost unknown in the Iron Age but commonplace in the Neolithic and Bronze Ages hint at long-enduring traditions. Yet, true or not, this did not justify the translation of a merciless priesthood into an academy of amiably romantic druids.

The result was to distort not only druids but also stone circles and rows which became fantastically ingenious druidical machines. They were imagined to be megalithic calendars; or landscaped images of the sun or moon; or colossal representations of the deity. Eighteenth- and nineteenth-century descriptions of Callanish in the Outer Hebrides reflect these whims.

Callanish is a small stone circle but an impressive one with a tall central stone, a well-preserved avenue at its NNE, and with short rows at the east, south and west. Explanations for the complex have varied over the centuries, confirming Jacquetta Hawkes's dictum about another site that 'Every age has the Stonehenge it deserves – or desires'.[22]

In 1703 Martin Martin published the first plan of the ring and its rows, 'The Form of Yᵉ Heathen Temple', very schematic and notorious for the fact that the number of stones in the avenue and in each row is wrong, a matter that deceived commentators for almost a hundred years. Yet Martin did include a fair sketch of the slim, L-shaped stone inside the circle, 'like the Rudder of a Ship', an observation which resulted in even more confusion.[23]

John Toland, a free-thinking deist whose book, *Christianity Not Mysterious* of 1696, was ordered to be burned by the House of Commons in 1697, was fascinated by druids. He was impressed by Callanish's central stone, tall, slender, rectangularly elegant but jutting broadly outwards near its base as though designed for steering a boat of stone. This pillar persuaded Toland, who had obviously read Martin, that the circle was an astronomical temple, the nineteen stones on either side of

> the avenue betokening the [moon's] Cycle of nineteen years. I can prove it to have been dedicated principally to the Sun; but subordinately to the Seasons and the Elements, particularly to the Sea and the Winds, as appears by the rudder in the middle.[24]

William Borlase, although he never saw the ring, enlarged upon this idea:

> One observation occurs to me relating to this curious Monument, which is, that the number of Stones in the Avenue is 39, and the Circle 13, in all 52, and the detached Stones to the South, East and West is twelve; whether these numbers happened to be so compleat by accident, or whether (as I rather imagine) they were intended to express the number of weeks and months in one whole year, I submit to the learned.

He added that Thomas Carte, historian and Jacobite, believed that the avenue was patterned on the lunar cycle of nineteen years and the stone circle was 'an emblem of the Zodiac.[25]

Conversely, William Stukeley, a great British fieldworker and an enthusiast for Stonehenge and other stone circles, was obsessed with the fancy that rings and avenues had been designed as megalithic versions of God and His Son. 'The circle meant the fountain of

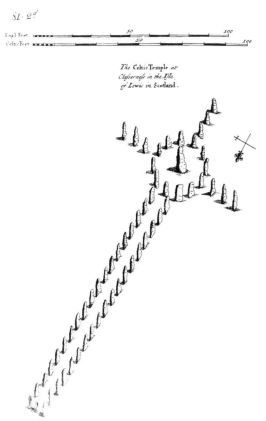

Sl. 2ᵈ

The Celtic Temple at Clasternis in the Ile of Lewis in Scotland.

Fig. 1 Callanish, Isle of Lewis. A drawing by William Stukeley, from his *Iter Curiosum II*, London, 1776, Plate 81.

all being, the invisible Supreme, who had no name. The serpent symboliz'd the Son, or first emanation from the Supreme'.[26] Such snakelike avenues became known as *Dracontia* from the Latin *draco*, 'serpent'.

This fictitious landscaping happened to accord well with the fortuitous layout of the circle at Avebury and the sinuous line of its Kennet Avenue but Stukeley was disconcerted to discover that plans of the Callanish avenue displayed it as unacceptably straight (Fig. 1). He rejected this. 'I took a drawing of it from *Mr Lwydd's* travels, but he was a very bad designer ... He did not discern the curve of it',[27] unsurprising as the avenue extends directly NNE from the circle for a full 272 ft (83 m) with no more than the tiniest wobble in either of its sides.

In those early decades of the eighteenth-century any mention of astronomy in stone rows and circles referred only to the belief that these were places where druids had worshipped the sun or moon. No one surveyed the monuments for solar or lunar sightlines. But by the end of the century when the development of bigger and better telescopes was stimulating interest in celestial studies comments about astronomy became more scientific. Druids, however, continued to occupy their megalithic temples.

By 1808 the Rev. James Headrick, an antiquarian, could write that a big stone at Callanish

is seen from the center [*sic*] through the avenue of stones, to be exactly south. This seems to have been an altar, where they probably offered sacrifices when the sun was in the meridian ... We are perfectly satisfied that these circles were intended to serve the purpose of rude astronomical observatories.[28]

Stone rows struggled between druids, serpents, war memorials and heavenly bodies for years. In 1805, describing the miles of standing stones at Carnac in southern Brittany, the Count Maudet de Penhouët decided they were records of battles. So did the Chevalier de Fréminville in his *Antiquités de la Bretagne* of 1827. But by 1826 de Penhouët had changed his mind and the Carnac rows became as dracontian as the Kennet Avenue at Avebury.

Serpentine landscaping gradually gave way to astronomical theories. Already, in 1805, Jacques de Cambry was sighing that had Carnac been near London its stones would have been as famous as Stonehenge because they were druidical astronomical observatories. 'Ce monument sans doute appartenait à l'astronomie (comprenez: astrologie); il était un thème céleste'.[29] And during the nineteenth century more and more writers felt certain that the ancient rows and rings were astronomical monuments.

One of the first signs of this awareness that lines of standing stones might have been orientated towards a solar or lunar event came from Daniel Wilson, Professor of History at University College, Toronto, who declared that:

The peculiar arrangement of the Callernish [*sic*] group, with its northern avenue, and cardinal rows of columns, strongly confirms the conviction, that we have here a memorial of primitive astronomical knowledge: of the observation of that one ever-resting polar star ... and of the study of the motions of the heavenly bodies in connexion with native rites of worship in prehistoric times.[30]

Six years earlier Henry Callender, Fellow of the Society of Antiquaries of Scotland, had remarked on the meridional alignment of Callanish's south row.

This coincidence is so exact, that it can hardly be supposed to be accidental, and affords, perhaps, the only trace we have of the knowledge possessed by the stalwart Druids who raised these old-world structures ... here we see them, as it were, watching the motions of the heavenly bodies.[31]

Two criticisms must be made. The first is that Wilson's 'Pole Star' had no connection with the south row at Callanish. At the time when Callanish was built Polaris, α Ursae Minoris, was rising over 20° away from True North, more than five miles (8 km) along the horizon from the north-south alignment of the south row. It did not reach its present position near True North for another three thousand years. Nor, in early prehistoric times, was there any other bright star visible at the north, only faint bodies such as Thuban, α Draconis, a dimmish star, merely one of many in the cluttered constellation of Draco.

The second point is that neither Callender nor Wilson suggested why their 'stalwart Druids' should be concerned with stars or other heavenly bodies except for an nebulous association with 'native rites'. More positive attempts to answer the mystery would come only in the twentieth century.

One of the difficulties that hindered investigators once they suspected a sightline in a stone row was the absence of good plans for the majority of lines. Ideally, surveys would be made on site but preliminary work could be undertaken in the study if a plan were sufficiently detailed and accurate. Until the mid-nineteenth century this was rarely so.

Then, around 1860, following an excavation at Callanish in 1857 during which five feet (1.5 m) of accumulated peat was removed from the circle and its rows, revealing the original heights of the stones, the Royal Commission for Ancient Monuments in Scotland made a plan of the complex.[32] This was followed by others, equally good, in 1867 and 1885. Surveys of the major Carnac alignments: Ménec, Kermario and Kerlescan among them, were undertaken by two Englishmen, Sir Henry Dryden and the Rev. W.C. Lukis between 1864 and 1872. Dryden was so meticulous a surveyor that it is reliably reported 'that having on one occasion found a discrepancy of half an inch [13 mm] in his measurements of an archaeological monument in France he made a journey of 200 miles [322 km] for the sole purpose of rectifying the error'. Not quite so painstakingly, the rows of Kermario were also plotted by James Miln, a Scot, in 1881.[33]

Elsewhere in Britain and Ireland increasing numbers of people were visiting the rows, measuring them, taking their bearings. The growth of County Archaeological Societies led to expansive reports about groups of standing stones, in particular the spectacular lines on Dartmoor that were described in a series of papers by R.N. Worth between 1892 and 1918.

Astronomy flourished. Sightlines were claimed. Around 1874 du Cleuziou declared there were solstitial and equinoctial alignments towards solar risings and settings in the long Carnac rows. He appears to have been the first person to be so definite.[34]

Archaeologists were more reticent. Although rejecting astronomical theories they offered few alternative hypotheses about stone rows. Druids lingered. Learned journals still had Indexes referring to 'Standing stones, druidical', and it was not until well into the twentieth century that those unreal spectres finally faded from the stones. Delusion was succeeded by illusion. Like the genial Dr Jekyll's transfiguration into the undesirable Mr Hyde, the druid did not vanish. He changed. Abandoning religion he mutated into

a scientific astronomer-priest obsessed with lunar mechanics.

Archaeologists continued reluctant to offer anything constructive about the purpose of stone rows. 'Avenue' was a favoured word, hinting at processions but for what reason and towards what was seldom explained. 'It is possible, therefore', wrote the Rev. W.C. Lukis when describing the cromlechs and rows at Carnac, 'that groups of pillars arranged in lines and in circles, and associated together, may have served a purpose in some way connected with the funeral rites or solemnities that preceded interment'.[35]

As many avenues and rows did not lead to circles this was not very helpful, a point taken up by Fergusson when discussing the two pairs of lines at Merrivale on Dartmoor (Pl. 8). 'They are not procession paths, inasmuch as both ends are blocked up; and though it is true the sides are all doors, we cannot conceive any procession moving along this narrow gangway hardly three feet [1 m] in width'.[36] Instead, he concluded, the rows represented two armies 'drawn up in battle array', a belief little different from that of Tudor antiquaries three centuries before. And what the short rows were no one asked.

So the megalithic lines entered the twentieth century, better recorded, slowly losing their druids, tinged, if not tainted, by astronomy, still keeping their silence.

(d) Archaeology and Astronomy in Stone Rows. The Twentieth Century

The opening of the twentieth century found stone rows affected by two separate approaches which, if not in opposition, were certainly very different in their intentions. Engaged by the newly-instituted County Inventories of the Royal Commissions of England, Scotland and Wales surveyors compiled gazetteers of prehistoric and historic sites. Since 1911 these corpora have been primary reference sources and despite errors, omissions and misinterpretations in the early volumes they are indispensable for research.

In Northern Ireland there were surveys by Chart et al (1940), and Jope (1966), and in the Republic of Ireland there has been an informative succession of different regional gazetteers: Buckley (1986), Cuppage (1986), Gosling (1991), Lacy (1983), Moore (1987), Power et al (1992) and Stout (1984). Curiously, given the megalithic marvels of Brittany, there was no up to date gazetteer of prehistoric monuments in either French or English until Burl (1985) and Bender (1986).

Astronomers had not been idle. At the beginning of the century, almost at the same time as the first Royal Commission volumes, Sir Norman Lockyer, Director of the Solar Physics Laboratory, having become interested in the orientations of Egyptian pyramids and of Stonehenge, turned his attention to Neolithic chambered tombs, stone circles and lines of standing stones. He analysed several rows on Dartmoor,

Pl. 8 Merrivale Centre, Dartmoor. The avenue from the WNW.

others in Wales and Scotland, and corresponded with French colleagues in Brittany, Gaillard in Morbihan, and Devoir in Finistère several of whose plans he reproduced.[37]

His interests, though more restricted, were complementary to those of archaeologists and at Callanish the two approaches yielded quite different data. The Royal Commission volume cited the dimensions of the diameter of the circle, the lengths of the avenue and rows, the heights of the stones, provided a general plan of the complex and a large-scale plan of the little passage-tomb squashed tightly inside the ring.

Lockyer wrote little about such matters.[38] Instead, he calculated the azimuth or compass-bearing down the passage of the chambered tomb which he considered had been constructed to face the rising of the

Pleiades in 1330 BC, a blazing galactic cluster, 'The Seven Sisters', and one of the loveliest sights in the night sky.

Lockyer believed that ancient observers had realised that when those stars rose above the skyline they acted as a signal that sunrise on May Day, the festival of Beltane, was imminent. In Eygpt he had discovered 'that stars far out of the sun's course . . . were observed in the dawn as heralds of sunrise – "warning stars" – so that the priests might have time to prepare the sunrise sacrifice'. Such useful stars rose about an hour before the sun giving the priest ample time for his preparations. Lacking sufficient warning 'he might go very wrong, and be either too early or too late at the moment of the rise of the great luminary.'[39]

According to Lockyer's computations the Pleiades

were used for the same purpose at sites as distant in miles as the Merry Maidens circle in Cornwall and the Stenness circle-henge in the Orkneys, and as far apart in years as Stonehenge in 1950 BC and Avebury in 1110 BC.

Lockyer calculated that the avenue at Callanish, extending to the NNE from the circle, 270 ft long and 27 ft wide (82.3 × 8.2 m), had an azimuth of 7°. At that latitude this pointed to the rising of the bright star Capella, α Aurigae, in 1720 BC. The alignments were wrong, the date was wrong, and the measurements were wrong because Lockyer had relied on other people's reports rather than visiting Callanish for himself. Nevertheless, it was a pioneering study and his book, *Stonehenge and Other British Stone Monuments Astronomically Considered* of 1906, revised in 1909, attracted an eager response from many professions – astronomy, architecture, engineering amongst them – but not archaeology. It was the start of an unreasoned antagonism that even today has not entirely vanished.

One of Lockyer's most competent followers was a naval officer, Boyle Somerville, who surveyed in both Scotland and Ireland where he recorded several prehistoric lines including the Three-Stone row at Newcastle in Co. Cork. Lacking archaeological guidance he misidentified some other sites, the ruined Five-Stone circle at Pluckanes in the same county, and what may have been tumbled field-divisions by the Drumhallagh Upper court-cairn near Lough Swilly in Co. Donegal. Despite these lapses Somerville's work was of a high standard and many of his plans, including one of Callanish, remain of value today.[40]

Sadly, the enthusiasm of other seekers for sightlines in megalithic monuments was greater than their surveying skills and during the 1930s the discipline of archaeoastronomy as it has come to be termed, the study of ancient astronomy, was derided by archaeologists who found it easy to scoff at the uncritical 'findings'. Archaeologically, considerable compensation for this recession appeared in several wellconducted field-surveys that recorded the existence of previously unsuspected stone rows.

In Caithness Gunn (1915) described the multiple lines, some parallel, some in fan-shaped complexes, unlike any others in Britain or Ireland. Years later Myatt (1980 *et seq*), with the assistance of Freer, produced scrupulous notes and plans about these and similar settings in Sutherland. In central Scotland the isolated concentration of pairs of standing stones was noted by Stewart (1966).

In south-west Ireland Conlon (1916 *et seq*) compiled lists of the 'rude stone monuments', the circles and short lines in the hills of Cork and Kerry. His invaluable records have been expanded and greatly improved by O'Nuallain after years of assiduous fieldwork (1984a, 1988). Without the latter's meticulous surveys and scholarship the present book would be much the less.

For Dartmoor Richard Hansford Worth (1967) continued the enjoyable labours of his father, R.N. Worth, tirelessly walking the moor, measuring the rows, checking their orientations and deciding that astronomy had not been of prime concern to their builders. Lockyer had suggested that a double row at Trowlesworthy, a row with a decided bend in it, had been constructed in two phases, the south section having been aligned on the star Arcturus, α Boötis, in 2130 BC, the north on the same target in 2080 BC. Worth was scathing.

> It pointed to Arcturus in, say, 2100 BC, we are told. If so, why is there a circle at the north (or Arcturus) end? Elsewhere we are led to believe that the circle was the place occupied by the observer; it should therefore be at the south end. But in any case the matter is unimportant, for it is the fact that each end of the avenue is invisible from the other, a rather startling circumstance in any monument used as a pointer.[41]

Emmett (1979), undertaking further fieldwork on Dartmoor and studiously analysing the rows' dimensions, orientations and development, was equally dismissive. 'The rows exhibit a wide variety of form, often suggesting several phases of construction, the final results of which are incompatible with theories involving ancient astronomy ... It is difficult to avoid the *un*-shattering conclusion that the rows merely run roughly downhill, towards the limits of the granite, and that the orientation is the result of such casual siting'. As a background to his exhaustive treatment of the Dartmoor rows Emmett compiled the first provisional gazetteer of long rows in Britain and Northern Ireland, adding 52 sites to the 62 he listed for Dartmoor.[42]

Other information came from a few excavations which yielded an inconclusive assemblage of artefacts and radiocarbon assays. Investigations at the Kennet Avenue, at Broomend of Crichie, Moor Divock and other avenues discovered Late Neolithic and Early Bronze Age pottery: beakers, Grooved Ware and food-vessels. Excavations at simpler rows located organic material from which C-14 determinations offered a range of dates from 1605±45 bc (UB-23), about 1930 BC, at Beaghmore in Co. Tyrone down to 715±50 bc (GrN-9172), around 840 BC, at Cashelkeelty in Co. Kerry. It will be argued that both are too late for the general *floruit* of stone rows in Britain, Ireland and Brittany.

The most recent development in the history of stone rows came with the statistical and astronomical publications of the late Professor Alexander Thom. This Scotsman, an engineer by profession, had been intrigued by megaliths since first seeing Callanish in 1933.[43] For over forty years he and his son, Archie, visited stone rows and circles, making excellent plans of them, and Thom became convinced that the rings and lines had been laid out by 'Megalithic Man' using a standardised, national unit of measurement, the Megalithic Yard of 2.72 ft (0.829 m). Thom argued that there was statistical evidence for the employment of such a yardstick in sites like the Kennet Avenue and the Carnac rows which he, with teams of surveyors, planned between 1970 and 1974.

Before Thom René Merlet had written in 1935 that a Gallic 'pied' of 0.3175 m (1 ft 0½ ins) had been used in the layout of some Breton cromlechs and of Stonehenge.[44] Such a 'foot' was not integral to Thom's Megalithic Yard and arguments in favour of either unit of measurement remain contentious.

Between eighty and ninety rows are listed in Thom's book, *Megalithic Sites in Britain*, 1967, Table 12.1. It is impossible to be more specfic as the catalogue contained 'rows' some of which were a form of stone circle known as 'Four-Posters'[45] (sites P1/18, W8/3), or mediaeval boundary-stones (S1/2). The avenue at Rhos y Beddau (W6/2) was listed as three lines and the three rows and avenue at Callanish (H1/1) were categorised as five alignments. It is disappointing that Thom was offered no guidance or help by archaeologists who could have advised him against these unnecessary blunders.

As his researches developed Thom became certain that many short rows contained very refined lunar alignments, and that multiple settings in northern Scotland as well as some in Brittany had been designed as delicate extrapolation sectors for determining the extreme rising and setting positions of the moon even when that body was not visible.

Archaeological reaction to the yardstick, the geometry and the astronomy was not always favourable. The Breton prehistorian, Giot, complained that the ideas were neither new nor convincing:

Some antiquaries were writing of zodiacs or calendars at the very beginning of the nineteenth century. In 1874 H. du Cleuziou, instructed to make an official plan of the Carnac alignments, suggested they were oriented to solar risings and settings at the solstices and equinoxes, so that these sites have been bedevilled by archaeoastronomy ever since; and in 1894 (and especially in 1904) R. Kerviler made calculations about the units of the megalith builders which have generated contrary views from scholars ever since. After more than a century of diverse hypotheses and efforts to try to demonstrate them, we do not appear to have made much advance.[46]

Advances are not made by negative thinking. Thom's conclusions remain controversial and they will be discussed in the chapters that follow. What is unquestionable is that his work forced a revision of long-accepted concepts in archaeology, most of all in the study of stone rows. Now that a comprehensive gazetteer exists for these lines, with excavations of some, and with many archaeological and astronomical surveys of individual sites, the rows need no longer linger in neglect.

CHAPTER THREE

THE DISTRIBUTION OF STONE ROWS

One class of megalithic monument which seems to be completely absent from Ireland is avenues of standing stones or alignments.

Adolph Mahr, *PPS 3*, 1937, 363.

INTRODUCTION

Since the time of that statement by the President of the Prehistoric Society well over three hundred rows ranging from unobtrusive paired stones to elaborate lines and avenues have been recorded in Northern Ireland and the Republic (Table 1). In an island so rich in megalithic tombs, circles and standing stones it would be astonishing if there were no linear settings.

To the contrary, there are outstanding sites such as the long, splayed rows at Beaghmore in Co. Tyrone and the cupmarked Three-Stone row at Ardamore in Co. Kerry. Not many miles to its north are the three curvaceous pillars at Cloonsharragh like leaping dolphins turned to stone, the survivors of a line of five just to the east of Brandon Mountain, 'Cnoc Gear', the dangerous hill.[1]

There the mountain slopes are an abundance of free-lying rocks, jumbles of boulders below shattered slides of scree, and it was the availability of easily-obtained stones like these that determined the presence or absence of prehistoric stone rows. Their distribution in Britain, Ireland and Brittany was determined almost exclusively by geology.

THE GEOLOGICAL IMPERATIVE

On occasion the writer has been asked why there are no megalithic sites, circles or rows, in regions of known Neolithic and Bronze Age occupation, like Kent, East Anglia or the Yorkshire Wolds. The answer is simple. There is no suitable stone. Prehistoric people did not go far in search of building material, preferring to use what happened to be in the locality. The obvious exception, Stonehenge, erected on the chalklands of Salisbury Plain, is exactly that, an exception for which its makers were prepared to haul cumbrous stones many miles because of a fanatical determination to create an enduring, awesome structure.[2]

Other people used whatever was most accessible, stone in the hills of the west, earth in the deep soils of the south and east, timber in forested country. Almost certainly where there were trees there were lines of upright posts, perhaps painted and carved, but the wood has rotted leaving nothing but invisible, earth-filled and grassed-over postholes to be discovered by chance.

At Kilham, near Great Driffield on the stoneless chalks of the Yorkshire Wolds, the excavation of an earthen long barrow uncovered a 22 ft (6.7 m) wide avenue of postholes leading to the burial mound. The holes, 8 ft to 11 ft (2.4–3.4 m) apart and arranged in two parallel lines, were traced for some 60 ft (18 m) before erosion of the chalk had destroyed further signs. A radiocarbon assay of 2880±125 bc (BM-293), c. 3640 BC, is an indication that funerary approaches such as this may have had an ancestry deep in the early Neolithic Age.[3] If so, it is strange that there are no comparable megalithic avenues leading to the stone-chambered long cairns and barrows of western Britain and Ireland.

Only six miles (10 km) west of Kilham an excavation at the Kemp Howe long barrow came upon a similar timber avenue, 130 ft (40 m) long, the postholes set 9 ft to 12 ft (2.7–3.7 m) apart. The spacing was very like that at Kilham but there was no evidence in either avenue of a unit of measurement being used.

A quern recovered from Kemp Howe and some sherds of Neolithic pottery akin to the Windmill Hill style of southern England suggests that the long mound and avenue were also constructed in early times. A previous excavation in 1878 by John Mortimer showed that the avenue had led to a timber mortuary house at the south-eastern end of the barrow, and that this had been burned down.[4]

Similar avenues of upright posts may have led to other burial sites but excavators have rarely had the time or the finances to search far beyond the limits of the barrow itself. It is known, however, that, centuries after the Neolithic Age, people were erecting avenues to some Early Bronze Age round barrows. One was linked to the causeway of a barrow inside a ring of

TABLE 1. *Provisional Tabulation of Stone Rows in Britain, Ireland and Brittany*

	England	France (Brittany)	Northern Ireland	Republic of Ireland	Scotland	Wales	Totals
Entrances and Portals	9	0	5	0	2	1	17
Avenues	27	4	3	1	9	0	44
Tangential and Detached Avenues	2	0	7	0	0	2	11
Long Double Rows	56	4	0	0	3	1	64
Long Single Rows	73	40	42	4	4	8	171
Multiple Rows	20	22	0	0	23	0	65
4–6 Stone Rows	11	27	7	47	21	13	126
3-Stone Rows	13	26	25	81	41	16	202
Paired Stones	29	22	15	131	105	31	333
TOTALS	240	145	104	264	208	72	1033

For more details see the County Concordance.

posts at Poole in Dorset. Excavation in 1949 obtained charcoal that produced an assay of 1260±50 bc (GrN-1684), c. 1550 BC. An adjacent barrow had a line of postholes stretching towards it from the south-east.[5]

A recent excavation of three of four ring-ditched barrows on Ogden Down in Dorset, one inside a concentric circle of timber uprights, discovered an avenue of posts, about 215 ft long and 11 ft wide (65 × 3.3 m) connecting two of the sites and set approximately at right-angles to the nearby Dorset cursus.

Lines like these may have been intended as solemn approaches for a cortège but not all double rows associated with barrows need have had a ritual function. Under a round barrow at Swarkeston in Derbyshire two buckled lines of stakes had been hammered into the ground. On a WNW–ESE axis this 'avenue' was about 40 ft (12 m) long, 7 ft (2.1 m) wide at its western end but narrowing to 2 ft 6 (0.8 m) at the east. 'The rows . . . appear to form a structure for animal use. In plan they form the shape of a long tapering tunnel, which suggests a bird trap . . . and the apparently flimsy nature of the structure rules out the possibility of cattle use'. The excavator had second thoughts. 'In its humble way it resembles an avenue, comparable in miniature to the West Kennet Avenue.'[6]

Other avenues of posts were less ambiguous. During the excavation of a round barrow on the Noordse Veld near Zeijen in the Netherlands 'traces have been discovered of two parallel rows of posts leading to the barrow and calling to mind the *alignements* of Brittany and the Stonehenge Avenue.'[7]

The avenue at Stonehenge itself is further proof that people used what was to hand. On Salisbury Plain it was the soft chalk. Gangs trenched parallel ditches 75 ft (23 m) apart for rubble to raise banks that led downhill exactly straight for a quarter of a mile. Two C-14 assays from antlers discarded in the ditches show that this avenue had been laid out around 2050 BC. As its construction appears to have been contemporaneous with the erection of the concentric bluestone circles inside the Stonehenge earthwork it is

puzzling that stones were not also set up along the course of the avenue. John Aubrey thought that they had been (Fig. 2), referring to 'the remaines of the avenue, or Entrance to this Temple . . . the imaginarie Walke of Stones which was there heretofore.'[8]

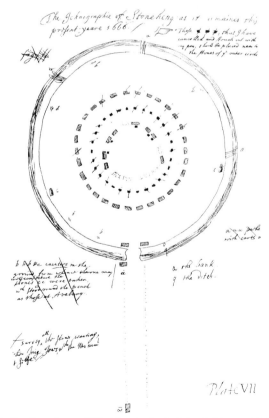

Fig. 2 Stonehenge, Wiltshire. A plan by John Aubrey in 1666, from his *Monumenta Britannica I (1665–93)*, Milborne Port, 1980, 80. The possible avenue is shown at the bottom of the drawing.

The question remains unresolved and will be discussed later. But as the Welsh bluestones had probably been lying quite near to Stonehenge[9] this unproven avenue would not be an exception to the rule that prehistoric workers sensibly used whatever lay conveniently close.

Other non-megalithic avenues and rows confirm this. It was true of two quite different avenues in the Milfield basin of Northumberland, one of earth, another of wood.[10] The gravel terraces of the River Till offered not stones but easily-dug soils and stands of trees that Bronze Age agriculturalists steadily cut back. A series of henges were built there in a rough south-east–north-west line. A ditched-and-banked avenue straggled inelegantly along part of the group, swerving past Marleyknowe henge, squeezing through the south and north entrances of Coupland henge, by-passing the little Milfield South henge, finally petering out over a mile (1.6 km) from where it began.

Nearly 600 ft (180 m) north-east of this earthen avenue the postholes of a second were detected by aerial photography. It consisted of pairs of timber uprights quite regularly spaced and running west-east in an interrupted line some 260 ft (80 m) long. Termed a 'pit-alignment', if stones rather than posts had stood there it would have been called a megalithic avenue or double row.

Sherds of Grooved Ware (Pl. 9), a Late Neolithic/Early Bronze Age style of pottery often associated with ritual monuments, a flint flake and some cremated bone had been deposited in one of the postholes. Charcoal, together with more from pits inside the Milfield South henge, produced six assays averaging 2050 BC, the same period as the avenue at Stonehenge.[11] Other 'pit-alignments' like this have been recognised in eastern England.

The one 'avenue' that would seem to contradict the geological argument is the rock-cut ditch and bank with no standing stones that bends from the southern entrance at Arbor Low in the Peak District, Derbyshire. This circle-henge, a henge with an internal stone circle, contains a tumbled ring of coarse limestone blocks.

Their presence seemingly implies that they had been lying in the immediate vicinity of the monument, or maybe even quarried from the bedrock during the digging of the henge's deep ditch. This was not so. The scrappy bits of rubble extracted from the ditches of the henge and the 'avenue' were piled up for the banks of those structures. This broken bedrock was 'very different in colour, texture and composition from that of which the slabs were formed.'[12]

Like the Stonehenge bluestones the Arbor Low pillars had been brought from a source nearby, possibly added to an already-old henge. The 'avenue', prehistoric from the finds of flint artefacts and flakes in its ditch, may have been left unfinished, just a single line from one side of the henge entrance with no sign

of its intended counterpart. Any intention of enhancing the avenue with standing stones was never fulfilled. By coincidence, a late extension to the Stonehenge avenue was also abandoned with only one of its sides completed.[13]

There is no mystery about the imbalance in the distribution of stone rows in Britain and Ireland. Even Stonehenge was a mixture of local timber and earth with the addition of some imported 'foreign' stones. Everywhere else the composition of prehistoric monuments reflected the geology of their immediate environment.

THE DIFFERENT TYPES OF STONE ROW

It is in the west of England, along the western coasts of Wales, in the Western Isles, in northern Scotland, in north-east and south-west Ireland, and in the granites and schists of Brittany that stone-row building flourished (Pl. 10). When this was is still somewhat uncertain although a time during the Bronze Age is likely for the majority of settings.

Even in those stone-littered countrysides there are unexpected gaps. Although geological considerations

Pl. 9 Grooved Ware. A type of Late Neolithic pottery whose origins are unknown but which has frequently been discovered in stone circles and henges. Devizes Museum.

Pl. 10   The impressive multiple rows of Ménec near Carnac.
From the south-west.

prevented their construction in the chalks, gravels and soils of the lowlands this does not explain the absence of rows from several megalithic regions. Only avenues are known in Wessex despite the presence of great circles like those at Avebury and Stanton Drew. In Cumbria with its many stone circles and associated avenues there is only one pair of stones, and that one dubious, at the Giant's Grave near Kirksanton. In north-eastern Scotland where over a hundred recumbent stone circles have been identified the only certain avenue was at Broomend of Crichie with one stone pair near Castle Fraser stone circle. Three-Stone rows, Four- to Six-Stone rows, long single, double and multiple rows are entirely absent.

This becomes understandable when it is realised that each type of row occupies areas that overlap but seldom coincide with other regions in which there are dissimilar lines. To understand the reasons it is necessary to categorise the architectural distinctions between the groups. Emmett did this for the Dartmoor rows, Type 1 being the single row; Type 2 the double lines; Type 3 the settings of three rows; and Type 4 the rare multiple arrangements of lines. For south-west Ireland O'Nuallain separated the pairs of standing stones from the rows of three to six stones that are common in the counties of Cork and Kerry. In the present wider study with its inclusion of types of row not to be found on Dartmoor or in south-west

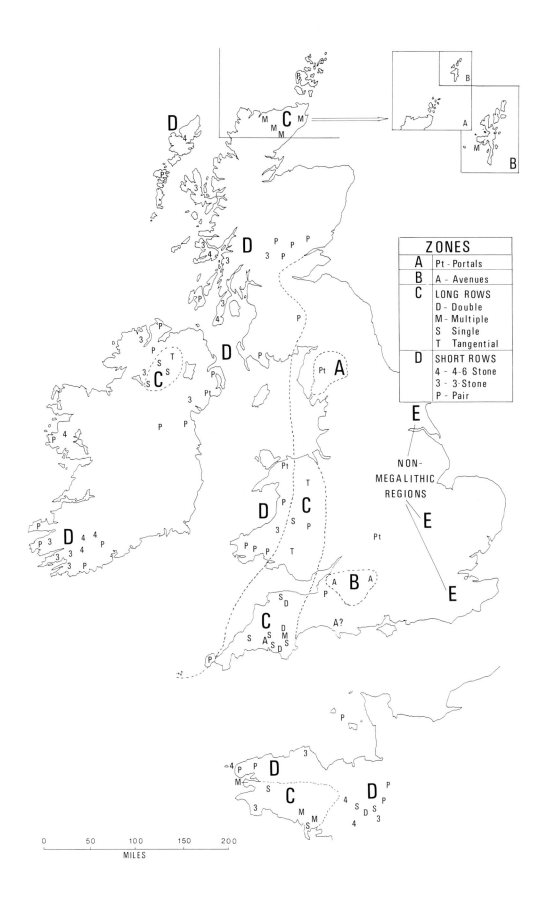

Ireland a more elaborate system is required (Fig. 3).

The first group consists of the simplest of all 'lines', the paired stones studied in detail for Perthshire by Margaret Stewart. They are followed by the rows of three stones. These were set up mainly along the coasts of the Irish Sea.[14] Settings of four to six stones, their distribution comparable to that of the Three-Stone rows, are alloted a separate class. Then there are longer lines, single and double, some of them attached to round cairns. Avenues are differentiated from the double lines by their direct connection with stone circles. Lastly there are the multiple rows of three or more lines in parallel or fan-shaped settings. With the exception of a few on Dartmoor these complexes are almost confined to southern Brittany and the northern Scottish counties of Caithness and Sutherland.

There are decided differences in distribution, art, astronomy and, presumably, function between the 'short' lines – the pairs, Three-Stone and Four- to Six-Stone rows – and the longer settings.

THE CHRONOLOGY OF THE ROWS

It will be argued that the long Dartmoor-type rows developed centuries after the construction of imposing stone circles. This hypothesis is given credence by the fact that the only other major form of stone row in England, the double-lined avenue, is always attached to a spacious megalithic ring.

Whether in the north-west in Cumbria – Cumberland, Lancashire and Westmorland, or in Wessex – Dorset, Somerset, Wiltshire – these twinned lines of standing stones lead up to enormous circles like Avebury or Stanton Drew. That they are not linked to the putatively earliest rings of all, from about 3200 BC, such as the splendid enclosures of Castlerigg and Swinside in the Lake District, may be an indication that the long avenues were embellishments added to stone circles of the middle period. The tentative dating, around 2400 BC, for the building of the Kennet Avenue at Avebury, a ring itself unlikely to have been begun much before 2800 BC, would accord with this thesis. There are archaeological reasons for believing that the even shorter lines in the far west of these islands were the final manifestations of this long-lived linear megalithic tradition.

The sequence in Brittany is likely to be similar but with an earlier chronology, the cromlechs, or megalithic rings, beginning around 3500 BC, early rows two or three centuries later, and the short rows in vogue from approximately 2000 BC.[15] A tentative 'chest-of-drawers' chronology, based on C-14 determinations and artefactual evidence[16] can be constructed (Table 2).

Fig. 3 The distribution of different types of stone rows and avenues in Britain, Ireland and Brittany.

If taken to an irrational conclusion it would follow that the single standing stones of Britain and Ireland and the menhirs of Brittany would be the last of this megalithic sequence. As will be noted later in this chapter, many of them may have been. It is known, however, that in Brittany several were erected long before passage-tombs. This is proved by early Neolithic carvings on standing stones such as Kermarquer and St-Samson-sur-Rance and by decorated menhirs that were thrown down and broken to be incorporated as capstones in chambered tombs like Mané Rutuel, the Table des Marchands and in the Carnac Mound of Mané-er-Hroek.[17] Lacking artefactual association, however, the dating of any isolated standing stone is almost impossible and they have been excluded from this study.

THE DISTRIBUTION OF THE ROWS

(a) England

The most spectacular linear settings in England are the avenues. These double lines of megaliths can be found leading to stone circles in the Lake District and in Wessex where the famous avenues at Avebury and Stanton Drew had less well-known counterparts in Dorset and at the north-eastern corner of Dartmoor.

Other types of row are even more localised. Except on the isolated uplands of the south-west peninsula stone rows are uncommon in England. Pairs of standing stones, Three- and Four- to Six-Stone rows are virtually non-existent, the linear settings of the Devil's Arrows and the Five Kings in north-east England being isolated examples of these short lines.

There is also a noticeable difference in distribution between the long stone rows and large stone circles which may imply a chronological distinction between them although this cannot be proved in our present state of knowledge.

The greatest concentration of long lines occurs on Dartmoor in Devon, Exmoor in Somerset and in

TABLE 2. A Provisional Chronology for Stone Rows in Britain and Ireland

	bc	BC
Late Neolithic, 3400 BC–		
Portals	2600–?	3300–?
Avenues	2150–1650	2600–2000
Early Bronze Age, 2200 BC–		
Detached Avenues	1900–1500	2300–1800
Double Long Rows	–	–
Single Long Rows	1750–1350	2100–1600
Middle Bronze Age, 1700 BC–		
4–6 Stone Rows	1500–1000	1800–1200
3-Stone Rows	1500–1000	1800–1200
Late Bronze Age, 1300 BC–		
Pairs of Stones	1100–900	1400–1000

Cornwall. These three regions contain three-quarters of all the long, wandering lines in England. In many the majority of stones are small enough to have been erected by just two or three people.

Even between these three enclaves there is regional divergence. On Dartmoor, where by far the greatest number occur, the rows, whether single or double, are frequently associated with a cairn surrounded by a stone circle at the upper end and a tall terminal stone at the lower. Such hybrid monuments do not exist on Exmoor where, although they are often near a cairn or barrow, the rows never approach a megalithic ring. Instead they mingle with unusual geometrically-designed rectangles and triangles that remain almost uninvestigated even though these idiosyncratic megaliths were known as early as the seventeenth century. Camden described them:

> The head of this river [Exe] lies in *Exmore*, a filthy barren ground near the Severn-sea; the greatest part whereof is in Somersetshire; where some monuments of antiquity are still seen; namely, stones set in the form of a triangle in some places, in others in the form of a circle.[18]

No mention, however, was made of the stone rows on Exmoor. It is to be remarked that the only great stone circle in the county stands well to the east of Exmoor at Stanton Drew near Bath.

In Cornwall until recently it was believed that the Nine Maidens near St Columb Major was the only long stone row in the county. Several others have now been discovered on Bodmin Moor and elsewhere but none is connected to any of the stone circles. It is possible, therefore, that the great megalithic rings of Stannon, Fernacre and the Stripple Stones preceded the building of lines of standing stones.

At the extreme of the south-west peninsula, on Land's End, there is a sudden concentration of pairs of stones, almost the only appearance of these minute rows in the whole of England. Perhaps not by coincidence two pairs are also suspected in Guernsey and Jersey a hundred miles to the south-east across the English Channel.

(b) *Brittany*
The distribution of stone rows in Brittany is essentially a coastal one, and more specifically one which is densest along the south and north-western coasts. There are some rows on the north coast and to the north and east where Brittany borders Normandy and Maine but these are occasional sites, ungrouped and isolated from others.

In this the rows mirror the distribution of Neolithic passage-tombs grouped on the granites of the south coast with coastal scatters to the south- and north-west.[19] Inland, once known as the *Argoat*, 'the wooded land', there are very few rows, An Eured Van 32 km (20 miles) from the sea in Finistère, some short rows

in the Montagnes-Noires, and, miles from any chambered tomb, the four startling rows at Médréac near St-Méen-le-Grand. Just to their north and south are solitary menhirs. The Médréac lines are not level with each other but overlap as if, though close together, they had not been intervisible. Even today hedges and trees prevent a clear view of the complex. Converging irregularly these jagged quartz rows have been likened to 'four rowing skiffs racing towards the winning-post of the northern menhir'.[20]

Médréac is a lonely wonder. It is for its southern rows that Brittany is best-known, the almost indescribable multiple files at Carnac by the Gulf of Morbihan. Here in a region of less than fifty-two square km (20 square miles) are some of the most astonishing rows in the world, line after line of ponderous stone at Ménec (Pl. 10), Kermario, Kerzerho and others intermingling with some almost unheard-of groups such as Ste-Barbe. This Carnac enclave accounts for two-thirds of the Breton multiple rows. Today those outside the area are in poor condition or even utterly destroyed like the four great lines at La Madeleine in southern Finistère.

Quite separate geographically and architecturally are the long single rows erected by the western coasts of that *département*. There were some uncommon multiples here also such as the devastated lines at Lostmarc'h but more typical were the geometrically intriguing single lines of Lagatjar and others on the Crozon peninsula. Many of them were unusually laid out, some with rows at right-angles to each other, Leuré, also destroyed, having been a good example.

Over a quarter of all the Breton rows were in Finistère, and two-thirds of all the single lines. The concentration is, or was, so great that a connection between western Brittany and the rows of south-western England, particularly those on Dartmoor, must be considered. The regions are not far apart.

> From Ushant to Scilly is thirty-five leagues
> Anon, *Spanish Ladies*

Archaeologically, links between Brittany and southern England are well-attested for the centuries of the Early Bronze Age.[21] There is no question of the ability of early people to undertake cross-Channel voyages. In the fourth century AD the Roman poet, Avienus, described the abilities of the seamen of north-west Brittany:

> Skilled and expert, continually engaged
> In trading in ships not built of wood but sewn ...
> Not from pine nor maple do they frame their keels
> But deftly fit together skins and hides
> On which to sail across the vast seas.
> Rufus Festus Avienus, *Ora Maritima*
> ['The Sea Coast']

The possible relationship between the stone rows of Finistère and the south-west peninsula of England can be stressed by pointing out that the three eastern and northern *départements* of Brittany, Ille-et-Vilaine, Loire-Atlantique, and Côtes-du-Nord, contain hardly a fifth of the Breton stone rows. Finistère alone, however, has over half, and of these a third are short lines – pairs, Three-Stone and Four- to Six-Stone rows – settings occurring never more than sporadically elsewhere in Brittany but commonplace across the Channel in Cornwall.

(c) *Northern Ireland*

Stone rows in the mainland of Ireland fall into two distinct regional categories and these are concentrated in the extreme north-east in Northern Ireland, and in the south-west of the Republic. At the north-east are the irregular, longish lines of small stones that lead up to cairns alongside many of the stone circles of Northern Ireland. The best-known are those at Beaghmore in Co. Tyrone.

At the south-west of the Republic, chiefly in the counties of Cork and Kerry, are rows of three to six tall stones in lines which are much shorter than those of Northern Ireland. Such rows are frequently monuments in their own right, unattached to any other structure.

In Northern Ireland there is a conspicuous disharmony in the distribution of stone rows. Almost every type of row exists there but in unbalanced blends, short lines separated from long, the coasts almost free of rows, the gently-swelling hills of the Sperrins in the interior filled with them. Where there are large stone circles there are no rows. Where there are diminutive rings the rows are numerous, many of them tangential, nudging against the circles in p- and q-shaped patterns.

Excellent examples of these peripheral lines can be seen at Drumskinny in Co. Fermanagh and Tremoge in Co. Tyrone, both of them miles away from the coast. There are also tangential avenues at sites such as Altaghoney in Co. Londonderry and Davagh Lower in Co. Tyrone. Adding to this mélange is the short avenue at Knocknahorna in the same county, and there seems to be an entrance of two tall stones in the stone circle of Ballygroll, Co. Londonderry. Except for the absence of any multiple settings Northern Ireland is a megalithic and minilithic pot-pourri of stone rows.

At the extreme north-east and east there is a flurry of Three-Stone rows. To their west, especially in Co. Tyrone, these short settings are frequently set alongside a stone circle. More often in that county, however, the rings of low stones have long rows leading to them and these have sometimes been misinterpreted as avenues. At Beaghmore, the celebrated complex of seven stone circles and rows, it has been suggested that funnelled avenues run up to the rings. More careful examination shows this to be mistaken. The lines are not identical. Instead, they consist of tangential, long low rows approaching cairns between the circles. Alongside them are taller, short rows. This mixture of the long and the short is typical of Co. Tyrone, the heartland of the known rows of Northern Ireland including four-fifths of the long single rows.

The conglomeration of all kinds of rows from pairs of standing stones in the eastern county of Down, almost the only lines there, to the outburst of long lines in the central counties make Northern Ireland unique amongst the countries studied here. Reasons for such a disparate collection of rows will be considered.

(d) *The Republic of Ireland*

In stark contrast to Northern Ireland there is hardly a long row in the whole of the Republic, a fallen line at the embanked stone circle of Castleruddery in the Wicklow mountains, a hotch-potch of ten standing and fallen stones at Roosky in Co. Donegal, a dubious avenue by Lough Gur in Co. Limerick, a very questionable single row at Dromavally on the Dingle peninsula of Co. Kerry, and a bewilderment of standing stones in the Timoney Hills of Tipperary.

No one has been able to discern any coherent layout in the Timoney Hills although an occasional optimist has claimed to see an alignment leading tangentially to a ruinous stone circle. Near Roscrea several hundred stones are spread confusingly across acres of fields and Timoney remains a megalithic perplexity. Locally there is a tradition that the stones are the result of mediaeval land clearance but why many are erect is not explained by this answer.

Archaeologists have remained cautious . . . and baffled. 'Numerous standing stones of which nearly 300 have been counted. The stones are small and form no recognisable patterns except for one circle of sixteen stones . . .', wrote Professor Estyn Evans. 'A number of stones, spread over a number of fields, but they do not form any apparent plan', observed Peter Harbison ruefully. 'The alignment of uprights marked on the map surveyed in 1934 is no longer present. They appear irregularly spaced on the map and do not run in a north-east/south-west axis which is a feature of the south-west of Ireland examples', noted Geraldine Stout in her excellent gazetteer.[22] Given such uncertainty the Timoney 'stone row' must be regarded as doubtful.

With the exceptions of Castleruddery and the four other debateable 'lines' the remainder of the stone rows in the Republic, over two hundred of them, are short, more than half of them simple pairs of standing stones.

Their distribution is markedly concentrated in the south-western counties of Cork and Kerry with outliers in Galway and Donegal. Outside those counties stone rows are virtually unknown. A line drawn from Sligo at the NNW down to the western borders of Waterford at the SSE has nineteen counties to its east, over half the entire area of the Republic. Despite the vastness of this region the Gazetteer lists few rows in it, amongst them the improbable Timoney 'line'.

(e) *Scotland*

Scotland has an outstanding diversity of stone rows. Over two hundred lines are recorded here and there must be others that wait recognition on the ground or rediscovery in old archaeology bulletins.

Pairs of stones predominate, chiefly in the south-west of the country and in Perthshire where they are an almost exclusive form of row. At Orwell near Kinross human cremated bones in a stonehole pointed to dedicatory practices when the two stones were erected. Elsewhere the differing heights or shapes of the paired uprights have led to suggestions that the pillars represented male and female principles associated with fertility rites.

Cupmarks carved on the pairs and Four-Poster stone circles in this part of Scotland are more common than in any other area of Britain, Ireland or Brittany.

Three-Stone rows in particular, with Four- to Six-Stone rows also, are numerous in the west of Scotland. Painstaking fieldwork by Royal Commission surveyors, and by the Thoms have recorded scores of these short settings. Continuing research, including excavations such as that at Glengorm in Mull, is revealing something of the ceremonies enacted at these short rows.

Long single and double rows are almost unknown. Undoubted avenues at the Hebridean stone circle of Callanish on Lewis and at Broomend of Crichie in Aberdeenshire are unique Scottish examples of those 'English' attachments to stone circles. Less certain are several other sites in the latter county where avenues may have led to some of the recumbent stone circles of the region.

The most striking of all the rows, however, are the multiple lines of Caithness and Sutherland in the far north of the country. These aggregations of lines of small stones are often set in fanlike arrangements. Commonly the lines climb up a shallow rise, presumably because they were directed towards the focal point of a small cairn or a natural mound at the head of the slope. Although well-known sites such as Mid Clyth in Caithness and Learable Hill in Sutherland may possess ten or more lines there are also Four- to Six-Stone rows in the same area at Broughwin SW in Caithness, and Kildonan SE in Sutherland.

Interestingly, this custom of putting up several adjacent rows had outlying examples as far north as Lumbister and the Giant's Stones on Shetland but appears to have by-passed the Orkneys altogether. In those islands there are only two three-stone rows and six pairs.

(f) *Wales*

Stone rows are rare in Wales although not as uncommon as has sometimes been claimed. In a country divided by steep hillsides, mountain ranges and fast-flowing rivers it could be anticipated that quite distinct regional fashions would develop, the strongest being towards the western seaboard.

What Wales lacks in number however it compensates for in variety. Almost every type of row can be seen here, pairs of standing stones, Three-Stone and Four- to Six-Stone rows – many of them of breath-taking boulders – single rows and tangential avenues.

The most common type is the single pair, particularly in the western counties of Dyfed and Gwynedd, with Four- to Six-Stone and Three-Stone rows almost as plentiful. Such short rows are manifestly of the Irish Sea tradition. The fact that similar monuments are numerous in south-west Ireland, south-west Scotland and in north-east Ireland points to a tradition popular along the western coastlands.

Single lines of many stones are scarce in the country, tending to lie in a north-south band down the centre of the country. Not surprisingly, if theirs was an origin emanating from the south-west of England where similar lines are abundant, the most striking Welsh examples are in the south-west, the best-known being the now-damaged line at Parc y Meirw near Fishguard.

In eastern Wales there are indications of influences from the east in the form of tangential avenues at the stone circles of Cerrig Duon and Rhos y Beddau in Powys. What Three-Stone rows are to be found there are of aberrant type with one enormous erect block like that of Maen Mawr at Cerrig Duon, and two tiny stones set in line with it.

(g) *Islands*

Although there are hundreds of stone rows on the mainlands of Britain, Ireland and Brittany it was a tradition that, with the important exception of the Western Isles of Scotland, affected outlying islands only very weakly.

There are few rows in either the Shetlands or the Orkneys and only one pair on Arran. At Ballakilpheric on the Isle of Man where there are two standing stones 'two others are known to have been near them in such a position as to suggest that they formed the remains of a large circle'.[23] Being so close to the spaciously grand megalithic rings of Cumbria it is more likely that the Ballakilpheric stones were the survivors of a great circle than a pair of standing stones or the relics of a ruined Four-Stone row.

No stone rows are known on any Irish island or the Isle of Wight and only one Three-Stone row has been discovered in the Scillies. In the Channel Isles Guernsey and Jersey appear to possess no more than one pair each. There is a similar paucity on the many islands of Brittany, one or two ill-recorded rows in the islets off Finistère and one good Three-Stone row at Brouel on the Île aux Moines.

A reason for this non-adoption of stone rows was not an absence of population. Chambered tombs on many of the islands attest to prosperous settlement there centuries before stone rows came into being. The answer may lie in that fact. Established communities, contented in their sea-circled isolation, unenthusiastic about foreign cults, may have preferred to retain their old traditions, continuing to perform rites in and around the ancient megalithic tombs, by now more probably temples than burial-places, rejecting the introduction of anything as novel and untried as a line of standing stones.

But if there are few rows on these islands what do exist are standing stones, bleak, unworked pillars that possibly belong to the final centuries of the second millennium BC. They can be found at the far north of Scotland and to the farthest south of Brittany.

At Bordastubble on Unst in the Shetlands there is a colossal pillar of gneiss 12 ft 6 (3.8 m) high, weighing over thirty tons, looming like a chilled watchman on the bare slopes overlooking the sea. The Devil is said to have thrown it from a distant hill.

Nearly a thousand miles (1600 km) away in the Atlantic Belle Île lies eight miles (13 km) off the Quiberon peninsula of Brittany. On it two menhirs, Jean and Jeanne Runelo, stand a quarter of a mile apart, Jean a lean needle of red schist, Jeanne a smaller granite block. Legend testifies that they were lovers, the man a lapsed druidical bard, fleeing for their lives but petrified by the Celtic priesthood for Jean's apostacy.

There are similar stones in the Scillies. In the eighteenth century Borlase saw one on the islet of Gugh, 'a large stone-erect nine feet high by two feet six inches wide' [2.7 × 0.8 m]. There are standing stones in the Channel Islands, monoliths of granite and sandstone on Arran, there is the tall Giant's Quoiting Stone on the Isle of Man. Worked flints were discovered near it.[24]

Erected on remote islands where there were few circles and even fewer rows, without art or artefact, these forlornly weathered stones may be the last descendants of a linear megalithic tradition already two thousand years old.

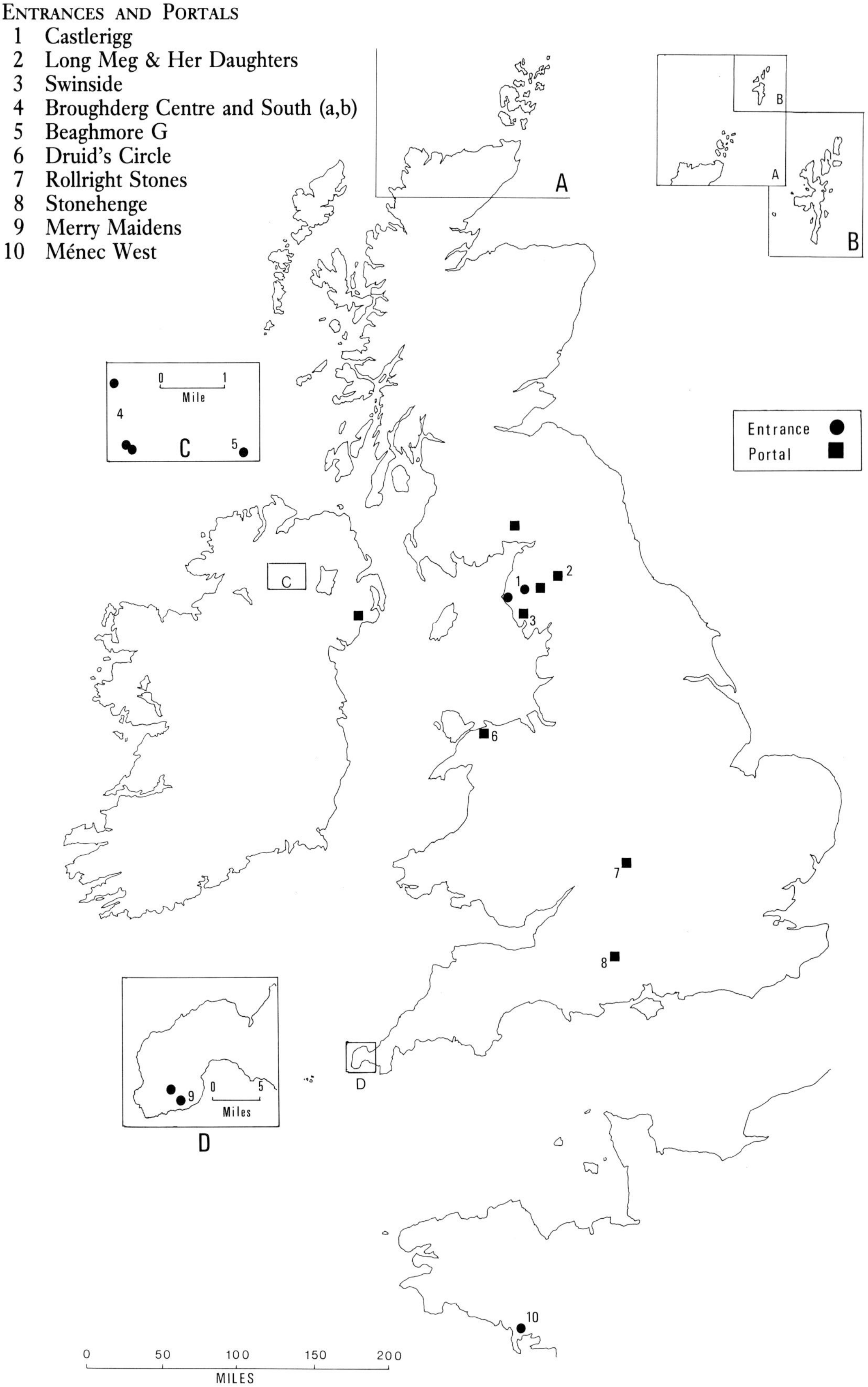

Entrances and Portals
1 Castlerigg
2 Long Meg & Her Daughters
3 Swinside
4 Broughderg Centre and South (a,b)
5 Beaghmore G
6 Druid's Circle
7 Rollright Stones
8 Stonehenge
9 Merry Maidens
10 Ménec West
Entrance
Portal
A
B
C
D
0 1 Mile
0 5 Miles
0 50 100 150 200
MILES

CIRCLES, ENTRANCES AND PORTALS 3300 BC–?

At the entrance [of Swinside stone circle] are four large stones, two placed on each side at the distance of six feet. The largest on the left hand side is five feet six inches in height and ten feet in circumference. Through this you enter into a circular area 29 yards by 30. This entrance is nearly south-east.

William Camden, *Britannia*, 3rd ed., 1806, 432

INTRODUCTION

Long stone rows may have been developments from the avenues that led to stone circles (Fig. 4). And avenues may have had an ancestry in the elaborated entrances of stone circles in the Lake District of England, at Castlerigg, Long Meg and Her Daughters, Swinside and others in the mountainous north-west corner of Britain.

At Castlerigg near Keswick there is no avenue but the wide entrance to the ring is defined by two massive pillars, their heights emphasised by the much lower stones that flank them. In some rings an extra pair of impressive stones was set up outside such an entrance as portals to the enclosure. These monumental 'gateways' of four high stones standing at the towering corners of a rectangle can be seen not only in Lake District rings but others related to them, at the Girdle Stanes forty miles (64 km) north of Keswick in Dumfriesshire and at Ballynoe, Co. Down, across the Irish Sea.[1]

It is greatly to be regretted that in Brittany the cromlechs have been so badly damaged by the removal of stones that it is impossible to be sure of any entrance. At the western end of the Ménec rows near Carnac the egg-shaped ring was once a vast megalithic enclosure measuring 300 ft by 230 ft (91 × 70 m). Its north-east and south-west arcs have been entirely robbed but at its east where the rows of standing stones run up to it there is a 33 ft (10 m) wide gap between two closely-set stones to the north and others to the south (Pl. 11). A similar space exists at the yet-more ravaged eastern cromlech. Here in the surviving north-west arc there is a 43 ft (13.1 m) wide gap.

A long mile to the north-east an examination of the sub-rectangular cromlech at Kerlescan is even more of a disappointment. Eighteen stones, some almost

touching each other, remain standing on its straight 255 ft (78 m) long eastern side. Halfway along there is a 13 ft (4 m) space flanked by tall menhirs, a gap bigger than that between most of the other stones. But as there is an even wider one immediately to its north its qualification as an entrance is not convincing.[2] Other cromlechs are in worse condition.

LATE NEOLITHIC DISRUPTION

The beginnings of stone rows and avenues are obscure but not irrecoverable. If not directly related to the avenues of posts leading to Yorkshire long barrows such as Kilham and Kemp Howe the first may have developed during the social upheaval that occurred in the late centuries of the fourth millennium BC.

It was a time of crisis. The Neolithic period had never been static, its social structure, its intermeshing trading systems, its burial practices always undergoing transformation but it had been consistent. The family group had been its basis, a stone economy its background, and a cult of ancestors its spiritual strength. Over the years they all became more complex but they continued to be the framework of existence. Then there was change.

Old cults waned and new ones replaced them. Chambered tombs were abandoned. Open-air enclosures were constructed. And where there had been no tombs and no ancestors to venerate the changes came earlier.

The earliest British stone circles, spacious rings of closely-set pillars, may have been erected around 3200 BC in the English Lake District. There, unlike other more settled regions, there were no strong megalithic traditions to overcome when Neolithic prospectors commenced exploiting mineral sources in the Langdale mountains for the production of stone axes.

That the farming inhabitants of the earlier Neolithic Age had prospered is proved by the steady increase in the number of C-14 determinations from 3500 to

Fig. 4 Distribution map of stone circles and cromlechs with entrances or portals.

Pl. 11 Ste-Barbe, Plouharnel near Carnac. The surviving stones of the cromlech from the west. A few stones of its rows can be seen in the background. Any avenue amongst them has been destroyed.

2600 bc, about 4450 to 3200 BC, as more land was cleared more settlements developed, more tombs were built, more sources of stone were discovered. Then, around 3200 BC, the number drops. A graph of radiocarbon dates records a decline from 2500 bc until 2300 bc,[3] a period from before 3200 to 2900 BC in real years, several centuries of a Dark Age when conditions deteriorated and when traditional rituals seemed to be failing.

Analysis of pollen from cultivated areas shows a regeneration of woodland with scrub and weeds spreading across deserted fields. Chambered tombs like Gwernvale in Powys were blocked up.[4] Defended villages with heavy gateways and walls were thrown up at Carn Brea in Cornwall, Hambledon Hill in Dorset, Crickley Hill in Gloucestershire, signs of a collapse of confidence between societies.[5]

Explanations for the disruption have included the possibility of over-use of land causing the failure of crops. Famine has been suggested, plague, even a population that had become too large for the limited supply of food. There may also have been a more insidious, apparently trivial agent, a worsening of the weather.

Examination of the annual growth-rings in Irish oaks has revealed a contraction of their widths around 3190 BC, a sign of cooler summers and winters. The evidence complements other data from Greenland where around 3250±80 BC ice-sheets received deposits of acid rain from volcanic eruptions. Similar

outbreaks in modern times have preceded long periods of low pressure with colder, wetter conditions for several years coupled with the waterlogging of poorly drained soils.

The bad weather was the result of clouds of volcanic dust that shaded the sun. The effects were disastrous. In the west of Ireland blankets of smothering peat can be attributed to this phenomenon. The stone-walled fields of Beldberg Beg in Co. Mayo were slowly choked.[6] Nearby, almost a square mile (2.6 km^2) of fields at Behy/Glenrula was covered by the encroaching bog. The consequences for unprepared, uncomprehending prehistoric societies must have been drastic.

We have to envisage the possibility of failed harvests, famine – and no doubt plague and pestilence as well . . . vast tracts of land rendered uninhabitable. In such circumstances the survivors would have been those who were more warlike than their neighbours.[7]

A historical correlation between similar eruptions and an outbreak of plague seems confirmed by a comparable narrowing of tree-rings in AD 540 together with acidulous ice-cores and records of a European 'mystery cloud'. It was the time of the pestilence during the reign of the emperor Justinian, 'the first authenticated visitation of bubonic plague in Europe'.[8]

It seems unlikely, however, that even several years of cold and rain would have affected Neolithic communities so devastatingly unless those societies had already been precariously poised between security and disaster. A combination of factors is more feasible, the temporarily worsening climate exacerbating a social discordance that may have begun some centuries before 3200 BC. Whatever the answer, as life slowly returned to stability it was returning with innovations, new pottery styles, new cults, and new assembly-places, the open-air henges and stone circles of the Late Neolithic period.

HENGES, STONE CIRCLES AND CROMLECHS

Late in the fourth millennium BC the custom of enclosing open-air circular areas many paces across, bordered by earthen banks in the lowlands, by standing stones in the west, gradually became widespread. There was no sudden outburst. Radiocarbon assays from early henges such as Stonehenge in its first phase, 2460±60 bc (BM-1583) and 2440±60 bc (BM-1617); 2470±50 bc (GU-1670) from Balfarg Riding School in Fife; from stone circles, 2356±65 bc (SRR-350 at Stenness in the Orkneys and 2525±80 bc (GU-1591) from the Lochmaben Stane near Dumfries, now just a gross, fallen boulder but in the last century one of 'a number of white stones placed upright circling half an acre in an oval form'; and 2550±250 bc (Gif-280) from the horseshoe-shaped cromlech of Tossen-Keler, Côtes-du-Nord, from material probably post-dating the ring, show that the construction of such enclosures in Britain, Ireland and Brittany was established centuries before 3000 BC. A 'date' of 2790±150 bc (NPL-220) from Llandegai NE, a destroyed henge close to Bangor, offers the possibility that a few earthen rings in Britain had been built as far back as 3500 BC.[9]

(a) *Entrances*

It is the entrance to a Late Neolithic ceremonial enclosure, whether henge, stone circle or cromlech, that is relevant to a study of stone rows and avenues. The banks of the first henges had only one or two breaks through them leading to causeways across the inner ditch. As if in imitation of these nearly-continuous walls early stone circles, especially those in the Lake District, were composed of a multitude of stones crowding closely together with just one wider space offering access to the interior.

These openings to a 'sacred' area were of ritual importance and were enhanced by ritual and by architecture. Remains, usually of women, were buried beside them. At Stonehenge the bodies of adults and children were deposited in pits at both entrances. By causeways elsewhere a woman's skull was interred at Gorsey Bigbury, a malnourished girl at Marden, a female dwarf by the south entrance of Avebury's earthwork enclosure. Invisible to the living world these burials, perhaps sacrifices, may have been thought to give power and protection to the henge.[10]

On occasion the bank of a henge such as Hutton Moor in Yorkshire was piled higher at the entrance, looming above anyone who entered. In stone circles two tall pillars served the same purpose. Such exceptional flankers straddling a notably wide gap can be accepted as entrance-stones. Much less certainty attaches to a space in the ring which happens to be wider than the distances between other stones. Doubts can sometimes be resolved by considering the positions of these 'entrances' because, in indisputable cases, Castlerigg being one, the entrance was laid out in line with one of the four cardinal points or towards a calendrical event such as midwinter sunset.

Astronomical sightlines were not a novelty. In Neolithic chambered tombs such as the Clava Cairns of Inverness-shire builders planned the passages to face in the general direction of the sun or moon. The same was true of the mounds of earthen long barrows like those on Salisbury Plain.[11] The lines were approximate, often accurate to no more than a degree or two. But by Late Neolithic times observers were more particular, sometimes aligning stones on elusive solar and lunar events (see Chapter 5). This increasing refinement is manifest in the laying-out of entrances to Castlerigg and other stone circles in north-west England.

Castlerigg, on a hill near Keswick at the heart of the Lake District, is one of the enticements of megalithic Britain. It is frequently misnamed the 'Carles' as though the stones were husbandmen petrified for some forgotten sin but the error comes from a misreading of Stukeley who, after visiting the ring in 1725, wrote, 'They call it the Carfles, and corruptly I suppose, Castle-rig. There seemed to be another larger circle in the next pasture toward the town.'[12] If it ever existed this second ring, whether a stone circle or an earthen henge, has disappeared.

Castlerigg is enclosed by some forty morosely grey stones – standing, leaning and tumbled.

> Scarce images of life, one here, one there,
> Lay vast and edgeways; like a dismal cirque
> Of Druid stones, upon a forlorn moor,
> When the chill rain begins ...
> John Keats, *Hyperion*, II, 33–6.

On average just over 3 ft 4 (1 m) high, and of local metamorphic slate, the boulders huddle together with a gap 12 ft (3.7 m) across at the precise north. This cardinal position is emphasised by two large stones, 5 ft 6 and 5 ft 8 (1.7, 1.7 m) high, standing astride the entrance, their size exaggerated by the little stones outside them (Pl. 12). The pillars are not only taller but much bulkier, heavy boulders as sombre and immoveable as a gateway to the world of death.

The ring may be one of the first stone circles in Europe, possibly connected with the manufacture and distribution of Neolithic stone axes. The source of the epidotised tuff used for the axes was only a few miles

Pl. 12   Castlerigg, Keswick, Cumbria. The wide entrance of the stone circle. From the north.

to the south in the Langdale mountains. In 1875 an unpolished stone axe was found inside Castlerigg, and in 1901, at Portinscale two and a half miles (4 km) to the west, four half-shaped rough-outs and a polished axe were discovered in peat near a pile of chippings and a long, thick stump with a battered top, a collection which its finder believed was an axe-maker's workshop,[13] a place where the unfinished stones were flaked and smoothed into the long, graceful Cumbrian axes.

Axes recovered from other Lake District stone circles and circle-henges such as Mayburgh make the connection between the industry and the rings more likely as does the 'date' of 2525±80 bc (GU-1591) from the Lochmaben Stane circle, a time around 3250 BC when the Langdale 'factories' were in full production.[14]

The northern gap at Castlerigg can be classed as a deliberately-fashioned entrance because of the combination of three factors: its exceptional width, the heights of the stones flanking it, and its location at a cardinal point. The first feature by itself would not be adequate. Even two would leave doubt.

Sixteen miles (26 km) west–south-west of Castlerigg on a level stretch of moorland alongside the

Ennerdale Bridge road is the pleasant little circle of Blakeley Raise (Pl. 13). Its twelve stones are quite evenly spaced but there is a bigger gap at the south–south-east, once wide enough for picnicking motorists to drive in. Happily, the deterrent of a line of sharp-edged kerbstones at the roadside has ended this conversion of a ritual circle into a napkin ring.

The opening at Blakeley Raise is defined by the tallest stones in the circle, 3 ft 3 and 3 ft 8 (1, 1.1 m) high. Thom suggested that looking from the taller, eastern stone across the ring's centre towards Screel Hill in Dumfriesshire a prehistoric observer would have seen the most northerly moon setting down the slope of the hill.[15]

In the opposite direction, however, using the tall pillar as a foresight, the nearby mountains obscure all lunar and solar sightlines so that the 'entrance' is astronomically useless. A further objection is that several stones were taken from the ring in the early twentieth century and replaced, rather haphazardly, in 1925. The 'entrance' may therefore be nothing more than a fortuitous gap, as questionable in status as Castlerigg is convincing.

Yet it is unlikely to be coincidental that not far from a cairn-circle a concentric ring of posts at Oddendale

Pl. 13 Blakeley Raise, Cumbria. From the south. The wider gap between the two low stones in the foreground may be an accident of twentieth-century restoration rather than an intended prehistoric entrance.

had a wide gap at the south of the outer ring. Nor may it be fortuitous that both the inner and outer circle consisted of twelve uprights, a number noticed at Blakeley Raise and in several later stone circles in and around the Lake District hinting at elementary numeracy there.[16]

Outside Cumbria, uncertainty attaches to the long stone lying in the SSE entrance of Arbor Low circle-henge in the Peak District. 'The narrow SSE entrance has the stump of a portal stone in it, the other wider entrance has a pit where a second may have been removed. It is possible that both entrances had pairs of portals originally'[17]. Without excavation this must remain surmise.

The construction of spectacular megalithic entrances was a specialism of Lake District communities. There are other rings, distant and unconnected, with entrances emphasised by conspicuous uprights but they are few. Two great shiningly white quartz blocks lie at the entrance of Castleruddery circle-henge in the Wicklow mountains of Ireland. Huge boulders front the passage through the bank of the Grange circle-henge in Co. Limerick. Massively high stones marked

the terminals of the Breton 'horseshoes' of Tossen-Keler in Côtes-du-Nord, and Kergonan, lost in a wilderness of apple-trees, bramble and undergrowth, on the Île aux Moines in Morbihan. Larger gaps between stones at the Merry Maidens and Boscawen-Un, circles a few miles apart on Land's End in Corn-wall, may also have been erected as entrances. Facing east and west respectively both rings regard cardinal points but the flanking stones are not outstandingly tall or broad, nor are the 'entrances' especially wide.[18]

Similar gaps, but bordered by stones twice the height of others in their rings, occur deep in the Sperrin mountains of Co. Tyrone where there is a small concentration. At Broughderg, a tight group of three inconspicuous concentric ovals, the majority of their stones no more than 1 ft (30 cm) high, huddle together on a hillside eleven miles (18 km) WNW of Cookstown. That these are genuine entrances is made likely by the presence of a fourth oval nearby, this having not only an entrance but an avenue leading to its eastern side. Only a mile or so away there are other probable entrances at Clogherny Butterlope and at the westernmost of the seven Beaghmore stone circles.

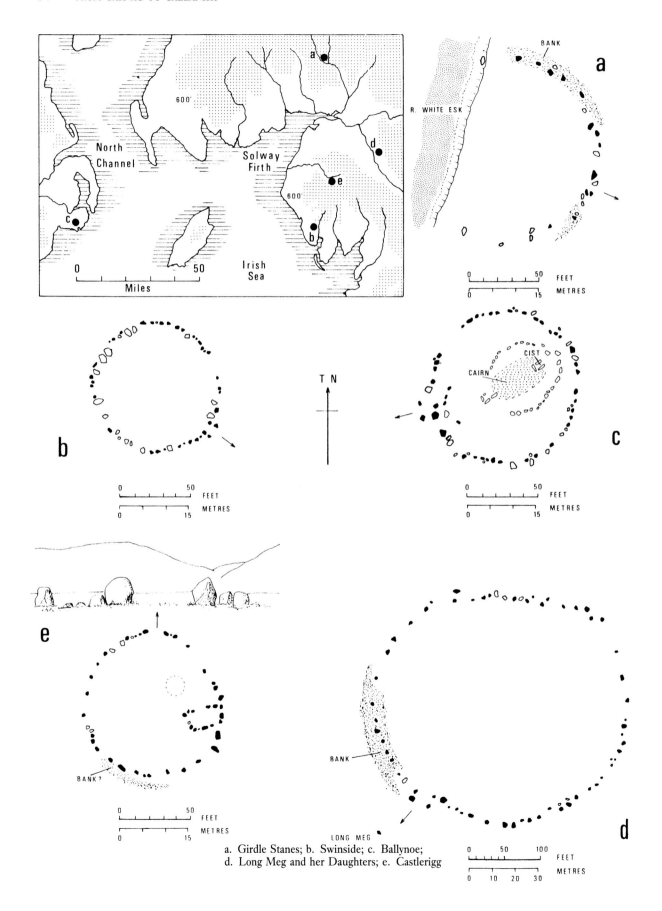

a. Girdle Stanes; b. Swinside; c. Ballynoe;
d. Long Meg and her Daughters; e. Castlerigg

The recumbent stone circles of Cork and Kerry, rings with a stone placed on its side in the south-west quadrant, had two conspicuously tall pillars opposite the recumbent. At Drombeg and Bohonagh, where the flankers are 7 ft 11 and 9 ft 5 (2.4, 2.9 m) high, there were areas of dark trodden turf and trampled-in pebbles around these portals where it seemed that people had walked or danced. It is doubtful, however, that the settings had originally been conceived as entrances.

Evidence suggests that these rings were late versions of Scottish recumbent stone circles whose architectural components were retained but rearranged in Ireland. In Scotland the two tallest pillars stand hard against the recumbent leaving no gap for even a playful terrier to wriggle through. In Cork and Kerry these flankers were put up not by but opposite the recumbent creating a fortuitously convenient entrance. The ancestry of the Irish recumbent rings is Caledonian rather than Cumbrian and in the circles there is nothing to indicate even a remote connection with Lake District traditions.[19]

Nor do the majority of henges in Britain and Ireland contain such associations. Most henges, lying in landscapes free of stones, were unlikely ever to have had any megalithic embellishment although a stone once lying at the entrance to Maumbury Rings in Dorset may have been the relic of such a setting. It has gone and excavation failed to locate any stonehole for it.

Timber-built entrances were more probable in henges. Two holes for posts were found on the east side of the entrance at Woodhenge but 'their purpose is enigmatical' the excavator regretted. At Gorsey Bigbury it was believed that a pair of holes, perhaps the remains of gateposts for the Late Neolithic enclosure, had been thrown down by hostile Beaker incomers. 'The takeover implies a disregard of the original communal or religious purpose'. Not far away at the line of henges at Priddy three holes, for stones not posts, lay in the entrance of the south site. Their layout was so irregular that no explanation was suggested for them.

Near Garstang in Lancashire a spacious timber stockade at Bleasdale, dated to 1810±90 bc (NPL-69), c. 2150 BC, had an entrance at the south-west about 12 ft 6 (3.8 m) in width framed by two massive posts. Inside the stockade was a smaller ring of oak posts with an eastern entrance. It surrounded a central grave with two urns, one of them containing a tiny accessory vessel of the Early Bronze Age.

It is perhaps significant therefore that, except for Stonehenge, the only indisputable evidence for a henge with a pair of stones at its entrance is in the Lake District itself, King Arthur's Round Table near Penrith. Eleven miles (18 km) to the north, near a group of stone circles, the hengelike ringwork of Broomrigg 'E'

had a large, isolated stone on one side of its entrance. A portal stone at the circle-henge of Balfarg in Fife also lacked any sign of a partner.[20]

King Arthur's Round Table had entrances at the SSE and NNW, the latter destroyed when the construction of a lane levelled the northern side of the henge. In the seventeenth century, however, Sir William Dugdale saw it while compiling data for his subsequently unpublished 'Visitation of Cumberland'.

John Aubrey transcribed some of the notes, describing the henge 'the diameter of which Levell [the interior] is about 160 foot. The entrances into it lyeing north and south, are in widenesse about 15 foot a piece. That toward the North having two huge [stones] (viz: on each side one) of about five foot in thicknesse'.[21]

Aubrey compensated for the omission of 'stones' by drawing a plan showing the two uprights just outside the entrance. What is instructive is that King Arthur's Round Table is only 300 yards (274 m) east of a colossal circle-henge, Mayburgh, which may once have possessed not two but four stones standing in the opening through its bank, two pairs set at the corners of a rectangle, an example of the imposing portalled entrances for which the Lake District rings are justly renowned (Fig. 5).

(b) *Portals*

Mayburgh, 'the stony mound', is an astounding pile of hundreds of thousands of cobbles, each 'not much bigger than a man's fist', over 360 ft (110 m) from crest to crest of its tree-grown bank which averages 14 ft (4.3 m) in height and 120 ft (37 m) across at its base (Pl. 14). This monstrous enclosure surrounds an area 287 ft (88 m) across with a single entrance at the exact east.[22] The effort involved in building it was strenuous and protracted.

Pl. 14 Mayburgh, Penrith, Cumbria, from the south. The remaining pillar of a small ring or rectangle inside the enormous cobbled bank of the circle-henge.

Fig. 5 Five 'entrance' stone circles around the North Channel.

Pl. 15   Long Meg and Her Daughters near Penrith, Cumbria. From the west. The huge boulders of the portalled entrance are to the right of Long Meg, the sandstone outlier of one of the biggest stone circles in Britain.

Pl. 16   Swinside, Cumbria. The narrow portalled entrance at the south-east of one of the finest stone circles in western Europe.

In 1890 Dymond estimated that if a thousand men had toiled continuously eight hours day after day drudgingly carrying basketloads of stones from the nearby River Eamont, dumping their burdens onto the bank the project would have taken six months to complete. In reality it would have taken longer, only possible when the river was low enough and when there was no other work. It is also questioable whether there were as many as a thousand labourers available.

Demographic calculations about the size of pre-historic populations are subject to so many variables that conclusions are little more than guesses. Even so, the internal area of a circle or henge may provide a clue if one assumes that the larger the space the more participants it was meant to hold. In the Lake District it is noticeable that the smaller rings are in regions that are only lightly populated today: Castlerigg, an average-sized ring, stands close to Keswick with a population in AD 1971, of some 5000 inhabitants; the tinier circle of Grey Croft is near Gosforth with about 1000; and the immense Long Meg and Her Daughters (Pl. 15) sprawls in the vicinity of Penrith with almost 12,000.[23]

On the arbitrary assumption that the 8596 sq. ft (799 m^2) of Castlerigg could comfortably accommo-date one hundred people a crude projection for the population of the Lake District in its Late Neolithic heyday produces the figures given in Table 3.

The estimate of 750 for Mayburgh is not greatly short of Dymond's 1000. What it does not indicate, however, is who was allowed into the enclosure, whether women and children were excluded, whether the congregation contained members of other settle-ments, or even strangers participating in arcane rituals of gift-exchange for the prized axes.

Little information comes from the architecture of Mayburgh. There are seventeenth-century reports of an internal rectangular setting of four stones, possibly a version of a 'Scottish' Four-Poster stone circle. There are less reliable statements about four stones in the entrance. Aubrey mentioned only one 'very great stone' there but drew two standing outside the bank. Stukeley in 1725 wrote of stones being 'blown to pieces with gunpowder', adding 'some more lie at the entrance within side, others without, and fragments all about'. Forty-four years later Pennant claimed that 'four again stood on the sides of the entrance, viz. one on each exterior corner, and one on each interior'. Dymond was sceptical but admitted a possibility that 'the avenue of approach was flanked by at least two great stones on each side.'[24]

All but one of the hypothetical eight stones have disappeared, some blasted, others rumoured to have been removed in the fifteenth century to repair Eamont bridge a quarter of a mile (40 m) away. The destruc-tion has left the question of Mayburgh's portalled entrance unanswered although the known portals at Swinside and Long Meg in the same region make a similar setting at Mayburgh feasible.

Reaffirming the belief that these rings were in some way connected with the axe industry Stukeley was informed of 'a brass Celt', a bronze axe, being ploughed up inside Mayburgh. In 1879 a stone axe was unearthed from the entrance itself, possibly a deposit as de-liberate as the human remains at Stonehenge and Avebury, concealed in the ground as an amulet or offering to safeguard the enclosure. It is unlikely to be coincidental that an axe from the Langdales was buried by the entrance of another henge, the coastal Llandegai South-East near Bangor in north-west Wales.

Heavy portalled settings of four head-high pillars would have made the entry into a ritual area, 'sacred space' as it is termed in alliterated sociological jargon, even more awesome. It might be asked what need there was for such elaborately-treated entrances. The reason may have existed in the desire of builders of early stone circles to emulate the banked enclosures of the first henges, the earthen walls of the latter and

TABLE 3. *Estimated Late Neolithic Populations in the Lake District*

Name	Type of ring	Diameter		Area		Hypothetical Population	Population in AD 1971*	
		Ft	M	S.Ft.	M^2			
Brats Hill	Stone Circle	105 × 97	32 × 30	8,125	755	90	Drigg	446
Castlerigg	Stone Circle	108 × 98	33 × 30	8,596	799	100	Keswick	5,169
Elva Plain	Stone Circle	113	35	10,029	932	120	Bassenthwaite	437
Grey Croft	Stone Circle	89 × 83	27 × 25	5,961	554	70	Gosforth	922
Grey Yauds	Stone Circle	156?	48?	19,113	1,776	220	Alston	3,344
King Arthur's Round Table	Henge	167 × 148	51 × 45	19,412	1,803	230	Penrith	11,299
Long Meg & Her Daughters	Stone Circle	359 × 311	109 × 95	87,454	8,125	1,030	Penrith	11,299
Mayburgh	Circle-Henge	287	88	64,692	6,010	750	Penrith	11,299
Studfold	Stone Circle	110	34	9,503	882	110	Distington	2,093
Swinside	Stone Circle	94	29	6,940	645	80	Broughton-in-Furness	1,139

TOTAL POPULATION 2,800

(* of the nearest town)

the closely-grouped stones of the rings obscuring the inner precinct from the profane world outside, barriers interrupted by only a single and obvious entrance.

There is considerable difference between the megalithic rings of the Lake District, including the regions its traditions affected, and the circles of the Early Bronze Age. In general these were smaller, more open, with about twelve stones fairly evenly spaced 13 ft 9 (4.2 m) apart, around a ring 60 ft (18.3 m) across. There were as many 'entrances' as there were stones.[25]

Even omitting the statistically-distorting dimensions of the enormous Long Meg and Her Daughters the Lake District rings were bigger in area and size of stone but more cramped in the spacing of their uprights. They averaged 110 ft (34 m) across with some fifty-nine pillars around the perimeter and, allowing 2 ft (0.8 m) for the width of the pillars, no more than 4 ft 2 (1.3 m) from each other, a whirligig of stone quite unlike the open stateliness of the later rings (Table 4).

With so many narrow gaps a definite entrance was needed. At Castlerigg this was achieved by setting up two high stones as flankers. In other circles two portals were erected outside a pair of circle-stones to form a rectangular gateway (Pl. 16). Even in ruin these settings remain impressive.

At Long Meg and Her Daughters, a huge flattened circle erected on ground falling quite sharply from south to north two massive boulders, each weighing about thirty tons and requiring over a hundred men or more to move them into place, were set up just outside the ring at the south-west. High and heavy they formed the outer side of a portalled entrance 25 ft wide by 10 ft deep (7.6 × 3 m). Two other gigantic blocks marked the ENE–WSW ends of the ring's long axis. They seem to have been planned to point towards the midpoint between the south-west midwinter and north-west midsummer sunsets. Had the western horizon been level such a line would have pointed due west but the pronounced slope caused the midwinter sun to set behind the hills a little south of

south-west making the midpoint not west but slightly west–south-west.

This typical cardinal alignment was matched by a calendrical one. The western stones of the portals stood in line with a tall, shrivelled sandstone outlier, Long Meg, a long-forgotten witch turned to stone with her many daughters for their necromantical practices.

From the centre of the ring the two stones and outlier stood neatly in line with the midwinter sunset, and this explains why it was the side rather than the entrance itself that was used for observations. With Long Meg's wide entrance an observer 183 ft (56 m) away near the ring's centre would have had a 'window' nearly 8° wide to the distant horizon, far too inexact for an astronomical alignment. A line of two or three stones provided a much finer sighting device.

At Swinside in the south-west corner of the Lake District the circle has a thin, high needle of stone at its north and a portalled entrance, 6 ft wide and 8 ft deep (1.8 × 2.4 m), at the south-east. Its two northern stones stand in line with sunrise at the beginning of November, anticipating the Iron Age festival of Samain by over two thousand years. It was the time of year when the Celts believed the dead rose from their graves and it is still celebrated as the pagan Hallowe'en and the Christian All Saints Day. Across the Irish Sea the ring at Ballynoe was almost identical to Swinside in size and architecture except that the northern stones of its portals were set up towards the equinoctial sunset.

A little-known yet attractive Scottish circle is the Girdle Stanes, lined with trees and standing against the River White Esk which has undercut its western side tumbling a third of the ring into its waters. David Christison, one of the Secretaries of the Society of Antiquaries of Scotland planned it in 1897. He noticed a taller 'double stone' at the south-east with another large block standing 11 ft (3.4 m) away, presumably the remains of an entrance. They were 4 ft 4 and 4 ft 10 (1.3, 1.5 m) high respectively and arrested 'the eye of an onlooker from their size and proximity to each other'.[26] A long slab lay between Christison's

TABLE 4. *Stone Spacing and Entrance Widths in 'Lake District' Circles*

	Diameter		Perimeter		Approximate No. of Stones	Average Spacing Between Stones		Width of Entrance	
	Ft	M	Ft	M					
Ballynoe	108	33	339	104	72	2 ft 9	0.8	7	2.1
Brats Hill	105 × 97	32 × 30	319	97	52	4 ft 1	1.3	?	
Castlerigg	108 × 98	33 × 30	327	99	42	5 ft 10	1.8	12	3.7
Druids' Circle	84 × 80	26 × 24	259	79	30	6 ft 7	2.0	9	2.7
Girdle Stanes	128	39	402	123	56	5 ft 3	1.6	11	3.4
Grey Yauds	156?	48?	490?	151?	88?	3 ft 7	1.1	?	
Rollright Stones	108	33	339	104	72	2 ft 8	0.8	6	1.8
Swinside	94	29	295	91	60	2 ft 11	1.1	6	1.8
AVERAGES	110	34	346	106	59	4 ft 2	1.3	9	2.7

stones N and P, perhaps one of the outlying portals. Despite the ruinous state of the ring it is conceivable that the 'double' southern stones, like Swinside, once stood in line with the November sunrise.

The design of other more distant rings also seems to have been influenced by this custom of putting up portalled entrances. The strangely beautiful Pobull Fhinn on North Uist in the Hebrides, overlooking a loch and distances of grassy machair with water lilies, marsh marigolds and orchids, overflown by lapwings, thinly whistling dunlins and shrieking oystercatchers, has broad entrances at the ESE and WNW ends of its axis.

In Wales, on the headland of Penmaenmawr above Conway Bay and close to the axe-factory at Graig Llwyd the furtive Druids' Circle crouches in a hollow alongside an ancient trackway. The 'circle' is actually an irregular oval, grim but grandiose despite the stone-robbing and explosions it has suffered. 'In 1846 the circle still retained some large monoliths that have now disappeared ... [and] some of these may have stood upright at the entrance'.[27] There were tall stones at the north. At the south-west was a portalled entrance, one stone of which now lies a full 13 ft (4 m) inside the ring.

Even farther from the Lake District are the ragged limestone blocks of the Rollright Stones in Oxfordshire, savagely weathered, wrote Stukeley, 'by the harsh jaws of Time'. Until recently it was thought the ring had only twenty-two stones, the other lumps and fragments being no more than pieces broken from them but field-surveys and excavations between 1982 and 1984 showed instead that this had truly been a 'Lake District' ring, large, with seventy or more closely-set stones and a portalled entrance, now fallen, at the south-east.[28] The northern portals were in line with the major southern moonrise.

There is a seeming contradiction between the spaciousness of these rings and the narrowness of the access to them. Most entrances are no more than 8 or 9 ft (2.4, 2.7 m) wide. Even Long Meg, capable of containing four-hundred uncrowded people, has an entrance only 25 ft (7.6 m) across. The compactness of all these portals implies a intention to have a controlled approach to the rings. Rather than a untidy mob straggling through gaps between stones there is an impression of order, a procession no more than two or three abreast, passing ceremoniously between the four great stones.

This applied even to the sarsen ring of Stonehenge's last phase. It is not suggested that the builders of that lintelled circle, raised a thousand years after Castlerigg and Swinside, were influenced by Cumbrian traditions. But a surviving stone, historical records and excavation show that the north-eastern entrance through the bank of the henge was once dominated by four towering pillars so closely-set that access to the interior was very constricted.

The one survivor, Stone 95, popularly known as the Slaughter Stone, lies just inside the entrance. It is 21 ft 6 long, 6 ft 9 wide and 2 ft 9 thick (6.6 × 2.1 × 0.8 m), nearly thirty tons of coarse sarsen. It once had a partner almost as big. Excavation in 1920 came upon 'a very large hole roughly 10 feet in diameter by 6½ feet deep' (3 × 2 m) only 8 ft 6 (2.6 m) north-west of the Slaughter Stone, a space six times narrower than the avenue that led up to it.[29]

Inigo Jones, the royal architect, who visited Stonehenge in 1620 when all four portal stones were still upright considered the ring was a Roman temple with three entrances. He wrote of 'The great stones which made the entrances from the outside of the Trench [the henge ditch] seven foot broad, three foot thick and twenty foot high' (2.1 × 1 × 6.1 m), measurements for the Slaughter Stone which accord very well with those of Herbert Stone 304 years later.[30]

Jones was in error concerning the number of entrances but not about the four stones. His nephew, John Webb, had access to Jones's posthumous notes. In a book defending his uncle's mistaken theories Webb recorded only one entrance and sketched it

1. *The Trench.*
2. *The Entrance thereat from the North-East.*
3. *The two Pyramids thereof, on the outside of the Trench.*
4. *The other two on the inside.*
5. *The Pylasters of the outward Circle, or Supporters of the open Gallery, as G. Cambrensis hath it.*
6. *The Architraves incumbent on them.*
7. *The Perpendicular Stones of the inner Circle.*
8. *The Pylasters of the greater Hexagon.*
9. *The Architraves that adorn them.*
10. *The Pylasters of the lesser Hexagon.*

Fig. 6   Stonehenge, a drawing by John Webb in 1665, from his *Stone-Heng, a Roman Work and Temple*, London, 1725, 141. It shows the four portal stones at the north-east entrance.

showing the four great portals (Fig. 6). These stones, several times the height of a man, rose high above the ends of the bank, monumental, a majestic threshold to the stone circle beyond.

The chronology of entrances and portals is insecure. The production of Cumbrian stone axes endured for many centuries, from as early as 3700 BC to as late as 2200 BC,[31] and it might be no more than guesswork to place the erection of great stone circles at any precise point within that period.

Fortunately, there is the guidemark of a radio-carbon assay, 2525±85 bc (GU-1591),[32] the approximate equivalent of 3300 BC, quite early in the history of the stone axe industry. It came from the mutilated site of the Lochmaben Stane near Gretna Green. This ring, once a spacious oval but now reduced to one large stone and a possible companion, stood on the northern fringe of the Lake District stone circle complex and there are reasons for believing it to be somewhat later than the majority of the megalithic rings at the heart of the axe production region.[33]

If the supposition is correct, and if the C-14 determination is reliable, then, although mainly confined to the Lake District and never numerous, the custom of constructing portalled entrances to stone circles was probably well-established before 3000 BC. The addition to these portals of one or two more pairs of standing stones would have created a short avenue.

CHAPTER FIVE

AVENUES AND STONE CIRCLES 2600–2000 BC

*From the south entrance [at Avebury] runnes a Solemne Walke, with Stones pitched on
end about seven foot high+, wch goes as far as Kynet wch is (at least) a measured mile from
Aubury . . . The distance of the stones in this Walk, and the breadth of it, is much about the
distance of a noble Walk of Trees of that length: and very probable this Walke was made
for Processions*

John Aubrey, *Monumenta Britannica I*, 1665–93, 37

INTRODUCTION

Other than in England avenues are uncommon in
Britain, Ireland and Brittany. And other than in
Cumbria, where they began, and in Wessex, including
Dartmoor to its west, they are rare even in England.

Just as the Lake District had been the birthplace of
portalled entrances to stone circles so, at one time, it
also contained several long avenues of standing stones
leading to other rings (Fig. 7). So many of these
approaches have been dismantled or utterly effaced
that it is difficult to appreciate how numerous and
magnificent these lines once were.

Megalithic avenues are parallel settings of three or
more pairs of upright stones attached to a circle.
Earthen avenues existed, the worn-down banks of one
just discernible over the final hundred yards or so at
Stonehenge. What timber lines there were have long
since decayed. Even avenues of heavy boulders have
been so vulnerable that hardly any have survived the
centuries. In Brittany they have been obliterated. In
Ireland, Scotland and Wales they were few and widely
dispersed. In England mediaeval peasants at Avebury
piously buried the pagan stones. Eighteenth-century
landlords blew up the boulders or ripped them out to
clear the land, often superstitiously replacing them,
albeit inexactly, when the new field refused to yield
crops. With the Enclosure Acts what had been occasional demolition became wholesale disruption as
tenant farmers exploited every inch of their holdings.
Only at Avebury and Callanish do avenues endure in
anything like their former condition, both of them
preserved by the unintended protection of man and
nature. Even the Kennet Avenue's 'measured mile'
may be deceptive. It may have started as a much
shorter setting.

ORIGINS. THE SHORT AVENUES

Just as a simple entrance consisting of a wide gap and
tall flankers could be enhanced by the addition of two
portals so, it seems, the portalled entrance itself could
be embellished by the introduction of further outlying
pairs that transformed the portals into short avenues.
Examples can be seen at Stanton Drew in Somerset,
apparently influenced by the architectural traditions of
north-west England.

Even though over two hundred miles (322 km) of
the Pennines and the Midland Plain separated them
there need be no surprise that Cumbria and northern
Wessex should be culturally related. By Late Neolithic
times contacts between them were well-established.
Stone axes from the Lake District prove this.

Axes from both Cornwall and Cumbria are plentiful
in Wessex but an east-west line dividing south from
north Wiltshire reveals a clear difference in their
distribution. To the south around Salisbury Plain in
Wiltshire, in Dorset and Somerset eighty per cent of
the provenanced tools come from either Cornwall or
south-west Wales. To the north of the line around
the Marlborough Downs and in Gloucestershire and
Oxfordshire the proportion falls to forty-five per cent.
Conversely, only thirty of the known 151 axes in the
southern counties came from the north.

But for axes from north Wales near the Druids'
Circle and from the Langdales the ratios are emphati-
cally reversed.[1] Well over half the stone axes in north
Wiltshire came from those sources proving the links
that existed with Cumbria and Wales (Table 5). The
discovery of Group VI Langdale axes in Oxfordshire
might also explain the presence there of the 'Cumbrian'
circle of the Rollright Stones only forty miles (64 km)
north of Avebury.

Six miles (10 km) south of Bristol the three stone
circles at Stanton Drew stand in meadowland by the
River Chew, their unworked stones mostly of local
breccia (Pl. 17). The rings lie on a twisted NE–SSW
axis. The north-east ring once had eight stones, the
south–south-west ring, badly ruined, perhaps twelve.
The great central circle, about 368 ft (112 m) in diam-

AVENUES
1 Callanish
2 Broomend of Crichie
3 Milfield
4 Shap
5 Broughderg
6 Arbor Low
7 Stanton Drew
8 Avebury
9 Stonehenge
10 Shovel Down
11 Yellowmead
12 Trowlesworthy Warren
13 Landaoudec
14 Kergonan

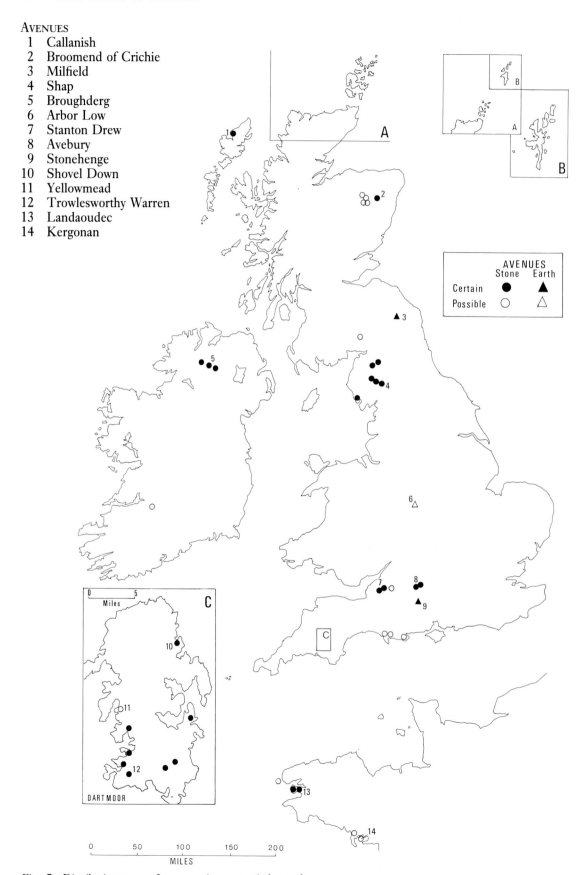

Fig. 7 Distribution map of avenues in stone circles and cromlechs.

Pl. 17   The tumbled stones of the Stanton Drew Centre and North-East circles, Somerset. From the north-east.

eter, is the largest stone circle in western Europe after the Outer Circle at Avebury.

Two short, devastated avenues extend westwards uphill from the river. One leading west–north-west to the north-east ring may have been composed of eight stones, one now missing and only three standing, in four pairs of an avenue 108 ft long and 28 ft wide (33 × 8.5 m). A shorter avenue of three pairs approached the central circle. Five stones remain, three standing, in a line 164 ft long and 34 ft wide (50 × 10 m).[2]

Although the entire complex is in disarray with monstrous blocks gnawed, rutted and overgrown in such a confusion of stone that little certain can be claimed about the original layout these settings appear to be additions to the circles. It is noticeable that the avenue of the great circle has pillars of siliceous breccia different from those of the ring, and that its stones are graded in height, the tallest 8 ft (2.4 m) high, much higher than those of the ring. Its companions decline in height to a mere 3 ft 2 (1 m) down the slope.

The mineralogy of the other avenue also is different from that of its circle. Although the stones nearest the ring are large, 10 ft and 12 ft 6 (3, 3.8 m) long the rest of the avenue is so displaced that it would be overconfident to claim grading for them.

Had the two short avenues been extended eastwards they would have intersected about 300 ft (90 m) from the circles. Such an arrangement seems meaningless unless the intention had been for the lines ulti-

TABLE 5. *The Distribution of Stone Axes in Wiltshire and Neighbouring Counties*

Source	S. Wilts	Dorset	Somerset	Total	N. Wilts	Gloucs	Oxon	Total
Cornwall and S.W. Wales	43	52	26	121	46	17	16	79
Lake District	7	6	6	19	22	23	26	71
North Wales	2	3	6	11	12	11	4	27
TOTALS	52	61	38	151	80	51	46	177

Pl. 18   The Kennet avenue, Avebury, from the south.

mately to merge into one stone-lined way descending to the river 130 yards (120 m) away down the slope, a Y-shaped setting unique in megalithic history.

At Avebury thirty miles (48 km) to the east the meandering mile and a half (2.4 km) of the Kennet Avenue may also have originated as a short avenue of high stones on an alignment unlike that of the later extensions. Today there is one tall stone, no, 4b, 9 ft 8 (3 m) high, and some ugly, hiphigh concrete obelisks just outside Avebury's SSE entrance and it is only when one has walked over the brow of the gentle rise that the first pair of stones, nos. 13a and b, is reached, nearly 300 yards (274 m) from the entrance. From there the avenue stretches south-east and then SSE in a series of straightish sections (Pl. 18).

Once there were four pairs of towering sarsens, nos. 1a to 4b, leading directly from the entrance in a short avenue, NNW−SSE, 200 ft long and 45 ft wide (60 × 14 m). Spaced 50 ft (15 m) apart the pairs were set much closer together than the 80 ft (24 m) average of the longer stretches of avenue. John Aubrey saw these tall stones in 1649 and was later informed that one had fallen. 'The great stone at Aubury's townes end, where this Walke begins, fell down in Autumne 1694, and broke in two, or three pieces: it stood but two foot deep in the earth'. The same sacrifice of stability and safety for the sake of spectacular effect was accepted by the builders of Stonehenge.[3]

There is little doubt that the four now-lost pairs formed the first part of the Kennet Avenue. An attempt was made to link the later lines of stone with them. 'There is a sharp, awkward turn with 5a and b but no satisfactory junction is effected with the four pairs at the entrance'. A minor mystery remains. Nothing is known of what happened to the sixteen stones, nos. 5a to 12b, filling the long gap between the short avenue and the long. 'There is no clue as to the fate of these [eight] pairs; none was visible in Stukeley's time and excavation revealed only the holes in which they had stood, but no evidence for burial or burning'.

From John Aubrey's plan and notes it appears that the stones 'where this Walke begins' were still standing in September, 1663. 'From the south *Part* entrance runnes a solemne Walke, sc, with Stones pitched on end about seven foot high+'. It may be that being so close to the entrance they were too dangerously tall and heavy for mediaeval villagers to risk toppling. Certainly it was the smaller stones of the Avebury rings that they superstitiously buried.

The first avenue pairs may have remained *in situ* until the later part of the seventeenth century when 'About 1694, *Walter Stretch* . . . found out the way of demolishing these stones by fire'. In 1723 Stukeley also recorded that from the south entrance 'Twenty four stones on both sides, next following, are carried off'.

During Keiller's excavations it was noticed that 'some of the stoneholes were thought to have been cut into by metal spades so that the stones . . . may have been overthrown and dragged away bodily to be broken up elsewhere'. It is unproveable. The fate of these missing stones is yet another megalithic mystery.[4]

No prehistoric region was a perfect copy of another. The short avenues of the two Wessex circles were like aggrandised versions of Cumbrian portalled entrances but unlike those portals there were no astronomical sightlines in them. Such absence is not unexpected if, as suspected at Stanton Drew, the avenues were additions to existing rings in which there were no celestial alignments. There was none in either of Avebury's north and south circles nor in its outer ring. The Kennet Avenue, moreover, began not at the inner circles but outside the overpowering bank of the surrounding earthwork, built dauntingly as a defensive work rather than as an observatory.[5]

Only the ruins remain. Once the stones of these short avenues stood as stiffly erect as soldiers of an honour-guard at the gates of a palace. Now they sag and slump like the aftermath of a firing-squad. Sometimes they cannot even be recognised.

At many circles these short approaches may have become no more than parts of later elongations of the avenue, the first stones indistinguishable from the later, and it was possibly by such accretions over the decades rather than by initial design that some avenues became as long as they are.

That avenues were lengthened, extending them section by section for a mile (1.6 km) or more, is hinted at by the obvious changes of direction that some have. The Shap avenue in Westmorland led northwards from Kemp Howe stone circle then abruptly swung towards the north-west, perhaps as a single line, as though, years after the construction of the avenue, people decided to link it with the distant cairn at Skellaw. The earthen avenue at Stonehenge in its beginning around 2200 BC extended exactly straight for a quarter of a mile (0.4 km), ending near the bottom of a shallow valley. Over eight hundred years later an extension was added, swinging the avenue suddenly eastwards for a mile or more towards the River Avon. Revealing the interruptions that were commonplace in prehistory the project was never completed.[6]

Further evidence that these long avenues were composed of successive segments comes from the northern third of the Kennet Avenue, the sole avenue to be systematically excavated. Its stones, religiously toppled and buried in the fourteenth century, were disinterred and re-erected between 1934 and 1939 under the direction of Alexander Keiller, a wealthy amateur archaeologist who subsidised several important excavations around Avebury. Places where stones had been broken up or removed were indicated by effective but unevocative concrete markers.

Keiller and his colleague, Stuart Piggott, noticed that the course of the avenue 'was tortuous but not

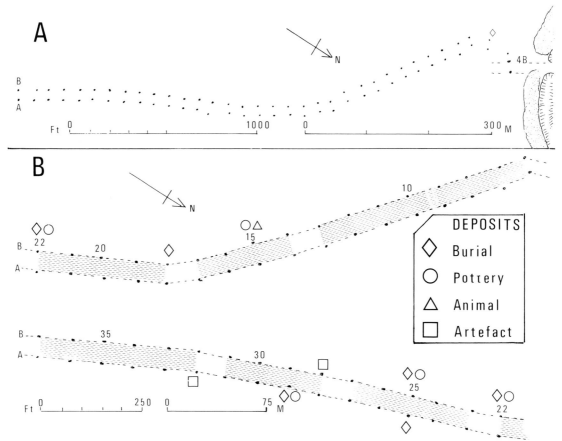

Fig. 8   The straight stretches of the Kennet avenue, Avebury, and the deposits alongside the stones. (A) after Keiller & Piggott. (B) after A. & A.S. Thom.

sinuous, being laid out in a series of relatively straight sections of various lengths'. Years later Alexander Thom and his son made a characteristically accurate survey and deduced 'that the six sections ... identified in the figure were intentionally straight.'[7]

The avenue stones are numbered 1a to 37b, 1a being the tall sarsen that once stood on the east of Avebury's south entrance, 1b its partner on the right-hand side looking from the earthwork. Their counterparts, 37a and 37b, were at the far end of the avenue where a shabby layby and swing-gate provide entry to the stones. Because of missing stones the Thoms plotted only from pairs 6a, b, two concrete obelisks, to 37a, b, two sarsens. They concluded that there were six straight segments: pair 6 to 14, 627 ft (191 m) long; 15 to 17, 202 ft (62 m) long; 18 to 22, 397 ft (121 m); 23 to 27, 349 ft (106 m); 28 to 32, 343 ft (105 m); and 33 to 37, an inconclusive stretch that terminated at unexcavated ground (Fig. 8).

There are clumsy joins where sections meet, particularly between pairs 5 and 6, and 17 and 19 but the Thoms' plan accords well with that of Keiller and

Piggott and it is likely that the interpretation of the stretches and the joints is correct. It is significant that in each new section prehistoric people deposited offerings. In the stonehole of 5b there was the head of a human legbone, in 5a a flint arrowhead and ox-bones. At 15b there was a sherd of Grooved Ware, eight flint flakes, a pig's jawbone, and ox bones and ribs; at 18b, a crouched human burial, probably of a man; and at the end of that line in 22b an intact Grooved Ware bowl and a human burial. Nothing was found in pairs 23 or 24. In 25b there were the remains of three individuals and a broken beaker. The burial was part of the stonehole, the grave dug after the stone had been set up 'but while it was artifically supported'. Part of a human skull lay by 25a.

At the start of the next stretch in 28b were seventy-seven flint flakes and some native Peterborough sherds. In 29a was a grave with the shattered bits of an early beaker in it. Stonehole 32a contained a polissoir, a sarsen block used as a rubbing-stone for sharpening axes. Not one find of significance came from any one of the other forty-four stoneholes.

The final part of the avenue was disturbed by an occupation site between pairs 28 and 32 with broken pieces of native pots, hearths and rubbish-pits, flint knives and scrapers and a broken stone axe from north Wales. And at the very end of the avenue, nearly 1600 yards (1460 m) to the south-east, where it led up to the Sanctuary stone circle on Overton Hill, Maud Cunnington recovered 'fragments of bone' from four of the eight stoneholes she opened there.[8] From this, it seems that like the specially-treated entrances to henges the extensions to avenues also were enhanced by deposits at the time that the stones were put in place.

As the result of additions and of later destruction, especially amongst the slighter lines, very few short avenues remain unaffected and recognisable. Hundreds of miles north-west of Avebury, in the Sperrin mountains near Strabane, the little Irish ring of Knocknahorna, 'barley hill', is thick with undergrowth and cut by a barbed-wire fence. Its stones are low but at the south-east two portals set at right-angles to the perimeter are 4 ft (1.2 m) high. Outside them are two or three pairs of grass-high stones in a line 8 ft (2.4 m) long and perhaps half as wide, a setting aptly described by Frances Lynch as a 'false portal'.[9]

Nothing is known about the contents or date of this lonely ring. Its remoteness, its size, its tiny stones all suggest a considerable distance in time from the Late Neolithic avenues at Avebury and Stanton Drew. Its short avenue may have been one of the last to be set up. Before then many much longer avenues had been erected in Cumbria and Wessex.

DISTRIBUTION OF THE LONG AVENUES

There was never an abundance of avenues, short or long. Of more than a thousand known stone circles and cromlechs in Britain, Ireland and Brittany fewer than fifty may have had those approaches and fourteen of these are not confirmed. An avenue of postholes is known from Dorset. Three earthen avenues are recorded including the dubious line at Arbor Low, the erratic banks at Milfield in Northumberland, and the best example, the nicely laid-out Stonehenge avenue.

Of the thirty-two confirmed megalithic avenues, if allowing only one, the southern, at Shap, five are in Cumbria and six in Wessex, over a third of the total. If the ten certain avenues on Dartmoor at the western edge of Wessex are included the proportion rises to sixty-six per cent increasing the likelihood that the lines had an origin in the Lake District and a secondary development in south and, ultimately, south-west England. No other region contains more than three undisputed avenues and no other region is close to another. Even in Brittany the départements of Finistère and Morbihan were separated by the central wooded hills of the Argoat. Between the Crozon pen-

insula and Carnac were 125 km (78 miles) of forest and river or an easier but longer 240 km (150 miles) of tortuous coastline.

(a) *England*
   (i) *Cumbria*
Of the two major regions of avenues in England, Cumbria and Wessex, not a single site in the north has survived the destructive avarice of man. Lacra NE, Moor Divock, Grey Yauds, others, it is a catalogue of such devastation that, apart from local studies, archaeological books no longer mention the lines that existed here. Only a stone or two are their relics, a pillar at Grey Yauds, a few footballish boulders of the avenues that led to the north-eastern of the four Lacra circles on a bleak hill above the sea, almost undetectable in the windblown sour grass and the moorland stones littered thickly amongst them.

With the eye of faith one can see an avenue extending ENE from the battered ring for 150 ft (46 m) while to the WSW is a second avenue in even more turmoil. An Early Bronze Age collared urn was found upside down and buried inside the circle, perhaps fashioned around 1800 BC.[10] The avenues may be later still.

The erstwhile avenue on Moor Divock near Pooley Bridge is even worse. Stukeley would have welcomed its snakelike twisting and curling, first NNW then northwest, finally WSW as it strayed from kerb-circle to kerb-circle, one of them 'a charming little prehistoric gem' in which, on 30 May 1866, a complete Early Bronze Age food-vessel, of the same general period as the Lacra urn, was discovered. About 160 yards (145 m) to the north was a collapsed cairn from which an urn was dug out. It was 'of the rudest manufacture, sun-dried'. Its rim was intact but almost instantly fell to pieces and the fragments were thrown away. It is possible that the hut-circles and cairns not far to the west were also of the Bronze Age, the homes and burial-places of the community that raised the rows and circles.

The Moor Divock avenue of low stones, 20 ft (6 m) wide and in 1885 estimated to be 540 wandering yards (494 m) long has gone. 'There is now no trace of this avenue, and its former existence has been questioned'.[11] The scepticism was as unwarranted as the destruction, much of it caused by cairns and kerb-circles being converted into shooting-hides. The avenue stones were removeable nuisances.

Nothing more displays the reduction of Cumbrian avenues than the fate of the lines of massive boulders at Shap in Westmorland. There, twenty mountainous miles (32 km) ESE of Castlerigg, were nearly two miles (3.2 km) of stones, some many tons in weight. Today there are no more than a few desolate pillars, so far from each other, so trapped in walled fields, that it is impossible to visualise how the complex once looked.

In the sixteenth century Camden noticed part of it,

Fig. 9 The Shap avenue, Cumbria. A sketch by Lady Lowther, 1775. From *TCWAAS 15 (O.S.)*, 1898–9, Plate II. From the south.

'large stones in the form of Pyramids (some of them 9 foot high and 14 thick) set almost in a direct line, and at equal distances, for a mile together'.

Formerly there may have been three separate lines at Shap, one a dubious avenue, maybe one thousand yards (915 m) long, aligned north-westwards on Skellaw cairn, 'the place of skulls'. Only a few western stones survive. A single row to the west and further north extended beyond the concentric cairn-circle of Knipe Scar. A more definite avenue of lower stones ran south from Shap over land known as Karl Lofts for three quarters of a mile (1.2 km) up to the large stone circle of Kemp Howe. Perhaps as wide as 70 feet (21 m) and with uprights spaced about 35 ft (11 m) apart it probably contained well over two hundred local granite stones and erratics (Fig. 9).

When Stukeley saw 'the great Celtic temple' in 1725 many of the stones had already been broken up. 'It proceeds northwards [from Kemp Howe] to the town [Shap], which intercepts the continuation of it, and was the occasion of its ruin; for many of the stones are put under the foundations of houses and walls ... or blown up with gunpowder'. Mistaking the northern 'avenue' and the single row to its west for the remains of an interrupted extension to the southern avenue he said that the line curved westwards, claimed it was serpentine, saw the immense Goggleby Stone, but was prevented from drafting what would have been an informative plan by rain that has so often accompanied attempts to make surveys of avenues. A later draft, made at Stukeley's request by Thomas Routh in 1743, has been lost.

As late as 1800 there was still much to be seen. Sir Richard Colt Hoare, the Wiltshire antiquarian, riding

from Shap wrote, ' ... on the left of the great road leading to Kendall over the moors is a most curious and singular piece of antiquity. It consists of a long avenue of large stones, placed at different intervals and extending nearly two miles. One end seems to have terminated in this common, as the avenue closes with a row of stones placed in a semi-circular form [presumably the already-slighted Kemp Howe stone circle]. This end stands nearly south and from thence the avenue takes a curve inclining to the west. The line of these stones may be traced to the village of Rasgill where I saw one of them. Many of these lying in corn and meadow lands have been blown up and removed. Enough however are left to ascertain the direction they took. The stone resembles red granite. They are all unhewn. I have not yet heard any account given of this singular piece of antiquity'.

More damage to the southern end of the avenue was reported in 1824. 'Both rows were tolerably perfect till the enclosure of the common in 1815.' Near their end a small cairn of cobblestones, quite unlike the local limestone, also was levelled.

Today there is little left. Knipe Scar has gone. Kemp Howe, already spoiled, was further mutilated by railway construction in the nineteenth century and today it is a wreck of tumbled pinkish boulders lying in confusion by the train-line.

Some avenue stones were enormous. A survivor, the Goggleby Stone, is 7 ft (2.1 m) high and weighs some twelve tons. This top-heavy triangular granite boulder may have stood opposite a rectangular block. 'The pairing of tabular stones with triangular ones is not unknown in analogous sites where the two shapes are thought to represent male and female forms.'[12]

The same has been claimed for the sarsens in the Kennet Avenue. The Shap avenue must have been comparable to it.

(ii) *Wessex*
The avenue of stones leading southwards from the circle-henge of Avebury is the most famous of these linear settings, once some one hundred pairs of stones along a zigzagging course about one and a half miles (2.4 km) long, turning south-eastwards up Overton Hill to the Sanctuary stone circle.

Perhaps because they were regarded superstitiously as part of a pagan ring some stones may have been uprooted and buried in the early fourteenth century before the Black Death of 1349 left too few villagers for further megalithic exorcism. When John Aubrey saw the stones in 1649 many were still erect and he noticed how Avebury was connected to the 'Walke and the lesser Temple [the Sanctuary] appendant to it'. Perceptively he added that it was 'very probable this Walke was made for Processions'.

In the early eighteenth century scores of stones were broken up for houses. William Stukeley saw the continuing destruction of the avenue when only seventy-two stones could be seen of the original two hundred. Further demolition in the nineteenth century followed. By 1908 only thirteen stones were visible, four upright and nine fallen but between 1934 and 1939 many stones in the northern half were disinterred and re-erected.

On average the avenue was 49 ft (15 m) wide, its pairs set laterally about 80 ft (24.5 m) apart. They were local sarsens from the Marlborough Downs four miles (6.4 km) away. Two shapes are recognisable, a tall, thin pillar and a squatter lozenge. These were erected alternately down each side of the avenue and also set opposite each other across the row. Although their shapes are entirely natural the obvious selection and disposition of the two types has led to their interpretation as representations of male and female fertility symbols. The stones are not remarkably large, seven to eight tons in weight, and 5 ft to 14 ft (1.5–4 m) long, rising in height as they approached Avebury's SSE entrance.[13]

There the space between the pinnacles of sarsen contracted to 45 ft (14 m) and beyond the bank the causeway was as narrow as 20 ft (6 m) before the ditch's chalk rims eroded,[14] another instance of a constricted entrance.

It is ironical that whereas the reconstructed Kennet Avenue is now one of the best-preserved settings its companion, the Beckhampton Avenue at Avebury's western entrance, has almost entirely gone.

No discussion of avenues would be complete without reference to this controversial line. William Stukeley in 1722 was the first antiquarian to realise what the few prostrate stones in the village street had been. Others had been broken up for walls and bridges and houses, their holes leaving 'marks yet to be seen in the Corn'.

Only three remained standing, the Devil's Quoits, or Adam and Eve or the Longstones as they are still called. One was destroyed in Stukeley's time. When another fell in 1911 it was re-erected the following year. A skeleton was found by it with a beaker of the same period as those in the Kennet Avenue.[15]

As the three stones were in the fields a good three-quarters of a mile (1.2 km) south-west of Avebury doubts have been expressed about the reliability of Stukeley's interpretation, even of his integrity. He had gradually persuaded himself that the avenue had been a landscaped replica of the tail of the sacred serpent, Avebury being its body and the Kennet Avenue and the Sanctuary circle its neck and head. He is known to have falsified distances to suit his theories and it has been argued that credulously, with wishful thinking, he accepted sarsens lying casually in the meadows as evidence of the avenue he needed for the tail of his 'serpent'.[16]

It is more feasible that the opposite is true, that it was only after his recognition of the actual Beck-hampton Avenue and his planning of its course that he became aware of how snakelike it and the Kennet Avenue were. In 1722 he was not yet a biassed convert to dracontia. He found no difficulty the next year in accepting the unsnaking Stonehenge avenue. 'Stone-henge strait avenue from the gate to the valley is 1400 cubits'.[17] But by 1724 he was full of serpents.

Geo-physical examination in January 1989 of the avenue's suspected course failed to produce incontrovertible proof of stoneholes but this may have been due to the unresponsive nature of the ground.[18] What is little appreciated is that there is impartial confirmation of the avenue. The Rev. Thomas Twining, vicar of Wilsford and Charlton eight miles (13 km) south of Avebury, an exact contemporary of, but possible stranger to, Stukeley, made several visits to Avebury in the early 1700s while writing a book to prove that Romans had built the circle and avenues. Like Stukeley he also saw not only the Longstones but other fallen stones of the Beckhampton Avenue.

'Hence the large Stones to the West, the Remains of the Discus [part of the avenue] are still call'd the Devil's Coits . . . a part of the Discus, *as other Stones lying in the same Field do show* [my italics] to justifie the Figure I have assigned the Whole', referring to his plan of the Avebury complex.[19] His unprejudiced statement owed nothing to Stukeley's quite independent researches.

Stukeley himself sensibly confirmed his ideas by questioning villagers about missing stones. '*Richard Fowler* shew'd me the ground here, where he took several stones and demolish'd them'. '*Mr Alexander* told me he remember'd several stones standing by the parting of the roads under *Bekamton*, demolish'd by *Richard Fowler*.' As other buried stones have been located the former existence of a long, sarsen-lined avenue leading to Avebury from the west is probable if not proven.[20]

It, the Kennet Avenue and the Avebury Outer Circle may have been prototypes for other double-avenued rings such as Lacra in Westmorland – but four-hundred times bigger. Both at Lacra and at Stanton Drew, Broomend of Crichie and perhaps at Callanish two or more avenues may have been intended. The Beckhampton Avenue would not have been unique.

Other Wessex avenues are more problematical. The two banks of one put up at Stonehenge, arguably by users of beaker pottery around 2200 BC, are not in dispute. Forty ft (12 m) wide this earthen avenue led unswervingly for a quarter of a mile up to the north-east entrance of the earthwork. What is debateable is whether there was an avenue of standing stones inside or even on its banks.

Aubrey, who did not notice the banks, thought the Heel Stone was a survivor of a megalithic setting. 'Northeastward from Stoneheng is a Stone a good distance off which seemes (to me) to be the remaine of it'. Stukeley, the first to detect the weathered banks, was undecided. In 1723 he wrote and then deleted, 'there is not one stone left thereof, yet a curious eye without difficulty will discover a mark of the holes whence they were taken ... this magnificent Walk or Entry is made by two rows of Stones containing fifty on a side'. Seventeen years later in his book, *Stonehenge*, he made no reference to the missing stones. His friend, Roger Gale, reproved him for the omission. 'The avenue up to the chief entrance was formerly planted with great stones, opposite to each other, upon the side banks of it, for I very well remember we observed the holes where they had been fixed.'[21]

Doubt is justified. Gale's 'stones' on the banks would have lined an avenue about 55 ft (17 m) wide. Geophysical examination in the Octobers of 1979 and 1980 failed to resolve the question. Anomalies that may have been stoneholes were recorded but they were few and ambiguous.[22]

The Heel Stone and its lost partner, Stone 97, inside the avenue are irrelevant to the problem. Together with the Slaughter Stone and its missing companion at the north-east entrance they once formed a narrow 9 ft wide, 100 ft long (3 × 30 m) rectangle through which the midsummer sun shone at its rising. It was a setting within a setting but one that was centuries later than the avenue. The manually-smoothed surfaces of the Slaughter Stone suggest that it was erected during the sarsen rather than the bluestone phase of Stonehenge. Stonehenge's earthen avenue is certain. Without excavation its stone equivalent must remain more mythical than megalithic.

The same is true of Little Mayne, a dubious site near the south coast. Roger Gale described it to Stukeley.

A mile S.E. of Dorchester, at Priors Maen, was a circle of stones lately broken to pieces by the owner of the ground, called Tallbot. The stones were very large and rude.... There were two avenues pitcht of stones leading up to it, one from the South, the other from the East, as I could perceive from their remains, like those at Abury.

Tempting though it may be to equate Little Mayne with other Wessex circles possessing two avenues the surveyors of the Royal Commission were entirely unconvinced. To them the stones were nothing more than a natural scatter of sarsens near the farm, and one of the 'avenues' was 'certainly a mediaeval road.'[23]

Two other Dorset rings are just as unsatisfactory. A few miles west of Little Mayne the small and much disturbed circle of Hampton Down had a 4 ft (1.2 m) wide track leading to it from the north but if this had been an avenue it was a very poor one. Equally, the damaged and overgrown circle of Rempstone near Corfe Castle may have had an associated avenue but its credentials are suspect. Two parallel lines of buried stones on Rollington Hill half a mile west of the ring had been dug out by a farmer to avoid damage to his plough. The 'avenue' was 9 ft (2.7 m) wide, its pairs set 15 ft (4.6 m) apart. There were very few other stones within 30 yards (27 m) of the lines of which about 112 yards (100 m) had been uncovered. The direction seemed 'to be following the easiest gradient up a slight incline which if continued would pass just in front of Rempstone Hall.'[24] The setting was destroyed in September, 1957 with no excavation or detailed plan.

(iii) *Dartmoor*

What scanty evidence there is for early Neolithic settlement on Dartmoor indicates a few limited territories on patches of heath amongst forested hills. Cattle could be grazed in the clearings and red deer hunted in the surrounding woods. Scatters of leaf-shaped flint arrowheads and tools, a few long chambered tombs such as Corringdon Ball, give an impression of small communities on the very edge of the upland, 'farming groups gradually enlarging their clearings in the woodland and setting up ritual structures which both served a spiritual need and demonstrated their stable prosperity.'[25] The settlements were probably limited in number and dispersed.

It may have been the disruption of the Late Neolithic, of an epidemic, or pressure on land caused by an expanding population, that forced some families away from Wessex. The lands to the east and south were already taken. To the north was a lack of stone. If ceremonial rings were set up there they were of perishable timber of which no signs have been recognised. But the west was open.

A dramatic, probably over-dramatic, picture has been drawn of the exodus. 'It is probable that the early inhabitants of Dartmoor were driven into these bleak and barren regions from pleasanter and more fertile lands ... and that the parallelitha [stone rows] and

Pl. 19   The Shovel Down avenue, Dartmoor, from the north.
A double row can be seen beyond it.

circles . . . were built in humble imitation of more splendid temples in the lower country'. There was a paradox. Although these settlers were numerous they were also feeble and impoverished 'yet their puny works have survived the gigantic Abury.'[26]

The truth was probably more prosaic, straggles of men, women, children, cattle, sledges, on a long, slow uncertain trek westwards, cautiously exploring the foothills of Dartmoor, avoiding settled areas, seeking unclaimed land.

Large free-standing stone circles had already been erected at Dartmoor's north-eastern corner, the driest, most-sheltered region, and the nearest to Wessex. The smaller 'avenue-circles' were built at the farther sides of the moor apparently by later incomers laying claim to land on less productive but unoccupied hillsides.

Along those western fringes there are nine little circles with avenues, Yellowmead being a questionable tenth. They consist not only of a ring and an avenue but also of a burial-cairn inside the circle. They appear to be hybrid monuments of the Bronze Age in which several traditions combined, one of them the custom of erecting double lines of standing stones leading to megalithic rings. Not one of the large stone circles on Dartmoor has an entrance or portals or an

avenue, and it is likely that the smaller cairn-circles with avenues belong to a succeeding period when the avenue tradition was influencing western regions a century or centuries after the first great circles were put up. They occupy different areas.

The large open circles, Scorhill, Buttern, Grey Wethers and others, concentrate at the north-east.[27] Standing near rivers, averaging 85 ft (26 m) in diameter, these spacious rings cluster within four miles (6.4 km) of each other with only scattered sites such as Sherberton at the east or Brisworthy at the south-west standing in distant isolation. The distribution of the avenue-circles is different. Unlike many rows on the moor itself[28] the majority are at its very western edge in a seven mile (11 km) south-north line from Trowlesworthy East up to Merrivale Centre. The rings are about 30 ft (9 m) across.

A site remote from the others, the avenue and circle at Shovel Down (Pl. 19) is less than a mile from Scorhill at the north-east. Its avenue of parallel lines 596 ft (182 m) long and 3 ft 6 (1 m) wide leads south-wards up an easy slope to an unusual stone circle. The ring, no more than 28 ft 8 (8.7 m) across, encloses three others, the innermost a mere 8 ft (2.4 m) in diameter. This multiple stone circle is one of ten

Pl. 20 The Ringmoor avenue, Dartmoor, from the east. Its stone circle can be seen at the top of the slope.

recorded on Dartmoor,[29] several others being covered by low cairns for which the rings acted as stabilisers.

One at Yellowmead thirteen miles (21 km) SSW of Shovel Down is on the other rim of the moor. Restored in 1922 it has a possible avenue, short and aligned not to the centre of the circle but towards its eastern side. An adjacent arc of three low stones, however, and two other slabs at the southern edge of the ring suggests that the Yellowmead 'avenue' may instead be the first stages of a circle with multiple rows.

Shovel Down's avenue is not equivocal even if some of its stones are little more than 4 ins (10 cm) high. They rise unsteadily in height until, abutting the circle, the avenue ends in two monsters, both fallen, one a thick, flat-topped block, 7 ft 4 (2.2 m) long, its partner a long slim column a full 11 ft 6 (3.5 m) in length. When erect they would have formed a majestic portal to the ring. This pairing of a pillar and a lower, broader block is reminiscent of the 'male and female' stones of the Kennet Avenue, a comparison that the location of Shovel Down on the fringe of Wessex does nothing to diminish.

The farther to the west they are the fewer similarities the Dartmoor avenues have to those in Wiltshire and Somerset. At Ringmoor (Pl. 20) the row, which for much of its 1740 ft (530 m) length is single but which originally may have been double, has a tall terminal or 'blocking' stone at its lower northern end. From it the

avenue of calf-high stones trails up the slope to a circle 41 ft (12.5 m) across with a weathered cairn at its centre. A pit under it was empty, any contents destroyed by the intense acidity of the soil. The circle was restored in 1909.

Only a few miles south of Ringmoor the avenue and circle on Trowlesworthy Warren (Pl. 21) stand in an area of dense prehistoric population with several spacious cattle-pounds whose collapsed walls are still up to 9 ft (3 m) thick, Here in the steeper, wetter south and west parts of Dartmoor it was pastoralism rather than agriculture that was practised, seemingly by family groups. Inside the pounds are up to six hut-circles 15 to 26 comfortable ft (4.6–7.9 m) wide and once with stone walls, paved floors and turf roofs.

Some of these settlements may have been occupied by builders of the avenue-circles at a time when the oak forests were being cleared and before the growth of blanket-bog left the land uninhabitable. 'Scattered patches of heath and bog were spreading and joining up; Dartmoor was coming into being. At some stage in the earlier part of the first millennium BC a wetter climate probably accelerated the process.[30] As the miles of reaves, stretches of wall that demarcated large tracts of moor, are known to post-date these circles, one of them built between the avenue and rows at Shovel Down, running only a little away from the circle but respecting it, and as the reaves themselves must pre-date the peat, a period centering on 1800 to

Pl. 21 Two views of the Trowlesworthy stone circle and avenue on Dartmoor.

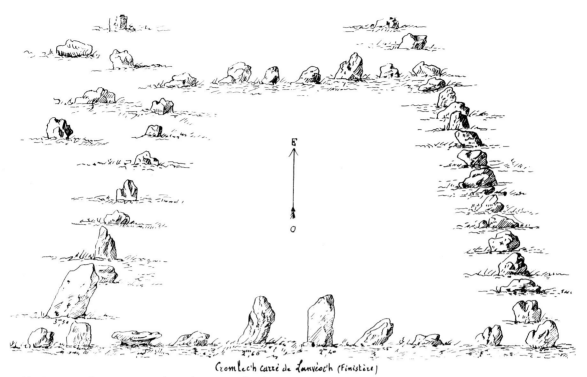

Fig. 10 Lanvéoc, Finistère, an eighteenth-century drawing.
From P. du Chatellier, *Les Époques Préhistoriques et Gauloises
dans le Finistère...*, Quimper, 1889. End paper. The rectangular
layout was popular in Finistère.

1400 bc (c. 2200–1700 BC) can be suggested for the
Dartmoor avenues.

The deliberate introduction of rabbits in the thir-
teenth century AD – hence the 'Warren' – as a commercial enterprise that competed with tin as Dartmoor's
main source of income meant that many of the pounds
and hut-circles at Trowlesworthy Warren are in poor
condition. The ground was further disturbed by the
digging out of a leat, a canal-like flume of water to
drive the wheel of the Lee Moor china clay works a
mile to the south.

Despite this the 23 ft (7 m) circle still stands as does
the 426 ft (130 m) of its 5 ft (1.5 m) wide avenue.
Although slightly damaged by labourers in 1859 and
interrupted by the banked leat it merits a visit, especially as the tallest stone in the ring, 4 ft 2 (1.3 m)
high, not only stands where the avenue joins the circle
but is set radially to the circumference like one side of
an embryonic entrance. The ring is known locally as
The Pulpit. From its perfect circle the avenue follows
a concave line down the slope.

Before leaving these Dartmoor avenues it should be
noted that with an average breadth of 5 ft (1.5 m) they
were quite wide enough for people to pass along them,
in single file maybe and perhaps only a few men and
women, but capable of acting as a processional way
gently rising to the circle and its burial-cairn. It is also
to be remarked that the narrowest of these approaches,
only 2 ft 10 (86 cm) wide, is the cramped Merrivale
Central avenue, idiosyncratic in layout and noticeably
farther to the west on the moor than any of the others.

(b) *Brittany*

There are few true avenues in Brittany unless they
were the earliest pair of a medley of identical lines
later erected on either side of them, absorbing and
concealing the original setting. In the multiple rows at
Carnac the phalanxes of lines are not evenly spaced
apart as one would expect had they all belonged to a
single phase of construction. They consist, moreover,
of a series of straight sections very like the additions to
the Kennet Avenue.[31] If, however, primary avenues
were disguised by an accumulation of extra rows at
Carnac and elsewhere it is unlikely that they will ever
positively be identified. To this negative conclusion
must be added the negative fact that the few that are
known to have existed have been destroyed. Even their
cromlechs have vanished.

Cromlechs in Brittany are not like the stone circles
of Britain and Ireland. They are larger and of unusual
designs, not only ovals and egg-shapes but also horseshoes, rectangles and squares.[32] Even in Finistère, the
département nearest to England, there were, for they
have all been removed, rectangles at Lanvéoc (Fig. 10)

Fig. 11 Île Beniguet, Finistère. A drawing of the 'English' cromlech by the Chevalier de Fréminville in the early nineteenth century. From B. le Pontois, *Le Finistère Préhistorique*, Paris, 1929, 126.

and Parc ar Varret, 'the field of the dead'. There was an enormous polygon, 60 × 30 metres (200 × 100 ft) at Le Conquet, a fishing village from which travellers today embark for the islands of Molène and Ushant, and there was a rectangle, the Phare du Creach, on Ushant itself. By the east coast of the island at Pen-ar-Land there is a restored megalithic horseshoe.

These great settings are so different from those across the English Channel that it is unexpected to come upon a reference to an 'English' stone circle with an avenue (Fig. 11) on the island of Beniguet 5 km (3 miles) out to sea from Le Conquet. Like many other Breton rings it has been uprooted but an early nineteenth-century sketch shows it had up to twelve well-spaced stones in an oval about 25 by 15 metres (82 × 49 ft).[33] In size, shape, spacing and pillarlike uprights it was dissimilar to Breton cromlechs but very like oval rings in Cornwall such as Tregeseal East and Boscawen-Un and could also be compared to the Merrivale oval in western Dartmoor, a pleasing ring a hundred or so yards (90 m) south of the Merrivale Centre avenue.

Early contacts between Brittany, Britain and Ireland are firmly attested. Finds of comparable pottery, the architecture of chambered tombs, Breton stone axes in Wessex,[34] all suggest communication between the three countries. 'From Ushant to Scilly is thirty-five leagues' (c. 170 km) has already been quoted but is worth repeating to stress that prehistoric Britain and Ireland were not isolated from the European mainland.

By archaeological good fortune the *Ora Maritima*, a doggerel poem by a pre-McGonagall Latin versifier of the late fourth century AD, plagiarised the *Massaliote Periplus*. This lost work was a mariner's handbook of the voyages of a sea-captain from Marseilles in the sixth century BC giving details of the cross-channel route between Finistère and Cornwall.

From the Pointe du Raz, a jutting peninsula 'against which the breakers foam, with high, overhanging cliffs within whose cavities, when the north wind blows, the waves resound like the hoarse roar of cannon-shots',[35]

merchants in their skin-sided boats passed along 'the widely scattered isles' of the Ushant archipelago, Beniguet, Quéménès, Molène, Bannec and Ushant. This, the largest of the islands and with sixty metre (200 ft) high cliffs, was a summer haven. Gales, the currents, reefs and fog deterred thoughts of any winter voyages.

Given good weather crews in long wicker-framed curraghs capable of carrying ten men could reach the trading-post of St Michael's Mount in two days. 'The seaborne traders, in distrust of mainland native treachery, conducted their business on offshore islands where they would be safe from attack on their persons and from plundering of their cargoes.' The Cassiterides or 'Tin Islands' of the Scillies or St Michael's Mount, 'accordingly, contained only the tin that was brought to them to be bartered on their neutral territory.'[36]

This might explain the location of the megalithic ring on Île Beniguet, an island sanctuary for seamen from south-west England and a place where tin or other commodities could be safely exchanged. If it were tin the circle could be dated to the Early Bronze Age but this is speculation rather than supposition.

Two parallel lines of stones were believed to have joined the ring but only a brief and uninformative note mentions them. The sketch of the circle does not show them and nothing more can be claimed for Île Beniguet. Much the same lack of detail applies to two other very un-English complexes on the Crozon peninsula 20 km (12½ miles) south-east of Beniguet. Little remains of either.

The first, at Ty ar c'Huré, 'the house of the curate', amongst Morgat's pine forests and expensive modern houses has been destroyed. In the nineteenth century two sinuous lines, 1500 metres (¾ mile) long, of large and small stones, raspingly coarse lumps of Armorican granite quite regularly spaced, led to a curved enclosure beyond which a second cromlech surrounded a three-sided rectangular paved area edged with stony banks. It was open to the east and the steep cliffs of the Pointe de Morgat.

Five kilometres (3 miles) to the north, beyond

Fig. 12   Landaoudec, Finistère. A plan of 1830. From B. le Pontois, *Le Finistère Préhistorique*, Paris, 1929, 116. It shows the complex layout of the avenue and cromlechs.

Crozon, the site of Landaoudec was even more elaborate. Until 1840 over 300 stones were in place and it was possible to make a plan of the lines and the cromlechs (Fig. 12). Now there is hardly a stone to be seen. At the north, not far from the tall menhir at Kervéneuré, there was an arc of low stones with the Breton name of *Karneliou*, 'the charnel-house' or 'mass-grave'. Scattered slabs lay near it. To the east were several much bigger menhirs near a windmill. Just to the south, between the row and the menhirs was the major setting at Landaoudec.

At its north-west end two parallel lines with huge pillars at their head 'formaient une sorte d'avenue'. This extended to three cromlechs in a fantastic conglomeration of a warped triangle, a loaf-shaped rectangle beyond it and, abutting the rectangle's eastern side, a semi-circle of small stones which encapsulated an earlier dolmen with a brutish capstone over its chamber. Analogous absorptions of chambered tombs are known in the Carnac region. One, Lann Mané, 'the mound on the heath', stands at the end of the great rows of Kermario. Another is buried under the Carnac Mound of the Tumulus St-Michel.

Except for two or three high menhirs draped in undergrowth and huddling together like cloaked way-farers in a blizzard Landaoudec has gone. Like other geometrical megaliths on the Crozon peninsula of which Lagatjar is the most famous the reasons for such strange juxtapositions of shapes is unknown but the double association with death hints at rites of fertility performed at the turning times of the year.[37]

In southern Brittany, not many kilometres east of the spectacular cromlechs and multiple rows at Carnac an avenue may have existed on the Île aux Moines, a long island in the Gulf of Morbihan. There is a large horseshoe-shaped cromlech at Kergonan, surrounded by houses, pitifully neglected, lush with wild flowers and weeds. Vague nineteenth-century reports mention 'deux files des menhirs' and 'deux rangées des menhirs' nearby at Parc Hir. In 1832 Bathurst Deane noted that a double row just south of Kergonan 'was formerly traceable in the direction of the island from south to north; but when we saw it there were very few stones remaining; sufficient, however, to convince me of the nature of the temple'. Except perhaps for a big stone, Pierre Colas, embedded in the foundations of a nearby house, nothing remains of what may have been an excellent example in Brittany of an avenue leading to a cromlech.

Of another 'avenue' little need be said for it is almost certainly spurious. On the Kerpenhir peninsula just south of Locmariaquer in Morbihan is a gross, weathered and ivy-wreathed menhir, 'La Pierre Jaune'. There are claims that it stands on the site of a former cromlech from which two lines of rough blocks curved away to the NNE. La Pierre Jaune exists. It is doubtful that the cromlech and the avenue ever did.[38]

(c) *Ireland*

The west was slow to adopt the custom of erecting lines of standing stones. There are no avenues attached to stone circles in Wales. They are also uncommon in any part of Ireland. There is a possible example in the Republic and two or three rather unusual variations in Northern Ireland.

In Co. Limerick, just west of Lough Gur and the fine Grange circle-henge in which beakers were discovered, there is a worn-down circular bank about 230 ft (70 m) from crest to crest, almost the same dimensions as the Grange bank 150 yards (140 m) to the south-east. Known as Lough Gur E the site may also have been a circle-henge but, if so, all its stones have been taken.

Leading to it from the south-east are two vaguely parallel lines of fallen stones, 3 ft to 7 ft (1 − 2 m) long, twelve on the western side, three only on the east 25 ft (7.6 m) away. These may be the prostrated sides of an avenue but the blocks have also been interpreted as the kerbstones of a demolished long chambered tomb. The site is ambiguous.

There is less uncertainty about three rings less than twenty miles (32 km) apart in Co. Tyrone, the short avenue at Knocknahorna already described, and two others at Broughderg North and Castledamph South.

Broughderg is an imperfect oval of low boulders, none more than a foot (30 cm) high. Significantly it is only just north of the group whose entrances have been mentioned. An untidy avenue crawls up to it from the east, 50 ft (15.2 m) long, one side composed of stones 1 ft 6 (0.5 m) high, the other so low that its line can only just be made out in the turf. In this the avenue is very like another at Castledamph nine miles (15 km) to the north-west, a morning's walk through the wooded hills, along the north bank of the Owenkillew River, north up the Barnes Gap and then along the Glenelly River to Castledamph.

This circle near Plumbridge, also one of a group, lies on the steep western slopes of Mullaghterrive mountain overlooking the lazy Glensass Burn. The stones are almost hidden in the clumps of stalky grass but excavation in 1937 uncovered a central cairn and

cist. An avenue 70 ft (21.5 m) long approached the circle uphill from the south. Like Broughderg its eastern side was formed by 16 tallish stones 3 ft (0.9 m) high whereas its western stones were virtually buried in the ground. Pits at its extreme end were thought to be postholes.

Avenues like these with one side markedly, and presumably intentionally, higher than the other have counterparts elsewhere in Co. Tyrone although those settings are not attached to a circle. They have no architectural affinities with the classical English avenues. Instead, in miniature they have a disconcerting resemblance to the avenues on the Crozon peninsula, Finistère, over 400 miles (645 km) south where the lines at Ty ar c'Huré and Landaoudec also had sides of different heights. To increase perplexity, those Breton avenues can be compared to the double row on the Grée de Cojoux, St-Just, in Ille-et-Vilaine, where the Alignements du Moulin had one side of tall grey menhirs and the other of squat quartz blocks. As St-Just and Crozon are over 100 km (62 miles) of forest apart the similarity is puzzling.

The origins of the Breton 'little and large' lines may lie with the uneven kerbstones of some of the tombs known as allées-couvertes, long megalithic galleries roofed with slabs and edged with slight banks. Near Mur-de-Bretagne in Côtes-du-Nord the site of Notre Dame-de-Lorette possesses this high-and-low trait, the south side of eighteen tall pillars of schist, the north of twelve smaller blocks of quartz (Pl. 22). The

Pl. 22 The 'high-and-low' sideslabs of the allée-couverte of Notre Dame-de-Lorette, Côtes-du-Nord. From the east.

long mound of the Tertre de la Croix-St-Pierre near St-Just has one side of little dark schists, the other of big quartz slabs. It is an architectural style unknown in Britain and southern Ireland.

It has been suggested that not far from the Tertre there is a version of a Scottish Bronze Age Four-Poster stone circle at the Château-Bû,[39] its stones at the corners of a small rectangle on top of a mound covering a Neolithic transepted passage-tomb.

Whether such a putative association between regions as distant as Scotland and Brittany, caused by movements of people or by trading networks, can be extrapolated to explain the likeness between avenues in Finistère and Northern Ireland is at present a subject only for conjecture. Architecturally it is not impossible.

Contacts between Brittany and Ireland have been claimed for a period far back into the Neolithic, as early as 3500 BC or before. Comparisons have been made between passage-tombs such as Kercado near Carnac and Newgrange in Co. Meath. Flotillas of Breton immigrants, even invaders, into Ireland have been proposed although it should be noted that the doyen of Breton prehistory, P.-R. Giot, has written, 'I don't believe in a word of this lovely picture.'[40]

More persuasive is the considerable likeness in building forms between the much later allées-couvertes and Irish wedge-tombs of which some four hundred are known, densest in the south and west but with others in the north. One, Largantea in Co. Londonderry, yielded the first beaker to be discovered in Ireland, a late long-necked form termed dully, S3/W, S for southern, 3 for the third phase of beakers, W for western. Two other beakers, S2/W and N3, came from the Lough Ash tomb in Co. Tyrone in which county the wedge-tomb at Clogherny was only two and a half hilly miles (4 km) north-west of the Castledamph avenue.[41]

However enticing the argument that avenues and rows in northern Ireland were the result only of Breton architectural fashions it remains too weak to be elevated to the status of a hypothesis. Later contacts between Brittany and south-west Ireland are likely but if there were earlier dominant Breton influences on the northern counties proof is unavailable. There is an intriguing similarity between the rows but like all intrigue it should be regarded with suspicion.

It is more likely that the unusual avenues of northern Ireland were hybrid monuments, the product of two traditions, one from Cumbria, the other from Brittany, commingling in the centuries after 2500 BC. Neolithic contacts between Ulster and northwest England are known through the discovery of Lake District stone axes in the counties of Antrim and Down,[42] and also through the construction of 'English' stone circles in Ireland such as the portalled Ballynoe in Co. Down. Centuries later, beakers of the Northern style are recorded both in the Eden Valley of Cumbria and in Co. Londonderry and Co. Tyrone,[43] deep into the previously unsettled hills of the Sperrin mountains.

The characteristic ritual monument of these incomers, a combination of circle and avenue, seems to have been something of a late megalithic mongrel. Rings such as Castledamph, hardly 60 ft (18 m) across, surrounding a low cairn and composed of even lower, close-set stones half-lost in the grass, have no resemblance to the great Neolithic circles of Cumbria but they are remarkably similar to succeeding rings with internal cairns such as Oddendale and Gunnerkeld to the south-east of the Lake District and to the Bronze Age sites of Lacra and Moor Divock to the west with their avenues. Cumbrian antecedents are plausible for the northern Irish rings but not for the alternating heights of the rows in avenues there. A separate tradition may have been involved.

Breton influence in the same regions west of the River Bann, just where the circles and avenues occur, has been proposed[44] on the basis of wedge-tombs in those areas and on the similarity between the native Kilhoyle pots and comparable vessels in the allées-couvertes of Brittany. From this it is feasible that the construction of avenues, albeit short and diminutive, developed from cross-North Channel associations, their architecture modified by the 'high-and-low' Breton tradition.

(d) Scotland

Avenues are scarce in Ireland and they are hardly more numerous in Scotland with its nine candidates, three certain, one questionable and five dissimilar from any other approach.

At the Girdle Stanes, a 'Lake District' stone circle near Langholm in Dumfriesshire, a straggling and broken line of prostrate stones, none of them long or broad, winds around a knoll to the Loupin' Stanes ring 600 yards (550 m) to the north. Here and there may be touches of an accompanying line even more interrupted and indefinite. The joining of a small circle to a larger, as at the Sanctuary and Avebury in Wiltshire, offers a tentative parallel with the Girdle Stanes line. If this had been an avenue, however, it did not lead from the south-east entrance of the Girdle Stanes but tangentially from the northern sector of the circle where there is no pair of taller stones or wider gap or break in the surrounding bank.

A better record exists of the erstwhile avenues at the circle-henge of Broomend of Crichie 160 miles (260 km) to the north in Aberdeenshire. The ring inside its double-entranced earthwork is small and despoiled. When excavated in 1855 it was found to contain urns and a sandstone battle-axe of the Early Bronze Age.

Lying on the outskirts of Inverurie the site has been subjected to sand-quarrying, disturbed by the laying of a railway line, damaged by road widening and almost destroyed by the felling of trees and levelling of a field. What was a combination of a long avenue, a circle-

Fig. 13 Beakers from Broomend of Crichie circle-henge, Aberdeenshire. From *PSAS 17*, 1882–3, 456–7. Top left, N2/L; top right, N3 both from Cist 2. Bottom. Both N2 from Cist 3.

henge and a shorter avenue leading northwards to a recumbent stone circle now consists only of a reduced ring inside its henge and three stones of its southern avenue. Yet the dismal activities at Broomend actually produced some benefits.

Once there had been two parallel lines of standing stones 450 yards (410 m) long running from the south near the River Don to the circle-henge, the thirty six pairs of stones forming an avenue 60 ft (18.2 m) wide, rising in height as the stones neared the ring. The avenue can be presumed to be postdate the circle. At its southern end, just west of the last known pair, four stone-slabbed cists were discovered in a high bank of sand in 1866. One was empty but the others, their corners neatly luted with clay, their floors bedded with pebbles, contained skeletons, flints, a horn ladle and four beakers, three of the Middle, one of the Late phase of the short-necked Northern beakers (Fig. 13).

Although the urns from the circle at Broomend of Crichie cannot be used to date the ring's construction because they could have been deposited by the stones years later the beakers, like those of the Kennet Avenue, can be supposed to postdate the avenue, their burials placed close to the lines of stones. As two

cremation urns of the same period were found against avenue stones during field trenching in 1850 and 1851 it is reasonable to envisage the avenue being erected early in the Bronze Age at a time before 2000 BC.[45]

From its description in 1757 as a 'long avenue of about 200 yards enclosed with a row of large stones erected on each side, it leads from the south to the lesser circle, and having crossed the same, continues its short passage to the larger' Broomend can be classified as a double avenue with affinities to others in England. The presence of a few Cumbrian stone axes in Aberdeenshire with many more from northern Ireland as well as evidence of a vigorous bronze industry demonstrates that north-east Scotland was far from being a backwater, isolated from the south of Britain.[46]

Also in Aberdeenshire five recumbent stone circles within six miles (10 km) of each other below the eastern slopes of the Correen Hills and on the very western fringes of the main concentration of rings had what may have been local versions of avenues. As they and their 'causeways' were all destroyed in the midnineteenth century one can only note what was stated about them.

Their approaches were not lined with standing stones but floored with rough, flat slabs 'so close that they were difficult to pick'. At Bankhead of Clatt the paving stretched thirty yards (27 m) north-eastwards and then curved north and petered out. There were similar paths at Crookmore, Nether Balfour, and at Druidsfield just north of the River Don where the 'road' was reputed to be at least one hundred yards long and forty wide (90 × 37 m), almost three times the width of the circle itself.

Handled stone ladles or 'paterae', ritual dishes used for libations or carrying ceremonial fire, were dug up in 1828 at Druidsfield 'under an ancient causeway leading from a circle of standing-stones on Donside in the parish of Tullynessle.' Reputedly another was unearthed at Callanish. 'Certain it is they have repeatedly been dug within the charmed area of those long-deserted fanes' being 'vessels originally consecrated to the mysterious rites of the so-called Druidical temples, or megalithic circles.'[47] Two comparable cups were found at Crookmore in the same year. Chronologically they are unhelpful:

> These stone cups appear to be mostly of Iron Age dates, or even later. They have not been found with interments, but there are several instances of their occurrence in brochs, in one case by the mouth of a well in the interior court of the broch.[48]

But what is of interest in a discussion of the anomalous Aberdeenshire pavings is that the causeway at Hillhead of Clatt led to a field 174 yards (160 m) to the ESE in which there were cairns, graves and cists, the central pits of some mounds covering cremations and urns. Such conjoining of a burial area with a stone

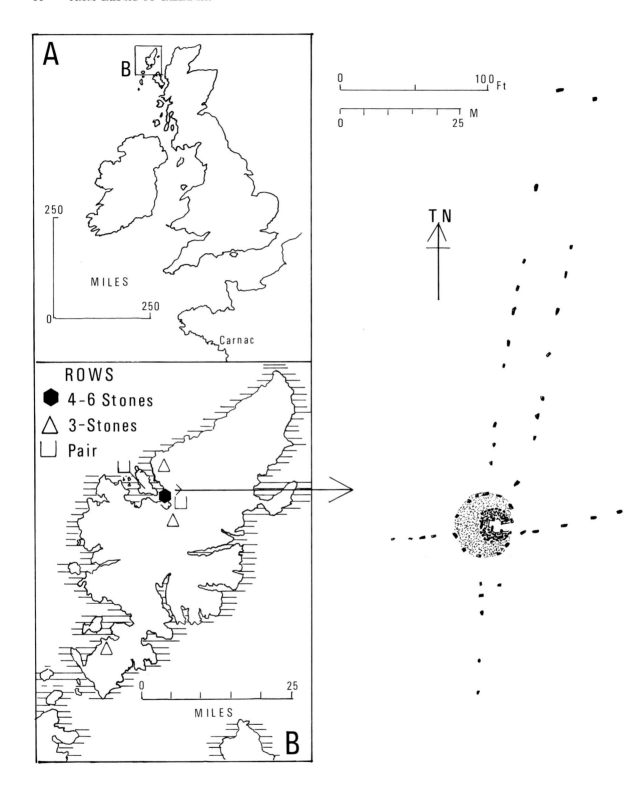

Fig. 14 Plan of Callanish, Isle of Lewis. Outer Hebrides. The stone circle, avenue and short rows.

circle by means of an artificially constructed approach suggests that the Aberdeen causeways if not avenues in a megalithic meaning may have been enigmatic variations on them.

No reservations are necessary for the avenue at Callanish in the Outer Hebrides almost two hundred miles (320 km) from Broomend of Crichie. No other avenue exists between them. It is strange that the two rings should be so far to the east and west of Scotland but whereas Broomend could pass for one of the English avenues Callanish is not a replica, being splayed rather than parallel. Today it is not perfect. Crofters settling nearby around AD 1790 may have removed some easily-shifted stones nearest the village. Nevertheless, this is the finest of all avenues, preserved by the fortune of 5 ft (1.5 m) of late-prehistoric peat decomposing and oozing thickly up its pillars.

The lines lead to a cramped circle of elegantly high slabs with three short rows of stones to the east, south and west. The cruciform setting is unique and has been likened to a Celtic cross but, if so, one that has been dropped once or twice, the south and west rows unaffected but the east row buckled to the ENE and the avenue jarred to the NNE. The rows will be discussed later.

The avenue is an imposing structure of thin, graceful stones, nine on its east side, ten on the west where, at the far end, it culminates in a tall pillar, 11 ft 7 (3.5 m) high. The avenue's sides are fanlike, wider by 4 ft (1.2 m) at its NNE than at its SSW against the ring where it contracts to 19 ft 7 (6 m). It is some 273 ft (83 m) long (Fig. 14). The stones of Lewissean gneiss may have come from a cliff at Na Dromannan a mile away. As the heaviest, the circle's tall central pillar, 15 ft 9 (4.8 m) high, weighs only seven tons no great body of workers was needed. Thirty or forty men would have sufficed.

It is possible that theirs was a project that was never completed. Gaps on both sides of the avenue may have been for intended stones that were not erected rather than evidence of eighteenth-century robbing. It is also arguable that this also had been a short avenue that was later extended. For 138 ft (42 m) from the circle the avenue stones steadily decrease in height from 7 ft 7 and 6 ft 4 (2.3, 1.9 m) down to 4 ft 4 and 4 ft 7 (1.3, 1.4 m). But from that point onwards and for almost exactly the same distance away from the ring the stones increase in stature to the two terminal pillars 7 ft 10 and 11 ft 7 (2.4, 3.5 m) high, the latter having its rediscovered, broken tip restored in 1978.[49] Such double grading, causing the avenue to sag like a hammock at its middle, is unknown elsewhere and may be the result of an added section.

Even more significant but unremarked is the realisation that the avenue, two hundred miles (320 km) north of Co. Tyrone and over three times that from Brittany, possesses the Breton-Irish 'high and low' trait, the stones on its eastern side consistently being

only three-quarters as tall as their western counterparts. The respective average heights are 5 ft 3 on the east and 6 ft 10 (1.6, 2.1 m) on the west.

Since this fashion of putting up tall stones opposite low ones was a characteristic not only of avenues in Northern Ireland but also of double rows and juxtaposed single lines there it is reasonable to see the architecture of the Callanish avenue partly as the result of Irish influence. The discovery on Lewis and North Uist of porcellanite axes from Tievebulliagh in Co. Antrim[50] shows that early links between the north of Ireland and the Outer Hebrides did exist.

The dignified and attractive avenue at Callanish appears to be a multi-phase composition of splaying, grading, short setting, extension and lopsidedness. As though this were not sufficient its rigid projection from the circle has led to interpretations of landscaped male sexual symbolism even though the lines contain no attempt to alternate tall, thin pillars with squatter, rounder slabs. 'It has been suggested that it is a relic of Phallic worship but this is altogether fanciful.'[51]

Theorists have not been idle about Callanish. To Pinkerton in 1814 the circle had been a gothic court, 'the avenue &c. being mere pieces of rude magnificence'. Thomas Wise, years later, was politer and more imaginative deducing that the avenue had been a military way for soldiers, with the lesser east, south and west rows used by merchants, peasants and priests respectively. This was less improbable than Tom Lethbridge's far-fetched theory that the stones were built as a landing-mark for Martians who also happened to be Beaker Folk.[52]

It is the astronomers, however, who have most enjoyed the challenge. Since 1726 when John Toland, misled about the number of stones, concluded that Callanish had been a temple of the sun and moon, 'the nineteen stones on each side the avenue betokening the [lunar] Cycle of nineteen years, I can prove it to have been dedicated principally to the Sun', astronomers have multiplied – and calculated.

In the nineteenth century Callender thought the site had been laid out to the cardinal points, 'The north being indicated by the double row or avenue', an error of 9°. Ignorant of the lapse Wilson agreed. 'This megalithic group has been expressly arranged with reference to the cardinal points by astronomical observation.'

(e) Archaeoastronomy
The study of ancient astronomical practices, archaeoastronomy, is a contentious discipline. In spite of the evidence of alignments in chambered tombs such as Newgrange and Maes Howe, in Cumbrian stone circles and Stonehenge, in stone rows like Ballochroy, many archaeologists remain reluctant to believe that prehistoric people ever looked upon the sun or moon as anything other than sources of light. It is a scepticism deriving partly from ignorance of astronomy

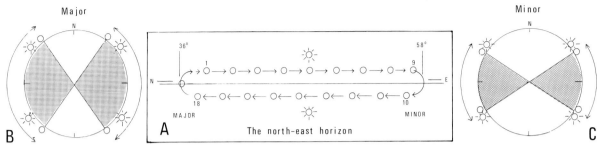

Fig. 15 Diagram to show the 18.61 year cycle of the moon. Latitude 53°. (A) The 18.61 year lunar cycle along the north-east skyline. Similar cycles occur at south-east, south-west and north-west. (B) The monthly swing of the moon from north to south to north at its major position. (C) At its minor position.

and largely from the early, uncritical and obviously absurd claims of enthusiasts such as Callender and Wilson.

Today, chiefly through the scholarly analyses of Alexander Thom and Clive Ruggles, the question has become not whether sightlines were built into some pre-Christian ritual monuments but why they were laid out and how precise they were. It is not the existence of alignments but the reasons for their existence that has to be debated. Acceptance of this, however, must be based on an understanding of the cycles of the sun and moon (Fig. 15).[53]

In western Europe, with rare exceptions, there are no instances of stars being used as celestial targets.

It is important not to confuse what the modern astronomer knows with what prehistoric observers thought. They would have no comprehension of why the sun rose and set, only that it did and was wonderful. In Neolithic and Bronze Age times people would notice how the sun and moon moved day by day along the horizon. The skyline would have been familiar to people living in the countryside, their lives regulated by the changing seasons. They would see that the rising and setting positions of the sun and moon slowly altered over the course of a year. From the inherited lore of their forefathers they would know that although it was easy to predict where the sun would be from year to year the positions of the moon were less simple to anticipate.

The sun never rose farther up the horizon than the north-east. When it was there daylight lasted longer, the weather was warmer and trees were in leaf. For three or four days the sun rose in the same spot, its 'standstill' or solstice, and then day by day it rose a little southwards until after six full moons of ever-darkening months it reached its south-eastern winter solstice. Men would soon associate the summer solstice with light and warmth and the winter solstice with darkness and cold. The sun provided a helpful calendar for the seasons despite its disadvantage that one could not look directly at it.

What prehistoric communities would not realise

was that solstitial extremes differed according to the latitude. In northern Britain the winter days were shorter and the summer days longer than in the south. In Cornwall daylight on midsummer's day lasted about seventeen hours but in the Orkneys, over six hundred miles (1000 km) north, there were almost two extra hours of light because the sun rose and set nearer to the north, remaining visible longer. Nowhere in Britain is the difference between summer and winter more incongruous than in the Shetlands. During June the 'Simmer dim' gives nights with little or no darkness but in winter the daylight lingers hardly more than four hours. Modern archaeoastronomers have to know the latitude of monuments as well as the compass-bearing or azimuth of any alignment.

The sun's annual passage from north to south is a regular one, but the moon is complex. It moves along the skyline just as the sun does but whereas the sun's cycle is a year long the moon's is contained within a month, the time it takes to circle the earth. Its risings and settings move quickly from one extreme to another in a fortnight, waxing and waning from full moon to a right-facing crescent then vanishing altogether only to reappear a few nights later with the points of its crescent now to the left. Such swift transformations may have seemed magical, perhaps godlike, to the prehistoric mind.

There were other complications. Sometimes the moon rises in daylight so that when darkness comes it can be high in the sky. Another difficulty is that there can only be a full moon when it is opposite the sun which provides its reflected light. At midwinter, when the sun is at the south a full moon will be at the north. The rapidity of the moon's movements, its changing shape and its periodic disappearance must have intrigued, perhaps awed prehistoric people. Even Sir Isaac Newton, mathematician and genius, 'used to say that accounting for the motions of the Moon was the one thing that made his head ache'.[54]

The moon is easily seen at night and capable of being looked with the naked eye but it has a third, very considerable handicap. Unlike the sun's predictably constant standstills the moon's farthest risings and settings at the four quarters of NNE, SSE, SSW and NNW do not always return to the same place annually but steadily expand and contract over a metronomic cycle of 18.61 years, moving from an extreme 'major' position to a 'minor' then back to the original 'major' place on the horizon.

The width of this major-minor arc, the sun being central to it, depends on the latitude and the date. At Carnac in 2500 BC the major northern moon rose around 44° from True North. Some nine years later at its minor standstill it rose near 62°, a swing of 18°. At Callanish, more than 10° of latitude to the north, the major and minor lunar risings were much farther apart from about 23° to 52°, nearly 30° of arc, far wider than that of the Breton moon.

So involved is this lunar cycle, together with the added confusions of the fast monthly movements and frequent daylight ascents that it would have taken years of observations, maybe generations, for prehistoric people to know exactly where the extreme lunar standstills occurred.

There is yet another astronomical problem, the question of the height of the skyline. It is only seldom that it happens to be at eye-level with a monument. Usually there is a hill or a valley higher or lower than the site and the closer they are the more difference they make to the compass-bearing (azimuth) of an alignment.

The sun and moon rise and set in graceful curves. If their ascents or descents are obscured for a while by a hill the azimuths of where they appear above the horizon will be affected. A modern surveyor must therefore take into account not only the azimuth and the latitude but also the skyline altitude. The combination of the three factors is known as the *declination*. In 2500 BC the midsummer and midwinter declinations of the sun were +23°.979 and −23°.979 respectively. The moon's major declinations were ±29°.129. Nine years later its minor declinations were reduced to ±18°.829. For practical purposes these solar and lunar positions have remained constant because they change by less than one-tenth of a degree, a mere six minutes of arc in any thousand years.

Knowledge of astronomy is not enough. Archaeological constraints must be imposed because individual sites are untrustworthy. The longer face of a single standing stone, the orientation of an isolated stone row that happens to be in line with a solar or lunar event cannot be taken as proof that the alignment was intended. It could be no more than coincidence. Confident statements about sightlines in prehistoric structures like Callanish are most readily acceptable if they are repeated time after time in a group of similar monuments such as stone circles in north-eastern Scotland in which the ponderous recumbent stone was always placed in line with the southern moon.

Other alignments can be assumed if they are defined by an otherwise inexplicable architectural feature such as the 'roofbox' above the entrance of the Newgrange passage-tomb, a kind of megalithic letter-box that admitted the light of the midwinter sunrise. A variation of this in the Orcadian chambered tomb of Maes Howe had a neatly shaped doorslab whose height was intentionally made too low so that it did not completely block the entrance. The narrow gap left above it created a 'window' through which the light of the midwinter sunset shone down the passage and into the chamber.[55]

A third indication that people had astronomical interests occurs in monuments of radiating design such as the cairns around the perimeter of American indian medicine-wheels, arguably in line with significant stars such as Rigel, Sirius and Aldebaran.[56] The spokelike avenue and rows at Callanish may belong within this category.

(f) *Callanish*

It was not until the twentieth century that astronomical analyses became sufficiently exact for confidence to be placed in them. Paradoxically they also became more contradictory. In 1909 there were two conflicting conclusions. Sir Norman Lockyer, relying on Sir Henry James's faulty plan of 1867, estimated that for Callanish the avenue pointed northwards towards the rising of the bright star Capella (α Aurigae) in 1720 BC. Somerville, who had made his own survey of the site concurred but dated the alignment to 1800 BC. Over fifty years later Thom revised this to 1790 BC.

In 1965 Gerald Hawkins criticised the stellar interpretation, observing that 'a star as viewed at sea level even under the very best conditions, is less bright by at least six magnitudes than it is when viewed higher in the sky and Capella at its rising would be faint and inconspicuous'. If, instead of gazing northwards, an observer had more logically looked in the opposite direction towards the circle and the SSW he would have seen the midsummer moon setting at its major southern extreme down the slope of Mount Clisham sixteen miles (26 km) away. The moon, not Capella, was the target.

Thom accepted this, noting that the sides of the avenue would have recorded the minute 'wobble' of the moon at its maximum. 'The discovery of this small variation in the inclination of the moon's orbit was made by Tycho Brahe [the celebrated Danish astronomer, 1546–1601]. Is it possible that its effect was known in the Outer Hebrides in 1800 BC? Certainly the necessary observing apparatus for detecting the effect was there'. Thom remarked that as the site was surrounded by slopes and a rocky knoll this made it 'difficult to see where there was room for any extrapolation to be done.'[57] In 1984, the Pontings added a grace-note that the avenue defined not only the major

Pl. 23 The avenue at Callanish, Isle of Lewis. The tall central circle can be seen in the distance.

moon but also the midwinter sunset sinking behind a mountain.[58]

The avenue at Callanish (Pl. 23) does seem to define lunar and solar alignments. It is credible that these were intended by the Callanish people but it is almost unbelievable that references to the sightlines should exist in a first-century BC classical text. The Greek historian Diodorus Siculus [of Sicily] quoted from a lost history by Hecataeus of Abdera, a verse-chronicle with later interpolations. Part appears to claim that an early voyager around northern Britain had seen a lunar 'spherical temple' on an 'island no smaller than Sicily'. In its path across the sky 'the moon as viewed from this island appears to be but a little distance from the earth' an event unique to the latitude of Callanish.[59] Diodorus added that 'the god' visited 'the island every nineteen years', the 18.61-year cycle of the moon.

The latitude of 58° N is critical. Nowhere farther south in Europe could the major moon between its rising and setting seem to skim the horizon. It would rise much higher in the sky. Not until 58° south of the equator, around Cape Horn, does the same lunar phenomenon occur. A Mediterranean voyager must have seen such a low moon at Callanish or some other

'spherical temple' at that northern latitude – and to the writer's knowledge there is none in Norway or southern Sweden, just one or two megalithic rings in Scotland, Guidebest in Caithness, the Ring of Brodgar on Orkney, both of them several miles inland from the coast.

'No smaller than Sicily' presents an insoluble problem. The British mainland is almost ten times larger than Sicily so that 'no smaller' would be an exceptional example of litotes. Conversely, although the island of Harris and Lewis is less than a tenth the size of Sicily the archipelago of which it is a part covers an area almost exactly that of the Italian island. As the Orkneys and the Shetlands are much smaller and Greenland, Iceland and Ireland all much bigger there is no convincing alternative claimant for the island.[60]

Stonehenge has repeatedly been identified as the 'temple' but this is wrong. Its latitude is five hundred impossible miles (800 km) too far south for the moon ever to brush the skyline. Moreover, if, as has been supposed, the information about the 'temple' derived from observations by the mid-third-century BC Greek explorer, Pytheas, it is unlikely that that he ever travelled far enough inland to see Stonehenge.[61]

There are other reasons to disqualify the ring. It

had been converted from a lunar to a solar monument at least 1700 years before Pytheas. And by his time the ring had been abandoned for a thousand years. All these militate against the acceptance of Stonehenge as the 'place where the priests of Alba worship in a circular temple'.[62]

Callanish, because of the area of the Outer Hebrides and Skye, its latitude, and its lunar alignment is a better candidate for the monument that some adventurous seafarer saw. With his ship hugging the safety of the coasts of western Scotland, following its inlets, the tall stones of Callanish would have been as dramatically visible as they were to Alexander Thom over two thousand years later.

In August 1933, Thom sailed into Loch Roag. 'As we stowed sail, I well remember looking up and seeing the full moon rising over the low land and there, silhouetted against the orb, were the Stones of Callanish.'[63] The same stark stones may have astonished a Greek crew around 250 BC. Diodorus states 'that certain Greeks visited the Hyperboreans [people of the far north] and left behind them costly votive offerings', not an unusual practice for strangers in a possibly hostile land. If so, it implies that as late as the Iron Age natives of Lewis remembered, perhaps even still celebrated, the times when the midsummer moon reached its southern extreme.

The astronomy is enigmatic. Diodorus wrote that when 'the god [the moon] visits the island every nineteen years', it would dance 'continuously the night through from the vernal equinox until the rising of the Pleiades'. This has been considered astronomical nonsense because at the time of the Spring equinox the Pleiades were in conjunction with the sun 'and would rise *unseen* shortly *after* sunrise'.[64] But as will be seen when considering the short rows at Callanish there may be some truth in the words of Diodorus.

CHAPTER SIX

AVENUES – AGE, SOCIETY AND PURPOSE

We cannot be certain for what purpose the [Stonehenge] Avenue was designed ... For 600 yards [it] heads straight for the centre of the monument, and for that distance follows precisely the path of the sun's rays on Midsummer morning. It is difficult to escape the conclusion that it was some sort of processional path, and that its direction was intentional.
R.H. Cunnington, *Stonehenge And Its Date*, 1935, 52

INTRODUCTION

The variety of architecture amongst avenues is important because it can reveal contacts between distant regions. The question of whether astronomical sight-lines were built into some avenues is also important because it would provide information about the ritual practices of some communities. But more important than either of these are the three problems of: when, how and why the standing stones were put up. Central to the solution of these difficulties is an understanding of the societies that erected the avenues.

DATING

Radiocarbon assays and finds from the few excavations show that the custom of erecting avenues leading to stone circles flourished in the centuries between 2600 and 2000 BC during the transition from the stone-using Neolithic to the metalworking of the Early Bronze Age.

There are only four C-14 assays that are derived directly from an avenue rather than from the circle to which it is attached. All come from Stonehenge. Two are related to the second phase of the monument when the building of a concentric stone circle was started inside the earthwork. Two others are from the time when a half-hearted attempt was made to extend the ditches and earthen banks of the avenue down to the River Avon.

Two antlers excavated by Hawley in 1923 from the bottoms of the avenue's outer ditches close to the henge entrance gave dates of 1728±68 bc (BM-1164), c. 2100 BC, and 1770±70 bc (HAR-2013), c. 2150 BC. Other assays of 1765±70 bc (BM-1582) from a nearby skeleton in the earthwork's ditch, and 1720±150 bc (BM-46) from a third antler inside the enclosure combine to indicate a period around 2150 BC for the construction of the stone circle and avenue.[1]

Two further determinations of 1070±70 bc (BM-1079) and 800±100 bc (I-3216) from antlers in ditches three-quarters of a mile (1.2 km) east of the first, straight section of the avenue suggest that an unfinished extension was begun and then abandoned around 1100 BC.[2]

The erection of circles of Welsh bluestones inside Stonehenge and the construction of the avenue have traditionally been attributed to users of beaker pottery, and it is of interest to note how frequently this ware has been discovered when avenues have been excavated: the Kennet and Beckhampton lines at Avebury, at Broomend of Crichie, at Callanish, and at Stonehenge itself.

It is not suggested that these people were the creators of avenues to stone circles. Finds from the circles themselves show them to be native monuments, not the products of continental incomers. The ancestry of avenues in the indigenous entrances and portals to circles confirms this. There is no sign of a Beaker takeover at Avebury or anywhere else. But standing stones appear to have attracted the makers of these vessels who often buried their dead alongside them, quite unaware that four millennia later the practice would provide a typological chronology for the rows.

A broad timescale has been devised for the various styles of beaker. On the reasonable assumption that a stone was standing when the grave was dug at its foot the discovery of a particular beaker points to a time before which the stone must have been erected, whether by a year or a century, a *terminus ante quem* for which the beaker is the indicator.

Until recently there was no argument about the users of beakers. The makers of these fine, well-fired vessels were Beaker Folk, European invaders, stocky, round-headed archers, skilled metal-workers, builders of the first stone circles, who gave their dead individual burial with valuable grave-goods under novel round barrows. They were of Nordic stock, speaking a form of Indo-European language from which our own is descended. Linguists no longer accept this.[3]

Skeletal evidence from their burials showed that these aliens were physically different from the small, dark natives, seemingly anatomical proof of an invasion of foreigners.

Today, every item of 'evidence' for overseas intruders has been reinterpreted as an episode caused not by warlike incomers but by a novel cult.[4] According to this re-thinking there were no Beaker people, only beaker pots, no invasion, only the gradual percolation of an idea, a 'package' of ritual objects and practices that was taken up enthusiastically from Kent to Caithness and from Suffolk to Sligo.

The writer remains to be convinced. People must have brought the first beakers to Britain, maybe introducing strange rites, but it was people who introduced them, not the pots. Nor do pots have enemies. Yet early Beaker burials on Salisbury Plain were interred well away from Stonehenge and native long barrows as though pioneering Beaker groups were tolerated only in an uneasy co-existence.[5]

There may never have been more than a few pioneering bands who settled on land well away from the natives. It is also feasible that over the decades as incomer and native mixed new rituals developed and variant styles of 'beaker' pots were made by native women.

The dating of such vague events is equally vague. Years ago there was a simple scheme to explain beaker history through their shapes, Abercromby in 1912 suggesting that because long-necked versions, his 'A' group, were prevalent in southern England, presumably the first region to be invaded, these were the earliest beakers. They were later succeeded by lower, squatter vessels, type 'B', and finally, in the far north of Britain which was the last area to be settled, beakers had short necks, type 'C'.[6]

In 1963, because of the close similarity of Abercromby's 'B' or 'Bell' beakers to others on the continent, Piggott amended the order to B, C, A. Seven years later Clarke, although accepting the sequence, proposed a more detailed scheme in which there had been two primary waves of intruders around 2500 BC followed by five later invasions of these islands over several centuries. By 1972 Lanting and Van der Waals were arguing that there had not been seven invasions but seven developmental steps which varied in four major regions of Britain: Wessex, East Anglia, Yorkshire, and north-east England and Scotland.

This interpretation had no more than a brief acceptance. Whether one believes in Beaker people or a beaker cult, and the writer believes in both with small groups of Beaker people gradually intermingling and merging with the native population over a century or so, it is now generally accepted that there had been the simplest of progressions, three stages of Early, Middle and Late much as Piggott had suggested. 'The straight-

Pl. 24   A 'European' (E) beaker. One of the first forms of this kind of pottery in Britain, perhaps as early as 2500 BC. Devizes Museum.

forward classification of Case (1977) is followed here, because it is so simple that any disagreements about it will be on what it has omitted rather than included.'[7]

In the Early phase from about 2500 BC there were two main types of beaker, both with profiles like upturned low, plump bells, one decorated all over with cord impressions (AOC), the other similar to pots known on the European mainland (E; Pl. 24). Unfortunately for chronological analyses both styles, especially the AOC, remained in fashion throughout all three phases of the beaker tradition.

In the Middle phase, from approximately 2350 BC, beakers became taller, more slender, more graceful, patterned in zones and bands of geometrical motifs. Relevant to the question of the dating of avenues is the W/MR style, Clarke believing that incomers from the Middle Rhine region had settled in Wessex. Also pertinent are N/MR beakers common in northern Britain, and BW for 'barbed-wire' decoration, and N2, a developed stage of northern beakers with short necks.

Finally, in the Late phase, c. 2000–1750 BC, in the full Early Bronze Age, the final short-necked forms appeared, N3, N4. In the south there was a trend towards pots with longer necks, increasingly ill-shaped, S1 to S4 (Pl. 25), and even beakers with handles, SH, like ceramic beer-mugs.

Using this pottery framework avenues can be placed in time, the first some decades before the Early phase, and the vogue enduring until the end of the Middle, some six centuries from 2600 to 2000 BC. Wessex may

Pl. 25   Two late beakers. On the left is a long-necked (S2/W)
vessel. The other (FP) has been decorated with rough finger-
pinching. Bristol University.

have seen the earliest of the long, extended avenues.
No dating material has come from the short lines at
Stanton Drew but Avebury's Kennet avenue is more
productive. As well as some indeterminate beaker
sherds from three of its stoneholes two vessels were
found in good enough condition to be identified. One
by stonehole 29a near the end of the excavated stretch
was a European (E) beaker of the Early phase. It could
have been made as long ago as 2500 BC but as the style
continued in fashion for centuries and as the pot lay
against one of the later extensions of the avenue it is
unsafe to accept so early a date.

The disturbed sherds of a Middle phase N2 beaker
are more trustworthy. They came from the filling of
the pit in which stone 25a stood. A corpse had been
buried there 'after the erection of the stone, but while
it was still supported by baulks.'[8] A period between
2350 and 2000 BC is likely for the interment and as it
was discovered in what was possibly the fifth extension
to the avenue the first short segment of stones 1a to 4b
by the entrance may have been set up as far back as
2400 BC when Avebury's colossal bank and ditch were
constructed.

The discovery of a rare Grooved Ware burial by
stone 22b, and other Late Neolithic pottery of indigenous Windmill Hill and Peterborough styles elsewhere in the avenue does nothing to contradict this
supposition. Nor does the presence of a Middle phase
BW beaker inside the Sanctuary stone circle at the
other end of the Kennet avenue, or an N/MR beaker

of the same phase excavated from a grave by the
Longstones of the Beckhampton avenue.

It is also possible that half a mile to the west of the
Longstones an overgrown sarsen and a beaker burial
were once part of this line of ruined standing stones.
During the ploughing of downland near Beckhampton
Grange in 1948 a large slab was found half-lying over
a child's skeleton. Round-skulled and lying on its back
the five-year-old had an N2 beaker by its left shoulder,
and by its right was a hand-sized decorated chalk
plaque. Its smoothed surface had five long grooves
gouged into it. 'The chalk seems to have been carved
in imitation of a hand ... and that it was meant to
represent the right hand of the child in the grave is
highly probable.'[9]

This beaker and Grooved Ware evidence makes it
likely that the Kennet and Beckhampton avenues were
spasmodically added to between 2600 and 2000 BC
after the completion of Avebury itself. Laid out in a
jerky series of straight segments beakers and other
deposits have been discovered at its junctions. Knowing
of a dedicatory burial, even sacrifice, at the Sanctuary
there is a chance that human offerings were made to
ensure the stability and potency of the stones.

Radiocarbon determinations suggest that the avenue
at Stonehenge was rather later than those at Avebury.
Its earthen banks edged by outer ditches were probably piled up between 2200 and 2100 BC. An early
S2/W beaker was of that general period, and the sherds
of a W/MR vessel were unearthed from the rubble that

was created when Stonehenge's north-eastern entrance was widened by levelling part of the bank and pushing the débris back into the ditch, filling it.[10]

Because of this reconstruction the axis of the monument, once passing through the midpoint of the narrow causeway, veered some degrees eastwards becoming almost but not quite in line with the midsummer sunrise. Lockyer believed that this had been the intention and there is evidence, tenuous but not imaginary, that if there really had been a Beaker cult it was a solar one unlike the native lunar rites suspected for Stonehenge during its first centuries.[11]

Other than in Wessex avenues were built during the Late phase of the beaker tradition. The three N2 vessels and one N3 pot recovered from the cists at the river end of the Broomend of Crichie avenue make it probable that the stones were in place just before 2000 BC. Urns from the same site were also of the Early Bronze Age.

At Callanish both beakers, N3 and N4, were of the Late phase and the existence of an AOC vessel, arguably fired late in the sequence, from the circle would not militate against the idea of the avenue belonging to a period after 2000 BC. But it must be remembered that beaker evidence is almost always *terminus ante quem* evidence indicating no more than a time before which the stones were put up. The gap could have been as wide as two centuries or even more.

Despite this necessary caveat a food-vessel from a kerb-circle at Moor Divock can be presumed to be earlier than the avenue leading to its cairn, implying that the stones were not set up before the Early Bronze Age. A similar argument can be applied to the collared urn excavated at the foot of a stone in the Lacra D circle. Belonging to what is termed the Primary Series it, like the food-vessel and the N3 and N4 beakers, would have been hand-coiled, hardened and fired in a bonfire in the kiln-less years around 2000 BC.[12]

Overall, avenues can be regarded as very late Neolithic and quite early Bronze Age phenomena, concentrated mainly in Cumbria and Wessex, the tradition spreading to Dartmoor, with more distant, later outliers in northern Ireland, from which there is as yet no dateable material, and the eastern and western coasts of northern Scotland.

SOCIETY

The structure of any prehistoric society will always be difficult to reconstruct. Lacking documents or pictorial representations, without descriptions by literate outsiders, only the most general deductions can be inferred from the surviving, indiscriminately preserved and imperfect material remains of such communities. Death helps. The communal burials of men, women and children in the long barrows of the early Neolithic

very slowly gave way by the Late Neolithic to the interment of a single adult male, often with prestigious articles of aggression, a flint club, a heavy antler macehead. By the Early Bronze Age such leaders were being buried with metal daggers and axes beneath large round barrows.

It was a transition from the family tomb to the chieftain's grave, from a community of equals to a society of grades and ranks. For powerful members there was woven clothing in place of garments of skin. There were copper and bronze instead of bone, flint and stone. The impression is of early Neolithic families gradually grouping into clans, and middle Neolithic clans merging into sub-tribes in which there were leaders, warriors and commoners.

Territories were demarcated. In Wessex these may have covered scores of square miles and contained many hundreds of people with petty chieftains in allegiance to one overlord. In less fertile regions a similar person may have been little more than the head of a few families.

Whatever their precise nature these were native societies. Whether Beaker Folk or beaker pots there is no sign of foreign invasion and conquest. If there were newcomers they soon became integrated into long-accepted ways of life. If a solar cult had been introduced it did not eradicate older lunar beliefs.

Even the pottery known as Grooved Ware, appearing as early as 3500 BC in northern Scotland and becoming widespread by 2700 BC, is not associated with any infiltrating bands of strangers.[13] Of unclear, possibly Irish ancestry, these poorly-fired vessels with channelled geometrical and spiral motifs reminiscent of the megalithic carvings in Irish passage-tombs, have often been found in henges and stone circles suggesting that the pots were part of a mystic cult involving the deposition of chosen objects in selected places.

At Stonehenge, before the arrival of any beakers, a Grooved Ware bowl was put in a pit on the major south-west – north-east axis in line with the northern moonrise. Bodies of adults and children were buried by both entrances, and antlers were left there. By the south entrance a ball of chalk and long flint flakes were concealed in pits with Grooved Ware sherds. By the bank at the south-east the cremated bones of a child were buried with a beautifully-polished, perforated macehead, an offering that from the centre of the henge was aligned on the southern moonrise.[14] It was a cult of association, objects placed together, objects kept apart.

> All things counter, original, spare, strange,
> Whatever is fickle, freckled (who knows how?),
> With swift, slow; sweet, sour; adazzle, dim . . .
> Gerard Manley Hopkins, *Pied Beauty*

The centuries around 2600 BC were times of change and adjustment as societies became larger and more formalised, their ceremonies more ostentatious, performed in ageing open-air enclosures. One manifestation of these developments was the building of avenues.

DESIGN AND CONSTRUCTION

If there were subtleties in the planning and erection of avenues the nuances are unapparent. The stones were not exotic imports but those that happened to lie nearby, sarsens at Avebury, granite glacial erratics at Shap, Lewissean gneiss at Callanish, and, on the stone-free expanses of Salisbury Plain, earth and chalk at Stonehenge.

Having been dragged to the site the stones were put up by experienced workers who probably had a local unit of measurement that varied from region to region, a 'Beaker Yard', a 'Perth Yard', a 'Megalithic Yard',[15] and others as yet undefined, all apparently based on bodily dimensions, a foot, an outstretched arm, a stride. There were rarely niceties of precision in the use of such yardsticks. The crudity of a sarsen prevented any meticulous positioning. Near enough was good enough, and stone by stone the line of the avenue was set out, often deviating when a further section was added. It was improvisation without refinement, Dixieland jazz rather than Mozart. But, as Avebury shows, the effort and determination were immense.

The Kennet and Beckhampton avenues were awesome undertakings. Hundreds of gigantic blocks, the heaviest over thirty tons in weight, had to be back-strainingly pulled over miles of rough ground from the upper slopes of the Downs. Men rather than slow and obstinate oxen may have towed the slabs.

Using ropes of wood-fibre, lashing the stone onto a hardwood sledge, dragging the load along moveable rails of squared oak trunks that could be taken up and moved forward once the sledge had passed a hundred or more workers could shift a sarsen step by step towards Avebury. In an experiment in 1979 at Bougon near Niort in central France 170 persons pulled, thirty more levered, tugging a thirty-one-ton block in exactly this manner in a series of short hauls and frequent rests.[16] The pace was laboriously slow, hardly a hundred yards (90 m) a day.[17] A similar crawl for the Kennet and Beckhampton stones would have entailed weeks, even months for the project.

The work-force would consist of the most able-bodied of a population of a thousand or more people, far more than the likely inhabitants of a single prehistoric settlement. A communal effort was demanded. 'It is much more likely that such imposing monuments were the work of a population scattered amongst several villages within the tribal territory around the structure, a place of veneration for a whole people'.[18] It is noticeable that Avebury stood in the Kennet valley at the centre of a prehistoric concentration of Neolithic megalithic and earthen long barrows, an area well-settled in the Neolithic and Early Bronze Ages.[19]

Once at the site the stone was dragged to its prepared hole, a pit with a sloping side down which the pillar's base could be manoeuvred. Greasy stakes, stripped of their bark, were hammered in against the back of the hole to lubricate the heel of the sarsen as it slithered downwards. The bottom of the hole may have been deeply packed with wet clay. At the Goggleby Stone in the Shap row of Cumbria, 'the purpose of the clay introduced by the original builders was to hold the stone in position until it could be pulled upright.'[20] Comparable lumps of clay were found at Callanish and in the Kennet avenue.

With sturdy oak bars the sarsen was levered very slowly upwards until at 70° from the perpendicular it had to be hauled upright with ropes.[21] At that angle the force required to move it was one-fifth its dead weight. Heaving at the lines men could each, for a short while, exert a pull of 100 lbs. For an average avenue stone of four tons the equation for the work-force would have been:

$$= \frac{4 \times 2240 \text{ lbs}}{5} = 1792 \div 100$$
$$= 18 \text{ labourers}$$

The heaviest, however, demanded as many as 130 workers.

More men were needed to prop the stone from behind with others hurriedly jamming packing-stones between the pit's sides and the sarsen to wedge it firmly into place but the size of this hypothetical workforce is feasible, being no larger than the gang that brought the stone from its source. The organisation, however, was prodigious, involving the disruption of ordinary life, providing food and temporary shelters for the team, older people taking over the domestic chores of the young men. With some two hundred stones in each of the two avenues the undertaking could have taken years.

It has been estimated that 300,000 man-hours were needed for the completion of the Avebury avenues.[22] With 150 men working eight hours a day, with no interruptions for bad weather or the harvest or festivals, the two avenues would have taken eight months to construct. The reality was probably much longer, drawn-out, slowly finishing the long rows of sarsens that led up to the stone circles inside Avebury.

FUNCTION

As Crossing drily reported, there have been many explanations of what stone rows were: for rites connected with the Flood, or gymnasia, landscaped sacred serpents, druidical paths, race-courses, shelters whose roofs had decayed, imitations of armies, trackway markers, astronomical observatories, open-air duplicates of the passages in megalithic tombs. 'From these hypotheses it certainly should be possible for the visitor to select one to his mind.'[23]

Most of these suggestions were preposterous and short-lived but some have persisted obstinately. Stukeley's belief in *dracontia* (Fig. 16), that Avebury had been laid out as an image of the sacred snake, was repeated as late as 1838 by the Rev. W. Bowles who was 'inclined to think the stones [of the Kennet and Beckhampton avenues] represented the form of the two serpents', being British versions of ancient Egyptian motifs. Another advocate of megalithic vipers went beyond the Near East, claiming that Avebury was composed of a snake, a large and two smaller circles, 'all of which are Buddhistic emblems.'[24]

Yet it was surely the Rev. C.H. Hartshorne who proved to be the most dedicated devotee of landscaped *dracontia*, fantasising a two-mile long winding outline of the serpent between the Shropshire stone circles of Marsh Pool and the Whetstones. Not one stone of this 'avenue' existed:

It is true that here we no longer see the stones on each side forming an avenue of communication with the *Body of the Serpent* but knowing the tendency of stones to become obliterated by moss, to sink into the soil, or their chances of destruction from the wicked spirit which has always prevailed among

ignorant cultivators of the land . . . we shall not be at a loss in accounting for their deficiency . . . If with such a deficiency, the enquirer can recognise DRACONTIA, he will be well repaid for a visit to the dreary and impressive region where these mysterious objects are scattered.[25]

It was a delusion. The circles were wrecks. Marsh Pool had been damaged by the fireworks of wedding parties. The Whetstones were blown up. And no avenue ever connected these sad rings.

Even today Avebury has not entirely slothed its serpent's scales. But it has shed its antique Eqyptian and Indian connections in favour of sexual intercourse. 'The [Kennet] avenue represents a snake on its way from hibernation in the Sanctuary to copulation at the henge'. Who its partner was is not clear. Certainly not its counterpart at Beckhampton. Being female the Kennet avenue 'came to to the place appointed for copulation with her jaws ajar and forty-nine stone teeth showing, ready to swallow down the phallic extension of the male Beckhampton avenue'.[26] Draconian if not dracontian.

Such ophidian fantasies are bores that constrict the truth. Other, more reliable observations can be made

Fig. 16 Avebury circle-henge and its Beckhampton (west) and Kennet (south-east) avenues. A drawing by William Stukeley, from his *Abury, a Temple of the British Druids* . . . , London, 1743, 14, Plate VIII. Stukeley believed the complex was a landscaped version of the sacred serpent.

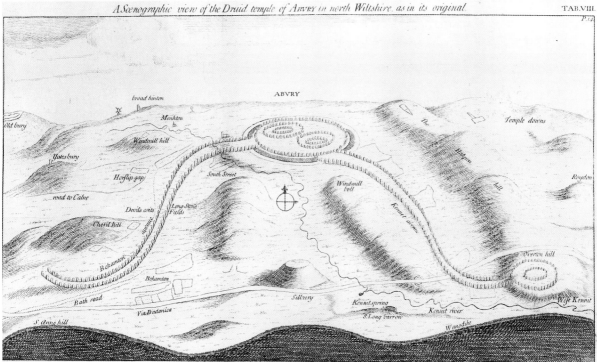

A Scenographic view of the Druid temple of Abury in north Wiltshire, as in its original. TAB.VIII.

Praehonorabili Dño. Dño. Philippo Dño. Hardwick summo magnæ Brittanniæ Cancellario tabulam. L.M.D. *W. Stukeley,*

about the purpose of avenues. On the assumption that they did develop as elaborated entrances to a circle a chronological sequence can be proposed:

   i. A wider space was left between the closely-set stones of a ring to permit access to the interior.
   ii. This could be enhanced by the addition of two more stones outside the circumference, creating an unequivocal entrance.
   iii. Later, three or four extra pairs of standing stones erected beyond the entrance formed a short avenue.
   iv. Further extensions resulted in longer, architecturally-planned lines.

The common feature to all four phases was a controlled approach to a megalithic ring, confirming what John Aubrey had decided about the Kennet Avenue three centuries ago. 'Very probable this Walke was made for Processions'.

The 1989 geophysical examination of that avenue found indications of trampling both inside and outside the stones. Explanations could be as numerous as the sarsens. The avenue may have been the privileged ground of an élite from which commoners were excluded; or the sacred way for funerary processions when approaching Avebury; or any one of many alternative causes.[27]

There are reasons for believing that avenues were not lengthened merely to make them more distinguished. Instead, it seems that the extensions were constructed with the intention of connecting once-separate places, linking major ritual centres with lesser but vital elements such as rivers or mortality. Avenue after avenue led from water to a stone circle: Broomend of Crichie from the River Don; Callanish from the direction of Loch Roag; the short Stanton Drew avenues from the River Chew; the extension at Stonehenge from the River Avon; the Kennet avenue from the springs and streams in the Kennet valley. The Beckhampton avenue crossed the Winterbourne brook. What rites were involved in these hydrographic associations remain unknown. Rituals of purification and fertility are not unlikely.

Even more obvious, especially in the later avenues, is their function as paths that joined stone circle and death together, sometimes from a funerary monument to a ring, more frequently as a stone-lined way to a later circle that contained a human burial within it. A miniscule passage-tomb was inserted into the already small circle at Callanish. There were burials inside the circle-henge of Broomend of Crichie. Dartmoor rings with avenues such as Merrivale and Shovel Down surrounded cairns. It is easy to imagine, though forever impossible to prove, people moving along the lines bearing the cremated bones of the person whose burial was to consecrate the stone circle. 'We must suppose', wrote Stukeley, 'the intent of the avenue was to direct the religious procession to the temple.'[28]

An increasing desire to combine a place of death

with an open stone circle may explain the unnecessarily buckled course of the Kennet avenue. There is good evidence that what became one long avenue once consisted of two sections, one the Kennet avenue leading north-westwards from water towards Avebury, the other climbing south-south-eastwards up Overton Hill to the Sanctuary, a ring that has been interpreted as a megalithic version of an earlier timber mortuary house.[29] There is a clumsy bend in the mile-and-half long (2.4 km) Avebury-Sanctuary avenue at its lowest point at West Kennet hamlet. From there the stones of each avenue rise in height; both avenues follow rising ground; both narrow in width as they near their circles; and both circles had short avenues which were later extended before the final unification.

The features of the mile-long (1.6 km) Kennet avenue have already been described. At its southern end John Aubrey noticed how it veered eastwards. 'West Kynet stands in the angle where the Walke from Aubury hither, and that from the top of the hill [the

Fig. 17　The Kennet avenue leading south from the Sanctuary stone circle. A plan by John Aubrey, from his *Monumenta Britannica I, 1665–93*, Milborne Port, 1980, 51. The plan shows the short kink against the ring.

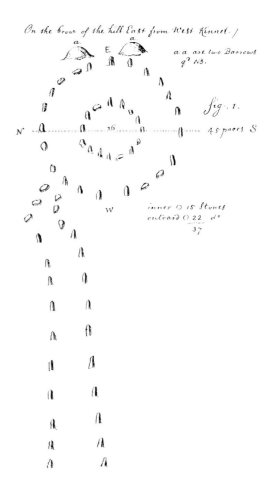

Two pairs of opposed sarsens in the Kennet avenue. The female' lozenge in the foreground stands opposite a 'male' pillar. The stones have not been shaped.

Pl. 26   Stones 33b and 33a are the fifth pair from the south.

Pl. 27   Pair 26 is near the top of the rise towards Avebury.

Sanctuary], did joine.' Years later Stukeley commented on 'the two great curves it makes to imitate the figure of a snake.' By his time, 1723, most of the Sanctuary's avenue had been demolished.[30]

By the twentieth century nearly all its stones have been buried, taken away or destroyed but its grading is still detectable. A sarsen at the bottom of the hill is 'very small . . . still in existence, lying by its stone-hole'.[31] Halfway up the hillside, however, another, discovered in 1921, was 10 ft 7 (3.2 m) long and would have stood 8 ft 6 (2.6 m) high.[32] The avenue also decreased in width from 28 ft (8.5 m) at its lower end to 18 ft (5.5 m) against the circle.[33] Its grading, its uphill course to a circle, its narrowing, all indicate that this had once been an independent avenue.

Aubrey was the last chronicler to see the Sanctuary circle intact (Fig. 17) before its destruction in 1723 although Samuel Pepys on his way to London from Avebury in 1668 mentioned seeing the ring, 'one place with great high stones pitched round . . . in some measure like that of Stonag'. Aubrey made a plan. This showed that there had been an initial short north-west – south-east stretch of the avenue at whose north-west end the next section swung abruptly westwards down the slope. Aubrey had no reason for inventing such a sharp bend, a change of direction as sudden as that of the Kennet Avenue near Avebury's southern entrance. Maud Cunnington's 1930 excavation partly confirmed his plan, discovering the holes of three, perhaps four pairs of stones leading north-west from the circle for about 50 ft (15 m). Regrettably, the excavation area did not extend beyond this but subsequently some stoneholes of the avenue's extension were located just over 100 ft (30 m) from the last of Aubrey's short avenue,[34] at first at a WNW angle (285°) to it then gradually curving north-westwards.

It would appear that at the Sanctuary a timber mortuary-house, transformed into stone, was ultimately attached to the centuries-old Avebury stone circles by the merging of two avenues. The same may have happened at Shap. Avenues became the means by which death and a ritual centre could fuse into one, no longer apart as they had been in the past but conjoined by the path that bound them together.

Whatever rituals were performed in these long, processional paths the participants had no need of megalithic art. There is none. At Shap an improbable cup-and-ring mark and a cupmark were reported on a large, leaning stone 155 yards (140 m) north-west of the Goggleby Stone and a very questionable cupmark on the Goggleby Stone itself. It is likely, however, that these gross boulders, decorated or not, were parts of a northern single row, Camden's 'large stones in the form of Pyramids . . . set almost in a direct line', rather than members of an addition to the avenue of lower blocks leading to the Kemp Howe stone circle.[35]

In the Kennet Avenue Keiller wrote that two

stones and possibly a third were found to bear ornament of 'cup and ring' type – circles made in 'pocked' technique usually but not invariably surrounding a central spot. Two well-preserved examples show irregular double concentric circles surrounding a pair of depressions, of which in each instance one is a natural hole in the sarsen and the other artifically worked.

These markings on the back of Stone 25b are now recognised as being natural. Other stones, nos. 19b and 32a, were used as polissoirs for sharpening axes. Such grooves are not artistic symbols.[36] No art is recorded in any other avenue.

Nor were the builders of the long avenues astronomical watchers of the skies although the extensions they added may obscure earlier sightlines. The first avenue at Stonehenge was laid out approximately in line with the midsummer sunrise and this seems deliberately planned by its builders.[37] Far less proveable is the possibility that the initial short avenue outside Avebury's southern entrance with an azimuth or compass-bearing of about 143° was set up towards the southern moonrise, an alignment similar to that at Callanish. It is possible. But no comparable sightline existed at the Sanctuary or at Stanton Drew, and although it has been suggested that the parallel rows at Merrivale on Dartmoor could have been used to predict lunar eclipses the argument is not persuasive.[38]

The devious course of most avenues was not conducive to astronomical observation. It is more likely that such paired rows were what they have long thought to have been, megalithic approaches to a ritual enclosure, the stones themselves perhaps symbolising life and death or male and female principles. This has been proposed for the sarsen pillars and lozenges of the Kennet Avenue (Pls 26 and 27), and at Shap the Rev. James Simpson noted that in what was left of the southern end 'it appears to me that every alternate stone stood on its narrow end'.[39]

Over the years, to the west of Cumbria and Wessex, the avenue became a process in its own right. Parallel lines of stone were erected. Occasionally such double rows were set by the side of a circle. More frequently they were independent of any ring.

The association that did prevail, even intensified, was the link with death. At site after site the rows led uphill to a cairn that was no longer contained inside a ring of standing stones. That this development was directly derived from the avenue tradition is shown by the distribution of these new lines.

CHAPTER SEVEN

DETACHED AVENUES AND DOUBLE ROWS 2300–1800 BC

There are, however, two special groups [of circles], those with alignments and those with three large stones. In the former the alignment is either tangential, or it meets the circle not far from the tangential point, or, failing to cut it, overlaps it a short way. The alignment-stones are normally taller and more massive than those of the circle.

Oliver Davies, *UJA 2*, 1939, 2

INTRODUCTION

Davies's observations about the double lines of stones associated with northern Irish stone circles illustrate how circle and avenue ultimately became separated. By the onset of the Early Bronze Age around 2200 BC three quite distinct architectural styles were developing. One saw the reduction of the avenue to a single line that often led to a circle surrounding a burial-cairn. These elementary rows will be discussed in the next chapter.

Other variations retained the open circle. Some avenues either stopped well short of the ring or were tangential to it. Such detached avenues, never numerous, appear to have been Cumbrian in origin and were set up in eastern Wales and northern Ireland.

A third version saw the total abandonment of the stone circle. The double row of the avenue kept its function as an approach but now customarily extended from a tall terminal stone up a slope towards an unimposing kerbed cairn. These parallel lines are most plausibly interpreted as derivations from Wessex and are best known from their comparative density on Dartmoor. Each of the three developments, however, retained the link between the lines and a place of burial (Fig. 18).

There is no direct dating evidence for any of these unusual avenues or rows but their distribution is informative. They occupy not only the same areas as conventional avenues but are also found just to the west and north of them. Inferentially this suggests that their chronology overlapped that of the later avenues, perhaps over the centuries between 2300 and 1800 BC around the commencement of the Early Bronze Age.

DETACHED AVENUES

(a) *Cumbria*

So many of the former avenues and rows of north-western England have been destroyed that they have generally been overlooked in any discussion of megalithic monuments. And yet, to the north-east and south-east of the Lake District, in areas peripheral to the central zone of great stone circles such as Castlerigg, even in the last century there were many lines of standing stones. There were single rows at Newton Reigny beyond Penrith, at the nearby Newbiggin and at Carlatton. At Broad Field not far from Carlisle there was 'an avenue of erect stones'. 'This line of stones seems to have been originally composed of a double row . . . and they would have defined or edged a long narrow path, perhaps 3 or 4 feet wide.' There were nineteenth-century rumours that a similar setting had been joined to one of the largest of all the Cumbrian stone circles, the destroyed ring of Grey Yauds.[1]

Miles to the south-east around Crosby Ravensworth where the Aire Gap through the Pennines linked Cumbria and north-east England there were 'remnants of former alignments of megaliths'. As well as the writhing avenues of Moor Divock and Shap there were others. At Penhurrock 'a line of fallen stones stretches . . . up the hill in a N.N.E. direction for a distance of 112 yards [102 m].' A heavy stone marked its lower end.

Expectedly, the site most clearly showing the ultimate disruption between circle and avenue was the one farthest from the source of avenues. Just north of Ulverston a ring at Kirkby Ireleth, twenty five direct but mountainous miles (40 km) south of Castlerigg, retains some elements of a detached avenue. Sometimes called a stone circle 'The Kirk' is in reality a ring-cairn, an embanked enclosure with an open, stone-lined interior. A full 100 ft (30 m) to its north-east is a pair of low stones. Beyond them are two other pairs in an arc curving northwards towards an overgrown and mutilated cairn in which a cist and cremated bones were found.

It is impossible today to decide whether the pairs are relics of a truncated avenue, whether they led to or

DETACHED AND TANGENTIAL AVENUES
1 Altaghoney
2 Aughlish NW
3 Aughlish N
4 Davagh
5 Moymore
6 Formil
7 Cavancarragh
8 Broad Field
9 The Kirk
10 Rhos y Beddau
11 Cerrig Duon

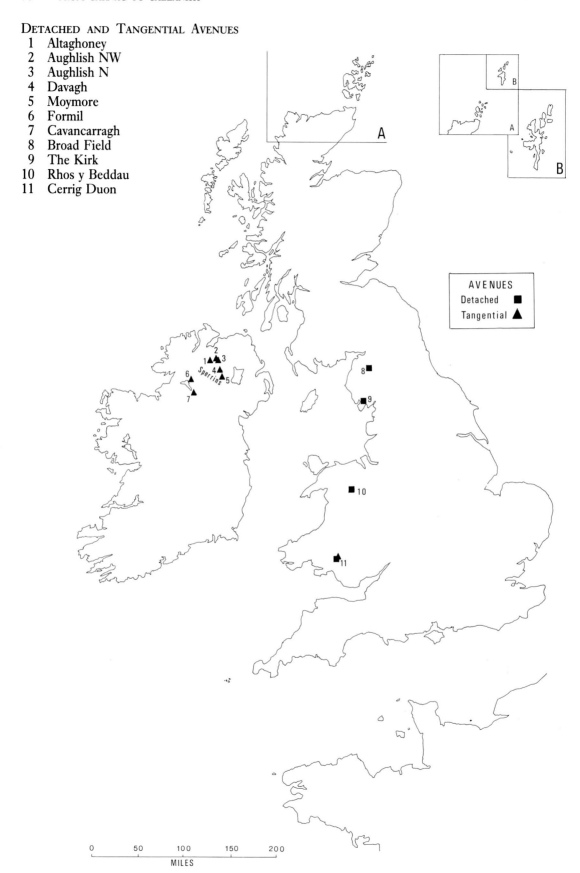

AVENUES
Detached ■
Tangential ▲

0   50   100   150   200
MILES

from the cairn, to or from the ring-cairn, or perhaps were no more than a stone-set way between two places of death. One reticent observation has been made about the line. 'It is interesting to note, although it may be of little significance, that the avenue leading to the north-east aligns with a notch in the hilly profile on the horizon (51°). This is close to, if not at, the actual position where the sun would be seen to rise at the summer solstice.'[2] Knowing of the interest in the sun shown by the builders of Cumbrian stone circles[3] such an alignment may have been intended. If so, it was not precise.

(b) *Wales*

At the very east of the Welsh mountains are two avenues, one detached, the other tangential, both excellent examples of the avenue's increasing independence of the circle.

A hundred miles (160 km) south of The Kirk, across the hills south-west of Llangollen, is the stone circle and avenue of Rhos y Beddau. It is easy today to forget that a modern journey by car along motorways and dual carriageways from Kendal to Llangollen, a comfortable hour and a half of driving, could be as much as a week's wearying, often dangerous travel in prehistoric times. Neither news nor customs were transmitted quickly. Between The Kirk and Rhos y Beddau were forests and wild animals, suspicious natives, rivers, rough trackways and the woods and swamps of the Mersey Basin, now a tedium of treeless flatness. Beyond was the marginally less threatening land around Malpas which, even as late as the Middle Ages, was known as the 'bad and unpleasant passage':

> It must always have been a difficult country to cross [but] it was not such a barrier as Mersey marshes. Instead there was at least one important, natural crossing, leading from the Cheshire Central Ridge at Malpas to Whitchurch, thence via the open Prees Heath to the sandstone outcrops of North Shropshire.[4]

The hardships of prehistoric travel are emphasised not because they deterred travellers. They did not. But it is necessary to remember that isolation rather than contact must have been the rule for most small Bronze Age communities. New ideas and fashions arrived only slowly and intermittently, and in conservative societies were probably rejected. Nor were there mandatory designs for megalithic tombs, stone circles or avenues. Each region, each group accepted what it wanted and adapted it to its own desires. The people of Rhos y Beddau were no different. Within the limits of their technical competence they built what they desired as best they could out of the materials they had to hand.

Four miles (6.4 km) south-east of Llandrillo, up a

long dreary valley, is Pistyll Rhaiadr, the highest waterfall in Wales, a cataract that drops sheer into a basin of rock through whose arch it spurts and cascades onto the boulders below, 'an immense skein of silk agitated and disturbed by tempestuous blasts' wrote George Borrow in *Wild Wales*. Yet this fierce foaming tumble, one of the Seven Wonders of Wales,[5] emanates from a mild mountain stream, the Afon Disgynfa, dribbling across a shelf in the hills 240 ft (73 m) above today's viewing-point. It is as unremarkable as the fall is spectacular. Near it, Rhos y Beddau, 'the moor of the graves', is just as unobtrusive.

To reach the circle entails a mile of Sherpa-like trudging up the mountainside and, at the top, a search amongst the rushes and wild grass to locate the stones in the boggy ground. The ring is an almost perfect circle about 42 ft (13 m) in diameter and in fair condition but its stones are low and overgrown and so are those of its avenue. They average less than 10 inches (25 cm) in height, eliciting the comment that the 'site is important because of the comparative rarity of stone rows in Wales, but it is of interest only to the enthusiast'.[6]

Despite this visually-justified jeremiad there are several reasons why the avenue is worth visiting. It is not joined to the ring. It is not aligned on its centre. A third of the way along it changes direction. It is splayed. And its southern stones are taller than those to the north.

Leading from the ENE the 162 ft (49 m) long line stops 27 ft (8.2 m) short of the circle, its axis pointing at least 7 ft (2 m+) south of the centre. 'There is no obvious reason on the ground for the choice of this position which does not seem to have been dictated by considerations of topography'.[7] Nor was astronomy involved. Thom suggested that with its azimuth of 79°.1 towards the ENE and the looming mountains the line could have been directed towards the rising of the bright star Spica (α Virginis) in 2000 BC, and in the opposite direction (259°.1) towards the sunsets of early March and late September.[8] The year is reasonable but the stones supposedly indicating the star are so tiny and dark that they would have been invisible at night, quite useless as a stellar sighting device.

A more likely explanation for the misalignment of the avenue is that though its builders knew that circles and avenues went together they treated them as individual structures. It was an early stage in a process that would conclude by detaching an avenue completely from a circle, a fission suspected for other prehistoric structures and artefacts. In their Irish counterparts the integrated elements of circle, flanking stones and internal ring-cairn of Scottish recumbent stone circles were retained but rearranged.[9] On British Iron Age coinage the chariot, charioteer and galloping horses derived from realistic images on Macedonian gold staters were 'exploded'. 'The Celtic artists took the basic Classical coinage and changed it . . . [to dis-

Fig. 18   Distribution map of tangential and detached avenues.

play] the legs of horses which have become detached from their bodies, chariot-wheels trundling along on their own'.[10] Similarly, what had been a unitary composition of circle and avenue was transmuted at Rhos y Beddau into two isolated features.

It is noticeable, however, that some aspects were retained. The part of the avenue nearer the circle, aligned 73°–253°, is about 62 ft (19 m) long. It narrows from 12 ft 6 to 6 ft 3 (3.8–1.9 m) as it approaches the ring. At its distant eastern end it veers some 5° southwards in a probable later extension about 100 ft (30 m) in length in two crudely parallel rows 11 ft (3.4 m) apart, close to four of Thom's Megalithic Yards of 2.72 ft (10 ft 10½ or 3.3 m).

Many stones are missing or sunk in the peat, especially in the north row, but careful inspection reveals that its eleven measurable uprights are on average only two-thirds the height of the twenty stones of the south row, under 7 inches contrasted against the more than 11 inches (17, 28 cm) of its companion.[11] It is, in Lilliputian style, the 'high and low' trait noticed previously in the avenues of northern Ireland and at Callanish.

Seventy miles south of Rhos y Beddau the circle of Cerrig Duon, described in Chapter One (p. 4), is even more exaggerated in the separation of its splayed avenue and circle. Climbing a hillside from the River Tawe the 148 ft (45 m) long NNE–SSW avenue contracts from 21 ft to 16 ft 6 (6.4 – 5 m) near the ring. Whoever laid it out had no intention of merging it with the circle. It ends 20 ft (6 m) before the ring's north side and, if extended, would have missed the circle to its west by at least 25 ft (7.6 m). So marked is this avoidance of the ring that it must have been deliberate.

But the function as a processional approach was not impaired. The avenue took the most convenient line up the gentle slope from the river. This combination of circle, avenue and water has been noticed elsewhere.[12]

(c) Northern Ireland

Little could more convincingly demonstrate the results of diffusion than the 'pebble-in-the-pond' pattern of widening ripples resulting from the expanding distribution of entrances and avenues in the Sperrin mountains of the counties of Fermanagh, Tyrone and Londonderry.

Whereas the four circles with entrances or portals cluster in a short half-mile (0.8 km) arc ten miles (16 km) south-west of Draperstown those with avenues are dispersed across sixteen miles in a line that stretches north-westwards towards Strabane. It is noticeable that the ring and avenue at the south-east end, Broughderg North, is very close to the entrance-circles in the same townland.

Almost predictably the tangential avenues are even more spread out around the distant edges of hills and mountains, and the farther they are from Broughderg

the longer and more idiosyncratic they become. Many of them, however, share the 'high and low' characteristic of their probable predecessors.

What may be a ring-cairn rather than a stone circle[13] at Davagh, the site nearest to Broughderg, has a short tangential avenue that ends a few paces to the north of the ring. At Moymore, 'the great plain', six miles (10 km) to the south a gaggle of nine circles are tightly packed together like doughnuts on a baker's tray. A squashed avenue no more than 46 ft (14 m) long buckles between seven of them, four to its west, three to the east, the stones in its west row half as tall again as the low ones opposite. At the southern end of the avenue it is joined at right-angles by a Three-Stone row of tall pillars.

Ten miles (16 km) north of Broughderg the two Aughlish circles have shortish tangential avenues of similarly 'up and down' sides, and at Altaghoney to the west a splendid avenue, laid out ESE–WNW and 110 ft (34 m) in length has lower stones in its north row. The lines pass by the southern arc of the circle, ending just beyond it to the west.

Thirty miles (48 km) WSW of Broughderg and not many miles north of Lough Erne the ruined circle of Formil had a long, splayed and tangential avenue with high-and-low rows. The farthest site of all, Cavancarragh in Co. Fermanagh, possessed a small circle of tiny stones with a single row at a tangent to its east. Alongside this were two parallel lines of standing stones. Some 46 ft (14 m) apart they formed a broad avenue at least 223 ft (68 m) long and reputedly once twice that length but with neither circle nor cairn at either end. In the vicinity there are other cists and cairns. 'They are said to have contained food-vessels and traces of cremations',[14] but their chronological relationship to the Cavancarragh circle and avenue is unknown.

DOUBLE ROWS

Double rows, which are not invariably parallel, consist of two lines of standing stones adjacent to each other but not leading to an open stone circle or a henge. Over sixty are known and eighty-six per cent of them are on Dartmoor or on Exmoor immediately to the north. With avenues in Dorset, Somerset and Wiltshire, all within ninety miles (145 km) of Dartmoor, it is plausible that those megalithic settings were the prototypes of the smaller avenues and double rows of Dartmoor. Farther away, in Wales and Scotland, there are few double rows and, in Brittany, only four well to the east in Ille-et-Vilaine (Fig. 19). Such an unbalanced distribution strengthens the belief that it was from the English avenue tradition that the double and single rows developed.

Fig. 19   Distribution map of double rows.

DOUBLE ROWS
1 Learable Hill
2 Mattocks Down
3 Yelland
4 White Ladder
5 Fernworthy
6 Watern Hill
7 Merrivale
8 Trowlesworthy Warren
9 Glasscombe Ball
10 Bazouges-la-Perouse

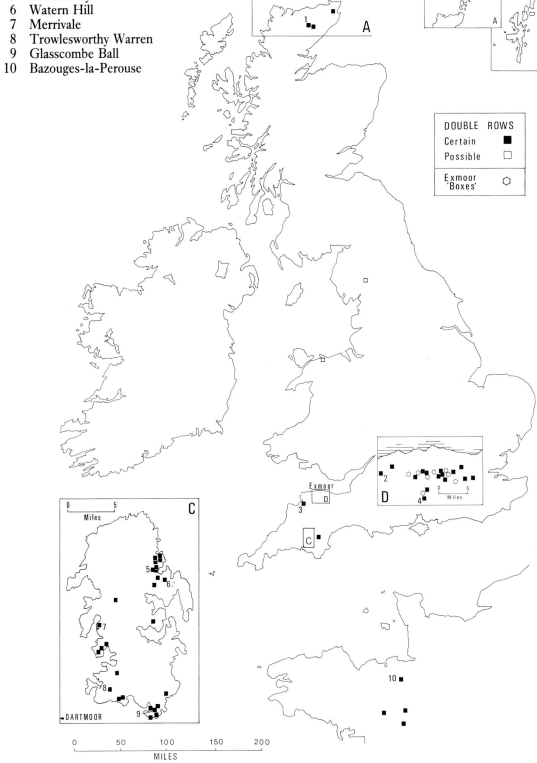

DOUBLE ROWS

Certain ■

Possible □

Exmoor 'Boxes' ⬡

Pl. 28   The wandering lines of the Shovel Down double row, Dartmoor, alongside the circle and avenue to its right. From the south.

Pl. 29   Assacombe double row, Dartmoor, from the NNE. The tallest stone stands against the overgrown mound of an encircled cairn.

(a) *Dartmoor*

These are the best-known of all British rows. The double lines there have a wider distribution than the avenue-circles on the moor, some overlapping the latter's enclave in the west but others laid out at the south and south-east with even more at the north-east where their builders took up land adjacent to the great open circles. The Shovel Down rows (Pl. 28) were hardly a mile from Scorhill though separated from it by the River Teign. The three Fernworthy double rows stretched to north and south of a large megalithic ring. It was as though the borders of Dartmoor were being enclosed in a noose of circles and rows with only the north-west remaining free. And for the first time people built further into the moor, at Laughter Tor, Conies Down, and at the very heart of the upland, at White Tor.

The rows vary in length from as little as 24 ft (7 m) at Penn Beacon SW up to a possible 950 ft (290 m) at Black Tor. Removing these extreme sites from the statistics the rows on average are 362 ft long (110 m) and 4 ft 2 (1.3 m) wide. With the exception of White Ladder the dispersed rows on Exmoor are much shorter.

On Dartmoor some rows, not many, are very constricted, no more than 1 ft (30 cm) across, leaving a space hardly enough for one of Stukeley's serpents. And it is like the slothed skins of enormous grey-spotted adders that the rows lie on their hillsides, most of them with impressive standing stones at their lower end and a small cairn at their head.

(i) *Features*

The terminal menhirs are often big, the Longstone at Shovel Down 10 ft 5 (3.2 m) high and so conspicuous that as long ago as AD 1240 it was used as a boundary marker. The re-erected stone at Laughter Tor now stands 8 ft 8 (2.6 m) high. Not as tall but the most prominent of all these terminals is one in the Challacombe multiple rows, 5 ft wide at its base and a good 6 ft in height (1.5 × 1.8 m). Like many others it is set at right-angles to its rows, spreading heavily across the open end like a broad, blocking slab.

At the upper end of most rows is an unobtrusive round cairn or barrow. It is seldom more than 19 ft in diameter and 2 ft high (5.8 m × 60 cm) but it is, nevertheless, the focus of the complex, and it is not unusual to find the tallest stones of the row standing by it. Fine examples have survived at Watern Down, known locally as the 'burying stones', and Assacombe (Pl. 29). 'In general, the stones nearest the grave give evidence of selection, being for the most part larger than the avenue; and no comparatively small or insignificant stones are used in this position'.[15]

Favouring the belief that these rows perpetuated the tradition of being processional ways the majority follow the easiest gradient along a slope. The builders of the Merrivale lines chose the 'best piece of level ground anywhere close to the Walkham'.[16] Even at

Assacombe, the steepest of all the rows where the ground rises sharply one foot in every six,[17] although the ground curves down from the triple-circle at its head the triangular terminal stone is still visible from the ring. Emmett noted that most rows occupied ground rising at a ratio of less than 1:10, adding that 'the gradient was only one in several factors' affecting the choice of site.[18]

Like any group of prehistoric monuments the Dartmoor double rows although basically similar repeatedly demonstrate the improvisations of their builders. No professional gangs with stone-row pattern-books touted for custom amongst the settlements. Nor was a standardised megalithic yardstick used. To the contrary, there were as many variations in the layout of a row as there were rows and nowhere are these departures from the norm of 'Bottom-of-the-Slope Terminal Stone + Graded Row + Upper Cairn-with-Cist' more evident than in the rows deepest in the moor.

At Laughter Tor the tall terminal may originally have been a single menhir. It is at the head of the slope with a double row leading uphill from a barrow (Pls. 30 and 31). The pillar is 'playing-card' in shape and a good 8 ft 8 (2.6 m) high even after its re-erection. The reconstruction may account for its longer axis being at an angle of some 10° from the 113°–293° of the row.

Conies Down, at 1660 ft (506 m) above sea level the highest of all the rows, also has a terminal stone at the top of the slope. At Trendlebere Down near Manaton, isolated and about to fall off the eastern edge of Dartmoor, the ruined rows have a cairn at either end. The Yelland row near Exmoor, regularly submerged at high tide, has neither terminal stone nor barrow. Discrepancies such as these make archaeological classifications no more than warnings that Neolithic and Bronze Age communities were not copyists. They were more akin to post-impressionists than to pattern-bound Roman mosaicists.

It is even possible that some double rows were left unfinished. The Drizzlecombe SW row 'is in part double, in part single, and it is doubtful whether it was ever wholly double'. Just to its north another row 'is single throughout, except for one pair of stones by the menhir'[19] as though men had laid out a template between barrow and terminal stone but never completed the infilling.

Conversely, not many miles away, the long avenue on Ringmoor Down whose attractively simple stone circle was restored in 1909 is mainly single but possibly was once double. Without excavation it is impossible to determine whether one is looking at an abandoned project or at twin lines that have been disastrously robbed of their stones, perhaps plundered for the reaves that pass near them.

Questions such as these are compounded at Glasscombe Ball NE where the row, 5 ft 5 (1.7 m) wide, has an eastern line 368 ft (112 m) long with its low stones spaced 7 ft 5 (2.3 m) apart. Its western partner is dif-

Laughter Tor, Dartmoor.

Pl. 30   Remains of the double row.

Pl. 31   The tall terminal at its wsw end.

ferent, no more than 212 ft (65 m) in length with stones at 10 ft 1 (3.1 m) intervals. 'It is perfectly clear that the north [western] part has lost no stones'.[20] With ravaged cairns at either end 'possibly the double row was erected first, leading up to a cairn in the normal way, and the lower cairn and single row added later. The specific significance is obscure'.[21] This suggestion that rows could be added to and 'improved' is currently the most feasible interpretation of these internally disparate settings and offers the best explanation for the multiple rows of Brittany and northern Scotland.

(ii) *Construction*

Despite the great lengths of some rows very few demanded great effort for their construction. Most stones were small, between 1 ft 6 and 3 ft (15 cm– 1 m) high, light enough for three or four men to lift. An average double row contained about 150, easily collected from the collapsed granite clitter of a nearby tor.

Crossing was unimpressed by these unspectacular lines. 'The stones in many of the rows rise only a foot or so above the turf. This is the more surprising seeing that in so many parts of the moor stones of large size and of suitable shape are scattered abundantly over the surface of the ground', and went on to point out that the builders of the Merrivale lines could have obtained impressive menhirs from Mis Tor to the north.[22]

This was to misunderstand the attitudes and numbers of the people concerned. The massive boulders of Mis Tor lie on a steep slope over a mile

(1.6 km) to the north with lesser stones strewn densely between them and Merrivale. A granite pillar of ten tons that had to be dragged downhill at a gradient of 1 in 6 required a work-force of nearly a hundred labourers,[23] maybe even more because the intervening clitter would have rendered sledges or rollers unusable. More sensibly the Merrivale workers chose less cumbersome stones from the lower slopes of King's Tor hardly a quarter of a mile to the south where tumbles of slabs weighing two to three tons could be manhandled across level ground by nine or ten workers. The resulting rows were less imposing but much easier to put up.

Relevant to this question of a work-force but as yet unanswered is the number of inhabitants of any community. Frequently the collapsed drystone walls of small round hut-circles, most thought to be of the Bronze Age, lie close to stone rows. Three survive near the Watern Hill row but the acid soil, as elsewhere, has eaten away bone, wood and pottery leaving nothing to show whether those homesteads were occupied by the builders of the rows. Perhaps 4000 hut-circles once existed on Dartmoor. Some stood inside compounds, most were unenclosed. With dimensions of about 15 to 16 ft (4.6–4.9 m) across they could comfortably accommodate five or six people. Except for occasional instances of large settlements such as Grimspound or Kestor an average cluster contains up to a dozen huts, not all of which may have been contemporary. With groups of three to ten huts family groups of twenty to sixty people may be assumed.[24]

Pl. 32 The double row of Watern Down, Dartmoor, also known as the 'burying stones'. From the NNE.

Computations can be made of the minimum number of people needed to erect heavy stones like the 9 ft 6 (2.9 m) high pillar against the Down Tor stone circle. Weighing about five tons it could have been set up by the efforts of twenty five to thirty men. Such a stone is in the minority amongst the Dartmoor rows. With less ponderous challenges ten to twenty able-bodied adults would have been sufficient for the work. Their communities, including the elderly, infirm and children, may have been no larger than fifty or sixty individuals. And if kinship groups co-operated in the construction of a row then individual societies may have been smaller still.

(iii) *Dating*

The problem is aggravated because there is no clear dating evidence for any of the rows. Nothing has come from their stoneholes, and the discovery in 1897 of a fine B/W beaker in a cist 250 yards (230 m) NNE of the Watern Hill row (Pl. 32)[25] provides no more than an interesting association. Nor does the presence of a S2/W beaker in the proximity of the Fernworthy stone circle and rows. A flint barbed-and-tanged arrowhead of beaker type at Yelland is even more ambiguous. It was found in an area of modern disturbance 90 ft (27 m) to the east of the rows' end.[26] It is certainly worth noting, however, that where pots have been found close to rows on Dartmoor the vessels have usually been beakers, an association similar to that which existed between beakers and avenues.

From these tantalising hints, for they are no more, it is arguable that the juxtaposition of rows and beaker material, but nothing earlier or later, suggests that the rows belonged to the Early Bronze Age centuries between 2300 and 1800 BC.

The landscaped lines of reaves, walls running for miles along the boundaries of Dartmoor, add something to this argument. There is evidence that these were laid out in the Bronze Age, starting around 1700–1600 BC, well before any Iron Age activity on the moor but post-dating the stone rows.[27] Fleming has shown that the walls sometimes overlie or interrupt rows such as Yar Tor and Sharpitor Tor East. The centre of the Watern Hill row is run through by the walls of a D-shaped enclosure attached to a reave to the west of the row. At other sites reaves seemingly avoid a row with some care leading just east of the Merrivale lines or passing between but not through the Shovel Down rows.[28] Rows such as these affected by reaves must predate them and probably be earlier than 1600 BC.

The picture is of small communities in neighbouring territories, their cattle grazing on pasture richer than today's impoverished soils. It has been thought that at a time when metal-working was developing these pastoralists may also have engaged in tin-mining. There have been confident claims that tin-streaming on Dartmoor took place in prehistoric times.[29] Many of the hut-circles are near running water which affords 'evidence of the activities of the mediaeval tin-workers'. It may be significant that in north-west Dartmoor where the rivers of West Okemont and Redaven offered excellent pasturage hut-circles are scarce. There is a similar absence of signs of tin-streaming.[30]

(iv) *Layout*

There are indications that sometimes a stone row was laid out in geometrical harmony with another, creating what has been variously termed a ritual centre, a sanctuary or a sacred landscape. Such complexes appear to have been deliberately planned by people with a desire for symmetry. Their motivations may have been astronomical, or directional towards a focal monument, or maybe based on nothing more than the satisfaction of achieving symmetry for its own sake.

Sometimes the connections were illusory. In one of his most charmingly eccentric and imaginative books Tom Lethbridge remarked on the relationship between two distant rows and tin-mining. The compass-bearing, he claimed, from

> Black Tor when projected cuts another row at Warren House, in an area seamed and scarred with very ancient tin workings. It may be a coincidence, but these two lines could have given you a cross-bearing on rich deposits of tin, long before maps are supposed to have existed. In any case how did anybody know that there was tin in Britain without long and elaborate prospecting?[31]

Prospecting for tin is proven. Neolithic miners had been seeking and exploiting sources of durable stone for over a thousand years, and in the Early Bronze Age deposits of tin, copper, even gold were sought all over Britain and Ireland. Lethbridge's supposition founders not on the unlikelihood of exploration but on the geographical fact that his two stone rows, Black Tor and Challacombe are over nine miles (15 km) apart with tors, valleys and marshes between them. It is inconceivable that their builders ever aligned one upon the other.

Trowlesworthy is different. Although now in poor condition there were once two double rows amongst a confusion of clitter, hut-circles and compounds for cattle. The eastern row is in better condition, its two gently curving lines from the SSW approaching a small stone circle known as The Pulpit. Lockyer thought the avenue had been aligned upon the rising of the star Arcturus, α Boôtis, between 2130 and 2080 BC.

About 350 ft (107 m) to the west of the circle is the head of the western row, once double, now single, extending from the WSW to the questionable remains of an encircled cairn. It is the easterly alignment of this row that is of interest for it seems that its builder had orientated it upon the stone circle. 'The line of the row, projected beyond the cairn, leads directly to the cairn at the head of the eastern row'.[32]

Embryonic though it may be the setting at Trowlesworthy in which a later line may have intentionally been designed to point to an earlier has affinities with the more involved design of Drizzlecombe to be described in the next chapter. Like Glasscombe Ball the converging rows at Trowlesworthy may have been two of the forerunners of the multiple rows on Dartmoor and elsewhere.

(v) *Art and Astronomy*

No carvings, whether elaborate motifs or simple cup-marks, have been recognised on any stone of the Dartmoor rows although cups, rings and grooves have been noticed on isolated boulders at Dunstone, Holming Beacon and Brisworthy.[33] Nor have many claims been made that the lines were put up astronomically to mark the risings or settings of the sun or moon. Only the dubious targets of sundry stars have been proposed.

Early in the twentieth century Lockyer[34] examined several of the straighter rows on Dartmoor, concluding that many been laid out towards the rising of bright stars such as Rigel (α Centauri), Arcturus (α Boôtis) and the loveliest of star clusters, the Pleiades, 'The Seven Sisters', of which the brightest star is Alcyone (η Tauri).

Unlike the midsummer and midwinter positions of the sun and moon which have remained almost unvaried over the millennia, many stars move across the heavens rapidly,[35] changing their risings and settings at predictable rates. As an example, at the Dartmoor latitude of 50°.5 Capella's risings moved some 25° from ENE (52°) to NNE (27°) between 3500 BC and 1400 BC. Lockyer therefore felt able to propose dateable stellar targets for some double rows: Challacombe aligned on α Centauri rising in 3600 BC; rows at Fernworthy on α Centauri rising in 1720 BC, 1670 BC and 1610 BC; the three Merrivale rows at on the risings both of Arcturus in 1860 BC, and the Pleiades in 1580 BC and 1400 BC; Shovel Down on α Centauri rising in 2900 BC; and Trowlesworthy on Arcturus rising in 2130 BC.

Despite the assurance of his findings a range of dates from 3600 BC to 1400 BC, a time span from the Middle Neolithic down to the Late Bronze Age is archaeologically unpersuasive. Nor is the wandering design of these rows explicable if they had been intended as astronomical sighting devices.

Worth wrote a detailed criticism of Lockyer's findings.[36] Having spent years fieldwalking on Dartmoor he noted that a majority of the lines had general alignments either north – south or north-east – south-west but 'in other cases the direction seems to be governed by the form of the ground'.[37] Emmett was even more dismissive. Except for a gap at the south-east – north-west segment of the horizon the rows were orientated to almost every point of the compass. For the double rows, 'there is invariably a different alignment for each line of stones'.[38] The rows on Dartmoor, he wrote, 'merely run roughly downhill, towards the limit of the granite, and . . . the orientation

Pl. 33 The east end of the Merrivale North double row, Dartmoor. In the background is the Merrivale Centre avenue.

is the result of such casual siting'. Worse, like his own driving of a golf-ball, 'not only do most of the stone rows go in the wrong direction, furthermore they do not even go straight in the wrong direction'.[39]

Denials that the Dartmoor double rows were ever designed as astronomical indicators are supported by their grossly different lengths. Averaging more than a hundred yards (90 m) of stuttering stones which one could comfortably take two minutes to walk, the rows far exceed the optimum distance between a backsight and foresight, about 50 to 100 ft (15–30 m). The presence of a thick terminal stone at their lower end effectively precluded any well-defined sighting along the line. The rows, moreover, usually ended uphill at a burial cairn, squat, broad and completely unsuitable as a foresight.

Despite the validity of these objections there is one complex that might appear to contain eligible candidates for deliberate astronomical alignments, the straight rows of the Merrivale avenue, double row and single line. Lockyer was enthusiastic.

The rows at Merrivale, 'the pleasant valley', at the far west of the moor, are elegantly disposed (Pl. 33): a double row at the north nearly 600 ft (180 m) long and running almost east–west; an avenue some 90 ft (27 m) to its south over 850 ft (260 m) long and, again, almost east–west; with a shorter single row and cairn im-

pinging on its southern side at an acute angle from the SSW with 'all the appearance of an afterthought', wrote Worth.[40]

The avenue is not quite straight. Its extension to the east of the central stone circle is kinked slightly farther to the north than the western sector 'which had neither barrow, menhir nor any other formal termination'.[41] It may be inferred that the western row was the original avenue to the circle, and that the eastern double row and terminal stone were appended later.

Because the avenue and the double row were not parallel to each other but somewhat skewed, the row angled 262°10′–82°10′, the avenue rather more to the north, 260°30′–80°30′, Lockyer suggested they had been set up as sightlines towards the rising of the Pleiades in 1580 and 1400 BC respectively. The star cluster had been chosen not for its beauty but because it was heliacal, its rising giving warning that the May Day sunrise was imminent.[42] The rows were therefore 'used as a processional road, a *via sacra*, to watch the rising of the Pleiades'. The single row performed the same admonitory purpose towards another heliacal star, Arcturus, in 1860 BC. 'This row, like the others, could have been of no *practical* use to anybody. It is interesting to note that this single row of stones is older than the double ones; this seems natural'.[43]

Lockyer's conclusions were wrong. The compass-

TABLE 6. *Hypothetical Stellar Alignments in the Merrivale rows, Dartmoor*

Site	Corrected Declinations	Lockyer	Alternative Targets
Merrivale North (D)	6°.33	Pleiades 1580 BC (1800)	Procyon 1800 BC; Spica 1200 BC; Altair 1350 BC
Merrivale Centre (A)	7°.60	Pleiades 1400 BC (1575)	Spica 1420 BC; Altair 2100 BC
Merrivale SW (S)	40°.69	Arcturus 1860 BC (1650)	Vega 1650 BC

bearings are incorrect by over a degree in each case.[44] Ironically, this changes Lockyer's dates of 1580 and 1400 BC, each very late for the rows, closer to megalithic reality, converting them to 1800 and 1575 BC.

Critically, there is no justification for preferring the Pleiades and Arcturus to other, equally appropriate stars (Table 6). There are many stellar options for Column B, the few cited being only the brightest. In the absence of evidence that one particular star was chosen for a majority of Dartmoor rows there is no statistical reason for accepting one and rejecting the alternatives. The same objection can be made to Lockyer's other 'astronomical' rows for all of which there are several choices of star.

An even more arcane astronomical interpretation of the Merrivale complex was put forward in 1975 when Penny and Wood[45] argued that the regular spacing of stones revealed that three distinct units of measurement had been employed in the layout, and that the rows together with outlying features such as standing stones formed a series of right-angled triangles and quadrilaterals. 'These complex and strange geometrical relationships, incorporated many times into the stone-row site at Merrivale, are not accidental'.[46] The patterns could be used for lunar observations and, by extrapolation, for calculating where the moon would set even when that phenomenon occurred in the invisibility of daylight.

The complications involved in fashioning such a device are discussed in Chapter Nine when considering the multiple rows of Caithness and Sutherland. Here it suffices to remark that if the erratic Merrivale rows were set up to predict lunar events the blueprints seem to have been devised by a prehistoric Heath Robinson rather than a Bronze Age Galileo.

(vi) *Function*

(a) *Dartmoor*

'When Col. Hamilton first saw the Merrivale parallelithons he immediately recognised their resemblance to monuments which he had visited in India, and pronounced them avenues or processional paths of the Druids. Dr Fergusson sees no better explanation than that they may represent the position of two armies.'[47] One must be grateful that the abomination of 'parallelithon' never became part of archaeological terminology.

In spite of Hamilton's pronouncement there has been almost unanimous agreement that the double rows were not pathways. Emmett noted that the uneven, sometimes extremely narrow width of the rows did not accord with the supposition that these were processional ways. 'The irregularity, which implies casual setting out, is inconsistent with a formal pathway. There are sites where the 'path' is less than 0.5 m [1 ft 6] and others where it narrows to a similar figure between some pairs of stones'.

This followed Worth's equally negative observation. 'Six inches is a restricted width for either a racecourse or a processional path, uses to which some would have believe that the stone rows were placed.'[48] Fergusson concurred. Referring to Merrivale he stated that 'They are not processional paths, inasmuch as both ends are blocked up', which is untrue, and '... we cannot conceive any procession moving along their narrow gangway, hardly three feet [1 cm] in width.'[49]

The width is correct. Yet it could be that these constricted double rows with their 'casual setting out' were put up by people simply following an ancient tradition of erecting two lines side by side, lines to the dead person whose cremated bones lay the cairn at the head of the row. It must be stressed that such cramped rows are exceptions. The average width of the rows is 4 ft 2 (1.3 m), quite wide enough for anyone to walk between in comfort and dignity.

What previously has not been considered are the likely origins of these rows and the custom of constructing approaches to a venerated circle or burial-place. Once understood, the reason for the twinned lines becomes explicable. Avenues led to stone circles. Double rows led to round cairns or barrows. But prehistoric studies are three-dimensional in space and time, and time can blur tradition. 'Useless' double rows could be built, too narrow for any physical passage, because over long generations such lines had always been put up.

The double rows on Dartmoor are connected to burial mounds. In twelve instances the upper ends of the lines join cairns, eight lead to encircled cairns and one, at Fernworthy, ends at an encircled cist.[50] That

Two views of the Merrivale avenue.

Pl. 34   The flat-topped stones at the WNW end.

Pl. 35   The triangular terminal at the ESE.

the rows themselves possessed a ritual significance is shown not only by their heightening as they near the cairn but also by the pairing of a taller pillar and a lower, flat-topped slab.

This feature has already been noticed at the Shovel Down avenue. Less than three miles (5 km) to the SSE, on Chagford Common, the double row on Watern Hill has similar features, its stones rising from tiny shafts of granite no more than 6 ins (15 cm) in height up to a slender, head-high needle alongside the cairn. Opposite this pillar is a low, wide stone. Other, smaller pairs in the rows also consist of flat-topped columns and triangular blocks which have been considered to be male and female symbols.

There are others at Assacombe and Har Tor North.[51] In the Merrivale avenue the last pair at its western end consists of a tall pillar and a low, wide block (Pl. 34). At the eastern end is a wide-based triangular terminal 4 ft 2 (1.3 m) high (Pl. 35). The northern double row has a thin, flattish-topped pillar of similar height. The Challacombe multiple rows have a triangular blocking-stone at their south, and a broader, flat-topped slab at the north. The Trowlesworthy West row has a substantial triangular terminal at its lower end and an even heavier flat-topped block bulking at its east against a plundered cairn.

None of these selected stones was fashioned. To the primitive mind, living in an animistic world where all things, clouds, trees, streams, rocks, had life, it may have been that to change a stone physically was to diminish it spiritually, reducing its potency. Nature formed it. Man used it. People took what was available, finding significance in the shapes, placing them in special positions. The integration of fertility symbolism and death is a theme repeated in many prehistoric ritual monuments and could be anticipated in the rows on Dartmoor.

The rows were not astronomical. Their ancestry lay with the great avenues of Wessex, their architecture determined by the size of the groups who raised them and by the weight of stones that could be manipulated. Their focus was the cairn:

> The 'single graves' of the Beaker and Food-Vessel peoples were concealed generally by an inconspicuous small mound. An interesting local development of this very simple funeral monument occurs on Dartmoor, where some sixty little cairns have settings of rows of stones . . . stone-lined paths to the tombs.[52]

(b) *Exmoor*

'Dartmoor for wildness, Exmoor for beauty'. Few adjoining regions could be so different. Contrasted with the harsh austerity of Dartmoor Exmoor is green with rounded hills that end abruptly at the steep cliffs between Porlock and Ilfracombe. The countryside is heather and bracken, slopes and valleys, dangerous bogs west of Brendon Two Gates, but quiet moorland, not jagged, almost somnolent. And, unlike Dartmoor

with its broken tors, boulders are scarce. Exmoor is not granite. It is splintering slate and grit, veins of quartz, sandstone. Outcrops only patchily provide large blocks for standing stones.

The moor is a prehistoric mystery. Although only thirty miles (48 km) north of Dartmoor it has, until recently, been almost an archaeological *terra incognita*, perhaps because it is divided between north Devon and west Somerset. Its distance from large cities has hindered surveys by organised fieldworkers. And the monuments have contributed to their own neglect. Whereas many Dartmoor rows are romantically megalithic those on Exmoor are minilithic, dwarfed in grassy tussocks and weeds, tiny and fragile shafts of slate that can be overlooked from even a few yards away, sunken in peat and unalluring.

Yet the sadness is that these delicate stones are arranged in geometrical patterns, almost without parallel in Britain and Ireland but with larger counterparts in Brittany, designs that, amazingly, have been recognised since the early seventeenth century. Camden was not flattering but he did record their existence. His first English translation of 1610 stated, 'This river [Exe] hath his head and springeth first in a weely barren ground named *Exmore* . . . wherein, there are seen certaine monuments of anticke work, to wit, stones pitched in order, some triangle wise, others in a round circle'.[53]

Triangles of standing stones are not exclusive to Exmoor. There are some on the Yorkshire Moors, one near Robin Hood's Bay of three stones up to 6 ft (1.8 m) high. Provocatively, midway between Exmoor and the Yorkshire Moors there is certainly one, if not two, megalithic triangles on Anglesey. One at Llanrhwdrys with 'sides' 500 yards (460 m) long is too big for acceptance as a planned monument. The second, at Llanfechell just south of Cemaes Bay on the north coast, is better. On top of a low hill three gigantically heavy pillars from 6 ft 3 to 7 ft (1.9, 2.1 m) in height stand at the corners of a triangle (with sides measuring 11 ft by 8 ft by 9 ft 6 3.4 × 2.4 × 2.9 m).

It is to be wondered whether such settings were not rough and ready 'Coves', free-standing Bronze Age representations of the three-sided chambers in Neolithic tombs. Such a continuing tradition of funerary rites would not be unlikely. The stones at Llanfechell are within a quarter of a mile (0.4 km) south-east of a wrecked dolmen that may have been their prototype. There is a claim that their position was chosen so that from the tomb's ruin the triangle would stand in line with the midwinter sunrise.

Sun, death and standing stones cling closely together. As Elgee wrote of the sites in Yorkshire:

> It is certainly curious that our triangles also belong to a culture characterised by cremations, flint arrow-heads and urns, for it cannot be doubted that they were erected by the [Bronze Age] urn people whose barrows they adjoin.[54]

On Exmoor as well as triangles there are rectangles and parallelograms and rhomboids like a series of Euclidean exercises. In 1879 R.N. Worth commented that 'The antiquities of this district have never received the attention they deserve, and the Forest may therefore be commended to the attention of zealous and discreet archaeologists'. Apart from the studious attentions of his son and the Rev. J.F. Chanter in 1905 and 1906 and a few recent exceptions the neglect continued until the admirable survey and inventory by the Royal Commission in 1992.[55]

Angular megalithic geometry was unusual in Britain and Ireland but not in Finistère where, amongst others, a quadrilateral is known on Ushant, an oblong at Ty ar c'Huré, a square at Lanvéoc on the Crozon peninsula, even a polygon at Kermovan near the fishing-port of Le Conquet.[56]

Brittany, almost three hundred sea miles (500 km) south of the Severn estuary, would seem an implausible candidate as the ancestral home of the Exmoor rows. Dartmoor was much closer. Less than thirty miles (48 km) separated Ramsley, the most northerly of the Dartmoor rows, from White Ladder near Kinsford on the southern slopes of Exmoor and of all Exmoor double rows the most similar to those on Dartmoor. Its length of 1300 ft (396 m) is more than twenty times that of the average Exmoor line. But like Yelland on the west coast near Barnstaple, it is isolated, the shorter rows being four miles (6.4 km) to the north with the dreadful barrier of The Chains between them, a long, bleak ridge surrounded by mires and marshes. It was not impassable but the passes between its hills were treacherous.

White Ladder, a mixture of quartz and sandstones, is yet another example of the observation that the farther a monument was from its origins the more it would differ from the original. Like rows deep on Dartmoor such as Trendlebere Down and Laughter

Tor it possesses all the elements of a 'classical' Dartmoor double row but in a modified or rearranged form. It is well over three times as long as the average but only three-quarters as wide. It is connected with water and has a cairn and terminal stone but the cairn is at the lower end and the stone at the upper alongside the marshy source of Kinsford Water, a name supposedly related to an ancient Indo-European word for 'spring' or 'well'.[57] Its stones are so low, however, that in wet weather the swelling peat completely conceals them.

The row has the distinction of containing a hypothetical alignment towards the midwinter sunrise around 2000 BC. The orientation is right though possibly coincidental. The date is feasible but the almost imperceptible shifting of the sun along the horizon, less than 24' of arc between 3000 and 1000 BC, or hardly a minute in a century, makes any precise estimate of age dubious. To a terrestrial observer the sun appears to be over half a degree wide making it almost impossible to determine its skyline position within the precision of two or three minutes – or centuries.[58]

The inconspicuous setting of White Ladder exemplifies the changes that could occur in stone rows over the distances of space and time. They could also differ in their origins. The majority of the Exmoor rows are architecturally different from White Ladder and lie to the north of The Chains in an five-mile (8 km) long east–west line, spaced a mile or two apart, within four miles of the coast. Mattocks Down is on the same straight line but detached from the others, seven miles (11 km) west of its nearest neighbour on Ilkerton Ridge.

The distribution of these rows is significant. They are not only near the coast but close also to tributaries of the East Lyn River, alongside the Badgworthy, Hoccombe and Farley Waters, and the River West

Fig. 20   Mattocks Down, Exmoor. A plan by T. Westcote, c. 1630. From Chanter and Worth, 1905, 78.

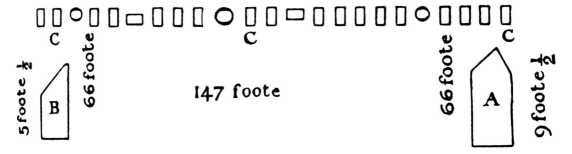

Lyn. It is as though voyagers had beached at the estuary by Lynmouth's red-streaked cliffs and made their way inland to the sheltered valleys between the hills, perhaps in search of ores, more probably looking for good land. What may be hut-circles and remains of field-systems have been suggested at the nearby sites of Shallowford Common and West Pinford with its adjacent short stone row.

The double rows of these hypothetical incomers differed from those on Dartmoor being both short and broad. Because massive boulders were virtually unobtainable the stones were small, 'about 14 in. wide by 6 in. thick by 22 in. high [36 × 15 × 56 cm] would be fair average dimensions.'[59] Even allowing a further eight inches (21 cm) below ground these slate slabs weighed no more than 250 lbs, not difficult for two or three men to sledge across a hillside.

Often of no more than four stones these unobtrusive quadrilaterals are sometimes termed quincunxes if there is a fifth stone at their centre. Such quincuncial settings are not uncommon on Exmoor, occurring at Brendon Two Gates, Chapman Barrows, Trout Hill and elsewhere. Short in comparison to the Dartmoor rows, none of the double lines is more than 150 ft (46 m) in length. The longest was on Mattocks Down. When described in the early seventeenth century one side of the double row had two tall quartz stones, 5 ft 6 and 9 ft 6 (1.7, 2.9 m) high, east–west of each other and 147 ft (45 m) apart. 66 ft (20 m) away to the north was a parallel line of twenty three much lower stones about 1 ft (30 cm) high, the 'Giant's Quoits'. Only the taller menhir survived the eighteenth-century enclosures. Two stone circles that may have stood nearby were also destroyed.

Before its dismantlement Mattocks Down had probably been a 'high and low' double row from which many tall stones in the south line had been robbed before 1630 (Fig. 20). 'The destiny of many of the larger stones of the spoliated monuments is easily traced',[60] five in a nearby field wall, six in another, thirteen in the foundations of a cottage. 'Careful search would probably discover many more'. This 'up-and-down' architecture is so reminiscent of rows in Brittany and Northern Ireland that the origins of Mattocks Down might have lain there.

The rows to its east are much smaller but share the same characteristics of shortness and width. On Dartmoor the relative length and breadth of a double row, 362 ft to 4 ft (110, 1.2 m), had a ratio of 91:1. At Mattocks Down it was barely 2:1. The eastern rows were comparable, averaging 53 ft (16 m) in length and 16 ft (5 m) in width, a ratio of just over 3:1, formations easily construed as oblongs and rectangles rather than double rows.

Proportions like these in which the ratio between length and width is so similar suggests that instead of 'double rows' such settings might better be referred to as 'boxes'. It is an architectural ambiguity com-pounded by the question of the sites' antecedents. Because the uncertainty has no present solution the rectangles of Tom's Hill, West Pinford and others have been included in the gazetteer of double rows.

A major trait amongst them is that their builders aligned them towards cardinal points, often north–south, sometimes east–west, directions presumably obtained by bisecting the risings and settings of the sun. No astronomical analysis has been undertaken.

Two rows in particular are of interest in this study of the development of avenues and stone rows. One on Tom's Hill, north–south, 48 ft by 22 ft (14.6 × 6.7 m), was formed of three stones in each line. Less than a mile to the SSW there is almost a duplicate at West Pinford, east–west, 30 ft (9.1 m) long, 13 ft (4 m) wide, with three tiny stones on each long side.

One might foresee in these brief rows the reduction of lengths and number of stones that would culminate in the short rows of Britain, Ireland and Brittany. Comparison could be made with the site of Ardnacross on Mull in western Scotland. There also are two parallel rows, each of three stones, each line a short 33 ft (10 m) in length. But at Ardnacross the rows are 120 ft (37 m) apart and are most sensibly regarded as two separate Three-Stone rows.

(c) *Scotland and Wales*

Double rows far from Dartmoor and Exmoor are scarce, widely dispersed, and their origins are debateable. The fact that the three in Caithness and Sutherland are very close to multiple, fanlike settings like others on Dartmoor is a teasing indication that there may have been a movement of people from south-west England to northern Scotland, a coastal migration of over five hundred miles (800 km).

There are tenuous architectural affinities between the two regions. The Scottish rows are much shorter than those on Dartmoor, no more than 112 ft (34 m) at Broughwhin and as abbreviated as 25 ft (7.6 m) at Kildonan, the stones are low, but they are associated with cairns or, sometimes, lead towards natural mounds that resemble round barrows. The rows at Learable Hill North have neither cairn nor terminal stone but at Kildonan 'two rows of large boulders of local stone . . . rise steeply to the west towards the top of a small hillock . . . On top of the hillock is a low rectangular mound about 8 m × 4 m [26 ft 3 by 13 ft 2] with a number of small stones around its periphery'.[61] Apart from the shape of the mound it is a description that could be applied to several double rows on Dartmoor.

The one Welsh site, Hwlfa'r Ceirw, is on the north coast of Great Orme's Head in Conway Bay. The two lines are some 300 ft (90 m) long, of small stones that climb from the foot of a slope towards a hollow in the cliffs. It cannot be certain that this is a prehistoric structure. Whether its location by the sea on the route between Dartmoor and Caithness is significant is even more unsure.

PART TWO
From Circles to Lines

CHAPTER EIGHT

THE SINGLE ROWS 2100–1600 BC

*The 'stone row' is almost invariably associated with cairns and kistvaens, and clearly had
some relation to funeral rites. The stone settings are often single, sometimes double…
Usually the largest stones are planted near the cairn, and they dwindle in size to the
blocking-stone, which is of respectable size.*

S. Baring-Gould, *A Book of Dartmoor*, 1907, 60

INTRODUCTION

Although over 170 long, single rows of seven or more
standing stones are known in Britain, Ireland and
Brittany they are not evenly spread (Fig. 21). They
are concentrated in three major areas that have to
be considered individually: south-west England and
south-west Wales (thirty-nine per cent); Northern
Ireland (twenty-five per cent); and Brittany (twenty-
three per cent) where almost half are in Finistère.
There are hardly any long rows in Scotland or in the
Republic of Ireland.

Dartmoor contains twenty-eight per cent of these
rows. Neighbouring it are smaller groups in Cornwall,
Exmoor and south-west Wales. With Dartmoor they
account for almost four in ten of all the known lines.

Long rows only intermingle with the short lines of
three to six stones in the north of Ireland. Even there
the long single lines, some forty of them, are confined
to the Sperrin counties of Fermanagh, Londonderry
and Tyrone. Although short rows also occur there it
is hardly ever against a long line, Beaghmore, Culvacullion, Moymore and Tremoge being exceptions.
That the short settings are independent structures is
shown by their presence in Counties Antrim, Armagh
and Down where there is no long row and hardly a
stone circle.

Stones in single rows are rarely high. On Dartmoor
and Bodmin Moor and in Northern Ireland some are
so low as to be almost completely concealed in the
shin-high grass. They tend, however, to increase in
height when approaching a circle or cairn.

Lengths vary greatly in the two major regions. Even
excluding the exceptionally long Stall Moor and
Butterdon rows and two small rows at Merrivale the
lines on Dartmoor average over 600 ft (183 m) in
length. This is more than six times that of similar rows
leading to cairns and stone circles in Northern Ireland
where, omitting the aberrant Dooish line in Co. Tyrone,
reputedly once an imaginative 1700 ft (520 m) long,
the average length is only 92 ft 7 (28.2 m).

There has been speculation that the lines on Dartmoor owed their development to Breton prototypes.[1]
Architecturally this is improbable and it is more credible to think of the avenues of Wessex as the antecedents of rows such as Down Tor and Butterdon. It
could be argued, just as fallaciously, that it was the
English tradition of erecting lines of standing stones
that was taken up across the Channel by the inhabitants
of north-west Finistère.

This is equally unlikely. In their designs the unique
Breton rows differ from those in Britain and Ireland.
Frequently they consist of lines at right-angles to each

LONG SINGLE ROWS
1 Tormsdale
2 Beaghmore
3 Shap
4 Timoney Hills
5 Parc y Meirw
6 Culbone Hill
7 Merrivale
8 Down Tor
9 Drizzlecombe
10 Stall Moor
11 Nine Maidens
12 An Eured Ven
13 Cordon des Druides

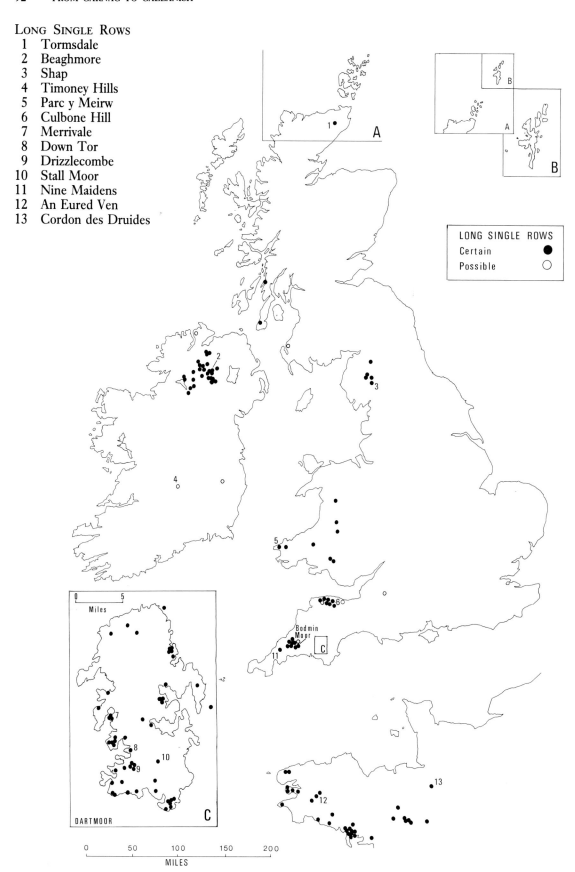

other or meeting tangentially in peculiar geometrical layouts like the alignment and its attached arcs at Lagatjar. Present knowledge indicates that the long rows of south-west England and Brittany were of independent origin though perhaps with comparable progenitors in the megalithic approaches to stone circles in England and to cromlechs in Brittany.

As the tradition of setting up lines of standing stones affected regions in England ever farther to the west the divergencies from an architectural norm became greater.

SOUTH-WEST ENGLAND

(a) Dartmoor

Erected at the time when the massive sarsen circle of Stonehenge was new, when Early Bronze Age heroic societies of axe- and dagger-bearing warriors came to power in Wessex (Pl. 36), when amber and jet and gold ornaments replaced antler and bone for the élite in their novel woven garments, in the centuries from 2100 to 1600 BC, nearly fifty single lines were raised on Dartmoor. They were less uniform than the double rows and there was less consistency about their connections with stone circles, cairns and terminal stones. Even where there was an association it was often a loose one. Sometimes the row pointed to a cairn but stopped some distance from it. At Butterdon the row was joined to a circle but was not in line with its centre. Such deviations make it likely that some of these settings were monuments of several phases, rows being added to circles, to cairns, even to other rows.

Following the excavation of the Cholwichtown row in 1961,[2] a row with the tallest stone at its middle, a trait known also in Brittany, there was evidence that the line had been set up in a clearing. Like other rows it may have been laid out while wide areas of the landscape were still tree-covered with clearances gradually opening the countryside. Pollen analysis there and at Shaugh Moor a mile away suggests that by 2000 BC the Neolithic oak forests were being slowly replaced by hazel scrubland and heath. Blanket bog was already ominously developing on the higher, thinner soils.[3] The quite regular spacing of the rows also intimates that by necessity during the Bronze Age Dartmoor was being apportioned into territories.[4] Cereal pollens at Cholwichtown, 'the coldest town', and Trowlesworthy tell of cultivation while rows were in use although pastoralism remained the principal means of livelihood.

The distribution of rows widened. Three-quarters of the single lines are in the south and west but even the previously empty north-west has possible sites at Arms Tor and West Mill Tor. Nearby, on the raw, cluttered slopes of Oke Tor, a devastated line of stones is 'placed in such a manner as to suggest a stone

Fig. 21 Distribution map of long single rows.

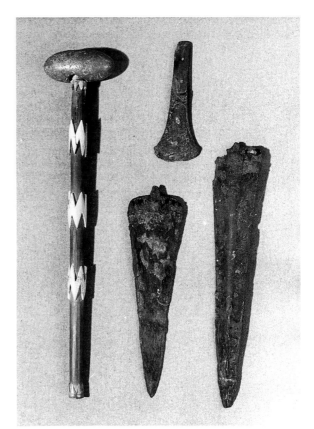

Pl. 36 Bronze daggers, axe and macehead of a Bronze Age Wessex chieftain. The weapons and regalia are from Bush Barrow, near Stonehenge, Wiltshire. Devizes Museum.

row'.[5] Lying a full three miles (5 km) into Dartmoor it is not the only row to be deep into the upland. There are others at Two Bridges, Drizzlecombe, Trowlesworthy, and farthest of all, at Stall Moor, a startlingly long line that ends miles from anywhere at Green Hill, a hill that 'affords the best pasturage in this part of the moor'.[6] With good land around the edges of Dartmoor already claimed later settlers may have been compelled to move farther inland onto higher, colder, wetter areas. Over long centuries it was their clearances, the endless felling of trees that affected natural drainage, resulting in the acidic soils of the moorland and the bogs of today.[7]

During this period single lines were also added to some of the existing double rows on the eastern side of Dartmoor. The resulting multiple settings of three lines are the subject of the next chapter.

In the west the single rows are shorter, longer, less straight than the double rows. The average length of the latter, 362 ft (110 m) is greatly exceeded by the 602 ft (184 m) of the single lines, but this conceals the extreme discrepancies between the lengths of the single rows themselves, the shortest a mere 16 ft (5 m) at Ringhill, and what was once the longest certain row, Butterdon, 6280 ft (1914 m), nearly a mile and a quarter of interrupted, rambling stones.

Eight of the Dartmoor single rows are shorter than 200 ft (61 m) (Pl. 37). All but one lie across the east-west waist of Dartmoor from Holne to Yelverton where the moor contracts like a misshapen eggtimer. Only Penn Beacon SE is outside that buckled rectangle.

Conversely seven rows exceed 1000 ft (305 m) in length. They are nearly all at the far south of the moor, from the Green Hill cairn at the northern end of the Stall Moor row, southwards to Burford Down a few miles from Ivybridge. Down Tor at the west and Natsworthy at the east are exceptions. The former is one of the best-preserved of all the rows (Pl. 38). Some 1145 ft (349 m) long it extends south-westwards from a terminal stone near pounds and hut-circles up to a fine stone circle. The stones of the row rise in height as they approach the ring, the closest being a full 9 ft 6 (2.9 m) high. Worth remarked upon the carelessness of the row's earlier reporters standing as it does not on Down Tor but Hingston Tor, not pointing towards a pound as the Ordnance Survey claimed, and not being either six hundred or eight hundred yards (549, 732 m) long as two of its chroniclers stated.[8]

On the other side of Dartmoor Natsworthy, about 990 ft (300 m) long is less spectacular, its stones low and fallen. Not far to its east where the Ashburton road crosses a green path (SX 733 799) is the quiet grave of Kitty Jay, a young girl, seduced, who committed suicide in the eighteenth century and was buried at an unconsecrated crossroads. Fresh flowers still commemorate her grave.

My cold green days surrounded
By lines and by perimeters. Life curled
In cairns, huts, pounds. My granite hours bounded
By stone rows.

Margaret Calloway, *Jay's Grave*[9]

Anyone wishing to see some of these astonishing Dartmoor rows should walk along the lovely Erme Valley from Harford, where the church contains unusual monumental brasses, one a painting on copper of the amiable John Prideaux (1578–1650), Bishop of Worcester, his wife and ten children.

Beyond Tristis Rock is Burford Down. 'All about it is the mysterious antiquity of stone avenues'.[10] The north-south row there is a third of a mile (0.5 km) of

Pl. 38   The circle and row of Down Tor, Dartmoor, from the north-west.

Pl. 37   The row of Lakehead East, Dartmoor, from the ESE. It is only 40 ft (12 m) long.

Pl. 39   The tall stones of the Staldon row, Dartmoor, from the SSW.

little stones, over a hundred of them, near a wrecked stone circle. The line peters out across Yadsworthy Waste. A mile (1.6 km) from there, past hut-circles, undulating moorland, by pounds and more hut-circles, at the head of the hill on Staldon Down is another row (Pl. 39). It also is long, also north-south, composed of some of the tallest stones on Dartmoor, many fallen, others jutting briskly from the tussocks, advancing jerkily to cairns at both ends of the row.

A further mile and a quarter (2 km) north of this proud setting is the stone circle known variously as The Dancers or Kiss-In-The-Ring. It stands overlooking the west bank 'of that turbulent torrent, the river Erme'.[11] The ring is not exceptional, 54 ft (16.5 m) across, with 26 stones from 2 ft 6 to 5 ft (76 cm, 1.5 m) high, around traces of a cairn, but the incredible row leading to it is certainly an exception. Northwards from the circle to the small barrow on Green Hill are two and a quarter miles (3.6 km) of small, determined stones. In 1879 the meticulous Rev. William Collings Lukis, after studious measurements, declared the line to be exactly 11,239 ft 8 ins (3425.89 m) long! R.H. Worth amended this to 11,150 ft (3399 m), but subtracted nothing from the prehistoric fanaticism that created this maverick.

The row is not megalithic. Indeed, in stretches of deeper peat the stones are engorged in it, tips just visible, and once, in hazy weather, the writer and nine students well spaced out in line abreast, walked right through it without noticing a single stone. The line stretches northwards for 1400 yards (1280 m), the stones becoming even smaller, concealed in blackened heather, sometimes detectable only by the feeble trail alongside it like a thin, white scar across the moor.

The row drops to the Erme, starts again beyond the river, reaches Red Lake stream whose clear water is coloured by its bed of red pebbles, crosses the brook and climbs uneasily up Green Hill, becoming a staccato of gaps and groups that veer from NNW to north and finally stop at an isolated stone about 200 ft (60 m) south of a tiny, savaged barrow whose cist and kerbstones lie in tumbled disorder around it.

The Stall Moor row is the longest known, longer than the Breton multiple lines of Kerzerho at Erdeven near Carnac, ten interrupted rows that spread across 6906 ft (2105 m) of gorse-covered heath, longer than any of the famous Carnac lines: Kerlescan, 978 ft (298 m), Petit-Ménec, 1149 ft (350 m), Kermario, 3777 ft (1151 m), even Ménec, three-quarters of a mile (1.2 km) of multitudinous granite pillars that probably were once two groups, one attached to a western cromlech, another batch of lines marching and rising in the opposite direction towards a cromlech at the east.

A group of rows on Dartmoor best revealing such additions and with a well-planned design exists at Drizzlecombe by the River Plym, below the large Whittenknowle Rocks settlement of hut-circles. The complex is so informative about the development of multiple rows that it is considered in detail at the end of this chapter.

Multi-phase activity may also have affected Stall Moor. Possibly an original line led southwards from the Erme to the stone circle almost a mile away. A second line, 1450 ft (442 m) long, may have started north of Red Lake towards Green Hill and its barrow. It is even possible that these individual rows were ultimately linked by the erection of a third stretch across the lower slopes of Brown Heath between Red Lake and the Erme, 600 yards (550 m) of minute blocks in a sector trickling across the dark and marshy ground from one water to the next.

The concentration of exaggeratedly long lines in the south of Dartmoor is strengthed by the presence of the Butterdon row hardly a mile to the east of Burford Down. Partly denuded in 1803 it once consisted of well over a mile of two thousand stones across the moor. As long ago as AD 962 it was known as the 'old way with the white stones'.[12] The fallen 8 ft 6 (2.6 m) long Longstone terminal lies at its northern end and there is an encircled barrow at its south, idiosyncratically 70 ft (21 m) lower down than the Longstone. Like Burford Down, Staldon and Stall Moor the row is roughly aligned north-south but in this it does no more than follow the lie of the land.

The sinuous nature of the Dartmoor rows argues against their having been used astronomically whereas the path they take, avoiding precipitous river-banks and steep slopes as the Stall Moor row does around Stingers Hill, makes a good case for thinking of them as processional ways, 'stones set up as memorials or tributes of respect to the dead man who is buried at the head of the row', wrote Baring-Gould, an author who felicitously compared the stones to 'a procession of cricketers in flannels stalking over the moor'.[13]

These obsessive lines demonstrate traditions that had almost forgotten their origins, lengths becoming important for their own sakes. To the north and west of Dartmoor in outlying rows on Exmoor, Cornwall and south-west Wales the differences became even more pronounced.

(b) Exmoor

'Even less explicable, and apparently peculiar to Exmoor, are the curious geometrical patterns of small stones, almost certainly Bronze Age work . . . They are usually made of slabs of dark sandstone, which stand about knee-high and are placed along, not across, the line they define . . . Perhaps some day somebody will find a setting which explains them all.'[14]

There are few long single rows on Exmoor. Almost all that are known or suspected are spoiled. At Brockenburrow Lane there is one low stone, 'the last remnant of a stone row which formerly existed at this point'. Other rows such as Wood Barrow are just as devastated but as if in compensation in the Chains

Valley near Exe Head there is a fine run of stones 162 ft (49 m) long, 'more nearly recalling the *Dartmoor* stone rows than any other group we have seen on *Exmoor*.'[15] And at Culbone Hill near the north coast just west of Porlock is another indisputable line. Discovered as recently as 1975 it shares all the characteristics of what seem to be the latest rows on Dartmoor, extreme length and idiosyncratic terminals.

Over 1200 ft (366 m) long but with no more than a score of local sandstone slabs remaining along it the row extends east–west but curves at its centre by at least 10°. At the west it stops well short of a round barrow. A second barrow, severely robbed, can be seen a little way from the other end. The row is not aligned precisely on either mound.

The decorated Culbone Stone with its incised ring-cross of the middle Saxon period leans 130 ft (40 m) south of the row's western end (Pl. 40).[16] Very similar in appearance and size to the other stones it is arguable that the 3 ft (1 m) high pillar was removed from the line and christianised in the sixth or seventh century AD to be set up by a trackway leading downhill to Culbone church, 'probably the smallest complete parish church in England [that] clings, like a wren's nest, to the wooded cliffs.'[17] The words were published in 1940, just a few months after the Culbone Stone had been found and re-erected. Almost 150 years earlier, in 1798, Coleridge was composing *Kubla Khan* at Ash Farm close by until interrupted 'by a man from Porlock'.

One remarkable aspect of the Culbone Hill row is that its line was erected not on level ground but over a ridge, its two distinct alignments meeting at the crest and its ends not intervisible. This suggests that it once consisted of a pair of separate lines, each of them unusually descending towards a Bronze Age round barrow.

(c) *Cornwall*

Unlike the concentration of stone rows on Dartmoor in Devon such long lines are rare in the adjoining county of Cornwall. Indeed, until the recent discovery of others on Bodmin Moor, some surprisingly conspicuous, the Nine Maidens near St Columb Major was the only line known west of Devon.

Over twenty miles (32 km) separates the row of Fox Tor at the east of Bodmin from Merrivale on western Dartmoor, and ten of those miles were obstructed by the River Tamar and the prehistoric forests and swamps surrounding it. Migrants may have followed the high ridge from Tavistock to Gunnislake, Hingston Down, crossing the River Lynher near North Hill. Close by are the two rows of East Moor and Fox Tor.

These and others skirt the eastern and southern fringes of Bodmin, and it is only at the east that they occur near a stone circle, Craddock Moor three-quarters of a mile (1.2 km) west of its namesake, and Fox Tor overlooking the Altarnun ring half a mile

Pl. 40   The christianised Culbone Stone, Exmoor.

(0.8 km) to the north-west. Elsewhere rows and circles are far apart. The great stone circles of the Trippet Stones, the Stripple Stones, the two at Leaze, Fernacre, Stannon all stand freely amongst the tors of western Bodmin with no row nearer than Trehudreth Downs, a long line of little stones nearly two miles (3 km) south of the Trippet Stones and separated from the ring by hills, streams and marshes.

The Bodmin rows share the same traits as the later lines on Dartmoor, their lengths increasing, their stone heights dwindling, and their blocking-stones and cairns disappearing. Whereas the long single rows on Dartmoor averaged 602 ft (184 m) in length the Bodmin lines are longer still with a mean of 883 ft (269 m), ranging from a mere 180 ft (55 m) at the uncertain setting of Langstone Downs up to 1837 ft (560 m) at East Moor, one of the closest rows to Dartmoor and with a large terminal stone and two cairns at its SSW end. Other rows lack such obvious features.

Often their stones are low, 'protruding just above the ground' at Leskernick Hill, tiny at Trehudreth, close-set and only a foot (30 cm) above the peat at Craddock Moor. Yet it is puzzling that no one before the 1980s commented on the four good-sized pillars about 5 ft (1.5 m) high at Colvannick Tor or the stones between 1 ft 6 and 4 ft 6 (0.5–1.4 m) in height at East Moor.

The rows have no consistent orientation, arranged north – south, north-east – south-west, ENE–WSW, even north-west – south-east, and they seem devoid of astronomical sightlines although an alignment has been claimed for the 800 ft (244 m) of eighty-five low, cramped stones on Craddock Moor near the headwaters of the River Fowey.

This row has some very interesting alignment features. At right-angles to the NE end of it there is a very direct alignment to an embanked avenue ... consisting of 2 parallel banks of stones and then on to the Craddock Moor stone circle and finally the Hurlers South stone circle. This is a major alignment feature marking the Beltane/Lughnasad sunset (Samhain/Imbolc sunrise) and running on to a cairn on Caradon Hill.[18]

Samain, Beltane and the others were important Celtic festivals and there is reason to believe that they had Neolithic origins.[19] Solar alignments commemorating them would not be improbable but long-distance sightlines such as this, extending over two miles (3 km) of undulating countryside, must be suspect. Instead of a sharply defined foresight there is only the broad outline of one of several very large barrows on Caradon Hill. There are no good grounds for accepting the one that happens to fit an alignment at the expense of seventeen others that do not, especially as the 'target' of the cemetery is now badly mutilated.[20]

Beyond Bodmin Moor the tradition of setting up long lines of standing stones petered out. Ten miles (16 km) to the west is the isolated and marred row of the Nine Maidens, reputedly 'maids turned into stones for dancing on the sabbath day, as the country folk will tell you',[21] a legend attached to some stone circles in the same region, Boscawen-Un, Boskednan and the Merry Maidens at Land's End, Belstone on Dartmoor. By some arithmetical quirk they too are nicknamed the Nine Maidens, presumably because nine (3 × 3) was so mystical a number[22] that superstition disregarded the reality that the Cornish rings contained at least nineteen stones. The hermaphroditic Belstone was known not only as the Nine Maidens but also as the Seventeen Brothers because of its eight additional slabs. For believers in its feminine ancestry the girls are supposed to return to human form each day and can be seen dancing at noon 'when the conditions are favourable'.[23] Despite several visits the writer has never been fortunate.

Such folk-tales about the 'christianisation' of pagan sites, widespread in Britain, Ireland and Brittany, may be no more than two hundred years old. The notion that the granite pillars of Boscawen-Un were the ossified bodies of dancing girls is not mentioned in any of the seventeenth- or early eighteenth-century descriptions of the ring by writers such as Camden, Aubrey, Toland or Stukeley. Even as late as 1769 the Cornish antiquarian, William Borlase, referred to it only as a place 'for the Election of some considerable Prince'.[24]

The Nine Maidens stone row is a series of maltreated quartz blocks on St Breocks Down. Arranged SSW–NNE up a shallow slope and 352 ft (107 m) long the row consists of nine stones of which five are erect, 5 ft 3 to 6 ft (1.6–1.8 m) high, one nearly fallen, two stumps, and a ninth prostrate and split. A tenth is a recent intrusion. The stones are not evenly spaced. Two at the lower end are only 15 ft (4.6 m) apart but 26 ft (7.9 m) separates the central stones.

Until the late nineteenth century there was a very tall stone, 7 ft 6 (2.3 m) high, standing at the top of the ridge 656 yards (600 m) to the NNE. Known as the Magi Stone, the Fiddler, or the Old Man, it may have been a terminal pillar towards which the row was directed. It was toppled and smashed between 1885 and 1902 and only its broken lower half, 6 ft (1.8 m) long, survives. It was to that elevated column, enclosed in a ring of low stones, that people may have proceeded for their ceremonies. At what time or times of year is unknown. The Nine Maidens has no solar or lunar orientation.

Except for one near the middle, the stones stand in a straight line and Lockyer, relying on a plan by Lukis instead of his own fieldwork, concluded that the row with a bearing of 28° had been directed towards the rising of Capella (α Aurigae) in 1480 BC. A much better survey by Alexander Thom corrected the azimuth to 26°.1. Its declination of 36°.5 was that of the bright star Deneb (α Cygni) rising in the centuries around 2000 BC (c. 1620 bc).[25] Such a date fits well archaeologically with the proposed chronology of long rows. Unfortunately both Deneb and Regulus (α Leonis) are the only first magnitude stars on which precession had very little effect with the result that their risings and settings shifted almost imperceptibly over the centuries making Deneb useless for accurate dating.[26]

The Nine Maidens, a line standing at the most distant edge of the distribution of long stone rows, is particularly interesting because of its comparative shortness, its small number of stones and their wide spacing. Rows to its west would have even fewer stones, six, three, even close-set pairs on the peninsula of Land's End.

WALES

If there were an origin other than an indigenous development for the few long single rows in Wales it is most plausibly the megalithic linear tradition of southern England. The concentrated south-western distribution of the Welsh rows and their architecture supports this.

From Bideford Bay to the sheltered coves and inlets of Dyfed (Pembrokeshire) is no more than sixty miles (97 km) of fair sailing, and knowing of the structural affinities between Dartmoor stone circles like Brisworthy and Fernworthy and the Welsh ring

Pl. 41 Saith Maen NW row, Powys. From the south-west.

of Gors Fawr near the Preseli mountains[27] a similar relationship between the stone rows is not improbable.

The eight long rows in Wales occur predictably in the southern corner of the country, the area closest to the Dartmoor settings and with no comparable rivals westwards in southern Ireland. Inland, at the heart of the mountains is Mynydd Llanbyther whose extended line of eighteen stones is a 'well-known landmark to pedestrians and shepherds',[28] but the best-known row is Parc y Meirw, 'the field of the dead', near Fishguard, for long thought to be the only long row in Wales. It is within a few miles of the sea.

Four of the eight tall stones in this unusual row still stand, trapped in a field-wall, two of them now gate-posts. Thom suggested that the line, 131 ft (40 m) long, was laid out downhill towards the WNW and the minor northern moonset just north of Mount Leinster ninety-one miles (147 km) away across the Irish Sea. The row was the most southerly of his reliable lunar sites. 'Because of rising ground it cannot have been intended for use to the south-east'.[29]

Astronomically this could be true but archaeologically it is more probable that, like most Dartmoor rows, its focal point was up the slope to the ESE. The row stands on ground rising in that direction and its stones also rise in height towards the tallest there, 11 ft (3.4 m) high. Characteristically it stood in line with a megalithic tomb, Coetan Arthur, 'Arthur's Quoit', possibly a heavily-capstoned portal dolmen which was destroyed in 1844 for a house which brought the owner no luck. 'Stories are told of a ghostly lady in white being seen near here', maybe a folk memory of the ancient funerary associations of the row and the tomb.[30]

The short length and limited number of stones in the row is a feature of other 'long' Welsh rows. Fifty to sixty miles (81–97 km) to the east in Powys are the three widely-separated Saith Maen, 'seven stones', rows (Pl. 41). The northernmost in the mountains by Rhayader, was surveyed by the indefatigable Thoms who would 'never have found this very short row had we not been taken to it by an obliging shepherd'.[31] No more than 22 ft (6.7 m) long only two of its low stones stand.

Another Saith Maen, thirty miles (48 km) to the south by the River Tawe and not far from the Cerrig Duon stone circle is well worth a climb from Craig-y-nos castle. It also is short but with five of its tall pillars upright. Both rows and Parc y Meirw are mentioned because, as with the Nine Maidens in Cornwall, they are geographically – and probably chronologically – at the outer limits of long rows. The lines of stones to follow them would be shorter. It is noticeable that close to the northern Saith Maen is a Four- to Six-Stone row at Rhos-y-gelynan, and a few miles farther north the long row of Cwm y Saeson, 'the Englishman's valley', had the short row of Cae Garreg erected in its vicinity. Reasons for such economical settings may have been no more esoteric than the reluctance of later people to put up anything more than the most basic of megalithic lines.

NORTH-WESTERN ENGLAND

Little is to be seen today of the long single rows that once stood at the far eastern and southern outskirts of the Lake District. In 1886 Taylor reported that 'remains of former alignments of megaliths may still be made out elsewhere, in various localities in the district around Penrith', referring to vestigial lines of standing stones at Newbiggin, Newton Reigny, and at Carlatton near Carlisle. They have gone.

> I have seen old people who remembered the removal of many of the stones at the beginning of this century . . . These lines may have been in connection with the barrows and stone circles, of which the dilapidated remains and half buried relics are frequent in this locality.[32]

Hardly anything is known about them or their associations. 'According to local tradition [the Carlatton row] leads to Grey Yauds',[33] but the row is as demolished as the great stone circle two unlikely miles (3 km) to its SSE. At Lowther Woodhouse a row supposedly led to a cairn near Yanwath Wood but this is hearsay without confirmation. Only at Shap seven miles (11 km) farther south is there anything left of what some centuries ago was a noteworthy assemblage of long rows in Cumbria.

Leland visited Shap in the early sixteenth century, mentioning the abbey, the only one in Westmorland, but not the stones. Some years later Camden, although missing the overgrown avenue crossing the Karl Lofts common south of the village, did notice the massive boulders to its north, 'large stones in the form of Pyramids (some of them 9 foot high and 14 thick) set almost in a direct line and at equal distances, for a mile together'.[34] This must refer to the 'almost' straight setting of granite stones from the Goggleby Stone to the pillars north of the prostrate Thunder Stone almost a mile to the north-west.

Pl. 42 The Goggleby Stone, Cumbria, from the south. Shap village is off the picture to the right.

Most of the boulders were huge erratics of which there were many in the locality. 'How such immense blocks (several being from 3 to 4 yards [2.7–3.7 m] in diameter) could be carried and placed in the regular manner they were it is difficult to form an idea.' Some were enormous, weighing twenty or thirty tons. Yet when the last upright, the Goggleby Stone (Pl. 42), fell and was re-erected in 1975 its stonehole was found to be less than 1 ft 6 (45 cm) deep, so shallow that it must have been easy to topple and drag away other such unstable giants.[35]

Since Camden subsequent visitors, Stukeley, Pennant, Colt Hoare, Simpson, Fergusson, Lukis and others have reported the progressive, unhindered destruction of the rows and it is impossible now to establish exactly what the disposition of the stones was. There are three reasonable hypotheses.

One is that the setting had consisted of one extensive avenue over two miles (3.2 km) long, leading south-eastwards to Shap and then sharply south to Kemp Howe stone circle. Stukeley was happy with this megalithic snake, suggesting that a 600 yard (550 m) gap at its middle was the result of its proximity to the iconoclasts of Shap village.

Objections to this theoretical long avenue arise not only from that break in the stones and the noticeable difference in heights between the low slabs of the south and the tall boulders of the north but also from the quite unnecessary 'remarkable turn' of some 40° WNW that the line makes north of Shap. It was noted by Routh, Stukeley's surveyor, who also remarked on the attractiveness of the stones of 'a very particular sparkling grit, with large veins of a reddish colour, and 'tis said will take a very beautiful polish'.[36] It is still used as ornamental stone today.

A more plausible interpretation would have a single line north-west of Shap with a second avenue to its east starting at the Goggleby Stone and running north-west for about two-thirds of a mile (1 km) to Skellaw Cairn. The Goggleby Stone is a bulbously triangular boulder standing on its head like an up-turned avocado. In 1834 the Rev. Bathurst Deane scoffed at the 'ridiculous name of the "Guggleby" stone, given to it by a facetious farmer some years ago, to exercise the ingenuity of antiquarians'. As, over a century before, Stukeley had referred to 'one particularly remarkable, called Guggleby stone' Deane appears to have been misled.[37]

In support of the belief that there had been a second avenue is the fact that the Goggleby Stone and another boulder 3200 yards (293 m) to its north do not align on the centre of Skellaw Cairn but to its west. A rectangular block set in a wall east of the Goggleby Stone may have been its opposite partner in the avenue. 'The pairing of tabular stones with triangular ones is not unknown in analogous sites where the two shapes are thought to represent male and female forms'.[38]

A third possibility, and one favoured undogmatically by the writer, is that to the north of the Kemp Howe avenue there had been two single lines, the eastern beginning at the Goggleby Stone, the other starting about 1000 feet (300 m) to the WNW and stretching north-westwards for some 900 yards (820 m), passing alongside the Knipe Scar enclosed cremation cemetery with its burnt human bones. Near the line's north end was a fallen glacial erratic, the Thunder Stone.

There are inconclusive reasons for preferring the idea of two single rows. A second 'avenue' would have been extraordinarily wide, about 200 feet (60 m) across if the Goggleby Stone's counterpart is in its original position. The Goggleby Stone, moreover, stands at right-angles to the line like a blocking stone whereas the leaning stone to its north once stood axially like the pillars in other single rows. Both stones are mistakenly claimed to be cupmarked.[39]

Sadly, what had been composed of almost five hundred stones in organised lines has been reduced to an incomprehensible scatter. 'When the antiquary now views the remains of this remarkable monument, he cannot but regret at what, perhaps, he may call the barbarous treatment it has met with.'[40]

The long rows were the end of a tradition in Cumbria. If there were any short rows they have gone except for the questionable pair of pillars at the Giant's Grave at Kirksanton and the nearby Lacra Three-

Stone row. It was only across the Irish Sea that long rows flourished.

NORTHERN IRELAND

The lines of standing stones at Beaghmore in Co. Tyrone are the best-known of all rows in Ireland. They are also the most misleading. Sometimes termed avenues, in reality they are an assemblage of connected, tangential and detached wriggling lines, long and short, high and low, parallel and splayed, linked to megalithic rings that are parodies of circularity. It is a collection untypical of the long, single rows of Ulster.

The distribution of those lines is uneven with not one in the eastern counties of Antrim and Down, and only one very questionable in Donegal at the north-west, a mixture of ten stones at Roosky, some standing, some leaning, two prostrate and a pile of four loose blocks. Three of the erect stones are out of line. The 'row' is not convincing and may be no more than the wreckage of a field-wall.

Even in the central regions between east and west the distribution is unbalanced with few rows in London-derry to the north or Fermanagh at the south. It is in Co. Tyrone that they concentrate on the undulating slopes of the Sperrin hills and mountains, spreading out from the more localised areas of avenues and double rows.

Their dating is uncertain. Four C-14 assays from the complex at Beaghmore provide only the broadest indications of age. One of 2185±80 bc (UB-603), from a hearth at the end of Circle E's row, approximately 2650 BC in the Late Neolithic, appears to relate to earlier occupation of the site. Three others of 1605±45 bc (UB-23), 1535±55 bc (UB-11) and 775±55 bc (UB-163) were obtained from material not directly related to the rows, the first from charcoal with a hoard of flints just east of the row that leads between circles F and G. The second derived from charcoal underneath a cairn at the south-west end of that row, and the third from organic material at the bottom of the ditch surrounding the cairn. 'The earliest possible date of construction of the stone circles is given by the charcoal under the cairn, the latest date by the lowest organic material in the ditch'.[41] This bracket of between 1880 and 950 BC is not very helpful but its upper limit does fall within the period of 2100 to 1600 BC suggested for the long single rows.

The discovery of some vaguely Western Neolithic sherds and flint scrapers from an excavation at Drum-skinny, Co. Fermanagh, in 1962, tallies with this general time-span. At Beaghmore the minute cairn between Circles A and B contained a stone axe from Tievebulliagh mountain in Co. Antrim. Production of these implements may have endured for almost two thousand years, petering out around 2000 BC. The flattened sides of the Beaghmore axe are typical of Bronze Age styles, and its abraded condition suggests that it was old when buried in the tiny cist of the cairn, perhaps not before 1700 BC.[42]

Despite the variety of megalithic monuments in the north of Ireland the single rows are associated strongly with only one type, the stone circle. Occasionally a row runs near a chambered tomb or a standing stone, a few, but very few, are close to a cairn, the squat stones of Doorat actually joined to one but this is unusual. Just as uncommon is the neighbouring presence of a short row, only two Four- to Six-Stone rows at Beaghmore and four Three-Stone rows, including one against a stone circle at Tremoge where a second circle has a long line.

In direct contrast, the relationship between the rows and the circles of numerous low stones is repeated at site after site, reaffirming the ancestry of the lines in the avenues and portalled entrances of Late Neolithic megalithic rings. But it is a strained relationship. Of the thirty-six sites where the position of the row is known only two lines are actually connected to a circle, one being Corick in Co. Londonderry. The other, Copney, Co. Tyrone, is a complex of nine ragged rings, a cairn and a standing stone. One circle has a shortish line of little stones running up to it.

Such a straightforward association is atypical. Of the remaining thirty-four rows twenty-four are tangential and ten are completely detached as though their builders were aware of the traditional link between stone circle and row but now regarded the row as an independent structure. The little-known but important group at Corick with its attached row reflects this fission.

By the east bank of a stream in the shadow of Slieve Gullion mountain with a passage-tomb high on its summit, the circles and rows at Corick are intriguing. Revealed by nineteenth-century peat-cutting, at a height almost 800 ft (244 m) above sea-level, the remains of four inconspicuous stone circles, one with a central pillar, an overgrown chambered tomb and six tallish stone rows lie on a bare, boringly flat moor within a few strides of each other.

A little distance south-west of the centre-stone ring are three stone circles. The west has the attached row. The middle and eastern have long south – north tangential rows nudging their east arcs. To the north a shorter line lies south-east – north-west with no ring, tomb or standing stone as its focus. A longer, arranged north – south, is also unattached. By its southern end another row leads ESE – WNW almost at right-angles to the end of the attached row but with no obvious target of its own. It is a combination of lines that in their disposition are reminiscent of the rows at angles to each other in Finistère. Perhaps more importantly, the collection of rows at Corick indicates the manner in which the multiple rows of Brittany and northern Scotland may have developed. In this respect, Corick is more significant than Beaghmore. But for the emergence of short rows the importance of Beaghmore is greater.

Despite their fame the monuments at Beaghmore,

'great birches', have only been fully appreciated since 1945. 'It is now known that they extend over several acres and the area already uncovered has revealed a complex system of circles, small cairns, and alignments' (Pl. 43).[43] The site is a conglomeration of seven circles, A to G, six of them in pairs and two, E and G, hypothetically egg-shaped. There are also six long, single rows, two short Four- to Six-Stone rows, a Three-Stone row and a set of tiny cairns, four of them intimately fused with long rows. Crude sightlines are contained in the long rows. It is a mixture as yet unknown elsewhere and for this reason its idiosyncracies require separate consideration.

The whole of Beaghmore is a contradiction. There is no impression of unitary planning. Like a mediaeval parish church the accumulation looks like a long-drawn-out series of additions and modifications from maybe as early as 1800 BC to as late as 1200 BC. And the series may include an upside-down chronology with cairns preceding circles, and short rows of tall stones preceding long rows of squat boulders.

A tentative sequence would see Circle G with its entrance, close to the other entrance-circles at Broughderg, as the first of a batch of rings that were put up, one at a time over the years, around a cemetery of little cairns. Careful inspection of the excavator's plan shows how the circumferences of Circles A and B flatten as they straddle their cairn. Circle D, a finely designed ring, abuts its cairn but its partner, C, is hideously distorted as though its eastern arc had been bashed against D. Circle E half-engulfs its cairn but the ends of its perimeter stop short of it and are not in line with each other. Quite differently, there is a symmetry to the cairns, four in a straight 220 ft (67 m) north-east – south-west line, another line, 150 ft (46 m) long, of three others lying WSW – ENE.

The evidence of the plan (Fig. 22) suggests that at Beaghmore the long rows were later than the short and that, contrary to the norm, it was the long rows that were astronomically aligned. It is the short rows of three or four high pillars that stand in line with the centres of the cairns whereas the long, low rows bend and twist as they squeeze past a circle, curving towards its cairn, hooking sharply inwards at Circle E like an awkward afterthought to a complex already centuries old.

The group, overlooked by an adjacent high mound from which ceremonies may have been directed, was constructed on an area that had previously been occupied during the Late Neolithic around 2700 BC. Traces of field-walls are still visible. The megaliths followed. Excavations between 1945 and 1949 and limited investigations afterwards have left the circles standing inside a peat-walled hollow like rings of children's spades in a sandpit. The effect is dramatic but distracts from the importance of the diminutive cairns.

Rows of low stones crawl up to them from the

Pl. 43 Aerial view of the Beaghmore stone circles and rows,
Co. Tyrone. From the south-east.

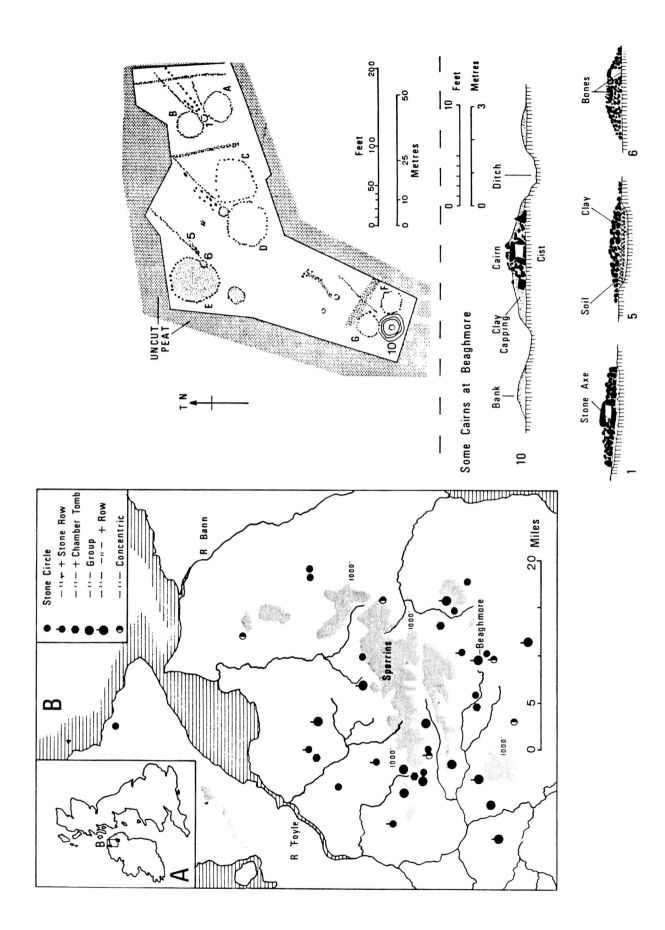

B

Stone Circle
—''—+ Stone Row
—''—+ Chamber Tomb
—''— Group
—''—+ Row
—''— Concentric

R Bann

R Foyle

Sperrins

Beaghmore

1000'
1000'
1000'
1000'

A

20 Miles
5
0

N T

UNCUT PEAT

A
B
C
D
E
F
G
5
6
10

Feet
0   50   100   150   200

Metres
0   10   25   50

Some Cairns at Beaghmore

Bank   Clay Capping   Cairn

Ditch

Cist

Feet
0   10

Metres
0   3

10

1   Stone Axe

5   Soil   Clay

6   Bones

north-east. The wording is important. Although the rows do 'run tangentially from the circles in a north-easterly direction',[44] in essence they flow in the opposite direction like nearly every row in Britain, Ireland and Brittany, not downslope away from but upwards towards the cairns that were their foci. Every long row has a cairn. It also has an astronomical alignment. With the exception of the line tangential to Circle A five of the six long rows at Beaghmore are aligned north-east – south-west within a few degrees of each other, centred on 42°–222°. It is a consistency not shared by the majority of rows in northern Ireland.

McConkey[45] has shown that those point to almost every part of the compass with only the slightest preference for a north-east – south-west alignment, statistically a very weak bias accounting for no more than eight of the twenty-eight rows cited. The proportion rises when only tangential rows are considered, six out of fifteen, or forty per cent, but as four of the six are from Beaghmore it can be seen how extraordinary the orientation of those lines was. It might also suggest that they were relatively late, revealing an incipient interest in sightlines that was not shared by builders of earlier rows.

Having been invited to make a study of Beaghmore Dr Archie Thom examined the six slightly dog-legged long rows and found the astronomy coarse and inconclusive. Because the higher south-western skyline was too close for him to determine any precise declinations he surveyed only towards the north-east horizon (Table 7).[46]

TABLE 7. *A.S. Thom's Solar Alignments for Long Rows at Beaghmore*[47]

North eastwards from	Thom's line	Azimuth	Horizon height	Declination
A. Tang row	11	63° 50′	41′.7	15° 21′
A + B. Cairn	10	45° 30′	−4′.5	23° 50′
B. Tang row	7	41° 00′	49′.0	26° 36′
D. Cairn	5	37° 36′	49′.3	28° 00′
E. Cairn	2	39° 00′	51′.7	27° 28′
F + G. Cairn	1D	42° 30′	−0′.5	25° 13′

Around 1800 BC at the latitude of 54°40′ the midsummer sun would have risen between about 45° and 50° depending on the height of the horizon. Only Line 10, the central row between Circles A and B, was at all close to that. None of the others indicated any important solar or lunar orientation causing Thom to wonder, 'were the erectors beginners and learning about the moon's movement or were the rows put there for other reasons?'[48] The explanation is different.

Over the centuries after the erection of the circles and rows the felling of trees and intensive grazing slowly created an open countryside but it was not always so. The evidence of pollen analysis suggests an

earlier darkly-wooded landscape.[49] Given the slope of the ground at Beaghmore even low-growing hazels a hundred yards (90 m) away would have raised the south-western horizon to an altitude of 3°. The discovery of an oak branch, 'part of a tree of considerable size' in one cairn, and birch twigs in another show that much heavier trees stood nearby.[50] A forest of moderately-sized oaks and birches no nearer than several hundred yards from Beaghmore would have produced a skyline of similar height. A mature 100 ft (30 m) or higher stand of oaks could have been as far away as half a mile.

With a raised horizon to the south-west the reversed astronomy of the long rows reveals unsuspected sightlines. Four rows, 2, 5, 7 and 9, have declinations between −23°.3 and −24°.9, clumsily directed towards the midwinter sunset. The declinations of two others, 1D and 10, are −22°.7 and −21°.6.

Archaeologically, south-west was the right direction, uphill and towards a target. Every one of the long rows ran purposefully up a slope towards a cairn at its south-western end. Although, because Beaghmore was ill-drained, the acidic, peaty water had destroyed much organic material in the cists the partly-preserved cremated bones of an adult skull, spine and limbs in the cairn of Circle E and fragments of bone elsewhere proved that the cairns were burial-places.[51] Like the Three-Stone row at Ballochroy in Argyllshire the lines were roughly aligned not only on a burial-place but also on the midwinter solstice.[52] Such juxtapositions between death and the sun or moon are commonplace in the megalithic monuments of western Europe.

The exceptional declinations, −21°.6 and −22°.5, are subtle. In his analyses of many rows in the west of Scotland Ruggles discovered that there were several declinations around −22° 'for which there is no obvious solar or lunar explanation.'[53] This declination, however, would indicate sunset in early December and could have warned observers that the winter solstice was close.

Line 9, a short row to the cairn between Circles A and B, also indicates the winter solstice, an astronomical characteristic of many short rows in western Scotland. It is possible, therefore, that the mixed long and short rows at Beaghmore were put up during the long transitional period between rows as processional ways and shorter lines of tall stones as calendrical indicators.

There are hints of an interest in cardinal points, something noticed in the great stone circles of Cumbria. The base of the cist between Circles A and B had an artificial north–south groove in it. A saddle-shaped stone inside Circle E had a comparable runnel, and two reddish stones of gneiss in the same ring were set up on an identical line.[54] The significance of these 'alignments' is elusive and may be illusory.

Beaghmore is an attractive place, one of the many megalithic wonders of Ireland but so far from being a

Fig. 22 Plan of the Beaghmore complex.

template for the other stone rows in the Sperrin mountains its intriguing eccentricities suggest that it was a late variant rather than an early model. Deep in the mountains of northern Ireland it is an amalgam of elements that have more in common with Cumbria than with Wessex. It may not be coincidence that some of those elements also existed in Brittany.

REPUBLIC OF IRELAND

Other than the dubious row at Roosky, Co. Donegal, already mentioned as possibly being a wrecked field-wall, there are virtually no long rows in the south of Ireland. A disturbed line of stones near a round cairn at Dromavally in Co. Kerry may also be the vestiges of a wall. At the circle-henge of Castleruddery in the Wicklows a collapse of boulders leads up the eastern entrance in vague imitation of the rows and avenues of Cumbria. But if ever there were a true megalithic mystery a challenging claimant would be the hundreds of stones strewn over a sprawl of fields in Timoney Park near Roscrea in Co. Tipperary. They lie, lean and stand in confusion.

Despite optimistic claims for an enormous stone circle amongst them at their north-east, a ring forty times the area of the average circle in southern Ireland, and for a tangential row to its west, there is no pattern to the litter. 'Unfortunately [they] do *not* form an Irish Carnac'.[55] They are unlikely to be an eighteenth-century folly because many of the northern sandstones and conglomerates are loose or prostrate. Belief in mediaeval land clearance is equally questionable as many in the south are erect. Haphazardly scattered, suspiciously confined within the boundaries of Cullaun and Timoney Hills townlands, the collection remains as baffling as it did in 1833 when a surveyor remarked on 'the upright stones all over the place'.

Stout concluded 'that the evidence against this complex being a prehistoric ritual site far outweighs that evidence which attests its authenticity.'[56] Nothing can be added.

SCOTLAND

Long rows are as sparse in Scotland as in the Irish Republic. Three lie in the south-west like outliers

Fig. 23 Plan of the Tormsdale single and multiple rows, Caithness, by Freer and Myatt. From Myatt, 1988, 296.

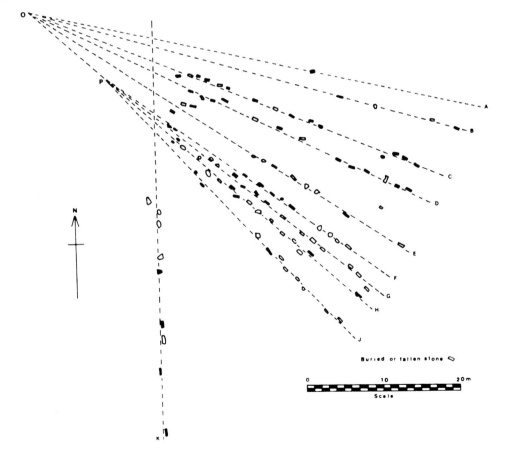

of influences from the south. 'The Grey Stanes o' Garleffan' by the Stinchar Water in Ayrshire make an unconvincing row. The mixture of conglomerates, granite and greywacke does not form a straight line and the stones may be a composition of shorter rows and standing stones.

Of more interest is the robbed 56 ft (17 m) long 'row' on Crinan Moss in Argyll. Known locally as 'The Small Stanes' several pairs of uprights, well-spaced, stand across a line that aims like a dart at a distant pair set axially to them. The arrangement of coupled stones at either end of a long row is akin to the famous setting, wrongly known as Temple Wood, at Slockavullin in the Kilmartin Valley (pp. 195–6) only three miles (5 km) NNE of Crinan Moss.

Southern beakers have been discovered in the valley. 'There can be little doubt that the main attraction for the southerners was copper, for several copper-deposits are known to have existed in the Kilmartin neighbourhood.'[57] The Early Bronze Age date and the infiltration from the south are credible and might explain the presence of the anomalous long row on Crinan Moss.

More than two hundred miles (320 km) north is an isolated long line at Tormsdale in Caithness (Fig. 23). It has a precise meridional alignment with the tallest of its low stones at the south, and it is tangential to one of the north Scottish multiple fans suggesting a distant relationship to some of the Dartmoor multiple settings.

BRITTANY

The question of the antecedents of the long single rows in Brittany presents a problem. In Britain and Ireland an ancestry for such lines can be inferred from the nearby presence of double rows and avenues. In Brittany avenues are almost unrecognisable. It has been surmised that these approaches to cromlechs may have been built only to be surrounded and masked by the erection of subsequent rows on either side of them. The supposition is reasonable. Proof is slippery.

The differing distributions of cromlechs and single rows, however, does offer some support for the hypothesis. Just as the Late Neolithic allées-couvertes in Brittany are to the north and west of the earlier passage-tombs in which their origins partly lie so the single rows stand well to the north and west of the main concentration of cromlechs and multiple rows near Carnac. Every cromlech may have had an avenue. Possible entrance gaps have been supposed at Ménec and Kerlescan (supra, p. 29), and an actual avenue was reported at Kergonan cromlech on the Île aux Moines (p. 56). Avenues may have existed at Ty ar c'Huré and Landaoudec (pp. 55, 56) on the Crozon peninsula, Finistère, a region of single rows, and on Île Beniguet.

Dating is vague. What scant evidence there is points to a Late Neolithic development for cromlechs with

rows being set up some centuries later.[58] There is one C-14 assay of 2550±250 bc (Gif-280), around 3300 BC, at the Tossen-Keler cromlech from material later than the ring. A similar period would accord with the Conguel pottery and artefacts discovered at Er-Lannic in the Gulf of Morbihan.

With such limited and fragile data it would be unsafe to offer anything more than the most general of periods, the Early Bronze Age, for the long, single Breton rows. At Penhoat near Rosporden some Bronze Age weapons were dug up at the base of a terminal stone but the offering could have been deposited years after the erection of the stones. At the Alignements du Moulin, St-Just (Pl. 44), the opposed splayed lines of schist pillars and quartz blocks, intermixed with timber posts, were associated with early beakers at a time between 4475 and 2500 BC. A chronological 'window' almost two thousand years wide is of little assistance.

Distribution is more helpful. It is noticeable that there are only three or four single rows in the Carnac region despite the plethora of megalithic monuments including multiple rows there. Instead, there are several in central Brittany to the north of Redon, five close together at St-Just. Far from them, over 80 kilometres (50 miles) to the north-east, is the lonely line of quartz boulders of the Cordon des Druides in the Forêt de Fougères. Most rows, however, are to the west of Carnac, a pattern akin to that in Britain, a thin straggle, 10 to 20 kilometres (6–12 miles) inland, along the bleakness of the Lande de Lanvaux, one or two in the Montagnes-Noires, and then a huddle of sites in the Crozon peninsula and on the coastline to its north. Not one is known in the extreme north along the coasts of Côtes-du-Nord.

The architecture is different from that in Britain and Ireland. Like those the Breton rows are composed of local stone, harsh and jagged quartz being favoured at the Alignements du Moulin, and at An Eured Ven, Lagatjar and others, but unlike the British and Irish there is a tendency for the tallest stone to be at the middle of the line. This can be seen at the Cordon des Druides where the pillar stands at the head of a rise with stones leading up to it from north-east and south-west (Pl. 45). Elsewhere, on a prickling dismal heath at An Eured Ven near Brasparts, quartz blocks meander through the undergrowth from ENE and WNW to a leaning stone at least 2 metres (7 ft) long. It is against a roundish patch of bracken, the only one to be seen, perhaps once the place of a cairn whose stones have long since been removed.

Such a focal point is not usual. It is said that a shortish row at Toulinguet, Camaret-sur-Mer, Finistère, was linked to a rectangular cromlech but the testimony is unconfirmed. At St-Lyphard in Loire-Atlantique ten stones were aligned on the terminal of the tall Pierre Fendue, 'the split stone', but the line has been destroyed. Other terminals existed

Pl. 44   The Alignements du Moulin, St-Just, Ille-et-Vilaine.
From the ESE. The dark schist pillars of the west row.

Pl. 45   The low quartz blocks of the Cordon-des-Druides row,
near Fougères, Ille-et-Vilaine. From the south-west.

at Plouguin, Finistère and perhaps at Kerpenhir by Locmariaquer, where the Pierre Jaune still stands in ivy-smothered silence.

The trait that most clearly characterises the Breton single row was the custom of setting up lines at sharp angles to each other. The 'high and low' Alignements du Moulin on a heath near St-Just had two lines, one tall and grey, the other of low, bulbous quartz blocks, narrowing towards each other with a third, shorter and ruinous, almost at right-angles to their head. Not far away at Grée de Bocadève two lines crossed each other. There was a similar intersection at Les Pierres Droites in central Brittany, one line arranged north-south, the other traversing it WSW – ENE. In the Carnac region itself there is only one of these angled rows, the enormous line of menhirs near the multiple rows of Kerzerho, 'the marchers'.

In contrast, nowhere were the angles more exaggerated than in the region farthest from Carnac, the Crozon peninsula in north-west Finistère where Lagatjar and others resemble multiple rows hurled into wild disarray. Paired lines at Leuré and Raguénès-Kerglintin ran at right-angles to each other, and at Lagatjar the main row had two satellites jutting from it with a third, detached and spoiled, on the far side (Fig. 24).

Sites like these with two or three rows set obliquely to each other are sometimes difficult to distinguish from splayed, multiple settings, another fact that contributes to the belief that very few, if any, of the multiple complexes were single-phase monuments rather than groups in which single and double rows accreted over decades and centuries. The scattered and lagging lines at Lampouy near Médréac could be mistaken for four individual rows were it not that they share a similar alignment and have a common target of a high menhir at the head of their slope. The criterion applied in the present book is that an assemblage is accepted as multiple if its three or more rows do not lie at acute angles, much more than 45°, to each other.

It might be thought that the reason for geometrical combinations of single rows arranged in different directions was to record astronomical events, one line perhaps towards midsummer sunrise, another to the major moonset or to a cardinal point but the recorded surveys, despite the enthusiasm of the surveyors, are not reassuring. Work by Gaillard in Morbihan was criticised by Lockyer for showing 'compass bearings only'. Devoir in Finistère studied many sites using a plane-table but admitted 'the orientations are exact to one or two degrees'. Today's archaeo-astronomer would demand an accuracy of a few minutes of arc before claiming an alignment.[59]

Few meticulous astronomical analyses were under-

Fig. 24 Plans of three 'angled' rows, in Brittany. (A) Monteneuf, Morbihan; (B) Leuré, Finistère; (C) Lagatjar, Crozon peninsula, Finistère.

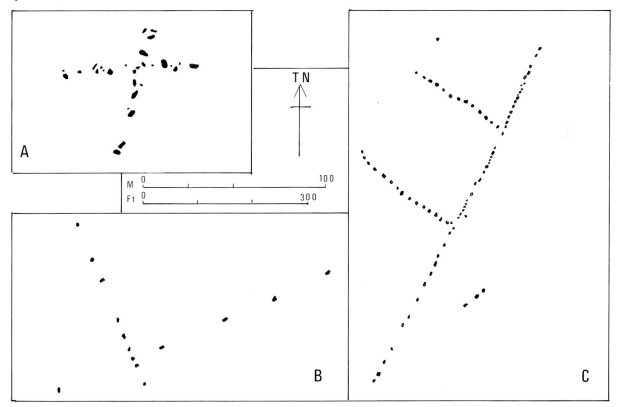

Pl. 46   View of the rows at Lagatjar, Finistère. From the ESE.

taken before the intricate Breton lines were severely damaged or destroyed but some do seem to have been celestially orientated. The lines at Leuré now gone, had possible alignments towards the May Day sunrise. Calendrical sightlines to midsummer sunrise, the equinoxes, to early May and November and the festivals of Beltane and Samain, and to midwinter were calculated for other lines. The sadly ravaged rows at Lagatjar were believed by Devoir and Lockyer to contain directions towards the midsummer sunset, the midwinter sunrise and Capella rising in 1600 BC, an improbably late date. Fieldwork by the writer leads him to the unconfident conclusion that the longest line was of no astronomical interest. The two shorter rows, aligned south-east – north-west, may have been directed towards midsummer sunset although the fact that the ends of both bend like cornstalks in a breeze makes this questionable. More convincingly, there is a Three-Stone row to the east and this does appear to be set towards the midwinter sunset like many others in Britain and Ireland.

Lagatjar, 'the fowl's eye', a nickname as whimsical as Klud-er-Yer, 'the fowl's perch', a single row near a passage-tomb in Morbihan, is one of the last rows to survive in fair condition in western Finistère (Pl. 46). Restored in 1928 the longest line, NNE – SSW, of lowish stones, is now about 200 m (660 ft) long. In 1830 it was almost 600 m (1970 ft) and there is a story that it once extended as far south as the hamlet of Kerbonn a kilometre (1100 yds) away.

From the restoration of 1928 came flimsy hints of the rites at Lagatjar. The two taller rows, both of local Armorican sandstone with bright quartz inclusions, run towards the north-west. A stone just to their east had been used as a polissoir for sharpening axes 'during the ceremonies that unfolded here', according to the excavator, Pontois, and a deep groove in it was in line with the highest menhir, typically at the centre of the row. The alignment was north-south.

Halfway along the western row the hole of the tall eighth stone, known as the 'menhir de feu', contained wood-ash among its packing-stones and the menhir's pointed base had been reddened by fires that had burned 'au moment de certain rites'. To the sun and the north and fire and the sharpening of stone axes can be added the ritual deposit of a metal axe. A little south of the middle of the longest line there had been a 6 m (20 ft) high pillar, La Pierre du Conseil, broken up in the mid-nineteenth century. Devoir stated that 'a bronze axe was found underneath it.'[60]

The hints are faint but the association of axes, cardinal points and solar alignments has already been noticed in the great stone circles of Cumbria suggesting that this may have been a recurrent form of ritual in the Late Neolithic and Early Bronze of western Europe. It does not seem over-fanciful to imagine seasonal festivals when fires burned and when axes, symbols of power, maybe of the sun, perhaps even of a guardian spirit, were held high in rites of fertility and regeneration.[61]

The most impressive, almost oppressive, of all the long single rows in Brittany must be the monstrous rank angled just north of the multiple rows at Kerzerho near Erdeven eight kilometres (5 miles) north-west of Carnac (Pl. 47). It is 190 m (625 ft) long.

Everyone knows of the Carnac rows. But whereas

Kerzerho, Erdeven, Morbihan.

Pl. 47   The single row.

Pl. 48   Some of its enormous pillars, 6+ m (20 ft) high. The Table de Sacrifice is the flat basin on the right.

Pl. 49   The ruins of a hut-circle just to the north of the Drizzlecombe rows whose tall terminal stones can be seen beyond it. The homestead may have been occupied by users of the rows.

Pl. 50   The tall terminal pillar, 10 ft 6 (3.2 m) high, of the Drizzlecombe South row from the SW.

those lines have been likened to well-trained legionaries the Kerzerho pillars are like giants turned to stone, a ragged crowd of colossally rough titans stamping brutally towards the road, advancing on a vanished cromlech.

There are thirty-two of them, six collapsed, in extended and unkempt disorder plunging into thickets and trees at their far end. Two of these enormous, thickset stones are over 6 m (20 ft) high (Pl. 48), more than 20 tons of perilous granite whose erection demanded the strength of a hundred men pulling on a fan of ropes while others in even greater danger wedged timber props against the undersides of the monsters. Visitors are dwarfed by these grey relics of long-dead people.

One of the fallen columns, its upper surface hollowed into a vast basin, is known as the Table de Sacrifice, named at a time when the stones were believed to be a temple of the druids. Legends attach to other rows, An Eured Ven a wedding party that offended a priest, Kervelhoué eleven stones that once every hundred years stir on New Year's Day and go down to the River Etel to quench a century of thirst. The stories, like the rituals, are common to western Europe.

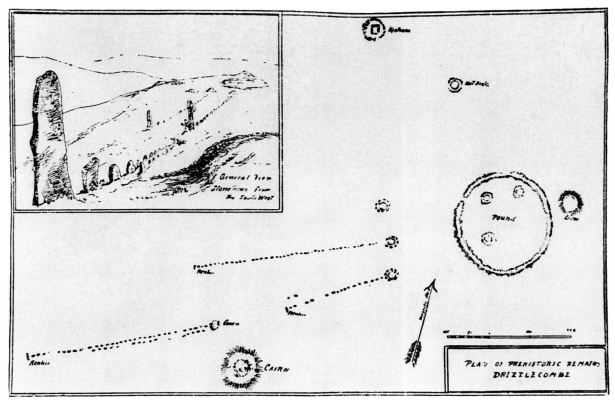

Fig. 25   Plan of Drizzlecombe, Dartmoor. From S. Baring-Gould, 1907, 60.

FROM SINGLE LINE TO MULTIPLE ROWS

One of the most elegant arrangements of rows and standing stones can be seen at Drizzlecombe on Dartmoor, a combination of four long lines by the River Plym overlooked by the crowded settlement of hut-circles on Whittenknowles Rocks. The complex on 'thrushel-' or 'throstle-combe' as it was known is a wonderment of megalithic monuments, some of which apparently were geometrically planned.

There are two great round cairns. The top of one, the Giant's Basin, was scooped into and left hollowed by treasure-seekers disheartened by the hard, unprofitable work. There is a ruinous kerb-circle and a splendid cist with a disturbed, heavy capstone. The relics of a row extend eastwards from it towards a short line of small round barrows. A little to their north, up the slopes of Hartor Tor, are the fallen walls of small pounds and turf-choked hut-circles (Pl. 49). There are also three long rows of little stones and a 'ghost' line (Figs 25 and 26). A partly double row, Worth's no. 19, lies at the south-east of the complex; there is a single row, to its north, no. 17; a single central line, no. 18; and a provisional row, never laid out, to the west of the others. These structures are dominated by three granite needles of very tall terminal stones at the south-west ends of the lines.

The fine pillar at the foot of the south-eastern row is 10 ft 6 (3.2 m) high (Pl. 50). It had been set up at right-angles to its row like a blocking-stone and from it a line of low stones led north-eastwards (48°) uphill to a small barrow. The row is a clear instance of the alterations that took place in prehistory and how multiple rows might grow, stretch by stretch, over the years.

At some time people began to add a second line. Many extra stones still run southwards near the barrow but peter out just over halfway down the row where the work was left unfinished. 'It is doubtful whether it was ever wholly double'. At Drizzlecombe the space between the twin lines was too narrow and irregular for any dignified procession, a reason for believing that the second, fragmentary row was set up nearer the end than the beginning of the custom of constructing an approach to a place of death. 'An examination shows this has at no time been an "avenue" throughout its entire length, but that the work of doubling the row was never completed.'[62] Similar optimistic enlargements, continued and fulfilled, would have produced a multiplicity of lines.

A hundred and fifty paces (c. 125 m) south of the row are the sideslabs of a desecrated cist from which two sherds were recovered in 1900. 'It is highly probable that pottery described as "bright red hard,

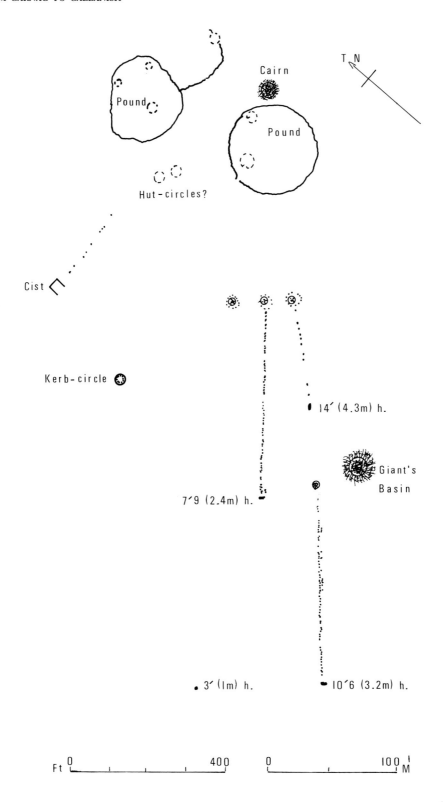

Fig. 26 Plan of Drizzlecombe, Dartmoor. The pounds and the hut-circles may be the settlements of the people who used the rows.

Pl. 51 The north-west cist at Drizzlecombe, Dartmoor. Too small for a corpse it was intended for a cremation.

one fifth of an inch in thickness"... was Beaker pottery.'[63] Otherwise, excavations in and around Drizzlecombe have produced only undateable flints and charcoal. It is by inference alone that the rows can be allocated a date late in the *floruit* of long single lines.

Fifty yards (46 m) to the north of the first row's barrow is a second terminal, the most spectacular of these towering pillars. It had fallen and when measured in July 1893, was found to be 17 ft 10 long and 4 ft wide at its base (5.4 × 1.2 m), seven tons of pointed granite, 'the largest recorded on Dartmoor'. After its re-erection in a hole deepened for safety it stood 14 ft (4.3 m) high, 'by far the finest in the West of England',[64] set in line with its 296 ft (90 m) row of widely-spaced low stones. This also ran north-east, (44°), to a small encircled barrow with a cist (Pl. 51).

This north-eastern row may have been the first. Although it is the shortest it has the tallest terminal. Its barrow, though small, only six paces across, retains the traditional stone circle, a diminished version of the fine megalithic ring on Down Tor only a mile and a half (2.4 km) away. The row is also the only one to contain an astronomical alignment.

From the combination of its latitude (50°28'44"), horizon height towards the ridge of Hartor Tor, al-lowing for atmospheric refraction, of 2°.2, and the azimuth of the row's bearing (44°) the declination can be calculated as +29°.2. This is very close to the moon's most northerly rising and it may have been lunar rites that were practised at Drizzlecombe.

The alignments of the other rows are of no astronomical interest. The south-east with an azimuth of 48° and a declination of +27°.1 looked towards neither sun nor moon. The central row, 52°, +24°.9, did point towards the midsummer sunrise but thousands of years before Drizzlecombe or any other megalithic monument. The putative western row, aligned 56° and with a declination of +22°.7 presumably only lay at that angle to be symmetrical with its partners. If the builders of these rows were concerned with lunar rites it would have been the north-eastern row that was the focus of their ceremonies.

The central row, no. 18, may, like the south-eastern, have been meant to be transformed into a double but, if so, only two stones of the second line were put up near the 7 ft 9 (2.4 m) high terminal. The completed line was almost exactly the length of the south row and also climbed to an encircled barrow whose stones had been quaintly but deliberately tilted outwards with packing-stones holding them firmly in place. Other examples of this unusual design exist on Dartmoor and there is a visually superb cairn-circle of outward-leaning pillars like a coronet at Bryn Cader Faner in Wales, its 'pointed stones like teeth or a crown of thorns'.[65]

A little to the north-west of the central Drizzlecombe barrow is a fourth, no bigger than the others but, unlike them, lacking a row. One gains the impression of an over-ambitious ritual precinct that had started at the east, perhaps with the tallest terminal pillar, row and barrow, and was slowly being extended to the west but with decreasing enthusiasm until, finally, the grandiose project was abandoned.

Although there is no row for the western barrow it may have been intended. About 963 ft (294 m) south-west of the barrow is an isolated slab, hidden in the long grass and no more than 3 ft (1 m) high. Being so low any interpretation of it as a terminal stone would be fanciful but its position at the geometrically correct angle to the barrow and its situation, in line with the terminal of the south row, suggests that it may have been a preliminary marker at the end of what would have been a fourth, very long row on the western side of a multiple setting. With such a row 'one has a completely symmetrical collection of rows, and this may have been contemplated'. The stone 'is in the right position to mark the beginning of such a row'.[66]

This is conjecture but it is speculation supported by the evidence of planning in a scheme that for reasons irrecoverable today never reached fruition. The layout was exceptionally neat in 'one of the few groups in which all parts can be seen from all parts, and perhaps this has had an influence on its symmetry'.[67] Certainly the distances and lengths of the rows and barrows were harmoniously blended.

The layout of the barrows, rows and terminals forms an enormous trapezoid like the outline of a kerbed long barrow. It is also an arrangement in which the narrow head, wider base and long sides were proportional to each other. The base, between the southern terminal and the 'marker-stone' is twice the length of the line of three barrows at the top of the plan. The sides are six times as long. The distances are not precise. Pacing or using a measuring-rod across yards of uneven ground and coarse grass inevitably caused errors. But about 160 ft (49 m) for the barrows, 330 ft (101 m) for the base, and 947 ft and 963 ft (289, 294 m) for the sides gives ratios of 1:2.1:5.9 and 6, surely too close to multiples of each other to be coincidence.

Drizzlecombe demonstrates how multiple rows could develop from simpler settings, how on occasion careful planning could precede their erection, and how prehistoric undertakings could be left unfinished. Deep on Dartmoor and well to its west this seems to have been a group of late long, single rows. They have the deviations from the 'classical' norm to be expected in lines erected towards the end of a tradition. They are connected with death but the burial-places are tiny whereas the terminal pillars are huge. And sporadically and incompletely they were being converted into double lines which, in the end, might have developed into a multiple setting.

CHAPTER NINE

MULTIPLE ROWS 3000–1500 BC

Garrywhin consists . . . of six rows, running north and south, and are like the headstones of a rude and old-fashioned burying-ground. The rows are narrow at one end, and get wider at the other or south end. A few feet from the narrow end was a round heathery knoll . . . Here there was also a stone coffin . . . in which were the enamel crown molars of a human being. The skeleton had long since mouldered away into dust. A bowl-shaped urn was found in the cist.

G. Gunn, *Trans Inverness Sci Soc 7*, 1915, 348

INTRODUCTION

The strangest, and rarest, of all linear complexes of standing stones are the sites composed of several lines. Such multiple rows, half of them arranged in the layout of a fan, vary greatly in their lengths and in the number of lines and stones, nearly 1200 gigantic boulders still standing in ten disrupted lines at Kerzerho.

The reason for such megalithic overkill puzzled antiquarians. One explained that Roman legionaries had set up the stones at Carnac to protect their tents from the wind, another that a medley of stones in Caithness commemorated warriors killed in an ancient battle. 'The theory of the stones being erected for this purpose is a plausible one, and it is confirmed by tradition'.[1] It is more probable that the multiplication of rows was the result of lines being added to lines.

The criteria used here to define a multiple setting are that there should be three or more lines approximately abreast of each other, of about the same length and not at acute angles. Over sixty such sites are known, their architecture ranging from as few lines as three at Yar Tor on Dartmoor to as many as twenty-three at Mid Clyth in Caithness; and, in length, as short as 32 ft (9.8 m) at Skelpick, Sutherland, to as long as 3094 ft (943 m) at Ménec, maybe even longer at Kerzerho where the rows wandered over 6906 ft (2105 m) of heathland if they once extended beyond Mané Bras as some reports claim.

The distribution of the rows is the most restricted of all megalithic lines (Fig. 27). Only Dartmoor and Exmoor, northern Scotland and Brittany have them. Not one is known elsewhere. None is recorded in Cornwall, Wales, Cumbria or Ireland. In those regions the tradition of long linear settings gave way to short rows with no more than six tallish stones in them.

The two major concentrations are 750 miles (1200 km) apart, in northern Scotland, thirty-eight per cent, with an identical proportion in Brittany where the most grandiose were erected. Between the regions there are other multiples in south-west England, twenty-three per cent, almost three-quarters of them on Dartmoor.

There is a mystery. Although it is most improbable that there was any direct connection between Carnac and Caithness the two regions contain not only similar multiple rows, unusual elsewhere, but also a second, tantalisingly comparable type of setting, equally unusual, the megalithic 'horseshoe'. Several of the cromlechs around the Gulf of Morbihan are 'les fers des chevaux', vast U-shaped monuments often open to the south-east. Near Carnac is Crucuny, Kerlescan and others, and in the Gulf itself Er-Lannic and Kergonan, a huge enclosure capable of holding more than a thousand people, its south-east – north-west axis towards its curved head and the midsummer sunset.

Such sites are almost non-existent in Britain but they do occur in Caithness, smaller and fewer but 'horseshoes' none the less, Broubster near Thurso and, fourteen miles (23 km) to the south, Achavanich, hardly a third the size of Kergonan but sharing the same open mouth, here at the SSE and with the SSE–NNW axis aligned on the major setting of the northern moon. The resemblance of multiple rows in Brittany and northern Scotland and the identical rare layouts of horseshoes with their astronomical sightlines hint at relationships between lands hundreds of miles of sea apart. Why this should be so remains an archaeological problem to which there is no facile solution.

In size the Breton lines, particularly those in the south near Carnac, by far exceed any others. The gigantic rows of Kerlescan, Kermario, Kerzerho –

MULTIPLE ROWS
  1   Garrywhin
  2   Mid Clyth
  3   Learable Hill
  4   Almsworthy
  5   Challacombe
  6   Corringdon Ball
  7   Lagatjar
  8   Medreac
  9   Kerzerho
10a   Menec
10b   Kermario
10c   Kerlescan

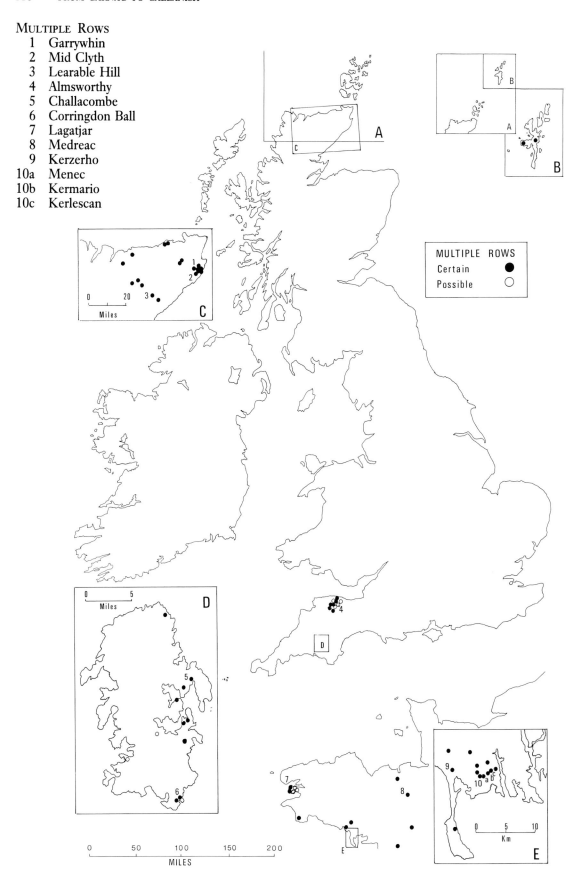

broken by huge gaps but once 2105 m (1.3 miles) of now uncomputable, massive blocks – Ménec, Petit-Ménec, together average ten rows of over 700 stones in lines 3179 ft (969 m) long.

In contrast, although the Caithness settings also have an average of ten rows their mean length is only 134 ft (41 m), a mere twenty-fourth of the stupendous Carnac alignments. To the south of Caithness in Sutherland the rows are lesser both in their number of lines and in length, only about 80 ft (24 m) from end to end. Unaccountably, although there are no rows on the Orkneys there are two small settings in Shetland sixty stormy sea miles (97 km) farther north.

Architecture differs from region to region. It is sometimes said that most Breton sites were set out in fans but this is not so. As many lie parallel to each other as converge. In northern Scotland the opposite is true. Only four parallel sites are known whereas at least twelve 'fans' have been recognised and planned by fieldworkers such as Sir Henry Dryden, George Gunn, Alexander Thom, and Leslie Myatt.

Many of the Breton rows lead uphill towards the huge megalithic enclosures of cromlechs, the stones in the rings almost contiguous unlike those in the rows which are set well apart. The fact that the lines, despite crowding together near the cromlech, do not all point to it[2] suggests that extra lines were later added to the first, narrower settings.

Excavation has proved of little assistance in the dating of any row. Domestic rubbish of flints, sherds, grinders and burnt stones was discovered during James Miln's 1877 and 1878 digging at Kermario. In Scotland a lost pot, either a Middle Phase beaker or a food-vessel, from the cist at the head of the Garrywhin rows in Caithness points to an Early Bronze Age origin for the burial there.

Wherever they are found in western Europe the purpose of these multiple rows remains unclear. Thom thought that some in Brittany and Caithness had been cleverly designed as extrapolation devices for detecting minor movements of the moon.[3] This will be discussed. For the present it is essential to keep two matters in mind when considering the rows' function. In Brittany there were associations with cromlechs. In northern Scotland the lines frequently focused upon a cairn, a cist or a small natural mound suggesting that the settings had been intended as parts of a monument for funerary rites. Secondly, whether parallel or splayed the lines are often unevenly spaced and angled as though some were aggregations.

Whatever their history the rows, particularly those at Carnac, are megalithic amazements. In 1827 the Chevalier de Fréminville, a French antiquarian, stared at the awesome Ménec rows.

Fig. 27   Distribution map of the multiple rows.

As I reached the top of the hill, the plain of Karnac [sic] suddenly spread itself out below me, and its wild heathland, the horizon fringed with pine woods, and above all the extraordinary view of that regiment of stones, the startling army of shapeless rock so symmetrically aligned, filled me with astonishment.

ENGLAND

Dartmoor and Exmoor

It will have been noticed how in Britain the custom of erecting lines of stones moved steadily westwards away from its origins, transmuting but not returning. There was no reflux. The people of Wessex with their avenues never put up single lines. The people of Dartmoor with their long rows never constructed short ones. Those would be raised only well to the south in Cornwall and well to the west in Ireland. After the long multiple rows no short lines would be built on Dartmoor.

The chronology of the English rows is unclear. No dateable finds have come from them. If some lines were associated with original avenues and double rows then a beginning around 2400 BC could be postulated with a conclusion around 1600 BC. Fleming has noted how some reaves must post-date the rows. 'The line of the southern terminal of the system across Holne Moor was probably determined to a large extent by the position of a triple stone row … which I think was deliberately left on the moorward side of this boundary'.[4]

The multiples were constructed almost exclusively along the eastern edge of the moor, the major Dartmoor region of stone circles, avenues and double rows. They concentrate in a narrow north-south rectangle about fifteen miles by three (24 × 5 km), Cosdon at its head, the rows of Corringdon Ball at its foot. The central limits were defined at the east by Challacombe with its high and triangular terminal block at the top of the slope (Pls 52–54), and at the west by Joan Ford Newtake. Only the unfinished Yellowmead was outside the zone, far away at the south-west corner of Dartmoor.

Contrasted against the average 602 ft (184 m) length of the single lines the multiples were not long, having an overall average of 447 ft (136 m). Subtracting the two abnormal Yar Tor rows, one a broken 1500 ft (457 m) of three convex lines between a barrow and a decapitated standing stone, the other three brief 50 ft (15 m) rows cut through by a disrespectful reave, the mean is reduced to 353 ft (108 m), almost half that of the singles but very close to the 362 ft (110 m) of the doubles, something to be expected if the multiples consisted of a double row to which an extra line had been attached.

It may not have been only double rows that were so affected. In several instances, at Corringdon Ball, Cosdon, Joan Ford Newtake, the rows lead to a stone

Challacombe, Dartmoor.

Pl. 52   The lower north end of the three rows.

Pl. 53   The detached triangular terminal stone at the southern head of the rows.

Pl. 54 'Male' flat-topped and thin, pointed 'female' stones at Challacombe, Dartmoor.

circle as though an avenue had been 'improved' by the introduction of a third row.

The number is significant. What has never been commented on is the consistent repetition of three in these settings, every one of the Dartmoor multiples from Challacombe to Yar Tor being of that number. There are no exceptions. Even to the north on Exmoor the number three predominates, at least seven of the nine recorded sites having three lines.

Composed of tiny stones many of the Exmoor settings have been badly damaged by cattle and vandals and there are several instances such as Horsen and Hoccombe where the original design can no longer be established. Other sites once claimed as multiple rows were misinterpreted, the rectangle and ring on Honeycombe Hill probably being no more than an abandoned and overgrown farmstead and weather-worn field-wall.[5]

Almsworthy, however, three-quarters of a mile (1.2 km) to the WSW of the hill, is genuine. It is also equivocal. When first noticed after peat-burning in 1931 the conglomeration of poky stones on the common was interpreted as the denuded circumferences of a triple oval ring measuring 129 ft by 94 ft (39.3 × 28.7 m). This was surely mistaken. There is little conformity to an ellipse in the disposition of the fourteen blotchy-red sandstones and the site, lying near an elaborate field-system, has been re-identified as the wreckage of six stone rows. This is rather less questionable:

> It contains 14 stones, but I doubt whether they were ever in the form of a circle, or even of the double oval which the late H. St. George Gray suggested. However, they are certainly the remains of a Bronze Age monument of some kind, presumably of religious significance.[6]

An eye of considerable faith is needed to see either a ring or a row at Almsworthy. One observable fact is that the tallest stone, a sharp-cornered, flat-topped cube, no more than 1 ft 10 (56 cm) high, stands at right-angles like a blocking-stone at the ESE and lower end of the longest 'line'. But the remainder on this quiet slope twist in a confusion of directions unlike most other rows.

Curiously, the Almsworthy 'circle/row' lies near the centre of a precisely straight, six and a half mile (10.5 km) long line from Porlock stone circle at the north to Withypool Hill stone circle at the south. Also curiously, the line passes within yards of a house called Ley on the B3223. Most curious of all, the line is never mentioned by ley-liners.

Almsworthy must remain a mystery. Too many stones have been removed. Solifluction, the gradual slithering of wet soil down a slope, may have shifted others, distorting the plan whether of an ellipse or six stone rows or, temptingly, two sets of three lines similar to Corringdon Ball fifty miles to the south, two contorted settings side by side, each of three lines like all the multiples on Dartmoor.

Even the Dartmoor concentric stone circle of Yellowmead, far from the others, possessed the embryo of a three-row multiple. It has the fragments of an avenue to its south with an adjacent arc of little stones. The circle was re-erected in 1925 by the Rev. H. Breton and some farm labourers:

> On the lower side, several stones are placed pointing inwards. Seven or eight seem to be the remains of a double row leading to the cairn. Next to this row three more are spaced out like the last stones of a treble row. Another two may indicate the line of single rows. It could be that this large Beaker monument, unparalleled on Dartmoor, originally had several rows leading to it up the slope from Yellow-mead Brook. It must have been a very important tomb indeed.[7]

Baring-Gould noticed how extra lines lay near an existing row. 'In several cases a second row starts from a small cairn in or close to the main row, and runs away in quite a different direction'.[8] If it had been placed parallel to a double row it would usually be indistinguishable from its companions. Yet in the splendid multiple at Cosdon (Pl. 55) on one of the highest hills on Dartmoor one of the three rows approaching a stone circle with two cists is taller and heavier than its partners. Restored in 1897 the rows

Pl. 55 The triple rows at Cosdon, Dartmoor, from the cairn at its WNW end. The north (left) line is taller than its partners.

had been vandalised, possibly in prehistory. 'About 120 paces N. of this monument, which presents a rather striking appearance, is a reave running like the row E. and W. It is very overgrown in places, but it can be seen that some large stones were used in forming it'.[9]

Not far away, over the brow of the hill, was another stone circle, now destroyed. Known locally as Sticklepath or Eight Rocks the stones were believed to dance when they heard the bells of South Tawton. This could not have been often. The church is out of sight and sound over the hill two windy miles (3.2 km) away.[10]

Emmett in his scholarly analysis of the stone rows on Dartmoor observed that in the doubles the stones were obviously paired and put up opposite each other but in the multiples there was 'variable spacing along their lengths, resulting in the stones of constituent rows being out of step',[11] another piece of evidence persuasively in favour of multi-phase construction.

One of the clearest examples of this and revealing how even more complicated settings could grow up lies on Corringdon Ball where the outline of a Neolithic long chambered tomb slumps conspicuously on the eastern skyline. On the moorland below it two treble rows, both of shakily parallel lines, creep uphill towards the sides of a cairn-circle, one to its northern half, the other to its south. Between them are two standing stones, 78 ft (24 m) apart, in line with the circle's centre.

To the north of the rows is a much longer single row running just north of the ring towards a round barrow but stopping short of it. Such an agglutination of seven rows, roughly in line and close to each other, with a possibly unfinished eighth, is a clearcut example of how a combination of once-separate lines could end by becoming an unanticipated multiple setting.

Some of these Dartmoor multiple rows were splayed. The plan of the Corringdon Ball complex shows that the lines converge slightly, surprisingly not towards the circle but away from it. The three Challacombe lines gather together as they converge on their triangular terminal stone. The lines on Shovel Down repeat the pattern.

Fifty-five stones of a 485 ft long (148 m) double row climb northwards up a calm gradient towards a despoiled cairn. At their lower end is a splendid standing stone, the Longstone, 10 ft 5 (3.2 m) high. To the east is a shorter single row. Its southern end is about 100 ft (30 m) from that of the double row but as it proceeds north-westwards up the slope towards the cairn it comes closer and closer to its neighbour, passing within 40 ft (12 m) of its head and bending inwards on towards the cairn to which another double row is attached from the north-west.

In a comparable complex to the north a double row runs south-eastwards up a steeper slope towards a stone circle. There it links with the avenue already described (p. 102), raggedly aligned south towards the same concentric ring. 'Thus the three rows of the southern group appear to have formed a roughly similar pattern to the northern group, i.e. all converging towards the top of the ridge.'[12]

The six rows were developing into a multi-phase complex whose main purpose was to draw attention to the burial-places. Had each setting been filled by two more rows the result would have been a near-replica of the Caithness fans.

SCOTLAND

Caithness, Sutherland and Shetland
The only multiple rows in Scotland are far to the north, 500 miles (800 km) north of Dartmoor, more than 750 miles (1200 km) from Brittany. In between there is nothing comparable in Scotland or in England, Ireland or Wales. Few other types of row whether avenues, long double or single lines or short rows stand near them. Only seven different rows occur in their locality, three doubles, a single at Tormsdale aligned north-south, one Four- to Six-Stone row and a couple of pairs of standing stones, quite insufficient in a thousand square miles (2600 km^2) of moor and mountain to account for the eruption of multiple rows in this remote region of Scotland. Callanish is 140 miles (225 km) to the west beyond the waters of The Minch. The Aberdeenshire avenue of Broomend of Crichie is a hundred miles (160 km) away, barricaded by the Grampian mountains. And neither avenue has any resemblance to the rows of northern Scotland. The multiple 'fans' of Caithness and Sutherland exist in cultural isolation. Readers wishing for detailed descriptions of them should refer to Myatt (1988) whose assiduous fieldwork and planning over the years have rescued these lonely settings from their centuries of neglect.

Twenty-one are known, some destroyed in living memory, twelve in Caithness, nine in Sutherland. There are two others in the Shetlands, none on Orkney. Distribution on the Scottish mainland falls into two major groups, a diffuse pattern to the east in Caithness with a cluster near the Loch of Yarrows, and a long, thin line in the west where the Sutherland rows weave through the mountains along river-valleys from Borgie in the north down to the vanished multiple and intact short double at Kildonan near Helmsdale at the south-east.

Rather unexpectedly their distribution does not correspond well with either the earlier Neolithic Orkney-Cromarty passage-tombs or the later Iron Age brochs. The former cluster in seven major groups from Betty-hill in the north-west to Helmsdale at the south-east.[13] Apart from some overlapping around the Loch of Yarrows there is little correspondence between the tombs and the rows (Table 8). Conversely the brochs, gracefully incurving drystone towers, have strong concentrations both at the low-lying north-east corner of Caithness[14] where, today, there is not a single row,

and along the east coast on lower land than the rows whose builders avoided the littoral and the mountains, preferring the gentle slopes of moorland between 250 ft and 500 ft (75–150 m) above sea level.

Splayed, inconspicuous, many running up to cairns, the rows rest on hillsides. Geographically they differ. On average the Sutherland multiples consist of seven shortish lines about 80 ft (24 m) long. The Caithness rows have more lines, ten, and are longer 134 ft (41 m), in settings ranging from four rows to twenty-three at Mid Clyth.

The trait that distinguishes these sites from any other group is that nearly all of them are arranged in fans, the sides contracting from a wide lower end to a shorter head as they climb a slope. They do not terminate in a sharp point. Instead, they stop abruptly in shapes similar to the outline of an upturned pail. Some rows on Dartmoor and in Brittany share this characteristic but they are never in the majority. At Camster, its stones lost in the heather, at Dirlot, Garrywhin with an explored cist and vicious autumn midges, Watenan, at the Loch of Yarrows, the feature is repeated. Nowhere is it more pronounced than at Mid Clyth, the 'Hill o 'Many Stanes' (Pl. 56).

These well-known rows were described as early as 1780 by the Rev. Charles Cordiner as 'a very singular collection, all well-shaped thick flagstones, standing erect, and from 4 to 6 feet high.' This was poetic but wrong. Although numerous, to be counted in scores, the stones are not high, up the knee rather than the thigh. Joseph Anderson was more circumspect, writing of 'a series of rows of small grey slabs, like the headstones of a country churchyard', a nice analogy paraphrased by Gunn as 'a rude and old-fashioned burying-ground.[15]

From the exiguous evidence the dating of the Scottish rows is likely to be deep in the Early Bronze Age. An excavation at Garrywhin in 1865 recovered the broken pieces of a 'bowl-shaped urn, ornamented with impressed markings of a twisted cord'. With it were two flint scrapers and some unburnt human teeth that had survived the acidic peaty waters of the moor. The shape of the pot and its decoration suggests that it had been a food-vessel but the inhumation offers the possibility that it had been a late and variant beaker. Another excavation near the rows on Learable Hill, Sutherland, found burnt bone and jet beads in the cist

TABLE 8. *Passage-Tombs and Stone Rows in Northern Scotland*

Area	No. of passage-tombs	No. of rows
Bettyhill	9	2
Loch Calder	20	1
Thurso	10–14	1
Loch of Yarrows	16	7
Dunbeath	9	0
Helmsdale	6	1
Strath of Kildonan	6 in 5 miles	4 in 13 miles

Pl. 56   Mid Clyth Caithness. From the north at the head of the slope.

of a diminutively kerbed round cairn lying just west of a standing stone. Buried alongside one of its kerb-stones was an inverted urn covering a cremation and a corroded bronze blade. A date around 1700 BC would not be unlikely.[16]

No diggings are recorded anywhere else, not even at Mid Clyth, the best-known of all the multiples. Like Beaghmore in Ireland it may also be the most mis-leading in the numbers of its rows and stones, in its location near the east coast, and in the astronomical interpretations that have been placed upon it.

Alexander Thom found it a challenge (Fig. 28). 'If the stone rows of Caithness have so far defied explanation, we are encouraged to believe that for at least some of them an astronomical use existed.[17] In 1971 he offered a solution. The fans with their convex bases, straight sides and shorter concave head like the pattern of an inverted windscreen wiper-blade had been designed as aids to determine the intricacies of the moon's movements. He cited Mid Clyth:

The site is certainly a lunar observatory. The chance is remotely small that these stones are situated by accident at a spot which provides fore-

sights for [the major and minor lunar stand stills] with perturbations, and provides them accurately. As has been pointed out, such a site is useless without a means of extrapolation.[18]

According to Thom these rows perhaps represent primitive stone computers used by the astronomer-priests to solve complex problems involving extra-polation which arises as a consequence that the Moon's maximum declination may be reached when it is not at its rising or setting point... The result is that the Moon may reach a maximum declination and then start to decrease again be-tween two observations which normally would be separated by at least an interval of a full day. Without recourse to some extrapolation method this could lead to an error up to 10′ of arc in an azimuthal fix when the astronomerpriests were attempting to fix an extreme lunar position by two (before-and-after) observations. Thom's inter-pretations of these fan-arrays perhaps represents the greatest degree of sophistication yet claimed for Megalithic man, and for good reason they have been referred to as 'Megalithic graph-paper.[19]

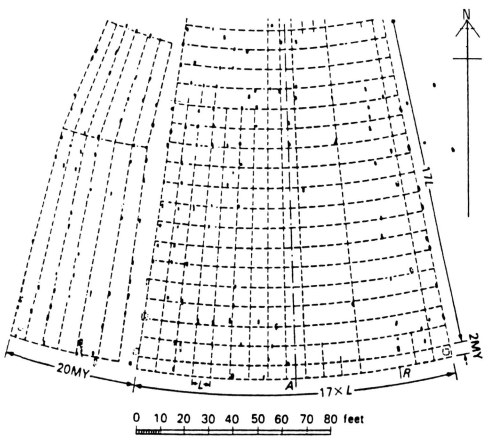

Fig. 28   Plan of Mid Clyth, Caithness, by A. Thom, 1967, 152.

'Perhaps' was discreet. The method was involved. Setting up a stake as a foresight and others as back-sights for observations on three successive nights towards the moon's rising or setting in a horizon notch the observers were able by a series of complicated – many would believe too complicated – calculations to compute the exact place where the invisible moon would be at its major position. The fan, the bottom sector of a triangle with sides 503 ft (153 m) long at Mid Clyth, was constructed as a template in which a person could move amongst the stones like a knight on a chess-board forward and sideways to a calculable backsight for a lunar event he could not see. Why people should wish to know this other than from the curiosity natural to man is unclear although they 'would be in a position to predict eclipses'.[20] Whether, inductively, they were capable of designing such a device is questionable. To lay out a practicable grid they must have comprehended the necessity of work-ing out a length known as 'G', a distance on the ground corresponding to the moon's declination de-ficiency in the sky.

To explain this for the general reader John Edwin Wood needed fifteen technical pages and nine dia-grams. For Mid Clyth Thom took thirteen pages, seven diagrams and eleven algebraic formulae 'but this gives no more than a hint as to how the genius who was ultimately responsible knew that this solution was in theory correct.'[21]

Objections must be faced by proponents of Thom's theory. Although eleven certain and two probable fans are known in Caithness and Sutherland only four: Mid Clyth, Loch of Yarrows, Dirlot and Camster, have layouts suitable for extrapolation and the two latter are in such poor condition that they cannot be properly tested. At Mid Clyth the sides of the in-itial theoretical triangular framework were over 500 ft (152 m) long, and the setting-out would have been difficult because of a considerable rise in the ground between one end and the other. The rise also partly blocked sight of the lunar notch almost two miles away. 'Thus the centres from which the lines radiate are not visible from the greater part of the sectors, nor is the notch. This would have made it more difficult to set out the rows.'[22]

The major criticism, however, is not astronomical

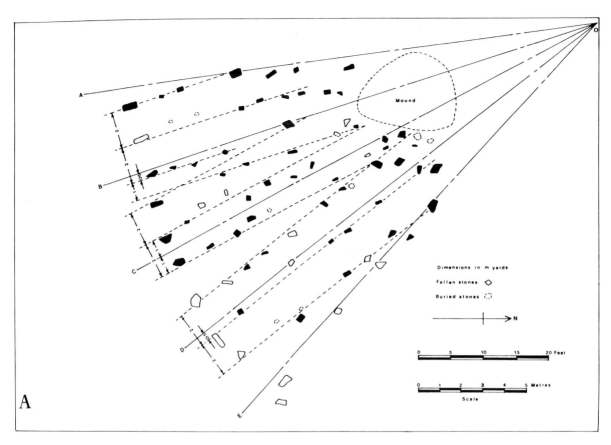

A

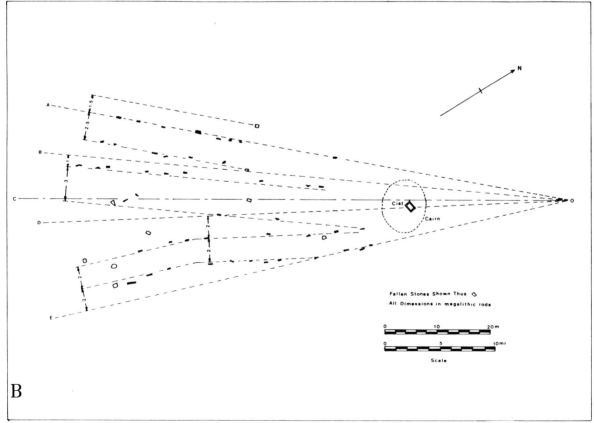

B

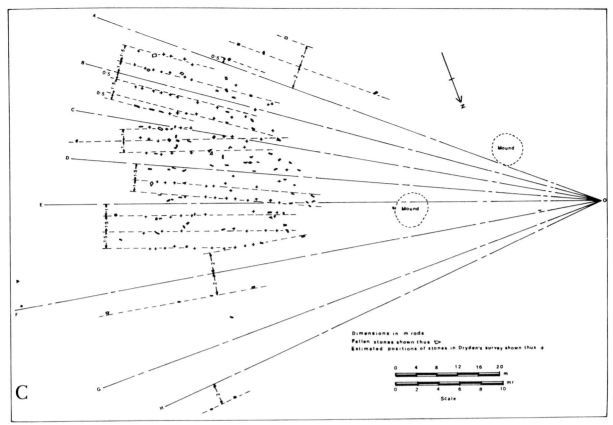

Fig. 29   Plans of three multiple rows in Scotland showing their groups of three rows. (A) Kinbrace, Sutherland; (B) Garrywhin, Caithness; (C) Upper Dounreay, Caithness, by Freer and Myatt. From Myatt, 1988, 304, 288, 298.

but architectural. Thom's hypothesis is predicated on Mid Clyth or any other setting being a unitary plan erected in a single phase and with a base the length of 'G'. There are several reasons for qualifying acceptance of this. Two questions should be asked: why the rows are multiple; and why they are splayed. The answer to the first contains the answer to the second.

If the fanlike arrangement of the lines was not because they had been planned as an extrapolation sector, and if it was not prehistoric art for art's sake, fashioning pleasingly harmonious patterns on a hillside then some other explanation is required. Examination of the good surveys of these rows by the Thoms and by Freer and Myatt reveals that the more lines there are the more fanlike the sites become. Settings of four or five lines are relatively parallel. Borgie, near Torrisdale Bay on the north coast of Sutherland, perhaps an early site, has three or four lines with the suspicion of a fifth. The rows narrow from their base 20 ft (6.1 m) across to 18 ft 8 (5.7 m) over a distance of 59 ft (18 m), a contraction as they worm uphill towards a peat-covered mound of hardly a quarter of an inch in a foot (0.6:31 cm).[23] The opposite is true of sites with many more lines.

The eight rows of Badanloch seventeen miles (27 km) to the south fan inwards from a base of 43 ft 7 (13.3 m) to a head only 11 ft 9 (3.6 m) wide 53 ft 6 (16.3 m) farther uphill, a convergence of 6 inches in every foot (15:31 cm). Kinbrace, four miles to the east, has ten rows narrowing 7 inches in the foot (18:31 cm). Mid Clyth in Caithness contains a similar constriction of about 5 inches for each foot of its length (12.7:31 cm).[24]

The majority of multiple rows had a target of a cairn or a cist, even a low natural hummock resembling a heather-covered burial-mound. Such a focus was not always at the crest of a ridge or knoll but it was always at the higher end of the rows. It is arguable that the rows are multiple and splayed because they are composite monuments in which there are separate groups of lines, often of three or four parallel rows, the earliest going directly towards its target, the later additions having to angle in towards the cairn, creating the stone fans for which northern Scotland is famous.

The outcome of this multi-phase activity can be seen at Kinbrace. The site is composed of three sets of three parallel lines (Fig. 29). The central and presumably the first, with an alignment of 243°–63°, goes straight to a low, overgrown mound. A second set of three parallel rows to the south-west of the first is skewed away from it, running towards the western side of the mound on an alignment of 258°–78°. The third set, to the east of the others, angles unsuccessfully inwards towards the mound, two of its lines missing it altogether on an alignment of 235°–55°.[25]

Comparably distinct and detached sets exist elsewhere: three sets of three lines at Garrywhin; four sets at Upper Dounreay, gaps between their ends, a central group of three parallel lines stopping short of a heathery hummock up the slope, a second set of three directed towards another mound to the west, and two outer sets of four rows each converging desperately on the same targets. At Badanloch there are two sets of four lines, one markedly narrower than the other, with an 8 ft (2.4 m) wide gap between their bases. Similar gaps between each of the sets can be seen at Tormsdale and Learable Hill.[26]

Solifluction, soil moving and slithering downhill in damp conditions, would certainly displace light and loosely-set stones as the untidiness of rows such as Yarrows displays, but it would not convert an evenly spaced fan of nine splayed rows into three neat sets of three parallel lines. Man, not nature, caused the groups.

A provisional Table can be constructed to show how the shapes of sites are affected by the number of rows they possess. It is provisional because solifluction has caused some stones to drift between rows leaving gaps and uncertainties behind them, and because others are buried beneath peat so that the lower ends of some rows may be visually truncated. For these reasons a line is accepted only if it is fairly straight and contains at least three stones. Because of these limitations some sites such as the fragments at Skelpick and Watenan and the badly-damaged Camster and Dirlot are omitted. It is an arbitrary exercise but the results are informative.

Simple arithmetical formulae can be constructed to demonstrate how an increase in the number of rows resulted in increasingly fanlike settings as the outermost rows angled inwards towards the focus of a small cairn. The percentage of such tapering is expressed by:

$$\frac{\text{Width of Base minus Width of Head}}{\text{Length of Row}}$$

As an example, a row 40 ft wide at its base, 23 ft across at its head and 62 ft long (12.2, 7.0, 18.9 m) has a percentage taper of 27.4 per cent, narrowing by over 3 ins (8.4 cm) for every foot of its length. Another of the same base and length but 35 ft (10.7 m) wide at its head would have a percentage taper of only 0.8, decreasing by less than an inch per foot. Whereas for each foot of their length the four rows of Borgie diminish in width by only a quarter of an inch the thirty-eight of Mid Clyth contract by almost 5 ins (6 mm : 11.8 cm). The settings with many rows have the higher percentage and are more fanlike. Those with only a few lines are almost rectangular (Table 9).

From the plan made by Ruggles the apparently aberrant Loch of Yarrows with seven parallel rows consists more probably, of two sets of three lines each lying north-south. Both groups have been severely affected by solifluction but a space about 11 ft 6 (3.5 m) wide still separates them.[27]

Except for Upper Dounreay high on the north coast of Caithness the western rows are all in Sutherland and they may have been the forerunners of those in Caithness, the area where some multiple rows may have been astronomically spaced: Dirlot and Camster,

TABLE 9. *Analysis of the Shapes of Multiple Rows in Northern Scotland*

Site	No. of rows	Widths		Length	Percentage of taper
		Base	Head		
Borgie	4	20 ft 6.1 m	18 ft 8 5.7 m	59 ft 18 m	2.3%
Loch Rimsdale	4	18 ft 8 5.7 m	8 ft 5 2.6 m	40 ft 8 12.4 m	25.2%
Loch of Yarrows	7? (3 + 3)	40 ft 5 12.3 m	33 ft 8 10.3 m	129 ft 3 39.4 m	5.2%
Badanloch	8	43 ft 7 13.3 m	11 ft 9 3.6 m	53 ft 6 16.3 m	59.5%
Learable Hill	8	55 ft 5 16.9 m	27 ft 7 8.4 m	71 ft 6 21.8 m	38.9%
Tormsdale	8	100 ft 0 30.5 m	34 ft 5 10.5 m	113 ft 10 34.7 m	57.6%
Kinbrace	10	48 ft 9 14.9 m	24 ft 4 7.4 m	41 ft 6 12.6 m	58.8%
Upper Dounreay	13	123 ft 0 37.5 m	80 ft 0 24.4 m	131 ft 3 40.0 m	32.8%
Mid Clyth	18	130 ft 0 39.6 m	76 ft 5 23.3 m	138 ft 8 42.3 m	38.6%

both of them ruinous and drowned in peat twelve miles (19 km) south of Thurso Bay, and the tightly-packed coastal group by Loch Watenan four miles (6.4 km) further east: Mid Clyth, Watenan, and Loch of Yarrows or Battle Moss. For reasons already given the latter can probably be excluded from the others and the state of Watenan, 'a rather ruinous site' in Myatt's words, bars it from being accepted as a celestial candidate. Despite a presumed length of 168 ft (51.2 m) with some twenty-two stones in each line, not one of the thirteen possible rows contains more than three standing stones. Thom placed a regular grid on his plan of this unsatisfactory site with radial lines at intervals of three of his Megalithic Yards, 8 ft 2 (2.5 m). He also remarked on the regular spacing of the rows at the bottom of Mid Clyth with 'a definite quantum of 7.7 ft', an implausible 2.83 multiple of his Megalithic Yard.[28]

From the location of these seemingly genuine fans it might be concluded that they were late settings in which it had become the custom to set up eight or more lines at one time. Before making too much of this it should be noted that even Mid Clyth has an annexe of seven more lines to its west and that two-thirds of the way up they incline inwards towards what may be a kerbed cairn at the head of the 23 rows.[29]

It should also be noted that only three rows in the main sector are directly aligned upon the mound and that these, lying almost precisely south-north, are more closely spaced than the others, only some 2 ft 6 (0.76 m) apart. The possibility must remain that Mid Clyth itself was a composite monument of at least three phases.

Whatever the truth, taken as a whole the rows of Caithness and Sutherland provide clues about their origins. On the negative side the absence of paired 'high and low' rows, and of rows in which the tallest stone stands at the centre argues against Ireland or Brittany as a source. The single angled row at Tormsdale is not necessarily of Breton ancestry. A similar line exists on Dartmoor where a single row runs up to the Merrivale avenue at an acute angle of about 25°.

If there has to be a region that supplied the motivation for the construction of multiple rows in northern Scotland Dartmoor has persuasive credentials. Its landscape is similar. It contains its own multiple rows, also in sets of three. They too ascend from terminal pillars to unobtrusive cairns. There are kindred cairns and tall blocking-stones at the ends of rows in Sutherland such as Badanloch, Kinbrace and Loch Rimsdale. Dirlot in Caithness has comparably bigger terminals.

Why and how this postulated connection was made between moors separated by 500 miles (800 km) of sea remains unclear. The 'why' may have been because land-pressure in the south forced migrations northwards. The 'how' is partly explained by other suspected long distance movements of people, between Neolithic Ireland and the Orkneys if the archi-tectural likenesses between the chambered tombs of Newgrange and Maes Howe are accepted, between north-east Scotland and south-west Ireland in the Bronze Ages if the recumbent stone circles of those far-flung localities were related.

Sea-travel along the western coasts of Britain had been established long before the later centuries of the Early Bronze Age, and as long as dangerous waters such as the Mull of Kintyre and the dreadful Gulf of Corryvreckan were avoided by overland portages the voyages could have been uneventful. From Ullapool at the north-western corner of Scotland parties could paddle to the Assynt peninsula and then 'to Lochinver or Eddrachillis Bay. The open sea passage between the two promontories could be made in a summer day, and at that season with reasonable assurance that the weather would hold; the tidal streams are weak. At Loch Laxford weather could be awaited for the unsheltered passage round Cape Wrath', a spectacular and perilous headland of bleak mountains and fierce cliffs, the highest sheer falls of rock in Britain. 'That rounded, shelter is to be found in the deep inlets which break the north coast of Sutherland'. A similar exodus from Somerset to the Hebrides has been proposed, and criticised, for the Iron Age builders of duns and brochs in the Western Isles.[30]

The journey was hard because of the slowness of the boats, fifty miles (80 km) on a good day, big timber-framed, skin-lined canoes like Eskimo umiaks, buoyant, flexible, steered by the winds, struggling against the tides and currents, but riding the waves as though part of them. It may have been in such vessels and in such conditions that tired groups of men, women and children eventually passed by Caol Raineach, anglicised as Kyle Rannoch, to the safety of Torrisdale Bay with its long sandy beaches where the River Naver flowed out to sea.

There were other landing-places to the east and it is likely that these were used by settlers in Caithness. But close to Torrisdale Bay are the rows of Borgie and Skelpick, perhaps the first of a line of sites in Sutherland whose builders took advantage of the con-venient bay. From there parties could travel for miles southwards down the long riverine valley of Strath Naver, seeking unoccupied farming land, trudging be-tween the mountains to a handful of lochs where they would turn south-east towards the sea at Helmsdale. Halfway down the valley with its rich alluvial soils before late prehistoric peat smothered them was Learable Hill. This amazing necropolis, ignored by most archaeologists, has the finest collection of rows in the whole of Scotland. To reach it one must cross the rushing Helmsdale river, tiptoeing across the tremors of a fraying suspension footbridge whose creaking struts would have terrified the peasants of San Luis Rey.

Learable Hill exemplifies the separation of the sacred from the secular that was a recurrent feature of prehistoric life in western Europe (Fig. 30). There are

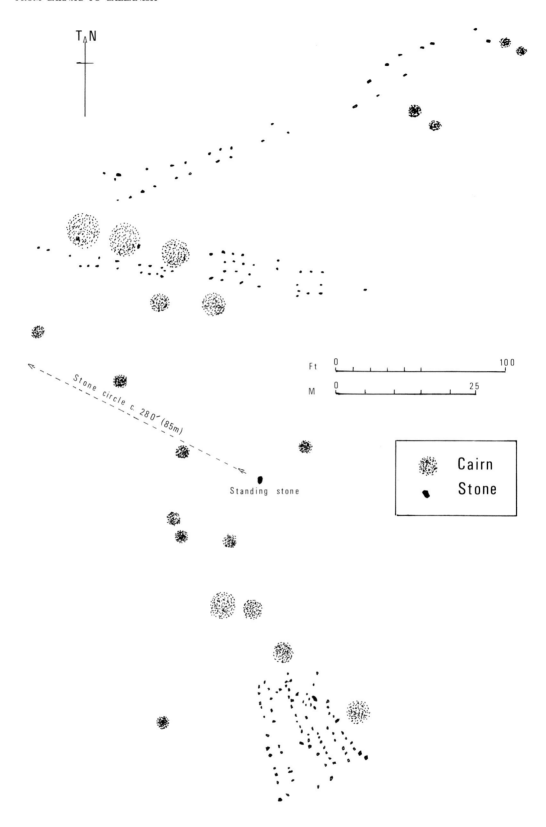

Fig. 30 Plan of the Learable Hill, Sutherland, complex. The
larger cairns may be burial-mounds. The smaller, more densely
stippled, are probably clearance cairns.

hut-circles to west and north on the lower hillsides near wood, water and pasture but none on the higher slopes. Under those open skies death and ritual intermix: cairns, rows, circles, and the focus of a tall standing stone christianised by the carving of a simple cross on its broad western side. Facing it twenty yards (18 m) away is the disturbed cairn where Anderson discovered an urn.

A score of round cairns, low, heather-lain, untouched, are scattered on the level hilltop. Some of them are clearance cairns heaped up when later people gathered loose stones and uprooted others from the rows to make grazing space for their cattle. Others are burial-places to which the rows extended, rows that were subsequently interrupted by the intrusive piles of cleared stones.

At the north is an irregular double row running towards the north-east and, if Thom's analysis of the line is correct, the Beltane sunrise of early May. This is more probable than his conclusion that five parallel rows to the south, at the centre of the complex, looked eastwards to the rising equinoctial sun. To the east the setting went downhill. It is more feasible that they were laid out the other way round where three large round cairns break the line of, perhaps significantly, three rows with two others parallel to them passing tangentially south of the cairns. These five rows and the double to the north point westwards in the general direction of a small, damaged stone circle, actually an oval, just below the summit.

There is more. Unrecorded by the Thoms but only about 30 ft (9 m) south of the central rows is the standing stone. To its south, some 150 ft (45 m) away, is the head of a fan of ten rows like stone droplets cascading down the hillside. Small round mounds lie by them but are 'not related in position to the geometry of the rows either in the fan or the plan of the parallel and intersecting rows shown by Thom'.[31] probably because they were the result of clearances rather than part of the original ritual complex.

The fan, like the sequence suspected in others, may consist of two sets of three lines with a further two lines to their west. With no obvious focus this must remain speculative. The central axis of the fan has an uphill azimuth of 324°.5. At Learable Hill's latitude and with a hilltop 3° skyline the row would be in line with the major northern setting of the moon, a matter of some interest because, in his analysis of the mean azimuths of the rows in Caithness and Sutherland, Myatt[32] demonstrated that with three exceptions the bearings lay between the risings and settings of the minor moon, astronomical positions so difficult to determine that this may be no more than coincidence. The approximate south-north alignments at Tormsdale, Mid Clyth, Watenan may also be due to chance alone.

Much work is needed for a proper understanding of the tantalising north Scottish rows, and it is poss-

ible that, stimulating though it was, the astronomical interest of the Thoms was a distraction rather than an advance. It is sad that archaeologists have virtually ignored the challenge, leaving research to dedicated fieldworkers such as Leslie Myatt who, almost single-handed, has studied and planned the known rows and discovered others. Learable Hill was no exception:

> Because of the complex nature of the Learable Hill site, with its numerous stone settings extending over a large area, a further detailed and accurate survey of the complete site is desirable. This would enable an analysis to be made of the interrelation between the individual settings, together with any further possible astronomical significance which the site may have.[33]

Before popular ignorance and commercial afforestation destroy further rows a programme of exploration, planning, even excavation where sites are threatened, should be instituted. After four thousand years the settings deserve wider attention.

BRITTANY

(a) *Distribution*

Of the twenty certain multiple rows in Brittany thirteen are at the south in Morbihan, eleven within 8 km (5 miles) of Carnac-Ville. It is unlikely to be chance that it is there that the greatest concentration of cromlechs exists. Attached to them are the most immense rows, vast lines of stones at Ménec, Kermario, Kerlescan, Kerzerho, once with outlying shorter and slighter settings, Hanhon and St-Cado near Ploemel, Coët-er-Hour by Kergroix among them, lying at the periphery of the region like lightweight, rustic afterthoughts. These vulnerable groups of small stones have almost disappeared.

Outside Morbihan the rows are scattered and varied in form. Two at Lostmarc'h (Pl. 57) on the Crozon peninsula of Finistère are like others in south-west England and may be related to them. There are wandering fans at Pleslin in Côtes-du-Nord (Pl. 58) and Langon in Ille-et-Vilaine where Les Demoiselles are reputed to be girls turned to stone for daring to dance on the Sabbath (Pl. 59). Others have been destroyed, Arbourg in Loire-Atlantique, and La Madeleine in south-west Finistère where four parallel lines once led for a kilometre (1100 yards) to a supposed cromlech. Hardly a stone can be seen today.

The most eccentric of the surviving settings stray like four lost rows in search of a cromlech at Lampouy just north of Médréac in Ille-et-Vilaine (Pl. 60). Reiterating the lack of standardisation in the work of prehistoric societies the rows are so bizarrely arranged that they could equally be considered independent single lines. They are accepted here as an embryonic multiple setting because of their common target of a menhir, La Roche Longue, at the top of the hillside.

Pl. 57   Lostmarc'h, Finistère. The ruined rows from the south.

Pl. 58   Champ des Roches, Pleslin, Côtes-du-Nord. From the north-west.

Pl. 59   The rows of Les Demoiselles, Langon. The remains of
a cromlech may exist at the head of the slope.

Pl. 60   Lampouy, Médréac. The eastern row.

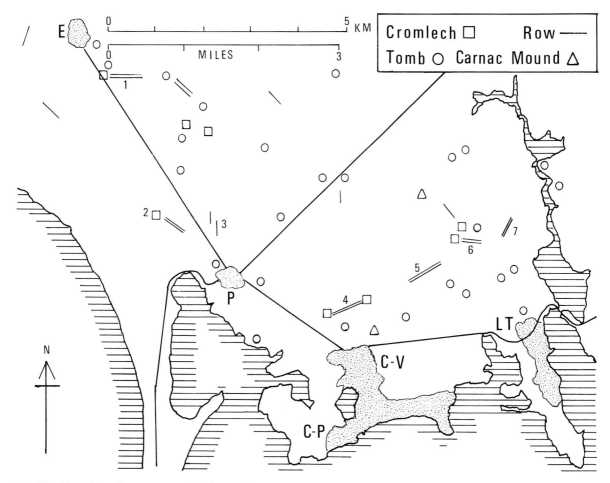

Fig. 31 Map of the Carnac region. C-P, Carnac-Plage; C-V, Carnac-Ville; E, Erdeven; LT, La Trinité-sur-Mer; P, Plouharnel. 1, Kerzerho; 2, Ste Barbe; 3, Vieux-Moulin; 4, Ménec; 5, Kermario; 6, Kerlescan; 7, Petit-Ménec.

Once likened by the writer to boat-crews racing towards the winning post of that tall red menhir, the westernmost is in the lead, the eastern splashing well off course behind its rivals, its white and red pillars standing, sagging and collapsed in a row some 30 m (100 ft) long. Far behind and below the lines is the starting point of a beautifully square and shiningly white quartz block, La Pierre Carrée, near Chenôt farm. The red and white colours seem deliberately chosen and placed just as the long burial mound of a tertre, Le Jardin aux Moines near Paimpont well to the south of Médréac is also composed of red slabs of local schist alternating with crystalline quartz and white pudding-stones brought from 3 km (2 miles) away. Added to the surprise of their colours the rows at Médréac contain hints of arithmetic in their respective numbers of stones, 9, 7, 9 and 7.

Similar niceties are encountered in the crowd of multiple rows around Carnac-Ville with the Quiberon peninsula to the west and the River Crac'h to the east.

Here there is the most famous collection of megalithic rows in the world (Fig. 31), rank upon rank of lines trailing so long and so far into the distance that even the greatest of their menhirs dwindles into obscurity.

(b) *Carnac: Architecture and Design*
The first impression is of immensity, of size, boulders of bulbous granite looming high and thick, many with a tiny plug of red concrete near their base showing they had been re-erected by le Rouzic in the early 1930s. The menhirs are huge and heavy. But then comes an awareness of space being crowded by an unending multitude of rows, a grey forest of pillars, stones, slabs, across, behind, beyond, in an expanse of lines sweeping down an incomparable landscape (Pl. 61).

The Scot, James Miln, was awed by the way in which the myriad of pillars and boulders at Kermario swept through the worndown ruins of Roman encampments, overshadowing and eclipsing them:

Independent of the emotions awakened by the view of these battalions of gray stones echeloned along the country, their presence excites the imagination to picture the events which have passed into history since their erection; and one is tempted to ask how it is that the Romans, the masters of the world, came and disappeared, whilst the race of the rude constructors still remains.[34]

In 1969 Alexander Thom was invited by Glyn Daniel, editor of *Antiquity*, to make a survey of the Carnac rows and between 1970 and 1974, equipped with theodolites, measuring-chains, ranging-poles and a dedicated team, he and his son, Archie, concentrated on the challenge of plotting over 3000 rough almost haphazard menhirs, many of them in the way of others, over a distance of 4 km (2½ miles).

Thom was dubious about foreign food and arrived in Brittany 'with buckets of porridge and pounds of haggis' but when taken to the crêperie at the end of the Ménec rows he developed a taste for the 'creeps'. For years the writer was asked by the proprietress about 'le professeur Thom'. Sadly, he is dead, and the crêperie is now closed. But the meticulous plans Thom produced of Ménec (Fig. 32), Kermario, Kerlescan, Petit-Ménec and others will endure for years as irreplaceable reference sources.[35]

Casual inspection of those plans suggests the rows are parallel. Careful inspection proves they are not. The lines are unevenly spaced, not straight, angling and twisting against each other, of differing lengths like rusting wire-netting, the work of men toiling with awkwardly cumbersome and rough boulders rather than the 'megalithic graph-paper' of theoretical geometricians.

The irregularities in these lines of bulky, weighty stones cannot be attributed to solifluction. Instead, they reinforce what has been suspected for multiple rows on Dartmoor and in northern Scotland, that these were composite settings, enlarged bit by bit over the years, their first simple rows engulfed and left indiscernible amongst the clutter of additional partners.

The Ménec rows are conventionally regarded as monuments of a single phase of construction. But their quite separate east and west sections as well as the satellite rows at Kermario and Petit-Ménec favour the idea that these megalithic compositions were accumulations, people adding more and more stones over the centuries.

There is only true fan among them, St-Pierre-Quiberon, once much longer, down to the shore and into the sea, so that its precise dimensions are impossible to reconstruct. Statistics taken from the most

Fig. 32 The Plan of the Ménec West cromlech and its rows, by A. and A.S. Thom, 1978, 63.

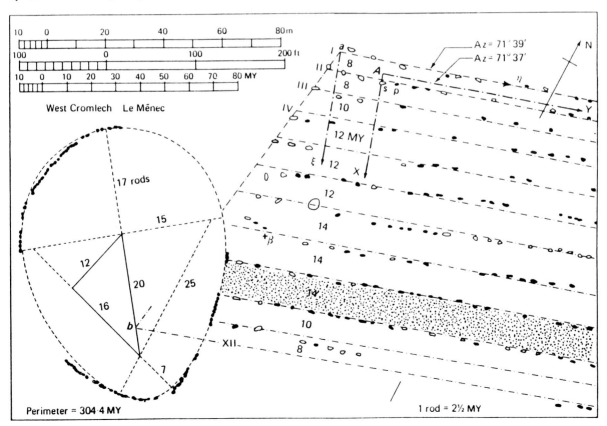

reliable surveys (Table 10), those of the Thoms between 1970 and 1974 differ considerably from those
of earlier researchers like le Rouzic but they are still
misleading because the rows are damaged.

Keriavel is so badly ruined that it has to be excluded
from the Table. So are the reputed eight rows at Ste-
Barbe despite the 'tradition...that these lines terminated in an enclosure made with stones arranged in
the form of a segment of a circle'.[36] Nearly all the rows
are toppled or dragged away and of the horseshoe-
shaped cromlech only two tall, thick blocks flanking a
lower remain standing in the fields (Fig. 33).

Like most statistics those in the Table should be
regarded as art rather than science. On the ground
arithmetical neatness disappears. There is no consistency between the numbers of rows in the sites, as
few as five at St-Pierre-Quiberon, as many as thirteen
at Kerlescan. Even the number of lines in a group is
debateable. So is their length. To walk down the
longest stretch of all, the four Carnac groups of rows
with only short breaks between them from Ménec in
the west to Kermario, on to Kerlescan and finally to
Petit-Ménec 3.8 km, nearly 2½ miles away, is to walk
down an illusion of megalithic tidiness. The reality is
different. The rows are prehistoric accretions whose
successive builders were not obsessed with exact-
ness. As Ménec shows, the lines are masterpieces of
improvisation.

There the eleven-or twelve-rows, usually cited as
1167 m (3829 ft) long, are in fact two linked settings
east and west of each other in a line no more than
943 m (1030 yds) long, each striding uphill towards a
cromlech, that at the west near Carnac vandalised but
recognisable, the east a fragment of stones, torn up, no
more than bits.

The writer has had the advantage of using the
Thoms' largescale 1:1000 plans[37] in his analyses.
They reveal the eccentricities in these supposedly
equidistant and parallel lines. At Ménec West (Pl. 61),
the rows nearest Carnac-Ville, the lines are numbered
I–XII from north to south. Despite leading to a
cromlech a full 91 m (300 ft) across (Pls 62 and 63)
the northernmost five rows would, if extended, miss
it completely (Fig. 34). The same may once have
been true at the south where stones were most easily
removed because of the proximity of the road. The
overall width of the rows, moreover, is one and a
quarter times that of the cromlech even ignoring any
former lines to the south. The probability is of rows
being added slavishly over decades, even centuries, to
an original much simpler setting.

The belief that such multiple rows were constructed
stage by intermittent stage is strengthened by the story
told to the antiquarian, Cambry, by a local man around
1800. 'Au mois de juin chaque année, les anciens
ajoutaient une pierre aux pierres déjà dressées'. It was

TABLE 10. *Statistics of the Multiple Rows near Carnac*

Site	P or F	No. of		Length	Widths		Cromlech
		Rows	Stones		Most	Least	
Kerlescan	F?	13	514	298 m 978 ft	125 m 410 ft	31 m 102 ft	√
Kermario, West	P	7	509	659 m 2162 ft	61 m 200 ft		?
Kermario, East	P	7	380	492 m 1614 ft	61 m 200 ft		√
Kermario, South (satellite)	F?	3	140	415 m 1362 ft	15 m 49 ft	5 m 16 ft	×
Kerzerho	P	10	1129	2.1 km 1.3 miles	64 m 210 ft		?
Ménec, West	P?	12?	516	455 m 1493 ft	99 m 325 ft	84 m 276 ft	√
Ménec, East	P	12?	553	488 m 1601 ft	61 m 200 ft		√
Petit-Ménec, North	P		3?	124 1148 ft	350 m 33 ft	10 m	×
Petit-Ménec, South (satellite)	F	6	79	99 m 325 ft	27 m 89 ft	15 m 49 ft	×
St-Pierre-Quiberon	(Originally 250m+ [820 ft+] long), F	5	23	55 m 180 ft	31 m 102 ft	23 m 76 ft	√
AVERAGES		8	397	561 m 1841 ft	55 m 180 ft	32 m 105 ft	

Fig. 33 The Ste-Barbe cromlech, Plouharnel, Morbihan. From A. Blair and F. Ronalds, *Sketches at Carnac (Brittany) in 1834*, London. The rows behind its ruin are so damaged by agriculture that their original design is irrecoverable.

Fig. 34 The possible original avenue to the cromlech at Ménec West, Carnac. The cromlech was erected around a slight knoll. The avenue points exactly to the cromlech's centre and highest point. (B) and (C) indicate sections which may have been additions to the original avenue (A).

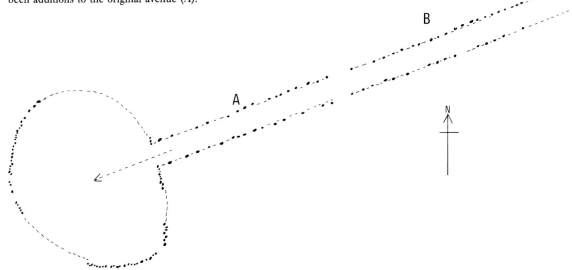

Pl. 61 Ménec West. The rows from the west.

repeated in a different form by Canon Mahé in 1825 that there was 'a verbal tradition that the alignments were added to each year in June. On the eve of the set day, all the stones were illuminated, at great expense to the people.'[38]

The theory of sporadic growth is encouraged by the variable spacing between the rows and by their irregularities. The gap between rows I and II is 6 m (19 ft 7) wide. Then, from II to XII the widths in metres are: 7, 9, 10, 9, 12, 11, 11, 8, 7 (23 ft to 39 ft 5). Even these figures are deceptive for they imply that the rows are straight whereas the outermost rows in particular expand and contract against each other like telegraph lines in a wind. Only the most perfunctory homage had been paid to precision.

Most significantly of all, the only truly parallel rows are lines IX and X, 11 m (36 ft) apart, that do run straight for about 120 m (395 ft) before losing shape. It is significant because, first, this pair of rows is markedly graded in height as it joins the cromlech Secondly, at that point in the ring there is a 10 m (33 ft) gap flanked by tall, close-set pillars. Thirdly, row IX is perfectly in line with the crest of the ridge on which the cromlech stands. If originally there had been a simple avenue leading to Ménec's western cromlech these surely were the two rows that formed it revealingly, in line with the centre of the ring.

The complex at Ménec was probably not only added to laterally but also extended, length by length like Avebury's Kennet Avenue, until eventually its rows merged at the bottom of a slope with those stalking uphill to the eastern enclosure. There is a change of direction where they meet of some 6° from WNW to ENE in a more moderate version of what Stukeley had termed the 'two vast curves contrary ways' where Avebury's Kennet Avenue linked with the rows going up Overton Hill to the Sanctuary stone circle.[39] The join at Ménec was ugly. From the west the southern line wriggles like a worm seeking its hole as it unites with its eastern partner.

There is a possibility that the lines and cromlech of Ménec East were the earlier. The rows are straighter

The Ménec West cromlech.

Pl. 62   Three closely-set stones of its eastern arc. The nearer stands at the north corner of the hypothetical entrance from the avenue.

Pl. 63   The south-west arc of stones, standing shoulder to shoulder unlike the separated stones of the rows.

though just as unevenly spaced, and, if the Thoms' reconstruction is accepted, the cromlech was considerably more spacious than that at the west.

A break of 340 m (370 yds) separates Ménec East from the rows of Kermario, 'the place of death' (Pl. 64). The western cromlech has gone, replaced by a carpark and a belvedere or viewing-platform, although three towering blocks like huge hooded figures may have been part of it. To their east are seven roughly parallel but badly spaced rows. Two unrelated lines drift to their south against a shorter third row. The main group deviates gently three times, passing a deserted windmill and, at La Petite Métairie, 'the smallholding', has the remains of an alien row standing at right-angles to it. Such a combination of disjointed lines merits the observation that 'il s'agit d'une juxtaposition d'ensembles différents'.[40]

The most southerly of the ten lines emphasises the disparity between the rows. Although adjacent to them it lies on a completely different bearing. The seven lines in the major setting, 659 m (721 yds) long, lead 61°–243° on a slight curve to the erstwhile cromlech. Rows VIII and IX follow nearly the same direction, 61°–246°. But the southern row is independent in azimuth, length and target. Its thirteen surviving stones in a line no more than 62 m (203 ft) long, lie 56°–236°

stopping 26 m (85 ft) short of the undifferentiated Neolithic passage-tomb of Lann Mané Kermario that stands in ruins at a bend in the road. It is presumably the earliest structure on the site. Its row may be the first at Kermario, a long single line whose identity is half-camouflaged by the rows alongside it.

At Kermario the linkage between the west and east settings is as inelegant as that at Ménec. The eastern group crosses the now-flooded Ravin de Kerloquet, near which in 1878 James Miln discovered sherds and burnt stones, and culminates in a dribble of broken lines where a cromlech once stood. 'At the eastern end of this group, a little beyond Manio, once can guess where it ends close against some remains of the arc of a semi-circle, because of the embankments, which seem to correspond with a structure visible in aerial photographs.'[41]

Beyond Kermario is Kerlescan with the best-preserved cromlech, usually accepted as a spacious, buckled rectangle lacking its north side (Fig. 35). This description of the ring with convex west and south sides and straight, exactly north-south, east side may be mistaken like much else at Kerlescan, 'the place of burning'. The ranks of stones to the east (Pl. 65), optimistically considered a 'fan', are megalithic chaos. Rows swerve, intersect and collide in 'alignments'

Fig. 35 Plan of the Kerlescan 'barrel' cromlech and its rows, by A. and A.S. Thom, 1978, 93.

Pl. 64 (*opposite*) The Kermario rows, Carnac, from the east.

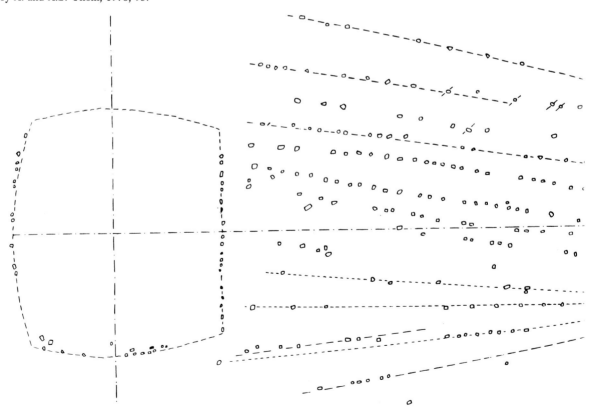

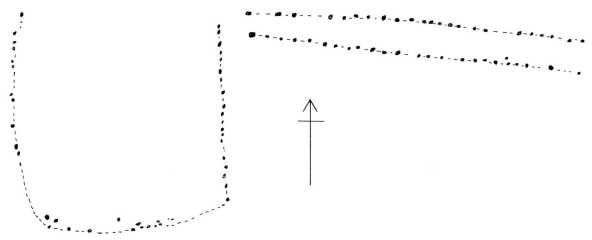

Fig. 36 Plan of the possible Kerlescan horseshoe and its oblique avenue. Notice the characteristic narrowing as it approaches the cromlech.

Pl. 65 The Kerlescan rows, Carnac. To the east and the hamlet.

lacking both symmetry and focus if the conventional interpretation is followed. At their west they spread so widely that the outermost overlap both ends of the 78 m (256 ft) long cromlech. At their east they contract and expire near the hamlet of Kerlescan whose predatory inhabitants years ago may have contributed to today's disruption.

There is no sign whatsoever of an avenue leading to a central entrance in the cromlech's eastern side even though it may be presumed that the 'rectangle' had been intended for assemblies. There are certainly gaps in that side but no lines go convincingly to them. The only parallel rows, and those of big stones, extend diagonally to the cromlech's north-eastern corner and it is arguable that this had been the approach, not to an enclosed rectangle but to a gigantic horseshoe of close-set stones open to the north (Fig. 36). Comparable horseshoes are well-known in Brittany.[42]

If the supposition, and it can be no more, is wrong then it is curious that not a single stone remains in the north 'side', the one farthest from the road, whereas there are clumps of contiguous pillars in the others, eleven in the west, eleven in the south, and eighteen in the east. The question could not be resolved without excavation but the putative 'avenue', Rows V and VI, is quantifiable, ESE–WNW, 125 m (410 ft) long, lightly splayed, contracting from 10 m (33 ft) wide at the east down to 7 m (23 ft) at the cromlech's north-east end.

Whatever uncertainties obtain at Kerlescan those of Petit-Ménec at the far end of the group are greater. Two or three mutilated lines 230 m (755 m) east of Kerlescan with the hamlet between them swing in a long, west–north-west curve to the north of a shorter batch of about six rows all higgledy-piggledy in the dappled shadows of pine woods. The farmers of Kerlescan were blameless. Between 1826 and 1835 hundreds of stones were methodically ripped up and carted to the nearby River Crac'h for the building of a lighthouse on the jagged coasts of the lovely Belle-Île far out to sea south of Quiberon.

Wrecked or unwrecked what almost all these rows have in common is their association with a cromlech and this offers clues about the date of the lines and their function.

(c) Dating

Wherever cromlechs and rows are joined it is the cromlech that stands at the top of a slope on level ground. The rows lead uphill to it, their stones increasing in height as they near the ring in the same manner as avenues in England. From this it is likely that the cromlech was the focus and that if there were a difference in time between it and the rows it is probable that the lines were the later. What excavations there have been tend to support this sequence.

Like the first British stone circles cromlechs were Late Neolithic phenomena. Investigations in 1963 of a large tumulus, some 60 m (197 ft) in diameter, at Tossen-Keler (p. 33) near Penvenan in Côtes-du-Nord discovered that it was bordered by an open-ended oval setting of heavy standing stones. These were too shallowly set to have been effective kerbs and the probability is that they had been a cromlech inside which the cairn had later been inserted.[43] At the end of the excavation the cromlech's stones were removed and taken 7 km (4½ miles) east to Tréguier for protection. They were re-erected and pleasingly planted with trees and bushes by the riverside.

At the centre of the mound two ritual hearths were discovered. Burnt wood and ash from one provided a radiocarbon determination of 2550±250 bc (Gif-280), approximately 3300 BC. From the date of the tumulus the cromlech of Tossen-Keler itself may have been a century or more older but this would be no earlier than the splendid rings, now marooned on an island bird-sanctuary in the Gulf of Morbihan, the flattened megalithic ring and submerged horseshoe of Er-Lannic. Once set on a low hill before the rising of the sea-level in historic times the cromlechs had been erected on an area of previous Middle Neolithic occupation but the presence of Late Neolithic Conguel ware in cists buried alongside the pillars shows that the circle was of a similar period as Tossen-Keler, maybe as early as 3500 BC.[44]

Nothing so clearcut is available for the rows. That they are likely to belong to the Early Bronze Age is hinted at by the fact that both at Kermario and Kerlescan an outer northern row was deliberately erected over the funerary mound of a low but very long Neolithic tertre containing numerous cists with hearths, stone axes and burnt material. At Kermario there were Chasséen sherds in the Manio tertre and the tertre tumulaire at Kerlescan also held fragments of Middle Neolithic pottery proving that the rows must be of a later period though whether of a year or of centuries is unknown.[45] The evidence is inconclusive.

Excavation has been only a little more helpful. Charcoal from a hearth against a stone in the three rows of Kersolan near Languidec 30 km (19 miles) north of Carnac 'ont permis de dater ces alignements d'environ 3300 ans avant notre ére', an early but not unacceptable date for the rows which may originally have been single lines leading, one directly, another tangentially to tertres at their east. Some of their stones were taken to be transplanted 'dans les jardins de la sous-préfecture de Lorient'.[46]

At Carnac just before 1872 the Abbé Collet dug at the foot of seven Ménec stones unearthing charcoal, nondescript sherds and flints. In 1877 and 1878 James Miln, a wealthy Scotsman who became enamoured with the Carnac region, excavated at Kermario, ending in 1878 near the middle of the rows at Kerloquet, 'the place of burning'. The previous year digging at the west end of the northern row 'we came upon a great number of burnt stones, charcoal, ashes, several stone hammers in quartz, numerous hand projectiles in granite, some flint chips, and several fragments of rude Celtic pottery belonging to vases which had been made with sea mud.' Constantly the work was interrupted by cries of 'douar losquet' from the workers, 'burnt earth'. 'After this we proceeded to the second and third alignments, but the only result obtained there was some charcoal ashes and flint chips at the base of the menhirs.'[47] Material such as this, rough flints, coarse undecorated pottery, is an archaeological nightmare. One can only remark that the sherds are very unlike the hard, well-shaped vessels associated with the Neolithic.

(d) Function

Whether at Carnac or in the bustling lines of Kerzerho where only a stone or two of the cupmarked cromlech survive (Pl. 66), the question that must be asked is for what purpose the rows were planned and built. People did not shift and haul thousands of boulders, incalculable tons of exhausting granite, without reason.

Astronomical alignments have been proposed. In the early nineteenth century Cambry believed the settings to be zodiacal patterns. Seventy years later du Cleuziou suggested the lines had been oriented on the solstitial and equinoctial sunrises and sunsets, an enticing idea but one contradicted by both the azimuths and the bends in the rows. And even though the many pine forests around Carnac are recent introductions to what in prehistoric times was a fairly open landscape conducive to celestial observations later theories by Gaillard, Merlot, even Thom himself, are not convincing. The rows were not essential elements of any solar or lunar observatory.[48]

The fan of five rows at Le Moulin de St-Pierre on the Quiberon peninsula demonstrates very clearly the hazards confronting any astronomical enthusiast. The rows are about 55 m (180 ft) long and 31 m (102 ft) wide at their ESE end (Pl. 67). The Thoms noted that 'In St-Pierre . . . there is part of a sector of which there is enough left to fix the radius as being at least 700 ft [213 m] and this is very close to the theoretical value required for extrapolation at this site, namely $4\,G = 720\,ft$' [220 m].[49]

Apart from one stone omitted from the western row their survey is correct and can be confirmed by anyone visiting the site. What the visitor will not realise is that much of the original layout has been lost. Between 1868 and 1872 the Rev. W.C. Lukis undertook extensive fieldwork in Brittany during which he saw the St-Pierre rows. He recorded that the five lines were then at least 193 m (635 ft) long but were being 'partially destroyed by the encroachment of the sea . . . [They] may be traced to the very edge of the beach, and even on the rocks when the tide is out'. Even assuming that the rows were never more than 200 m (220 yds) long this would produce a length of over 1400 m (1530 yds) for 4 G, 'an impossible distance to lay out nicely on the rugged ground of the peninsula.[50]

At Carnac the ravished rows of Petit-Ménec also

are theoretically fan-shaped but the design of the grid is not convincing as an extrapolation sector. The discrepancy between the projected value and the actual one for 4 G 'is uncomfortably large'.[51] As these rows may be no more than the lopped-off terminals of the larger Kerlescan group any extrapolation theory can be dismissed. Astronomy is not central to the problem of the rows in Brittany.

The cromlechs are the clue. The rows move towards them like queues shuffling towards the turnstiles of a stadium. As Giot, the leading Breton prehistorian, has written, 'incontestablement, les enceintes ou "cromlechs" sont les saints des saints, des haux lieux, des points focaux des systèmes...'; or as the previous doyen, Zacharie le Rouzic, thought, the rows 'étaient des voies sacrées où circulaient les fidèles. Les cromlechs étaient les sanctuaires où officiaient les pasteurs'.[52] Ian Hodder also saw the rows as pathways:

> The long lines of approach lead upwards towards a focal point, a 'centre'. Everything is channelled into a long, slow entry. Both the construction and use of these monuments formed large social entities through the linear ordering of space and through the domination and control of nature. The natural landscape had been transformed through massive, direct cultural intervention.[53]

People built the rows, added to them, using them as ever longer ways that gave pious access to the cromlechs.

If cromlechs, as is supposed for stone circles, were places of assembly what will never be known is the number of participants they were designed to hold. They are vast. Those in the Carnac region average $5000\,m^2$ (54,000 s.ft). If only half the space in the egg-shaped rings of Ménec, the wider lower base, was provided for spectators with officiants at the narrower focus of the head, and if the watchers were allowed a very comfortable body-space of 2 m (6 ft) around them, then an élite of some 250 people could have observed the ceremonies. If, instead, commoners were packed in like a football crowd on the terraces, shoulder to shoulder and chest to back, the congregation would increase nearly thirty-fold to a jostling mass of 7000. Nor is this the end of the equation.

Women may have been excluded. If so, this would entail doubling any computation of the Carnac population. There were, moreover, five, if not six or seven, cromlechs in the Carnac region. If each was independent of the others and if the figure of 7000 males is accepted, augmented by the absence not only of women but of the very old, the young and the infirm one might postulate as many as 100,000 to 200,000 men, women and children living there.

Demographic statistics are vulnerable to errors in every direction. It is easier to estimate how many angels could dance on the head of a mediaeval pin than to establish how many, if any at all, were the temporary occupants of a cromlech. Yet there is the

Pl. 66   Kerzerho, Erdeven. Taken from the site of the destroyed cromlech towards the rows approaching from the east.

Pl. 67   The rows of St-Pierre-Quiberon, Morbihan, from the ESE.

possibility that instead of several self-sufficient ritual centres within 4 km (2½ miles) of each other the cromlechs were part of a single system, used on different occasions for different purposes. This, especially if readmitting women, would reduce the Early Bronze Age population of Carnac to a more manageable 5000 to 10,000 people, about the same as the metaphysical number of dancing angels.

These are intangibles. It is interesting that the short axis of the Ménec West cromlech, an inverted egg, is in line with the midwinter sunrise and that the long axis of its eastern counterpart points in the direction of the midsummer sunset as though the two rings were complementary, each for celebrations at the year's ends.[54] From this one could speculate that other enclosures were for other festivals. It is noteworthy that the feast day of St-Cornély, Carnac's patron saint, the holy man who petrified the pursuing lines of pagan Roman legionaries, is in mid-September close to the autumnal equinox. If one knew that the Kermario cromlechs had been aligned on the times of Beltane in early May and Samain at the beginning of November these remarks could be transformed into a hypothesis.

Fires may have burned. Excavations have consistently recovered charcoal and ashes against the stones, at Carnac, at Lagatjar, at the bases of isolated menhirs where 'before the erection there was a ritual burial of objects or a ceremony in the trench. Remains of charred wood are always found, and stones reddened by fire'. As late as the nineteenth century a midsummer bonfire was lit on the gigantic tumulus of Mont St Michel overlooking the Carnac rows. Its Breton name was *tan heol*, 'the fire of the sun'.[55]

At the five ragged rows of the Champ des Roches, Pleslin, Côtes-du-Nord, early digging unearthed ashes and charcoal at the foot of many stones, 'trace d'une cérémonie de fondation assez générale'.[56]

Perceptions in the prehistoric mind of a correspondence between the flames of a fire and the brightness of the sun can be seen as early as 3000 BC in the Late Neolithic villages of Skara Brae and Barnhouse in the Orkneys. There, whatever the direction of the house entrances, the slabbed sides of the central hearths were invariably in line with a solstitial sunrise or sunset. It implies that the aligning of the rectangular fireplace was the primary stage in the laying-out of a building, an arcane necessity in an otherwise ordinary domestic area for cooking and warmth.[57]

In his *Golden Bough* Frazer, whose references are quoted for their facts if not for their conclusions, cites many instances of celebratory or protective bonfires in western Europe at seasonal times of the year. One wonders, also, if the names of Kerlescan and Kerloquet, places of burning, retain dimmed recollections of fires that once were lit there. Mahé certainly recorded a local story of fires by the rows, lit moreover in June, the time of year when they would have been least' needed unless in recognition of the summer solstice.

The Carnac rows lie in a great burial-ground, an area redolent with death. All around are passage-tombs: Kercado, Kerlescan North, Lann Mané Kermario. There are tertres at Kerlescan, Manio, Kermario. There are colossal Carnac Mounds with cremations and luxurious personal ornaments at Mont St-Michel and Le Moustoir. Like Stonehenge the rows occupy the heart of a necropolis and it would be surprising if their ceremonies were not in some ways connected with death.

For the less cautiously-minded, processions may be imagined, illuminated by flames in the darkness of night, throngs of people delighting in the warmth of summer, longing for the departure of winter, fearing death, desiring the regeneration and fertility of life. All these may have mingled, may even have lingered obstinately through centuries of Christianity. Until recently childless women would go to the Giant of Kerderff, a high granite menhir near the Ménec rows, and rub their bellies against it for fecundity. At the christianised chambered tomb of Cruz-Moquen or La Pierre Chaude in Carnac-Ville 'at full moon women would raise their skirts in front of the dolmen in the hope of becoming pregnant'.[58]

The rows of Carnac extend across nearly the entire land between the Baie de Plouharnel and the River Crac'h like a planned megalithic barrier separating the sacred from the profane. This also may have been one of their purposes.

But for the archaeologist in Brittany today there is a sad paradox. Both antique time and modern time are lost. Massive though they are the great rows are threatened. Like Stonehenge Carnac receives too many visitors, and the grass and the ground were being worn away. For their conservation parts of the lines have been barricaded by wire-meshing and one cannot stroll freely along them. Even the crêperie inside the remains of the Ménec cromlech, once the Mecca at the end of the long walk to Petit-Ménec and back, has gone and it is no longer possible to drink cool cider at its little tables. Glyn Daniel would have been shocked. 'The stones, which are of a delicate grey-green colour, rise like an army, in battalions, from the heather'. Not now. The soldiers have been interned.

At the west end of the Kermario rows, in place of the freedom to wander around the stones, an overbearing viewing-platform has been built with a small exhibition and bookstall. More ambitiously, for a few francs at Ménec West one can see a vivid and technically brilliant, if inconclusive, audio-visual presentation in the hideously modern Archéoscope against the car-park.

The consolation is the Miln-le Rouzic Museum in Carnac-Ville. The displays are well chosen, well lit, well explained. The museum is a delight to visit, preferably before going to the rows. There one can learn something of the people who raised the stones.

PART THREE

From Long to Short
1800 to 1000 BC

INTRODUCTION

THE SHORT ROWS

'Standing stones', often in groups of twos, threes, or more . . . abound in almost every district of Scotland. Of such megalithic monuments history is almost silent, and the associations which still hover about them in local folk-lore are of little value in determining their origin or purpose.

R. Munro, *Prehistoric Scotland*, 1899, 318

The distribution of short rows, lines with no more than six stones, is complementary to that of the long rows. Whether of six stones, three or two, they are to be found on the distant fringes of the longer rows, often in regions previously unaffected by the linear tradition. There appears to have been a slow diffusion spreading farther and later from its origins, and the greater the distance the fewer stones in the rows.

The two criteria used to distinguish them from collections of randomly placed stones is that there should not be more than about 100 ft (30 m) between any two stones unless they are clearly intervisible, and that the line in settings of three to six stones should be reasonably straight. The two stones at Llansadwrn near Cremlyn on Anglesey, for example, are excluded because they are little and over 250 ft (76 m) apart. The Royal Commission surveyors believed that with three other stones in Llandona they formed a Five-Stone row. As the alignment was not only far from straight but would have been nearly two miles (3.2 km) in length this was an unlikely proposition.

In their architecture short rows resemble the longer lines although in diminished form but they were for very different occasions. These abbreviated settings were not for great assemblies. They seem to have been for small groups, used at particular times of the year, and for this, unlike most long rows, many had calendrical alignments built into them (Pl. 68).

The concept of these shrunken lines being used for processions must be dismissed. Some, especially amongst the pairs of standing stones, are so short, no more than two or three paces apart, that even a group of lethargic sloths could have moved from one end to the other in a few seconds. The stones were no longer approaches. They had become centres for ceremonies signalled by the sun or moon's appearance beyond the stones, the focus of rituals that involved the deposition of arcane objects, rites in which fire was often important and with which death was frequently associated.

There is a great discrepancy between the location of these rows and the regions in which there are large tombs or megalithic rings. There are few rows near the passage-tombs of the Boyne Valley or the huge round barrows of the Yorkshire Wolds. It is a paucity repeated in the Orkneys, in Cumbria and Wessex, and southern Brittany, areas of impressive stone circles and spacious cromlechs.

Such concentrations of dominant ritual monuments

Four- to Six-Stone Rows
1 Callanish
2 Blanefield
3 Ballymeanoch
4 Beaghmore
5 Devil's Arrows
6 Eightercua
7 Vieux-Moulin
8 Grand Menhir Brisé

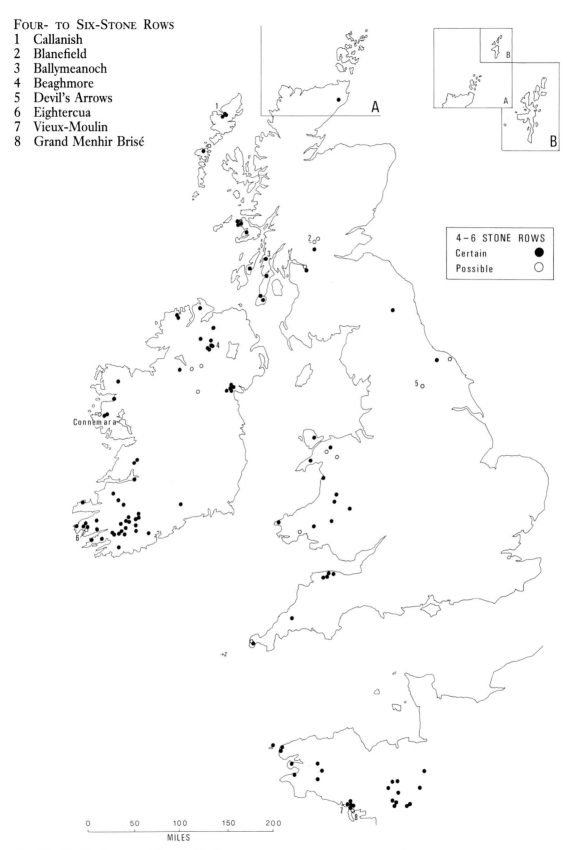

4–6 STONE ROWS
Certain   ●
Possible   ○

Fig. 37 Distribution map of Four- to Six-Stone rows.

THREE-STONE ROWS
1   Ballochroy
2   Barnes Lower
3   Beaghmore E
4   Lacra C
5   Plas Gogerddon
6   Harold's Stones
7   Dromatouk
8   Brouel
9   St-Just

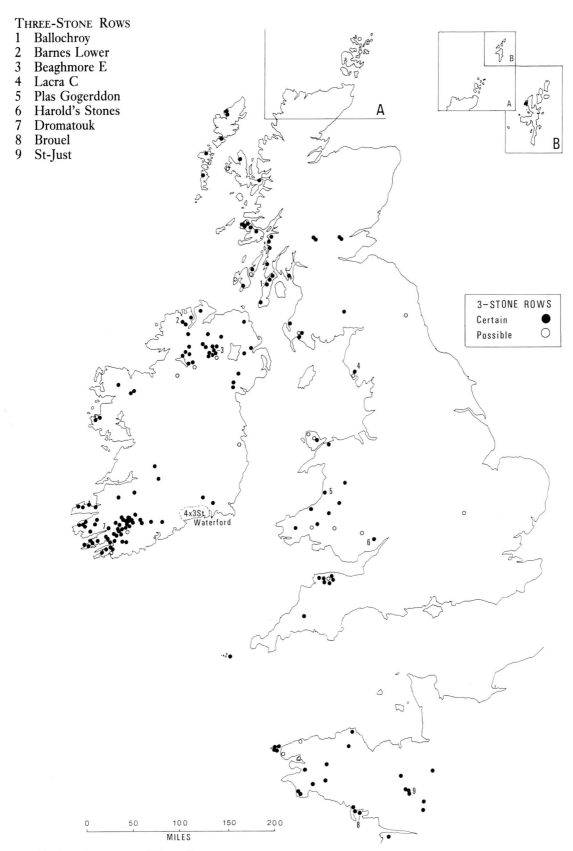

3-STONE ROWS
Certain   ●
Possible   ○

4×3St.
Waterford

0   50   100   150   200
MILES

Fig. 38   Distribution map of Three-Stone rows.

Pl. 68 A typical short row. Le Vieux-Moulin, Plouharnel, Morbihan.

may reflect high population densities and sub-tribal societies. The absence of short rows from those long-settled, heavily inhabited territories, and their presence in the more lightly occupied countryside and islands to the west, together with their own closely-packed distribution within a few miles of each other, suggest that they were the ritual centres of no more than a few Bronze Age families, simple and easily-constructed monuments on the outskirts of the megalithic world (Figs 37 and 38).

In England there are no short lines on Dartmoor despite the abundance of long avenues, double and single long rows there. There is none in Wessex, very few in Cumbria but some in Northumberland and Yorkshire, regions notable for the absence of earlier lines. In Wales some Four- to Six-Stone rows are coastal unlike the majority of Three-Stone and pairs which are to be found inland on the hillsides and mountain slopes of the interior. Similarly, eastern Brittany has several Four- to Six-Stone rows in the vicinity of Carnac in Morbihan but the Three-Stone rows appear more to the west, even to the north in

Côtes-du-Nord. Finistère to the west has almost a monopoly of paired stones.

South-west Ireland has hardly been mentioned in this account of the avenues and stone rows of Britain, Ireland and Brittany. Now, suddenly, scores of short rows appear. They developed unevenly. Although there are many primary Four- to Six-Stone rows in Co. Cork and Kerry they are increasingly outnumbered to the west by the Three-Stone and pairs in the Boggeragh mountains and on the hilly peninsulas around Bantry Bay. Pairs also predominate in the western counties of Galway and Mayo.

In northern Ireland all types of long and short row were erected in the Sperrins but to the east, in Antrim, Armagh, Down and Louth, where there had never been a long row there was every kind of short.

Scotland was no different. In the islands of the west, where only Lewis had an avenue and no other island had a long row there are over fifty short settings from the three rows of four and five stones at Callanish to the two tall granite pillars at Totronald on Coll, 'a Druidical temple' seen by Johnson and Boswell in 1773.[1]

Across the Scottish mainland from Argyll at the south-west to Aberdeen at the north-east there is the same pattern: Argyll with four Four- to Six-Stone rows, nine Three-Stone and sixteen pairs; then Perth with three, four and twenty-nine; and finally, at the far east, no Four to Six, no Three-Stone, only pairs in Fife (2), Angus (3), Kincardine (2), Aberdeen (1) and Moray (1). In the hills of the Cheviots the history is repeated with no Four to Six, a few Three-Stone but more of the apparently late, ultimate pairs.

So consistent is this distributional development, both in its detachment from the areas of longer lines and in the manner that the number of stones in the rows is reduced the farther away the sites are that the simplest interpretation is that the short lines developed from the custom of erecting longer lines of standing stones.

Alternative origins are not apparent. The possibility that these settings of a few tall pillars were vestigial imitations of the forecourts of neighbouring Neolithic chambered tombs, maintaining continuity of belief in a modified form, is not sustainable. Despite the ambiguity of one or two lines such as the row/forecourt at Blanefield in Stirling (p. 8) or Eightercua in Co. Kerry (p. 9) these are exceptions. The majority of short rows stand in regions where megalithic tombs had decidedly curved rather than flat façades, the concave forecourts of the court-cairns of the north of Ireland, and the Clyde-Solway tombs of south-west Scotland. The chambered Hebridean tombs of the Western Isles were enclosed in round, kerbed cairns. Even amongst the wedge-tombs of south-west Ireland, most of them ruined, wherever the façade is preserved it tends to be convex rather than straight.[2]

In the absence of convincing prototypes one must conclude either that short rows were megalithic innovations without forebears or that they were economical versions of the longer rows that existed in adjacent areas. The second is more likely.

CHAPTER TEN

FOUR- TO SIX- AND THREE-STONE ROWS 1800–1200 BC

In the Iland of Lewis beforemention'd, at the village of Classerniss, there is one of those Temples extremely remarkable . . . Directly south from the Circle, there stand four Obeliscs running out in a line: as another such line due east, and a third to the west, the number and distances of the stones being in these wings the same.

John Toland, *The History of the Druids*, 1814, 122

INTRODUCTION

From their closer proximity to the areas of long rows it is arguable that amongst the short rows those with four to six stones were the first. Well over one hundred are known with 200 Three-Stone rows overlapping and spreading into districts beyond them. It is possible that ultimately the two groups should be separated but for the present the similarity of their distributions, their architectural features and their related astronomical alignments make it sensible to combine them. To facilitate any future division, however, they have been given individual Gazetteers. Pairs of standing stones are considered in the following chapter.

The largest concentrations of short rows are in south-west Ireland and Scotland. Even as an assemblage England, Brittany, Northern Ireland and Wales have only forty-two per cent of the lines whereas Cork and Kerry alone contain twenty-seven per cent, and Scotland has nineteen per cent. Nearly half the Scottish sites are in the islands from Mull up to Lewis and Harris, reaffirming the density of these short Scottish settings around the North Channel and the western seaboards.

The paucity of short rows in other areas is remarkable, only fifty-three in all Brittany, fifteen in south-west England and Wessex, just four in northern England including the Devil's Arrows, and no more than four in north Scotland in Caithness, and the Orkneys and Shetlands.

Excluding atypically extended rows such as the 570 ft (174 m) of the Devil's Arrows in Yorkshire or the even longer 2100 ft (640 m) of the problematical Dunruchan Stones, Perthshire, the average length of a Four- to Six-Stone row is 34 ft (10 m) with a range from 73 ft (22.3 m) at the Five Kings on a Northumbrian hillside down to the 7 ft 6 (2.3 m) of the low granite blocks at Killadangan by the seashore in Co. Mayo, a stone circle against which it stood long since destroyed. In general, the Three-Stone rows are shorter, about 19 ft 3 (5.9 m).

Like Killadangan most rows are roughly graded often with the tallest stone in the south-west quadrant. In Connemara, however, the mountainous region between Galway Bay and Killary Harbour, the rows were arranged meridionally, rising in height towards the north. Several were built of vividly white quartz stones, and all of them stand in prominent hillside positions as though intended to be seen from a considerable distance.[3]

Amongst the rows eleven Four- to Six- and seven Three-Stone are decorated, setting them apart from the plain long lines. Fourteen sites, seven of them in Scotland, have cupmarks. Two others, Ballymeanoch, Argyll, and the Reyfad Stones, Co. Fermanagh, are distinguished by their unique cup-and-ring markings. No art of any kind appears in the south-west of Ireland and only the cupmarked row of Carragh a'Ghlinne on Jura is an exception in the Western Isles.

In Brittany one of the coarsely-grained pillars at St-Dénec, Finistère, has carvings of hafted axes, and the Grand Menhir Brisé, Morbihan, the gigantic but broken survivor of a lost row, has a similar though very eroded motif on the upper surface of its largest fragment. Such art is prehistoric unlike the Dark Age inscription on a pillar of the row in the churchyard of Gwytherin, Clwyd.

More research is required before firm statements can be made about the characteristic astronomical alignments in these rows, a second trait separating them from the longer lines, but preliminary comments are possible. For the first time there is clear evidence of purposeful sightlines in a group of stone rows. Qualification is necessary. Wherever the region much less interest was shown by the builders in movements of the sun than in the moon. Even here there were differences. In Scotland, particularly in the the Western Isles, several rows were directed towards the major southern setting of the moon. In Ireland the northern moonrise was preferred. If this is confirmed by further surveys it will strengthen the need to look at the

Pl. 69 A Three-Stone setting at Kerzerho. From the north.

Pl. 70 The shattered blocks of the Grand Menhir Brisé at Locmariaquer, Morbihan. From the north-east. When unbroken it was 20.3 m (67 ft) long. Stoneholes discovered near it suggest it was once part of a short row.

regional variations that almost certainly exist in the lines.

The *floruit* of the rows has not been clarified by unproductive excavations that recovered undateable pottery and undiagnostic flints but several radiocarbon assays from Wales and Ireland show that these short settings belong to the middle centuries of the Bronze Age, no earlier than 1800 BC and probably no later than 1200 BC.

BRITTANY

Short rows, whether of four to six or of three stones, are not numerous in Brittany. Those that are known usually exist near areas of longer lines. There were several complete rows and the remaining menhir of another in the Carnac region of southern Morbihan (Pl. 69) with others in the 'druidical' forest of Brocéliande near Paimpont. There are some in Ille-et-Vilaine and over a score in Finistère, one of them, Pen-ar-Land on Ushant, alongside a horseshoe-shaped cromlech for which lunar alignments have been claimed.[4] A Three-Stone row once stood on the seaweed-littered islet of Île Molène in the same archipelago.

Many of the Carnac rows are in dispute. None was suspected at Locmariaquer amongst the passage-tombs until a run of deep stoneholes was discovered during the excavations at the Table de Marchands. They led towards the fallen Grand Menhir Brisé, supposedly once the tallest menhir in France, now a shattered granite colossus (Pl. 70). Whether the pillar ever stood upright is extremely doubtful.[5]

Nearer to Carnac, at Plouharnel, in clear view just east of the road to Erdeven the six heavy pillars of Le

Pl. 71 The Trois Colonnes, St-Just, Ille-et-Vilaine. From the SSE

Vieux-Moulin form a short, north-south line. Lukis who saw them while a windmill stood nearby thought them 'the remains of destroyed lines. They are known by the name of 'Les trois pierres du vieux Moulin', another dispiriting example of peasant innumeracy. Giot believed them to have been part of a cromlech, '6 blocs d'une enceinte sub-circulaire'. Scouëzec concurred, 'les ruines d'un temple extravagent', and, more prettily, the phantoms of a slaughtered army.[6]

It is improbable that the menhirs were ever part of a longer line or of a cromlech. They stand on a slope, not on level ground. The row is short, composed of three tall pairs that shoulder together unlike the well-spaced uprights of the Carnac rows. It is significant that the two tallest stones, 3.4 m (11 ft 3) high, stand at the centre in an arrangement reminiscent of the earlier, longer lines.

Unremarked by most commentators some 75 m (82 yds) NNW at the crest of the low ridge is a second short row of four enormous boulders, one of them,

4 m (13 ft) long, toppled and shifted to make way for a farm track. This row is not in line with the first and its bearing is different. Rather than the remnants of a hypothetical long line or an eccentrically-situated cromlech it is more likely that these were two Four- to Six-Stone rows erected within 3 km (1¾ miles) of Ménec to the ESE and 4 km (2½ miles) from Kerzerho to the north-west.

Unlike the Grand Menhir Brisé there is no art at Le Vieux-Moulin but farther away in Morbihan, near Roudouallec amongst the Montagnes Noires of central Brittany, a high 'playing-card' slab standing by the roadside at Guernangoué has three others tumbled in a tangle of trees and bushes to the SSW. Two have fallen westwards. Close to them is the fourth lying in the opposite direction. On what had been its north-west face are five cupmarks. The density of the vegetation around this overgrown slab may explain why what had been a finely-arranged Four- to Six-Stone row has been mistakenly called 'trois pierres'.

Sixty kilometres (37 miles) to the south-west on the Pointe de Penmarc'h in Finistère what may have been a Three-Stone row, now ruined, at Plouguen-Bihan, cardinally graded, had a mass of cupmarks like a writhing Cross of Lorraine on its tallest stone at the north.

Quite different art of two hafted axes side by side occurs on a fallen stone in the row at St-Dénec near Porspoder on the coast of western Finistère. Roughly carved in high relief within a zone pecked out of the unresponsive granite the tools or weapons are not dissimilar to the axe on the Grand Menhir Brisé and on one of the slabs in the Tossen-Keler cromlech.[7] Such axe-carvings have been seen as representations of the armoury of a female guardian of the dead. If the interpretation is valid it would reinforce the idea that at least one function of a stone row was associated with funerary rites. With so few rows and even fewer carvings nothing is certain.

The dating of these Breton short rows is as inconclusive as that of the longer lines. In central Brittany the two Three-Stone rows of Les Trois Colonnes (Pl. 71) and Les Demoiselles near St-Just stand at the edges of a long-hallowed district as though they were the final megaliths in an area containing chambered tombs at Le Four-Sarrazin and Tréal, a horseshoe-shaped cromlech alongside the Tertre de la Croix St-Pierre, presumably a Late Neolithic structure, the three long single lines of the Alignements du Moulin associated with Middle Neolithic sherds and Early Bronze Age beakers, and what seems to be a Middle Bronze Age 'Scottish' Four-Poster stone circle at Château-Bû. The Three-Stone rows were presumably even later.

The four stones of La Roche de la Vieille at Campénéac in the Brocéliande forest are believed to have been uprooted to become the capstone and sideslabs of a Bronze Age tertre, the Tombeau des Géants. A Late Neolithic date between 3000 and 2500 BC has rather tentatively been proposed for the row.[8]

Coarse sherds, a quern and predictable charcoal were dug from the Kerfland Three-Stone row in southern Finistère. A similar row, Men Guen, at Brouel on the Île aux Moines, 115 km (72 miles) to the east in the Gulf of Morbihan, provided no better indication of its age. Now in a private back garden it suffered an excavation in 1877. As well as broken pottery, animal bones and, of course, charcoal and burnt flints two small pottery discs were found. Such objects, perhaps amulets or replicas of the sun or moon, have often been discovered with Neolithic and Bronze Age burials, another sign that stone rows had intimate links with death. One can also associate the charcoal and flints with comparable evidence from the multiple lines, material most simply regarded as the detritus of fire ceremonies.

The stones at Brouel are neatly graded towards the north where the tallest stone, 2 m (6 ft 6) high, tapers to a thin point (Pl. 72). Such a clearcut south-north orientation, as in many other short rows, suggests that the stones were set up in line with the sun or moon between their rising at the north-east and setting at the north-west.

Such meridional alignments are seldom commented on but they are too frequent to be accidental, several being known in the vicinity of Paimpont. They present three problems. First how the alignments were

Pl. 72 The three stones of Men Guen, Brouel, Île-aux-Moines, Morbihan. From the south-east.

achieved when there was no Pole Star. Secondly, why the 'alignments' are often 5° or more from True North or South. Thirdly, why prehistoric people should have been interested, almost obsessed, with areas of the sky where neither the sun nor the moon ever rose or set.

Centuries after Brouel's row was erected the bright Pole Star, α Ursae Minoris, still shone far away from north. The Greek explorer, Pytheas, stated as much. 'In fact there is no star at the pole but an empty space close to which lie three stars; these, taken with the point of the pole, make a rough quadrilateral, as Pytheas of Marseilles tells us.' Around 1500 BC the inconspicuous Kochab, β Ursae Minoris, flickered at the north supplanting an equally dim star, Thuban, α Draconis.[9] It was not until AD 200 that Polaris had drifted far enough in the heavens to become today's Pole Star. Yet from early prehistory orientations towards the cardinal points of north, south, east and west had been built into megalithic monuments such as Castlerigg stone circle, Kerlescan cromlech and long rows like Tormsdale in Caithness and the short Irish rows of Connemara.

In the absence of a brilliant Pole Star these orientations, especially those to north or south, were probably attained from a backsight by establishing the midpoint between the rising and setting of the sun or moon, setting up stakes in line with those events and then erecting a foresight halfway between them. If this indeed had been the practice it would explain what looks like careless inaccuracy today but what was, in reality, precision to the creators of the sightlines.

Rather than the geographical positions of cardinal points they seem concerned only with defining a central point between the emergence and disappearance of the sun or moon. True North or South were abstractions and matters of indifference, even incomprehension, to them. They were not geodetic surveyors. It was coincidental that had the surface of the Earth been of billiard-table flatness their foresight would have stood exactly at north or south.

Despite mediaeval beliefs the Earth is not flat. Rather than a level horizon it has skylines resembling tree-trunks gnawed by beavers, dented, gouged, torn and knuckled by hills and valleys, moors and mountain peaks (Fig. 39). They distort. If, as an example, at the latitude of the Solway Firth, 55°, halfway up Britain, a Bronze Age observer had looked southwards towards a nearly horizontal skyline at the level of his eyes he would have seen the major moon rise at 148° and set at 212°. Midway between those positions was 180°, True South.

This is hypothetical. A natural landscape would have a skyline of varying heights and this would affect how long the moon could be seen. With lowish moorland to the south-east 1° above the observer the moon would appear at 151°. But if to the south-west the summit of a steep hill was 4° above eye-level the moon would vanish behind it at 198°. Halfway between 151° and 198° would be 174°.5, SSE rather than south. Similar irregularities at other sites would account for the 'imprecise' sightlines to north or south.

The alignment at Brouel is good because the row faced north across the waters of the Gulf of Morbihan towards the featureless coast near modern Vannes. Most rows, however, were laid out amongst less amenable hills whose rugged horizons produced 'north' and 'south' orientations several degrees from 360° and 180°. The 'error' would not matter to planners of stone rows because to them it would not be an error. Their stones looked to the real target, the place in the sky midway between the rising and the setting of the sun or moon. It also explains why there are more lines to north or south than to east or west. North and south could be found in a day between sunrise and sunset, or in a night between moonrise and moonset. But east and west could only be found after six months between the midsummer and midwinter suns or in a lunar fortnight between the less predictable moonrises.

It would be misleading to write of sun- or moon-worship, even of solar or lunar cults. What those bodies meant to the societies that set up stones in line with their movements may never be known. Many rows, standing by pits in which wood had burned, led to cairns beneath which the dead were buried. The rows could be cenotaphs, calendars, assembly places for families, ancestral shrines.

Fig. 39 A diagram to show how the height of the horizon affects the place where the sun or moon appear on the skyline. Latitude 53°. 2000 BC. How the height of the horizon affects solar midpoints.
(A1). With a level skyline the midpoint between midsummer sunset at the north-west and the midsummer sunrise at the north-east is True North.
(A2). With a skyline higher at the north-west the midpoint is 'pulled' to the left.
(B1). With a level skyline the midpoint between midsummer

ENGLAND

Short rows are as rare in England as in Brittany and were raised only at the extremes of the country, in the north-east in Yorkshire and Northumberland where there were no long rows, and at the far south-west in Cornwall. There is even one off Land's End where in the Scilly Isles three stones form a wandering line on the beach of St Martin's.

Discrimination is needed. Some suspected rows may be no more than ruined field boundaries: Dunmore Hill in Northumberland with three or more stones in a curving line; Garleigh Moor with twenty-one stones in an irregular setting 120 ft (37 m) long; Old Byrness where one stone, cupmarked, may be the survivor of a now irretrievably lost row; the Eleven Shearers near Howman Rings just over the border in Roxburghshire, an insignificant line that Thom thought was 'a row of seventeen smallish stones' on 'almost exactly the declination of Megalithic Man's equinox' but more probably the foundations of a field wall like another at Crock Cleugh three miles away.

Across the Pennines at Kirksanton near Millom in south-west Cumberland a pair of high pillars, the taller cupmarked, standing on the Giant's Grave cairn, are said to have had a third by them. The cupmarks, and the situation of the stones, less than a mile from the coast and the Irish Sea around which

sunrise at the north-east and the midwinter sunrise at the south-west is True East.
(B2). With a skyline higher at the south-east the midpoint is 'pulled' to the right.
Finding A2 for the north or south midpoints between north or south might take only a day or two between sunrises and sunsets.
Finding B2 for the east or west midpoints would take at least six months between midsummer and midwinter. This may explain the paucity of equinoctial alignments.

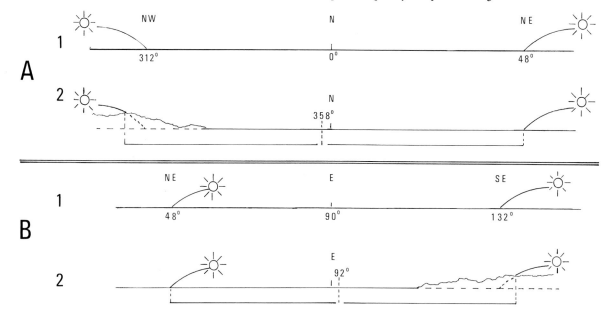

Pl. 73   Lacra SE, Cumbria. Once thought to be the remains of a small stone circle it is actually a fallen Three-Stone row. From the SSW.

there are many Three-Stone rows, are in the pair's favour but the cairn and a considerable doubt about the original number of stones militate against acceptance of the 'row'. In 1794 Hutchinson wrote that 'near adjoining to this monument, several other large stones stood lately, placed in a rude manner'.[10] The site could have been a stone circle.

Less doubts exist about the three fallen stones on Lacra hill three quarters of a mile (1.2 km) east and 300 ft (90 m) above Kirksanton (Pl. 73). Once thought to be the vestiges of a stone circle the stones of Lacra SE increase in height to the north-east. Excavation in 1947 found burnt bones by the tallest stone. An oyster shell was discovered at the other of the short row but whether from a prehistoric or later meal was uncertain.

Even more curious is the Devil's Jump Stone, the reputed survivor of three glacial boulders in Bedfordshire far to the east of any other row. Its name comes from the tale that this was where Satan leapt mockingly onto a man who was impiously playing leapfrog on a Sunday. The Devil has been connected with several other short rows but this is no guarantee that they are either genuine or prehistoric.

Clues to the origins of authenticated lines exist in their proximity to extended settings, Furzehill Common Centre on Exmoor only about 300 yards (275 m) from a multiple row on the same common, and, in Cornwall, the presence of the five tiny stones on Tolborough Tor within a mile or so of several long rows on Bodmin Moor.

Nearer to Land's End are the re-erected and artificially perforated blocks on Kenidjack Common and the pitifully disturbed row at Treveglos, one 8 ft 6 (2.6 m) high pillar standing against its prostrate and broken companions. Probably entirely by coincidence both Kenidjack and Treveglos were erected close to Logan Stones, massive boulders that by a glacial fluke were poised so delicately on others that they could be rocked up and down by hand. The most famous of these 'druidical stones' is near Treen on the headland of Treryn Dinas hillfort. In 1824 it was deliberately toppled by the orders of a naval lieutenant who was promptly commanded to replace it. He did. Imperfectly. Today great effort is needed to move the stone.

Druids were supposed to have balanced such boulders by magic. 'The Rocking-Stones, called in Cornwall, *Logan-Stones*, are also thought by some to be engines of the same fraud, and the Druids might probably have recourse to them, when they wanted to confirm their authority . . .'.[11]

The row on Kenidjack Common was associated with other superstitions. Close by was the Giant's Rock. Folklore claimed that a person walking nine times around it at midnight would be turned into a witch. A rather similar legend is attached to the three

Pl. 74 The Devil's Arrows, Yorkshire. The central and NNW pillar from the south-east. Both stones are deeply weathered.

tall stones of the Devil's Arrows in Yorkshire, thick and heavy bolts hurled maledroitly at Aldborough by the Devil who as usual missed the town by a long mile.[12] These towering pillars of millstone grit just south of the River Ure, now three but once four, even five great columns, stand on a slightly bent line 570 ft (174 m) long. It was said that anyone going around them twelve times, expectedly at midnight, would raise the Devil. An overseas visitor, perhaps fortified by Theakstone's extra-strong Old Peculier ale, boldly started on the two and a half mile (4 km) circuit. He gave up after the eleventh lap.[13]

Turning from fatuity to fact and the realities of prehistoric life it is clear that people accepted prolonged hardship to create this strenuous row of megalithic giants. That it exists is the proof.

Like Stonehenge on stoneless Salisbury Plain the Devil's Arrows should not be where they are (Pl. 74). The awesomely tall monoliths stand in a region where there were no glacial erratics. They jut from an unbroken landscape of sandstone in which there remained patches of Bronze Age forest but no clutters of boulders. It was a land whose monuments were the products of woodworkers. The nearest Neolithic long barrow to the row, Over Silton near Kepwick sixteen miles (26 km) to the NNE, had no burial chamber of large stones. There were no standing stones inside the six henges even at Cana less than four miles (6 km) from the Arrows.[14] Timber was the local material and

carpenters were the local craftsmen. Stones were unavailable.

Unavailable unless they were brought nine miles (15 km) from the south where the weather-loosened slabs and laminated outcrops at Plumpton Rocks near Knaresborough offered massive blocks of millstone grit. This was the most likely source. The Arrows could not have been dragged from the north. The Ure, a 200 ft wide river, 10 ft deep (60 × 3 m), without a ford, impassable for awkwardly long 30-ton stones, lay in between.[15] From the south, however, there were easy and unhindered gradients, and it was from here that the stones came, to be manhandled upright after their bases had been smoothed just as posts would have been shaped with flint adzes before erection. Sporadic excavations since 1725 have revealed the dressing, something to be anticipated if the Arrows were prepared by men accustomed to working in malleable but impermanent timber.

The project may never have been finished. Or perhaps the wide spaces between the stones were once occupied by carved and painted poles that have long since decayed. But the line contained all the features of earlier 'classical' rows. It was associated with water. At its lower end was a blocking-stone set at right-angles to its partners. The stones were graded in height, 18 ft, 22 ft, 22 ft 6 (5.5, 6.7, 6.9 m). They climbed a slight rise to the tallest pillar at the head of the slope. And the SSE angle of the line, about 152°, was quite well in line with the most southerly rising of the moon.[16]

It is noteworthy that in the early eighteenth century William Stukeley wrote that an annual fair was held there on St Barnabas's Day, the day of the mid-summer solstice. Like many other short rows the stones may have possessed a calendrical function, recording the times of festivals or gatherings at special times of the year.[17]

What is also noticeable about the Devil's Arrows and other 'short' rows in north-eastern England is their unusual length, even the Five Kings in Northumberland being over twice the national average. The explanation may lie in an ancestry from the extremely long lines on the far side of the Pennines where the avenues, double and single rows of Cumberland and Westmorland may have been prototypes for the few Four- to Six- and Three-Stone rows in Yorkshire and Northumberland.[18]

Stone rows, however, are so sparsely scattered in north-east England that it would seem that the inhabitants were unenthusiastic about such lines. What is not known, of course, is the number of impressive rows of great timber uprights that have decayed.

Pl. 75 Harold's Stones, Trellech, Gwent, from the wsw.

WALES

The short rows of Wales are dispersed, scarce, often of doubtful age. Commenting on the four tall stones at Pont Ddu, one of nine rows in the south-west of the country, Dyer observed that 'whilst many may be prehistoric, we should be under no illusion that they are all ancient in origin',[19] adding that some stones may have been put up in historic times for cattle to rub against.

As might be expected if the origin of these rows was ultimately from Dartmoor and subsequently from Welsh long single rows such as Parc y Meirw their distribution is a mixture of some coastal sites with more in the southern half of Wales. Very few were set up in the mountainous interior north of a line from Aberystwyth.

Some rows may have been both prehistoric and spectacular. The *meini-hirion*, 'long stones', at Llanbedr on the west coast just south of Harlech were 'once four or five broad stones, 8 foot high, standing upright' but now only two remain, 11 ft and 6 ft 6 (3.4, 2 m) high encircled by protective railings. Even here there is uncertainty. 'The smaller stone ... is quite possibly not ancient'.[20] The authors thought that the higher menhir, brought from some distance, might have been a navigational pillar set up at 'an important landing place from the sea' at the beginning of a long trackway inland, marked by standing stones along its path.

A strange feature of two rows near the north coast in Clwyd, Gallt y Foel, 'the wooded hill', and Llangwm, is the presence of a second row at right-angles to the main line. Had they been in Finistère this would cause no surprise but being in the Welsh hills the 'rows' may be only the gaunt remnants of field-walls.

Almost all these rows are to the west of the mountains separating one side of the country from the other, another reason for believing that theirs was a western tradition. Near Llanfihangel-nant-melan, however, Pedwar Maen, 'the four stones', is farther to the east. It is a row of good-sized stones graded in height towards the south-west and a little cairn. There are two other rows even farther away in south Wales although quite close to the Severn estuary a few miles to the south. Both are of three stones.

The name of Trellech, anglicised as Trelleck, a village once the capital of Monmouthshire, comes from 'tri-llech', 'the three stones'. On its outskirts is the well-known row of Harold's Stones (Pl. 75) whose three tall shafts of rasping puddingstone sway in a graded north-east–south-west line 39 ft (12 m) long. The tallest at the the south-west, is 15 ft (4.6 m) high. The surface of the central stone has been roughly ground for two large cupmarks to be carved on its south-west face which, with the row's azimuth of about 229°, looked towards the midwinter sunset. Just one other short row in Wales, Waun Oer, 'cold moorland', has a cupmark on its fallen slabs.

By the door inside the church at Trellech is a carving of the stones on the plinth of a weathered sun-dial (Pl. 76). Above them is written, MAJOR SAXIS, 'the

Pl. 76   Harold's Stones. The carving in the church.

great stones', and below them is HIC FUIT VICTOR
HARALDAS, 'Here Harold was conqueror', a lingering
memory in south Wales of Harold Godwinsson's
successful but little-known campaigns there in 1055,
1056 and, finally victorious, in 1063. That they should
be recalled as late as 1689, the date of the sun-dial, is
surprising. In a less regal conflict the mythical Jack
o'Kent won a hurling contest against the luckless
Devil when he threw the stones from Ysgyryd Fawr
mountain fourteen miles (23 km) away.

The same distance north-west of Trellech is the
hamlet of Trillech, also known as Great Triley, a
place-name suggesting that a Three-Stone row had
existed there also. There is no sign of it today. One
wonders if it is no more than a coincidence that the
mountain from which Harold's Stones were magically
flung is less than one mile east of Great Triley or
whether the legend arose from the similarity between
two far-distant Three-Stone rows. The name of
Trelach, a hamlet in the parish of Trelech a'r Bettws
eight miles (13 km) north-west of Carmarthen, may
record yet another lost row.

Informative place-names such as this are not confined to Wales. Several Featherstones in England,
corruptions of *feder-stan* or 'four stones', may be the
only memories of destroyed Four-Poster stone circles.
Fourstones near Hexham in Northumberland is actually only a few miles south of two, the Goatstones and
the Five Kings near Bellingham. Nor is 'Trellech'
unique. Near Enniskillen in Co. Down is the hamlet
of Trillick, *tri-liag*, 'three stones', close to the Three-
Stone row of Derryallen. Other names may even
retain whispers of ancient rites. The Three Sisters in
Co. Down are near the village of Greenan, *grianan*, or

'the place of the sun', and the row, like Harold's
Stones, may have possessed a solar alignment.

An unusual feature of some of the more remote
short rows in Wales is their combination of stones of
very different heights as though their builders had
over-emphasised the custom of grading. At Llech
Ciste, 'the slate chest', near Carmarthen a 10 ft (3 m)
stone stands between two much smaller with a fourth
some distance away. The row of Rhos y Gelynen south
of Rhayader also has one stone taller and bigger than
its neighbours. In the Brecon Beacons two Three-
Stone rows share the same ill-proportioned foible. By
the stone circle of Nant Tarw a long, fallen pillar has
two others a sixth its length standing alongside it. Not
four miles (6 km) to the SSW another circle, Cerrig
Duon, overlooking the River Tawe from which its
tangential avenue creeps, has the bulkily high outlier
of Maen Mawr, 'the great stone', just to its north.
Peeping behind this brooding mass are two tiny
uprights, dwarfed by the pillar and some feet away as
though intimidated by it. The resulting north-south
alignment is quite good but the malformed line lacks
the elegance of rows such as Brouel.

Like Maen Mawr many other short rows in Wales
are near stone circles or other rows, a pair of standing
stones against the Gors Fawr circle in the Preselis, and
amongst the Four- to Six-Stone rows at least two
alongside Three-Stone rows and six against pairs.
Similar groupings occur amongst Three-Stone rows.
Almost no research has been undertaken into these
combinations. They may have been due to people
moving to newly-built homesteads when the old became uninhabitable, or to an older row being deemed
obsolete, or to a solar alignment being set up against
an earlier lunar line much as Ruggles has detected
amongst the short rows of western Scotland.

Ignorance is compounded by the fact that apart
from casual and predatory diggings for treasure there
have been few investigations of the area around the
stones. The result is that what is known is normally
restricted to what can be seen above ground. That this
is a severe limitation was shown by a well-organised
and extensive excavation in 1986.

Plas Gogerddan, a site on a well-drained gravel
terrace above the flood-plain of the Afon Clarach
near Aberystwyth, had a ruined Three-Stone row.
Meticulous excavation, stripping off some 1000 sq. yds
(836 m^2) of turf and topsoil, proved that the stones had
been the focus of a multitude of pits and burials that
had been preceded by earlier Bronze Age occupation
and followed by a continuity of ritual practices from
late prehistoric into Christian times down to the nineteenth century.

Some crouched Iron Age burials had been succeeded by a score or more of coffin-graves aligned
east-west, some inside rectangular wooden mortuary
houses. One of these presumably Christian interments
gave a radiocarbon determination of AD 370 (CAR-

1045). What mediaeval activity there had been at Plas Gogerddan was unclear but by the late eighteenth century the ridge was being used as a race-course whose meetings left behind them beddings of marquees, snapped stems and bowls of clay pipes and 'vast amounts of broken wine bottles'. One stone of the prehistoric row was moved a little to the south-west to provide a better viewing point for the spectators.

The row itself, once about 500 ft (150 m) long, was damaged. Only two stones survived, that on the race-course and a second much farther to the west. But the excavation revealed that amongst the litter of centuries there were traces of Bronze Age settlement, a pit at the very edge of the uncovered area holding carbonised grain that provided an assay of 1580±70 bc (CAR-990), about 1950 BC. The stone some distance to the south may have been erected later.

Standing 6 ft 6 (2 m) high it was surrounded by the customary associations of death and burning: ditched round barrows, burials, an empty cist, and a scatter of pits to its north, one with a cremation dated to 1000±70 bc (CAR-993), approximately 1250 BC. As this pit was within 14 ft (4.3 m) of the stone, four times nearer than the one filled with grain, it is feasible that the stone row with its concomitant burials and pits belonged to a period towards the end of the second millennium.

Of especial interest at Plas Gogerddan when considering the possible antecedents of rows of standing stones was the discovery of an adjacent row not of stone but of timber. Although it is tempting to suppose that impermanent posts had been replaced by enduring stone the relationship between the two lines was problematical.

The wooden row had been impressive. From the width and depth of one hole its post had been at least 1 ft 6 thick and 15 or more feet (0.5 × 4.6 m) high. Its row, however, 30 ft (9 m) to the north of the standing stone, was on a completely different alignment, north-south, and much shorter, about 16 ft (5 m) long. With no connecting stratification between the two rows it could not be decided whether the posts were predecessors, contemporaries, or even replacements for the stone row.

The clustering of Christian graves around a heathen stone at Plas Gogerddan vividly demonstrates how the teachings of the Church only slowly, and never completely, eradicated the powerful, almost compulsive aura exerted by the old places. Nor did it prevent furtive gatherings at these ancient shrines. Persistent paganism led to several Papal edicts including one of AD 658 from Nantes, a city in the heartland of Breton megaliths, that bishops should 'dig up and remove and hide to places where they cannot be found, those stones which ... are still worshipped'. Despite this, marital vows and fertility rites around menhirs lingered in Brittany well into the nineteenth century.[21]

The race-course at Plas Gogerddan is a second

Pl. 77 The Queen Stone, Herefordshire. Alfred Watkins's excavation. The deep rain-runnels show how susceptible soft sandstone is to the weather. The depth of the stone below ground is the result of rising soil washed into the valley by the flood-waters of the River Wye.

example of the attraction prehistoric sanctuaries exercised, and it had a counterpart near Buttevant in Co. Cork. At Knockaunvaddreen, or Cnocan, there was a Bronze Age cairn and standing stone. In historic times an annual fair and the earliest recorded steeplechase in Ireland were held there with crowds assembling at the remote spot in the foothills of the Ballyhoura mountains. In 1870 a landlord ordered the meetings to be moved to the town of Ballyclogh. Deprived of the cairn and stone the fair's popularity dwindled. Finally the races were abandoned. Earlier, around 1824, the cairn, Cnocan na gCailini, 'the stone of the hag', had been pillaged for road-laying and a cist was discovered.

'It is clear why the foot-races had been held there year by year from the Bronze Age down to our own time. The old chief delighted in manhood when in life, so in death his spirit was honoured by the enactment of manly sports as the seasons revolved'.[22] Like the burials and the races at Plas Gogerddan it was another instance of the survival into recent centuries of how the hallowed stones of prehistory were respected long after their meanings were forgotten.

Plas Gogerddan has affinities with other short rows in Wales. One on a hillside at Banc Rhosgoch Fach near Cardigan had consisted of three great stones. Excavations, first in the 1930s and then more thoroughly and spaciously in 1989, uncovered two lines of charcoal-filled pits leading like a splayed avenue to the row. On the other side of the stones were flint flakes and signs of burning.

'Charcoal-filled pits are indeed a recurrent feature of these sites'.[23] But there had been no fires in the hollows at Banc Rhosgoch Fach where the oak-charcoal was buried. The wood had been burned elsewhere. Imagination, but not knowledge, may visualise fire-rituals east of the row, and later, at the conclusion of the ceremonies, the deposition of the cold ashes in carefully-positioned pits.

Even with what seems to be the most unhelpful of megaliths, the single standing stone, excavators have come across similar remains of burning and charcoal as well as cremations near to or even under the monolith. In Brittany such accompaniments were almost invariable. 'On y a presque toujours trouvé en effet des débris de charbons de bois et des pierres rougies par le feu.' In England, Ireland and Wales excavations at isolated menhirs have provided a range of dates from 1403 bc to 1140 bc (c. 1700–1425 BC). At least fourteen of the stones had burnt human bones by them[24] although the cremations may have been ritual deposits to enhance the stone rather than respectful burials. Nevertheless, the association with death persists even in these apparently uncomplicated monuments which consistently are found to be anything but uncomplicated.

The Queen Stone near Symond's Yat in Herefordshire is a weather-runnelled 7 ft 6 (2.3 m) high sandstone slab standing by the River Wye, its low-lying position accounting for the name which is probably a corruption of *cwm* or 'valley'. In 1926 the stone was dug around by Alfred Watkins (Pl. 77), author of the ley-liners' vade mecum, *The Old Straight Track*. He uncovered worked flints, a whetstone, broken quartzite pebbles and, inevitably, much charcoal, many bits of charred wood and burnt bone, further evidence of ritual fires and death.[25]

REPUBLIC OF IRELAND

(a) *The South-West*
In the Early Bronze Age south-west Ireland was an international staging-post and its megalithic monuments are late, cosmopolitan and magnificent. Their origins were diverse. The earliest, the wedge-tombs, probably derived from Brittany. They were followed by stone circles with a possible ancestry in north-eastern Scotland. Last of all came the stone rows, and here archaeology has been fortunate.

There are just three regions in the whole of Britain, Ireland and Brittany where lines of standing stones have been adequately studied: Dartmoor through the labours of the two Worths and Emmett; Caithness and Sutherland by Myatt; and the counties of Cork and Kerry where the assiduous fieldwork of O'Nuallain has been supplemented by the astronomical analyses of Ann Lynch and Clive Ruggles.

Only short rows exist, never with more than six stones. There were no long lines because there was nothing to stimulate their construction. No avenues or single rows were connected to the recumbent stone circles of Aberdeenshire from which the megalithic circles, Five-Stone rings and Four-Posters of Cork and Kerry are believed to descend. Instead, there was an outburst of short row building, almost thirty Four-to Six-Stone rows, nearly sixty Three-Stone rows, over a hundred pairs, all of them flourishing in the absence of rivalry from long, well-established lines, independent of other monuments, seldom found close to any stone circle or cairn. They were simple but they were structures in their own right.

Their distribution overlaps but is not identical to that of the wedge-tombs or circles. The major concentration of the tombs is in the north-west corner of Co. Cork on the southern sides of the Boggeragh mountains from Macroom north-eastwards to Mallow. There are others at the tips of the western peninsulas but none along the south coast from Clear Island to Cork harbour fifty miles to the east.

In contrast, the large stone circles do have a group there near the bay of Ross Carbery. Others farther inland, intermingling with the wedge-tombs, are smaller Five-Stone rings with four pillars and a supine slab, the recumbent. Some 'rings' lack it, little Four-Posters that have only recently been recognised in Ireland.

Geographically and chronologically the circles seem to be between the tombs and the rows. Many of the lines are contained in a broad north-east – south-west forty by ten mile (64 × 16 km) rectangle along the northern edges of the Boggeragh and Derrynasaggart mountains near both the wedge-tombs and the small circles. Others, however, particularly the Three-Stone rows, occur much farther to the west on the Beara, Dingle and Bantry peninsulas. Several also were put up in the south near Roaringwater Bay and the Mount Gabriel copper mines. It may be significant that the pairs of standing stones extend this pattern of western expansion.

Architecturally the short rows have features in common with lines elsewhere (Pl. 78), lengths ranging from 44 ft (13.4 m) at the Castlenalacht Four- to Six-Stone row down to 8 ft 10 (2.7 m) at the three stones of Currakeal. In Cork the Four- to Six- and Three-Stone rows average 24 ft 6 and 18 ft 4 (7.5, 5.6 m) in length, in Kerry, 25 ft 4 and 16 ft 10 (7.7, 5.2 m) respectively, none of them remarkably different from short rows in other parts of western Europe.

Pl. 78 A typical Irish Three-Stone row at Cullenagh, Co. Cork. From the south-east.

There was a preference for grading the heights of stones towards a particular orientation but never unalterably. From north-east rising to south-west was the general rule (61%) but half as many rows were graded in the opposite direction. Four lines had the highest stone at their centre and in several Three-Stone rows it was the lowest stone that was put there. An oddity, perhaps occasioned by the appending of one Three-Stone row to another, occurred at Derryinver in Co. Galway where near a small stone circle the northern half of a line was composed of three big granite boulders with three lower of schist to their south.

Arithmetical inconsistency was not confined to Britain and Brittany. At Gurranes a few miles south-east of Skibbereen in Co. Cork three stones stand on a littered ridge (Pl. 79) not far from Knockdrum ring-fort with its souterrain and heavily-cupmarked boulder. The stones are thin, backward-leaning pillars like silhouettes of emaciated Easter Island statues and they rise in stature towards the ENE where the tallest is a full 14 ft (4.3 m) high. It looks down on the long, lean broken slab of a fourth. A fifth was senselessly dragged away by a villager. This variability of three, four and five may explain the row's names of the Three Ladies and the Five Fingers.

The line is anything but straight, forming an arc that would fit perfectly on a circle over 60 ft (18 m) in diameter but there had been no ring. The uneven slope militated against one. More feasibly, like many other prehistoric work-gangs, precision was not an imperative to the builders of the row. Rather than laboriously quarrying stoneholes in the bedrock they opted to use convenient natural fissures, even if not quite in line, for the sockets. Near enough was good enough and the result was a spectacular compromise. As scrawny and shrivelled as a witch's claws it is appropriate that the palsied row should point to the Hallowe'en sunrise. Other lines in southern Ireland contain solar or lunar orientations. Why this should be is conjectural.

Lacking immediate geographical counterparts in western Britain or northern Ireland the origins of these short rows are obscure. So is the explanation for their profusion, over twice as many in the Republic as in the whole of Scotland, and many times the number of their English or Breton equivalents. There are reasons, however, for believing that influences from Brittany, possibly created by the demand for Irish copper ores, had become powerful in south-west Ireland during this period of the Bronze Age.

Comparisons between Neolithic passage-tombs in Brittany and Ireland have already been made when discussing the origins of the Irish avenues. But whereas the evidence of early contacts is ambiguous the similarities in design between Late Neolithic/Early Bronze Age Breton allées-couvertes and south-western Irish wedge-tombs are too close to be fortuitous. Even

their contents are comparable, intrusive beaker sherds being found in both groups.

In southern wedge-tombs such as Labbacallee and Lough Gur beaker material has been discovered 'but whether introduced by way of immigrants or by way of culture contact and through the existence of trading connections with Britain and the Continent, it is as yet impossible to say...'.[26]

Continental beakers, usually in secondary contexts, have also been discovered in Breton allées-couvertes such as Coat-Menez-Guen, Kerandrèze and Kernic. The tombs in Brittany, moreover, possess a feature unique to them and the Irish wedge-tombs, the existence of a three-sided, high terminal cell attached to the back of their long chamber. Yet despite the beakers and the cells it has been claimed that any megalithic connection between Brittany and Ireland is illusory because of the 'rectangular and consistently parallel sides of the Breton galleries' quite unlike the trapezoidal plans of the Irish wedge-tombs.[27]

This objection takes no account of Breton tombs intermediate between the early passage-tombs and the later allées-couvertes, megaliths that seem 'constituer des formes de passage entre les dolmens à couloir à chambre trapèzoïdale [my italics] et les allées couvertes'. Known as developed passage-tombs or 'sépultures en V' sites like Menn Iann on the Île de Groix, Morbihan, or Ty ar Boudiquet, Finistère, are undoubtedly V-shaped. So are those at Liscuis (Pl. 80) in west-central Brittany near the stone axe-factory of Plussulien, Sélédin, Côtes-de-Nord.[28] Dates of 3190±110 bc (Gif-3099), about 3950 BC, from Liscuis NW; of 2500±110 bc (Gif-3944) and 2220±110 bc (Gif-3585), averaging 3025 BC, for the remodelling of the terminal cell at Liscuis SW; and 2250±110 bc (Gif-4076) and 1730±110 bc (Gif-4075), approximately 2500 BC, from Liscuis NE, all three tombs wedge-shaped and rising in height to an open-ended terminal cell, indicate that these trapezoidal burial-places were in existence well before the period of wedge-tomb builders in south-west Ireland 'who arrived some time in late Neolithic or early Bronze Age times (i.e. centering on 2000 bc)', around 2500 BC.

Recently acquired assays from wedge-tombs in Co. Cork are in agreement with this picture: 1855±45 bc (GrN-11359), c. 2200 BC, from Labacallee; and as late as 1400 BC for the Island tomb with its three determinations: 1160±140 bc (D-49) and 1100±35 bc and 1140±30 bc, Groningen laboratory references unknown. None of the nine determinations from the Irish tombs is earlier than about 2200 BC. At Toormore, a wedge-tomb near Mount Gabriel, with a ritual deposit of a bronze axe and two pieces of raw copper near its entrance, five determinations ranged from 1445+35 bc to 590+70 bc (GrN-18492 to GrN-18496) and 'represent activity associated with the use of this tomb in the period c.1800–1400 BC, i.e. the later stages of the Early Bronze Age'.[29]

Pl. 79 Gurranes, Co. Cork. From the SSE.

Pl. 80 Liscuis SW, Côtes-du-Nord. From the SSW. A
chambered tomb overlooking the lovely Gorge de Daoulas in
central Brittany, erected c. 3000 BC its date, graded height,
trapezoidal shape and terminal cell make it a persuasive fore-
runner of the Irish wedge-tombs.

The finds, the dates, and above all, the architecture peculiar to the two groups, seeming 'n'exister que chez les allées couvertes armoricaines et les *Wedge Shaped Gallery Graves* d'Irlande' combine strongly to indicate the inter-relationships that existed between Brittany and Ireland from the mid-third millennium BC onwards.

It explains the emergence of the rows. Their catalyst was Irish copper. Their nexus was Cornwall and its tin. Their prototypes were Breton. In the absence of inhibiting longer lines that would have made their construction superfluous the short rows flourished, megalithic novelties erected by the natives of south-west Ireland.

What dates are available indicate that they belonged to the time when copper mines were being exploited. Charcoal from overlying peat at the Maughanasilly Four- to Six-Stone row in Co. Cork (Pls 81 and 82), yielded an assay of 1315±55 bc (GrN-9281), the approximate equivalent of 1600 BC, very late in the history of stone rows and avenues. A similar period, 1380±80 bc (GrN-9346), about 1700 BC, for the Dromatouk, Three-Stone row in Co. Kerry, and, inferentially, for Cashelkeelty, a Four- to Six-Stone row erected 'some centuries before the circle' against which it stood and which yielded assays averaging

960 BC, indicate a Middle Bronze Age development for short rows in the south-west of Ireland. Similar dates have been obtained from mines such as Mount Gabriel near the fuschia-hedged town of Schull.

Set amongst wild glaciated chasms and gorges the slopes of the mountain are pocked with short, unventilated tunnels from which copper ores were extracted by fire and water and broken up with heavy stone mauls grooved for rope handles. In the centuries when metal axes and knives were in demand sources of copper were found on other peninsulas, Staigue on Iveragh, Eyeries on Beara, even Horse Island in Roaringwater Bay. Fourteen assays from Mount Gabriel from 1500±120 bc (VRI-66) down to 1180±80 bc (BM-2336) suggest mining continued there from as early as 1800 BC to 1450 BC or later, another mine at Derrycarhoon being worked long before 1140 BC,[30] the same period as the short rows.

There is no reason to believe that the miners and the people of the rows were one and the same although 'rows or pairs are present in all the coastal copper-bearing areas where stone circles occur while isolated examples are found elsewhere near the deposits at Coad Mountain, Clear Island and Glandore'.[31] There are rows within a few miles of Mount Gabriel. It is not the industry, however, but the results of the industry

Pl. 81 Maughanasilly, Co. Cork, from the south-east. A Five-Stone row under excavation in 1977. Dated to c. 1600 BC. The tallest stone, 5 ft (1.5 m) high, weighs about 2 tons and could have been erected by some eight workers.

Pl. 82 Maughanasilly row after its reconstruction.

that caused the eruption of rows. Copper from Ireland, tin from Cornwall reached Brittany. Traditions from Brittany reached Cornwall and Ireland.

It has been estimated that the counties of Cork and Kerry alone produced some 370 tons of smelted copper yet the whole of Early Bronze Age Ireland contains only about three-quarters of a ton. From the entire country as many as 500 tons may have been exported.[32] A similar disproportion has been proposed for Cornish tin, some going inland, some farther abroad to the Low Countries and Germany, some to Brittany.

As long ago as 1932 Hencken stressed 'the importance of Cornwall in the Early Bronze Age as a halfway station from Ireland to Brittany', a maritime trade that led to long-lasting contacts. The voyages were long but not discouraging, about 100 miles (160 km) from Ushant to the Scillies, about 150 (240 km) from the Scillies to Cork, a few days' sailing in calm weather. Flat, chevron-patterned Irish axes of tin bronze have been discovered at Trenovissick in Cornwall. Beautiful articles of gold, Irish lunulae like glowing crescent moons, reached Cornwall and then Brittany. The decoration of one from Harlyn Bay near Padstow was identical to others at Kerivoa in Côtes-du-Nord and St Potan near Dinan, incised by the same craftsman. 'We can thus identify an itinerant smith plying his trade between Ireland, Cornwall and Brittany', demanding 'a journey over considerable distances, which involved sea travel . . . and some sort of political toler-

ance for him to work in areas which at present appear to be culturally separate on either side of the English Channel'.[33]

In reverse the practice of erecting short lines of pillars was adopted widely only in regions where there were no long rows. Simple alignments were never numerous in western Brittany either on the mainland or on the offshore islands in the Ushant archipelago except once on l'Ile Béniguet. Such an island may have an entrepôt for the exchange of goods but its size made any crowd of megaliths impossible.[34]

Beniguet, despite its cromlech, is a thin rectangle no more than 2.4 km long by 0.4 km wide (1½ × ¼ miles) with an area of hardly 95 hectares (235 acres). Molène 9 km (5½ miles) to the north-west is squarer but no bigger, 80 hectares (198 acres) of fields so tiny that it is said that a cow standing in one could graze in another and manure a third. There was no great collection of rows there, nor in Cornwall with its long lines, nor in the Scillies where rituals around chambered tombs persisted for centuries after similar tombs had been blocked up and deserted on the mainland. It was south-western Ireland with no earlier rows that welcomed the tradition and it is possible to detect how the layout of its innovatory short rows was influenced by previous customs, one facet of which was an increasing interest in the sun and moon.

In chambered tombs and long barrows orientations had been casual, only one of a number of factors affecting the design. In stone circles alignments be-

Pl. 83 Farranahineeny, Co. Cork. From the SSE. With its tallest stone at the south-west the row may have been aligned on the major southern moonset.

came more clearcut, more obviously directed to a particular celestial target. In short rows the sightlines were quite specific, perhaps now the most important element in the structure.

This development from the approximations of the Neolithic to the niceties of the Bronze Age is very apparent in the south-west. The entrances of wedge-tombs there faced westwards in a broad band from south-west to north-west, a range of almost 90°. The recumbent stones of the multiple circles and Five-Stone rings were set in the same direction but in a narrower arc from ssw to wsw over some 60°. The alignments of the short rows also lay between ssw and wsw but only from 200° to 243°. Examination shows that this arc is split by a gap at its middle on either side of two much thinner bands centred on 215° and 238° respectively. With a low horizon these would have been the azimuths of the maximum and minor settings of the southern moon.[35] Astronomical surveys could confirm or reject the supposition that such orientations were deliberate and here fieldwork has been informative.

Until Somerville's researches early this century little attention had been paid to alignments in the stone rows of Britain and Ireland and he was a pioneer in their study. By recognising the midsummer sunrise alignment in the Three-Stone row of Newcastle in Co. Cork, he anticipated Ann Lynch by seventy years. He discovered a similar orientation at Pluckanes, a pair of stones in the same county.

Between 1973 and 1976 Lynch plotted thirty-seven short rows in south-west Ireland. Applying the criteria that the rows should be both straight and have stones that were intervisible she tested them for possible alignments to the solstices and solar equinoxes, and to the major extremes of the moon (Pl. 83).[36]

Nearly all the lines were contained in two bands 43° wide spanning the north-east (20°–63°) and south-west (200°–243°). Of the thirty-seven rows Lynch determined that twenty-three contained significant alignments, twenty-one of them in one direction only, thirteen towards the north-east, eight to the south-west, with sightlines to the lunar extremes, to the solstices, and one to the solar equinoxes. These were the most exact results. If allowance is made for the visual coarseness of unshaped boulders many less precise but plausible sightlines appear in the great majority of the rows, giving totals of ten good and five fair alignments on the sun, and twelve good and fifteen fair ones on the major and minor moons (Pl. 84). Such lunar emphases support Thom's interpretations for rows in Britain, especially when coming from a region in which he had never undertaken fieldwork:

Looking at the results . . . there seems a slight pref-erence for lunar orientations, but whether solar or lunar, the events indicated are the more obvious from the observer's point of view, and do not imply a highly scientific group of alignment-builders . . . One may, however, speculate on the possible sym-bolic or ritualistic function of the alignments . . . Such observations as those claimed here, would not have required any detailed scientific knowledge on the part of the alignment-builders and there is nothing at present to suggest an organised systematic study of the movements of celestial bodies during Neolithic/Bronze Age times in SW Ireland.[37]

The disputed line of four stones at Eightercua (p. 9) overlooking Ballinskelligs Bay in Co. Kerry conforms to this astronomy. Sometimes seen as the remains of a wedge-tomb or even the entrance to a little and ruinous ring-fort on whose perimeter they stand the orientation of the pillars argues in favour of their being a genuine row. With the tallest stone 10 ft (3 m) high at the south-west the line has an azimuth of 227°17'. To have been the façade of a tomb the western entrance would have been at right-angles to that at 317°. Only one of the eighty-four recorded wedges in the counties of Cork, Kerry, Limerick and Tipperary faced as far to the north-west as that. Indeed, if every one of the known 465 wedge-tombs was included this would remain true, reaffirming the unlikelihood of Eightercua's stones being the survivors of a megalithic façade.[38]

Instead, its azimuth is entirely in keeping with that of an authentic short row. Combined with an horizon height of about 1° it produces a declination for the line of −24°.13, so close to an alignment on the midwinter sunset that it strongly supports the interpretation of the site as a real, if maltreated, short row.[39]

Only lunar and solar extremes were targets.

It is interesting to note that only one instance of an equinoctial orientation has been recorded at Gneeves [a Three-Stone row], Co. Cork. This is not surprising when one considers the amount of time and effort involved in counting the days between the solstices to arrive at their midpoint. It is clear however from this study that the alignment-builders were aware of the more obvious events in the solar and lunar cycles and it was on these events that they orientated their monuments.

Clive Ruggles came to the same conclusions for short rows in western Scotland. Later fieldwork by him in south-west Ireland confirmed the existence of similar sightlines, albeit imprecise, in many of the rows there.[40]

The settlements of the users of the rows are un-known and may have been far from the stones in sheltered, wooded valleys, covered in blanket peat today. Analysis of pollens has shown that around 2500 BC heavy oak forests were being cleared. For over a thousand years people tilled open patches of land, planted cereals while always the climate slowly but inexorably declined. Agriculture suffered and pastor-alism took its place. Soils became saturated. Remains of pondweed near the Cashelkeelty row must have come from standing pools of water. Oaks and birches gave way to damp-loving alders. By 1000 BC hazels and ash were growing amongst deserted, waterlogged fields. Hoards of Late Bronze Age weapons and gold ornaments in bogs and rivers may be indications of water cults to appease the spirits of the weather when the climate was worsening. The stone rows were abandoned.[41]

(b) *Other Regions of the Republic*

Outside the south-west corner of Ireland and the counties of Cork and Kerry stone rows of any kind are very scattered and very scarce in the Republic of Ireland (Pl. 85). Only seven are recorded in the south-east and only a few more in the west or north.

Amongst the hills and mountains of Connemara in Co. Galway, however, there is a remarkable set of Four- to Six-Stone rows built of carefully selected white quartz boulders. Like the south-western rows these also were astronomically aligned but not to any solar or lunar extreme. Instead, like Brouel in Brittany, they stand north to south. One on a glacial ridge at Derryinver was part of a large ritual area that included another alignment, a Five-Stone ring and a hengiform enclosure, the entire complex surrounded by field-walls that were ultimately engulfed by bog.[42]

To the east of Co. Cork in Co. Waterford there is one certain line of six stones and, predictably, a larger number of Three-Stone rows, two aligned north-east–south-west and two others north-south. One has a single standing stone close to it.

Apart from an occasional row in the counties of Mayo and Clare central Ireland is devoid of lines of standing stones. Then, in Co. Cavan, far apart along the south side of Upper Lough Erne, are two distinctive short rows. At the north-west, not many miles south of Belcoo are the three decorated pillars of St Brigid's Stones, one with a single cupmark, a second with four and the third with eleven. There have been suggestions that they were solar symbols.

Thirty miles (48 km) away are the bulbous blocks of Finn MacCool's Fingers on a bleak hill near Shantemon. Until recently harvest celebrations were held there. It is an interesting coincidence that the Feast Day of St Brigid at the beginning of February is also the time of the prehistoric festival of Imbolc or Oimelg. Harvesting at the beginning of August was once celebrated by the festival of Lughnasa. It is possible that modern events at the two rows retained wisps of tradition from forgotten centuries. Both, like the Four- to Six-Stone rows in Co. Louth near the east coast, seem to be outliers of the dense group in Northern Ireland. All the Louth rows are destroyed.

NORTHERN IRELAND (Ulster)

Ulster, including the Republican counties of Cavan, Donegal and Moneghan, is the only large region in which long and short rows intermingle and even here the shorter rows are in a considerable minority. No excavations are recorded and dating must be inferential. It has already been suggested that at Beaghmore in Co. Tyrone the short rows may have preceded the long. Only radiocarbon assays could confirm this.

In the north of Ireland there are four groups, all of them small, of Four- to Six-Stone rows: the lines in Cavan already mentioned; rows in the Sperrins; the destroyed lines in Louth; and three coastal sites in Donegal. Of the four Sperrin rows, one of them extremely dubious at Clogherny Butterlope, another tangential to a ring at Doorat, only two at Beaghmore are substantial. Both are connected with death. Between circles A and B is a long line of low stones. Just to its west and going directly to a cairn and cist is a row of four tall stones. An analogous arrangement of low and tall lines obtains between circles C and D where the four pillars lead to a cairn with a corbelled cist.

There was no close association between Four- to Six-Stone rows and stone circles. Of more than a hundred rings only three, all in Co. Tyrone, had such a row by them, and even amongst the more numerous Three-Stone rows only eight, again in Tyrone, stood by a circle. It can be assumed that these were additions to older rings. In most instances row-builders had no need of a stone circle.

The Four- to Six-Stone rows in Co. Donegal cluster around the sea-inlet of Lough Swilly near which Captain, later Admiral, Boyle Somerville believed were many solstitial and Beltane orientations in chambered tombs and standing stones. One court-cairn, the Giant's Bed at Drumhallagh near Croaghan Hill, faced the midsummer sunrise. Somerville thought five adjacent long rows were sighted on the same phenomenon. More probably these ragged, tumbled 'grievously ruined' lines were the results of field clearance. In the 1930s Somerville was murdered by terrorists for encouraging Irish boys to join the British Navy.[43]

One of the genuine Lough Swilly rows, the Reyfad Stones, consists of six fallen boulders, five of which have cup-and-ring marks on them. Such art is rare on Irish rows and it may be significant that it is only seven miles (11 km) to the south-west, beyond Lough Macnean Upper, that the decorated row of St Brigid's Stones stands.

Both the Louth and Donegal groups are very close to the sea and in the absence of obvious prototypes in Ulster it is arguable that the custom of erecting short lines of standing stones infiltrated Ireland across St George's Channel from the Mull of Kintyre where

Pl. 84 Beenalaght, Co. Cork. Also known as An Seisar, 'the six stones', the heavy row may have been aligned on the major northern moonrise.

Pl. 85 Graig, Co. Limerick. A rare Three-Stone row in the Republic outside the counties of Cork and Kerry. From the south.

some Four- to Six- and many more Three-Stone rows, including the famous line at Ballochroy, are known, others standing in south-west Scotland and on the islands of Jura and Islay close to the Irish coast.

The distribution of the Three-Stone rows in Ulster is in accord with this for they are to be found not only in the areas of Four- to Six-Stone rows, long rows and stone circles but in the counties of Antrim, Armagh and Down where there are no long lines, no Four- to Six-Stone rows and none of the typical 'Sperrin' circles of many, sub-contiguous stones. Traditions from overseas seem likely.

Reasons for the megalithic imbalance are clear. This cretaceous corner of Ireland had been settled centuries before the rows by Neolithic farmers whose court-cairns such as Annaghmare, Audleystown, Ballymac-dermot, still lie proudly on their hillsides. There are even some alien passage-tombs like Carnanmore at the very north-east tip of the country, its lintels bearing carved circles and cupmarks unknown in the native court-tombs. Tombs dominate the landscape.[44] The only large stone circles, of Cumbrian origins, are well to the south in Co. Down where the great ring of Ballynoe rests near Lough Strangford below the mountains of Mourne.

Any later incomers would have to bypass long-established territories, moving further inland into the unoccupied hills of the Sperrins. It was only when the tombs fell into disuse, some time after 2000 BC if two assays of 1710 ± 60 bc (UB-207) and 1565 ± 85 bc (UB-705) for the blocking-up of Ballymacdermot are trustworthy, and were no longer centres of ritual that new beliefs could be introduced. It was then that Bronze Age rows of three tall stones became acceptable.

There are nearly four times as many Three-Stone as Four- to Six-Stone rows, the majority of them composed of tall and heavy pillars. Oliver Davies described them, 'three large slabs, sometimes eight feet [2.4 m] high, set not contiguously and with their broadest faces aligned', noting that their infrequent juxtaposition to a stone circle might be fortuitous.[45] This was correct. Other than in the county of Tyrone the rows are seldom close to one. In that county eight of the eleven Three-Stone rows stand by a ring, the best-known being near the stone-studded circle of Beaghmore E. Whereas an adjoining long, low line hobbles towards a cairn embedded in the arc of the ring the three high stones point straight to a detached cairn covering pebbles, charcoal, some bone and two small flints.

As with short rows elsewhere there are few clues to the purpose of these settings in northern Ireland. Except for Dr Archie Thom's work at Beaghmore no systematic astronomical research has been undertaken. No excavations are recorded. Associations with stone circles, cairns, standing stones are infrequent. Art is almost non-existent. In this megalithic vacuum information from place-names is doubly welcome.

The three stones at Derryallen are within a few miles of the little village of Trillick in Co. Tyrone whose name derives from *tri-liag* or the 'three stones' like Harold's Stones at Trellech in Wales. In Co. Down the Three Sisters, perhaps lineally related to the Three Brothers at West Division in Co. Antrim, stand at the roadside by the hamlet of Greenan whose name comes from *grianan*, 'the place of the sun', hinting that here, as with several other short rows, there may have been midsummer and midwinter rituals. Otherwise knowledge and understanding is limited to what can be seen and what may cautiously be inferred from similar short rows in neighbouring parts of Scotland.

As Davies surmised half a century ago, 'It may be suspected that in this region other influences were at work, derived probably from Scotland'.[46] Sadly, since his brief observations there has been little further reference to these settings vital though they were to their users.

SCOTLAND

Although short rows, even those with only three stones, are not especially numerous in Scotland they are of much interest because of their art and their astronomical alignments.

(a) *Distribution*
Their distribution is essentially western and maritime along the coastlines of Argyll (Pl. 86) and Wigtown and on islands from Islay up to the Outer Hebrides. As usual, the Three-Stone rows outnumber those with four to six stones. They are also spread farther afield.

On the mainland the major concentration of short rows is along the Mull of Kintyre, that long, lovely promontory from Lochgilphead down to Campbeltown. At its north, beyond Lochgilphead, are the four stones of Ballymeanoch in the Kilmartin Valley. Halfway down the peninsula is Ballochroy, the most famous of all Three-Stone rows. Inland there are few of either type of row, a meagre scatter in central Scotland where the ambivalent stones of Blanefield in Stirling may be the denuded façade of a Clyde chambered tomb (p. 8). Miles beyond it are some Three-Stone rows, including St Madoes, near the east coast by the Firth of Tay. Other Three-Stone rows such as Torhousekie, Drumtroddan and Dyke were erected in Galloway and in the Southern Uplands far outside the ambience of Four- to Six-Stone rows.

On the islands there is the same dichotomy, more Three-Stone rows than Four to Six lines and occurring not only with them on Jura, Mull and Harris and Lewis but beyond them on Islay, Skye and South Uist. As pairs of standing stones in Scotland continue this expanding distribution into areas where not even Three-Stone rows exist it is feasible that the pattern reflects a progression not only in miles but also in years well into the Middle or Late Bronze Ages.

(b) *Excavations*

Except for the extremely dubious setting of Blanefield in Stirlingshire (p. 8) there is no radiocarbon assay for any short row in Scotland. And as the stones of Blanefield, unlike Eightercua, are probably all that survives of a Clyde chambered tomb's façade, something its determination of 2860±270 bc (Gx-2781), c. 3650 BC, suggests, the absolute chronology of the short rows remains unsettled.

This is because so few have been excavated. Investigations in 1977 at a fallen stone near the Ballymeanoch Four- to Six-Stone row in Argyll recovered three token deposits of burnt bone from one cremation. Two seasons of work in 1987–8 at Glengorm on Mull proved that a triangular setting of stones was a modern rearrangement of a prehistoric Three-Stone row. A post had also stood there, perhaps intended as a sighting-device. Eight miles (13 km) to the southeast, overlooking the narrow Sound of Mull, two Three-Stone rows, parallel but 120 ft (37 m) apart, at Ardnacross were excavated between 1989 and 1991. Both had been vandalised by pushing over all but their central stones. Between the rows were three half-demolished ring-cairns. Like another cairn near the Glengorm row they are further examples of the connection between short rows, death and fire. The undamaged stone of the north row at Ardnacross had fallen, permitting examination of its hole. Fragments of quartz and charcoal were found in it.

Pl. 86   A neatly arranged row at Inveryne, Argyll. From the WSW.

A pit close by contained a bronze bracelet. More significantly, the rows had not been set up on virgin ground. Long before their erection the land had been cultivated. Grooves of ards, a primitive form of ploughing, carbonised cereal grains and hazel charcoal showed that earlier people had farmed there. Then, after the rows themselves were abandoned, the signs of lazy-beds revealed that later settlers had come to the place, using the soil for a few years before they too departed. Of their homes nothing is known.[47]

(c) *Art*

Art, so noticeably lacking in the avenues and long rows, even in the majority of the short rows, is almost commonplace in Scotland. It is scattered, rare in the west, prolific in the east. Both regions contained earlier art, on stone circles in eastern Scotland, in tombs and on outcrops of rock in the west, and these long-established customs probably explain why cupmarks and cup-and-ring marks were so often ground into the surfaces of stones in the rows. Eastern and western art is different. Simple cupmarks predominate in the east, more intricate designs of cups, rings, and grooves or gutters are virtually exclusive to the west.

Perthshire, Tayside, was the eastern county most affected by the tradition of cupmarking stone rows. There, at Glenhead Farm, Doune, the second of four stones had twenty-three cupmarks on its top and four more on its west face. Tullybannocher, a wrecked setting which may have been a Four-Poster circle, had four carved on its south-east stone.

Three-Stone rows were still more lavishly ornamented. Kilspindie near Errol, a collapsed row of large boulders, had a rare cup with groove on its east stone but such austerity was not the norm. At Cowden, a lopsided site with one very tall pillar, so big that it was known as Samson, and two fallen stones, the ENE rock, coarse-grained, veined with quartz and half-buried, had at least twenty-six cupmarks, shallow, weathered, but clearly artificial. It is a profusion matched at St Madoes Stones near Pitfour Castle. This row was similarly assymetrical rather than graded, its NNW and central stones over 5 ft (1.5 m) high, the SSE only half as tall. It is the NNW that was cupmarked, its west face having ten carvings near the top, another at a corner of the stone, and twenty-eight near the middle of its east side.

So little research has been undertaken into the orientation of these short rows and pairs of standing stones in eastern Scotland that although cupmarks have been seen as symbols of the sun and moon it is not yet possible to point to any correlation between such art and solar and lunar alignments. It is a lacuna that may soon be resolved. Earlier monuments in north-eastern Scotland hint that celestial connections do exist. Amongst the recumbent stone circles of Aberdeenshire and neighbouring counties in Grampian cupmarks were found on stones in line with important lunar and occasional solar events. The pre-

Pl. 87 Ballymeanoch, Argyll. The cupmarked Four-Stone row
from the north-east. A pair of stones stand in the background.

Pl. 88 Roughting Linn decorated boulder, Northumberland.
The meaning of such art remains speculative.

sumably later Four-Posters also were cupmarked but the distance between stones in these little sites was too short to define any neat sightline.[48]

In western Scotland just one short row in the islands is known to be decorated, Carragh a'Ghlinne, the stone of the glen, on Jura. A substantial stone at the south-western end of a disturbed row had been cupmarked. 'Looking south-west... to the monolith, a small stone on the ridge is strikingly obvious, but whether this alignment is accidental or intentional is difficult to determine'.[49] The Thoms believed it to be significant. With an azimuth of 228° and with the ridge nearly 3° above the observer there is a crude alignment towards the minor setting of the moon. This, however, is a lunar position so elusive amongst a plethora of other lunar settings that though the astronomical analysis is correct the alignment may be coincidental.

It is in the Kilmartin Valley of Argyll with Temple Wood stone circle and its spiral motifs, with the rebated cists with axe-carvings and cupmarked capstones, and the abundance of richly-decorated rocks that one of the most attractive short rows is to be seen. Ballymeanoch is a megalithic delight.[50]

A mile (1.6 km) SSE of the strange Kilmartin paired stones and menhirs at Slockavullin for which meticulously-involved lunar alignments have been claimed[51] Ballymeanoch's four high 'playing-card' slabs form a 49 ft (15 m) long north-west – south-east line (Pl. 87). A pair of equally tall slabs on the same axis stands 135 ft (41 m) to the west. To their northwest and 176 ft (53.7 m) south-west of the short row is a single stone with a manmade 'hour-glass' hole in it 'just large enough to put the hand through' about 3 ft (1 m) above the ground.

The slab had split from front to back in antiquity and one half has gone. The remaining portion on which there are twenty cupmarks, all of them above the perforation, fell and broke into four pieces very late in the nineteenth century. Excavation in 1977 recovered three little deposits of burnt bone from its stonehole. Subsequently the fractured slab was dragged away and used as a drain-cover, its cupmarked surface uppermost, outrageously exposed to the weather.[52]

The short row has escaped such barbarism, fortunate because of the wonderment of art on its two inner stones. The northern of these, 9 ft high, 3 ft broad but only 12 ins thick (2.7 × 1 × 0.3 m) has a rash of thirty-eight cupmarks on its east face, two of them surrounded by rings, one near the top with a groove curving down from it.

To the south its taller partner is more remarkable still, 12 ft high, 6 ft 9 wide but a mere 9 ins in thickness (3.7 × 2 × 0.2 m). Its western side was decorated with at least fifty cupmarks spread from top to bottom and from side to side. Eleven are enclosed in circles or open-mouthed arcs. Downward-running grooves

were added to two or more of these eroded symbols.

Considering the diverse guesses about the motifs Morris, an authority on megalithic art (Pl. 88), recorded that 'One hundred and four theories... have been put forward in all seriousness from time to time by archaeologists and others to explain these mysteries.'[53]

Allotting the various ideas a probability score out of ten he was unenthusiastic about the proposition that the art was a record of sexual prowess, the leader of a community making 'a cup-and-ring to celebrate each female conquest he made'. Aware of the emasculating proliferation of cups at Ballymeanoch Morris awarded the fatuity 0/10. He gave full marks, however, to the art's association with death and the same for a link with standing stones. 'It has been pointed out that in most cases where a standing stone, whether one of a close-knit group or not, is carved, it forms part of an important seeming alignment on, say, the midwinter sunset, or the point where the moon sets at its most northerly setting point'. Morris gave a score of 9/10 for the art's connection with 'primitive, but accurate, astronomy – for such things as keeping the dates, for sowing correct, for predicting the ebb and flow of the tides, and, perhaps, even for predicting lunar and solar eclipses'.[54]

It is not necessary to accept ultra-precise alignments to obtain some insight into the reasons for the carvings at Ballymeanoch. One begins by asking why it was that only the two inner stones were chosen and why it was the east side of one and the west of the other that were treated.

The answer may lie in the alignment. The two outer stones, rising in height from 9 ft (2.7 m) at the northwest to 14 ft (4.3 m) at the south-east provided a sightline towards the midwinter sunrise and, in the opposite direction, because of a higher skyline, towards the major setting of the moon. Even with long-sided but thin slabs, ideal as sighting devices, neither alignment offers a declination much better than 1°, the northerly lunar line being the weaker.

It is possible, nevertheless, that the builders at Ballymeanoch had endeavoured to integrate extra astronomical phenomena at right-angles to their row, one to the south-west where the shadows of the midwinter sunset would fall on the batch of cupmarks on the first ornamented stone, the other to the north-east where the midsummer sunrise would have illuminated the more lavish art on the second slab. That such 'right-angle' settings could be intentionally constructed appears to be confirmed by the Three-Stone row of Ballochroy on the Mull of Kintyre less than thirty miles (48 km) south of Ballymeanoch.

(d) Astronomy
To the west of the Kintyre peninsula, across the Sound of Jura, the island's dark, hump-backed mountains loom against the sky. To the east of Kintyre the

Pl. 89   Ballochroy, Argyll. The Three-Stone row from the south-east. The island of Jura is in the background.

land rises from the coast in a series of raised beaches and on one of these terraces men set up the pillars of Ballochroy. Much of the peninsula consists of mica schists which split naturally into thin-ended, wide-sided slabs. Three were used at Ballochroy (Pl. 89).

It has been termed the most impressive prehistoric observatory in Britain. The stones were erected with their broader faces across the row in which the shortest stone, possibly broken, is at the north-east. The line is graded in height rising from 6 ft 6 to 11 ft 6 (2, 3.5 m) but the central stone is by far the broadest, 5 ft 6 (1.7 m) wide but only 6 ins (0.15) thick whereas the tall pillar at the south-west is almost square in section.

Looking south-westwards down the row, beyond a pillaged stone cist about forty yards (37 m) away, seven miles (11 km) in the distance is the islet of Cara. Turning to the north-west and looking along the stones' broad sides the mountain of Corra Bheinn, the most northerly peak in the undulating Paps of Jura, is outlined between the stones. These two views have intrigued astronomers because they appear to be aligned upon two sunsets, one to the south-west and the midwinter solstice, the other to the north-west and midsummer sunset.[55]

There has been an attempt to determine the age of the alignments by estimating the almost imperceptible drift of the solstitial sun along the horizon over the centuries, the north-western line towards Jura providing a tentative dating of 1640±70 BC, the south-western to Cara of 1580±100 BC.[56] In radiocarbon terms these would be the approximate equivalents of 1350 bc and 1275 bc, interestingly close to the hypothetical chronology for short rows in general.

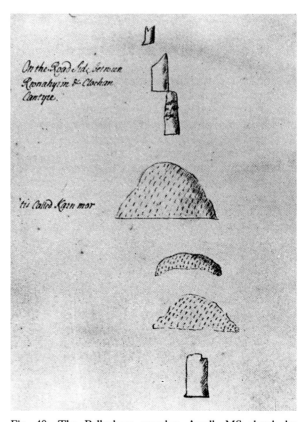

Fig. 40   The Ballochroy complex, Argyll. MS sketch by Edward Lhuyd, c. 1700. From J.L. Campbell and D. Thomson, *Edward Lhuyd in the Scottish Highlands, 1699–1700*, Oxford, 1963, Plate V. It shows how a great cairn, 'Karn mor', now levelled, would have blocked any sightline to the south-west.

Before surrendering uncritically to the astronomical conclusions two caveats should be considered. The first is that the south-west alignment was not a sight-line but a death-line. In either 1699 or 1700 the Welsh antiquarian, Edward Lhuyd, visited Ballochroy and recorded that just to the south of the row there was an enormous cairn, ' 'tis called Karn Mor', something that the name of Ballochroy, 'the farm by the cairn', repeats. The neighbouring farm, Cairnbeg, 'the little cairn', still has a mound 80 ft across and 12 ft high (24 × 3.7 m), intimating that the tumulus at Ballochroy had been mountainous.[57]

All that remains is its central cist. The cairnstones, a thousand tons of them, were removed for field-walls but when they were in place they would totally have obscured Cara island and the place at which the midwinter sun set (Fig. 40). It did not matter. To join death and the midwinter sunset, emphasising the association by aligning two smaller cairns and a further solstitial stone beyond Carn Mor, was the probable intention of the people of Ballochroy.

The sightline towards Jura and the midsummer sunset was uninterrupted, and knowing that the wide faces of the slabs were atypically angled across the row it is likely that the builders of the row quite deliberately set them transversely to establish the alignment, unaware of the lucky coincidence that theirs was the one latitude in Britain where the midwinter and midsummer solstices occurred at right-angles to each other. A few degrees to north or south would have rendered a comparable design unworkable.[58]

But what has hardly ever been remarked upon is that there is 'another surprise at Ballochroy. The line in reverse points along an elevated horizon to the extreme northerly position of the moon. An ingeniously neat combination of site selection and astronomical knowledge'.[59] From the row the land rises steeply to the north-east and an observer standing by the south-west stone would have seen the major moon rising quite close to the tip of the farthermost pillar. At Ballochroy, perhaps also at Ballymeanoch, men may have been constructing quite inventive megalithic settings to combine both solar and lunar events.

At Ballymeanoch where the short row points to the midwinter sunrise the pair of stones to its west is apparently aligned on the major northern moonset in one direction and to the most southerly moonrise in the other. Intriguingly, when the socket of the fallen single stone was excavated in 1977 it was found to lie ENE–WSW almost at right-angles to the other settings. The stone's broad eastern side would have faced the early May sunrise of Beltane.[60]

Elsewhere in western Scotland there appear to have been similar attempts. With the assistance of helpers between 1973 and 1978, and by himself from 1979 to 1983, Clive Ruggles surveyed some three hundred possible astronomical sites in western Scotland. Damage or destruction at some, the uncertain age and

nature of others, reduced the final number to 189.[61]

Among these, which included short stone rows and pairs, two preferences for orientations emerged, one north-south to cardinal points, the other north-west to south-east. From the data Ruggles deduced that amongst the short stone rows of western Scotland there was evidence of many unambiguous lunar orientations with others to the midwinter sun. There were no indications of any concern with the solar equinoxes in March and September. 'Indeed, declinations in the vicinity of the equinoxes are strongly avoided', an observation in keeping with the findings of Ann Lynch in south-west Ireland.[62]

Ruggles also discovered that the majority of rows were astronomically aligned in one direction only. It is essential for a surveyor to examine a line from both ends. It does not follow that if a row is aligned to the south-west and the midwinter sunset then in the opposite direction it will indicate the midsummer sunrise. Differences in horizon heights can make considerable differences to declinations.

Detailed computation showed that there were six important declinations, all of them within quite wide bands of $\pm 2°$: $-30°$, $+18°$, $+27°$, $-22°.5$, $-25°$ and $+33°$. The first three 'may indicate a specific interest in the edges of the lunar limiting bands (the lunar 'standstills') and would imply that organised observations were undertaken over periods of at least twenty years'.[63] It was noticeable, however, that there was little evidence for orientations towards the minor southern moon.

The declination of $-25°$ hinted at alignments towards the midwinter sun but there were no lines to the sun at midsummer. The sixth declination of $+33°$ 'is well outside those declinations attainable by the sun or moon'.[64] The declination of $-22°.5$ 'has no particular solar or lunar significance'.

Two comments should be made. The declination of $\pm 33°$ while well out of the range of solar and lunar extremes is well within the compass of the north cardinal point obtained by bisecting the limits of the southern sun or moon. Secondly, the declination of $-22°.5$, occurring in early December and January, may have 'marked the beginning and end of a four-week long ritual period as the sun approached and departed from its winter solstice'.[65]

Ruggles's subsequent analyses revealed distinct regional traits that provided fresh information about the beliefs of prehistoric societies. People on Mull and mainland Argyll erected their rows of stones in line with the southern moon whereas on the Kintyre peninsula the sun was the chosen target.

Several Three-Stone rows in south-west Scotland contain solar alignments, Ballochroy being the best known. Farther to the east on the rich, sandy soils of the Machars between Luce and Wigtown bays the row at Drumtroddan is set on a south-east facing slope its tall stones pointing uneasily to the midsummer sunrise but more convincingly past the heavier, higher south-west pillar towards the midwinter sunset. Eight miles farther north the three plump boulders of Torhousekie also increase in height and bulk to the south-west.

Proof of an interest in the moon comes from the places chosen for short rows on Mull. Level, well-drained terraces were preferred but sometimes the best were unsuitable because of their setting. There were compromises. As well as a natural platform a quite distant southern skyline was needed with two essential features, the first being a prominent peak to the east of south where the moon would rise. The horizon also had to extend openly to the west so that the moon, once risen, would remain visible until it set.

It is perhaps not too fanciful to suggest a scenario in which, as part of a ceremony around the time of summer solstice, the full moon, far down in the southern sky, is observed as it approaches a range of distant hills from the left and followed until it sets amongst them.[66]

That hills and mountains could be regarded as homes of the gods has long been suspected for prehistoric communities. Another unsuspected aspect of these short rows in western Scotland, particularly those in northern Mull and the Kilmartin Valley of Argyll, is that some seem to have been 'paired', a primary lunar row standing close to a 'secondary' line directed towards the sun.

The southern declinations indicated by the stone rows and aligned pairs in two important geographical concentrations in northern Mull and the Kilmartin area of Argyll seem generally to fit a clear pattern. Either they are oriented within about a degree of −30°, or else they are oriented within a degree or two of −24° and situated close to another row or pair which does indicate −30°.[67]

At Duncracraig [Ballymeanoch] they are only 40 m [130 ft] apart ... This suggests the idea that each of the structures in the Kilmartin area yielding a declination of around −24° is 'secondary' to another yielding a 'primary' declination of around −30°. The other sites indicate the primary direction only. The only fact which seems to run against this interpretation is that at Duncraicraig it is the four-stone row which indicates the supposed secondary declination and the aligned pair which indicates −30°.[68]

On the rugged island of Mull three Four- to Six-Stone rows stand in a long, warped line in the mountains and valleys near the north coast. The northermost, Dervaig or Maol Mor (Pl. 90), 'the great headland', 33 ft (10 m) long, was aligned on the major north moonset whereas Dervaig SSE or Glac Mor, 'the great hollow', a hilly mile (1.6 km) to the south, was set towards the major south moonrise. These could be considered settings connected with mid-winter ceremonies at the bleak north, and midsummer

rites at the warmer, sheltered southern row near Loch a' Chumhainn.

Unexpectedly, however, between these two lunar rows, within 200 yards (180 m) of Glac Mor but half-lost in a forest, is Dervaig Centre, 60 ft (18 m) long, only two of its five stones erect but graded in height from 3 ft at the SSE to 8 ft 6 (1–2.6 m) at the NNW.

With scrupulous caution the Thoms noted that Dervaig Centre:

points to a notch in the south-east and very nearly shows the rising moon at the major standstill but for this the horizon altitude seems to be a little high ... To the north the horizon seems to be slightly high to show the moon setting at the major standstill but as seen from the extreme south of the line it might be about right.

They added that resurveying was required.[69] Later Ruggles amended the south-east declination from the Thoms' −28°.5 to an arc between −25° and −26°, fairly close to that of midwinter sunrise. If this was the intention of the builders they were quite casual in their orientation. It is also puzzling that they looked to the south-east but graded their row markedly upwards to the north-west.

Many problems await any investigator into the

Pl. 90 Dervaig NW, Mull. From the NNW. Also known as Maol Mor, 'the great, bare rise', the row may have been aligned on the major northern moonset.

Pl. 91 Callanish, Isle of Lewis. From the north-east showing
the east, south and west short rows around the circle.

astronomy of these short rows but there is a tantalising
hint that sightlines were laid out, were remembered
centuries later and, almost unbelievably, were recorded in antiquity. Callanish stone circle on the Isle
of Lewis has not only an avenue to the NNE but three
short rows to the ENE, south and WSW. Somerville's
1909 plan indicated alignments towards the Pleiades,
to True South and to the equinoctial sunset.[70]

Diodorus Siculus, the Greek historian may have
referred to these short lines. Mentioning a 'spherical
temple', thought to be a vague concept of a stone
circle, a type of megalithic monument never seen by
Diodorus, he added that there '[The moon] dances
continuously the night through from the vernal equinox
until the rising of the Pleiades . . .'.[71]

This has been criticised as an impossibility because
at the time of the Spring equinox the Pleiades were so
close to the sun that their rising would have been
unobservable in its brightness[72] but the objection

misunderstands the passage. At Callanish the western
row with an azimuth of 266° was aligned not towards
the equinoctial sunrise but to the sunset, the slight
WSW bearing being caused by the higher skyline to the
north (Pl. 91).

Diodorus did not write that the Pleiades rose 'at' the
Spring equinox but that the moon danced from the
solar equinox 'until' the appearance of the lovely
cluster of stars, 'The Seven Sisters'. They would first
become visible 'at their dawn rising, which coincided
with Beltane, on May Day'. According to Frazer,
'In Hesiod's time Greek corn-reaping began on the
morning rising of the Pleiades, which then answered
to our 9th of May.'[73]

However corrupt the chronicles of Diodorus Siculus
they do appear to record that special significance was
given to the period of five or six weeks between the
equinox of late March and the beginning of May, the
time for the planting of crops and the welcoming of

the sun's returning warmth. The Pleiades, one of the most obvious of all stellar groups, have been observed and used world-wide by farmers because of their calendrical value, and 'in particular [people] have commonly timed the various operations of the agricultural year by observation of [their] heliacal rising or setting.'[74]

If the 'spherical temple' was not Callanish it is a remarkable conicidence that it was only the moon, the equinox and the Pleiades that Diodorus mentioned. Callanish seems associated with all of them. The avenue was directed towards the southern moonset; the western row was oriented on the equinoctial sunset; and although other stars are feasible targets the eastern row could have been aligned on the Pleiades, the third of the heavenly bodies specified by Diodorus.[75]

Somerville's plan was somewhat inaccurate. A survey by Glasgow University's Department of Geography in 1974 amended the azimuth of the east row from 77°.8 to 76°.5. The new declination of 7°.8 meant that the Pleiades were rising in line with the ENE row around 1550 BC (c. 1375 bc).[76] Excavations in 1980 and 1981 that recovered local Hebridean pottery, late beaker and Grooved Ware sherds, suggest that the circle was erected in the early centuries of the Bronze Age around 2200 BC.[77] The avenue may have been an addition. The three short rows may have been later still. A time for them around 1550 BC would not be unlikely in the chronological context of other short rows.

It is possible therefore, yet surely improbable, that the chronicles of Diodorus contained memories of ancient rites that had endured into the Scottish Iron Age, long after 'peat started to form over the site in the earlier half of the 1st millennium BC'.[78]

CHAPTER ELEVEN

PAIRS OF STONES 1400–1000 BC

At Sandville and Lisvidin in Co. Tyrone The E stone is . . . high and pointed; the other is a little shorter and has a flat grooved top . . . So many similar paired stones exist that they may be a distinct type of megalith, symbolising male and female.

Estyn Evans, 1966, 204

INTRODUCTION

There are many pairs of standing stones, the final manifestations of a linear tradition that had endured, always undergoing change, for almost two thousand years. Not all were megalithic. At Compton Bishop in Somerset (p. 3) the one stone still standing can hardly be seen in the long grass. What orientations exist are ill-defined by the rough and closely-spaced settings. But many of them, noticeably in Northern Ireland and Scotland, have the distinctive characteristic of setting stones differing in size and shape against each other. A flat-topped stone was matched against a pointed, a thin tall pillar against a low, fat block, a 'playing-card' slab against a broad boulder, a triangle against a oblong. It is not unusual to find one stone cupmarked.

Sometimes, in a 'classic' case, several such traits are combined. At Crofthead on the dismal Fowlis Wester moor near Crieff in Perthshire two stones, now fallen, stood on an ENE–WSW axis. The western near the stream has a flattish top, is rectangular and bears seven weathered cupmarks. The eastern stone is thinner, longer and pointed. When Fred Coles saw it in 1910 it was standing 8 ft 6 (2.6 m) high, 3 ft (1 m) taller than the other. It is customarily the higher, peaked stone that is at the east, but it is its lower companion that often acts as the clumsy foresight to some astronomical event.

As Evans speculated, opposites like these may have represented male and female principles, a visual symbolism that would be in keeping with the imagery of life, death and sympathetic magic in prehistoric times. It was not only the widely-reported Kennet Avenue at Avebury that had such 'fertility' couplings. There were many counterparts such as the pair at Crew Lower in Co. Tyrone and others in northern Ireland and Scotland.

Even at Stonehenge the two bluestones framing the north-east axis just inside the sarsen circle were similarly paired. Stone 31 to the east is broad with a low, rounded top. Stone 49 to the north-west is taller, narrower and tapers to a point. Their positioning at the entrance to the circle suggests a deliberate choice of shapes.[1]

Death was present in many pairs. Fred Coles wondered whether it would be worth excavating between the Crofthead pillars 'with the view of ascertaining if burials were deposited close to these Stones'.[2] He was percipient. Burials, or pits that once contained burials, have subsequently been found between other pairs.

Over 300 sites are listed in the Gazetteer, the most numerous of all the avenues and rows but the distribution is very uneven (Fig. 41). Major concentrations occur in south-west Ireland and central Scotland. There are more dispersed groupings in south-west Scotland and the Western Isles. Of the pairs thirty-nine per cent are in the Irish Republic, almost four in five in the south-western counties of Cork and Kerry. Scotland has thirty-two per cent, quite evenly divided between the west and the centre, mainly in Perthshire. Wales has nine per cent, Northern Ireland five per cent. Fewer than one in nine pairs occur in England, nine per cent, and Brittany, six per cent. Two-thirds of the English and Breton rows are in the west in Cornwall and Finistère.

It is a western and northern distribution spreading beyond the limits of the short rows and one which largely avoids regions of great megalithic rings. Despite the hundred or more recumbent stone circles in Aberdeenshire the county has only one recorded pair, the two pillars to the east of the Castle Fraser ring.

Occasionally one of the stones, frequently the taller, was cupmarked. Whether such carvings were associated with some celestial event is debateable. With heavy stones only about 10 ft (3 m) apart, an average of 10 ft 9 (3.3 m) in central Scotland, 10 ft 3 (3.1 m) in Co. Cork, an observer would have had a 'window' far too wide for any accurate sighting. One can only remark that surveys have registered crude and imprecise alignments towards the sun or the moon.

PAIRS OF STANDING STONES
1 Castle Fraser
2 East Cult
3 Orwell
4 Kilmartin
5 Barnes Lower
6 Crew Lower
7 Wren's Egg
8 Gors Llangynog
9 Higher Drift
10 Kergadiou

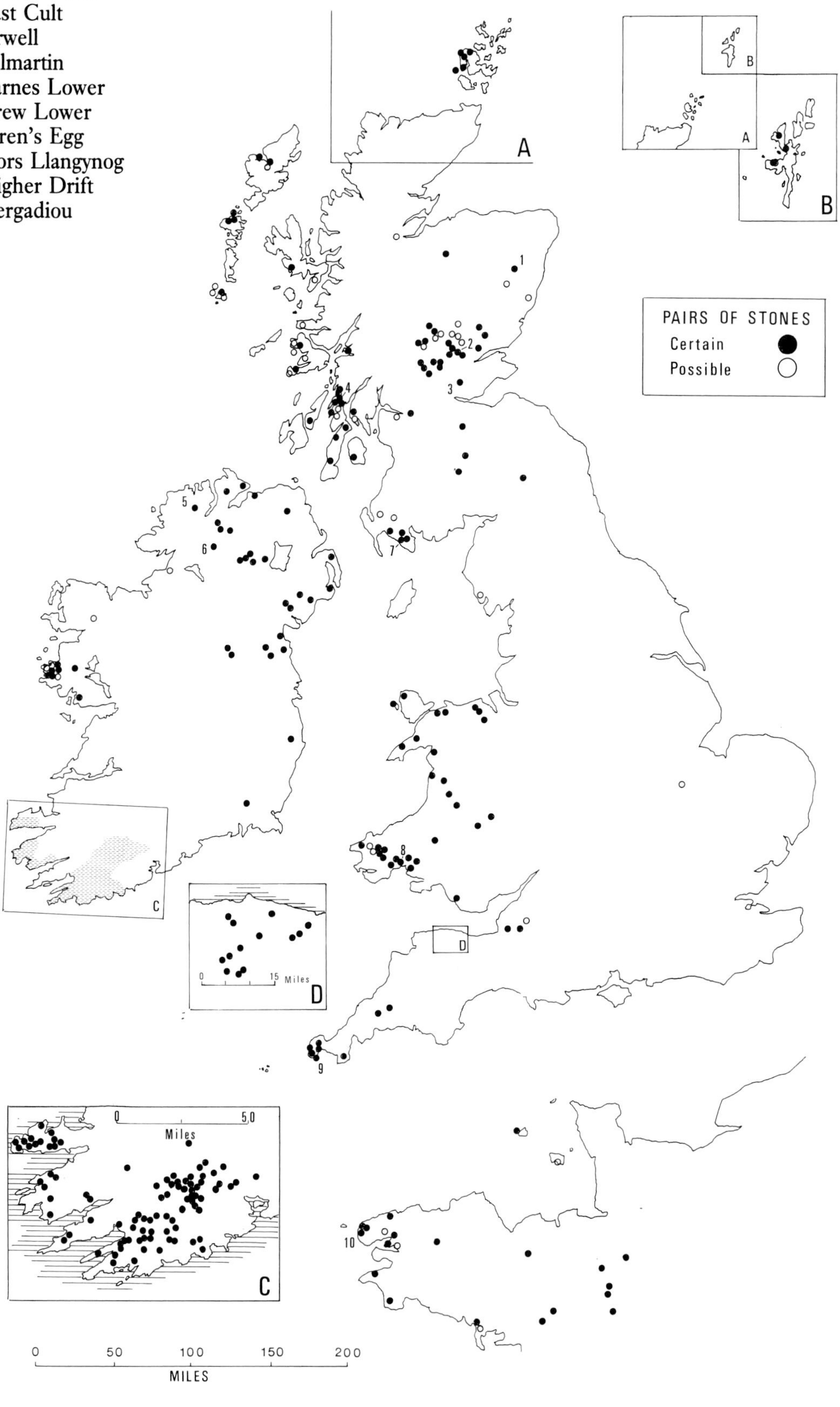

PAIRS OF STONES

Certain ●

Possible ○

More fieldwork and statistical analysis is needed before claims for unequivocal astronomical lines can confidently be made.

EXCAVATIONS AND DATING

Despite almost a score of recorded excavations between and around pairs of standing stones little information about their age or purpose has resulted. Half a dozen investigations were completely unproductive. From several others the only discovery was an empty pit between the pillars.

There is one C-14 assay, 1340±70 bc (CAR-957), around 1650 BC, from the south Welsh site of Gors a few miles east of St Clears near the Taw estuary. In its neighbourhood there are several Maen Llywd or Meinillwydion, 'brown stones'. At Gors only a prostrate limestone boulder remained of a possible pair when the area was excavated in 1985.[3] Nothing came from its stonehole but about 25 ft (8 m) to the southwest an isolated pit contained charcoal and burnt bone from which the assay was obtained, a date that provided a general time during which the site acted as the focus of ceremonies.

In an invaluable survey of standing stones in Wales and south-west England Williams concluded that 'most of the associated artefacts (from burials and other deposits) are ... of second millennium BC date'. His list of eighteen C-14 determinations recovered from Three-Stone rows, pairs and single stones confirmed this[4] ranging from an exceptionally early date of 2973±75 bc (BM-452), c. 3750 BC, from a pit preceding the erection of a menhir at Bedd Branwen to as late as 530±145 bc (NPL-241), c. 750 BC, from a cremation at Ystrad Hynod, a cairn that appeared to post-date a single pillar there. If the two highest and two lowest assays are removed from the list the remaining fourteen average 1212 bc, near 1400 BC, giving a crude indication of the Middle Bronze Age *floruit* of these elementary stone settings.

Artefacts offer little clarification. Sherds of an Early Bronze Age food-vessel and a broken slate disc came from Rhos y Clegyrn, a pair just west of the Preselis in south Wales. On Guernsey in 1857 indeterminate sherds and stone mullers or grinders were dug up by the Rev. W.C. Lukis at La Pierre Longue. A polished stone axe, pieces of quartz and a flint arrowhead were recovered from the disturbed site of Great Bernera on Lewis.

None of this provides an indication of the function of paired stones. Revelation comes from the prevalence of pits or cists between them, often empty, sometimes with a token cremation in the hole.

In the eastern stonehole at Orwell near Loch Leven people placed the cremations of men and women together with dog and pig bones before raising the

Fig. 41   Distribution map of pairs of standing stones.

stone above them. Other cremations close to the stones, and the presence of cists and pockets of burnt bone in the ground nearby, show that the pair remained the focus of ritual activity for many years. At other sites, however, excavations have revealed little more than pits, usually empty, and charred bone suggesting that the stones had acted as centres of funerary and fertility ceremonies.

Some time before 1872 digging at two widely separated stones at Achnabreac in Argyll unearthed 'human bones' at the foot of one. At Leafea on Orkney a farmer's dog scratched up bones from the base of two closely-set stones standing north-south 'in strict alignment'. Similarly, digging before 1833 at Tirgwyn,' the white house', where two pillars near Nefyn on the Lleyn peninsula also stood north-south, revealed a grave between them containing the bones of a large man.

Two large hollows just outside the stone circle of Croft Moraig by Loch Tay were interpreted as graves. During the 1965 excavation a student was persuaded to curl up in one to prove its adequacy. It would seem that late as these paired pillars were in the linear tradition they retained the persistent association with death.

REGIONS

(a) *Brittany*

The paired stones of Brittany are few and to be found at the extremes of the province, by the coasts of western Finistère, near the sea in Côtes-du-Nord, or in the far east of Morbihan at La Gacilly more than 70 km (44 miles) from Carnac's multitudinous rows.

What the pairs lack in number they compensate for in size. Their pillars stand metres high, rough gritted blocks at Les Roches-Piquées, La Gacilly; an 8 m (26 ft) high and pointed playing-card slab at Brigognan-Plage close to the shore, a tiny Christian cross added to its crown. Just to the north-east lies the gigantic Men-Marz, 'the miracle stone', on which St-Pol-de-Léon stood to repel the land-eroding tide. Local legend avers that its twenty-five-ton bulk was pulled upright by the saint's sister.

The greatest of these colossi is near Porspoder and the Atlantic. Kergadiou is the second tallest standing stone in Brittany (Pl. 92) excelled only by the menhir at Kerloas 8 km (5 miles) to the SSE. Like many of the stones in West Léon the Kergadiou obelisk, 8.8 m (29 ft) high and flat-topped was laboriously hammered and polished with stone mauls. It stands, elegantly smoothed, 80 m (260 ft) SSW of its deeply-leaning, tapered companion. That also had been scraped and ground but only on its upper surface as though the work was abandoned when the stone collapsed. Scatters of Neolithic flints and Bronze and Iron Age artefacts near these enormous stones were not sufficiently connected with them to offer clues to their date.

Pl. 92 Kergadiou, Finistère. From the south-west. The surfaces of both large, granite stones have been polished.

Pl. 93 Caillouan, Côtes-du-Nord. Although ruined the setting is typical of the 'high-and-low' pairs in Brittany. From the SSE.

The Breton pairs share the architectural traits of their British and Irish counterparts.

> Quite often they seem to be in pairs (if no other stones have been destroyed). These pairs are quite often of the 'Tweedledum-Tweedledee' type, a short one being associated with a tall one, or a large, broad menhir with a slender one. Usually the stones are a short distance apart, a few metres or tens of metres. Terms such as 'brothers' or 'twins' apply well to them, and the 'talkers' is also a colloquial name (Pl. 93).[5]

About 27 km (17 miles) SSE of Rennes and 10 km (6 miles) south-west of Janzé where many decorated Bronze Age bracelets have been ploughed up two tall stones are set 20 m (66 ft) apart. At the north-west the taller 3.3 m (10 ft 10) high is a lumpish grey granite block, its regular sides inclining towards a pyramidal point. Its partner is a raggedly rectangular thin slab, 2.5 m (8 ft 2) tall, flat-topped, gleaming white patches, perhaps of quartz, showing through the lichen that blotches it. With a variety of stones of differing shapes, lengths and colours within a short distance of the pair such a combining of opposites seems to have been intentional.

(b) England

Pairs of standing stones in England are almost exclusive to the south-west. And with the exception of two or three unspectacular specimens in Somerset and an erroneous claim for a fourth in the same county the settings are concentrated in Cornwall. Following the usual pattern of widening diffusion they stand at the farthest corner, at Land's End beyond the general distribution of other short rows.

Neither art nor astronomy were important. A single cupmark on the Giant's Grave in Cumbria (Pl. 94), either a vandalised Three-Stone row or a true pair, is the only known motif. The Thoms made the most diffident suggestion that the stones were aligned on the major southern moonset and were even less enthusiastic about the 'far uprights' of 'two menhirs 6 ft [1.8 m] high' just west of the Hurlers stone circles on Bodmin Moor. With azimuths of 76°.3 and 256°.3 the pair, known as the Pipers, could have been set in line with the sunrise and sunset of early April and mid-October respectively.[6] Neither seems probable.

Two hundred years earlier the great Cornish antiquarian, the Rev. William Borlase, was more down to earth. In a consideration of 'Monuments consisting of Two, Three or several Stones' he described the pair

Pl. 94   Giant's Grave, Cumbria. Either a pair or the remaining stones of a Three-Stone row. From the west.

Pl. 95   Higher Drift, Cornwall. From the south. An empty pit was found between the stones in 1752, the year when eleven days were deducted from September to adjust the calendar.

known as 'The Sisters' at Higher Drift, Land's End (Pl. 95), observing that 'one of the Stones stands nine foot [2.7 m] high out of the Earth, the other somewhat more than seven [2.1 m]; they are eighteen feet [5.5 m] distant, the line in which they stand pointing North-West'. He added that two miles to the north there was:

another of the same sort in the Tenement of Trewren Madern, the distance ten feet [3.1 m], the line of their plan lying E.N.E. Upon searching the ground between these two Stones (October 21, 1752) the diggers presently found a pit six feet six long, two feet nine wide and four feet six deep [2.0 × 0.8 × 1.4 m]; near the bottom it was full of black greazy Earth, but no bone to be seen. This grave came close to the Westermost and largest stone. . . .[7]

The same funerary vacuum was encountered by his great-great grandson, William Copeland Borlase. In the vicinity of the Merry Maidens stone circle are several isolated standing stones but nearly a quarter of a mile (400 m) to the north-east are the magnificent

Pl. 96 The oak effigy in Chew Magna church, reportedly of Sir John de Hauteville (1216–72) but more probably the memorial of John Wych who died in 1346, the year of the Battle of Crécy. The figure is contorted because it had been carved to fit into a cramped recess in a nearby chantry.

pillars popularly known as the Pipers because they were believed to be musicians petrefied for playing on the Sabbath.

Despite the north-eastern stone being the tallest in Cornwall, 15 ft (4.6 m) high, and its partner 317 ft (97 m) up the ridge to the south-west standing a clear 13 ft 6 (4.1 m) they are not intervisible so that their status as an intended pair must be questionable.

On 11 March 1871, Borlase excavated there. 'On digging carefully round each of these stones nothing remarkable was discovered'. He was more fortunate at Higher Drift. Trenching between the stones he 'came upon the end of a cavity cut with much precision in the hard natural clay'. It was a large, deep rectangular pit of much the same dimensions as that at Trewern. It lay midway between the pair but at right-angles to them and almost completely beyond the eastern side of the line. Nothing was found 'but the fine disturbed sub-soil of the neighbourhood'.[8] Across the English Channel the Rev. W.C. Lukis's investigations at La Longue Pierre, 'the witch's finger', recovered sherds, stone grinders and querns, a collection like the domestic material found in some of the Carnac rows. Empty graves and undateable pottery tantalise the imagination but do not inform the mind.

Even less evidence comes from the pairs in Somerset, all of them reputedly hurled, as inaccurately as ever, at churches or in contests by the Devil. None is enthralling. Compton Bishop is miniscule, the Devil's Quoits at East Harptree were removed last century, and the Whit Stones on Porlock Common are perhaps the remains of a more elaborate Exmoor setting, maybe even no more than outcropping bedrock.

Yet the most misleading of all these English paired stones lies physically shattered and wishfully fabricated on a ridge overlooking the Stanton Drew stone circles south of Bristol. Almost certainly an outlier of the Weddings as the rings are fancifully entitled the stone known as Hautville's Quoit was described by John Aubrey in 1664:

About a quarter of a mile from this Monument of the Wedding is a stone called Hakewell's Coyte ... which is a great roundish stone of the shape of a coyte, lies flatt, length of it is 10 foot 6 inches, Broad 6 foot 6 inches, thickness 1 foot 10 inches [3.2 × 2 × 0.6 m] ... The common-people tell this incredible story that *Hakewell* stood upon the top of *Norton*-hill, about halfe a mile off where the Coyte now lies, and coyted it down to this place.

Pl. 97   Penrhos-feilw, Anglesey. A fine pair of standing stones near Holyhead. From the SSE.

Nearly eighty years later John Wood confirmed the stone's dimensions, 'tho' greatly delapidated, is still ten Feet long, six Feet broad, near two Feet thick'.[9]

As Norton hill was more nearly a mile (1.6 km) away and as the sandstone slab weighed more than seven tons throwing it had been herculean. Aubrey added that Hakewell, or more properly de Hauteville, was buried in St Andrew's church, Chew Magna, 'where he hath a Monument' (Pl. 96).

The prostrate stone would have no place in this book were it not that William Stukeley visited Stanton Drew in 1723. Unlike Aubrey he asserted that there were 'two great stones, called Hautvil's Coyts' lying by the road. 'We measured that towards Pensford 13 foot long, 8 broad and 4 thick, [4 × 2.4 × 1.2 m] being a hard reddish stone',[10] transforming it into a 23-ton monster.

Stukeley was customarily a meticulous recorder but in 1877 Dymond found that the true Quoit was still 6 ft 6 long, 7 ft broad and 'about 2 feet' thick (2 × 2.1 × 0.6 m). 'If his [Aubrey's] figures were correct, the stone has since lost only about 3½ ft [1 m] of its length'.[11] As none of seventeen other antiquarians before and after Stukeley mentioned a second stone, and as Wood's figures agreed with Aubrey's, the likelihood must be that Stukeley erred, forgetfully confusing the Quoit NNE of Stanton Drew with a

larger stone lying nearby. If so, it has gone, probably broken up when the road was metalled. Hautville's Quoit, lying battered in a field, hidden behind the hedge and neglectedly overgrown, is the only surviving outlier of the low-lying circles by the River Chew.

As for Sir John de Hauteville (1216–1272), the exact years of the reign of Henry III, he fought bravely in the seventh Crusade.[12] A painted oak effigy in St Andrew's church, in plate armour, elbow on shield, left foot on an awkwardly kneeling lion, is wrongly attributed to this hero. Removed from the nearby chantry at Norton Hawkfield the monument is probably the memorial of John Wych. De Hauteville lies elsewhere, in death as evanescent as his legend.

(c) *Wales*

Paired stones in Wales are as widely scattered as the Four- to Six- and Three-Stone rows except at the south-west corner where there are small concentrations to the east and west of the Preseli mountains. There is also a thinner line along the north coast stretching from the east into Anglesey.

Information, limited but valuable, has come from some modern excavations. Earlier reports of a burial-cist between the two fine 10 ft (3 m) high stones at Penrhos-feilw on Anglesey (Pl. 97) are unconfirmed as are its contents of an unlikely spear- and arrowheads. But to the date of 1340±70 bc (c. 1650 BC) from a remote pit at Gors in Dyfed can be added the huddle of clay-filled hollows south-east of the remaining stone, a patch of cobbling, holes where stakes had been rammed into the ground and possible cavities for much heavier posts. There was no obvious pattern to the pits which could have been dug during a series of ceremonies spread over decades of ritual activity.

No date came from Rhos y Clegyrn twenty-seven miles (44 km) to the west on the far side of the Preselis but the site was a palimpsest of prehistoric life. What appeared to have been a temporary Neolithic settlement was succeeded by a Bronze Age complex in which a pair of standing stones stood between an embanked stone circle and a small ring. Spreads of sunken cobbles linked the sites amongst which were pits, some with 'miniature uprights of stone or wood'. Two pits 'had shelves, apparently for perishable materials'.[13] At the heart of this large ovoid area with its northern wall, paired features and axial layout, was a partial cremation, perhaps a dedication, surrounded by sherds of two or more broken vessels. Fragments of collared urn and food-vessel show that Rhos y Clegyrn was in use during the middle of the 2nd millennium BC. The setting also warns of the danger of interpreting sites simply from what can be seen on the surface.

The two stones at Whitford in Clwyd were close enough together to be re-utilised as gateposts. So were others at Berribrook in Dyfed. Some pairs were grotesquely different, as exaggerated in size and height as the Three-Stone row of Maen Mawr, Powys. At Carreg fawr nant jack, 'the great stone by the brook', near Llanstephen the boulder is a 5 ft 6 (1.7 m) high block of red sandstone. Fifteen feet (4.6 m) to the east is a small, grey granite stone no more than 1 ft (30 cm) high, so low that it is regularly covered by high tide in the Tywi estuary.

Other prehistoric pairs have been translated into history, those at Cwm gawr,' the rough valley', also being known as Cerrig meibion Arthur, 'the stones of the sons of Arthur' in the belief that they were a Dark Age memorial to his sons killed by a wild boar. The whole region is Arthurian country where the part-historical, largely mythical king is said to have hunted. The land is studded with standing stones, burial chambers and cairns, a natural outcrop known as Carn Arthur, a hilltop cairn called Bedd Arthur, 'Arthur's grave', and five miles south-east of Cwm garw the tomb of his dog, Gwal y filiast, 'the lair of the grey-hound bitch'. It is also known as Arthur's Table. His cauldron lies in the River Taf below.

Even closer to Cwm garw, only a mile and a half (2.4 km) to the SSE of the stones, is Dyffryn-fflibro from which the legendary war-leader, in an action reminiscent of Hautville's Quoit, flung Coetan Arthur, a thick megalithic capstone. And by Dyffryn is one of the most perfect stone circles in Wales, Gors fawr. Perhaps the very finest of the Welsh pairs stands close to it.

On the northern horizon outlined like a submerging Brobdingnagian tadpole is the dark shape of the Preselis looking down on the dreary common of Gors fawr, 'the great marsh', still wet and soggy today. Its circle is known locally as Cylch y trallwyn, 'the ring of the marsh'. The sixteen irregularly-spaced stones are not large, about 2 ft (60 cm) in average height although the growth of peat has reduced them by 18 inches (0.5 m). They rise slightly to the south.

The tall pair of stones 150 yds (137 m) to the NNE diminish them further. Standing 48 ft (14.6 m) apart on a south-west – north-east axis with their longer faces at right-angles to the circle the south-west pillar is 6 ft 2 high, its companion 5 ft 7 (1.9, 1.7 m). They differ. The south-west is a well-formed rectangular block, flat-topped, thick. The north-east is lower, scrawnier, tapering to a western point.

The pair is not aligned towards the ring but if extended would pass well to its west like an ultimate economy version of the earlier tangential avenues of Wales. Alexander Thom believed it to be a solar setting. His first survey suggested that the stones looked towards the midwinter sunset in one direction, to the midsummer sunrise in the other but a re-checking of the horizon altitude caused this to be amended to midsummer sunrise to the north-east and, perhaps, towards the early November sunset of Samain in the other.[14]

The circle and the pair, surely of widely-separated dates, may contain their own symbolism. Looking from the south between the two tallest stones of the ring, a thin triangle to the west, a lower hump-topped boulder to the east, the axe-factory outcrops of the Preselis are framed between the outlying pair of pillars.

There, prospectors for a few centuries exploited the Group XIII sources of preselite and dolerite for the fashionable shafted maceheads and battle-axes of the Early Bronze Age, bringing the roughed-out implements down from the spiky outcrops for shaping in the sheltered lowlands. The Preselis were also the slopes from which the famous Stonehenge bluestones came, moved onto Salisbury Plain not by man but glaciation. Suggestions by the writer and others that these were sacred mountains from which potent stones were superstitiously transported can no longer be sustained.

There is an archaeological irony. By the time that the two graceful pillars were set up at Gors fawr Stonehenge was in decay. Many of its bluestones were eroding. Yet while the best-known prehistoric ring in the world mouldered in neglect Gors fawr, a little-known bluestone circle, remained active. Like one stone at Cwm-gawr and another block in the embanked stone circle of Meini-gwyr nearby many of Gors fawr's boulders were of local spotted dolerite.[15]

Pl. 98 Typically 'high-and-low', flat-topped and pointed blocks at Foherlagh, Co. Cork. From the north-west.

The outlying pair, also of dolerite, chosen not for its magic but its convenience, was probably erected alongside the ancient ring in the fading centuries of the second millennium BC.

(d) Republic of Ireland

The Irish archaeologist, Sean O'Riordain, was well aware of how difficult it was to understand why ancient communities set up long lines of heavy and awkward boulders:

> Even less can be said of stone alignments than of standing stones. They consist of groups of standing stones arranged in one or more straight lines. They are neither very numerous in Ireland, nor are elaborate forms found here, but they are known elsewhere, as in Brittany and Scotland where very imposing examples occur . . . We can only conclude, probably correctly, that stone alignments are monuments connected with prehistoric ritual.[16]

(i) The South-West

Although the counties of Cork and Kerry occupy less than four per cent of the area of Britain, Ireland and Brittany they contain thirty-one per cent of the pairs of standing stones (Pl. 98).[17]

The widening expansion continued, to the west of Bear Island, to the east of Clonakilty Bay. The Dingle peninsula, jutting into the Atlantic, with just one line of five stones at Cloonsharragh and four scattered Three-Stone rows had a huddle of ten pairs stretching from Derrygorman at the east to the pairs at Ballineag-Castlequarter, embedded in a field-wall, and others at the extreme western tip around the low mountains of Croaghmarhin and Mount Eagle.

Amongst the group is Milltown North, 'The Gates of Glory', and, just to the south, Milltown South, two fallen stones. The eastern is a huge limestone block shaped like a battered guitar-case, a single cup-and-ring mark on the handle, the broad body covered with cupmarks and cup-and-ring carvings that possibly were made after the stone's fall. Not far to the southwest is a further standing stone known as Gallan na Cille Brice, 'The Milestone':

> We may without the least transgressing the bounds of reason, regard these three stones as the sole relics of an elaborate temple enclosure of wood. There are many standing stones in the neighbourhood which may or not belong to the same system . . . In considering megalithic monuments of any kind,

it must never be forgotten that what we see may be nothing but the skeleton of the original structure. There may have been mud, wicker-work, or wooden additions which were an essential element in their ritual use. These we have no data whatever to restore.[18]

Remembering the unsuspected features revealed at the excavations of the long single rows at the Alignements du Moulin at St-Just in Brittany and at the Gors pair in Wales these were sensible admonitions.

Unfortunately the few excavations in Co. Cork, at Carrigadrohid, Kealkil and Knocknakilla (Pl. 99) have produced nothing except for a scatter of quartz at the latter site. Nor is art common. Except for Milltown South, where the carvings are probably secondary, no row has any art. Decorated single stones exist, two half a mile (800 m) apart at Burgatia near Ross Carbery, one with over forty cupmarks on its northern face. There is another at Knockeenagearagh, and by the entrance to Knockdrum cashel by Castletownsend a prostrate boulder is covered with cupmarkings. But these are isolated pillars, not part of any row.

It is less likely that the art at Milltown South was an element of the original pairing than that it was added after the stone's fall. It is noticeable that the grooves from the cup-and-ring marks follow the downward slope of the east face much as the runnels from the

tops of the Devil's Arrows in Yorkshire are at angles to the vertical, hollowed by rains while the slabs were part of the bedrock millennia before the stone row was thought of.[19]

It has been suggested that some megalithic art was related to solar symbolism and devised to be at its clearest when the sun was at a particular position in the sky. For the west stone at Burgatia 'the carvings are best viewed during the sunset of a summer's evening when the sunlight at an angle to the face casts the shadows of the inscriptions into their best relief.' A comparable relationship between sunlight and visibility has been noticed at the menhir of St-Samson-sur-Rance in Brittany, and in Scotland where 'carvings show up best when the sun is at a low angle [causing] shadows to appear in them'. Further, 'where petroglyphs are found on standing stones, most of such carved stones are the principal stone in an astronomical alignment'.[20]

In their orientations the pairs of stones, though lacking art, may also have been set up in line with the sun. Over half the pairs in Cork and Kerry stand north-east – south-west, a preference far stronger than for any other of the fourteen bearings from north – south around to NNW – SSE, hardly one of which exceeded four per cent of the orientations.

One would imagine that this tendency to align towards the south-west was an indication of an interest

Pl. 99 Knocknakilla, Co. Cork. From the south. Beyond the pair's fallen stone are the remains of a Five-stone circle. The low stones of a radial cairn are just to the right.

in the midwinter sunset on the part of the builders. If so, it was the most general, the most easily-satisfied of concerns. Uncritically, at the latitude of south-west Ireland a south-west azimuth of 229° would broadly be towards the winter setting sun but the astronomical reality is against so simple an explanation. With an average length of 10 ft 3 (3.1 m) and with unshaped, rough-sided stones 3 ft (1 m) or more thick the setting created a visual arc of over 20°, one edge from the backsight to the south side of the farther stone, an alignment of 219° on the major southern moonset, or to its northern side an azimuth of 239° to the minor moonset. If the intention had been to align upon the midpoint of the 'window' and the midwinter sunset the people had not bothered, or were unable, to manufacture a refined viewing-mechanism, being content that the clumsy stones would indicate a point on the skyline where the sun would set at the dead of winter.

This indifference to megalithic accuracy is demonstrated at Lissyviggeen, a circle-henge and pair of stones not far from Killarney and the approach to the Dingle peninsula. 'Some idiot tried to punch his name on one of the pillars'.[21] Near a little stone circle called The Seven Sisters inside a henge two outlying stones stand east-west of each other only 7 ft 3 (2.2 m) apart. The easternmost is 7 ft 8 high, 5 ft 7 thick (2.3, 1.7 m)

and is flat-topped. Its partner to the west, in line with a distant gap between the mountains, is 6 ft 11 tall and 3 ft 3 (2.1, 1 m) wide. With its needlelike outline it would make an excellent gnomon or foresight except that the solid geometry of the stones, with an arc of vision over 25° across, prevents any nicety of observation. It offers, instead, a range of sunsets from early April to early September. The equinoctial sunsets of March and September occur between these dates, as vaguely defined by the stones as by the miles of space in the gap between the heights of Macgillycuddy's Reeks and the Slieve Mish mountains to their north.

A matter of positive interest amongst the numerous paired stones in south-west Ireland is their association with different kinds of monument. One or two are near other short rows or pairs. A few are close to boulder-burials, above-ground cists with enormous capstones but as most of those are low-lying by the coast whereas pairs in general are on higher ground up to 500 ft (150 m) above sea-level the connection, except for the presence of death, is not a striking one.

What does seem significant is the juxtaposition of a pair of stones to a circle, reaffirming the tradition of linear settings being conjoined to a ring. The pair at Lissyviggeen stand close to the Seven Sisters circle. At Coolcoulaghta and Glantane NE pairs were set up

Pl. 100 High-and-low, flat-topped and pointed stones at Cappaboy Beg, Co. Cork. From the north. A nearby radial cairn is hidden in the long grass.

within a few hundred yards of large megalithic rings architecturally akin to the recumbent stone circles of Scotland.[22] Emphasising this Hiberno-Scottish connection two pairs at Lettergorman and Cappaboy Beg are adjacent to Four-Poster 'circles' like others in Perthshire.

At Cappaboy Beg (Pl. 100) there is also a radial-cairn. Such cairns appear to be Irish versions of Scottish ring-cairns, an open central space for crema-tions encircled in Scotland by a low cairn edged with a continuous kerbing of upright slabs. In Cork and Kerry comparable cairns have 'kerbs' that instead of lining the perimeter of the mound protrude from its side like the ratchets of a cog-wheel.

Their pockets of cremated bone, like the deposits in boulder-burials such as that inside the Bohonagh stone circle, confirm the funerary associations that persisted even in monuments as late as pairs of stones. Several pairs were erected alongside Five-Stone rings, Baurgaum, Clodagh, Knockantota, Mill Little amongst them. At Cashelkeelty Five-Stone ring the burnt remains of a twenty-five to thirty year-old person lay in a central pit near a short row. Similarly, some pairs stood against both Five-Stone rings and radial-cairns.

At Kealkil a cairn and a Five-Stone ring excavated in 1938 lie within a few paces of a pair of towering pillars. This combination of pair, Five-Stone ring and radial-cairn is repeated at Knockraheen SW and at Knocknakilla. The latter site, also known as Muisire Beg, was dug into in 1931 uncovering evidence of trampling at the entrance to the ring where strewn quartz lay. Circularity, linearity and death were con-stant companions, perhaps fertility also if contrasting shapes, heights and girths had been selected as images of fecundity.

On the prominence of Foherlagh hill overlooking Roaringwater Bay is an impressive pair of stones. Both are big, the ENE, 6 ft 6 (2 m) high, broad, and sharply flat-topped. One long stride away the other is a slender, tapering slab, thin, a full 9 ft 3 (2.8 m) in height. Like many other pairs of standing stones these are 'untouched and lonely megaliths . . . and like sen-tinels of the past they await the passing of the ages as yet unrecognised for whatever they truly are'.[23] This need no longer be entirely true.

Weir[24] has drawn attention to the 'remarkably suggestive gateposts of Ulster' in which unnecessarily massive pillars flank narrow entrances to fields and lanes, some stones thick and with 'glandiform, conical caps (some quite phallic) . . . whereby the fertility of beasts was ensured by driving them between such – usually phalliform – stones'. Some pairs were mani-festly male and female, the latter denoted by a groove carved in it. Although the clearest instances of such discrimination are to be found in Northern Ireland the same symbolism may also have prompted the choice of disparate stones in the counties of Cork and Kerry.

(ii) *The remainder of the Republic of Ireland*
With the exception of Cork and Kerry and a few widely-dispersed sites along the south-east coast there are only three other and minor groups of paired stones in the Republic of Ireland, one in Connemara north of Galway Bay, another at the north-east of the country in the region of Carlingford Lough, and a third scat-tered in northern Co. Donegal whose pairs seem culturally related to others in south-west Scotland.

In Connemara, west of the Twelve Pins or Bens that radiate wildly and grandiosely in a series of quartzite peaks around the attractive fishing-port of Clifden, is a cluster of paired stones. As usual they are more numerous than the Four- to Six- and Three-Stone rows that hypothetically preceded them although 'a coastal extension northwards from the Clifden rows seemed indicated by the presence of a row of five stones, one prostrate, at Killandangan on the southern shore of Clew Bay'.[25]

The Connemara pairs, several of glittering quartz, favour a general north – south alignment, the orienta-tion varying from north-west – south-east (two sites) to north-east – south-west (one) with the three arranged most nearly to true north-south accounting for little more than a quarter of the assemblage. One site at Streamstown or Barratrough may be the ruins of a stray Four-Poster circle. To the east of two standing stones, one of them 7 ft (2.1 m) high, is a third upright with a fourth lying flat not far from it. If the site had been a genuine Four-Poster then it would be the westernmost of all those late and austere stone 'circles'.

The second group of paired stones is miles to the north-east, centred on the coastal countryside around Dundalk. A limited and tight cluster of Four- to Six-Stone rows there was extended in a wavering line northwards by some Three-Stone rows in Co. Down, the most distant of them standing in isolation at Ballyrushey near Strangford Lough.

The pairs repeat this distribution but they also spread thinly to the south entering Co. Louth and Co. Meath, the pattern angling westwards towards the Loughcrew hills with their prestigious passage-tombs stationed, like Slieve Gullion, on mountain tops. The later people who set up the more modest monuments of two stones were less ambitious, preferring the lower, less exposed slopes of the hills.

Paired stones in Co. Donegal near Lough Swilly and Lough Foyle with its long river-valley appear related to others in south-west Scotland, particularly those in the Kilmartin Valley of Argyll. Less than forty miles (64 km) of open sea separate the regions.

The art on the two stones at Barnes Lower in the foothills of Salt Mountain has close affinities with that on Scottish pairs such as Ballymeanoch. Standing not ten miles (16 km) from Lough Swilly the stones carry a profusion of cupmarks, arcs and grooves, the very motifs widespread in Argyll but not closely paralleled in the spirals and geometrical motifs of Irish passage-tomb decoration of which there is none in Co. Donegal.[26] The location of the art on standing stones and rock outcrops is the same in both Donegal and

Argyll. The cup-and-rings, arcs and gutters at Carrowreagh and Mevagh is mirrored on the stones and rock-surfaces in Argyll. As the carved stones in Donegal, like the pairs, are in the immediate vicinity of Lough Swilly and the sea the later Bronze Age links between north-west Ireland and south-west Scotland seem probable.

(e) *Northern Ireland*

Perhaps because of the discouraging presence of so many established long rows and avenues in Northern Ireland only a few short lines were built. Amongst them pairs are relatively sparse. There is one fair-sized group to the west of Lough Neagh and other sites, usually alone, near the north and east coasts. There, below the Mourne mountains where there had hardly been a standing stone before, pairs merge with others by Carlingford Lough in Co. Louth.

Well to their north a meandering twelve miles (19 km) of sites trickle westwards from Cookstown on the fringes of the Sperrins to Carrickmore. Two remote, unaccompanied pairs are still farther away, Crew Lower near Castlederg with Sandville and Lisvidin far away to its north on the plain of the River Foyle.

The Cookstown-Carrickmore stretch is a riverine distribution along the Ballinderry valley at the nervous edges of the uplands. Of all the pairs only Murnells is actually in the hills, standing within a few paces of the massive Cregganconroe court-tomb on the northern slopes of the mountain. The westerly route was an easy one. Today a good road penetrates into the heart of the South Sperrin moors with their abundance of prehistoric remains: stone circles, cairns, standing stones, wedge- and court-tombs. The chambered tomb of Dermot and Grania's Bed lies in wreckage at Dunnanmore not far north of Creggandevesky, the one pair to be set up close to a stone circle. Such an infiltration into the hills echoes the movement inland from the coast already noticed in the straggle of pairs in Co. Meath some sixty miles (100 km) to the south.

There have been no authorised excavations of pairs but investigations at the bases of single stones in Co. Down at Drumnahare and Carrownacaw came upon cremations. At the first the shallow stonehole held an adult's burnt bones with charcoal strewn around them. At Carrownacaw the 10 ft (3 m) high menhir stood against a circular ditch containing flint arrowheads and an undistinguished Bronze Age sherd. The discovery of such amorphous burials and deposits has evoked archaeological despair about such individual pillars. 'The only thing that is clear is that their real function still seems to remain a mystery.'[27] Fortunately, the settings of more than one stone are more enlightening.

No astronomical alignments have been claimed but the silence may be due to lack of modern research rather than an absence of prehistoric interest in the sun or moon. Nevertheless the rows are certainly too short to provide a sightline for any eclipse-seeking

astronomer-priest. Even allowing for the 30 ft (9 m) of Edentoit in Co. Tyrone the average length of a pair in Northern Ireland is no more than 9 ft (2.7 m) with some of the stones standing less than 3 ft (1 m) from each other.

What can be stated is that where orientations have been mentioned the two stones are set unusually east-west, three sites in Co. Down and six in Tyrone. No other direction is cited. How accurate these bearings are, and whether they resulted from an atypical concern with the equinoxes can only be resolved by proper surveys. Recalling the almost complete absence of such east-west bearings in the short rows of south-west Ireland (p. 169) and western Scotland (p. 177) it is an unexpected development. It becomes all the more intriguing because the same 'equinoctial' phenomenon occurs in many of the paired settings of central Scotland.

Amongst the northern Irish pairs art is almost non-existent. Only at Killybeg amongst a clutter of ruinous chambered tombs are any motifs reported, marks like 'four fingers and a thumb' causing the low and broad slab to be called Fion MacCumhall's Finger-Stone. Nearby is a second pair, one a small, square stone, the other pointed and with some possible cupmarks on its west face. They are not convincing. As decorated stones are very rare in Northern Ireland their identification as artificial must remain unconfirmed.

Conversely, it seems unquestionable that the pairs were quite deliberately composed of stones of disparate heights and shapes. Every one of the sites where an adequate description is available has a pointed stone opposed to one with a flat top. Even at Tully North in Co. Antrim where one stone has fallen it is square-headed unlike the 7 ft (2.1 m) high tapering pillar to its east. Whether the opposites do represent male and female principles as several writers have asserted is unprovable:

> Sometimes paired stones are quite obviously male and female (the latter with a grooved top). Good examples are at Boherboy (Dublin), Cabragh (Cork) and Sandville (Tyrone). Both phallus and vulva occur together at Boa Island (Fermanagh) where a famous double 'Janiform' torso (two carved pillars in one) is gouged female on one side (with protruding tongue: a universal symbol of coitus) and has a phallus carved in relief on the other.[28]

This is controversial. Not all the sites are pairs. The interpretation and age of the Boa Island carving are doubtful. 'It is difficult to state unequivocally that the two Boa Island figures are pagan, much less Celtic'[29] and it is even more speculative to associate them with pairs of standing stones that may predate them by over a thousand years. An objective physical fact is that the eastern stone is always the pointed one (7:0) and usually the taller (5:3). Sometimes the stones are of the same height with the western being wider. In three instances, all in Co. Tyrone, at Grange, Murnells

Pl. 101   A small pointed and flat-topped pair near the Wren's Egg boulder, Wigtownshire. From the east.

and Sandville and Lisvidin, the stone has a groove, perhaps manmade, on it. Sexual symbolism has been inferred, the phallic eastern pillar rising above the vulva-inscribed broad western slab. It is possible.

'That standing stones are recognised as resembling human figures is expressed in the name, "Fir Breagach", "False man", sometimes given to them.'[30] Identical names occur at a Scottish Three-Stone row, Na Fir Bhreage, 'the false men' at Blashaval on North Uist, and to a pair, Fir Bhreige, on the same island. The significance may be no more than that from a distance the stones look like a group of men. Comparable illusions led to the name of Grey Wethers for two contiguous stone circles on Dartmoor because from afar they could be taken for a flock of sheep. It is even rumoured that they were sold as such to a naive stranger.[31]

(f) Scotland

Scotland has been well-served in studies of its standing stones. Early fieldwork by Fred Coles was improved upon in accuracy and scope by the meritorious Royal Commission county volumes and by local descriptions in *Discovery & Excavation*. The pairs in central Scotland were catalogued and analysed architecturally by Margaret Stewart. Ruggles examined the astronomy of many short rows and pairs in Argyll and the Western Isles, supplementing the astronomical and geometrical surveys of the Thoms who worked both there and in other regions of the country.

From these researches two major and quite distinct patterns become apparent, one in the west and north, the other in central Scotland. That in the west ranges from the south-western corner of Galloway, is dense along the Mull of Kintyre and into north Argyll, rather more thinly scattered in the Western Isles but, almost for the first time, reaches Orkney and Shetland. A similar penetration into new areas also occurs south-east of Argyll in the Southern Uplands and the eastern Cheviots.

Although extending beyond the earlier limits this western and northern spread followed the earlier distribution of short rows and the pairs shared many of their traits. This was not true in central Scotland. The countryside around Loch Tay had hardly been affected by any linear tradition and the sudden eruption there of pairs of standing stones may have been the final emanation of these 'new' monuments. Their resemblance to others in Northern Ireland permits the suggestion of strong contacts between the two localities.

(i) The South-West, West and North

In western Scotland the densest concentration of pairs is in Argyll near Lochgilphead, in the Kilmartin valley with a hesitant line creeping into the Mull of Kintyre. To the south-east in Galloway and in the Southern Uplands to the east there are some widely separated sites. North of Argyll are others in the islands to the west, a few in the Hebrides and then an ouburst on the mainland of Orkney. As before, there was a steady increase in numbers over the short rows: four Four- to Six-Stone, eight Three-Stone and a score of pairs in south-west Scotland, a similar development, six, nine and twenty in the Western Isles and northern Scotland.

Reflecting the gradual waning of the linear tradition not all the pairs were of towering stones. Almost the southernmost of the Scottish pairs, the Wren's Egg in Wigtownshire, consists of two low stones standing ENE–WSW of each other, the eastern a tapering slab 4 ft 7 (1.4 m) high, its flat-topped partner 7 inches (17 cm) shorter (Pl. 101).

Twenty paces to the west on a low knoll is an enormous ice-borne boulder, the Wren's Egg, 160 cubic feet (4.5 m^3) of solid granite computed to weigh over ten tons. The wren being the smallest of common British birds the name of the stone is not a fitting one.

To the west the pair looks just north of the boulder towards a skyline which, being a little higher to the south, explains the row's WSW direction halfway between the solstitial sunsets. Eastwards the land also rises to the south. Had the intention been to indicate the place where the equinoctial sun rose the two stones would have been set WNW–ESE, a full 10° south of its present orientation.

A quarter of a mile to the SSE is another pair at Milton Hall. Its orientation, like that of the Three-Stone row at Drumtroddan half a mile away, is solstitial unlike the Wren's Egg, Drumtroddan to the midsummer sunrise, Milton Hall towards the midwinter sunset. Three sites so close together indicating the sun's midwinter, midsummer and equinoctial positions may have been used as a local calendar.

An excavation in 1977 at the Wren's Egg uncovered a patch of burning just east of the stones, a posthole by the south-east edge of the boulder, and sixty-four pieces of varied flints, 'meagre evidence of late third

and second millennium activity'.[32] Excavations elsewhere produced little more, some vague accounts of human bones at Achnabreac in Argyll and Galabraes near Clinkingstone Farm in West Lothian, a paved area, broken quartz, a polished stone axe and a flint arrowhead from the badly disturbed pair at Great Bernera on Lewis, a site where the intricate prehistoric activities may have been as intriguing and irrecoverable as those at Welsh pairs such as Rhos y Clegyrn, 'the heath of stones'.

Except for one small area megalithic art is unknown in these sites. But there, near Lochgilphead, in a three and a half mile (5.6 km) south-east – north-west line from Dunamuck by the River Add to the Kilmartin Stones is the only group of pairs of decorated stones in western Scotland.

On the edge of a fertile triangle of land below the eastern mountains the two uprights of Dunamuck, Mid stand 20 ft (5.7 m) apart, the NNW stone flat-topped, its taller counterpart with a sharply angled peak like an upturned guillotine blade. On its broad south-west side is a single cupmark. A hundred yards (90 m) away both the pillars of Dunamuck, South, 'the dancing stones', are prostrate. One has a cupmark.

Across the river at Torbhlarun, is a 'playing-card' slab. Both its wider surfaces are heavily cupmarked. Nearly three miles (5 km) to the north-west is the Ballymeanoch complex, the two inner stones of its Four-Stone row and the single stone to their southwest ornamented. The intervening pair lacks carvings.

A further mile (1.6 km) to the north at Slockavullin near the Temple Wood stone circles the Kilmartin Stones rise (Fig. 42), elegantly simple, in a long open line amidst the necropolis of a chambered tomb,

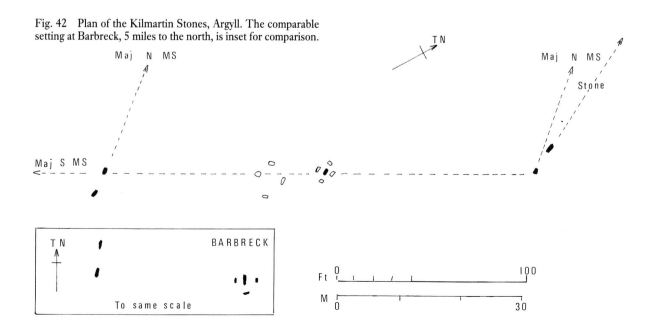

Fig. 42 Plan of the Kilmartin Stones, Argyll. The comparable setting at Barbreck, 5 miles to the north, is inset for comparison.

an extended cemetery of heavy round cairns and outcrops covered with cupmarks, cup-and-rings, arcs and grooves. The stones have carvings. Five slender pillars, all playing-card in shape, form a an almost unmatched layout of two thin and elongated triangles placed head to head in a NNE–SSW line with pairs of high stones for their narrow bases, even taller monoliths at their tips, the southernmost now missing.

The pairs stand at hard angles to the line. At the north the two stones, SSE–NNW, are not quite in line with each other but slightly hooked towards the north, the southern 8 ft 3 (2.5 m) high and pointed, the northern 8 ft (2.4 m), flat-topped and with four cupmarks on its southwest face. Although it is nicely aligned on an outlying stone 350 ft (107 m) to the NNW no celestial event is determined by the orientation. 'This line has no obvious astronomical significance in either direction, nor does it point to any notch on the horizon. We can conclude only that it had some other purpose'.[33] An alternative explanation will be suggested.

Well to the SSW of the pair the tallest stone, 9 ft 6 (2.9 m) high, has over forty cupmarks on its southwest face. From it, beyond the remains of a square of low slabs in which a second tall monolith may have stood, and 237 ft (72 m) from the first pair is a second, a mirror-image of the first for here it is the SSW stone that is the taller, 8 ft 9 (2.7 m) high, but flat-topped and with three cupmarks on its south-east side. Its partner is 3 inches (7 cm) lower and is pointed. With a bearing closer to the north than the other pair the stones define a good sightline to the major northern moonset.

The particular combination of height, shape and art in the Kilmartin pairs is not typical of pairs as a whole amongst which there is so much architectural diversity that no overall rule can be recognised. There is, nevertheless, a tendency for the backsight to be a tall, slim pillar that rises to a point, occasionally cupmarked, whereas the foresight is a thicker, lower block, rougher and devoid of art. In terms of celestial mechanics such a stone is so unsuitable for observations that to its prehistoric erectors it surely had meanings additional to a function as a sighting-device.

To extrapolate from this that the stones must have possessed a visually symbolic significance to the men and women who used them is as wasteful of time as a search for the snows of years gone by. To suggest that the taller stone was a phallic totem standing against a slab personifying the female body and spirit is to deduce too much. The conceptual imagery of ancient, pre-literate societies will always remain elusive, the beliefs and world-systems so far distant from our own social conditioning that they can never be understood. Like Salome the stones tease but do not satisfy.

Not only is the Kilmartin architecture unusual but claims have been made for refined lunar astronomy in this exceptional setting. The reality may be less exciting. Recalling the seemingly inexplicable non-alignment of the northern pair it too may have been intended to contain a lunar orientation but one that was spoiled either by maladroit workmanship or affected by some other need of the builders that resulted in a declination of +34°, several degrees too far north.

Plans can deceive. At the site itself it is noticeable that the stones are not in a straight line. With an azimuth of 321° the thin backsight is well directed towards the northern moonset. Its partner is not. Its longer sides are skewed almost 20° farther to the north causing the medial 'alignment' from one stone to the other to be a meaningless 151°–331°. Maybe the foresight has shifted. Maybe it was carelessly set up. Maybe it was a dog-legged compromise to integrate both a sightline to the moon and an alignment on what may have been an older, hallowed stone, the outlying pillar to the NNW that by misfortune stood several degrees north of the moonset.

That sightlines at Kilmartin were intended, rather imprecise, sometimes degrees rather than minutes of arc wide, but planned, is supported by the fact that the north and south pairs form a long NNE–SSW alignment to the major southern moonset.[34] The probability is further increased by the existence of an identical lunar sightline at Barbreck five miles (8 km) to the north, a half-version of Kilmartin that now has only one pair with a single standing stone to its ESE. It is the pair, also NNE–SSW, that looks towards the most southerly moonset.

Barbreck may originally have been a 'Kilmartin' twisted at 90° to its counterpart. In 1793 the landowner was safeguarding 'a cluster of rude obelisks . . . with a laudable respect for antiquity' but half a century later 'a large grey stone with others of smaller dimensions' was removed to make space for a new house. Barbreck and Kilmartin being so close together and so alike in design it is likely that the lunar alignment discovered in one confirms the comparable bearing in the other.[35]

At Kilmartin the placing of the cupmarks on the south-west and north-east broad faces of stones is suggestive of lunar symbolism in keeping with the sightlines established by the stones themselves. This is in accord with the preferred orientations of other pairs in western and northern Scotland, identical to those of the short rows. Of the pairs that have been subjected to accurate surveys forty-two per cent stand either south-east – north-west or south-west – north-east. A further twenty per cent were set north – south. Almost the same percentage appears with SSW – NNE and SSE – NNW settings in which 'cardinal' lines may have been attempted, distorted by irregular skylines. The orientations are indicative of an interest in lunar and solar extremes and, to a lesser extent, in the meridional positions between them.

Equinoctial positions were ignored. As with the short rows there is an almost complete absence of east-west lines. It seems informative that an exception, the Wren's Egg, is only a few miles across the North Channel from the 'equinoctial' pairs of Northern Ireland. Influences from there, reaching into south-western and central Scotland, can be inferred.

For the more characteristic pairs of the west there are sites beyond Argyll on the outlying islands although not greatly outnumbering the short rows on Mull, Skye and in the Outer Hebrides whose occupants may have continued to venerate the stones well into historical times. Martin Martin who made several visits to the Western Isles in the late seventeenth century noticed that on Barra 'There are several Instances of Heathenism and Pagan Superstition among the Inhabitants of the Islands . . . [although] only a few of the oldest and most ignorant of the Vulgar are guilty of 'em', adding that 'There is a Stone set up here, about seven foot high; and when the Inhabitants come near it, they take a religious Turn round it', to which the Cornish antiquarian, William Borlase appended the gloss, 'according to the ancient Druid custom!'.[36] The stone, now fallen, may have stood at Borve on the west coast, once the taller of a north-south pair.

This continuing respect for pagan stones was little different from the custom in Brittany, even in the nineteenth century, of men and women going to the stones in the belief that there was a power in them that could cure a wife of infertility. Taking a 'religious turn' around a stone in Scotland meant going around it 'deasil', clockwise, following the sun's path, never 'widdershins' in the other direction. One wonders whether this tradition was related to the long-forgotten associations of stone rows with the sun and moon.

North of the Hebrides Caithness and Sutherland were hardly affected by the maritime expansion. Few pairs were erected there. Instead, many appeared along the western coastline of Orkney mainland within a couple of miles (c. 3 km) of the sea with only Redland standing at the north-eastern corner of the island. They were megalithic novelties. No avenues, long or short rows had preceded them.

The same was almost true of the Shetlands where there were only two multiple and one Three-Stone row. Now came a tenuous stretch of three pairs from Gravlaba northwards to the Giant's Grave, two big stones of red granite standing south-north with a cairn of white granite between them. Another pair at Busta Brae had a massive twenty-ton pillar supposedly thrown by the Devil but, more prosaically, 'a useful sailing mark' standing where it did at the cliff-top.

These western Scottish settings are epitomised by the pair at Carse on the wooded hills of the Knapdale peninsula, Argyll (Pl. 102). The two stones stand in a classical combination of high and low, thin and broad, pointed and flat-topped in a north-south alignment. On a level stretch of fertile land a quarter of a mile (400 m) from the sea inlet of Loch Stornoway the southern pillar is a 'playing-card' slab, tapering to a 10 ft 6 (3.2 m) high tip. Against it is a lower, thicker flat-topped block.

Pl. 102   Carse, Argyll. The north stone is flat-topped, the south pointed. From the west.

A third stone leans 120 yards (110 m) to the WNW.

It has been claimed that looking westwards between the pair the equinoctial sun would be seen setting over this outlier but it is impossible. Both the Thoms and Ruggles calculated the declination to be not near 0° but about +10° where the sun would be setting in late August rather than late September but all three surveyors agreed that 'the two stone alignment is only 3° away from the meridian', an azimuth of 357° for the pair itself.[37]

The stones have a Late Bronze Age association. In 1864 some objects were donated to the National Museum of Scotland, 'Fragments of Bronze Plates found at the base of a Standing Sone on the estate of Carse, Argyleshire. These show traces of small projecting ornaments of Vandyke pattern, and knobs &c'.[38] The articles were mislaid. There is no mention of them even in early catalogues of the museum.

From the description they were probably small rectangles of lead bronze from a cauldron of the metallurgical Dowris phase around 900 BC, sheets that would be riveted together, decorated with embossed zigzags around the body. Another from Capecastle Bog near Ballycastle Bay, Co. Antrim, less than fifty miles (80 km) of coastal waters south of Knapdale, must have resembled it in design, ornamented with 'a series of triangles embossed in a similar manner forming a kind of vandyke collar round the vessel.'[39]

If the 'Bronze Plates' had been part of a cauldron, complete or unfinished, their discovery alongside one of the Carse stones is of interest because of the significance of the cauldron in late prehistoric times. In the first millennium BC the cauldron was used in rituals associated with Otherworld feasting, death and rebirth. 'The cauldron was a vessel of great magical power and ritual importance, and was frequently offered to the unseen powers by being deposited in a river or bog.'[40]

The deposition of such potent ware at Carse suggests that Bronze Age standing stones had not lost their power even in the Iron Age and could still be used for ritual. The stone at Carse, whether one of the pair or the outlier, may have been only a few centuries old when the offerings were buried at its foot.

(ii) *Central and Eastern Scotland*

West of Argyll there had been few short rows in central Scotland, one certain line of four stones at Glenhead Farm in Perthshire (Tayside) and four Three-Stone rows in the south of the county near the Firth of Tay. But pairs were abundant. Almost forty are known from Orwell, Kinross, to Castle Fraser near Aberdeen at the north-east. Between them was an eruption of sites in Perthshire, almost all of them in the lovely valleys of the Tay and Earn rivers and lochs.

From the architecture Irish influences are likely. Connections between Ireland and north-east Scotland had been established in the Neolithic when Group IX porcellanite stone axes from the Tievebulliagh axe-factory in Co. Antrim were taken as far east as Aberdeenshire. The links became stronger in the Early Bronze Age with the introduction of metal-working in the north-east by smiths probably using Irish ores from Cork and Kerry. Similarities between north-eastern Scottish and south-western Irish recumbent stone circles, Five-Stone rings and Four-Posters seem incontrovertible with the most likely direction of the transmission of ideas disseminating from Scotland to Ireland.[41] With the pairs of standing stones the reverse seems true with traditions from northern Ireland extending into the glens and hillsides around Loch Tay.

The distribution of pairs is virtually confined to the two river-valleys of the Tay and Earn, petering out east of Blairgowrie and the River Ericht along the littoral of Strathmore where forest may have inhibited settlement. 'The weight of the distribution of paired stones is westerly and this would encourage the idea that these monuments are an introduction from the west brought possibly from Ireland where pairs of standing stones are also known'.[42]

There have been few excavations, a fact compensated for by the finds from Orwell, two impressive stones standing on a ridge just north of Loch Leven. It is an 'Irish' setting with the east emphasised, as always, by the taller stone, 9 ft 8 (2.9 m) high and pointed, rising 2 ft 3 (0.7 m) above the lower, blunt angular pillar 47 ft (14.3 m) away. After the latter's fall in 1972 both stoneholes were examined.[43]

In the eastern was a peculiar set of cremations in two storeys. At the bottom were the remains of two women, one of whom had suffered from osteoarthritis. Mixed with the burnt bones were others of dog and pig. A stone slab rested over them and on it lay the cremation of a man about thirty years of age. In the western hole were the ashes of another woman. A rather similar deposit was dug up in the mid-nineteenth century at the foot of a standing stone at Easter Pitcorthie in Fife.

Flints and other cremations were found near the Orwell stones. In August 1904, Fred Coles visited the stones which:

for many years have attracted popular notice . . . In the same field stone coffins have occasionally been turned up by the plough; and about the beginning of the nineteenth century, the ground was in many places dug up by the neighbouring proprietor, when quantities of bones much decomposed and mixed with charcoal were discovered . . . Mr. R. Kilgour . . . showed me a fine partially flattened oval pebble of dark reddish quartzite, measuring 5 inches by 2⅞ inches [12.7, 7.3 cm] which he found in the ground between these two stones. The abrasion at each end clearly shows that this pebble has been used as a pounder.[44]

The cremations, burials, flints and domestic implement show that the pair, like others where excavations have been extensive, remained the focus of ritual activity for a long time with the stones acting as centres of funerary and fertility ceremonies.

Following her excavation of the Lundin Farm Four-Poster in 1963 Margaret Stewart made a detailed study of paired stones in Perthshire (Pl. 103).[45] Not far from the rectangular stone 'circle' were two prostrate stones. It is an irony that these, which prompted her to compile a catalogue of pairs in the county, were almost certainly not a genuine pair as she supposed but the wreckage of a second Four-Poster despoiled by a road which not only went right through the 'ring' but also passed alongside a thrown-down cupmarked stone from the north-east corner of the Bronze Age setting.[46]

The construction of Scottish Four-Posters flourished during the Bronze Age. A series of nine radio-carbon determinations from Park of Tongland, Kirkcud-bright[47] range from 1610±50 bc (GU-2382) down to 1090±50 bc (GU-2381), approximately the equivalent of a period from 2000 to 1400 BC. Finds of Bronze Age pottery and artefacts from other Four-Posters are in complete agreement with this chronological span. There is nothing to indicate that pairs of standing stones near the 'rings' belonged to an earlier period. The juxtaposition of a pair to a Four-Poster not only at Lundin Farm but also at Ferntower, and at the diminutive Glassel in Kincardineshire suggest that the earliest of the pairs may have been contemporary with the 'circles' with the latest erected perhaps centuries after 1400 BC.

Stewart defined two types of pairs in central Scotland. The first, her 'A' which she believed the earlier, consisted of stones 'playing-card' in shape with their broad sides along the axis of the setting which was usually east-west. In the 'B' sites the stones were coarser, often unshaped and set at right-angles to the axis. In both types some surfaces had been smoothed and some bases 'keeled' into a beak to facilitate the raising of the tall slabs.

Unlike the Irish pairs, in four cases out of five in Scotland it was the western stone that was higher (Pl. 104) and as this is a characteristic of the recumbent stone circles (RSCs) in Aberdeenshire it might be thought that such a fashion indicated that the origins of the pairs lay there.

It is unlikely. The orientations of RSCs are persistently between SSE and south-west, directed towards the southern moon. Stewart's 'A' settings are just as persistently between ESE–WNW, east-west and ENE–WSW like the 'equinoctial' pairs of the north of Ireland. It may be assumed that they were amalgams of two separate traditions, paired east-west like the Irish but with their heights reversed by the architectural customs of north-eastern Scotland. A comparable preference for placing the tallest stone at the west occurs in the Scottish Four-Posters.[48]

Amongst Stewart's 'B' pairs the orientations often

Pl. 103 Stare Dam, Perthshire. Flat-topped and pointed stones. From the south.

Pl. 104   New Tyle, Perthshire. At the bottom of a steep slope.
From the south.

Pl. 105   East Cult, Perthshire. From the west. The nearer
stone is higher and heavier.

veer from east-west, north-east – south-west at Cally, north-west – south-east at Pitfour and elsewhere as though the Irish custom was giving way to a stronger local choice of direction. Other differences between 'A' and 'B' were as great. At Dowally or Clachan More, 'the great stone', the slender pillars of an 'A' pair stand ESE – WNW, 9 ft (2.7 m) apart, the western 8 ft 4 (2.5 m) high, a foot (30 m) above the other. In contrast to this elegant setting the lumpish 'B' boulders, north-south, at Gellybank, 'both rough blocks of quartzose schist', neither of them more than 4 ft high but over 3 ft thick (1.2, 1 m) slump together with 'a space of only 8 or 10 inches [20, 25 cm] between their inner edges'.[49] The southern has a flattish top while its bigger partner climbs to a jagged peak.

There is no compelling astronomy in either type. What little there may be is either towards the equinoctial sun or to the southern moon as it was in the alignments of RSCs.

What do exist, unlike the austerity of the majority of western Scottish pairs, are cupmarks. Megalithic art had a long history in central and north-eastern Scotland, carved on westerly stones in lunar positions in RSCs but on eastern stones in Four-Posters.[50] The same easterly direction is repeated in the pairs. Simple motifs occur at Auchterhouse in Angus, and in Perthshire at Balnuaguard, Clach an Tuirc and Fowlis Wester NW. It is found most lavishly of all on a tumbled boulder to the east of the fine 'A' pair at East Cult near Blairgowrie.

East Cult's are secretive stones. The approach is difficult, along a discouraging forest track from the east, along a road marked 'Private' from the south, hidden in a tangle of lanes and steep wooded slopes below Newtyle Hill. But to persevere is to triumph.

The two stones of dull, greenish slate stand nearly east-west on a hill with a magnificent panoramic view (Pl. 105). As usual with a Perthshire pair the westernmost is the taller, 9 ft (2.7 m) high, broad and flat-topped. Some 35 ft (10.7 m) to its east is its pointed partner, 6 ft 11 (2.1 m) in height. A further 39 ft (11.9 m) to the east is a large, cupmarked stone, leaning severely to the north, almost prostrate and split across. It is not now in line with the standing stones but lies about 6 ft (1.8 m) north of their axis (Figs 43 and 44).

To the west the upright stones stand in line with a faint but definite V-shaped notch in the hilly skyline showing 'approximately megalithic man's equinox since the altitude to the west is about 2°.8'.[51] Such a bearing is in keeping with the pair's postulated Irish ancestry.

The decorated stone to the east is flat-topped, smooth and covered by over 150 cupmarks, two of them with radial grooves. The cups, in no discernible pattern, pack densely together in a central band, are scarce near the top and absent at the bottom where what seem to be packing-stones lie under the slab. These imply that the boulder once stood erect, its undecorated base concealed in a stonehole. If this is correct the pillar may have been the eastern upright of a Three-Stone row, its cupmarked surface looking towards the south.

East Cult is like the Three-Stone row at St Madoes, 'the supposed remains of [a] Druidical Temple', fifteen miles (24 km) to the SSE where two standing and one prostrate stone form a NNW–SSE line 18 ft (5.5 m) long. The row is graded up to the NNW pillar which is liberally cupmarked on both its east and west sides. Another richly carved boulder lies at Kincairney a mile and a half north-east of East Cult.

The stones of East Cult tantalise with their uncertainties. They are contradictions, Irish and Scottish, of debateable age, equinoctial unlike the majority of

Fig. 43 East Cult, Perthshire. Drawing by Romilly Allen in 1880. From *PSAS 15*, 1880–1, 81. The sketches show the pointed eastern stone and the taller, flat-topped west pillar. The cupmarked stone lies to the east.

Fig. 44 East Cult, Perthshire. A drawing by Fred Coles in 1907. From *PSAS 42*, 1907–8, 150.

Pl. 106 Castle Fraser, Aberdeenshire. From the south. As usual, the distant north-east stone is pointed and the south-west is flat-topped and heavier. Off the photograph in the same field is a splendid recumbent stone circle.

rows, their art undecipherable, the number of stones indeterminate. The site embodies the problems of stone rows.

Almost exactly one hundred miles (161 km) to the north-east across the southern Grampians is an equally enigmatic setting. Scores of miles from any other pair the two stones at Castle Fraser near Inverurie (Pl. 106) may be the last in Scotland, the culmination of the long-drawn out movement from the west. Of local granite, each about 7 ft (2.1 m) high the south-western is the bigger, almost rectangular in shape, flat-topped, ravaged by rain. The other is thinner, tapering sharply. They stand some 44 ft (13.4 m) apart 240 yards (220 m) east of a fine recumbent stone circle. The north-east stone stands neatly east of the ring's southern arc.

The circle's recumbent stone was aligned on the major southern moonset. It appears that the pair's azimuth of 22°–202° was directed towards the same lunar target. But what is at question is neither the astronomy nor the age nor the purpose nor the asso-

ciation with a stone circle but the original status of the two stones.

Charles Dalrymple, an antiquarian who excavated several recumbent stone circles in the mid-nineteenth century remarked on the pair. 'Another group of stones formerly stood about 400 y^{ds} to the Eastward of the Circle [at Castle Fraser], but the original number, which is uncertain, is reduced to two.'[52] The question remains. Are the two stones a true pair or are they the survivors of a short row or of a long line or even the beginnings of a tangential avenue?

If a pair, the stones may be the final manifestations of a linear tradition that began two thousand years before in the great stone circles of Cumbria. From the uncomplicated entrances to those rings developed the astonishing avenues and rows of Carnac and Callanish, of Caithness and Cork. It may be apt, therefore, that the late, perhaps last, pair of stones at Castle Fraser stand only six miles (10 km) south-west of the early avenue of Broomend of Crichie.

Without excavation it is premature to speculate further on these pairs of stones except to say that they look like the final and symbolic expression of a ritual avenue.

Margaret Stewart, 1966, 145

NOTES

If a particular book or article is frequently mentioned in the Notes only the author's name, date of publication and page number are cited. Full details will be found in the Bibliography (p. 271). As an example, in Chapter 1, Note 2, Grinsell, 1976, 99, refers the reader to: Grinsell, L.V. (1976). *Folklore of Prehistoric Sites in Britain*, Newton Abbot, in the Bibliography. Where a work appears just once or very rarely its author, title, date and page number are printed in full as in: Preface, Note 1. The full titles of abbreviations for learned journals such as *PDAS* in Chapter 1, Note 4, are given in the list that precedes the Bibliography.

PREFACE

1 E. Bray. *The Discovery of the Hebrides. Voyagers to the Western Isles, 1745–1883*, London, 1986, 10.

CHAPTER ONE

1 Thom, Thom and Burl, 1990. Three-quarters of this two-volume work was taken up with the Thoms' plans and astronomical comments about the standing stones of Great Britain. Supplementary to this was a preliminary gazetteer of rows in western Europe.
2 Grinsell, 1976, 99.
3 Dobson, 1931, 90, 237; Taylor, J., 85, SO 2.
4 For Corringdon Ball (SX 669 613), Cuckoo Ball (SX 659 581) and Butterdon Hill (SX 660 586) long chambered tombs see: Grinsell, 1978, 132; Pearce, 1981, 53; *PDAS 32*, 1974, 163–4.
5 *PSAS 63*, 1928–9, 154–5.
6 For Kilmartin see: *PSAS 16*, 1881–2, 110–12; Thom, 1971, 45–51; Heggie, 1981, 185–6. For Barbreck see: *PSAS 95*, 1961–2, 24, no. 159; Heggie, 1981, 185–6; Thom, Thom and Burl, 1990, I, 106–8.
7 Thom, 1967, 98, G8/9; 149, Fig. 12.9.
8 *RCAHM-S*, 1956, no. 409; Moir, 1981, 232; Baldwin, 1985, 147.
9 *PSAS 5*, 1862–4, 48–50.
10 Burl, 1987a, 174, 177.
11 Worth, R.H., 1967, 204.
12 Worth, R.H., 1967, 397.
13 Thom, 1967, S1/2 'Nine Stones', 100.
14 Norris, R. (1983), 'A solar calendrical indicator on Dartmoor?', *PDAS 41*, 123–5; 'Megalithic observatories in Britain: real or imagined?', (in: Ruggles, 1988, 262–76).
15 *TDA 66*, 1934, 319; Worth, R.H., 1967, 400.
16 Coles, 1911, 62–71 (quotation, 70–1).
17 The quotation is given in the 1982 edition of John Aubrey's *Monumenta Britannica, II*, 792–3. The original MS reference, in the Bodleian Library, Oxford, is Top. Gen. 25, 52. For a life of Aubrey see: Powell, A., *John Aubrey and His Friends* (2nd ed.), London, 1988. For an assessment of his work, see: Hunter,

M., *John Aubrey and the Realm of Learning*, London, 1975.
18 Plot, R., *The Natural History of Staffordshire*, Oxford, 1686. 432, Chapter 10, sections 63, 64. Also in Camden's *Britannia*, 1695, 534.
19 Smith, Cecil, *St Mary and All Saints Church, Checkley. A Guide*. n.d. no loc. 1.
20 *PSAS 77*, 1942–3, 34, no. 5.
21 Henshall, 1972, 367.
22 Thom, Thom and Burl, 1990, 169.
23 MacKie, 1975, 115.
24 Henshall, 1972, 491–4.
25 Selkirk, A., 'Duntreath', *Current Archaeology 36*, 1973, 7; MacKie, 1977, 118.
26 *JRSAI 32*, 1902, 331 'Templenakilla'.
27 Evans, 1966, 129.
28 O'Nuallain, 1988, 200.
29 Lynch, A., 1982, 207.
30 Burl, 1991, 5–6.
31 Le Roux, C., *Gallia Préhistoire 22*, 1979, 526–9; *ibid 24*, 1981, 395–9; Burl, 1985, 91–2.
32 Keiller and Piggott, 1936; Smith, I.F., 1965, 176–8; Burl, 1979, 37–8.

CHAPTER TWO

1 Thom, Thom and Burl, II, 1990, 374–540.
2 Fergusson, 1872, 23–6.
3 Long, W., *Abury Illustrated*, 1858, 54; Ucko *et al*, 1991, 8.
4 Brentnall, H.C., 'The Saxon bounds of Overton', *Marlborough College Nat Hist Soc*, 1938, 116–36. For other recensions of the charter, see: *WAM 42*, 1922, 57, 'Aethelferth's Stone'; *VCH Wilts I, 1*, 1951, 196, 'Coltas Barrow'.
5 Borlase, W., 1769, 189, 85. For a life of Borlase, see: Pool. P., *William Borlase*, Truro, 1986.
6 Eudes, 1981, 85.
7 Bord, J. and C., *Atlas of Magical Britain*, London, 1990, 171; Reader's Digest, *Folklore, Myths and Legends of Britain*. London, 1973, 431.
8 Spence, L., 1917, 44–5; le Rouzic, 1939, 18–19.
9 Scouëzec, 146; Scouëzec and Masson, 112–13.
10 Martin, 1716, 8.
11 Bord (note 7), 188; Grinsell, 1976, 191.

For St Ciaran, see: Attwater, D., *The Penguin Dictionary of Saints*, Harmondsworth, 1965, 86, 'Ciaran'; St Augustine's Abbey, Ramsgate, *The Book of Saints*, London, 1989, 333, 'Kieran'.
12 Borlase (note 5), 189.
13 Camden, 1695, 808.
14 Camden, 1610, 701; ibid, 1695, 734.
15 Aubrey, 1665–93, I, 129, 32.
16 This marginal comment is partly deleted on p. 37 of the 1980 edition of Aubrey's *Monumenta Britannica, I*. It can be seen in full in the Bodleian Library: MS Gen. Top. c. 24, 34.
17 Giot, 1983, 12.
18 Piggott, S., quoted on the back dust-cover of *Monumenta Britannica II*.
19 For Stanton Drew, Rollright Stones and Stonehenge, see: Aubrey, 1665–93, I, 67; Kennet Avenue: *ibid*, 37.
20 Kendrick, T.D., *The Druids*, London, 1927, 3.
21 Piggott, S., *The Druids*, London, 1963, 157. See also the same writer: *Ancient Britons and the Antiquarian Imagination*, London, 1989, 139. For an undiminished desire to perpetuate druids as workers of marvel see: Rutherford, M., *The Druids, Magicians of the West*, Wellingborough, 1983. For seventeenth- to nineteenth-century changing views about druids, see: Owen, A.L., *The Famous Druids. A Survey of Three Centuries of English Literature on the Druids*. Oxford, 1962.
22 *Ant 61*, 1967, 175.
23 Note 10, 8–9.
24 Toland, 1726, 122–3.
25 Note 5, 201–2.
26 Stukeley, 1743, 62. For the life and work of Stukeley, see: Piggott, S., *William Stukeley. An Eighteenth-Century Antiquary*. (2nd ed), London, 1985.
27 Stukeley, 1743, 62.
28 Headrick, J. (ed), Barry, G., *History of the Orkney Isles* (2nd ed), Edinburgh, 1808.
29 For early French investigators in Brittany, see: Michell, 1982, 66–8; Giot, 1983, 12–15.
30 Wilson, 1863, I, 167.
31 *PSAS 2*, 1854–7, 382.
32 Much of the information about the

early history of Callanish came from an unpublished MS by G. and M. Ponting, 'Carnac. The documentary record', 1979.

33 Michell, 1982, 72. For the work of Dryden and Lukis, see: Atkinson, R.J.S., 'Lukis, Dryden and the Carnac megaliths', in Megaw, J.V.S. (ed), *To Illustrate the Monuments: Essays Presented to Stuart Piggott*, Leicester, 1976, 111–24. For Miln, see: Miln, 1881, 3–11 *et seq.*

34 Giot *et al*, 1979, 425; Giot, 1983, 18.

35 Lukis, 1870, 13. See also: Lukis, 1875, 16–20, 27–8.

36 Fergusson, 54–7.

37 Lockyer, 1909, 96–106. Much of Devoir's work is reported in Pontois, 1929. Full references are: *Mannus I*, 1909, 71–82; *Bull. Soc. Archéologique du Finistère 38*, 3–38; *ibid 39*, 1912, 220–39.

38 For the two reports on Callanish see: *RCAHM-S, Outer Hebrides*, 1928, 24–7, no. 89; Lockyer, 1909, 344, 377.

39 For the two quotations, see: Lockyer, 1909, 108, 467.

40 Somerville, 1923, 200, 204. For Pluckanes, see: O'Nuallain, 1984a, 33, no. 58; for Drumhallagh: Lacy, 20–2, no. 23.

41 Lockyer, 1909, 161; Worth, R.H., 1967, 455–6.

42 Emmett, 94, 101. For his Gazetteer see pp. 112–13.

43 Thom, A.S., 'A personal note about my late father, Alexander Thom', in: Ruggles, 1988a, 3–13. 5.

44 Merlet, R. (1935), 'Valeur métrique du pied employé en Gaule, comme mesure de longeur, avant l'ère chrétienne', *Soc. d'Histoire et d'Archéologie de Bretagne 16*, 133–45.

45 Thom, 1967, 136–41, Table 122.1. For the statistical and astronomical views of Alexander Thom see his papers and books listed in the Bibliography.

46 Giot, 1988, 323.

CHAPTER THREE

1 Mersey, R., *The Hills of Cork and Kerry*, 1987, 130.

2 Burl, 1987a, 130–4, 175–7. See also; Patton, 1992.

3 *PPS 42*, 1976, 126.

4 *Annual Excavations Report*, HMSO, 1968, 13. Mortimer, J., *Forty Years' Researches in British and Saxon Burial Mounds in East Yorkshire*, 1905, 336–8, no. 209.

5 For the Poole barrows, see: Grinsell, L.V., *Dorset Barrows*, 1959, 48, 126, Poole 36, 37; *PPS 18*, 1952, 148–59.

6 For the Swarkeston barrow, see: *DAJ 80*, 1960, 17.

7 For Barrow 75 on the Noordse Veld, see: de Laet, S.J., *The Low Countries*, 1958, 119–20.

8 Aubrey, 1665–93, I, 76.

9 For the belief that bluestones lay near Stonehenge, see: Burl, 'Geoffrey of Monmouth and the Stonehenge bluestones', *WAM 79*, 1984, 178–83; ibid,

1987a, 130–5. Also: *PPS 57 (2)*, 1991, 103–58.

10 *PPS 47*, 1981, 87–135.

11 C-14 dates from the pit-alignment: 1790±50 bc (BM-1650); 1820±50 bc (BM-1652); 1655±80 bc (BM-1653). From Milfield South henge: 1740±80 bc (HAR-3068); 1590±100 bc (HAR-3040); 1950±110 bc (HAR-3071). The mean of the six is c. 1758±78 bc. Calibrated this would become approximately 2050 BC.

12 The excavation of the Arbor Low 'avenue' by H.St.G. Gray is reported in *Arch 58*, 1903, 482–4. For the source of the circle-stones, see: A. Bemrose, *DAJ 33*, 1911, 44.

13 Burl, 1987a, 220.

14 Burl, 1987b, 14–20.

15 Burl, 1985, 14.

16 Thom, Thom and Burl, II, 1990, 380–7.

17 For Kermarquer, see: *Bull. Soc. Poly. Morbihan*, July, 1969, 1–7; Burl, 1985, 117. For St-Samson-sur-Rance, see: Giot *et al*, 1979, 386–7; Burl, 1985, 43–4. For re-used menhirs, see: le Roux, 1985, 71–5; l'Helgouach, J., 'Monuments mégalithiques de Bretagne', in: *Probleme der Megalith-gräberforschung*, Berlin, 83–111, 96–9; Burl, 1985, 174 for references.

18 Camden, 1695, 29–30; Aubrey, 1665–93, II, 848–9. The geometrical formations are recorded in *TDA 37*, 1905, 375–97; *TDA 38*, 1906, 538–52.

19 l'Helgouach, J., *Les Sépultures Mégalithiques en Armorique*, Vannes, 1964, 14, 15; Giot *et al*, 1979, 172.

20 Burl, 1985, 87.

21 Burl, 1987a, 155–7.

22 Evans, 1966, 196; Harbison, 1970, 236; Stout, 1984, 18.

23 Kermode and Herdman, 30.

24 Shetland: Fojut, 58; Belle Île: Burl, 1985, 116, no. 142; Scillies: Ashbee, P., *Ancient Scilly*, 1974, 149; Channel Islands: Johnston, 63–136; Arran: *The Ancient Monuments of Arran*, HMSO, 1973, 33; Isle of Man: Kermode and Herdman, 30.

CHAPTER FOUR

1 For the relationship of the Girdle Stanes and Ballynoe to the Lake District circles, see: Burl, 1976, 57–9.

2 Thom and Thom, 1977, plans 1A (Ménec), 5 (Kerlescan).

3 Burl, 1979, 114.

4 Burgess, 1980, 234–7; Darvill, 1987, 75–7.

5 Bradley, R., *The Social Foundations of Prehistoric Britain*, London, 1984. 34–5.

6 Harbison, 1988, 34–5; O'Kelly, M.J., 1989, 65–7; Mitchell, F., 1990, 134–5.

7 Baillie, in: *Curr Arch 117*, 1989, 310. See also: *Arch Ire 2 (2)*, 1988, 71–4.

8 Howe, G.M., *Man, Environment and Disease in Britain*, 1972, 88.

9 For C-14 assays: Stonehenge, Burl, 1987a, 247, 'Dates'; for Balfarg, Llandegai and Stenness, Harding, 1987,

353, 331, 391; Lochmaben Stane, Crone, 1983, 18; Tossen-Keler, *L'Anthropologie 72*, 1968, 35; Giot *et al*, 1979, 273–6.

10 For possible female sacrifices in henges and stone circles, see: Hutton, 1991, 89–90.

11 For the developments in prehistoric astronomy, see: Burl, 'Pi in the sky', in: Heggie, 1981, 141–69; Burl, 1983. For Clava Cairns, see, Burl, 'By the light of the cinerary moon; chambered tombs and the astronomy of death', in: Ruggles and Whittle, 1982, 257–65. For the Salisbury Plain earthen long barrows: Burl, 1987a, 26–8.

12 Stukeley, 1776, 48.

13 Cowper, B., *TCWAAS 34*, 1934, 91–100.

14 Burl, 1988b, 181–4. An archaeological association between Lake District circles and stone axes was mooted as long ago as 1932 by R.G. Collingwood, *TCWAAS 33*, 1933, 178.

15 Thom, 1971, 71–3.

16 Burl, 'Intimations of numeracy in the Neolithic and Bronze Age Societies of the British Isles', *Arch J 133*, 1976, 9–32; Burl, 1988b, 190.

17 Barnatt, 1989, II, 364.

18 Lukis, 1885, Plates I, II.

19 For Drombeg, see: Fahy, E., *JCHAS 64*, 1959, 7, 25; Bohonagh, ibid, *JCHAS 66*, 1961, 94. For the Scottish-Irish connections, see: Burl, 1976, 217–18.

20 For Woodhenge, see: Cunnington, M., *Woodhenge*, 1929, 7; Gorsey Bigbury, *Proc Bristol Univ Spel Soc 11*, 1967, 119; Priddy, *ibid*, 109; Broomrigg, *TCWAAS 35*, 1935, 78; Balfarg, *PSAS 111*, 1981, 70.

21 Aubrey, 1665–93, I, 114; MS Top. Gen. c. 24, 70, 71, Plate XII.

22 Dymond, C.W., *TCWAAS 11 (O.S.)*, 1890–1, 197.

23 *Gazetteer of the British Isles*, Bartholomew, London, 1972. For the population figures, see under individual towns.

24 Aubrey, 1665–93, I, 113; Stukeley, 1776, II, 44; Pennant, T., *First Tour in Scotland*, 1769, 257; Dymond (Note 22), 195.

25 For the average diameter of a stone circle in Britain and Ireland, see: Burl, 1976, 40. For the average number of stones in a ring, see: ibid, 374–5.

26 Christison, D., *PSAS 31*, 1896–7, 288; Thom, Thom and Burl, 1980, 298–9, G7/5.

27 *PPS 36*, 1960, 314.

28 Lambrick, 1988, 121–4.

29 For the 1920 excavation, see: *Ant J 1*, 1921, 36. For the dating of the Slaughter Stone, see: Atkinson, 1979, 30–2, 69, 71, 77.

30 Jones, I., *The Most Notable Antiquity of Great Britain, Vulgarly Called Stone-Heng*, London, 1655, 57. Stone, E.H., *The Stones of Stonehenge*, London, 1924, 118–24.

31 Smith, I.F., 'The chronology of British stone implements', *Stone Axe Studies*,

1979, 13–22; Burl, 1988b, 183–4.
32 For the C-14 determination from the Lochmaben Stone, see: Crone, 1983, 18.
33 Burl, 1988b, 184.

CHAPTER FIVE

1 The statistics are extracted from *Stone Axes Studies, II,* 1988, 143–87. Each located source of axe-production has been allotted a Group number, Group I being a source near Land's End, Group VI, Great Langdale, Group VII, Graig Lwyd in North Wales. Groups I to V, XVI, XVII, XIX are the sources for Cornish axes; VIII, IX, XIII for S.W. Wales; Lake District, Groups VI, XI; North Wales, VII.
For distribution patterns of Cornish and Cumbrian stone axes, see: Cummins, W., *Ant 48,* 1974, 203–4; ibid, *PPS 46,* 1980, 58–9.
2 Dymond, 1896, 343, 35, plan, 40.
3 Avebury: Aubrey, 1665–93, I, 37; MS Top Gen. c. 24, 34; Stonehenge: Burl, 1987a, 185.
4 Smith, I.F., 1965, 206, 208–9; Stukeley, 1743, 25, 30.
5 Burl, 1979, 179, 188.
6 *WAM 68,* 1973, 42–56; Burl, 1987a, 140–1, 220.
7 Keiller and Piggott, 1936, 418; Thom and Thom, 1976, 195.
8 Smith, I.F., 1965, 229–43. Cunnington, M., *WAM 45,* 1931, 329; Bradley, 1993, 59–60.
9 *UJA 42,* 1979, 17.
10 For stone circle D at Lacra, see: *TCWAAS 48,* 1948, 5–13; Waterhouse, 1985, 49–52. For the collared urn: Longworth, 1984, 168, no. 213, 'Millom Without'.
11 Moor Divock: *TCWAAS 8 (O.S.),* 1885–6, 323–47; Waterhouse, 1985, 117–22. For the food-vessel, see: Abercromby, Hon. J., *A Study of the Bronze Age Pottery of Great Britain and Ireland, I,* 1912, 158, no. 164, 'Askham'; Greenwell, W., *British Barrows,* 1877, 400–1. For the urn, see: *PSAS 4,* 1860–2, 446.
12 For the Shap avenue, see: Clare, 1978. Also: Camden, 1695, 808; Stukeley, 1776, 62; for its serpentine course, Stukeley, 1743, 42; Colt Hoare, see: Thompson, M.W., *The Journeys of Sir Richard Colt Hoare, 1793–1810,* 1983, 138. Further destruction: *Gents Mag I,* 1824, 3. For 'male and female stones', see: Clare, T., *Archaeological Sites of the Lake District,* 1981, 16.
13 Kennet Avenue: Keiller and Piggott, 1936; Smith, I.E., 1965, 206–16, 229–42.
14 Gray, H.St.G., *The Avebury Excavations, 1909–22,* 1935, plate 43.
15 Cunnington, M., *WAM 38,* 1913, 1–8.
16 For Stukeley's falsifications: Piggott, S., *William Stukeley. An Eighteenth Century Antiquary,* 1950, 129; ibid, 1985, (2nd ed.) 106–7; Burl, 1979, 192–3. For doubts about the Beckhampton Avenue: Ucko *et al,* 194–9.

17 Stukeley, 1723, 97.
18 Geo-physical survey: Ucko *et al,* 196–9.
19 Twining, T., *Avebury in Wiltshire. The Remains of a Roman Work,* 1723, 15. There is a likelihood that Twining and Stukeley shared the acquaintance of the Earl of Winchelsea and of Lord Hertford. It is just possible, therefore, that the antiquarians met. See: Long, W., *Abury Illustrated,* 1858, 58–61.
20 Beckhampton Avenue: Stukeley, 1743, 34–6. Vatcher, F. and L. *The Avebury Monuments,* 1976, 38. Another eighteenth-century eye-witness, John Clements, a grocer at Avebury, 'could clearly point it out', *WAM 17,* 1878, 333, note 1.
21 Aubrey, 1665–93, I, 67, 76; Stukeley, 1723, 59; ibid, 1740, 13; Gale, R., *PSAL 7,* 1877, 268–71.
22 Pitts, M., *Archaeoastronomy Bulletin 4 (2),* 1981, 17–19. For the geo-physical survey: *PPS 48,* 1982, 92–3.
23 Little Mayne: Gale, R., in: Lukis, 1883, 128; *RCAHM-E, Dorset, II, S.E. (3),* 1970, 513.
24 Hampton Down: *PDNHAS 88,* 1967, 122–7; Rempstone: *PDNHAS 81,* 1959, 114–16.
25 Pearce, S., *Devon in Prehistory,* Exeter, 1978, 35.
26 Rev. John Bathurst Deane, 'Observations on Dracontia', *Arch 25,* 1834, 188–229. 200.
27 Burl, 1976, 107.
28 Emmett, 1979, 100.
29 *PDAS 39,* 1981, 33–6; ibid *44,* 1986, 166–7.
30 Fleming, 1988, 95.
31 For the spacing between rows at Carnac and the straight segments, see: Thom and Thom, 1978 – Ménec, 69, 70; Kermario, 77, 82.
32 Giot, *et al* 1979, 409–11.
33 For Île Beniguet, see: Gilbert, 1962, 225, no. 16; Pontois, 126.
34 For connections between Brittany and the British Isles see: Burl, 1987a, 147–9, 155–7. For pottery, see: Fox, 1973, 36; Ashbee, P., *Ancient Scilly,* 1974, 257. For chambered tombs: Fox, 58, 62; Ashbee, 285. For stone axes, see: le Roux, C.-T., in: *Stone Axe Studies,* 1979, 49–56; *Stone Axe Studies, II,* 1988, 274, Group X distribution. For trade in general: Fox, 81; Ashbee, 273; Darvill, 1987, 71. *PPS 54,* 1988, 203–21. 212; *PPS 56,* 1990, 291–4.
35 Carpenter, R., *Beyond the Pillars of Hercules,* 1973, 205. The quotation is from *Les Guides Bleus. Bretagne,* 1924, 647.
36 Carpenter (note 35), 207; Cary, M. and Warmington, E.H. *The Ancient Explorers,* 1963, 48–9, 55, 169–70. See also: Sir L. Scott, 'The colonisation of Scotland . . .', *PPS 17,* 1951, 20.
37 For Ty ar c'Huré, see: Pontois, 105, 115, 117; Gilbert, 1962, 225; Niel, 151–2. For Landaoudec: Pontois, 115–16; Sitwell, 1930, 123 'Kerdouanec'.
38 Kergonan: *Arch 25,* 1834, 212; Minot,

16, 17. Kerpenhir: Kergal, 1981, 55–7, 72, no.13.
39 Burl, 1988a, 56–7. See also, Burl, 1985, for the Alignements du Moulin, *et al.*
40 For early Brittany-Ireland links, see: Herity, M., *Irish Passage Graves,* 1974, 189, 192ff. For Giot: *Ant 49,* 1975, 233.
41 For *allées-couvertes* and wedge-tombs, see: Herity and Eogan, 1977, 121; O'Kelly, M., 1989, 115–22; Harbison, 1988, 91, 101.
42 *Stone Axe Studies, II,* 1988, 261–2.
43 Clarke, 1970, II, 540, 542, Map 6, 562.
44 Case, H. *UJA 32,* 1969, 22.
45 Broomend of Crichie, see: *PSAS 7,* 1866–8, 110–13; *ibid 18,* 1883–4, 319–25; *ibid 54,* 1919–20, 154–72. For its beakers, see: *PSAS 40,* 1905–6, 27; Clarke, 1970, II, 510. The chronology of beakers varies from region to region and no clearcut time-scale can be offered. See: Kinnes, I. *et al,* 'Radiocarbon dating and British beakers. The British Museum programme', *SAR 8,* 1991, 35–68. For the cultural problems, see: Burgess, 1980, 62–8. For north-east Scottish beakers, see: Shepherd, I.A.G., *Powerful Pots; Beakers in North-Eastern Prehistory,* 1986, 24–8.
46 *PSAS 54,* 1919–20, 168. For Cumbrian axes: *Stone Axe Studies, II,* 1988, 87, 238.
47 Wilson, 1863, I, 208–9.
48 *Catalogue of the National Museum of Scotland,* 1892, 59.
49 Details of stone heights and other statistics about the Callanish avenue come from the regrettably-unpublished documentary record by G. and M. Ponting, 1979, Appendix B, Fig. 9, Table 2.
50 *Stone Axe Studies, II,* 1988, 238.
51 Anderson-Smith, W., *Lewisiana,* 1874, 111.
52 Pinkerton, J., *An Enquiry into the History of Scotland,* 1814; Wise, T.A., *JBAA,* 1877, 158–69; Lethbridge, T., *The Legend of the Sons of God,* 1973, 36–7.
53 For detailed explanations of solar and lunar cycles and the question of alignments in megalithic monuments, see: Thom, 1967; ibid, 1971; Wood, J.E., 1978. For an elementary primer: Burl, 1983, 16–20.
54 Wort, R., *Stonehenge and Its Future.* Leeds, 1987, 12.
55 For the astronomical architecture of Newgrange, see: Patrick, J., 'Mid-winter sunrise at Newgrange', *Nature 249,* 1974, 517–19; O'Kelly, M.J., *Newgrange, Archaeology, Art and Legend.* London, 1982, 93–100, 123–6. For the entrance slab at Maes Howe, see: Henshall, 1963, 220. For its astronomical 'window', see: Burl, 1981, 124–6.
56 For medicine-wheels, see: Krupp, E.C., *Echoes of the Ancient Skies.* New York, 1983, 142–8.
57 Astronomical deductions: Lockyer, 1909, 344; Somerville, 1923, 203; Thom, A., *Vistas in Astronomy 7,* 1966, 49, H1/1; Hawkins, 1966, 185; Thom, 1967, 125; ibid, 1971, 68.

58 Ponting, G. and M., 1984, 52.
59 Diodorus Siculus, Book II (continued) 35–IV, 58, Loeb Classical Library, 1989. Ch. 47, 37–41; Hawkins, 1966, 185.
60 The area of Sicily is 9922 square miles. Other areas in square miles: British mainland, 88,546; Harris and Lewis, 824; Outer Hebrides, 1119; Skye, 643; Hebridean archipelago, including Skye, 8852; Orkneys, 377; Shetlands, 553; Greenland, 839,781; Iceland, 39,771; Ireland (North and Republic), 32,579. The figures are from *The Cambridge Encyclopaedia*, Cambridge, 1990.
61 It is often assumed that Pytheas's voyage was made between 310 and 306 BC when the Carthaginians had abandoned their blockade of the Straits of Gibraltar. See: Cary and Warmington (Note 36), 48; also, L. Casson, *The Ancient Mariners*, Princeton, 1991, 124–5. Carpenter's (Note 35) argument in favour of a time between 240 and 238 BC is a stronger one. The purpose of the exploration seems to have been to discover sources of British tin for the benefit of the merchants of Marseilles.
62 Acceptance of Stonehenge as the temple has ranged from the cautious to the confident. See: Hawkins, 1966, 128–31; Stover, L. and Kraig, B., *Stonehenge: the Indo-European Inheritance*, 1978, 78,130; Ashbee, P., *The Ancient British*, 1978, 154; Chippindale, C., *Stonehenge Complete*, 1983, 83. For Pytheas, see: (Note 35) Carpenter, 143–98; (Note 36) Cary and Warmington, 47–56.
    For the various phases of Stonehenge, its changing astronomy, and its abandonment, see: Burl, 1987a.
63 Thom, A.S., in: Ruggles, 1988a, 5.
64 Brown, P.L., *Megaliths, Myths and Men*, 1977, 113.

CHAPTER SIX

1 For the antlers, see: *Ant J 5*, 1925, 23; *Nature 275*, 1978, 50. For the skeleton, see: *WAM 78*, 1983, 22. For the C-14 assays, see: *Ant 41*, 1967, 64.
2 *WAM 68*, 1973, 42–56; *Ant 50*, 1976, 239–40.
3 Renfrew, C., *Archaeology and Language*, 1987, 86–94; Mallory, J., *In Search of the Indo-Europeans*, 1989, 168.
4 For revisionist views of beakers, see: Burgess, C. and Miket, R., 'The beaker phenomenon: some suggestions', in: Burgess and Miket (eds), *Settlement and Economy in the Third and Second Millennia BC*, 1976, 309–23; Mercer, R. (ed), *Beakers in Britain and Europe*, 1977; Harrison, 1980; Burgess, 1980, 62–70.
5 Burl, 1987a, 111.
6 Abercromby, Hon. J., *A Study of the Bronze Age Pottery of Great Britain and Ireland*, I, 1912, I, 9–92.
7 For interpretations of beaker pottery, see: Abercromby, 1912 (Note 6); Piggott, S., 'Abercromby and after . . .', in: *Culture and Environment*, 1963, 53–91; Clarke,

1970; Lanting and van der Waals, *Palaeohistoria 12*, 1972, 20–46; Case, H., 'The beaker culture in Britain and Ireland', in (ed. Mercer, R.), *Beakers in Britain and Europe*, 1977, 71–101; Harrison, 1980, 71–3.
8 Smith, I.F., 1965, 210.
9 *WAM 53*, 1950, 311–27. 323.
10 Hawley, W., *Ant J 4*, 1924, 30; Burl, 1987a, 140.
11 Lockyer, 1909, 314; Burl, 1987a, 64–79.
12 Longworth, 1984, 168, no. 213 'Millom'. Primary, NW IIIB.
13 Gibson, A. and Woods, A., *Prehistoric Pottery for the Archaeologist*, Leicester, 1990, 173–6.
14 Burl, 1987a, 99–101.
15 For the 'Perth Yard' of 3 ft½ (96 cm), see: Burl, 1988a, 7–8; for the 'Beaker Yard' of 2 ft 4¾ (73 cm), Burl, 1987a, 124; for the 'Megalithic Yard' of 2 ft 8¹⁶⁄₂₅ (0.829 m), see: Thom, A., 'The megalithic unit of length', *J.R. Stat. Soc. 125*, 1962, 243–51; Thom, 1967, 34–55; Davis, 1986. For the 'Druid cubit' of 20.8 ins (52.8 cm) see: Stukeley, 1723, 16; ibid, 1740, 11.
16 Mohen, 1989, 168–82.
17 Joussaume, *Dolmens for the Dead*, London, 1987, 103.
18 Note 17, 102.
19 Smith, R.W., *PPS 50*, 1984, 99–120.
20 Clare, 1978, 10.
21 Atkinson, R.J.C., 'Neolithic engineering', *Ant 35*, 1961, 292–9.
22 Note 19, 111.
23 Crossing, 1912, 36.
24 Bowles, Rev. W.L., *Hermes Britannicus*, 1828, 56; Stevens, E.T., *Gentleman's Magazine*, II, 1866, 68.
25 Hartshorne, Rev. C.H., *Salopia Antiqua*, 1841, 30, 31, 32.
26 Dames, M., *The Avebury Cycle*, 1977, 85, 144.
27 Ucko *et al*, 189.
28 Stukeley, 1740, 36.
29 Burl, 1979, 126–8.
30 Aubrey, 1665–93, I, 50; Stukeley, 1743, 33.
31 Smith, I.F., 1965, 207.
32 *WAM 43*, 1926, 341–3.
33 Note 31, 208.
34 Aubrey, 1665–93, I, plan, 51; Pepys, *The Diary of Samuel Pepys, IX. 1668–9*, 1976, 240–1; Cunnington, M., *WAM 45*, 1931, Plate 1; Note 31, 208.
35 *Arch 18*, 1861, 31; Simpson, 1867, 22–3, Plate XVII, fig. 4; *RCAHM-E*, 1936, 206, Stone (c); Camden, 1695, 808.
36 Keiller and Piggott, 1936, 420; Smith, I.F., 1965, 223.
37 Stonehenge: Burl, 1987a, 140.
38 Merrivale, see: Wood, J.E. and Penny, A., 'A megalithic observatory on Dartmoor', *Nature 275*, 1975, 205–7.
39 For Shap, see: *Arch J 18*, 1861, 28.

CHAPTER SEVEN

1 Broad Field: *Arch 10*, 1792, 105; *Arch J 27*, 1870, 200. Grey Yauds: Waterhouse,

1985, 151; *TCWAAS 35*, 1935, 171. Other rows: Taylor, M.W., 1886, 342–3.
2 Waterhouse, 1985, 83–5.
3 Burl, 1988b, 196–203.
4 Varley, W., *Cheshire Before the Romans*, 1964, 15.
5 George Borrow. *Wild Wales. Its People, Language and Scenery*. 1955, 345. The Seven Wonders are:

    Pistyll Rhaiadr and Wrixham Steeple,
    Snowdon's mountain without people;
    Overton Yewtrees, St Winifrid Wells,
    Llangollen Bridge and Gresford Bells.

6 Dyer, 1981, 360.
7 Grimes, 1963, 121.
8 Thom, 1967, 100. W6/2.
9 Burl, 1976, 213ff.
10 Ross, A., *The Pagan Celts*, 1986, 149.
11 Note 7, 120, fig. 23.
12 Note 9, 263.
13 Lynch, F., *UJA 42*, 1979, 17.
14 Evans, 1966, 114; *JRSAI 4*, 1876–8, 499–512.
15 Worth, R.H., 1967, 237.
16 Pettit, 156.
17 Note 15, 241.
18 Emmett, 103.
19 Note 15, 210.
20 Note 15, 235.
21 Note 16, 129.
22 Crossing, 95.
23 Atkinson, R.J.C., *Ant 35*, 1961, 297.
24 Pettit, 70; Worth, R.H., 1967, 99–132; Hamond, in Maxfield, V.A. (ed), 1979, 146–75.
25 B/W beaker: *TDA 29*, 1897, 67–71; Clarke, 1970, II, 479, no. 156 'Chagford Common'. S2/W beaker: *TDA 30*, 1898, 107–11; Clarke, 1970, II, 479, no. 158. ibid, I, 217, 218: remains of a wooden-hafted, pommelled bronze dagger was found with the beaker.
26 Rogers, 1947, 123.
27 Fleming, 1988, 103, 105.
28 Fleming, A., *PPS 44*, 1978, 109; Fleming, 1988, 8, 21, 42, 107.
29 Durrance and Laming (eds). *The Geology of Devon*, 1982, 126.
30 *TDA 64*, 1932, 380–2. See also: *TDA 120*, 1988, 91–5.
31 Lethbridge, T, *The Legend of the Sons of God*, London, 1973, 38.
32 Pettit, 132. Lockyer, 1909, 161–2. 'Row 15 points approximately to the circle at the head of Row 14', Worth, R.H., 1967, 209.
33 *PPS 55*, 1989, 88.
34 Lockyer, 1909, 145–65, 481–7.
35 Thom, 1967, 17.
36 Note 15, 452–7.
37 Note 15, 243.
38 Note 18, 101.
39 Note 18, 101.
40 Note 15, 216.
41 Note 15, 215.
42 Note 34, 108, 117, 147, 153–4, 483–4.
43 Note 34, 156.
44 Wood, J.E., 1978, 131.
45 Penny, A. and Wood, J.E., 'A megalithic observatory on Dartmoor', *Nature 257*,

205-7.
46 Note 44, 133-4.
47 Prior, 1872, 350.
48 Note 15, 214.
49 Fergusson, 1872, 54.
50 Note 18, 111, Column 15.
51 Note 16, 133.
52 Fox, 1973, 68, 74.
53 Camden, 1610, 203.
54 For Llanfechell, see: Baynes, 51, 65-6; Elgee, F., 1930, 105-6.
55 Chanter and Worth, 1905, 1906; RCAHM, see: Quinnell and Dunn.
56 Giot et al, 1979, 409-10.
57 Eardley-Wilmot, 1983, 24-5, 32, 43.
58 Stone, E.H.S., *The Stones of Stonehenge*. London, 1924, 30, Pl. 9.
59 Chanter and Worth, 1905, 389.
60 Note 59, 386. For details of Mattocks Down, see: Grinsell, 1970, 44-6, 158; Todd, M., *The South West to AD 1000*, 1987, 105-6.
6l Myatt, 1988, 300.

CHAPTER EIGHT

1 *Ant 12*, 1938, 461-2; *PPS 18 (1)*, 1952, 69; Eogan, 1964, 31-3.
2 Eogan, 1964.
3 Fleming, 1988, 100.
4 Note 3, 94, 97.
5 Crossing, 209.
6 Note 5, 374.
7 *PPS 35*, 1969, 214; Simmons, I. and Tooley, M. (eds), *The Environment in British Prehistory*, 1981, 243-5; Fleming, 1988, 110-11.
8 Worth, R.H., 1967, 212.
9 Toulson, S., *The Moors of the South-West*, II, 1984, 24; J. Galsworthy, *The Apple Tree*; Crossing, 295.
10 Mee, A., *The King's England. Devon*, 1938, 213. 'Harford'.
11 Buckingham, W.A., *Beliefs and Religious Symbols in the Bronze Age of England*, 1948, Malvern. 37.
12 *TDA 61*, 1929, 274.
13 Baring-Gould, 1907, 62, 60.
14 Eardley-Wilmot, *Exmoor Review 20*, 1979, 65.
15 Chanter and Worth, 1905, 397; 1906, 544.
16 Culbone Stone: *West Somerset Free Press*, 18 January 1940; Grinsell, 1970, 106; *Exmoor Review 24*, 1983, 67-9; Eardley-Wilmot, 1983, 33-4.
17 Mee, A., *The King's England. Somerset*, 1940, 153.
18 *Meyn Mamvro 14*, 1991, 13.
19 Burl, 1983, 34.
20 Hencken, H. O'N., *The Archaeology of Cornwall and Scilly*, 1932; Barnatt, 1982, 187.
21 Grinsell, 1976, 90.
22 Fraser, in the *Golden Bough. Pt. VIII*, 1912, 391, cites many instances of nine being treated as a special number including nine different kinds of wood being burned in Beltane and Midsummer bonfires, and of nine sorts of flowers being placed under a pillow on Mid-summer Eve for dreaming of the person

a girl would marry. See also: Grinsell, 1976, 61-3
23 Note 5, 222-3.
24 Camden, 1695, 5, 21; Aubrey, 1665-93, I, 70, 104-5, 226; Toland, c. 1726, 124-5; Stukeley, 1740, 54; Borlase, W., 1769, 205. For late fables about pre-historic stones see: Burl, 1991, 12-13.
25 Lockyer, 1909, 293; Thom, 1967, 100, S1/9.
26 Thom, Thom and Burl, 1990, I, 47.
27 Burl, 1976, 257; ibid, *Prehistoric Stone Circles*, 3rd ed., 1988, 20.
28 *RCAHM-W, Carmarthen*, 1917, 206, no. 604.
29 Thom, 1967, 159; ibid, 1971, 73-4; Thom, Thom and Burl, 1990, II, 362-3.
30 Parc y Meirw: *RCAHM-W. Pembrokeshire*, 1925, 173, no. 507; no luck, Grinsell, 1976, 250; megalithic tombs, *Megalithic Enquiries in the West of Britain*, 1969, 146; ghost, Barber, C., 1986, 11.
31 Thom, Thom and Burl, 1990, II, 366.
32 Taylor, M.W., 1886, 342, 343.
33 *TCWAAS 35*, 1935, 170-1.
34 Leland, VIII, fol. 69b; Camden, 1695, 808.
35 Hall, G., *Gent's Mag, Archaeology II*, 1886, 74; Clare, 1978, 12.
36 *Gent's Mag, Archaeology II*, 1886, 321, Note 8.
37 Deane, *Arch 25*, 1834, 201; Stukeley, 1776, II, 42.
38 Clare, T., *Archaeological Sites in the Lake District*, 1981, 16.
39 *Arch J 18*, 1861, 31; Simpson, 1867, 22-3, Plate XVII, fig. 4.
40 Hall, G., *Gent's Mag, Archaeology II*, 1886, 75.
41 Pilcher, 1969, 83. For the excavation report of Beaghmore, see: May, 1953.
42 May, 1953, 177-9, 192. For the dating of Tievebulliagh axes, see: Smith, I.F., in *Stone Axe Studies, I*, 1979, 14, 19-20.
43 O'Riordain, 1964, 88. Beaghmore is not mentioned in the first edition of *Antiquities of the Irish Countryside*, 1942.
44 *Ancient Monuments of Northern Ireland. Vol I. In State Care*, 1966, 103.
45 McConkey, 1987, Figs. 15, 16.
46 Thom, A.S., 1980, 17. Table 2. Solar lines.
47 Note 46, 16.
48 Note 46, 18.
49 Note 41, 85-6.
50 May, 1953, 183-4.
51 Note, 50, 184.
52 Thom, 1967, 151-5; Burl, 1987b, 11-12.
53 Ruggles, 1984, 271, 275-6, 305. For similar declination peaks of ±22°, see: Thom, 1967, 102, Fig. 8.1, 110.
54 Note, 50, 177, 184.
55 Mahr, A., *PPS 3*, 1937, 363.
56 Stout, 1984, 18.
57 Scott, J.G., *South-West Scotland*, 1966, 38.
58 Burl, 1985, 14, 25-8.
59 Lockyer, 1909: on Gaillard, 97; on Devoir, 100; on Breton alignments, 485-7. Also: Pontois, 1929, 95-121. For

Morbihan: Gaillard, F., 'L'astronomie préhistorique', *Les Sciences Populaires*, 1890. For Finistère: Devoir, A., 'Les grands ensembles mégalithiques de la presqu'île de Crozon...', *Bulletin de la Société Archéologique du Finistère 38*. 1911, 3-38.
60 Pontois, 1929, 111-15; Lockyer, 1909, 103-4.
61 Green, M., *The Sun-Gods of Ancient Europe*, 1991, 52-4; Gelling, P. and Davidson, H.E., *The Chariot of the Gods*, 1969, 27ff, 57-8; Burl, 1987a, 205-6.
62 Worth, R.H., 1967, 210, 401.
63 'Beaker' sherd at Drizzlecombe: Rogers, E.H., *Trans and Proc Torquay N.H.S. 8*, 1941-2, 182; also, Note 62, 193; Pettit, 160; Fox, 1973, 74.
64 *TDA 25*, 1893, 545; Crossing, 435.
65 Dyer, 1981, 343; Burl, 1976, 20.
66 Note 62, 210; Pettit, 159.
67 Note 62, 212.

CHAPTER NINE

1 Carnac: le Rouzic, 1939, 17-18; Caithness: Gunn, 1915, 347.
2 Thom and Thom, 1978, 63, 93.
3 Thom, 1971, 91-105.
4 Fleming, 59.
5 Eardley-Wilmot, 1983, 31-2.
6 Whybrow, 1970, 11.
7 Pettit, 102-3.
8 Baring-Gould, 62.
9 Crossing, 213.
10 Note 7, 213.
11 Emmett, 97.
12 Note 7, 153. See also: Worth, R.H., 1967, 219-22.
13 Henshall, 1963, Maps 6, 7, 8. For Caithness, see: Davidson, J. and Henshall, A., *The Chambered Cairns of Caithness*, 1991, 14-16.
14 MacKie, E.W., *PPS 31*, 1965, 99.
15 For Cordiner, see: Maclagan, C., *The Hill-Forts, Stone Circles and Other Structural Remains of Ancient Scotland*, 1875, 106; Anderson, 1886, 126; Gunn, 1915, 348.
16 Garrywhin: Anderson, 1868, 503. The beaker/food-vessel problem is not resolved by reference to Anderson's original report in *Memoirs Anthr Soc 2*, 1865-6, 226, which merely described the vessel as 'fragments of an urn, with the twisted string ornamentation'. Learable Hill: Anderson, 1886, 126.
17 Thom, 1967, 157.
18 Note 3, 95.
19 Brown, P.L., *Megaliths, Myths and Men*, 1976, 204.
20 Note 3, 19, 85.
21 Wood, J.E., 1978, 114-29; Thom, 1971, 83-95. For other discussions of the extrapolation theory, see: Heggie, D.C., *Ant 46*, 1972, 43-8; Heggie, 1981, 98-100, 192-5, 206-8.
22 Note 3, 94.
23 For a plan of Borgie, see: Myatt, 1988, fig. 12.17.
24 For plans of Badanloch and Kinbrace: Note 23, figs. 12.15, 12.14.

25 Kinbrace: Note 23, fig. 12.14.
26 For Garrywhin, Learable Hill, Torms-dale, Upper Dounreay: Note 23, figs. 12.5, 12.13, 12.10, 12.11.
27 For two plans of the Loch of Yarrows (Battle Moss), one with a grid super-imposed, the other showing the effects of solifluction, see: Thom, 1971, 98, fig. 9.7; Ruggles, 1981, 192, fig. 4.5 shows the two sets of three lines more clearly.
28 Thom, 1967, 157.
29 Myatt, 1988, 152, fig. 12.12.
30 For the sea route, see: Scott, Sir L., *PPS 17 (1)*, 1951, 33. For the English origin of brochs, see: Scott, Sir L., *PPS 13*, 1947, 21–9; MacKie, E.W., *PPS 31*, 1965, 134–7. For cautionary words, see: Ritchie, J.N.G., *Brochs of Scotland*, 1988, 39–42.
31 Note 23, 303.
32 Note 23, 314–15.
33 Note, 23, 303.
34 Miln, 1881, 67.
35 For Alexander Thom at Carnac, see: Daniel, G., *Some Small Harvest*, 1986, 407. Also: Thom, A.S. and Motz, H. in Ruggles, 1988, 9–10, and 19–20 respectively.
36 Lukis, 1875, 26.
37 Thom and Thom, 1977.
38 For Cambry, see: Giot, 1983, 8; For Mahé: Service and Bradbery, 56.
39 Stukeley, 1743, 33.
40 Giot *et al*, 1979, 422.
41 Giot, 1960, 123.
42 For megalithic horseshoes, 'fers aux chevaux', in Brittany, see: Burl, 1985, 25, 26, 40, 46, 92, 111, 114, 141, 164.
43 Briard, J. and Giot, P.-R., *L'Anthro-pologie 72 (1.2)*, 1968, 21, 35; Giot *et al*, 1979, 273–6.
44 Le Rouzic, 1930, 13–30, Plates 1–20; Burl, 1976, 130–4.
45 Tertres tumulaires, see: Giot, 1960, 36–42; l'Helgouach, 'Les tertres tumulaires', in: Giot *et al*, 1979, 212–18; Burl, 1985, 14, 17.
46 Kersolan: Abri, 56–7, no. 19; Giot *et al*, 1979, 406, 416.
47 For Collet, see: Giot, 1983, 21; for James Miln: Daniel, 1963, 124–5; For Miln's Kermario excavations: Miln, 1881, 25–32; *Catalogue du Musée J. Miln*, Vannes, 1894, 14–16.
48 Hadingham, E., 'The lunar observatory hypothesis at Carnac: a reconsider-ation', *Ant 55*, 1981, 35–42; Heggie, 1981, 194. For discussions of the possible astronomical alignments in the Carnac rows: Giot, 1960, 125–7; for sensible caution, Giot *et al*, 1979, 423–32; for uncritical reaction: Sitwell, 1930, 136–8. For enthusiasm: Kergal, 1978; 1979.
49 Note 2, 106–7.
50 Lukis, 1875, 29; le Rouzic, 1935, 22.
51 Wood, J.E., 1978, 145; Note 2, 93, 96–7; Heggie, 1981, 194.
52 Giot, 1983, 20; le Rouzic, 1935, 34–5; Pepper, E. and Wilcock, J., *Magical and Mystical Sites . . .*, 1977, 262.

53 Hodder, 1990, 239.
54 Kergal, 1978, 43; Burl, 1985, 155, 158.
55 Giot, 1960, 117. Mont St-Michel: Wors-fold, 7; Lockyer, 1909, 40.
56 *Livret-Guide . . . Bretagne*, 42.
57 Burl, 1985, 134, no. 173.

CHAPTER TEN

1 Boswell, J., *Journal of a Tour to the Hebrides with Samuel Johnson*. 1936, 262.
2 For wedge-tombs, see: de Valera and O'Nuallain, 1982. Fig. 4. Labbacallee and Island, Co. Cork; fig. 30. Shanballyedmond, Tipperary.
3 Gibbons and Higgins, 1988, 66.
4 Briard, 1990, 50.
5 For the Grand Menhir Brisé, see: Mer-ritt, R.L. and Thom, A.S., 'Le Grand Menhir Brisé', *Arch J 137*, 1980, 27–39; Hornsey, R., 'The Grand Menhir Brisé: megalithic success or failure?', *Oxford Journal of Archaeology 6 (2)*, 1987, 185–217.
6 Lukis, 1875, 26; Giot, 1960, 123–4; Giot *et al*, 1979, 410; Scouëzec and Masson, 176.
7 For St Dénec, see: Shee Twohig, E., *The Megalithic Art of Western Europe*, 1981, 57, 59, 65, 67, 68, 75, 189, no. 49, Fig. 168. For the Grand Menhir Brisé: ibid, 190, no. 52; Tossen-Keler: ibid, 191, no. 55.
8 Briard, 1989, 29–39, 107.
9 For Pytheas and the Pole Star, see: Casson, L., *The Ancient Mariners*, Prince-ton, 1991, 124. For the various polar stars, Kochab, Thuban and Polaris, see: Pickering, J., *1001 Questions Answered About Astronomy*, 1960, 178, no. 567; for Kochab, 296, no. 802; for Thuban, 234, no. 669; and for the changing declina-tions of Polaris over the centuries, see: Hawkins, G.S., *Astro-Archaeology*, 1966, 20, 'Umi Alpha'.
10 Hutchinson, 1794, I, 530.
11 Borlase, W., 1769, 143.
12 Burl, 1991, 12–13; Devereux and Thomson, 1979, 48–9; 187–9.
13 Burl, 1991, 13–14.
14 For Over Silton, see: Greenwell, W., *British Barrows*, 1887, 509–10, no. 227.
15 For transportation of the Arrows from the north, see: Note 13, 6–9; *Ant 65*, 1991, 68–9; from the south: *ibid*, 297.
16 Note 13, 14–16.
17 Lukis, W.C., *Surtees Society 73*, 1880, 358–9, 376; Stukeley, 1776, II, 74, Tab. 90.
18 Note 13, 20–3.
19 Dyer, 332.
20 For Llanbedr, see: Bowen and Gresham, 57; Barber and Williams, 143, no. 202.
21 For Plas Gogerddan, see: *Archaeology in Wales 26*, 1986, 29–31; *ibid 27*, 1987, 36.
22 For Cnocan (Knockaunvaddreen), see: Daniel, G., *Megaliths in History*, 1972, 19. For persisting paganism in Brittany, see: Burl, 1985, 172, 'Christianisation'.
23 For Banc Rhosgoch Fach, see: Thomas, J., *Archaeology in Wales 29*, 1989, 44–5; also, Ray and Thomas, 1989.

24 Excavations at single standing stones in Brittany: Giot *et al*, 1979, 398; in England, Ireland and Wales: Williams, 1988, with detailed lists: fires: 28, 73, 75, 83, 88, 104; charcoal: 65, 68, 71, 73, 74, 75, 79, 82, 88, 101, 102, 104; cremations: 63, 66, 68, 70, 71, 74, 75, 78, 83, 88, 100, 101, 102, 104.
25 Watkins, A., 'Excavations at the Queen Stone', *Trans Woolhope N.F.C.*, 1924–26, 189–93; Shoesmith, R., *Alfred Watkins. A Herefordshire Man*, 1990, 126–30. Unexpectedly, despite Watkins's con-fident statement that the stone was 'a mark stone at which at least three tracks crossed' the 'leys' are omitted from *The Ley Hunter's Companion*, Devereux and Thomson, 1979.
26 O'Kelly, M., 1989, 71.
27 Waddell, J., *Ant 52*, 1978, 124–5.
28 For the *Sépultures en V*, see: l'Helgouach, J., *Les Sépultures Mégalithiques en Armorique*, 1966, 189–99. For Breton radiocarbon assays, see: Hibbs, 1984, 322–3. For plans of the Liscuis tombs, see: *Livret-Guide . . . Bretagne*, Paris, 1976. Figs. 21–3.
29 'Wedge-tomb builders', see: Lynch, A., 1981a, 17. For radiocarbon assays from wedge-tombs, see: *JIA 4*, 1987–8, 13–20. For the two un-numbered Island dates, see: Kelly, M., 1989, 121–2. For Toormore: *JIA 5*, 1989–90, 9–17, 17. For the relationship between the Breton and Irish tombs, see; l'Helgouach, Note 28, 199. For contacts between Brittany and the British Isles continuing into the Middle Bronze Age, see: Burgess, C., 'Breton palstaves from the British Isles', *Arch J 126*, 1970, 149–53. For a general discussion of prehistoric Irish chrono-logy, see: Woodman, P.C., 'Filling in spaces in Irish prehistory', *Ant 66*, 1992, 295–314. Radiocarbon dates in the paper are cited in BP ('before the present', i.e. before AD 1950).
30 O'Kelly, M., 1989, 152–5; Mount Gabriel dates, *PPS 56*, 1990, 285. For prehistoric copper mines in West Cork, see: Power *et al*, 1992, 72–8, where thirty-six sites are described.
31 O'Nuallain, 1988, 190.
32 Jackson, J. *JIA 2*, 1984, 48; Harbison, 1988, 113–18.
33 Hencken, H. O'N., *The Archaeology of Cornwall and Scilly*, 1932, 81. See also: Fox, 1973, 95–6; Taylor, J., *Bronze Age Goldwork of the British Isles*, Cambridge, 1980, 34.
34 Hibbs, 1984, 296.
35 For the azimuths of wedge-tombs, see: de Valera and O'Nuallain, 1982, fig. 36; for stone circles, see: O'Nuallain, 1984a, 75, fig. 24; for short rows, see: Lynch, A., 1982, 210.
36 Somerville, 1923, 200; Lynch, A., 1981b; 1982.
37 Lynch, A., 1982, 212.
38 For the azimuths of wedge-tombs in Cork, Kerry, Limerick and Tipperary, see: de Valera and O'Nuallain, 1982,

109, fig. 36. For Co. Clare, see the same authors, *Survey of the Megalithic Tombs of Ireland, I. Co. Clare*, Dublin, 1961, 106, end figure. Ninety-nine sites have azimuths between 183° and 284°. For Co. Mayo, see: ibid, 1964, 113, fig. 71. nineteen sites, 215°–291°; *ibid, III Galway...Cavan*, 1972, 158, fig. 71, thirty-six sites, 200°–292°; *ibid, V. Co. Sligo*, 1989, 114, fig. 80, thirty-five sites, 204°–301°. For the amended total of 465 wedges, p. 114.

39 Note 37, 207.
40 Lynch, A., 1981b, 25–7; Ruggles, 1993.
41 For the effects of the climate in south-west Ireland see: Lynch, A., 1981a, 4–5 *et seq*. For the deposition of Irish hoards, see: Harbison, 1988, 134 *et seq*; O'Kelly, M., 1989, 184ff.
42 *Arch Ire 2, (2)*, 1988, 66.
43 For Boyle Somerville's researches around Lough Swilly, see: *JRSAI 39*, 1909, 192–202, 215–33, 343–9; for Drumhallagh, see: *Arch 73*, 1923, 204. For Somerville, see: Michell, J., *A Little History of Astro-Archaeology*, 2nd ed., London, 1989, 42.
44 For court-cairns and passage-tombs in Ulster, see: Mallory and McNeill, 1991, 56–65, 79–83.
45 Davies, 1939, 3–4.
46 Davies, O., *UJA 2*, 1939, 40.
47 Ballymeanoch: *PSAS 109*, 1987–8, 104–11; Glengorm: Ruggles and Martlew, 1989; Ardnacross: *D & E*, 1990, 32; *ibid*, 1991, 52.
48 For cupmarks in recumbent stone circles, see: Ruggles, C. and Burl, A., 'A new study of the Aberdeenshire recumbent stone circles', 2: interpretation, *Archaeoastronomy 8*, 1985, S25–S60, S54–S58; For cupmarks in Four-Posters, see: Burl, 1988a, 33–4.
49 *PSAS 66*, 1931–2, 149.
50 For rock-art in south-west Scotland, see: Morris, 1977; 1979; 1981. For decorated cists, see: Simpson, D. and Thawley, J., 'Single grave art in Britain', *SAF 4*, 1972, 81–104.
51 For Slockavullin, see: Thom, 1971, 45–51. 'Temple Wood'.
52 *PSAS 16*, 1881–2, 117. For the excavation of the single stone, see: *PSAS 109*, 1977–8, 104–11. For the stone's fate: *D & E*, 1982, 22; *ibid*, 1983, 22.
53 Morris, 1979, 15.
54 Note 53, 16.
55 Thom, 1967, 97, A4/4.
56 Few, R., Morgan, J., and Ruggles, C., 'A survey of three megalithic sites in Argyllshire', *Nature 253*, 1975, 431–3.
57 Campbell, J.L. and Thomson, D., *Edward Lhuyd in the Scottish Highlands, 1699–1700*, 1963, Fig. 5; Burl, A., *Rings of Stone*, 1979, 66–7.
58 Burl, 1983, 10–11.
59 Hawkins, 1977, 250.
60 *PSAS 109*, 1977–8, 105, Fig. 1.
61 Ruggles, 1984, 58.
62 Note 61, 304.
63 Note 61, 303.

64 Note 61, 304.
65 Burl, 1987b, 15–16.
66 Ruggles, Martlew and Hinge, 1991, S72.
67 Ruggles, 1988b.
68 Note 67, 243.
69 Thom, Thom and Burl, 1990, II, 268.
70 Somerville, 1923, 202–4.
71 Diodorus Siculus, Bk II (continued), 35–IV. Loeb Classical Library, 1987. Ch. 47, 141.
72 Brown, P.L., *Megaliths, Myths and Men*, 1977. 113.
73 Frazer, Sir J.G., *The Magic Art and the Evolution of Kings, I, 1*, 1911, 32; Krupp, E., *In Search of Ancient Astronomies*, 1979, 33.
74 Frazer, Sir J.G., *Spirits of the Corn and Wild, V, 1*, 1912, 122n. See also, 'The Pleiades in primitive calendars', 307–19.
75 If the ENE row at Callanish had been laid out to point towards a star the Pleiades were only one of several possible bright stellar targets. Aldebaran (α Tauri) and Procyon (α Canis Minoris) with dates around 550 BC and 880 BC respectively can be ignored as being too late. But Spica (α Virginis), c. 1475 BC, and Altair (α Aquilae), c. 2200 BC, have chronological declinations as well qualified as the Pleiades. It is only the latter's inclusion as one of the three heavenly bodies quoted by Diodorus Siculus that makes them the strongest of the contenders.
76 For the declination of the Pleiades, see: Hawkins, G.S., *Astro-Archaeology*, Smithsonian Institute Astrophysical Observatory. Special Report, no. 226, 1966. 22, 'Taurus Eta' [Pleiades]; ibid for Spica and Altair.
77 Ashmore, P., 'Callanish, 1980. Interim'. 5.
78 Bohncke, S.J.P., 'Vegetation and habitation history of the Callanish area, Isle of Lewis, Scotland', in: (eds) Birks, H.H. *et al, The Cultural Landscape – Past, Present and Future*, 1988. 460–1.

CHAPTER ELEVEN

1 For the two Stonehenge bluestones, 31 and 49, see: Petrie, W.M.F., *Stonehenge: Plans, Description, and Theories*, 1880, 10–11. (Reprinted in 1989. See: Petrie and Hawkins). Also: Stone, E.H., *The Stones of Stonehenge*, 1924, 7, Plate 6; Burl, 1987a, 201–2.
2 Coles, 1911, 87–8, no. 32. 'Crofthead'; Stewart, 1966, 144–5, no. 15. 'Fowlis Wester I'; Thom, Thom and Burl, 1990, II, 326, P1/11.
3 Williams, 1988, 72.
4 Note 3, 51. Also Appendix 1.7, 117–18.
5 Giot, 1988a, 322.
6 Thom, 1967: Giant's Grave, 99, 139, L1/11; Pipers, 100, S1/1.
7 Borlase, W., 1769, 187.
8 Borlase, W.C., 1872, 23–4.
9 Aubrey, 1665–93, I, 68; Wood, J., 1765, 149.
10 Stukeley, 1776, 169.

11 Dymond, C.W., *JBAA 33*, 1877, 300; ibid, 1896, 15.
12 For the Hauteville legend, see: Grinsell, L.V., *The Folklore of Stanton Drew*, 1973, 11. For the effigy in Chew Magna church, see: Fryer, A.C., *Wooden Monumental Effigies in England and Wales*, 1924, 23, 60. Priv. inf. I. Durham.
13 Note 3, 89–91.
14 Thom, 1967, 101, W9/2. Thom, Thom and Burl, 1990, II, 358–9.
15 Thorpe, R.S. *et al*, 'The geological sources and transport of the blue-stones of Stonehenge, Wiltshire, UK', *PPS 57 (2)*, 1991, 103–57. 114, 116, no. 13.
16 O'Riordain, S., *Antiquities of the Irish Countryside*, Cork, 1942, 44. (1st edition).
17 Areas in square miles: United Kingdom, 94,475; Republic of Ireland, 27,129; Brittany, 10,502, a total of 132,106. For Co. Cork, 2879, Co. Kerry, 1815, totalling 4694. Their ratio of 4694:132,106, is only 3.6 per cent of the whole. But Cork and Kerry have 104 of the recorded 333 pairs, 31.2 per cent, almost ten times what could geographically have been forecast.
18 Macalister, 1921, 305, 304.
19 Cuppage, 65, no. 191.
20 For Burgatia, see: Roberts, n.d., 36–7; for St Samson-sur-Rance: Giot *et al*, 1979, 386–8; for Scotland: Morris, 1979, 15; ibid, 1977, 14.
21 *JRSAI 16*, 1883–4, 307.
22 Burl, 1976, 216–18.
23 Roberts, n.d., 12.
24 Weir, 1990, 53–5.
25 O'Nuallain, 1988, 197.
26 Lacy, 98–101; Morris, 1977, 31–41.
27 Mallory and McNeill, 1991, 104.
28 Note 24, 55.
29 O'Kelly, M., 1989, 293.
30 Macalister, 1928, 105.
31 Note 22, 107.
32 For the excavation at the Wren's Egg, see: Masters, 1977; Stell, 1986, 167. For the astronomy there and at Milton Hall, confusingly conflated with the Wren's Egg, G3/13, and Drumtroddan, G3/12, see: Thom, 1967, 98.
33 Wood, J.E., 1978, 111.
34 The lunar astronomy of the Kilmartin Stones has been discussed, *inter alia*, by Thom, 1967, 97, A2/8 'Temple Wood'; ibid, 1971, 45–51; by Wood, J.E., 1978, 109–14; by Heggie, 1981, 174, 185–7; and, more generally for the rows in the Kilmartin valley by Ruggles, 1988, 239, 242–5. See also Hawkins, in: Petrie and Hawkins, 1989, 74–7.
35 For the layout and astronomy of Barbreck, see: Heggie, 185–6; Ruggles, 1984, 143, 148, 151 (Line 154), 279, AR3; Thom, Thom, and Burl, 1990, I, 100–1, A2/3.
36 Martin, 1716, xiv, 97; Borlase, W., 1769, 163.
37 Thom, Thom and Burl, 1990, I, 129, A3/6, 'Loch Stornoway'; Ruggles, 1984, 183, 186, 190, KT2.
38 *PSAS 5*, 1862–4, 345.

39 Sir John Evans, *The Ancient Bronze Implements, Weapons and Ornaments of Great Britain and Ireland*, 1881, 412–13.

40 For the quotation about cauldrons and late prehistoric feasting, see: Langmaid, M.J., *Bronze Age Metalwork in England and Wales*, 1976, 22. For other references to magical cauldrons, see: Green, M., *Dictionary of Celtic Myth and Legend*, 1992, 57–8; Ross, A., *Pagan Celtic Britain*, 1974, 57 *et seq*.

41 Burl, 1976, 213; ibid, 1988a, 27–8.

42 Stewart, 1966, 140.

43 *D & E*, 1972, 55–6; *Arch J 131*, 1974, 9, 27–9.

44 *PSAS 40*, 1905–6, 293–5, no. 2.

45 Note 42, 140–5.

46 Coles, 1908, 131–2, no. 22; Note 42, 127, 144–5, no. 19; Burl, 1988a, 181, 'Lundin Farm North-West'.

47 For the Park of Tongland C-14 assays I am grateful for information from Mr R. McCullagh, *priv. comm.* 16. 11. 88. See also: *PPS 58*, 1992, 312–23. For a general discussion of Four-Poster chronology, see: Burl, 1988a, 31–2, 137.

48 Burl, 1988a, 13.

49 Coles, 1911, 107.

50 For cupmarks in recumbent stone circles, see: *JHA 16*, 1985, S54–S56; in Four-Posters: Burl, 1988a, 34.

51 Thom, Thom and Burl, 1990, II, 335, P2/7.

52 Charles Elphinstone Dalrymple in a letter of 1 April 1855 or 1856, quoted in *PSAS 109*, 1977–8, 270.

COUNTY STATISTICS

1/ = Certain sites
/1 = Uncertain sites

County	(1) Ents	(2) Aves	(3) Tang	(4) Double	(5) Single	(6) Mult	(7) 4St	(8) 3St	(9) Pair	Totals
England										
Bedfordshire	–	–	–	–	–	–	–	1	–	1/–
Channel Isles										
Guernsey	–	–	–	–	–	–	–	–	/1	/1
Jersey	–	–	–	–	–	–	–	–	/1	/1
Cornwall	/2	–	–	–	8/2	–	2/1	1	8	19/5
Cumberland	3/1	2	/1	/1	3	–	–	1/1	1	10/4
Derbyshire	–	/1	–	–	–	–	–	–	–	/1
Devon (D'moor)	–	10	–	28	48	8/2	–	–	–	94/2
Devon (Exmoor)	–	–	–	12/1	2/1	5	1	3/2	2/2	25/6
Dorset	–	1/2	–	–	–	–	–	–	–	1/2
Huntingdonshire	–	–	–	–	–	–	–	–	1	1/–
Lancashire	–	–	/1	–	–	–	–	–	–	/1
Northumberland	–	1	–	–	–	–	1	1	–	3/–
Oxford	1	–	–	–	–	–	–	–	–	1/–
Scillies	–	–	–	–	–	–	–	1	–	1/–
Somerset	–	2/1	–	–	–	–	–	–	2/2	4/3
Somerset (Exmoor)	–	–	–	10/4	3/3	3/2	2/1	/2	7/2	25/14
Westmorland	/1	3/1	–	–	3	–	–	–	–	6/2
Wiltshire	1	3	–	–	–	–	–	–	–	4/–
Yorkshire	–	–	–	–	–	–	1/2	–	–	1/2
TOTALS	5/4	22/5	/2	50/6	67/6	16/4	7/4	8/5	21/8	196/44
France (Brittany)										
Côtes-du-Nord	–	–	–	–	–	1	–	2	1 –	4/–
Finistère	–	3	--	–	15/1	3/2	7/2	12/2	11/1	51/8
Ille-et-Vilaine	–	–	–	3/1	6	2	6	4/2	6	27/3
Loire-Atlantique	–	–	–	–	2	1	–	1	–	4/–
Morbihan	–	/1	–	–	15/1	13	10/2	3	2/1	43/5
TOTALS		3/1	–	3/1	38/2	20/2	23/4	22/4	20/2	129/16
N. Ireland										
Antrim	–	–	–	–	–	–	–	3	1	4/–
Armagh	–	–	–	–	–	–	–	2	–	2/–
Down	1	–	–	–	–	–	–	2	6	9/–
Fermanagh	–	–	2	–	8	–	1/1	3/2	1	15/3
Londonderry	–	–	3	–	10	–	–	2	–	15/–
Tyrone	3/1	3	2	–	23/1	–	4/1	10/1	7	52/4
TOTALS	4/1	3/–	7/–	–	41/1	–	5/2	22/3	15	97/7
Republic of Ireland										
Cavan	–	–	–	–	–	–	1	/1	–	1/1
Clare	–	–	–	–	–	–	1	–	–	1/–
Cork	–	–	–	–	–	–	21	47	76/1	144/1
Donegal	–	–	–	–	/1	–	3	5	6	14/1
Dublin	–	–	–	–	–	–	–	/1	–	–/1
Galway	–	–	–	–	–	–	2/1	2/1	6/6	10/8
Kerry	–	–	–	–	/1	–	8	12	27	47/1
Kilkenny	–	–	–	–	–	–	–	1	–	1/–
Limerick	–	/1	–	–	–	–	1	2	–	3/1
Louth	–	–	–	–	–	–	5	–	3	8/–
Mayo	–	–	–	–	–	–	2	3	1	6/–
Meath	–	–	–	–	–	–	–	–	3	3/–

COUNTY STATISTICS (*Continued*)

County	(1) Ents	(2) Aves	(3) Tang	(4) Double	(5) Single	(6) Mult	(7) 4St	(8) 3St	(9) Pair	Totals
Tipperary	–	–	–	–	/1	–	–	1	–	1/1
Waterford	–	–	–	–	–	–	1/1	4	–	5/1
Wexford	–	–	–	–	–	–	–	1	1	2/–
Wicklow	–	–	–	–	/1	–	–	–	1	1/1
TOTALS	–	/1	–	–	/4	–	45/2	78/3	124/7	247/17
Wales										
Clwyd	–	–	–	–	–	–	1/2	–	3	4/2
Dyfed	–	–	–	–	3	–	2/1	5/1	13	23/2
Glamorgan	–	–	–	–	–	–	–	–	1	1/–
Gwent	–	–	–	–	–	–	–	1/1	–	1/1
Gwynedd	1	–	–	1	–	–	2	1	6	11/–
Powys	–	–	2	–	5	–	4	2/2	5	18/2
Ynys Mona	–	–	–	–	–	–	1	1/2	2/1	4/3
TOTALS	1/–	–	2/–	1/–	8/–	–	10/3	10/6	30/1	62/10
Scotland										
Aberdeen	–	2/5	–	–	–	–	–	–	1	3/5
Angus	–	–	–	–	–	–	–	–	3	3/–
Argyll	–	–	–	–	2	–	4	9	14/2	29/2
Arran	–	–	–	–	–	–	–	–	1	1/–
Ayr	–	–	–	–	/1	–	–	1	–	1/1
Barra	–	–	–	–	–	–	–	–	2	2/–
Berwick	–	–	–	–	–	–	–	–	1	1/–
Bute	–	–	–	–	–	–	–	1	–	1/–
Caithness	–	–	–	1	1	12	1	–	2	17/–
Coll	–	–	–	–	–	–	–	–	1	1/–
Colonsay	–	–	–	–	–	–	–	–	1	1/–
Dumfriess	1	1	–	–	–	–	–	1	1	4/–
Fife	–	–	–	–	–	–	–	–	1/1	1/1
Islay	–	–	–	–	–	–	–	1/1	1/5	2/6
Jura	–	–	–	–	–	–	1	1/1	1	3/1
Kincardine	–	–	–	–	–	–	–	–	/2	–/2
Kinross	–	–	–	–	–	–	–	–	1	1/–
Kirkcudbright	–	–	–	–	–	–	–	–	1/1	1/1
Lewis	–	1	–	–	–	–	3/1	3	2/1	9/2
Moray	–	–	–	–	–	–	–	–	1	1/–
Mull	–	–	–	–	–	–	5	6/1	3/4	14/5
North Uist	1	–	–	–	–	–	1	1	3	6/–
Orkneys	–	–	–	–	–	–	–	2	6	8/–
Peebles	–	–	–	–	–	–	–	–	2	2/–
Perthshire	–	–	–	–	–	–	1/2	4	19/10	24/12
Ross	–	–	–	–	–	–	–	–	1	1/–
Roxburgh	–	–	–	–	–	–	–	–	/1	–/1
Shetland	–	–	–	–	–	2	–	1	3	6/–
Skye	–	–	–	–	–	–	–	2/1	1/1	3/2
South Uist	–	–	–	–	–	–	–	1	–	1/–
Stirling	–	–	–	–	–	–	1/1	–	–	1/1
Sutherland	–	–	–	2	–	9	–	–	–	11/–
Wigtown	–	–	–	–	–	–	–	2/1	3/1	5/2
TOTALS	2/–	4/5	–	3/–	3/1	23/–	17/4	36/5	76/29	164/44

COUNTY STATISTICS GRAND TOTALS

1/ = Certain sites.
/1 = Uncertain sites.

	(1) Ent	(2) Ave	Long Rows				Short Rows			Total
			(3) Tang	(4) Double	(5) Single	(6) Mult	(7) 4St	(8) 3St	(9) Pair	
England	5/4	22/5	/2	50/6	67/6	16/4	7/4	8/5	21/8	196/44
Brittany	–	3/1	–	3/1	38/2	20/2	23/4	22/4	20/2	129/16
N. Ireland	4/1	3/–	7/–	–	41/1	–	5/2	22/3	15/–	97/7
Eire	–	/1	–	–	/4	–	45/2	78/3	124/7	247/17
Scotland	2/–	4/5	–	3/–	3/1	23/–	17/4	36/5	76/29	164/44
Wales	1/–	–	2/–	1/–	8/–	–	10/3	10/6	30/1	62/10
GRAND TOTALS										
Certain	12	32	9	57	157	59	107	176	286	895
Unsure	5	12	2	7	14	6	19	26	47	138
TOTAL	17	44	11	64	171	65	126	202	333	1033

COUNTY CONCORDANCE OF STONE ROWS
AND AVENUES

Only grid references, type and main references are given in the Concordance. Details of architecture, finds and possible alignments are provided in the separate Gazetteers that follow the Concordance. Rows in italics are those for which no further information is available. They are not entered in the Gazetteers.

ABBREVIATIONS

A   = Avenue
D   = Double row
Det   = Detached avenue
Ent   = Entrance
EP   = Portalled Entrance
4St   = Four-, Five- or Six-Stone row
M   = Multiple row
P   = Pair of stones
S   = Long single row of many stones
StC   = Stone circle
Tang = Tangential avenue
3St   = Three-Stone row
*   = Uncertain site
[ ]   = Alexander Thom's reference

CHANNEL ISLANDS

GUERNSEY

*Crocq, Le, St-Saviour. P. Johnston, 1981, 101.

JERSEY

*Trois Roques, Les. P. Kendrick, 1928, 72; Patton, 75.

ENGLAND

BEDFORDSHIRE

*Devil's Jump Stone. SP 999 409. 3St. Dyer, 51

CORNWALL

Boscawen-Ros. SW 428 239. P. Barnatt, 1982, 229.
Boscawen-Un. SW 412 274. Ent? Barnatt, 1982, 159–62.
Buttern Hill. SX 169 815, S. *Bodmin Survey I.*
Carneglos. SX 198 773. S. *Bodmin Survey I.*
Colvannick Tor. SX 128 718. S. *Meyn Mamvro 14*, 1991, 12.
Craddock Moor. SX 239 720. S. *Bodmin Survey I.*
Crousa Common. SW 775 200. P. *Meyn Mamvro 8*, 1989, 12.
De Lank Quarry. SX 100 753. P. *Meyn Mamvro 9*, 1989, 2.
East Moor. SX 223 778. S. *Bodmin Survey I.*
Faughan, Paul. SW 452 282. P. Weatherhill, 49.
Fox Tor. SX 230 786. S. *Meyn Mamvro 14*, 1991, 1991, 13.
Higher Drift. SW 437 283. P. Borlase, W.C., 1872, 96.
*Kenidjack Common. SW 389 325. 4St. *Meyn Mamvro 14.*, 4.
*Langstone Downs. SX 253 737. S. *Meyn Mamvro 14*, 1991, 13.
Leskernick Hill. SX 187 798. S. *Bodmin Survey I.*

Longstone Farm. SX 362 803. 3St. *Bodmin Survey I.*
Merry Maidens. SW 433 245. Ent? Barnatt, 1982, 155–9.
Nine Maidens SW 936 675 – 936 676. S. Barnatt, 1982, 221.
Pipers, Land's End. SW 433 245. P. Borlase, W.C., 1872, 106–7.
Pipers, Bodmin Moor. SX 257 713. P. *JBAA 35*, 1879, 304.
Tolborough Tor. SX 175 778. 4St. *Meyn Mamvro 14.*, 12.
Trehudreth Downs. SX 124 729. S. *Bodmin Survey I.*
Treveglos. SW 453 388. 4St. *Meyn Mamvro 14*, 14.
Trewern. SW 429 313. P. Barnatt, 1982, 255–6.

CUMBERLAND

*Blakeley Raise. NY 060 140. Ent? Waterhouse, 1985, 68–70.
Broad Field. NY 425 445. Det. *Arch 10*, 1792, 105–13.
Broomrigg A. NY 548 467. A. *TCWAAS 53*, 1953, 5–8.
*Carlatton. NY 534 510. S. *TCWAAS 35*, 1935, 170–1.
Castlerigg. NY 291 236. Ent. Dymond, 1880, 50–5.
Giant's Grave . SD 135 810. P. *TCWAAS I*, 1872–3, 280.
Lacra SE. SD 150 810. 3St. *TCWAAS 48*, 1948, 3–5.
Lacra NE. SD 151 812. A. *TCWAAS 48*, 1948, 5–13.
Long Meg and Her Daughters. NY 570 372. EP. Dymond, 1880, 40–7.
*Newbiggin. NY 471 293. S. Taylor, 1886, 343.
Newton Reigny. NY 47. 31. S. Taylor, 1886, 343.
Penhurrock. NY 629 104. D. Taylor, 1886, 341–5.
Swinside. SD 171 882. EP. Dymond, 1880, 47–50.

DERBYSHIRE

Arbor Low. SK 160 036. A (earthen). *Arch 58*, 1903, 482–3.

DEVON (a. Dartmoor; b. Exmoor)

(a) DARTMOOR

Arms Tor. SX 536 863. S. Gibson. Priv. inf.
Assacombe. SX 660 826. D. Worth, 1967, 224–5, no. 43.
Bellever Tor. SX 643 765. Gibson. Priv. inf.
Black Tor NE. SX 572 714. D. Worth, 1967, 212–13, no. 21.
Black Tor NW. SW 667 634. S? Worth, 1967, no. 56.
Brent Fore Hill. SX 667 613. D. Worth, 1967, 234–5, no. 60.
Brown Heath. SX 641 653. A. Worth, 1967, 206, no. 4.
Burford Down. SX 637 601. S. Worth, 1967, 205–6, no. 3.
Butterdon Row. SX 654 608. S. Worth, 1967, 205, no. 2.
Cantrell. SX 662 609. D. Worth, 1967, 235 no. 62.
Cawsand Hill. see: Cosdon.
Challacombe. SX 689 809. M. Worth, 1967, 226, no. 46.
Cholwich Town Waste. SX 583 623. S. *PPS 30*, 1964, 25–38.

Cocks Tor. SX 530 760 S? Worth, 1967, 218, no. 31.

Collard Tor W. SX 558 621. S. Worth, 1967, 208, no. 11.

Collard Tor E. SX 559 621. S. Worth, 1967, 208, no. 12.

Conies Down. SX 586 791. D. Worth, 1967, 231, no. 55.

Corringdon Ball N. SX 667 612. S. Worth, 1967, 231–2, no. 57 (A).

Corringdon Ball Central. SX 667 612. M. Worth, 1967, no. 58 (B).

Corringdon Ball S. SX 667 612. M. Worth, 1967, 232–4, no. 59 (C).

Cosdon. SX 643 917. M. Worth, 1967, 218–19, no. 33.

Ditsworthy Warren. SX 58. 66. S. Gibson. Priv. inf.

Ditsworthy N. SX 5. 6. Gibson. Priv. inf.

Down Tor. SX 590 694. S. Worth, 1967, 212, no. 20.

Drizzlecombe NE. SX 592 671. S. Worth, 1967, 210, no. 18 (B).

Drizzlecombe NW. SX 593 670. S. Worth, 1967, 210–12, no. 19 (C).

Drizzlecombe S. SX 592 669. D. Worth, 1967, 209–10, no. 17 (A).

Drizzlecombe W. SX 591·672. S. *TDA 22*, 1890, 50.

Dunnabridge. SX 63. 64. S. Gibson. Priv. inf.

Fernworthy S. SX 655 841. D. Worth, 1967, 222–4, no. 40 (A).

Fernworthy N. SX 656 844. D. Worth, 1967, 224, no. 41 (B).

Fernworthy SX 655 841. D. Worth, 1967, 224, no. 42 (C).

Froggymead. See: Fernworthy.

Glasscombe Ball SW. SX 657 605. S. Worth, 1967, 206, no. 6.

Glasscombe Ball NE. SX 658 608. D. Worth, 1967, 35, no. 61.

Harford Moor N. SX 651 599. S. Barnatt, 1989, 519, no. 86.

Harford Moor S. SX 651 598. D. Barnatt, 1989, 519, no. 85.

Hartland Tor. SX 647 794. Gibson. Priv. inf.

Hartor N. SX 577 717. A. Worth, 1967, 213, no. 22.

Hartor S. SX 576 716. S. Worth, 1967, 213, no. 23.

Holne Moor. SX 675 709. M. Pettit, 1974, 131.

Joan Ford Newtake. SX 632 720. M. Barnatt, 1989, 519, no. 88.

Lakehead Hill E. SX 644 778. S. Worth, 1967, 229–30, no. 51.

Lakehead Hill W. SX 642 773. S. Worth, 1967, 230, no. 52.

Lakehead S. SX 645 776. S. Worth, 1967, 230, no. 53.

Langstone Moor. SX 550 788. S. Worth, 1967, 216–18, no. 30.

Laughter Tor. SX 653 753. D. Worth, 1967, 229, no. 50.

Leedon Tor. SX 565 715. S. Barnatt, 1989, 519, no. 84.

Merrivale N. SX 556 748. D. Worth, 1967, 215, no. 27 (A).

Merrivale Centre. SX 556 748. A. Worth, 1967, 215–16, no. 28 (B).

Merrivale SW SX 554 748. S. Worth, 1967, 216, no. 29 (C).

Merrivale SX 553 745. S. Barnatt, 1989, 519, no. 76 (D).

Merrivale SX 553 745. S. Barnatt, 1989, 519, no. 77 (E).

Natsworthy. SX 712 800. S? Barnatt, 1989, 519, no. 83.

Ogborough. SX 6. 6. Gibson. Priv. inf.

Oke Tor. nr. SX 560 734. S. Worth, 1967, 218, no. 32.

Penn Beacon NE. SX 598 627. S. Worth, 1967, 207, no. 8.

Penn Beacon SW. SX 595 625. D. Worth, 1967, 207–8, no. 9.

Penn Beacon SE. SX 599 625. D. Emmett, 111, no. 63.

Piles Hill NE. SX 655 611. S. Emmett, 111, no. 70.

Piles Hill SW. SX 649 610. D. Barnatt, 1989, 519, no. 82.

Ramsley. SX 651 931. S. Barnatt, 1989, 519, no. 79.

Ringhill. SX 647 795. S. Barnatt, 1989, 519, no. 89.

Ringmoor. SX 564 662. A. Worth, 1967, 209, no. 16.

Roundhill. SX 610 744. S. Emmett, 111, no. 64.

Sharpitor E. SX 561 709. D. Worth, 1967, 214–15, no. 26.

Sharpitor NW. SX 559 708. D. Worth, 1967, 213–14, no. 24.

Sharpitor NE. SX 564 708. S. Grinsell, 1978, 175.

Sharpitor W. SX 551 708. S. Emmett, 111, no. 67.

Sharpitor S. SX 559 707. S? Worth, 1967, 214, no. 25.

Shaugh Moor. SX 555 638. S. Worth, 1967, 208, no. 13.

Sherril Down. c. SX 687 734. A. Worth, 1967, 226–7, no. 47.

Shovel Down SX 660 862. A. Worth, 1967, 219–20, no. 34 (A).

Shovel Down SX 660 859. D. Worth, 220, no. 36 (C).

Shovel Down SX 659 862. D. Worth, 1967, 220, no. 35 (E).

Shovel Down SX 660 856. D. Worth, 1967, 220, no. 37 (G).

Shovel Down SX 660 857. S. Worth, 1967, 222, no. 39 (H).

Shovel Down SX 660 860. S. Barnatt, 1989, 519, no. 87 (I).

Shovel Down (Three Boys). SX 660 855. D. Worth, 1967, 220–2, no. 38.

Soussons Down. SX 676 799. M? Grinsell, 1978, 124 'Manaton 4'.

Spurrells Cross. SX 658 600. A. Worth, 1967, 206, no. 5.

Staldon SX 632 625. S. Worth, 1967, 206–7, no. 7.

Stall Moor – Green Hill. SX 636 678. S. Worth, 1967, 204–5, no. 1.

Stannon. SX 654 815. D. S. Worth, 1967, 225–6, no. 45.

Thornworthy Down. SX 663 849. S. Gibson. Priv. inf.

Top Tor. SX 735 764. S. Grinsell, 1978, 177.

Tor Royal Newtake. SX 623 734. S. Worth, 1967, 230, no. 54.

Trendlebere Down. SX 766 792. D. Worth, 1967, 227, no. 48.

Trowlesworthy E. SX 576 640. A. Worth, 1967, 209, no. 14.

Trowlesworthy W. SX 575 639. D. Worth, 1967, 209, no. 15.

Two Bridges. SX 610 744. S. Emmett, 111, no. 64.

Watern Hill. SX 673 825. D. Worth, 1967, 225, no. 44.

Westmill Tor. SX 589 907. S. Gibson. Priv. inf.

White Tor. SX 620 785. D. Emmett, 111, no. 71.

Yar Tor NW. SX 681 740. M. Worth, 1967, 227–29, no. 49.

Yar Tor SE. SX 682 738. M. Barnatt, 1989, 519, no. 75.

*Yellowmead. SX 574 676. M? Emmett, 111, no. 66.

(b) EXMOOR

Badgworthy Lees. SS 784 446. P. Quinnell & Dunn, 11.

Brayford NW. SS 719 388. P. Quinnell & Dunn, 7.

Brayford SE. SS 725 379. D? Quinnell & Dunn, 7.

Brendon Two Gates. SS 765 436. D. Quinnell & Dunn, 9.

Brockenburrow Lane. SS 661 424. S? Chanter & Worth, 1905, 397.

Chapman Barrows. SS 697 433. D. Quinnell & Dunn, 17.

Cheriton Ridge NW. SS 748 442. M. Quinnell & Dunn, 8.

Cheriton Ridge Centre. SS 751 437. S. Quinnell & Dunn, 15.

Cheriton Ridge SE. SS 754 433. M. Quinnell & Dunn, 9.

Clannon Ball. SS 759 436. D. Quinnell & Dunn, 10.

Furzehill Common SW. SS 734 439. 3St? Quinnell & Dunn, 24.

Furzehill Common Centre. SS 737 442. 3St. Quinnell & Dunn, 22.

Furzehill Common SE. SS 738 439. 4St. Quinnell & Dunn, 27.

Furzehill Common NE. SS 738 447. M. Quinnell & Dunn, 23.

Hoaroak. SS 739 437. D. Quinnell & Dunn, 23.

Hoccombe Coombe. SS 786 444. M. Quinnell & Dunn, 9.

Hoccombe Hill. SS 780 434. D. Quinnell & Dunn, 12.

Long Stone. SS 727 475. P? Quinnell & Dunn, 25.

Longstone Barrow. SS 707 425. 3St. Quinnell & Dunn, 17.

Mattocks Down. SS 601 438. D. Chanter & Worth, 1905, 542–3.

Pig Hill. SS 756 444. M. Quinnell & Dunn, 12.

Rooshitchen. SS 717 400. P? Quinnell & Dunn, 19.

Thornworthy Little Common. SS 712 438. S. Quinnell & Dunn, 27.

West Middleton. SS 648 458. 2 × D. Quinnell & Dunn, 31.

White Ladder. SS 733 370. D. Eardley-Wilmot, 1983, 24–5.

Winaway. SS 722 437. 3St. Quinnell & Dunn, 22.

Wood Barrow. SS 714 423. D. Quinnell & Dunn, 18.

Woodbarrow Hangings. SS 715 428. D. Quinnell & Dunn, 17.

Yelland. SS 490 330. D. Rogers, 1947.

DORSET

Hampton Down. SY 596 865. A (timber). *PDNHAS 88*, 1967, 122–7.

*Little Mayne. SY 721 870. A? *Ant 13*, 1939, 149.

*Rempstone. SY 994 821. A? *PDNHAS 81*, 1959, 114–16.

HUNTINGDONSHIRE

*Robin Hood and Little John. TL 139 983. P. Grinsell, 1976, 162.

LANCASHIRE

The Kirk. SD 251 827. Det. *Arch 53*, 1893, 417.

NORTHUMBERLAND

Five Kings. NT 955 001. 4St. Dyer, 202.

*Lordenshaw. NZ 052 991. 3St. inf: M. van Hoek.

Milfield. NT 943 323. A (earthen). *PPS 47*, 1981, 87–101.

OXFORDSHIRE

Rollright Stones. SP 296 309. EP. Lambrick, 1988, 41–3.

ISLES OF SCILLY

Higher Town, St Martins. SV 933 153. 3St. *Meyn Mamvro 14*, 1991, 14.

SOMERSET

(a) EXMOOR

Almsworthy. SS 843 417. M? Quinnell & Dunn, 37.

Beckham Hill. SS 806 423. M. Quinnell & Dunn, 46.

Bill Hill. SS 723 408. P. Quinnell & Dunn, 52.

Chains Valley. SS 749 417. S. Quinnell & Dunn, 40.

Codsend Moor. SS 882 411. D. Quinnell & Dunn, 35.

Culbone Hill. SS 834 473. S. *P. Som. ANHS 125*, 1980–1, 40–1.

East Pinford. see: West Pinford.

Hascombe. SS 769 383. M. Quinnell & Dunn, 40.

Honeycombe Hill. SS 856 420. S? *Exmoor Review 8*, 1967, 48–9.

Horsen. SS 790 373. M? Quinnell & Dunn, 39.

Hoscombe SE. SS 831 438. 3St? Quinnell & Dunn, 48.

Hoscombe NW. SS 830 441. P. Quinnell & Dunn, 49.

Kittuck. SS 820 438. D. Quinnell & Dunn, 47.

Lanacombe SW. SS 781 427. D. Quinnell & Dunn, 44.

Lanacombe Centre W. SS 784 428. 4St. Quinnell & Dunn, 44.

Lanacombe Centre E. SS 786 430. D? Quinnell & Dunn, 45.

Lanacombe NE. SS 786 431. 4St. Quinnell & Dunn, 45.

Long Chains Coombe SW. SS 743 420. P. Quinnell & Dunn, 42.

Long Chains Coombe NE. SS 745 423. D? Quinnell & Dunn, 42.

Madacombe. SS 831 425. S. Quinnell & Dunn, 52.

North Molton. SS 729 369. P? Quinnell & Dunn, 29.

Porlock Allotment NE. SS 840 447. P. Quinnell & Dunn, 61.

Porlock Allotment SW. SS 833 437. M. Quinnell & Dunn, 60.

Porlock Allotment Centre. SS 840 443. 4St? Quinnell & Dunn, 60.

Porlock Common NE. SS 846 461. S? Quinnell & Dunn, 78.

Porlock Common SW. SS 845 446. D. Quinnell & Dunn, 62.

Squallacombe Centre. SS 738 382. D. Quinnell & Dunn, 39.

Squallacombe NE. SS 739 382. P. Quinnell & Dunn, 49.

Swap Hill. SS 805 426. 3St? Quinnell & Dunn, 46.

Thorn Hill. SS 727 434. D. Quinnell & Dunn, 41.

Toms Hill. SS 801 432. D. Quinnell & Dunn, 57.

Trout Hill NW. SS 794 432. D? Quinnell & Dunn, 43.

Trout Hill SE. SS 795 431. D? Quinnell & Dunn, 43.

Twinhoe. ST 74. 59. S? *PSomNHAS 108*, 1963–4, 16.

West Pinford. SS 796 427. D. Quinnell & Dunn, 43.

Wester Mill. SS 822 409. D. Quinnell & Dunn, 37.

Whit Stones. SS 853 462. P. Quinnell & Dunn, 64.

Wilmersham Common. SS 856 419. D. Quinnell & Dunn, 55.

Yenworthy Common. SS 798 483 P. Quinnell & Dunn, 58.

(b) OUTSIDE EXMOOR

*Bathampton. ST 771 653. A. Dobson *Archaeology of Somerset*, 1931, 62.

Compton Bishop. ST 409 548. P. Grinsell, 1976, 99.

Devil's Quoits. c. ST 576 565. P. Grinsell, 1976, 138.

*Lower Tyning. c. ST 591 633. P? Dymond, 1896, 34.

Stanton Drew. ST 603 630. 2 × A. *JBAA 33*, 1877, 297–307.

*Twinhoe. ST 74. 59. 2 × S? *PSom ANHS 108*, 1963–4, 16.

WESTMORLAND

*Grey Yauds. NY 545 487. A? *TCWAAS 7*, 1907, 67–71.

Lowther Woodhouse. NY 52. 26. S? Taylor, 1886, 343.

*Mayburgh. NY 519 284. EP? *TCWAAS 11*, 1890–1, 195.

Moor Divock. NY 491 227. A. *TCWAAS 8*, 1886, 23–47.

Shap. NY 567 133. A or 2 × A or A + 2 × S. Waterhouse, 1985, 125–6.

WILTSHIRE

Avebury. SU 103 700. 2 × A. Burl, 1979, 137–8.
Stonehenge. SU 123 422. EP, A (earthen). Burl, 1987, 77–8, 140–1.

YORKSHIRE

Devil's Arrows. SE 391 666. 4St. Burl, 1991.
*Dunsley Moor. NZ 85. 11. 4St? Elgee, 1930, 106.
*High Bridestones. NZ 850 046. M? Burl, 1988, 74–5.
*Lower Bridestones. NZ 856 043. S? Elgee, 1930, 159.
Old Castle Hill. NZ 66. 10. 4St. Elgee, 1930, l06.

FRANCE (Brittany)

CÔTES-DU-NORD

*Caillouan, Plésidy. P? Scouëzec & Masson, 76.
Champ des Roches, Le, Pleslin. M. Burl, 1985, 32–3. no. 5.
Pergat, Louargat. 3St. Burl, 1985, 40, no. 20.
Poul ar Varquez. 3St. Giot et al, 1979, 414.
St-Jacut-du-Méné. P. Gilbert, 1964, 170, no. 481.

FINISTÈRE

An-Eured Ven, St-Michel Brasparts. S. Burl, 1985, 50, no. 39.
Bois du Duc. S. Giot et al, 415.
Brennilis. 4St. No details. Pontois, 1929, 124.
Croas-en-Teurec. 4St? Giot et al, 415.
*Délivrande ENE, Île-de-Seins. 3St. du Chatellier, 158.
*Délivrande WSW, Île-de-Seins. P. du Chatellier, 158.
*Difrout, Plouescat. 3St? du Chatellier, 91–2.
Feuillé, La, Huelgoat. P. du Chatellier, 129.
*Île Béniguet. A?. Giot et al, 1979, 415.
Île Glenan. S. Pontois, 1929, 121.
Île Molène. 3St. du Chatellier, 111.
Kéréléoc. P. Pontois, 1929, 124.
Kerfland, Plomeur. 3St. du Chatellier, 175.
Kergadiou, Porspoder. P. Burl, 1985, 60–1, no. 63.
Kerglas, Plougonven. 3St. du Chatellier, 80.
Kerguelven, Plonéour-Lanvern. P. du Chatellier, 149.
*Kérière, Douarnenez. 4St. du Chatellier, 140.
*Kerlaouentec, Crozon. M? du Chatellier, 124.
Kervelhué, Plouhinec. S. Burl, 1985, 118, 147b.
*Laené, Crozon. M? du Chatellier, 124.
Lagatjar, Camarets-sur-Mer. 3 × S + 3St. Pontois, 1929, 109–12.
Landaoudec, Crozon. A. Pontois, 1929, 115–16.
Landisiac'h, Plonévez-Lochrist. 3St. du Chatellier, 77.
Lesquivet, Plougastel-Daoulas. P. du Chatellier, 91.
Leuré, Crozon. 2 × S. Pontois, 1929, 115–16.
Lézaouréguan, Poullan. P. du Chatellier, 139.
Lostmarc'h NE. M. Pontois, 1929, 105–6; Bender, 89.
*Lostmarc'h SW. M? Burl.
Madeleine, La, Lestriguiou. M. du Chatellier, 28, 168.
Mehen. S. Pontois, 1929, 98.
Men Marz, Brigognan-Plage. P. Burl, 1985, 70, no. 81a.
Mezdoun, Porsporder. P. Scouëzec & Masson, 101.
Mont St-Michel, Montagnes d'Arrée. S. Pontois, 1929, 121, 122, 125.
Montagne Noire. S. Pontois, 1929, 122.
Moulin Blanc. S? Pontois, 1929, 105.
Palue, La. P. Pontois, 1929, 120.
Parc-ar-Menhir, Buzit. 3St. du Chatellier, 201.
Pen-ar-Land, Ushant. 4St, P + cromlech. Briard, 50.
Penhoat, Coray. S. Giot et al, 1979, 415.

Plomelin, Quimper. 3St. du Chatellier, 188.
Plouguin. 2 × S. Giot et al, 1979, 414.
*Porspoder-Lanildut. S? du Chatellier, 110.
Poulguen-Bihan. 3St. Pontois, 1929, 257–9.
Raguenès-Kerglintin, Crozon. 2 × S. Pontois, 1929, 106, 116–21.
St-Denec, Porspoder. 4St. Scouëzec & Masson, 102–3.
St-Laurent. 4St. Pontois, 1929, 122.
St-Nic, Chateaulin. 3St. du Chatellier, 119.
Toulinguet, Crozon. S? Pontois, 1929, 105, 120.
Traonigou, Porsporder. P. Scouëzec & Masson, 100–1.
Trémazan. 4St. Pontois, 1929, 121.
Tri-Men, St-Goazec. 3St. Giot et al, 1979, 415.
Troanigou, St-Douarzel. 3St. Pontois, 1929, 123.
Ty ar c'Huré, Morgat. A. Niel, 151.

ILLE-ET-VILAINE

Alignements du Moulin, St-Just. 3 × S. Burl, 1985, 91–2, no. 110d.
Baillerie, La, Chelun. P. Bézier, 129–30.
Bazouges-la-Pérouse. D. Bézier, 84–5.
Bellevue, Janzé. 4St. Bézier, 20.
Bois-Hervy, St-Just. 4St. Bézier, 197–8.
Bosné, St-Just. S. Rigaud, 1989, 214.
*Bouëxiere, La, Liffré. 3St? Bézier, 237–8.
Brignerault, Bazouges-sous-Hédé. P. Bézier, 13.
*Brossay, Le, Rénac. 4St? Bézier, 174–5.
Clos de la Grée, Langon. 3St. Bézier, 165.
Cordon des Druides, Le, Fougères. S. Burl, 1985, 85, no. 103a.
Demoiselles, Les, Langon. M. Burl, 1985, 82, no. 100.
Demoiselles, Les, St-Just. 3St. Burl, 1985, 92, no. 110f.
Forêt de Haut Sève, St-Aubin-du-Cormier. 4St. Giot et al, 1979, 413.
Grée de la Bocadève, St-Just. S. Rigaud, 1989, 214.
Guinois, Pléchatel. D. Bézier, 178–9.
Lampouy, Médréac. M. Burl, 1985, 86–8, no. 10.
Mâlon N, Guipry. 3St. Bézier, 192.
Mâlon S, Guipry. 4St. Bézier, 192.
Mont-Belleux, Luitré. P. Bézier, 76.
Musson, Langon. 4St. Bézier, 165.
*Nourais, Grand-Fougeray. D? Bézier, 181.
Rocher, St-Just. P. Bézier, 197.
Theil, Le, Rétiers. 3St. Bézier, 151–2.
Villozénes, Sixt. D. Bézier, 217.

LOIRE-ATLANTIQUE

Arbourg, Herbignac. M. Giot et al, 1979, 124.
*Grée Gallot, Soudan. S? l'Helgouac'h, 1984, 47.
Pauvredie, La, St-Père en Retz. 3St. Burl, 1985, 102, no. 123b.
Pierre Fendue, St-Lyphard. S. 10 st. l'Helgouach, 1984, 48.

MORBIHAN

Brouel, Île aux Moines. 3St. Burl, 1985, 115, no. 139f.
*Castellic. 4St. Kergal, 1980a, 58.
Clos Pernal. P. Kergal, 1980a, 58.
Coëpan, Guer. 4St. Briard, 1989, 107.
Coët-er-Hour, Kergroix. M. Le Rouzic, 1935, 21.
Crifol, Ménec. P. Le Rouzic, 1935, 22.
Crucuny. 4St. Kergal, 1980a, 61.
Forêt de Floranges, Korvenec, Camors. S. Scouëzec & Masson, 141.
Grand Menhir Brisé. 4St? inf: l'Helgouach.

Grand Resto. See: Kersolan.
Guernangoué, Roudouallec. 4St. Giot *et al*, 1979, 415.
Hanhon A, Ploemel. M. Le Rouzic, 1935, 21.
Hanhon B, Ploemel. S. Le Rouzic, 1935, 22.
Kerascouet, Erdeven. S. Burl, 1985, 146, no. 187b.
Kerderff, Carnac. S. Le Rouzic, 1935, 22.
*Kergonan, Île-aux-Moines. A. Minot, 16, 17.
Keriavel, Plouharnel. M. Burl, 1985, 151, no. 197b.
Kerlan. M. Sitwell, 1930, 122.
Kerlescan, Carnac. M. Burl, 1985, 141–2, no. 180d.
Kermario, Carnac. M. Burl, 1985, 144, no. 183b.
Kerpenhir. S. Kergal, 1981, 55–6.
Kersolan, Grand Resto, Languidec. M. Abri, 56.
Kerzerho, Erdeven. M + S Burl, 1985, 145–6, no. 187a.
Kerzine, Plouhinec. M. Burl, 1985, 118, no. 147a.
Klud-er-Yer. S. Sitwell, 1930, 123.
Lac, Kerlescan. S. Le Rouzic, 1935, 22.
Lann Granvillarac. 4St. Kergal, 1980a, 71.
Mané Bras, Erdeven. 2 × S. Sitwell, 1930, 122.
Mané Coh Clour. S. Kergal, 1980a, 80.
Ménec, Carnac. M. Burl, 1985, 157–8, no. 203b.
Men-Pleurit. S. Le Rouzic, 1935, 22.
Minardais, Carantoir. 4St. Briard, 1989, 107.
Moulin de St-Pierre-Quiberon, Le. M. Burl, 1985, 158, no. 204a.
Petit-Ménec, Carnac. M. Burl, 1985, 159–60, no. 207.
Pierre Drette, Comper. 4St. Briard, 1989, 35.
Pierres Droites, Monteneuf. 2 × S. Abri, 66.
Prise de Comper, Paimpont. S. Briard, 1989, 35.
Roche de la Vieille, Campénéac. 4St. Briard, 1989, 29–35.
Roches-Piquées, Les, La Gacilly. P. Burl, 1985, 123, no. 157.
St-Barbe, Plouharnel. M. Burl, 1985, 164, no. 213.
St-Cado, Ploemel. S. Le Rouzic, 1935, 22.
Trinité, Le, Le Lac. 3St. Kergal, 1980a, 68.
Trois Roches, Concoret. 3St. Briard, 1989, 107.
Vieux-Moulin, Le, N. Plouharnel. 4St. Fieldwork, 1991.
Vieux-Moulin, Le, S. Plouharnel. 4St. Burl, 1985, 166, no. 216.
Ville Guichas, St-Malon-sur-Mel. 4St. Briard, 1989, 107.

Note: In Brittany there are records of rows with no reliable details: FINISTÈRE. Kereven, Pontois, 1929, 121; Kernaveno, Pontois, 1929, 117; Kerprigent, St-Jean-du-Doigt, Giot *et al*, 414; Kerscaven, Giot *et al*, 404; Lespurit, Peumerit, Giot *et al*, 414; Roscanvel, Pontois, 1929, 117; Tremeran, Pontois, 1929, 113.

NORTHERN IRELAND

ANTRIM

Ballycleagh. D 251 333. 3St. Chart, 17.
Tournagrough. J 252 743. 3St. Chart, 57.
Tully North. D 082 252. P. Chart, 18.
West Division. J 338 887. 3St. Chart, 47.

ARMAGH

Aughadave. J 00. 19. 3St. Chart, 76.
Eshwary. J 02. 28. 3St. Davies, 9, no. 84.

DOWN

Ballyloughlin. J 392 342. P. Jope, 95, no. 289.
Ballynoe. J 481 404. EP. Jope, 1966, 97–9.
Ballyrushy. J 626 523. 3St. Jope, 95, no. 95, no. 290.
Castleward. J 569 499. P. Jope, 95, no. 291.
Killybeg. J 121 312. P. Chart, 149.

Moneyslane. J 254 399. P. Chart, 114.
Portavo. J 571 820. P. *UJA 39*, 1976, 37–42.
Saval Mor. J 122 312. P. Jope, 95, no. 295.
Three Sisters, Greenan. J 102 411. 3St. Jope, 95, no. 293.

FERMANAGH

Brougher. H 359 529. S + 2 × S?. Chart, 156.
Cantytrindle. H 22. 55. 3St. Davies, 12, no. 69.
Cavancarragh. H 306 435. Tang + S. *JRSAI 14*, 1878, 499.
Coolgarren. H 22. 55. 3St. Chart, 154.
*Drumacken. H 362 515. 3St. Chart, 157.
Drumskinny. H 201 707. S. Waterman, 1964.
Formil S. H 159 675. Tang. Chart, 145.
*Formil N. H 159 676. 3St. Chart, 145.
Montiaghroe NW. H 190 692. 3St. Chart, 144.
Montiaghroe Centre. H 194 693. S. Chart, 144.
Montiaghroe SE, H 197 690. 3St. Chart, 144.
Ratoran. H 326 465. 4St. Davies, l939, 12, no. 62.
Reyfad Stones. H 124 442. 4St. Chart, 158.

LONDONDERRY

Altaghoney. C 515 013. Tang. Davies, l939, 11.
Aughlish NW. C 662 043. Tang. McConkey, 52.
Aughlish N. C 662 043. Det. McConkey, 52.
Ballygroll. C 533 146. S. McConkey, 51.
Ballyholly W. C 572 118. 2 × S. Chart, 199.
Ballyholly E. S. Chart, 199.
Ballyholly. C 575 118. S. Chart, 199.
Clagan. C 583 054. 3St. Chart, 202.
Coolnasillagh. C 785 003. 3St. Chart, 208.
Corick. H 778 897. 6 × S + 3St. McConkey, 53–4.

TYRONE

Aghalane. H 495 920. S. Chart, 218.
Beaghmore. H 685 842. 7StCs. 6 × S + 2 × 4St + 3St. May, 1953.
Beaghmore A, B. H 685 842. 3 × S + 4St. May, 1953.
Beaghmore C, D. H 685 842. S + 4St. May, 1953.
Beaghmore E. H 685 842. S + 3St. May, 1953.
Beaghmore F, G. H 685 842. S, Ent. May, 1953.
Beleevna Beg td. H 693 827. 3St. Chart, 233.
Broughderg Centre. H 650 861. Ent. McConkey, 61.
Broughderg N. H 661 873. A. McConkey, 61.
Broughderg S (A). H 653 843. Ent. McConkey, 61.
Broughderg S (B). H 653 843. Ent? McConkey, 61.
Castledamph. H 522 925. A. *JRSAI 68*, 1938, 106.
Clogherny Butterlope. H 493 497. 4St. *UJA 2*, 1939, 36–43.
Copney. H 599 782. S. McConkey, 62–3.
Cornamaddy. H 685 698. 2 × S. Chart, 244.
Creevy Upper. H 25. 88. 3St. Chart, 219.
Cregganconroe NE. H 663 758. S. Chart, 223.
Cregganconroe SW. H 648 752. S. McConkey, 64.
Creggandevesky. H 636 740. P. McConkey, 65.
Crew Lower. H 315 848. P. Chart, 220.
Culvacullion. H 505 888. S + 3St. McConkey, 58.
Davagh Lower S. H 701 870. Tang. Chart, 226.
Davagh Lower N. H 707 867. 3St. Chart, 226.
Derryallen, Trillick. H 309 531. 3St. Chart, 250.
Dooish. H 314 697. S. Chart, 243.
Doorat. H 493 974. 4St. Chart, 216.
Dunbunrawer. H 48. 85. S. Davies, 1939, 7.
Edentoit. H 709 749. P. Chart, 238.
Glassmullagh N. H 387 805. 2 × S. Chart, 230.

Glassmullagh S. H 387 804. 2 × S. *ibid*, 231.
Glenmacoffer. H 530 862. 3St. Chart, 224.
Glengeen. H 383 555. S. Chart, 250.
Golan. H 66. 94. 4St. Chart, 219.
Grange. H 830 752. P. Chart, 240.
Knocknahorna. H 410 989. A. McConkey, 56.
Meendamph. H 458 976. S. McConkey, 56.
Moymore. H 712 745. Tang + 3St. Chart, 238.
Murnells. H 662 757. P. Chart, 238.
Oughtboy. H 59. 93. S. Chart, 218.
Sandville and Lisvidin. C 388 048. P. Evans, 204.
Tremoge NE. H 655 738. S + 3St. Chart, 239.
Tremoge SW. H 654 733. 3St. Chart, 239.
Tulnacross. H 705 801. P. Chart, 233.
Turnabarson. H 68. 69. S. Chart, 244.

REPUBLIC OF IRELAND

CAVAN

St Brigid's Stones. H 059 378. 3St. Evans, 67.
Shantemon. H 466 077. 4St. Evans, 67.

CLARE

Knockaroura. R 423 803. 4St. O'Nuallain, 1988, 240, no. 70.

CORK

Annagannihy. W 392 836. P. O'Nuallain, 1988, 242, no. 83.
Ardrah. W 069 544. 4St. O'Nuallain, 1988, 235, no. 40.
Ballindeenisk. W 723 819. 3St. O'Nuallain, 1988, 232, no. 14.
Ballinvarrig. W 648 789. P. O'Nuallain, 1988, 244, no. 101.
Ballycommon. V 976 437. P. O'Nuallain, 1988, 248, no. 137.
Ballyhalwick. W 252 521. P. O'Nuallain, 1988, 246, no. 123.
Ballyhesty. W 672 807. P. O'Nuallain, 1988, 244, no. 100.
Ballynagree. W 363 819. P. O'Nuallain, 1988, 243, no. 91.
Ballyvongane. W 380 759. P. O'Nuallain, 1988, 243, no. 95.
Barrahaurin. W 452 824. 4St. Macalister, 1921, 304.
Barryshall. W 462 425. 2 × P. O'Nuallain, 1988, 248, no. 139.
Baurgaum. W 023 469. P. O'Nuallain, 1988, 247, no. 126.
Bawnatemple. W 405 710. P. O'Nuallain, 1988, 245, no. 105.
Bawnmore. W 363 782. P. O'Nuallain, 1988, 243, no. 93.
Bealick. W 351 727. 3St. O'Nuallain, 1988, 233, no. 24.
Beenalaght. W 485 873. 4St. O'Nuallain, 1988, 232, no. 12.
Behagullane. W 275 567. 4St. O'Nuallain, 1988, 246, no. 117.
Cabragh. W 278 798. 4St. O'Nuallain, 1988, 232, no. 16.
Caherbaroul. W 363 782. P. O'Nuallain, 1988, 243, no. 94.
Cahermuckee. W 083 572. P. O'Nuallain, 1988, 245, no. 113.
Candroma. W 233 740. P? O'Nuallain, 1988, 252, no. 178.
Canrooska. V 936 583. 4St. O'Nuallain, 1984a, 39.
Canrooska. V 936 583. 3St. O'Nuallain, 1984a, 39.
Cappaboy Beg. W 095 604. P. O'Nuallain, 1988, 245, no. 111.
Carrig. W 422 450. P. O'Nuallain, 1988, 247, no. 134.
Carrigadrohid. W 418 726. P. O'Nuallain, 1988, 244, no. 103.
Carrigagulla. NE. W 371 829. 3St. O'Nuallain, 1988, 232, no. 10.

Carrigagulla SW. W 384 838. 3St. O'Nuallain, 1988, 232, no. 11.
Carrigaline. W 69. 50. 4St. Killanin & Duignan, 133.
Castlenalacht. W 485 612. 4St. O'Nuallain, 1988, 235, no. 36.
Caum. W 387 716. P. O'Nuallain, 1988, 244, no. 104.
Ceancullig. W 136 488. P. O'Nuallain, 1988, 247, no. 129.
Clashmaguire. W 278 789. P. O'Nuallain, 1988, 243, no. 90.
Clodagh NE. W 152 499. P. O'Nuallain, 1988, 246, no. 121.
Clodagh SW. W 152 499. P. O'Nuallain, 1988, 247, no. 131.
Clogagh. W 453 470. P. O'Nuallain, 1988, 247, no. 135.
Cloghboola Beg. W 305 853. 3St. O'Nuallain, 1984a, 31.
Cloghboola More. W 277 872. 3St. O'Nuallain, 1988, 231, no. 7.
Cloghvoula. R 158 143. 4St. O'Nuallain, 1988, 231, no. 1.
Clongaskan. V 644 446. 3St. O'Nuallain, 1988, 236, no. 45.
Cloonshear Beg. W 264 446. 3St. O'Nuallain, 1988, 234, no. 27.
Commillane. V 977 229. 3St. O'Nuallain, 1988, 237, no. 56.
Coolacoosane. W 323 789. 3St. O'Nuallain, 1988, 233, no. 18.
Coolavoher. W 191 753. 3St. O'Nuallain, 1988, 233, no. 21.
Coolcoulaghta. W 932 393. P. O'Nuallain, 1988, 248, no. 136.
Coolgarriff. W 413 769. P. O'Nuallain, 1988, 243, no. 96.
Cools. W 247 730. P. O'Nuallain, 1988, 244, no. 192.
Coomleagh NW. W 100 537. P. O'Nuallain, 1988, 246, no. 120.
Coomleagh SE. W 119 536. 3St. O'Nuallain, 1988, 235, no. 39.
Crumpane. V 657 495. P. O'Nuallain, 1988, 247, no. 125.
Cullenagh. W 116 053. 3St. Lynch A., 1982, 206.
Cullenagh West. W 160 526. P. O'Nuallain, inf. 1990.
Currakeal. V 937 582. 3St. O'Nuallain, 1988, 234, no. 31.
Curraghawaddra. W 396 795. P. O'Nuallain, 1988, 243, no. 92.
Cusloura. W 313 807. P. O'Nuallain, 1988, 243, no. 88.
Derrynagree. W 140 627. 3St. O'Nuallain, 1988, 234, no. 32.
Derrynasaggart. W 183 780. 3St. O'Nuallain, 1988, 232, no. 15.
Dooneens. W 382 815. 3St. O'Nuallain, 1988, 233, no. 19.
Dromasta. W 112 458. P. O'Nuallain, 1988, 247, no. 130.
Dromcarra N. W 278 681. 4St. O'Nuallain, 1988, 234, no. 28.
Dromdrasil. W 171 557. 4St. O'Nuallain, 1988, 236, no. 41.
Dromteewakeen. V 760 081. 4St. Lynch A., 1981, 103.
Eyeries. V 645 505. 3St. O'Nuallain, 1988, 236, no. 43.
Fanahy. V 651 448. 3St. O'Nuallain, 1988, 236, no. 44.
Farranahineeny. W 214 607. 4St. O'Nuallain, 1988, 235, no. 35.
Farranamanagh. V 825 385. 3St. O'Nuallain, 1988, 252, no. 175.
Foherlagh. W 062 355. P. O'Nuallain, 1988, 248, no. 142.
Foildarrig. V 684 467. 3St. O'Nuallain, 1988, 236, no. 46.
Garrane SE. W 477 908. P. O'Nuallain, 1988, 241, no. 77.
Garrane NW. W 478 912. 4St. O'Nuallain, 1988, 231, no. 5.
Garraneleigh. W 432 687. P. O'Nuallain, 1988, 245, no. 108.

Garranenamuddagh. W 442 650. P. O'Nuallain, 1988, 245, no. 110.
Garryduff. W 904 854. 3St. O'Nuallain, 1988, 252, no. 174.
Glandine. W 481 888. P. O'Nuallain, 1988, 250, no. 161.
Glantane E. W 235 828. P. O'Nuallain, 1988, 242, no. 81.
Glantane W. W 277 830. 3St. O'Nuallain, 1988, 231, no. 9.
Glenleigh. W 323 903. P. Inf: O'Nuallain, 1990.
Gneeves. W 469 928. 3St. O'Nuallain, 1988, 231, no. 4.
Gortloughra. W 112 59. P. O'Nuallain, 1988, 245, no. 112.
Gortyleahy. W 319 717. 3St. O'Nuallain, 1988, 233, no. 23.
Gurranes. W 175 315. 4St. O'Nuallain, 1988, 237, no. 55.
Gurteenaduige. W 205 392. P. O'Nuallain, 1988, 253, no. 179.
Gurteenard. R 397 023. P. O'Nuallain, 1988, 241, no. 76.
Island. W 604908. P. O'Nuallain, 1988, 242, no. 79.
Kealkil. W 055 555. P. O'Nuallain, 1988, 246, no. 119.
Keilnascarta NE. V 994 453. P. O'Nuallain, 1988, 247, no. 127.
Keilnascarta South. V 994 451. P. O'Nuallain, 1988, 247, no. 128.
Keilnascarta NW. V 993 453. 3St. O'Nuallain, 1988, 236, no. 48.
Kilcaskan. V 817 523. 3St. O'Nuallain, 1988, 235, no. 38.
Kilcrohan. W 882 374. P. O'Nuallain, 1988, 248, no. 140.
Kilcullen. W 451 813. P. O'Nuallain, 1988, 243–4, no. 97.
Kilmore. W 125 436. P. O'Nuallain, 1988, 248, no. 138.
Kinneagh. W 309 575. P. Inf: O'Nuallain, 1990.
Kippagh. W 225 883. 3St. O'Nuallain, 1988, 231, no. 6.
Knockagappul. W 346 831. 3St. O'Nuallain, 1988, 252, no. 173.
Knockane. W 339 644. P. O'Nuallain, 1988, 245, no. 109.
Knockantota. W 558 877. P. O'Nuallain, 1988, 242, no. 85.
Knockatlowig. W 320 443. 3St. O'Nuallain, 1988, 237, no. 51.
Knockawaddra E. W 271 460. P. O'Nuallain, 1988, 247, no. 132.
Knockawaddra W. W 269 460. 3St. O'Nuallain, 1988, 237, no. 50.
Knockeennagrough. W 806 830. P. O'Nuallain, 1988, 252, no. 177.
Knocknakilla NW. W 282 867. P. O'Nuallain, 1988, 242, no. 80.
Knocknakilla SE. W 297 841. P. *JCHAS 36*, 1931, 9–19.
Knocknanagh E. R 227 057. 4St. O'Nuallain, 1988, 231, no. 2.
Knockraheen NW. W 300 812. P. O'Nuallain, 1988, 242, no. 87.
Knockraheen SE. W 303 802. P. O'Nuallain, 1988, 243, no. 89.
Knocks. W 304 448. P. O'Nuallain, 1988, 247, no. 133.
Lackabaun. W 192 614. P. O'Nuallain, 1988, 245, no. 114.
Leitry Lower. W 138 488. 3St. O'Nuallain, 1988, 236, no. 49.
Lissaclarig W. W 039 367. 3St. O'Nuallain, 1988, 237, no. 53.
Loughane E. W 570 781. P. O'Nuallain, 1988, 244, no. 99.
Maughanasilly. W 044 585. 4St. Lynch A., 1981, 69–71, 107.
Maulinward. V 975 438. 3St. O'Nuallain, 1988, 237, no. 52.
Meenahony S. W 469 835. 2 × P. O'Nuallain, 1988, 242, no. 84.
Mill Little. V 989 565. P. O'Nuallain, 1988, 246, no. 118.
Monavaddra. W 195 623. 3St. O'Nuallain, 1988, 235, no. 34.

Murrahin N. W 029 365. 3St. O'Nuallain, 1988, 237, no. 54.
Newcastle. W 577 804. 3St. Lynch, A., 1982, 206.
Piercetown. W 690 593. 4St. O'Nuallain, 1988, 235, no. 37.
Rathcool. V 940 332. P. O'Nuallain, 1988, 248, no. 141.
Reanerre. W 204 727. 4St. O'Nuallain, 1988, 233, no. 22.
Reavouler. W 200 437. P. Roberts, J., 49.
Roovesmore SE. W 456 701. P. O'Nuallain, 1988, 245, no. 107.
Roovesmore NW. W 450 702. 4St. O'Nuallain, 1988, 234, no. 25.
Rossnakilla. W 324 658. 3St. O'Nuallain, 1988, 234, no. 29.
Scartbaun. W 003 461. 3St. O'Nuallain, 1988, 236, no. 47.
Shandagan W. W 408 694. P. O'Nuallain, 1988, 245, no. 106.
Shanlaragh. W 258 595. P. O'Nuallain, 1988, 246, no. 116.
Shehy Beg. W 145 591. P. O'Nuallain, 1988, 246, no. 115.
Slievereagh. W 181 803. P. O'Nuallain, 1988, 242, no. 86.
Teernahillane. V 639 457. P. O'Nuallain, 1988, 246, no. 124.
Toom. W 284 555. P. O'Nuallain, 1988, 246, no. 122.
Tooreenglanahee. R 174 207. 3St. O'Nuallain, 1988, 231, no. 3.
Tullig. W 318 872. 4St. O'Nuallain, 1988, 231, no. 8.
Turnaspidogy. c. W 188 670. 3St. O'Nuallain, 1988, 234, no. 26.

DONEGAL

Ballymagaraghy. C 605 472. P. Lacy, 75, no. 350.
Ballymunterhiggin. G 872 601. P. Lacy, 77. no. 354.
Barnes Lower SW. C 107 245. P. Lacy, 77, no. 356.
Barnes Lower NE. C 122 263. 3St. Lacy, 77, no. 358.
Carlan Upper. C 1. 3. Once 4St. Lacy, 90, no. 528.
Cloghfin. C 355 111. P. Lacy, 79, no. 382.
Killycolman. C 282 334. 3St. Lacy, 83, no. 435.
Knocknafaugher. C 039 344. 4St. Lacy, 83, no. 439.
Labbadish. C 238 096. 3St. Lacy, 83, no. 441.
Meenadoran. C 392 437. P. Lacy, 84, no. 458.
Portleon. C 172 233. 3St. Lacy, 85, no. 468.
Rashenny NW. C 418 482. 4St. Lacy, 85, no. 471.
Rashenny SE. C 422 476. 3St? Lacy, 85, no. 472.
Roosky. C 38. 45. S. Lacy, 86, no. 477.
Stroove. C 673 430. P. Lacy, 88, no. 489.

DUBLIN

*Dun Laoghaire. O 2. 2. 3St? Aubrey, I, 127.

GALWAY

Attidoddaun. L 590 576. P. Gosling, 1991, 25.
*Ballynew NW. L 621 590. P. Gosling, 1991, 25.
Ballynew SE. L 629 584. P. Gosling, 1991, 26.
Baunoge. L 701 563. 3St. Gosling, 1991, 26.
Cloonederowen. L 667 570. P. Gosling, 1991, 27.
Crocknaraw NE. L 664 561. P or 4S? Gosling, 1991, 28.
Crocknaraw SW. L 658 559. P. Gosling, 1991, 27.
Derryinver. L 688 608. 4St or 2 × 3St? *JGAHS 25*, 1953–4, 98.
Gleninagh. L 815 552. 4St. Gosling, 1991, 29.
Knockaunbaun. L 902 255. P. Gosling, 1991, 29.
Oorid. L 924 245. P. Gosling, 1991, 30.
Poundcarton. L 887 553. 4St. Gosling, 1991, 30.
Rosleague. L 687 574. P. Gosling, 1991, 31.
Sheeauns. L 625 581. 3S. Gosling, 1991, 31.

KERRY

Ardamore. Q 521 000. 3St. O'Nuallain, 1988, 238, no. 60.
Ballineanig-Castlequarter. Q 359 043. P. Cuppage, 40, no. 55.
Ballygarret. Q 685 101. 3St. O'Nuallain, 1988, 238, no. 59.
Ballineanig-Castlequarter. Q 359 043. P. Cuppage, 40, no. 55.
Ballygarret. Q 685 101. 3St. O'Nuallain, 1988, 238, no. 59.
Ballyrishteen. Q 489 027. P. Cuppage, 40–1, no. 56.
Beale Middle. V 885 475. 4St. O'Nuallain, 1988, 238, no. 57.
Bolus. V 396 630. P. Inf: O'Nuallain, 1990.
Caherpiece. Q 682 017. P. Inf: O'Nuallain, 1990.
Canburrin. V 504 773. P. O'Nuallain, 1988, 253, no. 182.
Cashelkeelty. V 747 575. 3St. Lynch A., 1981, 65–9, 76.
Clogher. Q 314 033. 3St. O'Nuallain, 1988, 240, no. 69.
Clogherane. V 788 556. P. O'Nuallain, 1988, 250, no. 160.
Cloonsharragh. Q 511 128. 4St. O'Nuallain, 1988, 238, no. 58.
Coomnahorna E. V 555 607. P. O'Nuallain, 1988, 250, no. 159.
Coumduff. Q 581 043. P. Cuppage, 41, no. 57.
Curraduff. Q 703 088. 3St. Cuppage, 40.
Curraghmore. V 801 819. 3St. O'Nuallain, 1988, 238, no. 62.
Derreenafoyle. V 794 688. P. O'Nuallain, 1988, 250, no. 158.
Derrygorman. Q 599 044. P. Cuppage, 41, no. 58.
Doory. V 546 710. 3St. O'Nuallain, 1988, 239, no. 64.
Drom E. Q 530 113. P. Inf: O'Nuallain, 1990.
Dromatouk SW. V 095. 071. 4St. Lynch A., 1981, 97–103.
Dromatouk NE. V 952 711. 3St. O'Nuallain, 1988, 239, no. 44.
*Dromavally NW. Q 590 063. S? Cuppage, 70, no. 221.
Dromavally SE. Q 593 053. P. Cuppage, 41, no. 53.
Dromkeare. V 50. 65. 4St. Lynch A., 1982, 206.
Dromod. V 552 704. P. O'Nuallain, 1988, 250, no. 156.
Dromteewakeen. V 761 808. 3St. Lynch, A., 1981, 104.
Eightercua. V 512 646. 4St. JRSAI 32, 1902, 330.
Fahan. V 351 975. P. Cuppage, 43, no. 68.
Fermoyle. V 453 724. 3St. O'Nuallain, 1988, 252, no. 176.
Garrane. Q 425 048. P. Cuppage, 41, no. 61.
Garrough. V 558 608. 4St. O'Nuallain, 1988, 239, no. 68.
Garrydine. V 543 837. P. O'Nuallain, 1988, 250, no. 155.
Gearha. V 775 735. P. O'Nuallain, 1988, 250, no. 157.
Gortacloghane. V 759 738. 4St. O'Nuallain, 1984a, 49.
Gortnagulla. V 568 836. 3St. O'Nuallain, 1988, 238, no. 61.
Gowlaneard. Q 530 021. P. Cuppage, 42, no. 62.
Kildreelig. V 408 637. 4St. O'Nuallain, 1988, 239, no. 67.
Kilnabrack Lower. V 663 914. P. Inf: O'Nuallain, 1990.
Kimego. V 450 808. P. O'Nuallain, 1988, 253, no. 181.
Knockavrogeen E. Q 425 045. P. Cuppage, 42, no. 63.
Lissyviggeen. V 997 906. P. O'Nuallain, 1988, 250, no. 154.
Milltown N. Q 429 011. P. O'Nuallain, 1988, 249, no. 148.
Milltown S. Q 429 010. P. Cuppage, 64–5, no. 191.
Minard W. V 536 991. P. Cuppage, 43, no. 65.
Reask. Q 367 046. P. Cuppage, 43, no. 66.
Teeromoyle. V 571 823. P. O'Nuallain, 1988, 253, no. 180.

KILKENNY

The Three Friars. S 606 277. 3St. O'Nuallain, 1988, 240, no. 71.

LIMERICK

Graig. R 457 308. 3St. Limerick Arch. Survey.
Lackanagoneeny. R 838 533. 3St. JCHAS 60, 1955, 68–9.
*Lough Gur E. R 638 411. A. PRIA 54C, 1951, 39.
Tomdeely N. R 329 524. 4St. O'Nuallain, 1988, 240–1, no. 72.

LOUTH

Balregan SE. J 027 000. P. Buckley, 1986, 19, no. 182.
Balregan NW. J 023 100. 4St. Buckley, 1986, 18, no. 176.
Baltray. J 144 851. P. Buckley, 1986, 19, no. 183.
Carrickedmond E. J 024 128. 4St. Buckley, 1986, 18, no. 177.
Carrickedmond W. J 026 128. 4St. Buckley, 1986, 18, no. 178.
Edenkill. H 978 123. 4St. Buckley, 1986, 20, no. 199.
Ravensdale Park. J 098 157. 4St. Buckley, 1986, 22, no. 219.

MAYO

Eskeragh. G 048 189. 4St. inf: O'Nuallain.
Derryhillagh. G 084 092. P. O'Nuallain, inf. 1990.
Killadangan. L 943 826. 4St. O'Nuallain, 1988, 197.

MEATH

Ballinvally. N 580 786. P. Moore, 1987, 42.
Farranaglogh. N 534 827. P. Moore, 1987, 43.
Grangegeeth. N 964 792. P. Moore, 1987, 43.
Millockstown. N 891 877. P. Buckley, 1986, 21, no. 203.

TIPPERARY

Barbaha. R 768 759. 3St. O'Nuallain, 1988, 241, no. 73.
*Timoney. S 194 837. S? Stout, G.T., 1984, 18.

WATERFORD

Tooreen West. S 245 117. 4St. O'Nuallain, 1988, 241, no. 74. See also the Four- to Six- and Three-Stone Gazetteers.

WEXFORD

Robinstown Great. S 811 291. P. O'Nuallain, 1984b, 17, no. 6.
Whitechurch. S 792 190. 3St. O'Nuallain, 1988, 241, no. 75.

WICKLOW

*Castleruddery. S 925 937. S? JRSAI 75, 1945, 266.
Giant's Grave. T 210 961. P. Price, 1934, 40.

SCOTLAND

ABERDEENSHIRE

*Bankhead of Clatt. NJ 529 270. A? NSA Aberdeen 12, 1845, 851.
Broomend of Crichie. NJ 779 196. A. PSAS 54, 1919–20, 154.
Castle Fraser. NJ 717 125. P. Coles, F., 1901, 197, no. 3.
*Crookmore. NJ 588 184. A? Keiller, 1934, 18, 19.
*Druidsfield. NJ 578 177. A? NSA Aberdeen 12, 1845, 449.
*Hillhead of Clatt. NJ 528 265. A? NSA Aberdeen 12, 1845, 851.
*Nether Balfour. NJ 539 172. A? NSA Aberdeen 12, 1845, 449.

ANGUS

Auchterhouse. NO 345 392. P. Burl, 1988, 103.
Corogle Burn. NO 348 601. P. Burl, 1988, 108–9.
Fletcherfield. NO 401 525. P. Coutts, 1970, 19.

ARGYLL

Achnabreac. NR 856 899. P. *PSAS 95*, 1961–2, 23, no. 155; 28, no. 191.
Balliemore. NS 056 845. P. *RCAHM-S, Argyll VI*, 1988, 126–7, no. 198.
Ballymeanoch. NR 833 964. [A2/12]. 4St + P. *PSAS 109*, 1977–8, 104–12.
Ballochroy. NR 730 524. [A4/4]. 3St. Burl, 1983, 7–11.
Barbreck. NM 831 064. P. Patrick, 1979, S80–S85.
Barcaldine. NM 963 421. P. *RCAHM-S, Argyll II*, 1975, 62, no. 111.
Carnasserie. NM 834 008. P. *PSAS 95*, 1961–2, 12, no. 70; 25, no. 166.
Carse. NR 742 615. [A3/6a]. P. *RCAHM-S, Argyll VI*, 1988, 131. no. 204.
*Clenmacrie. NM 924 285. 3St. *RCAHM-S, Argyll II*, 1975, 62, no. 114.
Clochkeil. NR 657 244. 3St. *RCAHM-Argyll, I*, 1971, 62, no. 137.
Cnoc Pollphail. NR 931 683. P. *RCAHM-S, Argyll VI*, 1988, 131, no. 207.
Crinan Moss. NR 808 941. S + P. *PSAS 95*, 1961–2, 26, no. 173.
Duachy. NM 801 205. [A1/4]. 3St. *RCAHM, Argyll, II*, 1975, 62, no. 116.
Dunamuck Mid. NR 848 924. [A2/14] P. *PSAS 95*, 1961–2, 27, no. 177.
Dunamuck N. NR 847 929. [A2/21]. 3St. *PSAS 95*, 1961–2, 27, no. 178.
Dunamuck S. NR 848 923. [A2/20]. P. *PSAS 95*, 1961–2, 26, no. 176.
Escart. NR 846 667. [A4/1]. 4St. *RCAHM, Argyll, I*, 1971, 63, no. 143.
Inveryne. NR 915 749. 3St. *RCAHM-S, Argyll VI*, 1988, 134–5, no. 218.
Kames. NR 971 714. P. *RCAHM-S, Argyll VI*, 1988, 135, no. 219.
Kilmartin. NR 827 979. [A2/8]. 2 × P. *PSAS 95*, 1961–2, 28, no. 187.
Loch Seil, NM 801 206. [A1/4]. 3St. *RCAHM-S, Argyll II*, no. 116.
Macharioch. R 736 093. 4St. *PSAS 64*, 1929–30, 319–20, no. 32.
Macrihanish. NR 644 206. [A4/15]. 4St. Ruggles, 1984, 53.
Mealdarroch. NR 877 680. 3St. *PSAS 53*, 1918–19, no. 4.
Salachary. NM 840 040. [A2/26]. 3St. *PSAS 95*, 1961–2, 224, no. 162.
Skeroblin. NR 706 273. S. *D & E*, 1982, 22.
South Muasdale. NR 679 391. P. *PSAS 64*, 1929–30, 306, no. 7.
Tarbert. NR 606 823 to 608 822. P? *PSAS 66*, 1931–2, 146–7.
Upper Fernoch. NR 727 860. P. *PSAS 95*, 1961–2, 29, no. 195.

ARRAN

Auchenar. NR 891 364. P. Bryce, T.H., 1910, 155.

AYR

Ballantrae. NX 087 818. [G1/4]. S or 3St. Thom, 1967, 137.

BARRA

Borve. NF 652 014. P. *RCAHM-S, Outer Hebrides*, 1928, 136, no. 461.
Brevig. NL 689 990. P. *RCAHM-S, Outer Hebrides*, 1928, 136, no. 460.

BERWICK

Brothers' Stones. NT 619 360. P. Baldwin, 1985, 164.

BUTE

Stravanan Bay. NS 085 553. [A9/7]. 3St. *PSAS 4*, 1860–2, 396.

CAITHNESS

Broughwin NE. ND 313 412. M. Freer & Myatt, 1982, 59–60.
Broughwin Centre E. ND 312 409. M. Freer & Myatt, 1982, 60.
Broughwin SW. ND 311 408. D. Freer & Myatt, 1982, 60.
Broughwin Centre W. ND 311 409. 4St. Freer & Myatt, 1982, 60.
Camster. ND 260 437. [N1/14]. M. Freer & Myatt, 1982, 62.
Dirlot. ND 123 485. [N1/17]. M. Freer & Myatt, 1982, 62.
Garrywhin. ND 314 413. [N1/9]. M. Freer & Myatt, 1982, 60.
Loch of Yarrows NW. ND 313 441. [N1/7]. M. Freer & Myatt, 1982, 61–2.
Loch of Yarrows SE. ND 316 432..P. Gunn, 1915, 349–50.
Loch Watenan. ND 318 411. M? Freer & Myatt, 1982, 59.
Mid Clyth. ND 295 384. [N1/1]. M. Freer & Myatt, 1982, 58–9.
Tormsdale. ND 148 497. M, S. Myatt, 1988, 295–7.
Upper Dounreay E. ND 012 660. [N1/3]. M. Freer & Myatt, 1983, 120.
Upper Dounreay W. ND 007 660. M. Freer & Myatt, 1983, 120–1.
Watenan. ND 315 412. M. Freer & Myatt, 1982, 59.
Watten. ND 223 517. [N1/15]. P. Thom, 1967, 139.

COLL

Totronald. NM 166 559. P. *RCAHM-S, Argyll III*, 1980, 71, no. 120.

COLONSAY

Drumclash. NR 367 949. P. *RCAHM-S, Argyll V*, 1984, 68, no. 96.

DUMFRIESSHIRE

Dyke. NT 084 036. [G6/4]. 3St. *RCAHM-S Dumfriess*, 1920, p145, no 426.
*Girdle Stanes. NY 258 965. [G7/4]. A? *RCAHM-S Dumfriess*, 1920, 78–9, no. 199.
*Skipknowe. NY 11. 94. P. *RCAHM-S East Lothian*, 1924, 212, no. 627.

FIFE

*Bandrum. NT 036 915. P. *RCAHM-S Fife*, 1933, 267, no. 489.

North Glassmount. NT 244 884. P. *RCAHM-S Fife*, 1933, 346.

ISLAY

Achnancarranan. NR 389 460. 3St. *RCAHM-Argyll V*, 1984, fig. 63a.
Ballinaby. NR 220 671. [A7/5]. 3St. *RCAHM-S, Argyll, V*, 1984, 63. no. 79.
*Beinn Cham. NR 349 679. P. Ruggles, 1984, 165.
*Clachan Cean Ile. NR 436 483. P. *RCAHM-S, Argyll V*, 1984, 65, no. 85.
Finlaggan. NR 392 685. P. *RCAHM-S, Argyll V*, 1984, 68, no. 97.
*Kilbride. NR 383 465. P. Ruggles, 1984, 180.
Knocklearoch. NR 398 648. P. *RCAHM-S, Argyll V*, 1984, 69, no. 108.
*Lagavullin. NR 395 462. P. *PSAS 48*, 1913–14, 404–7.

JURA

Carragh a'Ghlinne. NR 512 664. [A6/6]. 4St. *RCAHM-S, Argyll V*, 1984, 64–5, no. 83.
*Knockrome. NR 548 714 to NR 560 717. [A6/4]. 3St. *RCAHM-S, Argyll V*, 1984, 70–1, no. 116.
Sannaig. NR 518 648. [A6/3]. 3St. *RCAHM-S, Argyll V*, 1984, 116, no. 117.
Strone Farm. NR 507 637. P. *RCAHM-S, Argyll V*, 1984, 71, no. 120.

KINCARDINE

*Glassel House. c. NO 649 997. P. *PSAS 39*, 1904–5, 205.
*Kempstone Hill. NO 876 894. [B3/5]. P. Thom, 1967, 98.

KINROSS

Orwell. NO 149 043. P. *Arch J 131*, 1974, 8–9, 27–9.

KIRKCUDBRIGHT

Bagbie. NX 498 564. P. Burl, 1988, 135.
*Thieves. NX 404 716. [G4/2]. P. *RCAHM-S, Galloway II*, 1914, no. 367.

LEWIS

Airigh nam Bidearan. NB 234 298. [H1/5]. 3St. Ruggles, 1984, 81.
Callanish. NB 213 330. A + 3 × 4St. Ponting, G. & M. 1984.
Clach an Tursa. NB 204 429. [H1/16]. 3St. *RCAHM-S, Outer Hebrides*, 1928, 24, no. 87. 'Carloway'.
*Cnoc a Greana. NF 922 819. 4St. *RCAHM-S, Outer Hebrides*, 1928, 43, no. 134.
Cul a Chleit. NB 247 303. P. *RCAHM-S, Outer Hebrides*, 1928, 29, no. 95.
Great Bernera. NB 164 342. P. *RCAHM-S, Outer Hebrides*, 1928, 24, no. 77.
Nisabost. NG 041 973. [H2/2]. 3St. *RCAHM-S, Outer Hebrides*, 1928, 43, no. 135.

MORAY

East Port. NJ 03. 27. P. *PSAS 41*, 1906–7, 131–4.

MULL

Ardalanish. NM 378 188. P. *RCAHM-S, Argyll III*, 1980, 65, no. 88.
Ardnacross. NM 542 491. 2 × 3St (?A). *RCAHM-S, Argyll III*, 1980, fig. 18.

Balliscate. NM 499 541. [M1/8]. 3St. *RCAHM-S, Argyll III*, 1980, 65, no. 90.
Calgary. NM 384 523. P. *RCAHM-S, Argyll III*, 1980, 68, no. 104.
Cladh Chatain. NM 526 695. P. *RCAHM-S, Argyll III*, 1980, 66, no. 99.
*Craigaid. NM 402 390. P. *RCAHM-S, Argyll III*, 1980, 66, no. 100.
Dail na Carraigh. NM 370 218. [M2/7]. P. *RCAHM-S, Argyll III*, 1980, 88.
Dervaig Centre. NM 439 520. [M1/5]. 4St. *RCAHM-S, Argyll III*, 1980, 66, no. 101 (2).
Dervaig NNW. NM 435 531. [M1/4]. 4St. *RCAHM-S, Argyll III*, 1980, 66, no. 101 (1).
Dervaig SSE. NM 438 516. 4St. *RCAHM-S, Argyll III*, 1980, 67. no, 101 (3).
Dervaig E. NM 442 519. 3St. *D & E*, 1957, 9.
Glengorm. NM 434 571. [M1/7]. 3St. *RCAHM-S, Argyll III*, 1980, 68, no. 105; *JHA 20*, 1989, S137–S149.
*Gruline. NM 545 396 and 543 397. P. *RCAHM-S, Argyll III*, 1980, 68, no. 106.
Lag. NM 362 535. P. *RCAHM-S, Argyll III*, 1980, 68–9, no. 109.
Mingary. NM 413 552. 3St. *RCAHM-S, Argyll III*, 1980, 70, no. 111.
Quinish. NM 413 552. [M1/3]. 4St. Ruggles, 1984, 123 (ML2).
Scallastle. NM 699 382. 3St. *RCAHM-S, Argyll III*, 1980, 71–2, no. 121.
Uluvalt. NM 546 300. 4St. *RCAHM-S, Argyll III*, 1980, 72, no. 121.

NORTH UIST

Blashaval. NF 887 717. [H3/8]. 3St. *RCAHM-S, Outer Hebrides*, 1928, 82, no. 246.
Fir Bhreige. NF 770 702. P. *RCAHM-S, Outer Hebrides*, 1928, 85, no. 255.
Leac nan Cailleacha Dubha. NF 785 763. P. *RCAHM-S, Outer Hebrides*, 1928, 85, no. 258.
Na Fir Bhreige. See: Blashaval.
Pobull Fhinn. NF 844 650. EP. Thom, Thom & Burl, 1980, 310–11.
Skeal Traval. NF 853 707. 4St. *D & E*, 1986, 52.

ORKNEYS

Braeside. HY 564 371. 3St. *RCAHM-S, Orkneys II*, 1946, 53, no. 211.
Brodgar Farm. HY 300 129. P. *RCAHM-S, Orkneys II*, 1946, 304, no. 878.
Deepdale. HY 271 116. P. *RCAHM-S, Orkneys II*, 1946, 325, no. 922.
Leafea. HY 226 093. P. *RCAHM-S, Orkneys II*, 1946, 325, no. 923.
Redland. HY 38. 24. P. *RCAHM-S, Orkneys II*, 1946, 81, no. 273.
*St Tredwell's Chapel. HY 497 509. 3St. *RCAHM-S, Orkneys II*, 1946, 186, no. 543.
Spurdagrove. HY 255 246. P. *RCAHM-S, Orkneys II*, 1946, 22, no. 33.
Stanerandy. HY 268 277. P. *RCAHM-S, Orkneys II*, 1946, 22, no. 35.

PERTHSHIRE

Balmuick. NN 784 251. P. Burl, 1988, 145.

*Balnabroich. NO 092 566. P. Stewart, 1966, 142–3, no. 1.

*Balnaguard. NN 947 522. P. *D & E*, 1971, 34–5.

Bandirran. NO 208 311. P. Stewart, 1966, 142–3, no. 2.

*Broadmoss. NO 198 475. P. Stewart, 1966, 142–3, no. 3.

*Broughdarg. NO 138 671. P. Burl, 1988a, 189.

*Cally. NO 118 519. P. Stewart, 1966, 142–3, no. 5.

*Clach an Tuirc. NN 725 448. P. *D & E*, 1968, 33.

Comrie Bridge. NN 787 468. P. Burl, 1988, 157.

Cowden. NN 776 205. 3St. Stewart, 1966, 142–3, no. 6.

Craggish. NN 763 207. 3St + P. Coles, F., 1911, 56, no. 8.

Craigmakerran. NO 148 328. P. Stewart, 1966, 142–3, no. 8.

*Cramrar. NN 723 451. P. Burl, 1988, 160–1.

Croft Moraig. NN 797 473. P. *PPS 37*, 1971, 1–15.

Dalchirla. NN 824 159. [P1/1]. P. Stewart, 1966, 142–3, no. 10.

Dowally. NO 001 480. P. Stewart, 1966, 142–3, no. 11.

*Dunruchan Stones. NN 789 162 – NN 792 174. S. Coles, 1911, 663–71.

East Cult. NO 072 420. P. Stewart, 1966, 142–3, no. 12.

Ferntower. NN 874 226. P. Burl, 1988, 165.

Fincastle. NN 872 628. P. Stewart, 1966, 142–3, no. 14.

Fowlis Wester NW. NN 920 241. P. Stewart, 1966, 144–5, no. 16.

Fowlis Wester SE. NN 921 240. P. Stewart, 1966, 144–5, no. 15.

Gellybanks. NO 082 313. P. Stewart, 1966, 144–5, no. 17.

Glenhead Farm. NN 755 004. [Doune, P1/2]. 4St. *PSAS 16*, 1881–2, 87–8.

*Grantully Vale. NN 90. 52. P. Stewart, 1966, 144, note 1.

Keppoch. NN 879 252. P. Stewart, 1966, 144–5, no. 18.

Kilspindie. NO 175 248. 3St. *D & E*, 1973, 44.

*Kindrogan. NO 056 632. P. Coles, F., 1908, 99–100, no. 3.

Meikleour. NO 158 384. P. Stewart, 1966, 144–5, no. 20.

Muthill. See: Dalchirla.

New Tyle. NO 047 410. P. Stewart, 1966, 144–5, no. 21.

Pitcastle. NN 895 543. P. Stewart, 1966, 144–5, no. 22.

Stare Dam. NO 050 383. P. Stewart, 1966, 144–5, no. 24.

St Madoes Stones. NO 197 210. 3St. *PSAS 16*, 1881–2, 95–8.

*Taymouth. NN 801 477. P. Stewart, 1966, 144–5, no. 25.

*Tullybannocher. NN 755 225. 4St. Burl, 1988, 193.

Ross

*Windhill. NH 531 482. P. *PSAS 88*, 1954–6, 85, no. 58.

Roxburgh

Dere Street. NT 750 155. P. *RCAHM-S, Roxburgh*, 1956, 384, no. 812.

Shetland

Beorgs of Housetter. HU 361 854. P. *RCAHM-S, Orkneys III*, 1946, 93–4, no. 1360.

Busta Brae. HU 348 673. P. *RCAHM-S, Orkneys III*, 1946, 10, no. 117.

Giant's Stones. HU 243 805. M. *D & E*, 1985, 32–3.

Gravlaba. HU 325 558. P. *RCAHM-S, Orkneys III*, 1946, 103, no. 1403.

Hamna Voe. HU 243 806. [Z3/2]. 3St. Fojut, 58.

Lumbister. HU 487 964. M. Fojut, 56–7.

Skye

*Boreraig. NG 62. 162. P. *RCAHM-S, Outer Hebrides*, 1928, 214, no. 665.

*Clach Ard. NG 421 491. 3St. *RCAHM-S, Outer Hebrides*, 1928, 204–5, no. 637.

Clachan Erisco, Borve. NG 451 480. [H7/5]. 3St. *RCAHM-S, Outer Hebrides*, 1928, 204, no. 636.

Crois Mhic Jamain. NG 345 345. P. *RCAHM-S, Outer Hebrides*, 1928, 81, no. 243.

Soirnaichean Coir Fhinn. NG 414 526. 3St. Thom, Thom & Burl, 1990, I, 265.

Sligeanach. NG 73. 27. 3St. *RCAHM-S, Outer Hebrides*, 1928, 119, no. 406.

Trotternish. See: Soiraichean.

South Uist

Ru Ardvule. NF 727 286. [H5/3]. 3St. Ruggles, 1984, 106.

Stirling

*Craigmore Cottage. NS 529 799. P. *D & E*, 1957, 36.

Blanefield. NS 532 807. 4St. *RCAHM-S, Stirling, I*, 1963, 67, no. 58.

Middleton. NS 561 766. 4St. *RCAHM-S, Stirling, I*, 1963, 68, no. 63.

Waterhead. NS 657 839. P. Feachem, 1977, 86.

Sutherland

Badanloch. NC 782 351. M. Freer & Myatt, 125.

Borgie. NC 661 587. M?. Freer & Myatt, 1983, 121.

Kildonan SW. NC 955 185. M? Freer & Myatt, 1983, 132.

Kildonan NE. NC 966 189. D. Freer & Myatt, 1983.

Kinbrace. NC 827 322. M. Freer & Myatt, 1983, 125.

Learable Hill. NC 892 234. [N2/1]. D, 2 × M. Freer & Myatt, 1983, 126.

Loch Rimsdale. NC 716 348. M. Freer & Myatt, 1983, 121–5.

Skelpick. NC 722 574. M. Freer & Myatt, 1983, 121.

West Lothian

Kaimes. NT 130 665. P. *RCAHM-S, Midlothian*, 1929, no. 216.

Wigtown

Drumtroddan. NX 364 443. [G3/12]. 3St. *RCAHM-S, Galloway I*, 1912, no. 231.

Gillespie. NX 245 528. P. *RCAHM-S, Galloway I*, 1912, 126, no. 365.

*Laggangarn. NX 222 717. P. *TDGNHAS 52*, 1977, 41.

Milton Hall. NX 362 415. P. *RCAHM-S, Galloway I*, 1912, 12.

Torhousekie East. NX 384 565. [G3/7]. 3St. *RCAHM-S, Galloway I*, 1912, nos. 531, 532, 534.

*Torhousekie West. NX 381 565. 3St. Destr. *TDGNHAS 56*, 1981, 21–2.

Wren's Egg. NX 361 420. P. *TDGNHAS 52*, 1977, 28–43.

WALES

Anglesey, see: Ynys Mona

Clywd

Gallt y Foel. SH 80. 55. 2S. 4St. *RCAHM-W, Denbigh*, 1914, 144–5, no. 511.

Grey Stones. SJ 27. 62. P. *RCAHM-W, Flintshire*, 1912, 59–60, no. 175.

Gwytherin Stones. SH 877 614. 4St. Houlder, 69.

Llangwm. SH 97. 45. 4St. *RCAHM-W, Denbigh*, 1914, 128, no. 452.

Naid-y-March. SJ 167 753. P. *RCAHM-W, Flintshire*, 1912, 5, no. 17.

Whitford. SJ 152 766. P. *RCAHM-W, Flintshire*, 1912, 94, no. 270.

DYFED

Abergwili. SN 453 215 P. *RCAHM-W, Carmarthen*, 1917, 7, no. 8.

Banc Rhosgoch Fach. SN 435 541. 3St. *Arch in Wales 29*, 1989, 44–5.

Berribrook. SN 71. 38. P. *RCAHM-W, Carmarthen*, 1917, 16, no. 77.

Cae garreg fawr. SN 413 084 P. *RCAHM-W, Carmarthen*, 1917, 45, no. 146.

Carreg Bicca. SN 57. 30. 3St. *RCAHM-W, Carmarthen*, 1917, 139, no. 414.

Carreg fawr nant jack. SN 35. 10. P. *RCAHM-W, Carmarthen*, 1917, 192, no. 569.

Cefn Gwernffrwd. SN 737 492. 3St. *Arch Camb 124*, 1975, 111–13.

Cilmaen llwyd. SN 152 252. P. Barber & Williams, 108, no. 35.

Cwm gawr. SN 118 310. [W9/3]. P. Barber, C., 1982, 9.

Dolau Main. SN 158 313. [W9/8]. P. Thom, Thom & Burl, 1989.

Ffynnon newydd. SN 49. 21. P. *RCAHM-W, Carmarthen*, 1917, 116, no. 335.

Gors fawr. SN 134 294. [W9/2]. P. *RCAHM-W, Pembroke*, 1925, no. 731.

Gors, Llangynog. SN 312 140. P. Williams, G., 1988, 72.

Llech Ciste. SN 514 261. 4St. Houlder, 169.

Meini-Gwyn. SN 459 261. 3St? *Trans Carmarthen A.S. 5*.

Mynydd Llanbyther. SN 549 395. S. *RCAHM-Carmarthen*, 1917, 206, no. 604.

Parc y maen llyd. SN 385 163. P. *RCAHM-W, Carmarthen*, 1917, 149, no. 441.

Parc y Meirw. SM 999 359. [W9/7]. S. *RCAHM-W, Pembroke*, 1925, 173, no. 507.

Penmeiddyn. SM 930 357. 4St. *RCAHM-W, Pembroke*, 1925, 209, no. 642.

Penparke. SN 091 358. P. Barber & Williams, 125, no. 128.

Plas Gogerddan. SN 626 835. 3St. Williams, G., 1988, 29, 85–7.

Pont Ddu. SN 309 149. 4St. Dyer, 332.

Rhos-clegyrn. SM 913 354. P. *Arch Camb 123*, 1974, 13–42.

Troed y rhiw. SN 080 339. S. *RCAHM-W, Pembroke*, 1925, 258, no. 767.

Yr Allor. SN 142 266. 3St or P. *Arch in Wales 31*, 1992, 27–8.

GLAMORGAN

Cae'r-hen-Eglwys. SS 879 809. P. Barber & Williams, 161, no. 283.

GWENT

Harold's Stones. SO 498 052. 3St. Dyer, 340.

*Trillech. SO 314 175. 3St? *Arch Camb*, 1855, 122.

GWYNEDD

Bryn seward meini hirion. SH 583 270. P or 3St? *RCAHM-W, Merioneth*, 1921, 90, no, 250.

Bryn-y-chain, Llanllyfni. SH 468 494. P. Fieldwork.

Bwlch y ddeufaen. SH 715 717. P. *RCAHM-W, Caernarvon I*, 1956, 36, no. 173.

Caerhun. SH 742 718. P. *RCAHM-W, Caernarvon I*, 1956, 36, no. 174.

Druids' Circle. SH 722 746 EP. *PPS 36* 1960, 313–14.

Hwylfa'r Ceirw. SH 765 840. D. *RCAHM-W, Caernarvon*, 1956, 117, no. 380.

Llanbedr. SH 583 270. 4St. Bowen & Gresham, 64, no. 59.

Llyn creigenen issa stones. SH 601 103. P. *RCAHM-W, Merioneth*, 1921, 126, no. 408.

Moelfre. SH 721 746. 3St. Grinsell, 1976, 261.

Pont Ddu. SN 309 149. 4St? Dyer, 332.

Tir-gwyn. SH 344 390. P. *RCAHM-W, Caernarvon II*, 1960, 83, no. 1675, 1676.

Waun Oer. SH 617 112. 4St. Bowen & Gresham, 65, nos. 75–9.

POWYS

Cae Garreg. SN 963 777. 4St. *RCAHM-W, Radnor*, 1913, 145–6, no. 603.

Cerrig Duon. SN 852 206. [W11/3]. Tang. Grimes, 138–9. (see also: Maen Mawr. 3S).

Cerrig yr Helfa, Mynydd Dyfnant. SH 983 156. S. *Report No. 24*, Clwyd-Powys Archaeological Trust, 1992.

Cwm y Saeson. SN 964 776. S. *RCAHM-W, Radnor*, 1913, 142, no. 603.

Cwm y Saeson. SN 953 771. P. *RCAHM-W, Radnor*, 1913, 142, no. 586.

Garreg wen. SN 82. 88. P. *RCAHM-W, Montgomery*, 1911, 115, no. 592.

Kinnerton. SO 246 627. P. Barber & Williams, 168, no. 311.

Llanllugan. SJ 02. 02. 3St? *RCAHM-W, Montgomery*, 1911, 120, no. 608.

Llidiardau mawr. SJ 02. 02. 3St. *RCAHM-W, Montgomery*, 1911, 120, no. 608.

Maen Mawr, Cerrig Duon. SN 852 206. [W11/3]. 3St. Grimes, 138–9.

Nant Tawr. SN 820 258. 3St. Grimes, 1963, 136–7, nos. 26a, b.

Pedwar Maen, Llanfihangel. SO 156 568. 4St. *RCAHM-W, Montgomery*, 1911, 90, no. 355.

Pennybont. SO 11. 54. P. *RCAHM-W, Radnor*, 1913, 49, no. 187.

Pen y Garreg. SN 915 676. 3St? *RCAHM-W, Radnor*, 1913, 102, no. 406.

Rhos dyrnog. SH 829 005. P. *RCAHM-W, Montgomery*, 1911, 31, no. 158.

Rhos y Beddau. SJ 057 301. [W6/2]. Det. Grimes, 120–2.

Rhos y Gelynen Stones. SN 906 630. [W8/1]. 4St. *RCAHM-W, Radnor*, 1913, 101, no. 402.

Saith Maen NW. SN 833 154. S. Houlder, 157.

Saith Maen SE. SN 862 146. S. Barber & Williams, 181, no. 362.

Saith Maen. SN 949 602. [W11/1]. S. Thom, 1966, 45.

Trecastle Mountain. SN 833 311. [W11/2]. 4St. Grimes, 135–6.

YNYS MONA

Cremlyn. SH 571 773. 4St. *RCAHM-W, Anglesey*, 1937, 113a.

Llandona. SH 567 799. 3St? *RCAHM-W, Anglesey*, 1937, 45b.

Llanfairynghomwy. SH 33. 90. 3St. Lynch F., 1991, 152.

Llanrhwydrys. SH 334 906. P. Lynch F., 1991, 324.

Maen y Gored. SH 341 832. P? Baynes, 73.

Pentraeth. SH 530 782. 3St? *RCAHM-W, Anglesey*, 1937, 141a.

Plas meilw. SH 227 809. P. Lynch F., 1991, 152.

GAZETTEERS

The Avenues and Rows of Britain, Ireland and Brittany

There is a Gazetteer for each type of avenue and row. Sites are arranged alphabetically under countries, counties and *départements* for the Channel Isles; England; Brittany; Northern Ireland; the Republic of Ireland; Scotland; and Wales. Details for each site occur in the following order:

1. The name of the site, and alternatives.
2. The condition of the site:
   (1) Good. Worth visiting
   (2) Restored
   (3) Ruined but recognisable
   (4) Destroyed or unrecognisable
   (5) Uncertain status, including misidentified sites.
3. Grid reference.
4. Alexander Thom's (1967) reference no. where applicable.
5. Measurements in Imperial units. These are followed in brackets by their metric equivalents.
6. Architectural details, using the following abbreviations
   * = uncertain site
   [ ] = Thom's reference

A	Avenue
Alig	Alignment
Astr	Astronomy
Az	Azimuth
B	Barrow
CH	Circle-henge
ChT	Chambered tomb
Cm	Cupmark
Cn	Cairn
Cr	Cup-and-ring mark
Crem	Cremation
Ct	Cist
d	Diameter
D	Double row
Decl	Declination
Det	Detached avenue
E	Eastern
Ent	Entrance
Equi	Equinoctial
EP	Portalled entrance
Exc	Excavation
F	Fan-shaped
5	5-stone ring
4P	Four-Poster ring
4St	4–6 stone row
h	high
hor	horizon

l	long
M	Multiple row
Maj	Major
MdS	Midsummer
MdW	Midwinter
Min	Minor
MR	Moonrise
MS	Moonset
N	Northern
P	Pair of stones
Pl	Parallel
Pros	Prostrate
Q	Quartz
R	Row
Rad	Radial
RSC	Recumbent stone circle
RtL	Right-angle
S	Long single row
S/h	Stonehole
Sn	Southern
SR	Sunrise
SS	Sunset
St	Stone
St st	Standing stone
3St	3-stone row
T	Terminal stone
Tang	Tangential
Wn	Western
w	wide

7. Details of excavations, finds, C-14 assays with laboratory numbers.
8. Astronomical alignments. For reasons of space although astronomical interpretations for particular rows are provided the details of azimuths, horizon altitudes and declinations are given only for the most important sites such as Ballochroy (3St). Full data are available from the bibliographical sources provided.
9. Major references. These are given by the author's name if the work is cited in the Bibliography, adding a date if the author appears more than once. Other works are cited by volume and date.

ENTRANCE GAPS AND PORTALLED ENTRANCES

ENGLAND

CORNWALL

*Boscawen-Un. (1). SW 412 274. [S1/13]. E? StC 83 ft by 73 ft (25 × 22 m), 19 st, av spacing 15 ft 6 (4.7 m). 20 ft w (6.1 m) gap at exact W. No. of st, ent width, cardinal point position, similar to Merry Maidens 2¼ miles (3.6 km) to SSE. Thom, Thom & Burl, 1980, 96–7; Weatherhill, 1981, 20; Barnatt, 1982, 159–62; Barnatt, 1989, 395, no. 14.4.

*Merry Maidens. (1). SW 433 245. [S1/14]. Ent? StC 78 ft (24 m) d. 19 st, av spacing 12 ft 10 (3.9 m). At exact E a 20 ft (6 m) wide gap. Thom, Thom & Burl, 1980, 98–9; Weatherhill, 1981, 25; Barnatt, 1982, 155–9; Barnatt, 1989, 415, no. 14.53.

CUMBERLAND

*Blakeley Raise. (6). NY 060 140. [L1/16. 'Blakeley Moss']. Ent? StC 55 ft (17 m) d. Av spacing 14 ft 4 (4.4 m). Wider gap, perhaps fortuitous, at SSE a possible ent flanked by 2 taller st, each 3 ft 3 (1 m) h. Stones re-erected in 1925. Quine, R.H., *The Mystery of the Early British*, n.d., 22–5; *TCWAAS 23*, 1923, 263; *ibid 28*, 1928, 410; Thom, 1971, 71–2; Thom, Thom & Burl, 1980, 52–3; Waterhouse, 1985, 68–70; Barnatt, 1989, 341, no. 9.3.

Castlerigg. (1). NY 291 236. [L1/1]. Ent. StC 108 ft by 98 ft (33 × 30 m), av spacing 8 ft (2.4 m). At exact N 2 tall st 5 ft 6 and 5 ft 8 (1.7, 1.7 m) h flank 12 ft (3.7 m) w gap. Dymond, 1880, 50–5; Thom, Thom & Burl, 1980, 28–9; Burl, 1988b, 175, 183, 189, 198–9; Barnatt, 1989, 343–4, no. 9.8.

Long Meg and Her Daughters. (1). NY 570 372. [L1/7]. EP. StC 359 ft by 305 ft (109 × 93 m). Av spacing 15 ft (4.6 m). 2 massive outliers, up to 7 ft 6 h by 6 ft 6 thick (2.3 × 2 m) form portals of ent 25 ft w by 10 ft (7.6 × 3 m) deep. Dymond, 1880, 40–7; Thom, Thom & Burl, 1980, 32–3; Waterhouse, 1985, 99–102; Barnatt, 1989, 349–50, no. 9.22.

   Astr: The 2 western portals stand in line with outlier, Long Meg and MdW SS. Burl, 1988b, 177–8, 195–7.

Swinside. (1). SD 171 882. [L1/3. 'Sunkenkirk']. EP. StC 94 ft (29 m) d. Av spacing 5 ft 3 (1.6 m). At SE 2 portals form ent 6 ft w by 8 ft deep (1.8 × 2.4 m). Dymond, 1880, 47–50; Thom, Thom & Burl, 1980, 34–5; Barnatt, 1989, 353–4, no. 9.31.

   Astr: Alig through southern portals, MdW SR. Burl, 1988b, 195, 198; Thom, Thom & Burl, 1990, I, 29.

OXFORDSHIRE

Rollright Stones. (2). SP 296 309. [S6/1]. EP. StC 108 ft (33 m) d. Av spacing 4 ft 8 (1.4 m). At SE a ruined ent, 6 ft 7 w by 6 ft deep (2 × 1.8 m) with outlying portals. Thom, Thom & Burl, 1980, 98–9; Lambrick, 1988, 41–3; Barnatt, 1989, 436–7, no. 15.9.

   Astr: Alig through N portals, Maj S MR. Thom, Thom & Burl, 1990, I, 78–9.

WESTMORLAND

*Mayburgh. (3). NY 519 284. EP? CH, 383 ft (117 m) crest to crest of bank. Ent at exact E 15 ft (4.6 m) w. No stones now but may have had 4 st, 2 at front, 2 inside the entrance. Aubrey, 1665–93, I, 113–14; Pennant, T., *First Tour in Scotland*, 1769, 257; Dymond, *TCWAAS 11 (O.S.)*, 1890–1, 195; Burl, 1988a, 58–9.

WILTSHIRE

Stonehenge. (2). SU 123422. EP. CH 320 ft (98 m) d. NE ent through henge bank. The Slaughter Stone (Stone 95) pros inside at E of ent. In 1920 a s/h found 8 ft 6 (2.6 m) to its NW. In 1620 Inigo Jones recorded 4 st at ent, 2 outside, 2 inside of which only Slaughter Stone survives. I. Jones, *The Most Notable Antiquity of Great Britain, Vulgarly Called Stone-Heng*, 1655, 57; J. Webb, *A Vindication of Stone-Heng Restored*, 1725, 141; *Ant J 1*, 1921, 36; J.F.S. Stone, *The Stones of Stonehenge*, 1924, 118–22; Burl, 1987a, 188; Barnatt, 1989, 442–51, no. 15.14.

NORTHERN IRELAND

CO. DOWN

Ballynoe. (1). J 481 404. EP. StC 108 ft (33 m) d. Av spacing 5 ft 4 (1.6 m). WSW portalled ent, 7 ft w by 9 ft deep (2.1 × 2.7 m). Chart et al, 1940, 120–1; Jope, 1966, 97–9; *Palaeohistoria 18*, 1976, 73–104.

   Astr: Northern portal stones alig on equi SS. Burl, 1988b, 195, 197–8.

CO. TYRONE

Beaghmore G. (1). H 685 842. Ent. 7 StCs, A-G. F, G.2 StCs. S, NE-SW, between rings to ditched C. 2 tall st on SE circum of StC G, prob Ent. *JRSAI 83*, 1953, 174; Evans, 1966, 198; Thom, A.S., 1980; Burl, 1987b; McConkey, 60.

Broughderg Centre. (3). H 650 861. Ent. Conc st oval, 51 ft by 50 ft (15.6 × 15.1 m). Av ht 1 ft (0.3 m). 2 tall st on E side, 6 ft 6 (2 m) apart, 2 ft 8 (0.8 m) h. 'They appear to form an entrance'. McConkey, 61.

Broughderg South (A). (3). H 653 843. Ent. Oval StC 30 ft by 26 ft (9 × 7.9 m). E. Gap at W. McConkey, 61.

*Broughderg South (B). (3). H 653 843. Ent? Oval StC 30 ft by 26 ft (9 × 7.9 m). Gap at the W. McConkey, 61.

SCOTLAND

DUMFRIES-SHIRE

Girdle Stanes. (3). NY 254 961. [G7/5]. EP. StC 128 ft (39 m) d. 3/5 ruined. Av spacing 10 ft (3 m). At ESE remains of probable portalled ent with 2 tall st, 4 ft 4 and 4 ft 10 (1.3, 1.5 m) h. *PSAS 31*, 1896–7, 281–9; *RCAHM-S*, 1920, no. 198; Thom, Thom & Burl, 1980, 298–9; Barnatt, 1989, 333–4, no. 8.11.

   Astr: 2 southern portals alig on November, Samain, SR? Burl, 1988b, 192, 204.

NORTH UIST, OUTER HEBRIDES

Pobull Fhinn. (3). NF 844 650. [H3/17]. EP. 'The holy people'. StC 124 ft WNW-ESE by 92 ft (38 × 28 m). On an artificial shelf on the hillside. 50 st, 22 stand. Tallest 7 ft (2.1 m) h at the ESE. Fallen portals at either end of the long WNW–ESE axis.

Beveridge, 1911, 259–60; *RCAHM-S*, 1928, 83, no. 250; Thom, Thom & Burl, 1980, 310–11.

WALES

Gwynedd

Druids' Circle. (3). SH 722 746. [W2/1A. 'Penmaen-mawr']. EP. StC 84 ft 4 by 80 ft 3 (25.7 × 24.5 m). Av

spacing 8 ft 7 (2.6 m). Ruined SW portalled ent, 9 ft w and 6 ft 3 deep (2.7 × 1.9 m). *PPS 36*, 1960, 313–14; Thom, Thom & Burl, 1980, 372–3.

Astr: Southern portals alig on May, Beltane SS. Burl, A., 'Stone circles: the Welsh problem', *CBA Report No. 35*, 1985, 72–82. 79–80; Barnatt, 1989, 380–1, no. 13.17.

AVENUES

ENGLAND

CUMBERLAND

Broomrigg A. (3). NY 548 467. StC + A, 177 ft l by 115 ft w (54 × 35 m) to NW. *TCWAAS 35*, 1935, 77–8; *ibid 52*, 1952, 1–8; *ibid 53*, 1953, 5–8; Clare, 1978, 13.

Lacra NE. (3). SD 151 812. StC + 2A?. To WSW. 345 ft l by 50 ft w (105 × 15 m). Poss 2nd A, 152 ft (46 m) to ENE. Exc. 1947. *TCWAAS 48*, 1948, 1–22 (5–13). Collared urn. Longworth, 168, no. 213. 3St (Lacra C) to SW. *TCWAAS I (3)*, 1872–83, 278–80; Clare, 1978, 13.

DERBYSHIRE

*Arbor Low. (3). SK 160 036. CH + single earthen bank from S ent. 1050 ft (320 m) l. Slight bank, 1 ft 6 (45 cm) h. Ditch 8 ft wd by 3 ft deep (2.4 × 0.9 m). Exc 1902. Fl flakes, scrapers. Contemporary with CH. *Arch 58*, 1903, 466, 482–3; Barnatt, 1989, 364–5, no. 12.1.

DEVON (Dartmoor)

Brown Heath. Erme Pound. (3). SX 641 653. 540 ft (165 m) l. N–S. StC, 31 ft (9.5 m) d. B. *TDA 4*, 1871, 502; Worth, R.H., 1967, 206, no. 4; Emmett, 107; Barnatt, 1989, 398, no. 14.11.

Hartor North. (3). SX 577 717. 450 ft l. by c. 6 ft 6 w (137 m × 2 m). Over 40 pairs of st. ENE–WSW. StC, 29 ft (8.8 m) d. Worth, R.H., 1967, 213, no. 22; Barnatt, 1989, 408, no. 14.36.

Merrivale, Central. (1). SX 556 748. [S2/2]. StC + 2 × A 865 ft (264 m) l. 266 st st + R + C. On level ground. A. 75 ft to 100 ft (23–31 m) south of Merrivale North.

    (a) West A. 438 ft (134 m) l, 2 ft 10 (0.9 m) w. ENE–WSW (262°–82°). Pillar and slab at W end. StC, 12 ft (3.7 m) d. Internal barrow. Adj pits.

    (b) East A. 427 ft (130 m) l. ENE–WSW (81°–261°). Triangular T at E end, 4 ft 2 h by 3 ft 7 w at base (1.3 × 1.1 m). Top only 9 ins (23 m) w. Worth, R.H., 1967, 215–16, no. 28; Barnatt, 1989, 414, no. 14.51. 'Merrivale North'.

    Astr: Pleiades rising, May Day SR, 1400 BC, Lockyer, 1909, 309, 484; an extrapolation device. *Nature 257*, 1975, 205–7.

Ringmoor. (2) SX 564 662. StC, 41 ft (12.5 m) d + A, 1740 ft (530 m) l, mostly S. NNE–SSW. *TDA 73*, 1941, 234–5; Worth, R.H., 1967, 209, no. 16; Emmett, 98, 107, 111; Barnatt, 1989, 416, no. 14.56.

Sherril Down. (4). c. SX 687 734. c. 225 ft l by 8–9 ft w (69 × 2.4–2.7 m) w. N–S. N end, StC? Destr in 1898 for road. Worth, R.H., 1967, 226–7, no. 47; Baring-Gould, 54.

Shovel Down (A). (1). SX 660 862. 596 ft l. 3 ft 6 w (182 × 1.1 m). N–S. 2 tall fallen 'male and female' portals. M StC, 28 ft (8.5 m) d. *TDA 4*, 1871, 504–5; *TDA 24*, 391–2; *TDA 64*, 283–7; *TDA 73*, 1941, 237–8; Worth, R.H., 1967, 219–20, no. 34; Emmett, 97; Barnatt, 1989, 519, no. 34.

    Astr: α Centauri rising, 2900 BC, Lockyer, 1909, 484.

Spurrells Cross. (3). SX 658 600. 370 ft l by 3 ft 6 w (113 × 1.1 m). ESE–WNW. StC, 50 ft (15.2 m) d. *TDA 40*, 1908, 282; Worth, R.H., 1967, 206, no. 5.

Trowlesworthy East. (1). SX 576 640. 426 ft l by 4 ft 6 w (130 × 1.4 m). N–S. StC, 22 ft (6.7 m) d, 'The Pulpit'. 2 tall 'portals' set radially to head of row. *TDA 24*, 1892, 401; *TDA 73*, 1941, 232–3; Worth, R.H., 1967, 209, no. 14; Barnatt, 1989, 422–3, no. 14.70.

    Astr: Arcturus rising, 2080 BC, Lockyer, 1909, 483.

*Yellowmead. (3). SX 574 676. M StC 65 ft (20 m) d. A? 31 ft l by 3 ft w (9.5 m × 90 cm). From W to E side of ring. But irreg arc 37 ft (11.3 m) l to N of head of 'A'. More probably an uncompleted M? *TDA 54*, 1922, 70–2; Worth, R.H., 1967, 188–91; Emmett, 111, no. 66; Barnatt, 1989, 425–6, no. 14.77.

DORSET

Hampton Down. (4). SY 596 865. StC + A (timber). Exc. 1965. N–S. Length unknown. 4 ft w (1.2 m). *PDNHAS 88*, 1967, 122–7; Barnatt, 1989, 434–5, no. 15.5.

*Little Mayne. (4). SY 721 870. StC + A or 2 rows? R. Gale, in: Lukis, W.C., 1883, 128; *Ant 13*, 1939, 149; 50 pros sarsens scattered round Little Mayne farm. Natural? *RCAHM-E, Dorset, II, SE. Pt 3*, 1970, 513.

*Rempstone. (5). SY 994 821. StC. *RCAHM-E, Dorset, II, SE. Pt 3*, 1970, 513. ½ mile (800 m) to W 2 Pl rows of st st 9 ft (2.7 m) apart aligned some 12° N of the StC. Destr. *P Dorset Nat Hist & Arch Soc 81*, 1959, 114–16; Barnatt, 1989, 436, no. 15.8.

NORTHUMBERLAND

Milfield. Henge + A (earth). (3). NT 939335–943323. Two irregularly Pl ditches, c. 5662 ft l by 50 to 100 ft (1726 × 15–30 m) apart, earth-banked, N–S, pass through Coupland henge (NT 940 330) and lead just W of Milfield South henge (NT 939 335), ending to its N. *PPS 47*, 1981, 89–91, 100–1; Harding with Lee, 213–216.

SOMERSET

*Bathampton. (5). ST 771 653. *JBAA 13*, 1857, 105. St Cs + A; Dobson, *Archaeology of Somerset*, London, 1931, 62; Barnatt, 1989, 505, no. 15 b–c.

Stanton Drew. (3). ST 603 630. [S3/1]. 3 StCs (NE, Central, SW) + 2A.

    (a) From NE StC. WNW–ESE. 8 st? 108 ft l by 28 ft w (33 × 8.5 m).

    (b) From Great Central StC. WSW–ENE. Splayed. Now 6 st only. 164 ft by 34 ft w (50 × 10.4 m), narrowing to 30 ft (9 m) by circle. WSW–ENE.

    As would have joined 330 ft (100 m) ENE of Great Circle. Both towards River Chew. Wood, J. 1765; *JBAA 33*, 1877, 297–307; Dymond, 1896; Grinsell, L.V. (1956), *Stanton Drew Stone Circles*; London; *ibid*, (1973). *The Folklore of Stanton Drew*, St Peter Port, Guernsey; *Proc Univ Bristol Spelaeological Soc 11 (1)*, 1966, 40–2; Barnatt, 1989, 441–2, no. 15.11–13.

    Astr: NE StC to Gt StC. Az = 232°.7. hor = 1°.6. decl. = −21°.2. November SS; Gt StC to NE StC. Az = 52°.7. hor = 1°.3. decl. = +22°.9. SR, early June. Gt StC to SW StC? Az = 211°.4. hor = 1°.4. decl = −30°.9. Major S

MS. Thom, 1966, fig. 31; *ibid*, 1967, 100; Thom, Thom & Burl, 1990, I, 60–3.

WESTMORLAND

Crosby Ravensworth. (4). Near NY 65.11. Conc StC + A. 336 ft (102 m) l. SSW–NNE. Destr. *TCWAAS 27*, 1870, 200–3.

*Grey Yauds. (4). NY 545 487. StC destr. + ?A. 6 st (2 st, 4 pros). 'Local tradition claims that these two stones with the two on Carlatton Desmesne are the remains of a stone alignment' leading to Grey Yauds StC. *TCWAAS 7*, 1907, 67–71; *TCWAAS 35*, 1935, 170–1; Waterhouse, 1985, 151; Barnatt, 1989, 346, no. 9.13.

Moor Divock. (4). NY 491 227. StCs, Cns + As c. 1620 ft by 20 ft w (494 × 6 m).
  (i) StC, Site 4, (food-vessel). To SE 4 st st, remains of A?, (ii) Cairn, Site 5. A, Pl. 150 ft (46 m) to SE, remains of A, 336 ft (102 m) l.; (iv) StC, Site 6. 135 ft (41 m) to SE, A, P. 270 ft (82 m) l.; (v) StC, Site 9. 2 more st 105 ft (32 m) W of Site 9. Taylor, M.W., 1886, 23–47; Greenwell, *British Barrows*, 1877, 400; Fergusson, 1872, 130–1; *TCWAAS 1*, 1874, 164–6; *ibid 21*, 1921, 273; Clare, 1978, 13; Waterhouse, 1985, 117–20; Barnatt, 1989, 496–7, nos. 9. t–x.

Shap. (4). NY 567 133. StC + 2A, or 2A + S, or A + 2S.
  (a). S from Shap over Karl Lofts to Kemp Howe StC. Boulders. ¾ mile l by 70 ft w (1200 × 21 m). Barnatt, 1989, 347–8, no. 9.16.
  (b). To N, 2nd A + S, or 2 × S. Pyramidal stones. If A, SE–NW. c. 3150 ft (960 m) l. Ending at Skellaw Cairn. S to west. C/r and cm on N stone, cm on Goggleby Stone, all dubious. Camden, 1695, 808; Stukeley, 1743, 62; *ibid*, 1776, 42–3; Pennant, T., *A Tour in Scotland*, 1774, 258; Nicolson, J. & Burn, R., *The History and Antiquities of the Counties of Westmorland and Cumberland*, 1777, 477; *Ant J 18*, 1861, 25–38; Fergusson, 1872, 129–30; *TCWAAS 15*, 1898–9, 27–34; *Gent's Mag. Archaeology, II*, 1886, 72–5, 321–5; *PSAL 10*, 1893–5, 313–20; *RCAHM-E. Westmorland*, 1936, 206. Clare, 1978; Clare, T., *Archaeological Sites of the Lake District*, 1981, 15–16; Thompson, M.W., *The Journeys of Sir Richard Colt Hoare . . . 1793–1810*, 1983. 137–8; Waterhouse, 1985, 125–6.
  Astr: α Centauri rising, 3400 BC (c. 2600 bc), Lockyer, 1909, 484.

WILTSHIRE

Avebury. SU 103 700. [S5/3]. StCs + 2As:
  (a) Kennet. (2). 1½ miles l by 45 to 49 ft w (2.4 km × 13.7–15 m). SSE, possibly towards River Kennet, then SE to Sanctuary StC. Exc 1934, 1935. Stonehole 9, 2 sherds; s/h 18, E beaker; s/h 25b, N2; s/h 52, sherds; Windmill Hill pottery, s/hs 19, 31, 67; Grooved Ware, s/h 45. Keiller & Piggott, 1936, 417–27; Smith, I.F., 1965, 206–16; Clarke, 1970, II, 501. Aubrey, 1665–93, 48–51; Stukeley, 1743 29–33, 51; Thom & Thom, 1976b; Wood, 1978, 32–4; Burl, 1979, 69–70; Thom, Thom & Burl, 1990, I, 69, 70–2; Barnatt, 1989, 427–32, no. 15.1; *PPS 58*, 1992, 203–12.
  Astr: α Centauri rising, 3500 BC, Lockyer, 1909, 484.
  (b) Beckhampton. (4).c. 1½ miles (2.4 km) l. SW then W. Exc 1912. Longstone Cove. N/MR beaker, *WAM 38*, 1913, 1–8; Clarke, 1970, II, 501. Twining, T., *Avebury in*

Wiltshire . . ., 1723, 15; Stukeley, 1743, 34–6; Smith, I.F., 1965, 184; 216–17; Vatcher, F. & L., *The Avebury Monuments*, 1976, 38; Burl, 1979, 137–8; Ucko *et al*, 194–9.

Stonehenge. (3). SU 123 422. StC + A (earthen). (a) Phase I (Stonehenge II). ⅓ mile l by 68 ft w between ditches (530 × 21 m). SW–NE. Exc 1923, 1924. *Ant J 4*, 1924, 30; *Ant J 5*, 1925, 22–24. Antlers in ditch, 1728±68 bc (BM-1164), 1770±70 bc (HAR-2013), c. 2150 BC. Stukeley, 1740, 35–9; Atkinson R.J.C., 1979, 66–7, 72–3, 74; Burl, 1987a, 77–8, 140–1; Barnatt, 1989, 442–51, no. 15.14.
  Astr: Az = 49°.6. hor = 2°.7. decl = 23°.9. MdS SR, 1680 BC, Lockyer, 1909, 60, 63–8, 120, 482.
  Phase II (Stonehenge IV). Extended 1¼ miles (2 km) l. E then SSE, unfinished. Towards River Avon. Exc 1973. 2 Antler C-14 = 1070±180 bc (BM-1079), 800±100 bc (I-3216) c. 1465, 975 BC. *WAM 68*, 1973, 42–56.

FRANCE (Brittany)

FINISTÈRE

Île Beniguet. (4). 5 km (3 miles) offshore from Le Conquet. 12 man-high st. Probable ellipse 25 by 15 m (82 × 50 ft) d, stones up to 2 to 3 m (6 ft 6–10 ft) h. 2 lines of double row and cromlech till 1835. Pontois, 1929, 124, (sketch, 126); Gilbert, 1962, 225, no. 16; Giot *et al*, 1979, 415; Hibbs, 1984, 296.

Landaoudec, Crozon. (4). c. 400 m (1300 ft) l. c. 300 st. 'Axe-shaped', S leading to cromlech? Till 1840 300+ st. At SE ch t. S+. W end 2 Pl lines 'formaient une sorte d'avenue' to 3 enclosures: triangle, rectangle and semicircle. Pontois, 1929, 115–16. (plan, 116); Sitwell, 1930, 123 'Kerdouanec'; Giot, 1960, 125; Giot *et al*, 1979, 417. Scouëzec, 208–9 (sketch).

Ty ar c'Huré, Morgat. (4). 'Curate's house'. In nineteenth century 2 sinuous lines of large and small st, regularly spaced, c. 1500 m (¾ mile) l. SSW–NNE. veering SW–NE. Led to an oval cromlech from which a 2nd surrounded a 3-sided paved area edged with banks of long stones lying on smaller and entered down 3 rough steps. SW–NE side was 60 by 70 m (200 × 230 ft) l, with 2 sides NW–SE 20 by 15 m (66 × 50 ft) l. Open SE towards head of cliff and isolated st, 'Kador-ar-Person' (priest's chair). Du Chatellier, 31, 124; Pontois, 105, 115, (photo 117); Gilbert, 1962, 225, no. 18; Giot, 1960, 120; Burl, 1985, 79, no. 97a.
  Astr: May Day SR, MdW SR, Arcturus rising, 1550 BC, Capella rising, 1700 BC, Lockyer, 1909, 485–6; MdS SR, MdW SR, Pontois, 98.

MORBIHAN

*Kergonan, Île-aux-Moines. (3). Horseshoe. 'Cercle de la Mort', 'Er Anké', the 'notorious harbinger of death'. 31 st, 24 st st, 7 pros. Long axis NW–SE, 306°–126°. 101.5 m × 90 m (333 ft × 295 ft) across open mouth at SE. Open side (orig. closely-set st st across it?) marked at each end by tall menhirs. Axe-carving reported by le Rouzic impossible to find, weatherworn and vegetation. Exc 1864, quartz borer; 1877, fl flakes at bases of biggest stones. Majority of stones linked by a low drystone wall. Le

Rouzic & Péquart, 1, 45; Gilbert, 1962, 233–4, no. 30; Niel, 113; Giot *et al*, 411; Minot, n.d., 26–7; Burl, 1985, 114, no. 139a.

Astr: long axis to MdW SR, Kergal, 1981, 111, no. 248.

Possible avenue (4) to S 'was formerly traceable' S–N, destr. *Arch 25*, 1834, 212. 'Près de Kergonan, deux files de menhirs, au lieudit Parc Hir'. Minot, 14, 16, 17.

*Kerpenhir, Point de, Locmariaquer. (5). At the Point a st st, Men Melein, La Pierre Jaune', weather-grooved. On site of former cromlech? To S, possible to follow traces of double row of coarse blocks, N–S, curving to NNE. Kergal, 1979, 46–8; *ibid*, 1981, 55–7, 72, no. 13.

NORTHERN IRELAND

TYRONE

Broughderg North. (3). H 661 873. StC + A. E–W. N side taller. 7 st, 50 ft (15.2 m) l. S side very low. Near its centre, a quartz st. McConkey, 60.

Castledamph. (3). H 522 925. D. 2 contig StCs. E–W. Exc. 1937. 82 ft (25 m) to S is conc StC + A, 16 ft w (5 m). N–S. E side, 16 larger stones, 71 ft l (21.5 m). W side, lower stones, 71 ft (21.5 m) l. 3 postholes at S end. *JRSAI 6*, 1938, 106; Evans, 199; McConkey, 1987, 57, fig. 13. Chart, 21.

Knocknahorna. (3). H 410 989. StC + ?A or extended ent at SE with radial portals. 6 ft 3 l by 5 ft w (1.9 × 1.5 m). SE–NW. N side, 2 st, S side, 3 st + 1 adj. 7 ft (2.1 m) l. Davies, 1939, 7, fig. 2; Chart, 215; McConkey, 1987, 56, fig. 25.

REPUBLIC OF IRELAND

LIMERICK

*Lough Gur E. (3). R 638 411. Banked StC + A? or remains of court-cairn. c. 60 ft l by 30 ft w (18 × 9 m). NW–SE. 17 st. *JCHAS I*, 1895, 300; *PRIA 30*, 1912, 293; *PRIA 54C*, 1951, 39.

SCOTLAND

ABERDEENSHIRE

*Bankhead of Clatt. (4). NJ 529 270. RSC. Causeway led 30 yds (27 m) E then curved to N. *NSA Aberdeen, 12*, 1851; *ONB 14*, 1886, 26, 28; Coles, 1902, no. 51; Keiller, 1934, 18; Barnatt, 1989, 459, no. 6.117.

Broomend of Crichie. (4). NJ 779 196. [B2/12]. CH + RSC? + 2A?

(a) South. N–S, 1350 ft l by 60 ft w (412 × 18 m). Orig. c. 72 st. Now 3 only. To R. Don at S? At S end nr NJ 780 192, 4 cists. Exc 1858, 1866. Beakers: N2/(L), 2 × N2, N3, indet, Clarke, 1970, II, 510. *PSAS 7*, 1866–8, 110–13; *ibid 18*, 1883–4, 319–25; *ibid 35*, 1900–1, 219–25; *ibid 54*, 1919–20, 154–72; Thom, Thom & Burl, 1980, 216–17. Barnatt, 1989, 273–4, no. 6.17.

(b) North. May have led from CH to RSC 150 ft (46 m) N. Maitland, W. *History and Antiquities of Scotland, I*, 1757, 154.

*Crookmore. (4). NJ 588 184. RSC. Surrounded by area of flagstones. Paved road to SE (not NE as in Keiller, 1934, 18–19), c. 500 yds by 12 ft w (460 × 4 m). 1828, 2 stone paterae found under paving just W of ring. *PSAS I*, 1851–4, 116–17; Wilson, 1863, I, 207–10; *Catalogue of the National Museum of Scotland*, 1892, 59, nos. 10, 11; Evans, *Ancient Stone Implements*, 1897, 444–5; *PSAS 35*, 1900–1, 211; Barnatt, 1989, 460, no. 6.121.

*Druidsfield. (4). NJ 578 177. RSC. Considerable pavement, 100 yds l by 40 w (91 × 37 m). Stones from hill 3 miles away. 2 stone ladles or paterae. Paved road traced 600 yds (550 m) through bog, at far end 18 ft w (5.5 m), near circle 60 ft (18 m). Here ash-covered. *NSA Aberdeen*, 12, 449; Keiller, 1934, 18; Barnatt, 1989, 280, no. 6.33.

*Hillhead of Clatt. (4). NJ 528 265. RSC. Rudely paved causeway linked StC to tumuli with graves and cists. In field 174 yds (159 m) ESE of circle. Coles, 1902, no. 50; *NSA Aberdeen 12*, 1845, 851; Wilson, 1863, I, 111; *ONB 14*, 1866, 24, 25; Keiller, 1934, 18; Barnatt, 1989, 459, no. 6.118.

*Nether Balfour. (4). NJ 539 172. RSC. Causeway 60+ ft (18 m) l. Led NNE at 39°. Wilson, 1863, 159–60; *ONB 88*, 1867, 107; *PSAS 10*, 1872–4, 196; *NSA Aberdeen*, 449 (Tullynessle & Forbes); Keiller, 1934, 18; Barnatt, 1989, 463, no. 6.146.

DUMFRIESS

*Girdle Stanes. (4). NY 257 966 to NY 254 961. [G7/4]. 2 StCs and ?A. Irregular curving line, D?, of c. 15 low st between the StCs of the Loupin' Stanes and the Girdle Stanes. NNE–SSW. 1700 ft (520 m) l. Starts 140 yds (128 m) NE of the Girdle Stanes. *PSAS 31*, 1896–7, 283; Hyslop, J. & R., *Langholm As It Was*, Langholm, 1912. 17–46; *RCAHM-S. Dumfriess*, 1920, 78–9. no. 199; Barnatt, 1989, 333–4, no. 8.11.

LEWIS

Callanish. (1). NB 213 330. StC, A + 3 4–6. A = 272 ft l by 29 ft w (83 × 9 m). NNE–SSW. 19 st. Stone cup (Iron Age?) found. *PSAS I*, 1851–4, 117. Exc. 1980, 1981. Pottery: Hebridean; beakers: AOC, N3, N4; Grooved Ware. Toland, 1726, 122–3; Stukeley, 1743, 36, 62; *PSAS 3*, 1857–9, 110–12; *RCAHM-S, Outer Hebrides*, 1928, 24–7, no. 89; Burl, 1976, 148–55; *Callanish. A Map of the Standing Stones and Circles at Callanish, Isle of Lewis*, University of Glasgow, 1978; *D & E Scotland*, 1981, 49–50; Ponting, G. & M., *New Light on the Standing Stones of Callanish*, 1984; Ashmore, 'Callanish', in: *Studies in Scottish Antiquity*, Edinburgh, 1984, 1–31; Barnatt, 1989, 238–9, no. 3.2.

Astr: (1) Toland, 1726, 122; (2) Callender, H. *PSAS 2*, 1854–7, 382; (3) Wilson, 1863, I, 166; (4) Lockyer, 1909, 344 – Az = 9°. hor = 1°26'. decl = 32°26', Capella rising, 1720 BC; (5) Somerville, 1913; *ibid*, 1923, 203 – Capella 1800 BC; (6) Hawkins, 1966, 182–90, ibid, 1973, 239–40 – to predict eclipse seasons?; (7) Thom, 1967, 98, H1/1 – Az = 190°.1. Maj S MS, Azs = 9°.2, 10°.6. hors = 1°.5, 1°.6. decl = +32°.5. Capella 1790 BC; (8) Wood, 1978, 33, 41, 92; (9) Ponting, G. & M., 1984 (supra), 52 – Maj S MS, MdW SS.

LATER AVENUES: DETACHED AND TANGENTIAL

ENGLAND

CUMBERLAND

*Broad Field. (4). NY 425 445. StC destr. On mound. Exc 1789, 3 cists. Large stones 160 ft (50 m) to S, remains of Det A? *Arch 10*, 1792, 105; Hutchinson, II, 1794, 431–3; Clare, 1978, 13; Waterhouse, J., 1985, 153; Barnatt, 1989, 467, no. 9.34.

*LANCASHIRE

The Kirk. (3). SD 251 827. StC or ring-cairn, C, + Det A. 100 ft l by 9 ft w (30 × 2.7 m). NE–SW. *Arch 31*, 1846, 540; *ibid 53*, 1893, 417; Barnatt, 1989, 495, no. 9.p.

NORTHERN IRELAND

FERMANAGH

Cavancarragh. (3). H 299 449. StC + 2 rows + A, tang to E. NNW–SSE. W side, 223 ft, E side, 198 ft (68, 60 m) l. 21 st. 46 ft w (14 m). Davies 1939, 12; Chart, 164; McConkey, 1987, 47, fig. 12.

Formil. (3). H 159 675. StC + A/Tang. 2 converging lines ending at semi-circle towards W. 4 ft (1.2 m) apart at W, 10 ft (3 m) apart at centre. S line now 8 st at 7 ft (2.1 m) intervals, some pros, 5–8 ft (1.5–1.4 m) l. Long axis on alig. N line, 19 low stones, long axis at RtLs to alig. Once 111 ft (33.7 m) l. Davies, 1939, 11; Chart, 145; McConkey, 1987, 45.

LONDONDERRY

Altaghoney. (3). C 515 013. StC, A, tang. A 4 ft 6 (1.4 m) S of ring. Ends level with W arc. WNW–ESE. S side, 25 big st, 110 ft (33.5 m) l. N side, 26 low st, close-set, 82 ft (25 m) l. Av ht 1 ft 6 (0.5 m). 23 ft w (7 m). Davies, 1939, 11; *JRSAI 70*, 1940, 143; McConkey, 53, fig. 45.

Aughlish NW. (3). C 662 043. StC + A, tang. NE–SW. Taller side, 58 ft (17.7 m) l, 7 st, av ht 1 ft 6 (0.5 m). Lower side, 8 st, 47 ft (14.3 m) l. McConkey, 52.

Aughlish N. (3). C 662 043. Tang A between Aughlish NW and SE. Taller side, 10 st st, NW–SE, av ht 1 ft 3 (0.4 m). Lower side, c. 7 st, 6 ft (0.15 m) h. McConkey, 52.

TYRONE

Davagh. (3). H 701 870. Conc StC + A, tang, to N. ENE–WSW, 49 ft (15 m) l. S side, 9? st. N side, 44 ft (13.3 m) l. 11 ft 6 w (3.5 m). Davies, 1939, 8, fig. 5; Chart, 226; McConkey, 1987, 60, fig. 20.

Moymore. (3). H 710 745. 9 StCs + A + 3St. At NW of complex 4 StCs (nos 4–7) at corners of a square. To their S are 3 more rings (1–3). Between 4,5 and 2,3, an irreg tang A, NNE–SSW. W side, 11 large stones, 46 ft (14 m) l. E side, 8 small st, 26 ft 3 (8 m) l. 1 ft w (0.5 m). S of 5, tang 3St, E–W, joins tang A at RtLs. McConkey, 64, fig. 9.

WALES

POWYS

Cerrig Duon, (1). 'Black rock'. (Brecks). SN 852 206. [W11/3 'Maen Mawr', 'The great stone']. StC + tang and det A + 3St row. A is NE of StC, 47 ft (14.3 m) to E of circumference. SSW–NNE. 2 lines of st st diverge, 16 ft 6 (5 m) apart at SSW, 21 ft (6.4 m) at NNE. W side, 16 st, 148 ft (45 m) l. E side, 11 st, 81 ft (24.7 m) l. From River Tawe? 3St to N of StC. Grimes, 1963, 138–9, no. 27; Thom, 1966, 46, fig. 34; Burl, 1976, 262; Thom, Thom & Burl, 1980, 392–3; Barnatt, 1989, 377, no. 13.9.

Rhos y Beddau (1). (Montgomery). SJ 057 301. [W6/2]. 'The moor of graves'. StC + det A 27 ft (8.2 m) from StC. 162 ft l by 6 ft 3 to 12 ft 6 w (49.4 × 1.9–3.8 m). ENE–WSW. Afon Disgynfa flows past. *Arch Camb*, 1868, 176; Grimes, 1963, 120–2, no. 13; Thom, 1967, 149, W6/2; Burl, 1976, 262, 267; Thom, Thom & Burl, 1990, II, 357; Barnatt, 1989, 390, no. 13.43.

Astr: Spica rising, 2000 BC; sunsets in March and September, Thom, 1967, 100.

A possible 2nd StC is reported 450 yds (400 m) to N. *Arch in Wales 26*, 1987, 38.

DOUBLE STONE ROWS

ENGLAND

CUMBERLAND

*Penhurrock. (4). NY 629 104. StC? C. 336 ft l by c. 4 ft w (102 × 1.2 m). NNR–SSW. T. 'A line of fallen stones stretches away up the hill ... [it] seems to have been originally composed of a double row'. *Arch J 27*, 1870, 200–3; *TCWAAS 2(OS)*, 208; *TCWAAS 6 (OS)*, 1882, 179. Rev. Simpson. *TCWAAS 8 (OS)*, 1886, 341–45.

DEVON (A. Dartmoor; B. Exmoor)

a. DARTMOOR

Assacombe. (1). SX 660 826. 'Assycombe'. 430 ft l by 6 ft w (131 × 1.8 m). ENE–WSW. B. The steepest row on Dartmoor, climbing 60 ft in 420 ft (18 in 128 m). *TDA 26*, 1894, 298; Worth, R.H., 1967, 224–5, no. 43; Pettit, 130; Emmett, 98, 103, 107.
    Astr: Arcturus rising, 1720 BC (c. 1400 bc), Lockyer, 1909, 483.

Black Tor NE. (3). SX 572 714. 1 side in wall. 950 ft l (290 m). NE–SW. 66 st. *TDA 4*, 1871, 505; Worth, R.H., 1967, 212–13, no. 21.

Black Tor SW. (3). SX 677 634. 50 ft (15 m) l? NNW–SSE. C. Barnatt, 1989, 519, no. 56.

Brent Fore Hill. (3). SX 667 613. 410 ft l by 2 ft 6 w (125 × 75 cm). ENE–WSW. B. Worth, R.H., 1967, 234–5, no. 60.

Cantrell. (1). SX 662 609. 153 ft l by 7–12 ft w (47 × 2.1–3.7 m). NE–SW. C. *TDA 40*, 1908, 282; Worth, R.H., 1967, 235 no. 62; Emmett, 98.

Conies Down. (3). SX 586 791. 588 ft by 3 ft w (179 × 1 m) l. N–S. T. Ruinous. The highest row at 1600 ft (488 m) O.D. *TDA 25*, 1893, 543; Crossing, W., *Guide to Dartmoor*, 1912 (1965), 119–20; Worth, R.H., 1967, 231, no. 55; Pettit, 132; Emmett, 98.

Drizzlecombe S. (A). (1). SX 592 669. 488 ft l by varying w (149 m). NE–SW. B, 18 ft (5.5 m) d. T. *TDA 25*, 1893, 172; *TDA 72*, 1940, 194–6; *TDA 75*, 1943, 75 (cattle pound); Worth, R.H., 1967, 209–10, no. 17.

Fernworthy S (A). 'Froggymead'. (3). SX 655 841. C. To N–S, 210 ft l by 4 ft w (64 × 1.2 m). 72 ft (22 m) N of Cn, a StC, 64 ft 6 (20 m) d. Worth, R.H., 1967, 222, no. 40.
    Astr: Arcturus rising, 1720, 1670, 1610 BC, Lockyer, 1909, 483.

Fernworthy N (B). 'Froggymead'. (1). SX 656 844. Cn. 340 ft l by 4 ft w (104 × 1.2 m). NNE–SSW. Worth, R.H., 1967, 224, no. 41.

Fernworthy S. (C). 'Froggymead'. (3). SX 655 841. Cn. 104 ft l by 4 ft 10 w (32 × 1.5 m). NNE–SSW. Worth, R.H., 1967, 224, no. 42. Nearby Cn, S2/W beaker: Worth, R.H., 1967, 194; Clarke, 1970, II, 479, fig. 886, p. 387.

Glasscombe Ball NE. (1). SX 658 608. 580 ft l by 5 ft 5 w (177 × 1.7 m). [368 ft = D + 212 ft = S (112 + 65 m)]. NE–SW. StC. Cn. *TDA 24*, 1892, 434; Worth, R.H., 1967, 235, no. 61; Pettit, 129.

Harford S. (3). SX 651 598. 66 ft (20 m). NE–SW. Barnatt, 1989, 519, no. 85.

Laughter Tor. SX 653 753. 'Lough Tor'. (1). 657+ ft l by 4–6 ft w (200 × 1.2–2 m) ENE–WSW. B? T, 8 ft 8 (2.6 m) h at angle to row. *TDA 25*, 1893, 542–3; Crossing, 461; Worth, R.H., 1967, 229, no. 50; Pettit, 129–30.

Merrivale N. (1). SX 556 748. 2 lines, 596 ft l by 3 ft 6 w (182 × 1 m). ENE–WSW (84°–264°). 186 st. Triangular T at E end. Not Pl to the longer Merrivale Centre avenue to its S. E end is 75 ft 6 (23 m) N of the avenue, W end is 100 ft 4 (30.6 m) N of it. *TDA 4*, 1871, 507–9; *TDA 24*, 1892, 395–6; *TDA 25*, 1893, 541–2; *TDA 27*, 1895, 84–7; Worth, R.H., 1967, 215, no. 27.
    Astr: (1) Pleiades rising, 1580 BC, 1400 BC, Lockyer, 1909, 153–4; (2) lunar eclipse predictor. Wood & Penny, 1975; Wood, J.E., 1978, 129–39. (3) See also: Brown. P.L., *Megaliths, Myths and Men*, Poole, 1976. 77–80.

Penn Beacon SW. (3). SX 595 625. 24 ft l by 1 ft 10 w (7.3 m × 58 cm) NNE–SSW. B. Worth, R.H., 1967, 207–8, no. 9.

Penn Beacon SE. (4). SX 599 625. ?l. *TDA 50*, 1918, 402; Emmett, 111, no. 63.

Piles Hill W. (3). SX 649 610. 66 ft (20 m) l? E–W. Veers from Piles Hill East, a single row. Barnatt, 1989, 519, no. 82.

Sharpitor NW. (4). SX 559 708. 366 ft l by 5 ft w (112 × 1.5 m). ENE–WSW. Cn. T. Worth, R.H., 1967, 213–14, no. 24; Emmett, 98.

Sharpitor E. (4). SX 561 709. 120 ft l average 10 ins w (37 m × 25 cm). E–W. Worth, R.H., 1967, 214–15, no. 26; Emmett, 97.

Shovel Down, 'Three Boys'. (5). SX 660 855. South of the Longstone. 1 st survives, 4½ ft (1.4 m) h, of the 'Three Boys' that stood here. The others taken away for gateposts. Some intervening stones, remnants of row once c. 555 ft (170 m) l. *TDA 4*, 1871, 504–5; *TDA 64*, 283–7; *TDA 73*, 1941, 237–8; Worth, R.H., 1967, 220–22, no. 38.

Shovel Down, (C). (1). SX 660 859. 386 ft l by 5 ft w (118 × 1.5 m). NNE–SSW. B, 13 ft (4 m) d. *TDA 4*, 1871, 504–5; *TDA 64*, 283–7; *TDA 73*, 1941, 237–8; Worth, R.H., 1967, 220, no. 36.

Shovel Down, (E). (3). SX 659 862. 476 ft l by 4 ft w (145 × 1.2 m) wd. NNE–SSW. *TDA 4*, 1871, 504–5; *TDA 64*, 283–7; *TDA 73*, 1941, 237–8; Worth, R.H., 1967, 220, no. 35.

Shovel Down, (G). (3). SX 660 856. 485 ft l by 3 ft 3 w (148 m × 1 m). ESE–WNW. T. *TDA 4*, 1871, 504–5; *TDA 64*, 283–7; *TDA 73*, 1941, 237–8; Worth, R.H., 1967, 220, no. 37; Emmett, 98.

Stannon. (3). SX 654 815. 620 ft l by 1 ft w (189 × 1 m). N–S. B. Worth, R.H., 1967, 225–6, no. 45.

Trendlebere Down. (3). SX 766 793. 412 ft l by 3 ft 1 w (126 m × 95 cm). N–S. B. Worth, R.H., 1967, 227, no. 48.

Trowlesworthy W. (1). SX 575 639. Orig D, now S. 254 ft (77 m) l. ENE–WSW. Poss StC. T. 350 ft (107 m) W of Trowlesworthy East row and StC. In 1848, D. In 1871, 60 st on N side, 42 on S. T 4 ft (1.2 m) h, offset at end of S. *TDA 24*, 1892, 401; Worth, R.H., 1967, 209, no. 15; Pettit, 132.

Watern Hill. 'Hurston Ridge'. (1). SX 673 825. F. 473 ft l by 5 ft 10 w (144 × 1.8 m). 'Male and Female' stones by Cn? NNE–SSW. T. *TDA 26*, 1894, 305; Worth, R.H., 1967, 225, no. 44; Pettit, 127; Emmett, 97, 103. Slighted by a reave, *PPS 49*, 1983, 207–8.

White Tor. (3). SX 620 785. 331 ft (101 m) l. NNW–SSE. T. Emmett, 111, no. 71. Barnatt, 1989, 519, no. 71 'Great Whitton Tor'.

b. Exmoor

Brayford SE. 'Setta Barrow'. (3). SS 725 379. D? 3 st st + 1 pros. NE–SW. 54 ft (16.5 m) l. 26 ft 6 (8 m) w. Chanter & Worth, 1905, 395. Row not quite alig on kerbed round barrow, 96 ft d × 6 ft 6 h (29.3 × 2 m). On Devon-Somerset boundary. Grinsell, 1970, 46, 58. Quinnell & Dunn, 7. SS73 NW 3.

*Brendon Two Gates. 'Brendon Common'. (3). SS 765 436. 3 st + 1 pros. N–S. 40 ft l by 20 ft w (12.2 × 6.1 m). Chanter & Worth, 1905, 395–6, pl IX, 1; Quinnell & Dunn, 9. SS74 SE 13.

Chapman Barrows. 'Longstone Allotment'. (3). SS 697 433. Quincunx. Rect. c 60 ft (18 m) square. Challacombe Longstone, 9 ft 6 (2.9 m) h adj. Edward II may have licensed local lord to dig for treasure in adj barrow group. Chanter & Worth, 1905, 391; Whybrow, 1970, 13, 16; Eardley-Wilmot, 38: 'an old charm against weeds'; Quinnell & Dunn, 17. SS64 SE 2.

Clannon Ball. 'Benjamy?' (4). SS 759 436. D? Now a ruinous triangle. NW–SE. S side 37 ft (11.3 m) l. c. 10 ft (3 m) w. Chanter & Worth, 1905, 394; Quinnell & Dunn, 10. SS74 SE 86.

Hoaroak. (3). SS 739 437. N–S. 24 ft (7.3 m) l. W row = 5 st, E = 3 st. Rows converge to N, S = 22 ft (6.7 m) w, N = 16 ft (4.9 m) w. Chanter & Worth, 1905, 394, pl VII, 1; Grinsell, 1970, 189; Quinnell & Dunn, 23. SS74 SW 34.

Hoccombe Hill I. SS 780 434. D? (3). SS 795 433. 54 ft l and 2 ft w (16.5 × 0.6 m). 2 rows, 11 st, 8 st. Whybrow, 1966, 69–70; Whybrow, 1970, 12; Grinsell, 1970, 46, 189. Remains of a boundary wall? Eardley-Wilmot, 32; Quinnell & Dunn, 12. SS74 SE 86.

Mattocks Down. 'Maddocks Down'. (4). SS 601 438. 'Giant's Quoits'. 1 st st (east) 9 ft 6 (2.9 m) h. E–W. 2 tall st 147 ft (44.8 m) apart. 66 ft (20 m) to N, 23 small quartz st. 'High and Low'. Chanter & Worth, 1905, 376–86, figs. 383, 395, pl II; Grinsell, 1970, 45–6, 189.

West Middleton. (3). SS 648 458. 2 × D, converge to SE. Each c. 75 ft 6 (23 m) l, 5 ft 6 (1.7 m) w. 35 ft (10.6 m) apart at NW, 16 ft (5 m) at SE. 6 st irreg placed between rows at NW. Quinnell & Dunn, 31. SS64 NW 6.

White Ladder. (3). SS 730 373. c. 1300 ft l by 3 ft w (400 × 1 m) w. NW-SE. Prob orig c. 200 st, 1 ft (30 cm) h. 1/3 were Q. Uphill from low cairn at NW to spring.
    Astr: MdW SR? Eardley-Wilmot, 24–5; Quinnell & Dunn, 29. SS73 NW 20.

Winaway. 'Ilkerton Ridge'. (3). SS 722 437. 4 st. D. N–S. E row, 3 st 51 ft (15.6 m) l. W row, 1 st only. 26 ft 6 (8.1 m). Tallest st 2 ft 2 (66 cm) h. Chanter & Worth, 1905, 395, pl VII; Grinsell, 1970, 189; Quinnell & Dunn, 22 (SS74 SW 1).

Wood Barrow. 'North Regis Common'. (4). SS 714 423. NNE–SSW. 7 st, 4 on E side. c. 71 ft 6 l by 14 ft 9 w (21.8 × 4.5 m). Quinnell & Dunn, 18. SS74 SW 49.

Woodbarrow Hangings. 'Woodbarrow Arms'. SS 715 428. Quincunx. NNW–SSE. 24 ft by 20 ft (7.3 × 6.1 m). Chanter & Worth, 1905, 392; Quinnell & Dunn, 17. SS74 SW 15.

Yelland. (1). SS 490 330. Discovered, 1932. 113 ft (34.4 m) l. 6' (1.8 m) wd. Stones 7–7½' (2.1–2.3 m) apart. Orig 16 each side? Roughly E–W, 87°–267°. Exc. Barbed and tanged arrowhead found. E.H. Rogers. *TDAES 3 (3)*, 1947, 109–35. Grinsell, 1970, 43.

Somerset (Exmoor)

Codsend Moor. (4). SS 882 411. 320 ft (100 m) l by 160 ft (50 m) w. SE–NW. A tiny triangle is 320 ft (100 m) to NE. Quinnell & Dunn, 35. SS84 SE 20.

Corney's Row, see: Wilmersham Common.

East Pinford, see: West Pinford.

Honeycombe Hill, see: Wilmersham Common.

Kittuck. (4). SS 820 438. Only 2 st stand of 7 or 8. SW–NE. 120 ft l by 21 ft w (37 × 6.4 m). Small Cn at NE. Quinnell & Dunn, 47. SS84 SW 47.

Lanacombe SW. (3). SS 781 427. 133 ft l by 16 ft w (41 × 5 m). Small Cn at SE end. Quinnell & Dunn, 44. SS74 SE 49.

Lanacombe Centre E. (4). SS 786 430. D? NW–SE. c. 66 ft l by 13 ft w (20 × 4 m). A Cn at the SE. Quinnell & Dunn, 45. SS74 SE 51.

Long Chains Coombe NE. (4). SS 745 423. D? Orig a rectangle? 27 ft 6 SE–NW by 15 ft 9 (8.4 × 4.8 m). Quinnell & Dunn, 42. SS74 SW 94.

Porlock Common SW. (3). SS 845 446. Incomplete D. 39 ft l SE–NW by 3 ft (12 × 1 m). Alig on Cn to NW? Quinnell & Dunn, 62. SS84 SW 82.

Squallacombe Centre. (3). SS 738 382. SSW–NNE. 48 ft l by 10 ft 6 w (14.6 × 3.2 m). Quinnell & Dunn, 39. SS73 NW 18.

Thorn Hill. 'Five Barrows'. (3). SS 727 434. SW–NE. 49 ft l by 20 ft w (15 × 6 m). Chanter & Worth, 1905, 396; Quinnell & Dunn, 41. SS74 SW 9.

Toms Hill. 'Little Tom's Hill'. SS 801 432. (1). SS 803 434. 2 rows, Pl, 3 st each. N–S. 48 ft l by 22 ft w (14.6 × 6.7 m). Tallest 2 ft 6 (76 cm). Chanter & Worth, 1906, 542–3, pl IV. Setting similar to West Pinford, Somerset, ¾ mile to SSW. Grinsell, 1970, 46; Whybrow, 1970, 12; D. Quinnell & Dunn, 57. SS84 SW 1.

Trout Hill NW. (3). SS 794 432. D? Quadrilateral, WNW–ESE, 35 ft 6 by 26 ft (11 × 8 m). Chanter & Worth, 1906, 542; Quinnell & Dunn, 43. SS74 SE 1.

Trout Hill SE (4). Quadrilateral, damaged by army shell in 1976. WNW–ESE, 49 ft by 43 ft (15 × 13 m). Quinnell & Dunn, 43. SS74 SE 3.

West Pinford. 'East Pinford'. (1). SS 796 427. E–W. 2 rows, P, 3 st in each. 30 ft l by 13 ft w (9.1 × 4 m). Tallest st 2 ft 6 (76 cm). Like Little Tom's Hill, Devon. Whybrow, 1970, 12; Grinsell, 1970, 46, 189; Quinnell & Dunn, 43, (SS74 SE 7).

Wester Mill. (3). SS 822 409. Rectangle, E–W. 24 ft by 21 ft (7.3 × 6.4 m). Quinnell & Dunn, 37. SS84 SW 14.

Wilmersham Common. Corney's Row'. 'Honeycombe Hill'. SS 856 419. c. 190 ft + 48 ft l by 2 ft w (60, 14.6 m × 60 cm) w. SSW–NNE. Sinuous. On W-facing slope. T at each end 1 ft 7 (0.5 m) h. Stones 4 to 8 ins (10–20 cm) h. At NE end, stones graded in ht, triple extension to large T. *Exmoor Review 8*, 1967, 48–9; *ibid 9*, 42–3; Grinsell, 1970, 43–5; Whybrow, 1970, 12. A ruinous field-wall? Eardley-Wilmot, 31–2; Quinnell & Dunn, 55. SS84 SE 18.

FRANCE (Brittany)

ILLE-ET-VILAINE

Bazouges-la-Pérouse. (3). 38 st in 2 rows, local granite, 2 m (6 ft 6) h. 100 m l × 4 m w (110 yds × 13 ft). E–W. Bézier, 84–5.

Guinois, Pléchatel. Champ des Meules. (3). 2 rows, P. N–S. White quartz blocks. 100 m (110 yds) l. Bézier, 178–9.

*Nourais, Grand-Fougeray. 2 lines, E–W. 12 m (13 yds) w. Bézier, 181.

Villozènes, Sixt. (1). 2 rows, E–W. 8 Q in one, 2nd Pl with 5. 4 to 5 m (13 – 16 ft 6) apart. Bézier, 217.

SCOTLAND

CAITHNESS

Broughwin SW. (3). ND 311 408. Pl. SSE–NNW. Low stones. W row, 10 st, 112 ft (34 m) l. E row, 3 st, 79 ft (24 m) l. To W of Kenny's Cairn. C?. *RCAHM-S, Caithness*, 1911, no. 572; Freer & Myatt, 1982, 60; Myatt, 1988, 287.

SUTHERLAND

Kildonan NE. 'Torrish Burn'. (3). NC 966 189. Pl. 25 ft 3 l by 2 ft to 5 ft w (7.7 × 0.6–1.5 m). E–W. Towards low mound. Freer & Myatt, 1983, 132, no. 20, fig. 15; Myatt, 1988, 299–300.

Learable Hill N. (3). NC 892 234. Pl? 110 ft (34 m) l, 2 ft (0.6 m) w. SW–NE. Thom, 1967, 158; MacKie, 1975, 218–19.

    Astr: May Day SR. Thom, 1967, 100, N2/1.

WALES

GWYNEDD

*Hwlfa'r Ceirw. (5). SH 765 840. 300 ft (90 m) l. Small st st. NNE–SSW. Foot of scarp to hollow by cliff. *RCAHM-W, Caernarvon, III*, 1964, 117, no. 380.

SINGLE ROWS OF MANY STONES

ENGLAND

CORNWALL

Buttern Hill. (3). SX 169 815, 252 ft (77 m) l. NNE–SSW. 4 st st + 17 pros. Bodmin Survey I; *Meyn Mamvro 14*, 1991, 12.

Carneglos. (3). SX 198 773. 194 ft (59 m) l. N–S. 20 low st st + 14? pros. Bodmin Survey, I; *Meyn Mamvro 14*, 1991, 13.

Colvannick Tor, Cardingham Moor. (1). SX 128 718. NW–SE. 4 st st + 8 pros. 1250 ft (380 m) l. Well-preserved. Bodmin Survey, I; *Meyn Mamvro 9*, 1989, 2; *ibid, 14*, 1991, 12.

Craddock Moor. (1). SX 239 720. 800 ft (244 m) l. NE–SW. 85 close-set low st st. At RtLs to NE end an alig to embanked A. Bodmin Survey, I; *Meyn Mamvro 14*, 1991, 13.

East Moor. (3). SX 223 778. 1837 ft (560 m) l. NNE–SSW. 4 st st + ?17 pros. 1 ft 6 to 4 ft 6 (0.5–1.4 m) h. T? at SSW. Bodmin Survey, I; *Meyn Mamvro 14*, 1991, 13.

*Fox Tor. (5). SX 230 786. Some st st. *Meyn Mamvro 14*, 1991, 13.

*Langstone Downs. (3). SX 253 737. 15 very small st st. 180 ft (55 m) l. *Meyn Mamvro 14*, 1991, 13.

Leskernick Hill. (3). SX 187 798. 1040 ft (317 m) l. ENE–WSW. 27 very low st. Close to Leskernick N StC Bodmin Survey I; *Meyn Mamvro 14*, 1991, 12.

Nine Maidens. (3). SW 936 675–936 676. [S1/9]. 9 st NNE–SSW. 350 ft (107 m) l. 5 to 6 ft (1.7–2 m) h. 5 st st, 2 stumps, 1 leans, 1 pros and split. 10th st near NNE is recent addition. A T? 'The Old Man; The Fiddler, The Magi Stone', 650 yds (600 m) to NNE, was smashed between 1885 and 1902. Its stump, 6 ft (1.8 m) l survives. Borlase, W., 1769, 89; Lukis, 1885, 16, Plate 32; Bodmin Survey, 8; Barnatt, 1982, 221–3; Weatherhill, 1985, 119; *Meyn Mamvro 14*, 1991, 11.

    Astr: (1) Capella rising, 1480 BC (c. 1200 bc), Lockyer, 1909, 293; (2) Az = 26°.1. hor = 2°. decl = +36°.5. Deneb rising, 2000 BC (c. 1620 bc). Thom, 1967, 100.

    Legend: 19 girls turned to stone for dancing on the Sabbath.

Trehudreth Downs. (3). SX 124 729. 1509 ft (460 m) l. ENE–WSW. Small st st. Bodmin Survey I; *Meyn Mamvro 14*, 1991, 12.

CUMBERLAND

Carlatton. (4). NY 534 510. 6 st, granite and sandstone. 'According to local tradition [the line] leads to Grey Yauds'. *TCWAAS 35*, 1935, 170–1.

Newbiggin. (4). NY 471 293. 'A line of stones extends from Sewborrens over the Riggs Farm to Newbiggin'. Taylor, 1886, 343.

Newton Reigny. (4). NY 47. 31. A line of stones at the south end of Newton Reigny extends by Mossthorn, over Pallet Hill to Newbiggin. Some old folk remember removal of the stones'. Taylor, 1886, 343.

DEVON

a. (DARTMOOR)

Arms Tor. (5). SX 536 863. Poss row amongst hut-circles. Gibson. Priv. inf.

Burford Down. (3). SX 637 601. 1650 ft (503 m) l. N–S. StC. T. Worth, R.H., 1967, 205–6, no. 3; Pettit, 135.

Butterdon. (1). SX 654 608. 6280 ft (1914 m) l. N–S. Once over 2000 st. B, 35 ft (10.7 m) d. T. *TDA 24*, 1892, 402–3; *TDA 61*, 1929, 274, referred to in Saxon charter of AD 962, 'the old way with the white stones'; *TDA 73*, 1941, 229–31; Worth, R.H., 1967, 205, no. 2; Pettit, 135–6. Hobajon's Cross in destr part. Crossing, 395–6; Worth, 1967, 205, P. 93B.

Cholwich Town Waste. (4). SX 583 623. [S2/7. Lee Moor]. StC + S. 705 ft (215 m) l. 91 st. NNE–SSW. StC. Exc. 1961. No finds. *PPS 30*, 1964, 25–38. Erected in forest clearing. *PPS 35*, 1969, 203–19. *TDA 24*, 1892, 401; Worth, 1946, 290; Worth, R.H., 1967, 208, no. 10. Emmett, 96, 105, 107, 111, no. 10. 'A very fine single row'. Thom, Thom & Burl, 1990, I, 59.

Cocks Tor. (4). SX 530 760. Length unknown. *TDA 25*, 1893, 544–6; Worth, R.H., 1967, 218, no. 31.

Collard Tor W. (3). SX 558 621. 216 ft (66 m) l. N–S. B. Worth, R.H., 1967, 208, no. 11.

Collard Tor E. (3). SX 559 621. 275 ft (84 m) l. N–S. StC. Worth, R.H., 1967, 208, no. 12; Pettit, 132.

Corringdon Ball N. (3). SX 667 612. 507 ft (155 m) l. NE–SW. B. *TDA 24*, 1892, 404–5; Worth, R.H., 1967, 231–2, no. 57 (A); Emmett, 107.

Ditsworthy Warren. (5). SX 58. 66. Alleged row. Amongst conc. of hut-circles, 23 to square mile (2.6 km²). Gibson. Priv. inf. Worth, R.H., 1967, 100.

Down Tor. 'Hingston Hill'. (1). SX 590 694. 1145 ft (349 m) l. 160 st. ENE–WSW. StC 36 ft (11 m) d. T 7 ft 6 (2.3 m) h. *TDA 24*, 1892, 398–400; Worth, R.H., 1967, 212, no. 20; Pettit, 128.

Drizzlecombe E. (3). SX 591 672. 250 ft (76 m) l. E–W. To Cn. Fragmentary. *TDA 22*, 1890, 50.

Drizzlecombe NE. (1). SX 592 671. 491 ft (150 m) l. NE–SW. StC. T. *TDA 24*, 1892, 400–1; *TDA 25*, 1893, 172; *TDA 75*, 1943, 276–8 (cattle pound); Worth, R.H., 1967, 210, no. 18 (B).

Drizzlecombe NW. (3). SX 593 670. 276 ft (84 m) l. NE–SW. StC. T. *TDA 25*, 1893, 172; *TDA 72*, 1940, 194–6; *TDA 75*, 1943, 276–8; Worth, R.H., 1967, 210–12, no. 19 (C).

Drizzlecombe SE. see: Double Rows.

Drizzlecombe W. (3). SX 591 672. 250 ft (76 m). W–E. From Ct. *TDA 22*, 1890, 50; Grinsell, 1978, 167, no. 25.

Dunnabridge. (5). SX 63. 64. Nr 12 ft (3.7 m) B, Cts and pound. Gibson. Priv. inf; Worth, R.H., 1967, 173, 190, 334.

Glasscombe Ball SW. (3). SX 659 605. 276 ft (84 m) l. NE–SW. B. *TDA 24*, 1892, 403–4; Worth, R.H., 1967, 206, no. 6; Emmett, 98.

Harford Moor N. (3). SX 651 599. 651 599. 330 ft (100 m) l? SW–NE. Barnatt, 1989, 519, no. 86.

Hartor S. (3). SX 576 716. 165 ft (50 m) l. ENE–WSW. B.

TDA 24, 1892, 396–8; *TDA 73*, 1941, 233; Worth, R.H., 1967, 213, no. 23.

Lakehead Hill E. (2). SX 644 778. 44 ft (13.4 m) l. Curved. 'E–W'. StC? Ct. Worth, R.H., 1967, 229–30, no. 51.

Lakehead Hill W. (1). SX 643 778. 60 ft (18.3 m) l. ENE–WSW. Worth, R.H., 1967, 230, no. 52.

Lakehead S. (3). SX 645 776. 400 ft (122 m) l. N–S. Worth, R.H., 1967, 230, no. 53.

Langstone Moor. (3). SX 550 788. 330 ft (101 m) l. N–S. B. T. Level ground. *TDA 25*, 1893, 172; *TDA 27*, 1895, 83; Worth, R.H., 1967, 216–18, no. 30; Pettit, 131.

Leedon Tor. (3). SX 565 715. 790 ft (240 m) l. WNW–ESE. C. Barnatt, 1989, 519, no. 84.

Merrivale Central. See: Avenues; Merrivale N. See: Double Rows.

Merrivale (D). (3). SX 553 745. 16 ft (5 m) l. N–S. T. Barnatt, 1989, 519, no. 76.

Merrivale (E). (3). SX 553 745. 50 ft (15 m) l. E–W. StC. Barnatt, 1989, 519, no. 77.

Merrivale SW. (1). SX 554 748. 139 ft (42 m) l. NNE–SSW. 41 st. B. *TDA 4*, 1871, 507–9; *TDA 24*, 1896, 395–6; *ibid 25*, 1893, 541–2; *TDA 27*, 1895, 84–7; Worth, R.H., 1967, 216, no. 29; Emmett, 98.
Astr: for lunar extrapolation. Wood, J.E., 1978, 131–2.

Natsworthy. (3). SX 712 800. S? 985 ft (300 m). E–W. Barnatt, 1989, 519, no. 83.

Oke Tor. (4). c. SX 60. 89. S? Worth, R.N., 1894, 300–2; Crossing, 209; Worth, R.H., 1967, 218, no. 32. S only on W slope. StC + Ct? Remains of row WNW–ESE. T?

Penn Beacon NE. (3). SX 598 627. 66 ft (20.1 m) l. E–W. Worth, R.H., 1967, 207, no. 8.

Piles Hill NE. (3). SX 654 610. 1814 ft (553 m) l. E–W. Emmett, 97, 109, 111, no. 70; Barnatt, 1989, 519, no. 70.

Ramsley. (4). SX 651 931. Destr by Ramsley Mine workings. Gibson. Priv. inf.; Barnatt, 1989, 519, no. 79.

Ringhill. (3). SX 647 795. 16 ft (5 m) l. WSW–ENE. Barnatt, 1989, 519, no. 89.

Roundhill. (3). SX 610 744. Row leads to Ct. Pettit, 123; Worth, R.H., 1967, 173, 179; Emmett, no. 64.

Sharpitor NE. (1). SX 564 708. ? N–S. Grinsell, 1978, 175 'Walkhampton 23', no. 68.

Sharpitor W. (3). SX 551 708. 410 ft (125 m) l. NE–SW. Emmett, 111, no. 67.

Sharpitor S. (3). SX 559 707. S? NE–SW. *TDA 26*, 1894, 302–3; Worth, R.H., 1967, 214, no. 25.

Shaugh Moor. (1). SX 555 638. 587 ft (179 m) l. N–S. StC. Adj hut-circle, B. *TDA 50*, 1918, 403; Worth, R.H., 1967, 208, no. 13.

Shovel Down (H). (1). SX 660 857. 555? ft (169 m) l. NNW–SSE. T. *TDA 4*, 1871, 504–5; *TDA 24*, 1892, 391–2; *TDA 64*, 283–7; *TDA 73*, 1941, 237–8; Worth, R.H., 1967, 222, no. 39; Emmett, 96.

Shovel Down (I). (3). SX 660 860. 820 ft (250 m) l? S–N. Continuation of Shovel Down (H)? Barnatt, 1989, 519, no. 87.

Shovel Down (J). (3/4). SX 660 855. 'Three Boys'. 890 ft (270 m) l. S–N. T. Worth, 1967, 222; Barnatt, 1989, 519, no. 38.

Staldon (1). SX 632 625. StC. 1643 ft (501 m). Largest stones of any Dartmoor row. *TDA 24*, 1892, 402; *TDA 73*, 1941, 227–9; Worth, R.H., 1967, 206–7, no. 7; Pettit, 128–9; Emmett, 97.

Stall Moor – Green Hill. (1). SX 636 678. StC. 50 ft (15.2 m) d. 2 joined S? 11,150 ft (3.4 km) l. Varies NNE–SSW–NNW–SSE. B. Crosses River Erme. To Green Hill barrow. *TDA 29*, Fox, 1973, 70–4, fig. 17; 1897, 145–7; Simmons, 1961; Worth, R.H., 1967, 204–5, no. 1; Pettit, 136–7; Emmett, 105.

Thornworthy Down. (3). SX 663 849. S. Adj Cn (SX 667 843) with 2 Cts, flints, urn sherds? inf, Gibson; Worth, 1967, 170, 173, 196–7.

Top Tor. (3). SX 735 764. ? NNW–SSE. Grinsell, 1978, 177 'Widecombe 12', no. 69.

Tor Royal Newtake. (3). SX 623 734. 98+ ft (30 m) l. NNW–SSE. *TDA 30*, 1898, 97; Worth, R.H., 1967, 230, no. 54.

Two Bridges. (3). SX 610 744. N–S. Emmett, 111, no. 64.

West Mill Tor. (5). SX 589 907. Poss row with RtL bend. Or 2S? Inf Gibson.

b. (Exmoor)

*Brockenburrow Lane S. (4). SS 661 423. Destr. St st (Stone D) 3 ft (90 cm) h. 'The last remnant of a stone row which formerly existed at this point'. Chanter & Worth, 1905, 397, pl. IX.

Cheriton Ridge Centre. (3). SS 751 437. 7 st, N–S. 92 ft (28 m) l. Quinnell & Dunn, 15. SS74 SE 90.

Thornworthy Little Common. (3). SS 712 438. Row ENE–WSW, 16–22 st. 340 ft (104 m) l. Quinnell & Dunn, 27. SS74 SW 85.

Somerset (Exmoor)

Chains Valley. 'Exe Head'. (1). SS 749 417. SSW–NNE. 162 ft (49.4 m) l. Tallest at centre. 2 ft 11 (0.8 m) h. Once M? 'A collection of stones more nearly recalling the *Dartmoor* stone rows than any other group which we have seen on *Exmoor*. Chanter & Worth, 1906, 544; Quinnell & Dunn, 40. SS74 SW 2.

Culbone Hill. (3). SS 832 473. 1200 ft (366 m) l. E–W. 20+ st, 9 ins to 2 ft (22–60 cm) h. Local sandstone. Robbed. Curved by 10°, lines join at crest. Ends not intervisible. Round B 150 yds (137 m) to W. Another at E. Culbone inscribed stone, 130 ft (40 m) S of W end at SS 832 473. Once part of row? *PSomANHS 125*, 1980–1, 95–6, fig. 3; *Exmoor Review 24*, 1983, 67–9; Eardley-Wilmot, 32; Quinnell & Dunn, 62. SS84 NW 20.

Madacombe. (3). SS 831 425. 12 st, ESE–WNW. 938 ft (286 m) l. Quinnell & Dunn, 52. SS84 SW 125.

Porlock Common NE. (3). SS 846 461. S? 11 pros st. Quinnell & Dunn, 78. SS84 NW 28.

Somerset

*Twinhoe. (5). ST 74. 59. St st 'of no mean size' in line. Part exc. 1963. 3C Roman coin, glass, sherds. Meg alig? 2nd row by ruined farm. 'The farmhouse together with the stone alignments will be the subject of a later report'. *PSomANHS 108*, 1963–4, 16; *A Somerset Miscellany*, 1966, 7–12.

Westmorland

Lowther Woodhouse. (4). ?NY 52.26. A line of stones led from a cairn by Yanwath Wood. Taylor, 1886, 343.

Shap. (5). NY 560 150–553 158. c. 1800 ft (550 m) N of Karl Lofts ave a 2nd A or 2× S. Pyramidal stones. Ruined.

    (a) E. (4). From Goggleby Stone SE–NW to Skellaw Cairn. c. 1450 ft (440 m) l. Poss cm on Goggleby Stone, and c/r and cm on leaning stone to its N.

    (b) W. (4). S end c. 800 ft (245 m) W of (a). SE–NW. 2710 ft (826 m) l, incl. Thunder Stone, passing Knipe Scar conc StC. Camden, 1695, 808; Stukeley, 1743, 62; *ibid*, 1776, 41–2; *TCWAAS 15*, 1898–9, 27–34; *PSAL 10*, 1894, 313–20; *Gent's Mag. Archaeology, II*, 1886, 72–5, 321–5; Clare, 1978; Thompson, M.W. *The Journeys of Sir Richard Colt Hoare through Wales and England. 1793–1810*, 1983. 137–8; *RCAHM-E. Westmorland*, 1936, 206.

FRANCE (Brittany)

FINISTÈRE

An Eured Ven. (1). (La Noce des Pierres), 'The wedding party'. Montagne du Casque, Brasparts. Winding low Q stones. WSW–ENE. c. 335 m (1100 ft). Graded from both ends to highest point on moor. Nearest st, S side of Cn?, leans 30°, 2 m+ (7 ft) h. Du Chatellier, 131; Pontois, 1929, 121, 122, 125; Eudes, 18; Burl, 1985, 50, no. 39.

    Legend: A wedding party petrified for insulting a priest, 'condamné à l'immobilité éternelle'. Scouëzec & Masson, 112–13.

Bois Du Duc, Spézet, Pleyben. (4). Some stones cup-marked. Giot *et al*, 415.

Îles de Glénan, Concarneau. No details. Pontois, 1929, 121.

Kervelhué, Plouhinec. (3). 3 st st, 8 pros. Burl, 1985, 118, 147b; Giot *et al*, 1979, 416.

    Legend: Once a century on New Year's Day stones go to River Etel to drink. Scouëzec, 536.

Lagatjar, Camarets-sur-Mer, Crozon. (3). S + 2 Tang. c. 200 m (656 ft) l. Once 1 km (1000 yds) l. 60 st. NE–SW. Pontois, 1929, 109–15. Plan 110. St to N used as polissoir. Du Chatellier, 30, 123; Giot, 1960, 85; Gilbert, 1962, 226, no. 18; Giot *et al*, 1979, 414; Burl, 1985, 66–8, no. 74.

    Astr: MdW SR, Lockyer, 1909, 485.

Leuré, Crozon. (4). 2 lines almost at RtLs, main is SW–NE, 246°–66°, 2nd is 157°–337°. 160 m (525 ft) l. 'Slight elbow in the centre from which starts a short branch...', Sitwell, 1930, 123, 124. Pontois, 1929, 105, 115, 118, 119, plan 118; Giot *et al*, 1979, 414.

    Astr: (1) May SR, MdS SR, Lockyer, 1909, 485, 487; (2) May and Aug SR, Pontois, 1929, 105.

Mehen. (4). Astr: MS SR, Pontois, 1929, 98.

Mont St-Michel, Montagnes d'Arrées. (3). Alig. Pontois, 1929, 106, 121.

Montagnes Noires. No details. Pontois, 1929, 122.

Moulin Blanc, Quimperlé. No details. Pontois, 1929, 105.

Noce des Pierres, see: An Eured Ven.

Penhoat, Coray, Rosporden. (3). 13 Q st. Exc. Bronze Age artefacts. Giot *et al*, 1979, 415.

Plouguin, Ploudalmézeau. (4). 1 st, Locmajan, survives, 6 m (20 ft) h. Were 2 angled lines, one towards Castellourou, 2nd to Lannoulouarn menhir, destr, also used as polissoir near fibrolite outcrop. Giot, 1960, 80; Giot *et al*, 1979, 414.

*Porspoder-Lanilet, Ploudalmézeau. (3). Line of st st, orig part 'd'un vaste alignement'. Du Chatellier, 110.

Raguenés-Kerglintin, Crozon. (4). 2 lines. WSW–ENE. At RtLs. In 1900 8 fine st stones. Ruined. Pontois, 1929, 106, 116, 119, 121.

    Astr: Feb, Nov SR; MdS SR. Pontois, 1929, 98, 106, 116.

Toulinguet, Camaret, Crozon. (3). 17 m (58 ft) l. To rect cromlech, 65 by 18 m (70 × 20 yds), low stones, open to E? Gilbert, 1962, 226, no. 18; Pontois, 1929, 105.

    Astr: MdS SS, N–S, MW SR, Pontois, 1929, 98.

ILLE-ET-VILAINE

Alignements du Moulin, St-Just. (1). 2 × S + tang. F. ESE–WNW. South = 30 m (98 ft) l. Low Q and schist blocks. 13 m (43 ft) to N, 60 m (197 ft) l. Tall grey to S. Tallest st appears to be at centre of rows. 100 m (110 yds) To W at RtLs, Tang. N–S. 12 m (39 ft) l. Exc. 1978–80. Phase I, 3 Neolithic hearths: 3630±120 bc (Gif-5456), 3600±120 bc (Gif-5457), 3710±120 bc (Gif-5458), averaging 4475 BC. Phase 2, stone row and mound. Phase 3, early beakers + 2 pol axes. Phase 4, 1990±80 bc (Gif-5235) c. 2500 BC. MBA urn. *Gallia Préhistoire 22*, 1979, 526–9; *ibid 24*, 1981, 396. Burl, 1985, 91–2, no. 110d.

Bosné, St-Just. (3). A short line. Adj menhirs. Rigaud, 1979, 214.

Cordon des Druides, Le, Fougères. (1). 300 m (984 ft) l. 80 Q, 2 granite st. c. 1 m (3 ft) h. NE–SW. Up slope from both directions to tallest st. SW end, remains of 2 cromlechs, each of 6–7 little stones. Bézier, 75–6; Burl, 1985, 85, no. 103a; Giot *et al*, 1979, 413.

Grée de la Bocadève, St-Just. (3). Line of Q st, 500 m (550 yds) l. Cut transversely by 2nd line. Bézier, 211; Rigaud, 1979, 214.

Lampouy, Médréac. See: Multiple rows.

LOIRE-ATLANTIQUE

Grée Gallot, Soudan, Châteaubriant. (4). A few st survive. l'Helgouach, 1984, 47.

Pierre-Fendue, St. Lyphard. (4). 10 st with large terminal st. l'Helgouach, 1984, 48.

MORBIHAN

Forêt de Floranges, Korvenec, Camors. (1). NE–SW. 5 st st + 67 pros. 1 m to 4.5 m (3 ft 3–14 ft 9) l. Scouëzec & Masson, 141; Giot *et al*, I, 415, 'À Korvenec... une file... plus nette'.

Hanhon. 'Seulement en une seule ligne'. (4). Le Rouzic, 1935, 22.

Kerascouet, 1 km W Erdeven. (3). In trees and undergrowth. NNE–SSW. 30 m (100 ft) l. NNE st 2 m (6 ft 6) h, at RtLs to row. Pros, broken st, 4 pros, st 3 m (10 ft) h. Le Rouzic, 1935, 22; Sitwell, 123; Burl, 1985, 146, no. 187b.

Kerderff, Carnac. (4). 2 menhirs 5.4, 3.5 m (17 ft 9, 11 ft 6) h, orig part of line ESE–WNW to Kerbabichiche, Plou-harnel, 1100 m (1200 yds) l. WNW end menhir 3 m (10 ft) h. Exc. 1879, Miln, no finds. Taken to Carnac-Plage in 1923, in Square d'Alsace. Le Rouzic, 1935, 22; Kergal, 1980a, 74; Burl, 1985, 139, no. 178.

*Kerpenhir, Locmariaquer. (5). Cromlech, 'Men Leton-niec', only survivor a tall menhir, 'La Pierre Jaune'. To S a reputed line of stones N–S, then double, veers 4° or 5° from N. 200 m (220 yds) to S, a Cn. Kergal, 1981, 55–6; Lukis, 1875, 35.

Kerzerho, Erdeven. (2). SSW–NNE. 26 st st + 6 pros. 190 m (625 ft) l. 2 st 6 m+ h. 3rd st, cms. Pros st, 'Table de Sacrifice'. Restored, 1888. At RtLs to M rows 100 m (330 ft) to S. Lukis, 1875, 27–8; Le Rouzic, 1935, 21; Sitwell, 1930, 121–2; Giot *et al*, 1979, I, 419; Burl, 1985, 145–6.

Klud-er-Yer, Carnac. (3). 'Perch of the hens'. 8 pros st in line, W of group of burial sites. Le Rouzic, 1935, 21; Sitwell, 1930, 123.

Lac, Le, Carnac. 'Une seule ligne'. Le Rouzic, 1935, 22.

Mané Bras, Kervilor. (3). Mané Bras to Mané Groh. NW–SE. c. 1 km (1100 yds) l. In undergrowth. Stones 1 m to 1.5 m (3–5 ft) l, mostly pros. Kergal, 1978, 69–70, fig. 50; Scouëzec & Masson, 178–80. Possibly part of Kerzerho alig. 2 × S, one N–S (Mané Bras), 2nd E–W (Kerzerho). Sitwell, 1930, 122.

Mané Coh Clour, La Trinité. (3). Several little st in line. Kergal, 1980a, 80.

Men-Pleurit. 'Une seule ligne'. (4). Le Rouzic, 1935, 22.

Pierres Droites, Monteneuf. (3). 2 intersecting schist lines, N–S 55 m (180 ft) l; WSW–ENE, 78 m (256 ft) l. Now 22 st, only 3 st st. Exc. 1979, 1988. Abri, 66; Briard, 1989, 35, 107.

Prise de Comper, Paimpont. (3). Menhir 1.8 m (5 ft 10) h near line of small st st and natural blocks N–S. Briard, 1989, 35, 107.

St-Cado. (4). 'Une seule ligne'. Le Rouzic, 1935, 22.

NORTHERN IRELAND

FERMANAGH

Brougher. H356 529. (3). StC. To N large st st 6 ft 8 (2 m) h. Pl to its axis, 1 certain, 2? S, 2 to E, 1 to W. Chart, 156; McConkey, 46.

Cavancarragh. (3). H 306 435. Tang S + S + A. Cists and C. Once had StC and tang S of stones 3 ft (1 m) h. c. 150 ft (46 m) l. N–S. To SE, 2nd S. 100 ft (30 m) l. N–S. *JRSAI 14*, 1878, 499; Chart, 163; McConkey, 47, fig. 12.

Drumskinny. (1). H 201 707. StC + S. 49 ft (14.9 m) l. 24 st st. Cn. N–S. Tang to W side of StC. Points to centre of Cn. Exc. 1962. W Neo (?) sherds, flint scrapers. Waterman, 1964; Evans, 1966, 114; McConkey, 45; Harbison, 1992, 139–40.

Montiaghroe. (3). H 194 693, H 194 694. 3 StCs + 2S/Tang. Chart, 144; McConkey, 45.

LONDONDERRY

Ballygroll. (3). C 533 146. StC + S. 80 ft (24 m) l. E–W. Davies, 1939, 14; McConkey, 51. In ritual complex, Harbison, 1992, 88.

Ballyholly. W. (3). (a) C 572 118. StC + 2 × S. 1 is tang 45 ft (13.7 m) long. 10 ft (3 m) apart. Chart, 199. S; McConkey, 51.

   (b) (4) To SE 4 st st, ? part of 2nd StC. NW of this, a large StC + 30 ft (9.1 m)+ long alig. Chart, *et al*, 199.

Ballyholly E. (3). C 577 118. W side of hill. StC + S. 7 st. N–S. 35 ft (10.7 m) long alig. Chart, 199; McConkey, 50.

Corick. (3). H 778 897. 4 × StC + 6 × S (2 tang). 3 are P, unevenly spaced apart. N–S, 62 ft (18.9 m) l. Davies, 1939, 10; Chart *et al*, 211; McConkey, 1987, 53–4, Fig. 18.

TYRONE

Aghalane. (3). H 495 920. S. 3 ruined StCs. 300 yds (274 m) E, det alig. Ruinous. 4 st only. St st 35 ft (10.7 m) from StC, 4 ft (1.2 m) h. 130 ft (40 m) ENE are 3 st st, 14 ft (4.3 m) l, remains of row. NW–SE. Chart, 218; McConkey, 57.

Beaghmore. H 685 842. 7 StCs, A-G, with related aligs. May, 1953.

   A, B. (1). 2 StCs. 3 × S + 4St. A = long tang S to N arc. ENE–WSW. 40 ft (12 m) l. Low st. B = long tang S to E arc, NE–SW, 78 ft (24 m) l. Between StCs is Cn. S + 4St lead NE–SW to it. E = 12 low st, 2 ft 3 (0.7 m) h. 78 ft (24 m) l. W = short 4St, 4 ft 1 (1.2 m) h, 24 ft (7.3 m) l. 'Up and down'. 8 ft w, narrows to 1 ft 6 (2.4 × 0.5 m) between StCs. Ct in Cn had Gp IX axe.

   C, D. (1) 2 StCs. S + 4St. Long S, 136 ft (42 m) l, low st, tang StC C to Cn. NE–SW. Short 4St to W. 33 ft (10 m) l, tall st.

   E. (1). H 684 843. A StC. Long tang S to Cn in E circum. 100 ft (31 m) l, low st. Tall 3St on E, P.

   F, G. (1). H 683 842. 2 StCs. S + Ent. S, NE–SW, between StCs to ditched Cn just to SW. 68 ft (21 m) l, low st. To W, Ent. 2 tall st on E circum of StC G.

   Dating: Late Neo occ: 2185±80 bc, c. [2650 BC]. StCs: between 1605–775 bc [c. 1980–950 BC]. 1605±45 bc (UB-23), c. 1980 BC, from char in flint hoard nr Cn 9 to N of Circle G; 1535±55 bc (UB-11), c. 1880 BC, from Cn 10 between Circles F and G; 775±55 bc (UB-163), c. 950 BC, char from cairn 10. *JRSAI 83*, 1953, 174; Evans, 198; Pilcher, *UJA 32*, 1969, 73–91; *UJA 38*, 1975, 83–4; Thom, A.S., 1980; McConkey, 1987, 59–60, fig. 8; Thom, Thom & Burl, 1990, I, 90, 91–2.

   Astr: (1) MdS SR? c. 1800 BC?; Maj N MR? c. 1640 BC? Thom, A.S; (2) MdW SS, Burl, 1987b, 11–12, 16.

Copney. (3). H 599 782. 9 StCs, Cn + st st + S. 1 ring has row of 10 st st. ESE–WNW. 53 ft (16 m) l. Towards centre of ring. McConkey, 62–3, figs. 6, 7.

Cornamaddy. (3). H 685 698. 2 S/Tang. 2 StCs with tang aligs. Chart, 244, Killanin & Duignan, 398; McConkey, 66.

Cregganconroe NE. (3). H 663 758. S. ChT. By it, alig of 9 st. On gravel ridge. Killanin & Duignan, 399; Evans, 1966, 200–1; McConkey, 64. No mention of alig. Chart, 223. C.

Cregganconroe SW. (3). H 648 752. 2 StCs + ?tang, S. NW–SE. Tang to NE ring. McConkey, 66.

Culvacullion. (3). H 505 888. S/Tang. 4 StCs, ruined ChT. StCs of low stones. 1 StC has quasi-tang alig. E–W. 118 ft (36 m) l. Chart, 224; McConkey, 58.

Dooish. (3). H 314 697. S. C, 2nd C. 30 yds (27 m) E, ruined StC + alig of small st, 25–30 ft (7.6–9.1 m) apart. Can be traced for 686 ft (209 m) NW–SE to dyke then ploughed land before some stones 1000 ft (300 m) further on. Chart, 243; McConkey, 66.

Doorat SE. (3). H 495 966. 2 StCs + S. Remains of alig 150 ft (46 m) l between StC and a st st 4 ft (1.2 m) h. 35 st up to 6 ft (1.8 m) apart, 8 ins (0.2 m) h. WSW–ENE. At E end, small Cn? Killanin & Duignan, 398. Chart, 216; McConkey, 56.

Dunbunrawer. (3). H 48. 85. S/Tang. 3 StCs. 1 with tang alig. Davies, l939, 7; McConkey, 58.

Glassmullagh. (3). H 387 805. Killanin & Duignan, 393. In

small field a small, ruined ChT. To its W, remains of 4 StCs + 2 × S (tangs), NNE–SSW, NE–SW, + P. Chart, 230. Chart, 231; McConkey, 61.

Glengeen. (4). H 383 555. StC + S/Tang. Ruined StC, peat-covered quasi-tang alig. Chart, 250; McConkey, 67.

*Meendamph. (5). H 458 976. 2 StCs, Cn, st st 6 ft (1.8 m) h + S + poss S, tang and 2nd. McConkey, 56.

Oughtboy. (3). H 59. 93. S. 2 ruined StCs. 90 ft (27 m) W of W circle, alig 105 ft (32 m) long, N–S, not related to either StC. Most stones are low, thin slabs. 1 or 2 taller, St st nearly 3′ (1 m) h. 4′ (1.2 m) to W 40 ft (12 m) from N end. Chart, 218; McConkey, 58.

Tremoge NE. (3). H 657 736. 3 StCs + S, tang, 43 ft (13 m) l. NE–SW. 3St 246 ft (75 m) to NW is D. NNW–SSE. McConkey, 65.

Turnabarson. (5). H 68. 69. S. StCs, traces of alig. Killanin & Duignan, 398. 1 StC + alig? Chart, 244; McConkey, 66.

REPUBLIC OF IRELAND

DONEGAL

*Roosky. (5). C 38. 45. A mixture of 10 st st and heaps. NE–SW. Damaged. Lacy, 86, no. 477.

KERRY

*Dromavally. (5). NW. Q 590 063. 16+ st and pros st. E–W. 640 ft (195 m) l. 5 ft 3 to 1 ft 4 (1.6–0.4 m) h. Round Cn, 'Cuchullin's House', at W. Row is remains of wall? Cuppage, 70, no. 221.

TIPPERARY

*Timoney. (5). S 194 837. Possible tang alig to StC. 'Numerous standing stones of which nearly 300 have been counted. The stones are small and form no recognisable patterns...' Evans, 1966, 196; 'The alignment of uprights... surveyed in 1934 is no longer present... [it did] not run in a north-east/south-west axis which is a feature of the south-west of Ireland examples'. Stout, G.T., 1984, 18; Harbison, 1992, 314.

WICKLOW

*Castleruddery. (3). S 925 937. Ditched CH + 7 st of E–W row c. 50 ft (15 m) l. To 2 large Q st at entrance. JRSAI 61, 1931, 131–3; JRSAI 75, 1945, 266; Churcher, 1985, 11–12, 55–6.

SCOTLAND

ARGYLL

Crinan Moss. (3). NR 808 941. Robbed alig. S + 2 × P. Akin to Kilmartin Ps? 56 ft (17 m) l. NE–SW. 150 ft (46 m) to E is C. PSAS 95, 1961–2, 26, no. 173.
   Astr: May SS. Thom, Thom & Burl, 1990, I, 124–5.

Skeroblin. (3). NR 706 273. S. 24 ft (7.3 m) l. N–S? St st 1300 ft (400 m) to SSE. D & E, 1982, 22.

AYR

*Ballantrae. (5). NX 087 817. [G1/4]. 'The Grey Stanes o' Garleffan'. 5 st st + 2 pros in crude curve. NNE–SSW.

600 ft (180 m) l. Tallest 5 ft 4 (1.6 m) h. Smith, J., Prehistoric Man in Ayrshire, 1895, 222–3; PSAS 79, 1944–5, 87; Thom, Thom & Burl, 1990, I, 199.

CAITHNESS

Tormsdale. (1). ND 148 497. 98 ft (30 m) l, low st, tallest at S. N–S. Just S of M fan. Myatt, Caith F.C. Bull 4, 1985, 4–9; ibid, 1988, 296, fig. 12.10.

WALES

DYFED

Mynydd Llanbyther. (3). SN 549 395. 18 st E–W. Tallest are 3 ft (1 m) high. About 43 ft (13 m) apart. 360 ft (110 m) l. RCAHM-W, Carmarthen, 1917, 206, no. 604; Houlder, 173.

Parc y Meirw. (3). SM 999 359. [W9/7]. 'Field of the dead'. In hedgerow. 4 st st + 4 pros. NW–SE (tallest). 9 ft 6, 8 ft, 11 ft (2.9, 2.4, 3.4 m) h. 130 ft (40 m) l. Alig NW–SE on tallest st and Coetan Arthur Cn at SN 000 360, destr in 1844, Grinsell, 1976, 250. RCAHM-W, Pembroke, 1925, 173, no. 507.
   Astr: Az = 301°.4. hor = −0°.4. decl = +17°.8. Min N MS. Thom, 1967, 101, fig. 12.17; ibid, 1971, 73–4, fig. 6.19. To Mount Leinster, Ireland, 91 miles to NW. Thom, Thom & Burl, 1990, II, 362–3.

Troed y rhiw. (3). SN 080 339. 'Foot of the hill'. 24 low st. 40 ft (12 m) l. E–W. RCAHM-W, Pembroke, 1925, 258, no. 767; Barber & Williams, 125, no. 127.

POWYS

Cerrig yr helfa. (hunter's rock), Mynydd Dyfnant. (3). SH 983 156. 'Bryn Bras "Big Hill" Stones'. 8 st st. orig 14? 28 ft 6 (8.7 m) l. NNE–SSW. Graded, tallest near SSW end, 6 ft 6 (2 m) h. Poss Ct just NW of N end. Q. RCAHM-W, Montgomery, 1911, 98, no. 502; Report No. 24, 1992, Clwyd-Powys Archaeological Trust.

Cwm y Saeson. (4). SN 964 776. 'Englishman's valley'. 1 st st 8 ft 2 (2.5 m) h survives. Nearby was row of 8 st st. E–W. 96 ft (29.3 m) long. Stones now by river, 7 ft (2.1 m) long. RCAHM-W, Radnorshire, 1913, 142, no. 603.

Saith Maen NW. (Brecks). (3). SN 833 154. 'Seven stones'. 5 st st (2 lean) + 2 pros. NNE (tallest)–SSW. 5 ft, 2 ft 6, 3 ft 6 (1.5, 0.8, 1.1 m) h. Pros 9 ft 6 and 7 ft 6 (2.9, 2.3 m) l. Points to Cerrig Duon stone circle. Houlder, 157; Barber, C., 1982, 12; Barber & Williams, 181, no. 361.

Saith Maen SE (Brecks). (3). SN 862 146. On Y Wern, 1400 ft (427 m) O.D. '? st st, N–S. Barber & Williams, 181, no. 362, 'Ystradgynlais'.

Saith Maen. (Brecks). (3). SN 949 602. [W11/1]. 'Seven stones'. 2 low st st + 5 or 6 pros. WSW (taller)–ENE. 2 ft and 1 ft (0.6, 0.3 m) h. 25 ft 6 (7.8 m) l. PPS 2, 1936, 108, note.
   Astr: Az = 263°. hor = 3°.8. decl = −1°.4. Equi. SS. Thom, 1966, 45, fig. 33A; Thom, Thom & Burl, 1990, II, 366.

MULTIPLE ROWS

ENGLAND

DEVON

a. (DARTMOOR)

Challacombe. (1). SX 689 809. 3 rows, P, 4 ft 7 and 5 ft 10 (1.4, 1.8 m) apart. NNW–SSE. 528 ft+ (161 m). Robbed. E row, triangular T, 6 ft 9 h and 5 ft 2 w at base (2.1 × 1.6 m). *TDA 24*, 394–5; *TDA 25*, 1893, 546; *TDA 26*, 1894, 299; Buckingham, 1948, 38–9, 45; Worth, R.H., 1967, 226, no. 46; Pettit, 131–2; Emmett, 97, 98.

Corringdon Ball Central. (1). SX 667 612. 30 ft (9 m) SE of Corringdon Ball North (A) S. 3 rows, F, 7 to 9 ft (2.1, 2.7 m) apart. NE–SW. 260 ft (79 m). StC. *TDA 79*, 1947, 32–3; Worth, R.H., 1967, 232, no. 58 (B); Pettit, 134; Emmett, 106, 107.

Corringdon Ball South. (1). SX 667 612, 10 ft (3 m) SE of Central. 3 rows, F, 8 to 13 ft (2.4, 4 m) apart, NE–SW. 219 ft (67 m). *TDA 24*, 392–4. Worth, R.H., 1967, 232–4, no. 59 (C); Emmett, 106–7.

Cosdon Hill. (2). SX 643 917. 3 rows. 447 ft (136 m). P. 8 ft 10 (2.7 m) w. WNW–ESE StC. Double Ct. Level ground. Worth, R.H., 1967, 218, no. 33; Pettit, 131; Emmett, 97, 106, 107, Class 3.

Holne Moor. (3). SX 675 709. 3 rows. P? Cn. Robbed. 156 ft (48 m) l. WNW–ESE. Pre-date reaves immed to N, Fleming, 1988, 59–60. Phosphate in trial pit, burial?, ibid, 95. Pettit, 131; Barnatt, 1989, 519, no. 81.

*Joan Ford Newtake. (3). SX 632 720. 3 rows? 660 ft (200 m) l? SE–NW. StC, Cn. Robbed? Barnatt, 1989, 519, no. 88.

Soussons Down. (4). SX 676 799. 3 rows. 200 ft (60 m) l? N–S. Cn. Destr c. 1897. Pettit, 131, 'Red Barrows'; Grinsell, 1978, 155, 'Manaton 4'; Barnatt, 1989, 519, no. 65.

Yar Tor NW. (3). SX 681 740. 3 rows. P. NW–SE. 1500 ft (457 m). B. *TDA 73*, 1941, 237; Worth, R.H., 1967, 227–29, no. 49; Emmett, 111, Class III. Once led to Money Pit Cn. 2 reaves cross. *Dartmoor Atlas of Antiquities, I. The East*, 1991, 126–7.

Yar Tor SE. (3). SX 682 738. 3 rows? 50 ft (15 m) l? NW–SE. Barnatt, 1989, 519, no. 75.

*Yellowmead. (5). SX 574 676. M StC 65 ft (20 m) d. A? 31 ft (9.5 m) l. 3 ft (90 cm) w. From W to E side of ring. 3 + 2 st in irreg arc 37 ft (11.3 m) l to N of 'A'. An uncompleted M? *TDA 54*, 1922, 70–2; Worth, R.H., 1967, 188–9; Emmett, 111, no. 66; Barnatt, 1989, 425–6, no. 14.77; 519, no. 66.

b. (EXMOOR)

Cheriton Ridge NW. (3). SS 748 442. 3 rows, E–W. 4st in both outer rows, 2? st in centre. 75 ft 6 by 46 ft (23 × 14 m). Quinnell & Dunn, 8. SS74 SW 40.

Cheriton Ridge SE. 'Farley Water. (3). SS 754 433. 3 rows? Each 4 st. WNW–ESE. 53 ft 5 by 33 ft (16.3 × 10 m) w. Isolated st st at SW. Chanter & Worth, 1905, 396, pl IX, 2. Quinnell & Dunn, 9. SS74 SE 15.

Furzehill Common NE. (1). SS 738 447. 3 rows, N–S. 72 ft by 46 ft (22 × 14 m). An isolated st is 36 ft (11 m) S of central row. Chanter & Worth, 1905, 393, Pl. V; Quinnell & Dunn, 23. SS74 SW 35.

Hoccombe Coombe. (3). SS 786 444. Once termed a StC these are actually 3 or 4 rows, WNW–ESE. c. 92 ft by 43 ft (28 × 13 m). Quinnell & Dunn, 9. SS74 SE 6.

Pig Hill. (3). SS 756 444. 3 or 4 rows, WNW–ESE. 125 ft by 46 ft (38 × 14 m). Quinnell & Dunn, 12. SS74 SE 85.

SOMERSET (EXMOOR)

*Almsworthy. (5). SS 844 417. M/P. Orig thought to be a StC, the 13 st + outlier are poss 6 ruined lines, ESE–WNW. 129 ft (39.3 m) l by 94 ft (28.7 m) w. Discovered, 1931. *P Som ANHS 77*, 1931, 77–8; Whybrow, 1970, 11; Grinsell, 1978, 40–1; Eardley-Wilmot, 28; Quinnell & Dunn, 37. SS84 SW 3.

Beckham Hill. (3). SS 806 423. 3 rows, WNW–ESE. 43 ft by 30 ft (13 × 9 m). Quinnell & Dunn, 46. SS84 SW 18.

Hascombe. (4). SS 769 383. 4 rows, poss of 4 st each. SSW–NNE. 119 ft by 75 ft 6 (36.3 × 23 m). Quinnell & Dunn, 40. SS73 NE 36.

Horsen. (4). SS 790 373. Remains of poss 3 rows. Badly damaged. SW–NE? c. 36 ft by 23 ft (11 × 7 m). Quinnell & Dunn, 39. SS73 NE 11.

Porlock Allotment SW. (3). SS 833 437. 3 rows, SW–NE. 24 ft by 21 ft 4 (7.3 × 6.5 m). Quinnell & Dunn, 60. SS84 SW 27.

FRANCE (Brittany)

CÔTES-DU-NORD

Champ des Roches, Le, Pleslin. (1). 5 rows, F. 65 st. NE–SW. 80 m (263 ft) l, 33 m (108 ft) w at SW. Exc 19th cent: ashes and charcoal at foot of stones. *Livret-Guide*, 42. Giot, 1960, 124; Scouëzec, 472; Gilbert, 1964, 156–7, no. 472; Burl, 1985, 32–3. no. 5.

FINISTÈRE

*Kerlaouentec, Crozon. (4). Large group orig in middle of hamlet. Du Chatellier, 124.

*Laené, Crozon. (4). Former aligs. Du Chatellier, 124.

Lostmarc'h NE, Crozon. (3). 3 rows. F. SW–NE, 246°–66°. Centre 30 m (98 ft) l. 4 st st + 3 pros. av 4 ft (1.2 m) h. SE row, 1 st st 3 m (10 ft) h. NW row, 1 st 1.5 m (5 ft) h. Up slope, from NE st 30 m (100 ft) to heathery mounds. Pontois, 1929, 115, plan, 118; Giot, 1960, 124; Bender, 89.
   Astr: (1) May SR, Lockyer, 1909, 485; (2) MdS SR, Pontois, 1929, 105, 106.

Lostmarc'h SW. (4). 3 rows? 180 m (590 ft) SW of (NE). SE–NW. 6 m (20 ft) l. 30 m (100 ft) to NW kerbed Cn 14 × 0.6 m (45 ft w × 2 ft) h. Personal fieldwork, 1991.

Madeleine, La, Lestriguiou, Penmarc'h. (4). 4 rows, P, WNW–ESE, + cromlech around a windmill. 1 km (3300 ft) l. In 19th cent 500–600 st st. Middle gap 12 m (40 ft) w, two outer, 8–9 m (26–30 ft) w. Stones 50 cm to 3.5 m (1 ft 6 to 11 ft 6) h. 5, 6, 8 m (16, 20, 26 ft) apart. Du Chatellier, 28–9, 168; Forde, 1927, 19, 35; Pontois,

1929, 206, 117–21; Giot, 1960, 124; Kergal, 1979, 30; Burl, 1985, 70, no. 80.

Astr: MdS SS, MdW SR. Pontois, 1929, 124.

ILLE-ET-VILAINE

Demoiselles, Les, Langon. (1). 37 st in 6 rows, P. SE–NW. Bézier, 162–3; Giot et al, 1979, 415; Burl, 1985, 82, no. 100.

Lampouy, Médréac. (3). 4 rows, F. Staggered, not in line abreast. At N, La Roche Longue, single red menhir, 5 m (16 ft 5) h. In La Favelais near head of shallow terrace
(a) *West Row* 300 m (1000 ft) SSW, 29 m (95 ft) l. SSW–NNE, 190°–10°. 10 st, 9 pros, central st 2.5 m (8 ft 3) h. 19th cent exc, S of W row, ashes and char.
(b) *W Centre row*: N st is 10 m (33 ft) SW of S st of (c). 35 m (115 ft) l. SSE–NNW, 7 st. S st 3 m (10 ft) h. 10 m (33 ft) to NE of N st is S st of
(c) *E Centre row*: N st is 60 m (200 ft) ESE of N st of (a) 29 m (95 ft) l. 7 st. All pros, 3.5 to 6 m (12–20 ft) l. SE–NW, 144°–324°. 200 m (656 ft) SE of S st is N st of
(d) *E row*: 30 m (99 ft) l. SSE–NNW. 7 st, 4 pros. N = tall white pillar, 5.3 m (17 ft 4) h. S = triangular red block 5 m (16 ft 6) h.
500 m (1650 ft) down slope to SE, single white stone, La Pierre Carrée near Chenôt farm. Bézier, 227–30; Gilbert, 1964, 94–7, no. 424; Scouëzec, 389; Giot et al, 1979, 413–14; Burl, 1985, 86–8, no. 104; Scouëzec & Masson, 75–6.

Astr: from La Roche Longue to La Roche Carrée, MdW SR?

LOIRE-ATLANTIQUE

Arbourg, Herbignac. (4). 7 rows, 57 st. Giot, 1960, 124.

MORBIHAN

Coët-er-Hour. Le Moustoir, Carnac. (4). Lines of many small menhirs, some standing, some fallen. le Rouzic, 1935, 20–1, 'Lignol'; Sitwell, 1930, 122; Kergal, 1980a, 59.

Grand Resto, see: Kersolan.

Hanhon A. (4). 'Plusieurs petits menhirs couchés et debout et placés en lignes'. le Rouzic, 1935, 21.

Keriavel, Plouharnel. (3). 4 rows, P. N–S. 68 m (223 ft) l by 36 m (118 ft) w. le Rouzic, 1935, 21; Sitwell, 1930, 122; Kergal, 1980a, 70, 72.
Astr: (1) Az = 118°.2. hor = 0°.3. decl = −18°.6. Min S MR. Thom & Thom, 1978, 115–17. (2) Probably a N–S cardinal site. Burl, 1985, 151, no. 197b.

Kerlann, Carnac. (3). 'Many small menhirs, all fallen but placed in lines'. le Rouzic, 1935, 20; Sitwell, 1930, 122.

Kerlescan, Carnac. (1). 13 rows, 514 st, F? 298 m (326 yds) l. 1176 m (1286 yds) l, incl 230 m (252 yds) gap, if Petit-Ménec added. 125 m (137 yds) w. WNW–ESE. + horse-shoe cromlech open to N. Lukis, 1870, 7; Lukis, 1875, 17–18, 35; le Rouzic, 1935, 19–20; Sitwell, 1930, 119–21; Giot, 1960, 123; Daniel, 1963, 138; Niel, 138, 146; *JHA 8*, 1977, 52–4; Thom & Thom, 1977, 4a; 1978, 93; Wood, 1978, 146, 155; Batt et al, 24, 78; Kergal, 1980a, 63–4; Burl, 1985, 141–2, no. 180d; Scouëzec & Masson, 170.

Astr: equi SR, MdW SR, Pontois, 1929, 98, 103.

Kermario, Carnac. (1). 7 major rows + 3 subsidiaries, 1029

st, P. WSW–ENE. W, 659 m + E, 492 m, 1151 m (1259 yds) l. Exc 1877–8: flints, sherds, pol. axe, quern, burnt stones: Miln, 1881, 25–32. Lukis, 1870, 6; Lukis, 1875, 19–20, 35; le Beau, 1894, 14–16; le Rouzic, 1935, 18–19; Sitwell, 1930, 119; Giot, 1960, 122–3; Daniel, 1963, 137–8, 146; Niel, 137–8, 147; Thom & Thom 1977, 3a, 3b, 17, 19; 1978, 79–81; Batt et al, 27, 79; Kergal, 1980a, 65–6; Burl, 1985, 144, no. 183b; Scouëzec & Masson, 168–70.

Astr: (1) equi SR, MdS SR, MdW SS, Pontois, 1929, 98, 103, 105. (2). extrapolation sector? Thom & Thom, 1978, 91; Wood, 1978, 33, 145–6, 155–8, figs. 8.1, 8.7.

Kersolan, Languidec. (3). 3 rows, granite and Q st. P. WNW–ESE. N row 29 st, 217 m (237 yds) l; 41 m (135 ft) to Centre 69 st, 260 m (853 ft) l; 48 m (158 ft) to S 43 st, 35 m (115 ft) l. E end, 2 tertres, exc 1898, 1981. Adj hearth, 3380±80 bc (Gif-5765), c. 4200 BC. *Révue Archéologique*, 1898, 102–8; Giot et al, 1979, 416; Burl, 1985, 113, no. 135a; Abri, 56; Scouëzec & Masson, 140.

Kerzerho, Erdeven. (2). 10 rows, P. 1129 st. Damaged. E–W, 88°–268°. 2105 m (2302 yds) l if Mané Bras sector included. 64 m (210 ft) wd. W cromlech destr. Cms on its W st, 'les restes d'une des enceintes'. Restored, 1884. At RtLs, a long S, 29 st. 18th-century report of trilithons, *Livret-Guide*, 110. Lukis, 1870, 7; Lukis, 1875, 27–8, 35; le Rouzic, 1935, 21–2; Sitwell, 1930, 121–2; Giot, 1960, 124; Giot et al, 1979, 419. Batt et al, 26, 84; Burl, 1985, 145–6, no. 187a; Scouëzec & Masson, 178–80.

Astr: (1) May SR, Pontois, 1929, 105; (2) Equi SRs. Az 88°–89°, 'nettement dirigée vers les levers d'équinoxe'. Also MdW SR, Niel, 151.

Kerzine, Le Moulin de, Plouhinec. (3). 8 rows, c. 45 m (148 ft) l. c. 40 st. WNW–ESE. Lukis, 1875, 29–30; Giot et al, 1979, 416; Burl, 1985, 118, no. 147a.

Lignol. see: Coët-er-Hour.

Ménec, Carnac. (1). 12? rows, F. WSW–ENE. + 2 ovoid cromlechs. 1069 st. W, 455 m + E, 488 m, 943 m (1031 yds) l. 99 × 84 m (325 × 276 ft) w. Lukis, 1870, 5–6; Lukis, 1875, 20, 35; Pontois, 1929, 105; le Rouzic, 1935, 18; Sitwell, 1930, 117–18; Giot, 1960, 122; Daniel, 1963, 136–7; Niel, 137–41, 146; Thom & Thom, 1977, 1a, 1b, 13, 14; 1978, 63–7; Wood, J.E., 1978, 33, 54, 140–59; Batt et al, 22–3, 79–80; Kergal, 1980a, 74–5; Burl, 1985, 157–8, no. 203b. Scouëzec & Masson, 164–7.

Astr: (1) May, Nov SR, Lockyer, 1909, 98–9; (2) equi SR, MdS SR, Pontois, 1929, 98, 103.

Legends. (1) Lines were a memorial to a warlord – Spence, 1917, 43–4; stones raised by dwarfs, ibid, 98–9. (2) Roman soldiers chasing St-Cornély were turned to stone – le Rouzic, 1939, 18–20.

Moulin de St-Pierre-Quiberon, Le, Quiberon. (1). 5 rows, F. 23 st. ESE–WNW. + ovoid cromlech. 55 m (60 yds) l, but orig. 250 m (273 yds) l. 31 × 23 m (102 × 76 ft) w. Lukis, 1870, 8; Lukis, 1875, 29, 35; le Rouzic, 1935, 22; Giot, 1960, 124; Niel, 151; Thom & Thom, 1978, 107; Batt et al, 28; Burl, 1985, 158, no. 204a; Scouëzec & Masson, 215–16.

Astr: (1) Feb, Nov SR, Pontois, 1929, 98. (2) Extrapolation sector. Thom, Thom & Burl, 1990, I, 88.

Nignol see: Coët-er-Hour.

Petit-Ménec, Carnac. (3). 8 or 9 rows, P. c. 203 st. WSW–ENE. 350 m (383 yds) l. Perhaps part of Kerlescan rows.

Sitwell, 1930, 120; Thom & Thom, 1977, 4b; 1978, 93; Wood, J.E., 1978, 141, 145; Batt *et al*, 25, 77; Kergal, 1980a, 65; Burl, 1985, 159–60, no. 207.

Ste-Barbe, Plouharnel. (3). 4 rows, ?P. c. 50 st. ESE–WNW. 416 m (455 yds) longest. Ended in semi-cromlech. Lukis, 1875, 26, 35; le Rouzic, 1935, 20, 22; Sitwell, 1930, 121; Giot, 1960, 124; Burl, 1985, 164, no. 213; Bender, 157; Scouëzec & Masson, 176.

 Astr: Feb, Nov SR, Pontois, 1929, 98.

NORTHERN IRELAND

TYRONE

Beaghmore. H 685 842. StCs, A to G. See: 4-6-Stone Rows; Single; 3-Stone Rows.

SCOTLAND

Broughwin NE. (3). ND 313 412. M/F. Cn. *RCAHM-S, Caithness*, 1911a, no. 560; Freer & Myatt, 1982, 59–60, no. 4; Myatt, 1988, 286.

Broughwin Centre E. (3). ND 312 409. 4 rows, NE–SW. 108 ft (33 m) l. Cn. Ct, NE–SW. R 180 ft (55 m) to W. Anderson, 1868, 503–4; *RCAHM-S, Caithness*, 1911a, no. 561. Freer & Myatt, 1982, 60, no. 5; Myatt, 1988, 286–7.

Camster. (3). ND 260 437. [N1/14]. ?6 rows, F. S–N. 101 ft (31 m) l. Dryden, 1872, 530; Anderson, 1886, 129–30; *RCAHM-S, Caithness*, 1911a, no. 573; Gunn, 1915, 348; Wood, J.E., 1978, 128; Heggie, 1981, 193; Ruggles, 1981, 193; Freer & Myatt, 1982, 62, no. 9, fig. 6; Myatt, 1988, 292–3, fig. 12.8; Thom, Thom & Burl, 1990, II, 300.

 Astr: A site for lunar extrapolation. Thom, 1971, 99–100, fig. 9.8, 104.

Dirlot. (3). ND 123 485. [N1/17]. c. 14 rows, F. ESE–WNW. 148 ft (45 m) l. 2C. *RCAHM-S, Caithness*, 1911a, no. 165. Gunn, 1915, 352–4; Feachem, 73; Wood, 1978, 124–9; Heggie, 1981, 193; Wood, J.E., 1978, 128; Ruggles, 1981, 193; Freer & Myatt, 1982, 62, no. 10, fig. 7; Myatt, 1988, 293–5, fig. 12.9.

 Astr: a lunar site for 'both the major and minor standstills'. Thom, 1971, 95–8, fig. 9.5, 104.

Garrywhin. (3). ND 314 413. [N1/9. Wattenan]. 6–8 rows, F. SSW–NNE. 180 ft (55 m) l. Cn, 18 ft (5.5 m) d. Ct E–W, exc. 1865. Human teeth, 2 flint flakes. 'Twisted-cord' beaker or food-vessel sherds, Anderson, 1868, 503–4; Clarke, 1970, II, 516. *PSAS 9*, 1871–2, 444; Dryden, 1872, 529; *RCAHM-S, Caithness*, 1911a, no. 558; Gunn, 1915, 348; Thom, 1964, fig. 2; Feachem, 73; Freer & Myatt, 1982, 60, no. 7, fig. 3; Myatt, 1988, 287–90, fig. 12.5; Thom, Thom & Burl, 1990, II, 294–5.

Loch of Yarrows. (3). ND 313 441. [N1/7]. 'Battle Moss'. ?6 rows, very irreg. P or F. N–S. 131 ft (40 m) l. Dryden, 1872, 529; Anderson, 1886, 130–1; *RCAHM-S, Caithness*, 1911a, no. 570; Gunn, 1915, 350; Wood, J.E., 1978, 128; Ruggles, 1981, 192–3, fig. 4.5; Freer & Myatt, 1982, 61–2, no. 8, figs. 4, 5; Myatt, 1988, 290–2, figs. 12.6, 12.7.

 Astr: A possible lunar extrapolation site. Thom, 1971, 91, 98–9, 104; Thom, Thom & Burl, 1990, II, 292.

Loch Watenan. (3). ND 318 411. 4 rows. 94 ft (29 m) l. 36 ft (11 m) wd. N–S. *RCAHM-S, Caithness*, 1911a, no. 571; Freer & Myatt, l982, 59, no. 2; Myatt, 1988, 285.

Mid Clyth. (1). ND 295 384. [N1/1]. 'Hill o' Many Stanes'. 23 rows, F. N–S. 143 ft (44 m) l. Cn? Cordiner, Rev. C. (1780), *Antiquities and Scenery of the North of Scotland*. London. 84. *PSAS 9*, 1871–2, 444; Dryden, 1872, 529–30; Anderson, 1886, 131–2; *RCAHM-S, Caithness*, 1911a, no. 292; Thom, 1967, 95, 152, fig. 12.12, 156, fig. 12.16; Feachem, 73; MacKie, 1975, 226–7; Wood, J.E., 1978, 113, 124–9, fig. 7.8; Heggie, 1981, 49–50, 206–8; Ruggles, 1981, 193; Freer & Myatt, l982, 58–9, no. 1, fig. 1; Myatt, 1988, 282–5, fig. 12.3.

 Astr: For lunar extrapolation. Thom, 1967, 156–8; ibid, 1971, 91–5, 103, 104; Brown, P.L., *Megaliths, Myths and Man*, 1976, 203–5; Thom, Thom & Burl, 1990, II, 284–6.

Tormsdale. (3). ND 148 497. 9 rows, F. SE–NW. 121 ft (37 m) l. + 1 tang S, N–S. 98 ft (30 m) l. D & E, 1982, 49; Myatt, l985; 1988, 295–7, fig. 12.10.

Upper Dounreay E. (3). ND 012 660. [N1/3]. 'Craig Beac' (spotted rock). 13 rows, F. WNW–ESE. 131 ft (40 m) l. A 4–slab Ct above the rows provides a focus for them. *RCAHM-S, Caithness*, 1911a, no. 397; Gunn, 1915, 355; Thom, 1964, fig. 3; Feachem, 73; Freer & Myatt, 1983, 120, no. 11, fig. 8; Myatt, 1988, 297–9, fig. 12.11; Thom, Thom & Burl, 1990, II, 290–1.

Upper Dounreay W. (4). ND 007 660. Freer & Myatt, l983, 120–1, no. 12; Myatt, 1988, 299.

Watenan. (3). ND 315 412. ?12 row, F. NNE–SSW. 178 ft (54 m) l. Freer & Myatt, l982, 59, no. 3, fig. 2; Myatt, 1988, 285, fig. 12.4.

SHETLAND

Giant's Stones. (3). HU 243 805. Small st st form 1, prob 3 rows, S–N, SSW–NNE direction. N of Giant's Stones P near Hamna Voe. 17 st visible. *D & E*, l985, 32–3.

Lumbister, N Yell. (3). HU 486 962. 5 rows, P. Linear setting of small boulders. NE–SW. 395 ft (120 m) l. 66 ft (20 m) apart. 2nd row from E crossed by short line of larger boulders NNE–SSW, 148 ft (45 m) l. Exton, *Shetland Life 124*, 1991, 34–5; Fojut, 56–7; *D & E*, 1991, 75.

SUTHERLAND

Badanloch. (3). NC 782 351. 7 rows, F. S–N. 53 ft (16 m) l. Freer & Myatt, 1983, 125, no. 16, fig. 12; Myatt, 1988, 305–8, fig. 12.15.

Borgie. (3). NC 661 587. ?5 rows, ?P. SW–NE?. c. 59 ft (18 m) l. Freer & Myatt, l983, 121, no. 14, fig. 10; Myatt, 1988, 308–9, fig. 12.17.

Kildonan SW. (4). NC 955 185. 'Allt Breac' (trout stream). 14 rows? 66 ft (20 m) l. 2Cns. *RCAHM-S, Sutherland*, 1911b, 132, no. 379; Freer & Myatt, 1983, 132, no. 19; Myatt, 1988, 299–300.

Kinbrace. (3). NC 827 322. 'Ach'na h'Uai' (Field of the graves). 10 rows, F. SE–NW. 41 ft (13 m) l. Cn? Freer & Myatt, l983, 125, no. 17, fig. 13; Myatt, 1988, 303–5, fig. 12.14.

Learable Hill. (1). NC 892 234. [N2/1]. A complex of (a) North, 3 rows, (b) Centre, 4 rows, (c) South, 10 rows.

(a). *North*. 3 rows? P? SW–NE. 116 ft (35 m) l. Freer & Myatt, 1983, 126, no. 18, fig. 14; Myatt, 1988, 301.

Astr: Az = 61°.6. hor = 2°.4. decl = +16°.6 August SR Az = 75°. hor = 2°.2. decl = +9°.5. September SR Thom, 1967, 100, 153, fig. 12.13; 158; a calendrical site. Thom, Thom & Burl, 1990, II, 304–5.

(b). *Centre*. 4 rows, P. E–W. 172 ft (52 m) l. St st 5 ft 3 (1.6 m) h at hill summit 115 ft (35 m) south of rows has cross carved on W face. *PSAS 7*, 1866–8, 93; Anderson, 1886, 132; *RCAHM-S, Sutherland*, 1911b, no. 381; Gunn, 1915, 353; Feachem, 87; Thom, 1967, 153, fig. 12.13; MacKie, 1975, 218–19; Wood, J.E., 1978, 92, 95; Freer & Myatt, 1983, 126, no. 18. Fig. 14; Myatt, 1988, 301, fig. 12.13.

Astr: Az = 92°.8, hor = 2°.4, decl = 0°.3, equi SR.

Thom, 1967, 100.

(c). *South*. NC 892 233. 10 rows, F. SSE–NNW. 73 ft (22 m) l. 65 st. st + 17 pros. 72 ft (22 m) w at base, 33 ft (10 m) w at head. Cns at head of slope. Local st. St st 5 ft 3 ins (1.6 m) h 76 ft (23 m) to N. 4 low Cns may underlie the N side of fan.

Astr: St st aligned (?) on Maj S MR. Myatt, 1988, 301–3, fig. 12.13.

Loch Rimsdale. (3). NC 716 348. 4 rows, F. SSE–NNW. 43 ft (13 m) l. Freer & Myatt, 1983, 121–5, no. 15, fig. 11; Myatt, 1988, 308, fig. 12.16.

Skelpick. (4). NC 722 574. ? 5 rows, P. SSE–NNW. 97 ft (30 m) l? Myatt, 1975, *D & E*, 1975, 55; Freer & Myatt, 1983, 121, no. 13, fig. 9; Myatt, 1988, 309–11, fig. 12.18.

FOUR- TO SIX-STONE ROWS

ENGLAND

CORNWALL

*Kenidjack Common. (2). SW 389 325. 4 or 5 st, all holed. Re-erected. *Meyn Mamvro 9*, 1989 2, *ibid 14*, 1991, 14.

Tolborough Tor. (3). SX 175 778. By Cn. 5 tiny st st. *Meyn Mamvro 14*, 1991, 12.

Treveglos, Zennor. (3). SW 453 388. E–W. 4 st st. 8 ft 6 (2.6 m) h st + 3 low st, 1 broken, 1 pros. *Meyn Mamvro 14*, 1991, 14.

DEVON (Exmoor)

Furzehill Common SE. (3). SS 738 439. 4 st, SE–NW. 32 ft (10 m) l. Quinnell & Dunn, 27. SS74 SW 90.

NORTHUMBERLAND

Five Kings. [L3/3]. (1). NT 955 001. 4 st st + 1 pros. ENE–WSW. Pros (ENE) 5 ft (1.5 m) l. 6 ft 6, 6 ft, 4 ft, 8 ft (WSW) (2, 1.8, 1.2, 2.4 m) h. 79 ft (24 m) l. WSW st and next but 1 st set at RtLs. Row said to be five brothers who were kings. Grinsell, 1976, 177; Dyer, 202.

 Astr: Indicated foresight to st st on skyline. Az = 312°.6. hor = 21°.3. decl = +41°.1. Vega setting, 1820 BC (c. 1500 bc). Thom, 1967, 99. Thom, Thom & Burl, 1990, I, 41.

SOMERSET (Exmoor)

Lanacombe Centre W. (3). SS 784 428. 4 st, 1 ft to 1 ft 6 (30–45 cm) h, WNW–ESE. 108 ft (33 m) l. Quinnell & Dunn, 44. SS74 SE 50.

Porlock Allotment Centre. (5). SS 840 443. 4 st, 3 pros, SE–NW. 79 ft (24 m) l. 4 st, erect, is 36 ft (11 m) to SE, not quite in line with others. 3 pros may be collapsed 3St 43 ft (13.4 m) l. Quinnell & Dunn, 60. SS84 SW 81.

YORKSHIRE

*Devil's Arrows. (1). [L6/1]. SE 391 666. 'Three Greyhounds'. 'Three Sisters'. S. 3 st st. Possibly orig 5 st of an unfinished row. NNW–SSE (tallest). 18 ft, 21 ft, 22 ft 6 (5.5, 6.4, 6.9 m) h. 570 ft (174 m) l. NNW st to Centre st 200 ft (61 m). Centre st to SSE st 370 ft (113 m). Centre (south) st removed. Was c. 8 ft (2.4 m) from Centre (north) st. Millstone grit from 9 miles to S. Tops naturally weathered. Exc. 1725 onwards. Packing stones and clay, no finds. Stones roughly shaped. Leland, I, 95–6; Camden, 1610, 701; Aubrey, I, 108–12; Stukeley, 1776, 74; Hutchinson, 1794, I, 242; *PSAL 7*, 1876–8, 134–8; *Surtees Society 73*, 1887, 291–2. Lockyer, 1909, 365; Burl, 1991.

 Astr: (1) Az 155°, hor 1°, decl −32°.5. α Centauri rising, 3400 BC (c. 2650 bc). Lockyer, 1909, 484. 'Boroughbridge'; (2) Azs = 151°.5 and 152°.5, hor = 0°.5, decl = −30°.46. Maj S MR? Thom, Thom & Burl, 1990, I, 42–3; Burl, 1991, 14–16.

*Dunsley Moor. (5). NZ 85. 11. S. 5 st st, 2 with cms. Elgee, 1930, 106.

Castle Hill, (5). NZ 66. 10. S. 5 st st. WNW–ESE. 450 ft (137 m). Elgee, 1930, l06.

FRANCE (BRITTANY)

FINISTÈRE

Brennilis. No details. Pontois, 1929, 124.

Croas-en-Teurec, Montagnes-Noires. (3). 3 st st + pros. Giot *et al*, 415.

*Kérière, Douarnenez. (5). 2 st st, 3 pros, in adj fields. Du Chatellier, 140.

Pen-ar-Land, Ushant. (2). Horseshoe cromlech open to WSW. 13 by 10 m (43 ft × 33 ft). By cliff. Restored, 1988. 300 m (320 yds) S is 4-St row N–S. At end is P, E–W. 150 m+ (500 ft) to E is Q block.

 Astr: Axis of cromlech alig on MdS SR. 'Each stone marked a different sunrise over the course of the year, and also lunar movements'. Goffic, M. & J. le, 'Un observatoire préhistorique à Ouessant: l'enceinte de pierres de Pen-ar-Land', 1988; Briard, 1990, 50.

St-Denec, Porspoder. (3). 2 st st + 2 pros. SW–NE, 246°–66°. 2 m (6 ft 6) h. Rosy granite. Axe-carvings on pros st. Lockyer, 485; Pontois, 1929, 123; Burl, 1985, 74–5, no. 91; Scouëzec & Masson, 102–3.

St-Laurent, Crozon. No details. Pontois, 1929, 123.

*Trémezan, Landunvez. (5). 'Petit alignement'. Poss remains of a cromlech. Pontois, 128; Giot *et al*, 414.

ILLE-ET-VILAINE

Bellevue, Janzé. (3). 4 pros st, red schist. 100 m (110 yds) l. Menhir, Pierre des Fées, 4.4 m (14 ft 5) adj. Bézier, 20.

Bois-Hervy, St-Just. (3). 1 st st 3 m (10 ft) h. 4 pros. N–S. Bézier, 197–8.

*Brossay, La, Rénac. (4). Menhir, Pierre Rouge, 4 m (13 ft 2) h. 3 smaller st near, all Q. E–W. Bézier, 174–5.

Forët de Haut-Sève, St-Aubin-du-Cormier. (3). 4 st st. NW–SE. 2 adj menhirs. Bézier, 103; Giot *et al*, 1979, 413.

Malon S, Guipry. 4 st. (3). SE–NW. 20 m (66 ft) l. 2.7, 1.4, 2.1, 3.1 (8 ft 10, 4 ft 6, 6 ft 10, 10 ft 2) h. 20 m (22 yds) to N is 3St. Bézier, 192.

Musson, Langon. (3). 5 Q blocks. NE–SW. 15 m (49 ft) l. Bézier, 165.

MORBIHAN

*Castellic, Le. (3). 4 pros st. 2.8, 4.5, 2.7, 2.6 m (9 ft 2, 14 ft 9, 8 ft 10, 8 ft 6) l. Remains of cromlech? Kergal, 1980a, 58.

Coëpan Guer. (3). Short row, white Q. Briard, 1989, 107.

Crucuny. (3). 5 st in line. Kergal, 1980a, 61.

*Grand Menhir Brisé. (5). Axe-carving on largest frag. Exc., 1990, several large s/hs to menhir from the E. Inf: J. l'Helgouach. *Arch J 137*, 1980, 27–39; *Oxford J Arch 6*, 1987, 185–217.

Guernangoué, Roudouallec. (3). 1 st st, + 3 pros. All big. NNE–SSW. 18 m (59 ft) l. St st, NNE, c 4 m (13 ft) h. SSW, pros, 5 cms on W face. Giot, 1960, 125; Giot *et al*, 1979, 415, 'trois menhirs'.

Lann Granvillarac, Mané Kérioned. (3). 5 pros st, E–W. Kergal, 1980a, 71.

Minardais, Carantoir. (3). Short row. Briard, 1989, 107.

Pierre Drette, Comper, Paimpont. (3). Schist menhir 4 m (13 ft) h + 2 puddingstone and a schist st st. N–S. Briard, 1989, 35, 107; Geneste *et al*, 205.

Roche de la Vielle. 'Rock of the Old Hag', Campénéac. (4). 4 schist st st, N–S. Orig a Late Neo alig, 3000 BC?, destr for capstone and sideslabs of Bronze Age tertre 8 m (26 ft) to S, 'Le Tombeau des Géants'. Local red schist 'indicateur' menhir, 4.3 m (14 ft) h re-erected. Briard, 1989, 29–35, 107; Geneste *et al*, 205.

Tombeau des Géants'. See: Roche de la Vieille.

Vieux-Moulin, Le, N. Plouharnel. (3). 3 st st + 1 pros. All big. NNE–SSW. 18 m (60 ft) l. 2.5, 3 m (8 ft 2, 9 ft 10) h. c. 60 m (200 ft) N of Vieux Moulin South, but not in line. Fieldwork, 1991.

Vieux-Moulin, Le, S. Plouharnel. 'Les Trois Pierres'. (1). 6 st N–S. 14 m (46 ft) l. 2.5 to 3.4 m (8 ft 3 – 11 ft 3) h. 2 tallest at centre. Lukis, 1875, 26, 35; le Rouzic, 1935, 22; Giot, 1960, 123–4; Batt *et al*, 83; Burl, 1985, 166, no. 216. 'Les fantömes d'une armée decimée'. Scouëzec & Masson, 176.

Ville Guichas, La, 'Roche Trébulante', St-Malon-sur-Mel. (3). Menhir + 2 pros and one dressed, schist. Briard, 1989, 14, 107.

NORTHERN IRELAND

FERMANAGH

*Ratoran. H 326 465. (3). 4 large st. Davies, 1939, 12, no. 62.

Reyfad Stones. H 124 442. 6 large pros st, 5 have crs, 6th heavily hammered, 2 smaller embedded. Chart, *et al*, 158; Killanin & Duignan, 273; *JRSAI 13*, 1875, 453; *ibid, 15*, 1880, 380; *ibid 41*, 1911, 25.

TYRONE

Beaghmore. H 685 842. 7 StCs, A to G. May, 1953.
    A, B. (1). 4St + S between 2 splayed S. E = S, 12 low st. W = short 4St, 4 ft 1 (1.2 m) h, 24 ft (7.3 m) l. 'Up and down'. To Cn. Ct had Gp IX axe.
        Astr: 4St. Poss Maj N MR, Thom, A.S., 1980, 17, Line 9.
    C, D. (1). S + 4St. Pl. NE–SW. To Cn with empty corbelled Ct on N arc of StC D. E = S, low st. W = 4 tall st, 3 ft 2 (1 m) h. 27 ft (8.2 m) l. 'Up and down'. *JRSAI 83*, 1953, 174; Evans, 1966, 198; Thom, A.S., 1980; McConkey, 59; Burl, 1989. Thom, Thom & Burl, 1990, I, 90–3.
        Astr: 4St. MdS SR. Thom, A.S., 1980, 17, Line 4B.

*Clogherny Butterlope. (3). H 493 497. Remains of 5 StCs. Exc. 1937. 4 st to E of a ring, 1 broken, 1 pros. Av ht 1 ft 3 (0.4 m). Davies, 1939, 7; *UJA 2*, 1939, 36–43; Chart, 217; McConkey, 58.

*Doorat. (5). H 493 968. 2 StCs. Possible 4St, tang. NE–SW. 26 ft 3 (8 m) l. McConkey, 62.

Golan. (3). H 66. 94. S. 5 st st in line in dyke. 4 = c. 4 ft (1.3 m) h, 1 6½ ft (2 m)h, 3–6 ft (1–1.8 m) apart. Chart, *et al*, 219.

REPUBLIC OF IRELAND

CAVAN

Shantemon. 'Finn Mac Cool's Fingers'. (1). H 466 077. 4 st st, others pros. O'Riordain, 1964, 84; Evans, 1966, 67; Killanin & Duignan, 147; McNeill, 1962, 174.

CLARE

Knockaroura. R 423 803. 'Knocknafearbreaga Standing Stones'. (3). 5 st st + 1 pros. 37 ft (11.3 m) l. NNE–SSW. *PRIA 24c*, 1903, 96–9, pl. 5; O'Nuallain, 1988, 240, no. 70, fig. 36.

CORK

Ardrah. (1). W 069 544. S. 4 st st. High, low, high, low, like 2 conjoined Ps. 14 ft 5 (4.4 m) l. NE–SW (tallest). O'Nuallain, 1988, 235, no. 40, fig. 23.
    Astr: Az. 237°.1. hor 1°.8. decl. −18°.3. Min N MR, Min S MS. Lynch, A., 1982, 206.

Barrahaurin. (4). W 452 824. S. Once 5-st alig, 3, pros in 1916. 20 ft 9 (6.3 m) l? E–W. Killanin & Duignan, 166; Macalister, 1921, 304; ibid, 1935, fig. 14a; O'Nuallain, 1988, 232, no. 13. No fig.

Beenalaght. 'An Seisar', 'the six'. (1). W 485 873. S. 5 st st +1 pros. Av 9 ft (2.7 m) h. 36 ft (11 m) l. Tallest stones at ends. NE (tallest)–SW. *JRSAI 46*, 1916, 145–6, no. 125; Evans, 1966, 75; O'Riordain, 1964, 84; O'Nuallain, 1988, 232, no. 12, fig. 29; *ABM*, 3.
    Astr: Maj N MR. Lynch, A., 1981b, 26.

Behagullane. (3). W 275 567. 2 st st + 2 stumps. 21 ft (6.4 m) l. NE–SW. Rad-st Cn 53 ft (16 m) to SE. O'Nuallain, 1988, 246, no. 117, fig. 42. (Mistakenly listed as a pair).

Cabragh N. (1). W 278 798. S. 4 st, 25 ft 10 ins (7.9 m) l. NE (tallest)–SW. 10 ft 10 ins h. (3.3 m). Adj 5-StC. Killanin & Duignan, 345. O'Nuallain, 1988, 232, no. 16, fig. 26.
    Astr: Az. 228°.7. hor 0°. decl. −24°.4. MdW SS. Lynch, A., 1981b, 26; ibid, 1982, 206.

Cabragh S. (3). W 278 793. 4 st st + 2 pros. 31 ft 2 (9.5 m) approx l. E–W. O'Nuallain, 1984, 233, no. 17; O'Nuallain, 1988, no. 17, fig. 29; Killanin & Duignan, 365.

Castlenalacht. (1). W 485 612. S. 4 massive st st. 43 ft 7 (13.3 m) l. Longest row in Cork. ENE (tallest)–WSW. O'Riordain, 1964, 84; Killanin & Duignan, 97; O'Nuallain, 1988, 235, no. 36, fig. 22.
    Astr: Az. 238°.1. hor 0°. decl. −19°.2. Min S MS, Min N MR. Lynch, A., 1981b; ibid, 1982, 206.

Cloghvoula. (1). R 158 143. 3 st st + 1 pros. ? NNE–SSW. O'Nuallain, 1988, 231, no. 1, fig. 25.

Coolgarriff. (3). W 407 776. 3 st st + 1 pros. 20 ft 8 (6.3 m) l. NE–SW (tallest). O'Nuallain, 1988, 233, no. 20, fig. 20.

Derrymihan W. (4). V 696 461. Plan in Somerville papers, UCC shows 4 st st. ENE–WSW. 5th st removed, now in fence to N. O'Nuallain (*in litt*, 1990).

Dromcarra N. (1). W 278 681. S. 4 st st + 1 pros. 30 ft 10 (9.4 m) l. NE (tallest)–SW. Lynch A., 1982, 207; O'Nuallain, 1988, 234, no. 28, fig. 23.
    Astr: Maj N MR. Lynch, A., 1981b, 26.

Dromdrasil. (1). W 171 557. S. 4 st st. 17 ft 9 (5.4 m) l. NE–SW (tallest). Lynch A., 1982, 206; O'Nuallain, 1988, 236, No. 41, fig. 20.
    Astr: MdS SR. Lynch, A., 1981b, 26.

Farrannahineeny. (1). W 214 607. S. 4 st st + 1 pros. 26 ft 7 (8.1 m) l. NE–SW (tallest). 20 ft (6 m) SW, Ct?. Long views to S. Harbison, P., 1970, 55; O'Nuallain, 1988, 235, no. 35, fig. 25.

Astr: Maj N MR. Lynch, A., 1981b, 26.

Garrane. (3). W 478 912. S. 3 st st + 1 pros. 24 ft 11 (7.6 m) l. NNE (tallest)–SSW. Lynch A., 1982, 207; O'Nuallain, 1988, 231, no. 5, fig. 24.

Astr: Maj S MS. Lynch, A., 1981b, 26.

Gurranes. (3). W 175 315. S. 'Three Ladies', 'Five Fingers'. 3 st st + 1 pros. 5th removed. 34 ft 10 (10.6 m) l. ENE, tallest, 14 ft (4.3 m) h – WSW. *JCHAS 33*, 1928, fig. 2; O'Nuallain, 1988, 237, no. 55, fig. 12; Roberts, 14.

Astr: Samain (November) SS. Lynch, A. 206.

Knocknanagh E. (3). R 227 057. 4 st st. 24 ft 4 (7.4 m) l. NE–SW (tallest). *JCHAS 39*, 1934, 22; O'Nuallain, 1988, 231, no. 2, fig. 12.

Maughanasilly I. (3). W 044 585. S. 5 st st. 18 ft 9 (5.7 m) l. NE–SW. Lynch A., 1981, 69–71, 107. Exc. 1977. Fl. scraper. 1315±55 bc (GrN-9280) c. 1610 BC, Lynch A., 1982, 206.; O'Nuallain, 1988, 234–5, no. 33, fig. 23.

Piercetown. (3). W 690 593. 4 st st. 22 ft 7 (6.9 m) l. NNE–SSW. O'Nuallain, 1988, 235, no. 37, fig. 25; Killanin & Duignan, 133, 'Carrigaline'.

Reanerre. (1). W 204 727. S. 6 st st. 22 ft 11 (7 m) l. Row with narrowest gaps, only 8 ins (20 cm) w. NNE–SSW (tallest). Adj 5-StC. Lynch A., 1982, 207; O'Nuallain, 1988, 233, no. 22, fig. 30.

Roovesmore. (3). W 450 702. S. 1 st st + 5 pros. ? NNE–SSW. Killanin & Duignan, 166; O'Nuallain, 1988, 234, no. 25, fig. 31.

Tullig. 'Kerryman's Table'. (1). W 318 872. 4 st st. 16 ft 9 (5.1 m) l. ENE–WSW (tallest). O'Nuallain, 1984a, 46, no. 6; *ibid*, 1988, 231, no. 8, fig. 20; *ABM*, 3.

Astr: Min N MR. Lynch, A., 1981b, 26.

DONEGAL

Carlan Upper. (4). C1 . . 3 . . Location unknown. Once 4 st (3 pros) in N–S line. Lacy, 90, no. 528.

Knocknafaugher. (3). C 039 344. 5 st in line, central biggest. 4 ft 10 ins h (1.5 m), NNE–SSW. Row 8 ft 6 (2.6 m) l. Lacy, 83, no. 439.

Rashenny (A). (3). C 418 482. S. 5-St alig, NNE–SSW. From N, 1 st st, then 2 thin st side by side, 1 st st, 2 pros st. Lacy, 85, no. 471, fig. 34.

GALWAY

*Derryinver. 'Finn McCool's Fingers'. (5). L 688 608. 6 st st or 2 × 3St? N–S. 53 ft (16 m) l. 3 N st, granite, graded N–S, 5 ft 11, 4 ft, 2 ft 3, then 3 schist, N–S, 5 ft 3, 2 ft 3, 1 ft 8 (1.8, 1.2, 0.7, 1.6, 0.7, 0.5 m) h. Adj 5-StC? Evans, 118; *JGAHS 25*, 1953–4, 98; O'Nuallain, 1988, 195; Gosling, 1991, 28.

Gleninagh. (3). L 815 552. 6 Q st st. 28 ft 7 (8.7 m) l. NNE–SSW (tallest). 3 ft 2, 2 ft 3, 3 ft, 3 ft 4, 2 ft 3, 1 ft 10 (1, 0.7, 0.9, 1, 0.7, 0.6 m) h. O'Nuallain, 1988, 195; Gosling, 1991, 28.

Poundcarton. (3). L 887 553. 2 st st + 2 pros. All Q. N–S. 23 ft (7 m) l. Orig hts c. 2 ft 11, 2 ft 11, 4 ft 11, 2 ft 6 (0.9, 0.9, 1.5, 0.8 m). O'Nuallain, 1988, 195; Gosling, 1991, 30.

KERRY

Beale Middle. (3). V 885 475. S. 5 st st + 1 pros. 30 ft 6 (9.3 m) l? NNE (tallest)–SSW. Lynch A., 1982, 207; O'Nuallain, 1988, 238, no. 57, fig. 30.

Cashelkeelty. (3). V 747 575. 3 large st. 'The alignment originally consisted of four standing stones with the socket of the fourth lying to the east of the three now standing'. Lynch, A. 1981, 66. 20½ ft (6.3 m) l. E (tallest)–W. Adj 5-StC. Tallest st, 8 ft (2.4 m) h, is at the E. Exc. 1977. B/t a/h and fl scraper near alig. StC gave 2 C-14 dates: 970±60 bc (GrN-9173) and 715±50 bc, (GrN-9172), av. c. 960 BC. 'Stratigraphic evidence seems to indicate that the stone row was erected some centuries before the circle'. Lynch, A., 1981, 65–9, 76.; O'Nuallain, 1988, 240, no. 69, fig. 19.

Cloonsharragh. (1). Q 511 128. 3 st st + 2 pros. WSW (tallest)–ENE. 9 ft 2, 6 ft 10 and 6 ft 10 (2.8, 2.1, 2.1 m) h. 10 ft 9 (3.3 m) l. Just W 2 pros, 6 ft 3 and 7 ft 11 (1.9, 2.4 m) l. Cuppage, 1986, 38–9. Views to E. O'Nuallain, 1988, 238, no. 58, fig. 18.

Astr: MdS SR. Lynch, A. 1981b, 26.

Derrineden. (3). V 572 716. 4 st st. 21 ft 4 (6.5 m) l. NE–SW. O'Nuallain (*in litt*, 1990).

Dromkeare. (3). V 540 684. 4 st st. 24 ft (7.3 m) l. NE–SW (tallest). O'Nuallain, (*in litt*, 1990).

*Eightercua. (5). V 512 646. S. 4 st st, E–W, 28 ft 6 (8.7 m) l. 6–10 ft (1.8–3 m) h. St st at RtLs + 1 pros to W. Remains of ChT forecourt? Evans, 1966, 129; *JRSAI 32*, 1902, 330; Killanin & Duignan, 455; O'Nuallain, 1988, 200, 228, fig. 62.

Astr: Az = 227°.3. hor 1°. decl = −24°.1. MdW SS. Lynch, A., 1981b, 26; ibid, 1982, 207.

Feavautia. (3). R 065 235. 3 st st + 1 pros. NE–SW. O'Nuallain, (*in litt*, 1990).

Garrough. (3). V 558 608. 2 st st + 2 pros. 36 ft (11 m) l. NE–SW (tallest). Coad Mountain Bronze Age copper mines to NE. O'Nuallain, 1988, 239, no. 68, fig. 32.

Gortacloghane. V 759 738. S. 3 st st + 2 pros. O'Nuallain, 1984a, 49.

Kildreelig. (1). V 408 637. S. 4 st st. 16 ft 5 (5 m) l. High, low, high, low, like 2 conjoined Ps. ENE (tallest)–WSW. Evans, 1966, 130; O'Nuallain, 1988, 239, no. 67, fig. 33.

Astr: Az = 63°.2. hor = 14°.9. decl. 28°.1. Maj N MR. Lynch, A., 1981b, 26; ibid, 1982, 207.

LIMERICK

Tomdeely N. (3). R 329 524. 3 st st + 3 pros. 26 ft 7 (8.1 m) l. N–S. O'Nuallain, 1988, 240–1, no. 72, fig. 36.

LOUTH

Balregan. (4). J 023 100. Buckley, 1986, 18, no. 176.

Carrickedmond E. (4). J 024 128. Buckley, 1986, 18, no. 177.

Carrickedmond W. (4). J 026 128. Buckley, 1986, 18, no. 178.

Edenakill. (4). H 978 123. 5 st once. Buckley, 1986, 20, no. 199.

Ravensdale Park. (4). J 098 157. 4 st. Buckley, 1986, 22, no. 219.

MAYO

Eskeragh. (3). G 048 189. 4 st st. 16 ft 1 (4.9 m) l. NNE–SSW (tallest). O'Nuallain (*in litt*, 1990).

Killadangan. 'Gortbraud'. (3). L 943 826. S. 4 st st + 1 pros. 7 ft 6 (2.3 m) l. NNE–SSW. By seashore, Clew Bay.

Adj StC destr. de Valera & O'Nuallain, 1964, 98–9; O'Nuallain, 1988, 197; Killanin & Duignan, 456.

WATERFORD

Tooreen W. (1). S 245 117. 4 st st + outlier. 18 ft 5 (5.6 m) l. NNE–SSW (tallest). O'Nuallain, 1988, 241. no. 74, fig. 37. In Bronze Age ritual complex with ring barrow, other rows and StC. *Arch Ireland 6.1*, 1992, 17.

There may be a second row of 6 stones 'somewhat dubious since it is built into a field-fence'. Inf: M. Moore. See: 3 St Gazetteer.

SCOTLAND

ARGYLL

Ballymeanoch. (1). NR 833 964. [A2/12]. 4St + P + st st. 4St NW–SE, (tallest), 14 ft (4.3 m) h. Nos. 2, 3, have cms. Row 49 ft (15 m) l. P, NNW–SSE, 132 ft (40 m) to SW. *PSAS 16*, 1881–2, 114–17; *ibid 95*, 1961–2, 24, no. 158. Exc. 1977, 3 crems in s/h, *ibid 109*, 104–12; *D & E*, 1982, 22; *ibid*, 1983, 22; Ruggles, 1984, 149, (AR15).
 Astr: (1) Az = 321°. hor = 2°.6. decl = 29°.1. Maj N MS. Thom, 1971, 52–3; Thom, Thom & Burl, 1990, I, 106–8. (2) To SE, decl limits = −25°.8 to −23°.7. MdW SR. To NW, decl limits = 28°.3 to 29°.3. Maj N MS? Ruggles, 1984, 279; Ruggles, 1988b, 239.

Escart. (1). NR 846 667. [A4/1]. Impressive. NNE–SSW. 5 st now, 5 ft to 10 ft (1.5–3 m) h. 51 ft (15.6 m) l. Once longer. Wide gap between 2nd and 3rd stones from NNE. NE st at RtLs, 9 ft 6 (2.9 m) h. 5th st, SW, broken, 3 ft 7 (1.1 cm) h. *RCAHM-S, Argyll I*, 1971, 63, no. 143; Ruggles, 1984, 183 (KT5).
 Astr: (1) Maj S MS. Thom, 1971, 59–60; Thom, Thom & Burl, 1990, I, 134. (2) Maj S MS, Maj N MR? Ruggles, 1984, 279.

Macharioch. (3). NR 736 093. 3 st st + boulders + pros stones. *PSAS 64*, 1929–30, 319–20, no. 32.

Macrihanish. (4). NR 644 206. [A4/15]. Large Cn, exc. 1835. Once were st st to N. '. . . was able to assert that the central cist was in direct alignment with these stones'. *Arch Scot III*, 1831, 43. Wilson, I, 94; *PSAS 64*, 316, no. 23; Ruggles, 1984, 53 (KT38); Thom, Thom & Burl, 1990, I, 142.

CAITHNESS

Broughwin Centre W. (3). ND 311 409. 5 st on ridge. Freer & Myatt, 1982, 60 (IV).

JURA

Carragh a'Ghlinne. 'The stone of the glen'. (3). NR 512 664. [A6/6]. Impressive st st at SW 7 ft 10 (2.4 m) h + 3 pros 9 ft 2, 7 ft and 7 ft 11 (2.8, 2.4, 2.4 m) l. S. NE–SW. 16 ft (5 m) l. SW st has cms. Ruggles, 1984, 163, JU6, 'Craighouse'. *RCAHM-S, Argyll, V*, 1984, 64–5, no. 83.
 Astr: (1). *PSAS 66* 1931–2, 149; (2) Min S MS. Thom, 1966, fig. 8; Thom, 1967, 97; Thom, Thom & Burl, 1990, I, 159.

LEWIS

Callanish. [H1/1. Callanish I]. NB 213 330. StC, A + 3 × 4St.
 (a) East Row. (2). 5 st. 50 ft 6 (15.4 m) l. ENE–WSW.

Exc. 1980. 5th st found. Re-erected, 1982. Ponting, G. & M., 1984, 11.
 (b) South Row. (1). 5 st. 72 ft (22 m) l. N–S.
 (c) West Row. (1). 4 st. 29 ft 6 (9 m) l. E–W.
Burl, 1976, 148–55; Heggie, 1981, 209–12; Ponting, G. & M., 1984, 51–2; Ponting, M., 1988, 426–31. *Callanish. A Map of the Standing Stones and Circles . . .* University of Glasgow, 1978.
 Astr: East row. (a) To ENE. (1) Pleiades rising, 1330 BC (c. 1050 bc). Lockyer, 1909, 344, 484. 'Callernish'; (2) ibid, 1750 BC (c. 1450 bc). Somerville, 1923, 203; (3) Altair rising, 1760 BC (c. 1460 bc). Thom, 1967, 98; 1800 BC (c. 1475 bc)?, 124. (4) To WSW. Equi MS. Hawkins, 1966, 183, 186.
 South Row. (1) To True South. Somerville, 1923, 203; (2) To the meridian. Thom, 1967, 98, 123, 124–5; (3) Maj S moon in transit. Hawkins, 1966, 183, 186.
 West Row. (a) To W. (1) Equi SS. Somerville, 1923, 203; (2) ibid, Thom, 1967, 98. (3) To E. Equi SR. Hawkins, 1966, 183, 186.

*Cnoc na Greana, Berneray. (3). NF 922 819. 'Knoll of the Sun'. Large glacial boulder 5 ft h + 2 st st 3 ft 4, 2 ft 9 h (1.5, 1, 0.7 m) + pros st to the E 3 ft 2 (1 m) l. 'Placed so as to form the southern arc of a circle'. t 4 (1 m) h. *RCAHM-S, Outer Hebrides*, 1928, 43, no. 134.

MULL

Dervaig NNW. 'Maol Mor', 'the bare moor'. (1). [M1/4. Dervaig A]. NM 435 531. 3 st st + 1 pros. NNW–SSW. NNW, pros across row. 8 ft 2 (2.5 m) l. Then 6 ft 10 (2.1 m) h, 7 ft 2 (2.2 m) h, SSE 6 ft 10 (2.1 m) h. 32 ft 10 (10 m) l. Ruggles, 1984, 127 (ML9); Ruggles, 1988b, 237, 241; Ritchie & Harman, 143; *RCAHM-S, Argyll III*, 1980, 66–7, no. 101 (1). Thom, Thom & Burl, 1990, II, 267.
 Astr: (1) Capella setting, 1930 BC (c. 1580 bc). Thom, 1967, 99. (2) Maj N MS? Ruggles, 1984, 279.

Dervaig Centre. (1). NM 439 520. [M1/5. Dervaig B]. S. 2 st + 3 pros, all basalt, 4 in NNW–SSE line, 60 ft (18.3 m) l. 30 ft (9 m) to SSE of row, a st st 6 ft (1.8 m) h. Dervaig SSE 4-st row is 660 ft (200 m) to SSW. *RCAHM-S, Argyll III*, 1980, 67, no. 101 (2); Ruggles, 1984, 127 (ML10); Thom, 1966, 23, fig. 7c. Thom, Thom & Burl, 1990, II, 268.
 Astr: (1) probably to Maj S MS. Thom, 1971, 67. (2) Maj N MS? Ruggles, 1984, 279; Ruggles, 1988b, 237.

Dervaig SSE. 'Glac Mhor', 'the hollow in the moor'. (3). NM 438 516. [M1/6. Dervaig C]. 3 st st + 1 to ESE. NNW–SSE. 20 ft (6 m) l. 4th st now a gatepost, prob taken from row 33 ft (10 m) to its WNW. 3 ft 7 (1.1 m) h. *RCAHM-S, Argyll III*, 1980, 67, no. 101 (3); Ruggles, 127, 243 (ML 11).
 Astr: (1) Near Maj S MR. Ruggles, 1984, 125, 134, 168; Ruggles, 1988b, 279. (2) Maybe a lunar decl on Maj N MS. Thom, Thom & Burl, 1990, II, 269.

Quinish. 'Mingary'. (3). [M1/3]. NM 413 552. 3 st st + 1 pros. Once 5 st. NNW–SSE. St st 9 ft 2 (2.8 m) h. 33 ft (10 m) long. Ruggles, 1984, 123 (ML2).
 Astr: (1) Maj S MS. Thom, 1971, 66–7, 76; Thom, Thom & Burl, 1990, II, 266. (2) Maj S MS. Ruggles, 1984, 305; 1988b, 237.

Uluvalt I. 'Barr Leathan'. (3). NM 546 300. 260 ft (80 m) N of basalt st st 6 ft 3 (1.9 m) h was a 4-st row. Now 1 st st +

3 pros st. NW–SE. NW st, 7 ft 6 (2.3 m) l, 7 ft 10 (2.4 m) l, then st st, SE st 6 ft 6 (2 m) l. Row approx 33 ft (10 m) l. *RCAHM-S, Argyll III*, 1980, 72, no. 121; Ruggles, 128. (ML25).

    Astr: Near Min S MR. Ruggles, 1984, 279; Ruggles, 1988b, 125, 137, 268–9.

NORTH UIST

Skeal Traval. (3). NF 853 707. 6 st. 492 ft (150 m) l. SE–NW. *D & E*, 1986, 52.

PERTHSHIRE

Comrie, see: Tullybannocher.

Doune, see: Glenhead Farm.

*Dunruchan Stones. (5). NN 789 162 – NN 792 174. S. 4 st in alig SSW–NNE. 700 yds (640 m) l. 6¾, 8½, 9′¼, 5 ft (2.1, 2.6, 2.8, 1.5 m) h. Craigneich Stone is 450 yds (410 m) to N. A tall st, 11¼ ft (3.4 m) h, is 340 yds (310 m) to E. *PSAS 45*, 1910–11, 63–71.

Glenhead Farm. (1). NN 755 004. [P1/2, 'Doune']. 3 st st + 1 pros. NNE–SSW (tallest). 3 ft 6 h, 6 ft 6 l, 4 ft h, 6 ft 6 h (1.1, 2, 1.2, 2 m). 27 ft (8.3 m) l. Central st, 23 cms on top, 4 on W side. *PSAS 16*, 1881–2, 87–8; Thom, Thom & Burl, 1990, II, 322.

    Astr: Capella rising 1760 BC (c. 1725 bc). Thom, 1967, 100.

*Tullybannocher. (5). NN 755 225. [P1/8. Comrie]. 2 st st NW–SE. Each 4 ft 3 (1.3 m) h. 19 ft 6 (6 m) apart. Smooth E face of SE st, 4 cms. Orig 4 st. By 1890 only 3. Now 2. Once a 4-Poster? Coles, 1911, 50–1; Stewart, 1966, 144–5, no. 26; Burl, 1988, 34, 36, 193. Thom, Thom & Burl, 1990, II, 323.

    Astr: 'It might be lunar but it is not a convincing site. The stones do not lie along the line'. Thom, 1967, 100.

STIRLING

*Blanefield. 'Dumgoyach', 'Duntreath'. (5). NS 532 807. [A11/1]. St st 4 ft (1.2 m) h + 4 pros. NNE–SSW. 54 ft (17 m) l? Exc. 1972. Mesolithic flints? Charcoal = 2860±270 bc (Gx-2781), c. 3650 BC. *D & E*, 1972, 38–9. Prob façade of ruined Clyde ChT. *PSAS 40*, 1905–6, 301–4; Feachem, 87; MacKie, 1975, 114–15; *RCAHM-S, Stirling*, 1963, 67, no. 58. *Curr Arch 36*, 1973, 6–7.

    Astr: MdS SR. Thom, 1967, 98.

Dumgoyach. Duntreath. see: Blanefield.

Middleton. (4). NS 561 766. S. Was a line of st st, NW–SE, the largest at the NW, the 'Law Stone of Mugdock'. Cts discovered in same field. *RCAHM-S, Stirling, I*, 1963, 68, no. 63.

WALES

ANGLESEY: SEE YNYS MONA

CLWYD

*Gallt y Foel. (5). SH 80. 55. 4St + S? Row of 6 st st, 200 yds (180 m) l, 20–35 yds (18–32 m) apart, meets a 2nd of 11 st at RtLs. None more than 2 ft (0.6 m) h. *RCAHM-W, Denbigh*, 1914, 144–5, no. 511.

*Gwytherin Stones. (5). SH 877 614. In churchyard. 4 st, c. 3 ft (1 m) h, 6 ft (1.8 m) apart in a line c. 20 ft (6 m) l. Celtic inscription on the W stone, VINNEMAGLI FILI/SENEMAGLI, 'The stone of Vinnemaglus, son of Senemaglus', 5th or 6th century AD. Houlder, 69; Barber, C., 1986, 10; Laing, L. & J., *A Guide to the Dark Age Remains In Britain*, 1979, 183.

*Llangwm. (5). SH 97. 45. S. Row of 6 st st with 3 others at RtLs to it. *RCAHM-W, Denbigh* 1914, 128, no. 452.

DYFED

Llech Ciste. 'Slate chest'. (Carmarthen). (3). SN 514 261. 10 ft (3 m) h stone, 2 smaller on either side, 11½ ft (3.5 m) away. 4th 53 ft (16 m) further to SE. Houlder, 169.

Penmeiddyn. (1). SM 930 357. S. 4 st st. NE–SW. 2 are 3 ft (1 m) h. others 5 ft 9, 6 ft 3 (1.8, 1.9 m) h. 18 ft (5.5 m) apart. *RCAHM-W, Pembroke*, 1925, 209, no. 642; Barber & Williams, 120, no. 110, 'Manorowen'.

*Pont Ddu. (Cardigan). 'Black bridge'. (3). SN 309 149. A st st at SN 319 139. To its S is a st st at SN 312 141. A row of st 5–6 ft (1.5–1.8 m) h is to its W. Anthony, 46; Dyer, 332.

GWYNEDD

Llanbedr. (3). SH 583 270. 2 st st, each in railings. 10 ft and 6 ft 6 (3, 2 m) h. Once 'four or five broad stones, 8 feet high, standing upright'. *RCAHM-W, Merioneth*, 1921, 52, no. 139; Bowen & Gresham, 64, no. 59.

Waun Oer. 'Cold moorland'. 'Ynys Faig meini hirion' (island of standing stones). (3). SH 617 112. S. 3 st st + 2 pros. NE–SW. 200 ft (60 m) l. A c/m on pros st at NE. *RCAHM-W, Merioneth*, 1921, 127, no. 410; Bowen & Gresham, 62, 65, nos. 75–9.

POWYS

Cae Garreg. 'Stone Field'. (4). SN 963 777. c. 1890, line of st st toppled. E–W. 'Like tombstones'. On low mound, 90 by 20 ft (27 × 6 m). All faced N. Riverside stones, av ht 7 ft (2.1 m). In 1957, 1 st st 6 ft 1.8 m) h. *RCAHM-W, Radnor*, 1913, 145–6, no. 603; Barber & Williams, 176, no. 346.

Pedwar Maen. 'Four Stones', Llanfihangel-nant-melan. (Radnor). (1). SO 156 568. C. 4 st st nearby, NE–SW (tallest). 1 ft 6, 1 ft 6, 2 ft, 2 ft 6 (46, 46, 61, 76 cm) h. 13 ft (4 m) l. Of different kinds of stone. *RCAHM-W, Radnor*, 1913, 90, no. 355. Grimes, *PPS 2*, 1936, 138, Radnor 4; Barber & Williams, 173, no. 335.

Rhos y Gelynen Stones. 'Enemy's moor'. (3). SN 906 630. [W8/1. Rhosygelynnen]. 4 st st + 1 pros. 1 tall st st + 4 low st st. WSW–ENE. WSW = 2 ft 3, 2 ft 3, 4 ft 11, 7 ft 7 + pros (0.7, 0.7, 1.5, 2.3 m) h. 25 ft (7.6 m) l. *RCAHM-W, Radnor*, 1913, 101, no. 402; Thom, 1966, 45, fig. 33b; ibid, 1967, 100.

Trecastle Mountain. (Brecks). (3). SN 833 311. [W11/2. Y Pigwn]. 2 StCs + 4St ENE st missing, tang. NE StC 76 ft (23 m) d. 145 ft (44 m) to SW is 2nd StC, 25 ft (7.6 m) d. 54 ft (16.5 m) to its SW is row, now of 3 low st. ENE–WSW. 62 ft (18.9 m) l. Grimes, 1963, 135–6, nos. 25a, b; Thom, Thom & Burl, 1980, 390–1; Thom, Thom & Burl, 1990, II, 367.

YNYS MONA

*Cremlyn, Llansadwrn. (5). SH 571 773. S. 2 st st + 3 others, 'a row of 5 small stones 450 yards (410 m) long'. S st fell, 1977, Re-erected. Probably had replaced an orig post. *Trans Anglesey Ant Soc*, 1980, 117–24; *RCAHM-W. Anglesey*, 1937, 113a; Lynch, F. 1991, 325, 348–9.

THREE-STONE ROWS

ENGLAND

BEDFORDSHIRE

Devil's Jump Stone. (5). SP 999 409. A glacial erratic 2 ft (60 cm) h, 1 of 3 st once. Unusual for this region. Dyer, 51.

CORNWALL

Longstone Farm. (4). SX 362 803. Once 3 large st, head ht, widely spaced. Bodmin Survey.

CUMBERLAND

*Giant's Grave. (5). SD 137 811. [L1/11]. Near Standing Stones Farm 2 great st 10 ft and 8 ft (3, 2.4 m) h, NE (taller)–SW, 13 ft (4 m) apart. The NE has cms on inner face. A 3rd st is reputed to have stood here. 'Near adjoining to this monument, several other large stones stood lately, placed in a rude manner', Hutchinson, 1794, I, 529–30; *TCWAAS 1*, 1872–3, 280; Ruggles & Whittle, 1981, 208; Waterhouse, 1985, 46; Thom, Thom & Burl, 1990, I, 37.
    Astr: Maj S MS. Thom, 1967, 99.

Lacra SE. (1). SD 150 810. 3 pros st, SW–NE (longest). Mistakenly identified as remains of StC. 39 ft 2 (12 m) l. Exc. 1947. Oyster shell by SW, oak char near NE. *TCWAAS 48*, 1948, 3–5; Waterhouse, 49.

DEVON (EXMOOR)

*Furzehill Common SW. (3). SS 734 439. 3 st, E–W. 29 ft 6 (9 m) l. 4th st 16 ft (5 m) N of W st. Remains of rectangle? Quinnell & Dunn, 24. SS74 SW 59.

Furzehill Common Centre. (3). SS 737 442. 2 st + 1 pros. NE–SW (pros). 48 ft (14.6 m) l. Chanter & Worth, 1906, 544–5, Plate VII – shows NE pros. Quinnell & Dunn, 22. SS74 SW 32.

Longstone Barrow. (3). SS 707 425. 2 st st + 1 now missing. SE–NW. 30 ft (9 m) l. Quinnell & Dunn, 17. SS74 SW 47.

Winaway. (1). SS 722 437. 3 st st, N–S. 50 ft 3 (15.3 m) l. 4th st 26 ft 6 (8 m) to W at RtLs to S st. Chanter & Worth, 1905, 395, Pl. VIII (2); Quinnell & Dunn, 22. SS74 SW 1.

NORTHUMBERLAND

*Lordenshaw. (3). NZ 052 991. 3 low boulders. 25 ft (7.6 m) l. ENE–WSW. 60 ft (18 m) to SW, 2 c/m outcrops. 105 ft (30 m) to WSW a ruined Cn. Inf: M. van Hoek. Beckensall, 1983, 201–2.

SCILLY ISLES

Higher Town, St-Martin's. (1). SV 933 153. 3 low st st on beach. *Meyn Mamvro 14*, 14.

SOMERSET (EXMOOR)

Hoscombe SE. (3). SS 831 438. 2 st st + 1 pros, SE–NW. 59 ft (18 m) l. 4th st 50 ft (15 m) NE of SE pros st. Quinnell & Dunn, 48. SS84 SW 48.

*Swap Hill. (5). SS 805 426. 3St? 3 st st, SE–NW. 36 ft (11 m) l but spacing irreg. NW to centre st 11 ft 8 (3.6 m)

but centre to SE 24 ft 3 (7.4 m). Largish block 43 ft (13 m) E of central st. Small st 12 ft (3.7 m) NE of NW st. Orig a rectangle or a D? Quinnell & Dunn, 46. SS84 SW 39.

FRANCE (BRITTANY)

CÔTES-DU-NORD

Pergat, Louargat. (3). 3 st in NE–SW line. Tallest, SW, 10 m (32 ft) h at RtLs to row. 2 m to NE pros st, 6 m (20 ft) l, 9 m (30 ft) to NE 2 m (6 ft 6) h st. Track-marker out of valley? Giot, 1960, 119; Burl, 1985, 40, no. 20; Scouëzec & Masson, 86–90.

Poul ar Varquez, Port-la-Chaîne en Pleubian. (3). 3 st st in banked enclosure. Giot *et al*, 1979, 414.

FINISTÈRE

*Délivrande, Île-de-Seins. (3). 3 st st. Du Chatellier, 158.

*Difrout, Plougastel-Daoulas. (3). 3 st st 3.5, 1.5, 1.8 m (11 ft 6, 4 ft 11, 5 ft 10) h. Du Chatellier, 91–2.

Île Molène. (1). 3 st st. Du Chatellier, 111; Giot *et al*, 415.

Kerfland, Plomeur. (3). 2 st st + 1 pros. 4.4 m (14 ft 5) apart. 4.3, 4.4, 3.3 m (14 ft, 14 ft 5, 10 ft 10) h. NNE–SSW. Exc. Sherds, char and quern. Du Chatellier, 175; Pontois, 1929, 97; Giot *et al*, 415; Burl, 1985, 60, no. 62.

*Kerglas, Plougonven. (5). 3 st st. E–W. 100 m (330 ft) from each other. Du Chatellier, 80.

*Landisiac'h, Plouescat. (3). St st 2.2 m (7 ft 2) h + 2 pros, 4 m (13 ft) l. Du Chatellier, 77.

Parc-ar-Menhir, Scaër. (3). 3 st st. N–S. Du Chatellier, 201.

Pointe de St-Mathieu, Île Molène. (4). 3 st st. Du Chatellier, 111; Giot *et al*, 1979, 415.

Plomelin, Quimper. (3). 2 st st + 1 pros. Du Chatellier, 188.

Poulguen-Bihan, Penmarc'h. (3). 3 pros st, south (longest)–N. 7 m (22 ft 10) l. S st, 4.7 m (15 ft 4) l, 38 cms. Pros st 25 m (82 ft) to W. Pontois, 257–9.

St-Nic, Châteaulin. (3). 2 st st + 1 pros. Du Chatellier, 119.

Tri-Men, St-Goazec. (3). 1 st st, 2 pros. Du Chatellier, 122; Giot, 1960, 125; Giot *et al*, 1979, 415.

Trouanigou, St-Douarzel, Île Mélon. (4). Menhir 7 m (23 ft) h. 80+ tons. Dressed. Long sides look to 3St 1 km (1100 yds) NE. Pontois, 1929, 103, 123; Giot, 1960, 116; Giot *et al*, 1979, 393, 414.
    Astr: (1) May, Nov SR, Lockyer, 1909, 102, 'St-Dourzal'; (2) MdS SR. Pontois, 1929, 106.

ILLE-ET-VILAINE

*Bouëxière, La, Liffré. (3). At La Tertre st st 2.4 m (7 ft 10) h. Local Q. At base a pros st 2.6 m (8 ft 6) l. 20 m (22 yds) to SW a st st 1.1 m (3 ft 7) h. Bézier, 237–8.

Clos de la Grée, Langon. (3). 3 pros st, 3 m (10 ft) l. Q and schist. 6 m (20 ft) l. Bézier, 165.

Demoiselles, Les, St-Just. 'Les Roches Piquées'. (3). 2 Q st, 3 m (10 ft) h on an E–W axis. Adj 3rd pros. Bézier, 202; Burl, 1985, 92, no. 110f.

Malon N, Guipry. (3). 3 st st, 1 m, 2.7 m, 1.6 m (3 ft, 8 ft 10, 5 ft 3) h. 10.6 m (35 ft) l. Just to S a 4St row. Bézier, 192.

Theil, Le, Rétiers. (5). Menhir, Pierre de Rumfort, 3 m

(10 ft) h. 60 m (200 ft) to E, pros st 2 m (6 ft 6) l. Just to W, pros st 1.2 m (4 ft) l and 3rd pros. Bézier, 151–2.

Trois Colonnes, Les, St-Just. (1). By D65. 3 st st, N–S. 15.8 m (52 ft) l. S st 3 m, centre 4 m, N 2.8 m (10, 13, 9 ft) h. Schist. 3 adj artificial grottoes dedicated to saints. Scouëzec, 633.

LOIRE-ATLANTIQUE

La Pauvredrie, St-Père en Retz. (3). 3 great st lie in a NNE–SSW line, biggest, 5.8 m (19 ft) l, at NNE. Burl, 1985, 102, no. 123b.

MORBIHAN

Brouel, Île aux Moines. 'Men Guen', 'white stones'. (1). 5.1 m (16 ft 9) l row of 3 granite st. S–N. 1.6, 1.3, 2.1 m (5 ft 1, 4 ft 1, 6 ft 9) h. Exc. 1877: charcoal, sherds, animal bones and flints. Minot, 22–3; Burl, 1985, 115, no. 139f.

Lac, Le, Carnac. (3). 3 st st. Exc. 1890. Sherds, flints, arrowhead. Kergal, 1980a, 68.

Trinité, La. (3). 3 pros st, N–S. 4 m (13 ft) l. Kergal, 1980a, 68.

Trois Roches, Concoret. (1). 3 big st st, white Q. Briard, 1989, 107.

NORTHERN IRELAND

ANTRIM

Ballycleagh. (3). D 251 333. 2 massive st stand 18 ft (5.5 m) apart, 6 ft (1.8 m) h. 3rd is pros in fence by road. Chart, 1940, 17.

Tournagrough. (3). J 252 743. 2 pros st 10 ft (3 m) apart, 7 and 6 ft (2.1, 1.8 m) l. Orig a 3rd st, now buried. Chart, 1940, 57; Davies, 13, no. 77.

West Division. (3). J 338 887. 'The Three Brothers'. 3 large pros st in line 15 ft (4.6 m) l. Chart, 1940, 47.

ARMAGH

Aughadave. (1). J 00. 19. 3 st in line, the tallest 7 ft 6 (2.3 m) h. Chart, 1940, 76.

Eshway. (3). J 02. 28. 2 st st, 9 ft (2.7 m) apart, with a fallen st between them. Davies, 9. no. 84.

DOWN

Ballyrushey. (3). J 626 523. 1 st st + 2 pros. Silurian grit. 4 ft 6 (1.4 m) h. 6 ft 8, 4 ft (2, 1.2 m) l. 9 ft (2.7 m) l. Jope, 290.

The Three Sisters, Greenan. 'Place of the sun'. (3). J 102 411. 2 st st and 1 pros. Av ht, 5 ft 6 (1.7 m). 8 and 19 ft (2.4, 5.8 m) apart. Chart, 1940, 112; Jope, 293.

FERMANAGH

Cantytrindle. (4). H 22. 55. 3St with 2 st missing. St is 8 ft 3 (2.5 m) h. The missing st buried in 20th century. Davies, 12, no. 69; Chart, 1940, 154.

*Drumacken. (3). H 362 515. 2 large st st, 4 ft 3 (1.3 m) apart, 7 and 5 ft 6 (2.1, 1.7 m) h. 2 ft 9 (0.8 m) away is a 3rd st, 2 ft 9 (0.8 m) h. Chart, 1940, 157.

*Formil. (3). H 159 676. Just N of a StC with two converging S are 2 st st with 3rd to the E. Chart, 1940, 145.

Montiaghroe, NW. (1). H 190 692. StC + 3 st st, 5 ft 9, 4 ft 9 and 3 ft 9 (1.8, 1.5, 1.1 m) h. Chart, 1940, 144.

Montiaghroe, SE. (1). H 197 690. 3 st stand in a slight curve 6 ft 9 and 2 ft 3 (2.1, 0.8 m) apart. 8 ft 3, 5 ft 9 and 4 ft (2.5, 1.8, 1.2 m) h. Chart, 1940, 144.

LONDONDERRY

Clagan. (2). C 583 054. 3 tall schist st toppled by treasure-hunters in 1770. 1 re-erected, 2nd leans, 3rd, the largest, 12 ft (3.7 m) l, pros. The st is 10 ft (3 m) h. Chart, 1940, 202.

Coolnasillagh. (3). C 785 003. E of a conc StC is 3St of which only 1 st stands. It is 1 ft 6 (46 cm) h. Chart, 1940, 208.

TYRONE

Beaghmore. H 685 8484. 7 × StCs + 6 × S + 2 × 4St + 3St.

Beaghmore E. (1). H 684 843. S + 3St. NE–SW, S, NE–SW, long, of low stones. To E 3St, short, SW–NE, 20 ft (6 m) l. Tall pillars up to 5 ft (1.5 m) h. To Cn, exc. 1945–9, 2 crems. May, 1953, 184. McConkey, 60. Burl, 1987b, 11–12. Thom, Thom & Burl, 1990, I, 90–3. Astr: Decl. +22°.3. Thom, A.S., 1980, 17.

Beleevna Beg. (1). H 693 828. 3 st st 7 ft (2.1 m) apart, 4 to 5 ft (1.2–1.5 m) h. NW–SE. Graded hts: 4 ft, 2 ft 6, 1 ft 6 (1.2, 0.8, 0.5 m). Chart, 1940, 233; McConkey, 63.

Creevy Upper. (3). H 25. 88. 1 small st st and 2 others pros. Chart, 1940, 219.

Cregganconroe. (3). H 650 752. 3St tang to StC. Chart, 1940, 237, 'Giant's Grave'. Chart ref is misleading, also Davies, 1939, 7, no. 14. O'Nuallain (in litt, 1990).

Culvacullion. (1). H 505 888. Conc StC + S = + 2 contig StCs. 3 ft (1 m) SE a 3St. NW–SE. 28 ft 7 (8.7 m) l. 1 ft 3, 1 ft 2 and very low (0.4, 0.3 m) h. McConkey, 58.

Davagh Lower N. (3). H 707 867. By a ruined StC are 3 big st, 2 pros. Chart, 1940, 226.

Derryallen. (1). H 309 531. 3 st st, 4 ft (1.2 m) h and 9 ft (2.7 m) apart. Only 2½ miles (4 km) SSW of Trillick village whose name means 'tri-liag', 'the three pillar-stones'. Chart, 1940, 250; Joyce, 93; O'Connell, 79.

Glenmacoffer. (1). H 529 863. 3 st st, 6 ft (1.8 m) h. Once assoc with a StC. Chart, 1940, 224; Davies, 1939, Plate 1A.

Moymore, (1). H 710 745. 9 StCs + D + 3St. At NW of complex 4 StCs (nos 4–7) at corners of a square. To south are 3 StCs (1–3). Between 4,5 and 2,3, an irreg tang A. S of 5, tang 3St, E–W, joins tang A at RtLs. McConkey, 64, fig. 9.

Tremoge SW. (3). H 654 733. 2 × StC, 1 with a tang S of massive stones, the other with a 3St 25 ft (7.6 m) away. ENE–WSW. 11 ft (3.4 m) l. Graded: 2 ft 11, 2 ft 9, 9 ins (0.9, 0.6, 0.2 m) h. Chart, 239; McConkey, 65.

*Tremoge N. (3). H 655 738?. A ruined StC with 3 adj pros slabs. Chart, 1940, 239.

REPUBLIC OF IRELAND

CAVAN

*St-Brigid's Stones. (3). H 059 378. 3 erratic sandstone boulders. 1 st has 11 cms, a 2nd has 4, and the 3rd has 1. Evans, 1966, 67.

CORK

Ballindeenisk. (3). W 723 819. 1 st st, 2 pros. E–W. O'Nuallain, 1988, 232, no. 14, fig. 27.

Bealick. 'Laught Mahon'. (1). W 351 727. 2 st st, orig 3. 20 ft 9 (6.3 m) l? ENE–WSW. Tallest centre, 7 ft (2.1 m) h. To SE is single st st. O'Nuallain, 1988, 233, no. 24, fig. 16.

Canrooska. (3). V 936 583. 3 st, 2 erect, 1 pros, by a 5-StC. The biggest is pros. the others are 2 ft 3 and 1 ft 3 (70, 40 cm) h. O'Nuallain, 1984, 39; 1988, 234, no. 30, fig. 21.

Carrigagulla NE. (3). W 371 829. 3 st st, the 2 outer broken? 17 ft (5.2 m) l. NE–SW. Centre tallest. O'Nuallain, 1988, 232, no. 10, fig. 9.

Carrigagulla SW. (3). W 384 828. 2 st st + 1 pros. ? NE–SW. Conlon, 1917, 155, no. 173; O'Nuallain, 1988, 232, no. 11, fig. 16.

Carrigonirtane. (3). W 276 797. 2 st st + 1 pros. 12 ft 10 (3.9 m) l. NE–SW. Conlon, 1918, 136–7, no. 226. Conlon did not see central st in bog. O'Nuallain (in litt, 1990).

Cloghboola Beg. (3). W 305 853. 3 large st lie to the S of a 5-StC. O'Nuallain, 1984, 31.

Cloghboola More. (1). W 277 872. 3 st st. 15 ft 5 (4.7 m) l. NE–SW (tallest). O'Nuallain, 1988, 231, no. 7, fig. 15.

Clongaskan. (3). V 644 446. 1 st st, 2 pros. 34 ft 9 (10.6 m) l. NNE–SSW. ?adj boulder-burial. O'Nuallain, 1988, 236, no. 45, fig. 28.

Cloonshear Beg. (1). W 264 682. 3 st st in line. 16 ft 8 (5.1 m) l. NE–SW (tallest). O'Nuallain, 1988, 234, no. 27, fig. 8.
    Astr: MdS SR. Lynch, A., 1981b, 26.

*Comillane. (3). V 977 229. 2 st st + 1 pros. NNW–SSE. NNW is perforated. Conlon, 1918b, 58; O'Nuallain, 1988, 237, no. 56, fig. 13.

Coolacoosane. (1). W 323 789. 3 st st. 18 ft 9 (5.7 m) l. SSW–NNE. SSW off line. Centre tallest. O'Nuallain, 1988, 233, no. 18, fig. 9.

Coolavoher. (1). W 191 753. 3 st st. 10 ft 7 (3.2 m) l. NE (tallest)–SW. O'Nuallain, 1988, 233, no. 21, fig. 9.

Coomleagh East. (3). W 119 536. 2 st st + 1 pros. 13 ft 1 (4 m) l. NE–SW (tallest). Long view. O'Nuallain, 1988, 235, no. 39, fig. 13.

Cullenagh. (1). W 116 553. 3 st st. NNE–SSW. 16 ft 5 (5 m) l. O'Nuallain, 1988, no. 43, fig. 8. Largest alig in Ross Carbery area. It may mark the pass between N and S. Roberts, 58.

Cullomane West. (3). W 017 459. 2 st st + 1 pros. 19 ft 8 (6 m) l. NE–SW. A single st 72 ft 2 (22 m) NE of row. O'Nuallain (in litt, 1990).

Currakeal. (1). V 937 582. 3 st st. 8 ft 10 (2.7 m) l. ENE–WSW (tallest). O'Nuallain, 1988, 234, no. 31, fig. 7.

Derrynagree. (3). W 140 627. 3 st st. 16 ft 5 (5 m) l? NE–SW (tallest?). 59 ft (18 m) W is a banked enclosure c. 30 ft (9 m) d. O'Nuallain, 1988, 234, no. 32, fig. 14.

Derrynasaggart. (3). W 183 780. 3 st st on commanding site. 20 ft 7 (6.3 m) l. WNW–ESE (tallest). O'Nuallain, 1988, 232, no. 15, fig. 11.

Dooneens. (3). W 382 815. 1 st st + 2 pros on natural platform. ? N–S? Immediately E is small Cn with radially-set stones. O'Nuallain, 1988, 233, no. 19, fig. 28.

Dromnea. (4). V 840 382. E–W. 10 ft 6 (3.2 m) l. *O.S. Memoranda*, 1845, 458. O'Nuallain (in litt, 1990).

Eyeries. (3). V 645 505. 2 st st + 1 pros. 16 ft 5 (5 m) l. NNE–SSW. O'Nuallain, 1988, 236, no. 43, fig. 11.

Fanahy. (3). V 651 448. 1 st + 2 pros. NE–SW? Macalister, 1908, 7–9; O'Nuallain, 1988, 236, no. 44, fig. 15.

Farranamanagh. (3). V 825 385. 1 st st + 2 pros on terrace. O'Nuallain, 1988, 252, no. 175, fig. 34.

Foildarrig. (3). V 684 467. 1 st st + 2 pros overlooking Berehaven peninsula. 26 ft 3 (8 m) l? O'Nuallain, 1988, 236, no. 46, fig. 10.

Garryduff. (1). W 904 854. 3 st st, packing-stones exposed. 16 ft 1 (4.9 m) l. NE–SW (tallest). Extensive view to E. O'Nuallain, 1988, 252, no. 174, fig. 34.

Glantane East. (1). W 277 830. 3 st st overlooking Keel River. 18 ft 8 (5.7 m) l. ENE–WSW, 7 ft 6 (2.3 m) by far the tallest. O'Nuallain, 1988, 231, no. 9, fig. 7.
    Astr: Min N MR. Lynch, A., 1981b, 26.

Gneeves. (1). W 469 928. 3 st st set at RtLs to row like Ballochroy. 26 ft 6 (8.1 m) l. WNW–ESE (tallest). O'Nuallain, 1988, 231, no. 4.
    Astr: Equi SR. Lynch, A., 1981b, 26; ibid, 1982, 215.

Gortyleahy. (1). W 319 717. 3 st st. 15 ft 5 (4.7 m) l. ENE–WSW is just taller. O'Nuallain, 1988, 233, no. 23, fig. 11.

Keilnascarta. (3). V 993 453. 3 st st. 20 ft 9 (6.3 m) l. ENE–WSW Central is tallest. O'Nuallain, 1988, 236, no. 48, fig. 14.

Kilcaskan. (1). V 817 523. Low 3St row. 16 ft (4.9 m) l. NNE–SSW. O'Nuallain, 1988, 235, no. 38, fig. 10.
    Astr: Min S MS. Lynch, A., 1981b, 26.

Kippagh. (1). W 225 883. 3 st st, long view across River Blackwater basin. 16 ft 5 (5 m) l. N–S (tallest). O'Nuallain, 1988, 231, no. 6, fig. 7.

Knockagappul. (3). W 346 831. 1 st st + 2 pros on a saddle. O'Nuallain, 1988, 252, no. 173, fig. 35.

Knockatlowig. (3). W 320 443. 2 st st + 1 pros at top of slope. ? ENE–WSW. Extensive N–NE outlook. O'Nuallain, 1988, 237, no. 51, fig. 13.

*Knockawaddra. (5). W 269 460. 4St or 3St? 3 st st 22 ft 11 (7 m) l + 2 pros at SSW. NE (tallest)–SW. Long views to E and N. O'Nuallain, 1988, 237, no. 50, fig. 9.

Knockoura. (3). V 631 447. 3 st st. NNE (tallest)–SSW. A st st 7 ft 6 (2.3 m) to NW. O'Nuallain (in litt, 1990).

Leitry Lower. (3). W 138. 488. 3 st. 11 ft 3 (3.4 m) l. SW–NE. Centre tallest. Lower slopes of Nowen Hill. Long views to SW across river. O'Nuallain, 1988, 236, no. 49, fig. 10; Roberts, 56.
    Astr: MdS SS. Lynch, A., 1981b, 26.

Lissaclarig West. (3). W 039 367. In prominent situation. 2 st st in wall, 1 in wall across lane. ENE–WSW. O'Nuallain, 1988, 237, no. 53, fig. 15.

Maulinward. (1). V 975 438. 3 st st. 15 ft 1 (4.6 m) l. NE–SW. Poss kerb of Cn just to N. O'Nuallain, 1988, 237, no. 52, fig. 27.

Monavaddra. (1). W 195 623. 3 st st in peat. NE–SW (tallest). 10 ft 10 (3.3 m) l. O'Nuallain, 1988, 235, no. 34, fig. 9.

Murrahin North. (3). W 029 365. 2 st st + 1 pros on ridge. ENE–WSW. O'Nuallain, 1988, 237, no. 54, fig. 16.

Newcastle. (5). W 577 804. 3St or P? 3 st st 4 ft 6, 6 ft 6 and

8 ft 6 (1.4, 2, 2.6 m) h but 3rd st 24 ft 7 (7.5 m) NE of others. SW–NE. 33 ft (10 m) long. O'Nuallain, 1988, 244, no. 98, fig. 47.

   Astr: (1) 'On line of Summer solstitial sunrise'. Somerville, 1923, 200. (2) MdW SS, Mds SR. Lynch A., 1981b, 26; ibid, 1982, 206.

Pluckanes North. (4). W 536 845. 3 st st. ENE (tallest)–WSW. Site is 246 ft (75 m) NE of destr StC (O'Nuallain, 1984, 33, no. 58). O.S. Name Book, Sheet 51, 12; and Field Trace, 1904. O'Nuallain (in litt, 1990).

Rossnakilla. (1). W 324 658. A fine row. 3 st st with long views to N and W. 24 ft 3 (7.4 m) l. NE–SW. O'Nuallain, 1988, 234, no. 29, fig. 7.

   Astr: Maj N MR. Lynch, A., 1981b, 26.

Scartbaun. (1). W 003 461. 3 st st with long views to S and W. 12 ft 2 (3.7 m) l. NE–SW. O'Nuallain, 1988, 236, no. 47, fig. 7.

Tooreenglanahee. (4). R 174 207. Once 3 st st graded in height up to NE. Tallest 4 ft (1.3 m) h. Now 1 st st only. O'Nuallain, 1988, 231, no. 3, no fig.

Turnaspidogy. (3). c. W 188 670. 2 st st + 1 pros, on small platform on hillside. ? NE–SW. Long view southwards. O'Nuallain, 1988, 234, no. 26, fig. 13.

DONEGAL

Barnes Lower. (1). C 122 263, 3 st rising in height towards the NE. Heights: 4, 2 ft 9 and 6 ins (1.2, 0.8, 0.15 m) Lacy, 77, no. 358, fig. 32.

Killycolman. (3). C 282 334. 3 st in line, pros. Lacy, 83, n 435.

Labbadish. (1). C 238 096. A line of 3 st. N–S. The central st is 4 ft 3 (1.3 m) h, others are granite boulders. Lacy, 83, no. 441.

Portleon. (3). C 172 233. 2 st st, a 3rd removed, in a NE–SW line. Lacy, 85, no. 468.

Rashenny SE. (3). C 422 476. 1 st st 4 ft (1.2 m) h. To its W and SW are 2 partly buried st. The SW has 2 cms. Lacy, 85, no. 472.

DUBLIN

*Dun Laoghaire. (5). O 2.. 2.. 'Mr Thomas Henshaw R.S.S. tells me, that at Dun Lary, about two miles south from Dublin, doe stand three stones together eleven foot high'. Aubrey, I, 127.

GALWAY

Baunoge. (1). L 701 563. 3 st st. 18 ft (5.5 m) l. NNW (tallest)–SSE. 2ft, 2 ft 11, 5 ft (0.9, 0.9, 1.5 m) h. Gosling, 1991, 26.

Derryinver. 'Finn McCool's Fingers'. (1). L 688 608. 6 st st or 2 conjoined 3St? N–S. 53 ft (16 m) l. 3 N st, granite, graded N–S, 5 ft 11, 4 ft, 2 ft 3, then 3 schist just to S, also graded N–S, 5 ft 3, 2 ft 3, 1 ft 8 (1.8, 1.2, 0.7, 1.6, 0.7, 0.5 m) h. Adj 5-StC? Evans, 118; JGAHS 25, 1953–4, 98; O'Nuallain, 1988, 195; Gosling, 1991, 28.

Sheeauns. (3). L 625 581. 2 st st + 1 pros. NNW (pros)–SSE. 14 ft 9 (4.5 m) l. 3 ft 10 l, 1 ft 7 and 3 ft 3 h (1.2, 0.5, 1 m). A st st in line with row is 23 ft (7 m) to N. Robinson, 1990, 41; Gosling, 1991, 31.

KERRY

Ardamore. (1). Q 521 000. 3 st st. NE (tallest)–SW. 9 ft 10, 7 ft 2 and 7 ft (3, 2.2, 2.1 m) h. 23 ft 11 (7.3 m) l. 197 ft (60 m) to NE is st st 9 ft 6 (2.9 m) h. NW face has several

cms, crs, grooves. Adj boulder-burial destr. O'Nuallain, 1988, 238, no. 60, fig. 17; Cuppage, 38.

   Astr: MdW SS. Lynch, A., 1981b, 26.

Ballygarret. (3). Q 685 101. 2 st + 1 pros. ENE–WSW (biggest). ENE, split in three, vertical, 7 ft 2 (2.2 m) h. Centre 9 ft 2 (2.8 m) h. WSW pros, 10 ft 7 (3.2 m) l. 13 ft 10 (4.2 m) l. ENE–WSW. O'Nuallain, 1988, 238, no. 59, fig. 18; Cuppage, 38.

Clogher. (4). Q 314 033. St st + 2 pros. Cuppage, 40.

Curraduff. (4). Q 703 088. 1 st st + 2 pros. N–S. 36 ft 5 (11.1 m) l. N and Centre, 8 ft 10 and 11 ft 2 (2.7, 3.4 m) l. S st st 8 ft 2 (2.5 m) h. Destr. by 1945. Cuppage, 40.

Curraghmore. (3). V 801 819. 3 st st in peat, line not straight. 8 ft 11 (2.7 m) l. E (tallest)–W. O'Nuallain, 1988, 238, no. 62, fig. 19.

Derreenauliff. (3). V 632 624. 1 st st + 2 pros. A Cn 19 ft 8 (6 m) d is 16 ft 5 (5 m) to S. O'Nuallain (in litt, 1990).

Derrineden. (3). V 567 713. 2 st st + 1 pros. E–W. O'Nuallain (in litt, 1990).

Doory. (1). V 546 710. 3 st st. 26 ft 3 (8 m) l. Up to 12 ft 9 (3.9 m) apart. NE (tallest)–SW. 4th st, 6 ft 10 (2.1 m) h, alig 43 ft (13 m) to SW. O'Nuallain, 1988, 239, no. 64, fig. 31.

   Astr: Maj MdW MS. Lynch, A., 1981b, 26; ibid, 1982, 207.

Dromatouk. (1). V 952 711. 3 st st on hillock. ? NE–SW? Exc. 1977. 2 C-14: peat = 70±30 bc (GrN-9174); charcoal = 1380±50 bc (GrN-9346), c. 1700 BC. Lynch, A., 1981, 97–9; O'Nuallain, 1988, 239, no. 44, fig. 17.

   Astr: MdW SS. Lynch, A., 1981b, 26.

Dromteewakeen. (1). V 761 808. 3 st. SW tallest? Poss boulder-burial 80 ft (24 m) to N. Exc. 1977. Peat near row gave C-14 of AD 965±45 (GrN-9283) but 'a date of c. 1300–1000 bc [1575–1250 BC] is being suggested for the stone alignments ... there is nothing to suggest that Dromteewakeen was any later'. Lynch, 1981, 104–5; O'Nuallain, 1988, 238–9, no. 3, fig. 14.

Fermoyle. (3). V 453 724. Once 3 st st, today only 2. N–S. O'Nuallain, 1988, 252, no. 176, fig. 35.

Gortnagulla. (3). V 568 836. 2 st st + 1 pros. NE–SW. Ruinous adj circular enclosure, 10 ft (3 m) d, 26 ft (8 m) to W. O'Nuallain, 1988, 238, no. 61, fig. 17.

KILKENNY

The Three Friars, Smithtown. (1). S 606 277. 3 st st. 17 ft 5 (5.3 m) l. NNE–SSW (tallest). JKAS I, 26; Macalister, 1928, 106; O'Nuallain, 1988, 240, no. 71.

LIMERICK

Graig. (1). R 457 308. 3 st st, 23 ft (7 m) l. NNE (tallest)–SSE. 5 ft, 3 ft, 4 ft (1.5, 0.9, 1.3 m) h. Limerick Arch Survey, site no. 038167; Arch Ire 5.1, 1991, 9, 11.

Lackanagoneeny. (1). R 838 533. 3 st st. 9 ft (2.7 m) l. NNE (tallest)–SSE. 5 ft, 4 ft 4, 4 ft 10 (1.5, 1.3, 1.4 m) h. Cn, 30 ft d by 4 ft h (9 × 1.2 m) 108 ft (33 m) to SE. JCHAS 60, 1955, 68–9.

MAYO

Corlee. (5). G 329 086. 3 st st. 26 ft 11 (8.2 m) l. NNE–SSW. Poss a P with outlier or remains of 4St. Aldridge, 1963, 88 'N'. O'Nuallain (in litt, 1990).

Cuillonaghtan. (3). G 307 032. 1 st st + 1 pros + stump.

11 ft (3.4 m) l. N–S. O'Nuallain (*in litt*, 1990).

Dooleeg More. (3). G 031 188. 16 ft 11 (5.2 m) l. NNE–SSW (tallest). O'Nuallain (*in litt*, 1990).

TIPPERARY

Barbaha. (3). R 768 759. 3 st st. 25 ft 3 (7.7 m) l. NE–SW. O'Nuallain, 1988, 241, no. 73.

WATERFORD

There are four 3St rows in the county. Two N–S, others NE–SW. Details in the forthcoming County Survey. Inf: M. Moore.

WEXFORD

Whitechurch. (1). S 792 190. 3 st st. 21 ft (6.4 m) l. NE–SW (tallest). O'Nuallain, 1988, 241, no. 75.

SCOTLAND

ARGYLL

Ballochroy. (1). NR 730 524. [A4/4]. 3 st st. NE–SW (tallest). NE st 6 ft 6 h broken?, then 10 ft, 11 ft 6 (2, 3, 3.5 m) h. 16 ft 5 (5 m) l. Orig the site of a large Cn. Only the Ct remains. Once 2 smaller Cns and a st st in line to SW of large Cn. Stukeley, 1776, plate 95; *PSAS 44*, 1929–30, 302–3; Campbek, J.L. & Thomson, D. (1963). *Edward Lhuyd in the Scottish Highlands, 1699–1700* O.U.P., Fig. 5. Hawkins, 1973, 247–50; Wood, J.E., 1978, 84, 85, 89, 90, 107, 111, 197, fig. 5.3; Burl, 1983, 7–11; Ruggles, 1984, 185, 305, KT10.
     Astr: (1) Az = 226°. hor = −0°. Decl = −23°.6. MdW SS. Thom A., 1966, fig. 9; Thom, 1967, 97, 151–5, fig. 12.2; Thom, Thom & Burl, 1990, I, 132–3. (2) To SW, decl limits = −25°.5 to −24°.5 MdW SS. Ruggles, 1984, 279; (3) To Maj N MR. 'The line in reverse [to the NE] points along an elevated horizon to the extreme northerly position of the moon', Hawkins, 1977, 250.

Clenamacrie. (3). NM 924 285. 4-sided st st 4 ft 11 (1.5 m) h. Close at W 2 large boulders. *RCAHM-S, Argyll II*, 1975, 62, no. 114.

Clochkeil. (3). NR 657 244. 18 ft 8 (5.7 m) l line of 2 st st with a 3rd pros by them. The tallest st, WSW, is 6 ft 3 (1.9 m) h. *RCAHM-S, Argyll I*, 1971, 62, no, 137; Ruggles, 1984, 189 (KT27); *PSAS 64*, 1929–30, 308.
     Astr: Near MdW SS, MdS SR? Ruggles, 1984, 188–189, 194, 271.

Duachy, Loch Seil. (3). NM 801 206. [A1/4]. 4 st, 3 in NNW–SSE line. 4th a stump, 125 ft (38 m) to E. Line of 3 st st 16 ft (5 m) l. *RCAHM-S, Argyll II*, 1975, no. 116; Ruggles, 1984, 143 (LN22).
     Astr: (1) MdW SR. Thom, 1966, fig. 10; Thom, 1967, 97; Thom, Thom & Burl, 1990, I, 98; (2) Near Min S MR, Maj N MS? Ruggles, 1984, 143, 144, 272–5, 279; Ruggles, 1988b, 239.

Dunamuck North. (3). NR 847 929. [A2/21]. 'Dunamuck I'. 2 st st 8 ft 3 (2.5 m) h with a pros st 11 ft 3 (3.4 m) l between them. Row c. 16 ft (5 m) l. SSE–NNW. *PSAS 38*, 1903–4, 130–1; *ibid 95*, 1961–2, 27, no. 178; Ruggles, 1984, 161. (AR28).
     Astr: (1) Near Maj S MR, The bearing of NNW–SSE follows the line of local topography. Ruggles, 1984, 145, 158, 243, 268–70, 272, 275, 279; 1988b, 239.

Inveryne. (1). NR 915 749. 3 st st. NE–SW (tallest). Playing-card shaped. 2 ft 7, 3 ft 3 and 3 ft 7 (0.8, 1, 1.1 m) h. 13 ft (4 m) l. *D & E*, 1963, 10; *RCAHM-S, Argyll VI*,

1988, 134–5, no. 218.

Mealdarroch. (1). NR 877 680. 3 st st in straight line E–W. Flat faces at RtLs to line. 51 ft (15.5 m) l. *PSAS 53*, 1918–19, 109, no. 4.

Salachary. 'Bealach Mor', 'great birches'. (3). NM 847 040. [A2/26]. 2 st st 8 ft 3 (2.5 m) h and a pros st. c. 13 ft (4 m) l. N–S. *PSAS 95*, 1961–2, 24, no. 162; Ruggles, 1984, 148, (AR6). Thom, Thom & Burl, 1990, I, 126.
     Astr: Az = 356°.4 to 357°.8. Did not look to south where line could be towards Maj S MR. Ruggles, 1984, 144, 148, 152, 243, 281; ibid, 1988b, 239.

Upper Fernoch. (3). NR 727 860. 3 pros st, 9 ft, 9 ft, 8 ft 6 (2.7, 2.7, 2.6 m) l. 2 st st nearby. *PSAS 95*, 1961–2, 29, no. 195.

AYR

Ballantrae. (1). NX 087 818. [G1/4]. 3 st st NNE–SSW. Thom, 1967, 137.
     Astr: Deneb rising. Thom, 1967, 98, 105; Thom, Thom & Burl, 1990, I, 199.

BUTE

Stravanan Bay. 'Largizean Farm'. (1). NS 085 553. [A9/7]. 3 large st st. NW–SE (tallest). 20 ft (6 m) l. Same field, 3 rivetted bronze daggers. *PSAS 4*, 1860–2, 396; Thom, Thom & Burl, 1990, I, 163.

DUMFRIESSHIRE

Dyke. NT 084 036. 'Three Stannin' Stanes', 'Moffat'. (1). [G6/4]. 3 squat massive blocks, in a NNE–SSW line 28 ft (8.5 m) l, 3, 4 and 5 ft (0.9, 1.2, 1.5 m) h. *RCAHM-S, Dumfries*, 1920, 145, no. 426. Thom, Thom & Burl, 1990, I, 218, plan.
     Astr: (From Thom's plan). Maj S MR.

ISLAY

Achnacarran. (3). NR 389 460. 2 st st + pros central. N–S. N st, 8 ft 10 (2.7 m) h. Centre, pros across row, 10 ft (3 m) l. S st 9 ft 6 (2.9 m) h. 26 ft 3 (8 m) l. *RCAHM-S, Argyll V*, 1984, 63, no. 74. Ruggles, 180, 'Laphroaig'. (IS41).
     Astr: Az = 168°.4 to 169°.8. To SE, decl limits = −34°.5 to −34°.3. Unusually inaccurate. No target known. Ruggles, 1984, 167, 169, 279.

*Ballinaby. (5). NR 220 671. [A7/5]. Only 2 st st of 3 orig (Pennant, I, 257). Larger is SSW on crest, a huge st 16 ft 1 (4.9 m) h. 240 yds (220 m) to SSE a broken st st, 6 ft 6 (2 m) h. Missing st probably once in between 'placed nearly equidistant' according to Pennant. Wood, J.E., 1978, 105–6, fig. 6.4; *RCAHM-S, Argyll V*, 1984, 63, no. 79; Ritchie & Harman, 141.
     Astr: Maj N MS. Thom & Thom, 1978, 169–70; Thom, Thom & Burl, 1990, I, 160.

JURA

*Knockrome. 'Ardfernal'. (5). NR 548 714 to NR 560 717. [A6/4]. Poss 3St. 2 widely spaced st st. NNE–SSW. NNE leans, 4 ft 8 (1.4 m) h. 220 yds (200 m) WSW, a st st 5 ft 3 (1.6 m) h. 490 yds (450 m) WSW, a triangular boulder, 2 ft 11 (0.9 m) h. Prehistoric? Martin, 1716, 231; Ruggles, 1984, 163. JU3, JU4; *RCAHM-S, Argyll V*, 1984, 70–1, no. 116.
     Legend that stones were two Danish brothers who killed each other. Grinsell, 1976, 229.

Astr: (1) To Crackaig Hill. Maj S MS. Thom, 1966, fig. 10; Thom, 1967, 97; Thom, Thom & Burl, 1990, I, 154–5.

Sannaig. (3). NR 518 648. [A6/3]. 1 st st + 2 pros. NNE, pros, 8 ft 8 (2.6 m) l. Central st 7 ft 4 (2.2 m) h. SSW stump, 1 ft (0.3 m) h, a recumbent fragment immed to its S, 6 ft 4 (1.9 m) l. Flat slab adj to E of stump, poss a displaced Ct-cover. Row orig c. 16 ft (5 m) l. *RCAHM-S, Argyll V*, 1984, 70–1, no. 116; Ruggles, 1984, 165 (JU7). Thom, Thom & Burl, 1990, I, 158.

Astr: To SW decl. limits = −33°.1 to −32°.2. Maj S MS? This is an isolated row and an exception to the 'southern rule' of declinations between −19°.5 to −30°. Ruggles, 1984, 165, 166, 172–3, 272–4, 279.

LEWIS AND HARRIS

Airigh nam Bidearan. 'Shieling of the Pinnacles'. (5). NB 234 299. [H1/5. Callanish V]. 3 st st closely set, 2 ft 6 to 3 ft 6 (0.8–1.1 m) h. 30 ft (9 m) l. NNW–SSE. 4th st st 100 ft (31 m) to NNE. 5th low st 110 ft (34 m) SE of SSE st. Ruggles, 1984, 81, LH24; Ponting, G. & M., 1977, 28. Shieling close by at NB 232392. *D & E*, 1973, 48.

Astr: (1) Maj N MS. Thom, 1967, 98; Thom, Thom & Burl, 1990, I, 230–1; (2) Maj S MR, Maj N MS? Ruggles, 1984, 279.

Clach an Tursa. 'Stone of sadness'. (3). NB 204 429. [H1/16]. A st st 8 ft 3 (2.5 m) h and 2 pros st. NW–SE. c. 16 ft (5 m) l. Martin, 1716, 8–9; *RCAHM-S, Outer Hebrides*, 1928, 24, no. 87; Ponting, G. & M., 1977, 31; Ruggles, 1984, 77, (LH6) 'Carloway'; Thom, Thom & Burl, 1990, I, 236–7.

Astr: (1) Az. c. 153°. 'It could be lunar in either direction', Thom, Thom & Burl, 1990, I, 237; (2) 'The exact azimuth is uncertain within wide bounds', Ruggles, 1984, 77 (LH6).

Clach Mhic Leoid, see: Nisabost.

Nisabost. (1). NG 041 973. [H2/2. 'Clach Mhic Leoid'. 'MacLeod's stone']. St st 10 ft 6 (3.2 m) h. 8 ft 6 (2.6 m) to its W are 2 small st st at RtLs to its broad face. E–W. *RCAHM-S, Outer Hebrides*, 1928, 43, no. 135; Feachem, 78; Ruggles, 1984, 84, LH36, 'Horgabost'. For comparative settings see: Cerrig Duon and Nant Tarw, Powys, Wales.

Astr: Equi SS. Thom, 1967, 99, 129, 130, fig. 11.5d, 138; Thom, Thom & Burl, 1990, I, 237.

MULL

Ardnacross. (3). NM 542 491. [M1/9]. 2 × 3St. 1 st st + 5 pros in 2 Pl 3St rows, both vandalised. NNE–SSW. St st 7 ft 10 (2.4 m) h. Pros stones 6 to 10 ft (2–3 m) l. Each row about 33 ft (10 m) l. 3 large kerb-cairns between them, 18 ft and 13 ft (5.5, 4 m) d, with big kerbstones. Rows are 120 ft (37 m) apart. *D & E*, 1958, 7–8; *RCAHM-S, Argyll, III*, 1980, fig. 18. Exc. 1989–91. Pre-row cultivation, Q, pit with bronze bracelet. Thom, 1967, 99; Thom, Thom & Burl, 1990, II, 273; *D & E*, 1990, 32; *ibid*, 1991, 52. Ruggles, 1984, 127, 243 (ML12).

Astr: Near MdW SS. Ruggles, 1984, 279; Ruggles, 1988b, 125, 135, 279.

Balliscate. 'Sgriob-Ruadh' (the red furrow). (3). NM 499 541. [M1/8. Tobermory]. 2 basalt st st, 6 and 8 ft 3 (1.8, 2.5 m) h with a pros central st 9 ft (2.8 m) l. N–S. Row

16 ft 6 (5 m) long. *RCAHM-S, Argyll III*, 1980, 65, no. 90. Ruggles, 1984, 243, (ML4).

Astr: (1) Within 3° of meridian. Thom, Thom & Burl, 1990, II, 272. (2) 279. Near Maj S MS. 'Preferentially oriented upon the southern limit of the … "major standstill" moon'. Ruggles, 123, 124, 268, 272, 274–5, 279.

Dervaig D. (3). NM 442 519. 3 st st in wall, 1 broken. Apparently a row in line with Dervaig 4St row. *D & E*, 1957, 9.

*Glengorm. (2). NM 434 571. [M1/7]. 3 st st set in a triangle. In 1880s only 1 st st but 2 were re-erected by 1942. NW st 6 ft 10 (2.1 m) h. 13 ft (4 m) to 2nd st at SE, same height. 13 ft (4 m) to its ESE 3rd st, 7 ft 2 (2.2 m) h. Exc. 1987–8. Orig a 3St row. NNW–SSE. 30 ft 9 (9.4 m) l. 13 ft 9 (4.2 m) to S of SSE st, a small posthole. 'Observations would require the use of temporary markers'. Ruggles & Martlew, 1989, S137–S149. Once a poss adj Cn. *RCAHM-S, Argyll-III*, 1980, 58, no. 105; Ruggles, 1984, 123 (ML1); Thom, Thom & Burl, 1990, I, 270–1.

Astr: (1) Maj S MR? *T. Glasgow A.S. 9*, 1937, 128–34. (2) Close to Maj S MR. Ruggles & Martlew, 1989.

Mingary. (5). NM 413 552. *RCAHM-S, Argyll, III*, 1980, 70, no. 111. See: Quinish in 4St gazetteer.

Scallastle. (3). NM 699 382. A st st 4 ft (1.2 m) h and 2 pros st in a row 16 ft 6 (5 m) l. Ruggles, 1984, 128. (ML21).

NORTH UIST

Blashaval. 'Na Fir Bhreige', 'the false [illusory] men'. (3). NF 887 717. [H3/8]. 2 st st + 1 pros. E–W. E st, 85 ft (26 m) up slope, 2 ft 3 (0.7 m) h. Centre st, 1 ft (0.3 m) off line, pros. W st, 109 ft (33 m) down hill, 1 ft 10 (0.6 m) h. All in peat. Beveridge, E., *North Uist: Archaeology and Topography*, 1911, 261; *RCAHM-S, Outer Hebrides*, 1928, 82, no. 246; Ruggles, 1984, 99. (UI 19).

Legend that they are men turned into stone for deserting their wives. Grinsell, 1976, 194.

Astr: (1) equi SS, Thom, Thom & Burl, 1990, I, 243. (2) An anomalous declination in an isolated line. Ruggles, 1984, 103–4, 108, 279. (2).

ORKNEYS

*Braeside, Eday. (5). HY 564 371. 3 pros st just E of stalled Cn. 'Row' 300 ft (90 m) l. The Stone of Settar, 15 ft 6 (4.7 m) h is half a mile (800 m) to south, a focal point in the island landscape. Weathered and grooved. *RCAHM-S, Orkney & Shetland, II*, 1946b, 53, no. 211.

*St-Tredwell's Chapel, Papa Westray. (4). HY 497 509. 'A high stone standing behind which there is another stone lying hollowed in the form of a manger, and nigh to this there is another high stone standing with a round hole through it …'. *RCAHM-S, Orkney & Shetland, II*, 1946b, 186, no. 543.

PERTHSHIRE

Cowden. NN 776 205. (3). St st 6 ft 4 (1.9 m) h. 2 adj squat st, WNW–ENE, 8 ft (2.4 m) l. ENE st has 22 cms like P of East Cult (NO 023421). *PSAS 22*, 1887–8, 24; Stewart, 1966, 142–3, no. 6.

Craggish. (4). NN 763 207. Till 1891 line of 3 st + P in a field 220 yds (200 m) NE of Craggish Farm. *PSAS 45*, 1910–11, 56, no. 8.

Kilspindie. 'Commonbank'. (3). NO 175 248. 3 pros st, largest 6 ft 4 (1.9 m) l, E–W. E st has cm with groove. E of the row is a small circ area, edged with stones. *D & E*, 1964, 44; *ibid*, 1973, 44.

St-Madoes Stones. (1). NO 197 210. NNW–SSE. SSE st 2 ft 6 h, centre 5 ft 3 , NNW, 5 ft 4 (0.8, 1.6, 1.6 m) h. The last has cms on its E and W sides. *PSAS 16*, 1881, 95–8.

SHETLAND

Hamna Voe. 'The Giant's Stones'. (3). HU 243 806. [Z3/2]. 2 st st, 5 ft 10, 7 ft 10 (1.8, 2.4 m) h. E–W. The 3rd st has gone since 1774. Line is 240 ft (73 m) l. Fojut, 58; Thom, Thom & Burl, 1981, 367.

Astr: Row runs 20°.5 and 'is perhaps lunar'. Did not measure horizon. Thom & Thom, 1978, 164–5; Thom, Thom & Burl, 1980, 367; Thom, Thom & Burl, 1990, II, 348.

SKYE

*Clach Ard. (3). NG 19. 52. [H7/4]. Pros st 5 ft 2 (1.6 m) l. 7 ft (2.1 m) to NE are 2 boulders 13 ft 6 (4.1 m) apart, 3 ft 4 and 3 ft 2 (1˙, 1 m) l. *RCAHM-S, Outer Hebrides*, 1928, 204–5, nos. 636–7.

Astr: Capella setting, 1850 BC [c. 1525 bc], Antares rising, 1870 BC [c. 1540 bc]. Poor alig. Thom, A., 1966, 13.

Sligeanach. (3). NG 73. 27. St st 7 ft (2.1 m) h. 100 yds (90 m) NNW are 2 pros stones, lying on one another, 6 ft 6 and 6 ft (2, 1.8 m) l. 18 ft (5.5 m) ENE is 3rd pros st, 7 ft 6 (2.3 m) l. *RCAHM-S, Outer Hebrides*, 1928, 119, no. 406.

Sornaichean Coir Fhinn, Eyre. (3). NG 414 563. [H7/3]. 2 st st. NNW–SSE (taller). 5 ft 6 and 5 ft 8 (1.7, 1.7 m) h. 13 ft 6 (4.1 m) apart. Reputedly once a 3rd st. *PSAS 46*, 1911–12, 208–10; *RCAHM-S, Outer Hebrides*, 1928, 205, no. 638. Rumoured to be used for boiling Finn MacCoul's cauldron. Grinsell, 1976, 198.

Astr: Maj N MS. Thom, Thom & Burl, 1990, I, 265.

SOUTH UIST

Ru Ardvule. (Kildonan). (3). NF 727 286. [H5/3]. 1 st st and 2 pros st. Ruggles, 1984, 106. (UI 50).

Astr: (1) MdS SR. Thom, 1967, 133; Thom, Thom & Burl, 1990, I, 260; (2) Decl = +22°.3. Ruggles, 1984, 105, 272–3.

WIGTOWNSHIRE

Drumtroddan. (3). NX 364 443. [G3/12]. 2 st st, each 10 ft 2 (3.1 m) h. + central pros. Pros is 9 ft (2.7 m) l. NE–SW. 43 ft (13 m) l. Adj cr outcrops to NW at NX 362 447, NX 377 444, NX 373 440. *RCAHM-S, Galloway I*, 1912, no. 231; Morris, 1979, 46, 48, 93–6; Stell, 166; *TDGNHAS 52*, 1977, 41.

Astr: MdS SR. Thom, 1967, 98; Thom, Thom & Burl, 1990, I, 205.

Torhousekie East. (1). NX 384 565. [G3/7. Torhouse]. 3St. NE–SW (tallest). 2 ft 1, 3 ft 4 and 4 ft 2 (0.6, 1, 1.3 m) h. 16 ft 4 (5 m) l. 415 ft (127 m) E of StC. In wall on S of road 60 yds (55 m) E of StC is a boulder with 'an oval smoothed hollow' 13 ins across by 8 ins deep (34 × 20 cm). *RCAHM-S Galloway, I*, 1912, 185, no. 534; *TDGNHAS 56*, 1981, 19–20; Stell, 165; *D & E*, 1970, 51.

Astr: 'Probably solstitial'. Az = 224°. hor = −0°.1. decl = −24°.3. MdW SS. Thom, Thom & Burl, 1980, 274–5, ibid, 1990, I, 202–3.

*Torhousekie West. (4). NX 381 565. In 1896 3 pros st, all large, in line c. 15 ft (4.6 m) l. NW–SE? Removed by 1932. 3St or remains of 'a small circle some 30 feet [9 m] in diameter'. *PSAS 31*, 1896–7, 91; *RCAHM-S*, 1912, no. 532; *TDGNHAS 56*, 1981, 21–2.

WALES

DYFED

Banc Rhosgoch Fach, Llanarth (Carmarthen). (3). SN 435 541. 2 st st, 3rd gone. N–S. Excs, 1930s, 1989. Pits with char to W of stones. No finds. *Arch In Wales 28*, 1988, 49; *ibid 29*, 1989, 44–5.

Carreg Bicca. (4). SN 57. 30. 3St. 1 was Q. *RCAHM-W, Carmarthen*, 1917, 139, no. 414.

Cefn Gwernffrwd. (1). SN 737 492. StC, Cn, ring-cairn + 3 st st of local stone. E–W. 6 ft 6 and 1 ft 4 (2, 0.4 m) apart. *Arch Camb 124*, 1975, 111–13.

Astr: 6 aligs tested. 3St had poor aligs to MdW SS and MdS SR. *Arch Camb 125*, 1976, 162–4.

*Meini-Gwyn, (Carmarthen). 'The white stones'. (1). SN 459 261. All white Q. NW–SE (tallest). 8 ft 9, 9 ft 2 (2.7, 2.8 m) h. 360 ft (110 m) l. *Trans Carmarthen A.S. 5*; Houlder, 169.

Plas Gogerddan, (Cardigan). (3). SN 626 835. 2 st st 153 yds (140 m) apart. 3rd st gone. The st on the site is 6 ft 6 (2 m) h. Exc 1986. Carbonised grain from pit to N of st, C-14 1580±70 bc (CAR-990) c. 1945 BC, from earlier settlement site. Adj pits, a crem, empty Ct. Alig of 3 massive postholes, N–S. 14 ft 9 (4.5 m) l. Biggest 1 ft 6 (50 cm) d. Barrows to W. Charcoal = 820±60 bc, (Car-1073), crem, 200±60 bc (CAR-1072). *Arch In Wales 26*, 1986, 29–31; *ibid 27*, 1987, 36; Williams, G., 1988, 29, 85–7.

Yr Allor. 'The altar'. (3). SN 142 266. 2 st st, S flat-top, N triangular, 6 ft 6, 4 ft 11 (2, 1.5 m) h. 3rd st 66 ft (20 m) SSE, pros, 12 ft 9 (3.9 m) l. 210 yds (190 m) W of Meinigwyr StC. W of StC 'stand on end three other large rude stones', Camden, 1695, 628. Exc. 1991. N, E and S of stones were pits and p/hs but 'none of these pits was readily identifiable as the socket for Lhuyd's third stone'. Token crem near. *Arch in Wales 31*, 1991, 3–5; Barker, C.T., *The Chambered Tombs of South-West Wales*, 1992, 55.

GWENT

Harold's Stones, Trellech. (Monmouth). 'The Three Stones'. (1). SO 498 052. NE–SW. Local, pimpled puddingstone. Tallest at SW, 14 ft 4 (4.4 m) h. The middle st, 10 ft (3 m) h, is shaped and has 2 large cms on its SW face. The NE stone is 8 ft (2.4 m) h. 39 ft (12 m) l. All lean, NE 15° to N, centre 16° to SE, SW 18° to N. Village name derives from 'tri-llech', 'the three stones'.

On the plinth of a sun-dial dated AD 1689, orig in school-house garden but now in church, is a carving of the stones. Hts given as 8, 10 and 14 ft (2.4, 3.0, 4.3 m). Above is written, MAJOR SAXIS, 'the great stones', and below them is HIC FUIT VICTOR HARALDAS, 'here Harold was victorious'. Norman motte, Tump Terret, in farm-yard near church said to be burial-place of Harold Godwinsson's warriors killed in a battle against Gruffyd ap Llewellyn. Giraldus Cambrensis may have seen or heard of these stones in March, 1188. *Gerald of Wales. The*

Journey Through Wales . . . Trans. Thorpe, L., Harmondsworth, 1978. 266, notes 613, 615; *Arch Camb I*, 1855, 120–2; *ibid 9 (6th series)*, 1909, 67–71; Bagnall-Oakeley, Rev. W. & M.E., *An Account of some of the Rude Stone Monuments . . . in Monmouthshire*, 1889, 13–15, plan, Plate VI; Crawford, O.G.S. *Long Barrows of the Cotswolds*, 1925. 209–11 (plan); Barber & Williams, 36–40; Ekwall, 479.

Astr: Azimuth = c. 229°, hor = 0.5°, decl = −23°.5. Probably MdW SS Thom, Thom & Burl, II, 1990, 488.

*Trillech, Llantilio Pertholey. (5). c. SO 314 177. Name, also known as Great Triley, suggests a 3St. No sign today. *Arch Camb*, 1855, 122; *ibid*, 1861, 59.

GWYNEDD

Moelfre. (Caernarvon). (4). SH 721 746. 3 st st, red, white and blue, said to be women turned to stone for winnowing on the Sabbath. Graves, 1961, 70; Grinsell, 1976, 261.

POWYS

*Maen Mawr. (Brecks). 'The great stone'. (1). [W/3]. 3St + StC + A. 30 ft (9 m) NNE of Cerrig Duon StC a huge st st, Maen Mawr, rectangular. 6 ft (1.8 m) h by 4 ft 10 by 3 ft (1.5 × 0.9) in section. 11 ft (3.4 m) to N are 2 low st, 2 ft (0.6 m) apart, forming a N–S 3St 19 ft (5.8 m) l. Grimes, 1963, 138–9, no. 27; Thom, Thom & Burl, 1980, 392–3. For comparable anomalous settings, see: Nant Tarw, Powys; Nisabost, Lewis and Harris. Thom, Thom & Burl, 1990, II, 368–9.

Llidiardau mawr, Llanllugen. 'Cae y garreg fawr'. 'Field of great stones'. (4). SJ 02. 02. 3St, 4–5 ft (1.2–1.5 m) h. Destr. around 1870. *RCAHM-W, Montgomery*, 1911, 120, no. 608.

*Nant Tarw. (Brecks). 'The bull's brook'. (1). SN 820 258. [W11/4. Usk Water]. 2 × StC + 3St. ESE StC 68 ft (20.7 m) d. 364 ft (111 m) to WSW 2nd StC, 63 ft (19.2 m) d. 24 ft (7.3 m) to its W, tang to its N arc, a large pros st 10 ft (3 m) l. To WSW 2 low st st 1 ft 5 and 11 ins (0.5, 0.3 m) h. 11 ft (3.4 m) l. Grimes, 1963, 136–7, nos. 26a, b; Thom, Thom & Burl, 1980, 394–5. For comparable settings see: Cerrig Duon, Powys; Nisabost, Lewis & Harris. Thom, Thom & Burl, 1990, II, 370.

Pen y Garreg. 'The stony headland'. (3). SN 915 676. St st 2 ft (0.6 m) h + 2 pros in line, E–W, 12 ft (3.7 m) l. *RCAHM-W, Radnor*, 1913, 102, no. 406.

YNYS MONA

*Llandona. SH 567 799. (5). To W of ChT 2 low st in line 100 and 150 yds (90, 137 m) apart. Was a 3rd st to S. Baynes, 68; *RCAHM-W, Anglesey*, 1937, 45b, no. 6.

*Llanfairynghomwy. (5). SH 337 904. 2 st st, perhaps 3 orig. Lynch, F. 1991, 152, 324.

Pentraeth. 'Three Leaps'. (5). SH 530 782. 3 small st, c. 1 ft (30 cm) 12 and 15 yds (11, 14 m) apart. *RCAHM-W, Anglesey*, 1937, xlix, 141a, no. 18.

PAIRS OF STANDING STONES

CHANNEL ISLES

GUERNSEY

Crocq, Le, St-Saviour. 'La Longue Pierre'. 'The Witch's Finger'. 'La Pierre de l'Essart'. (2). WV 271 795. 10 ft (3 m) h granite st st. St st 75 ft (23 m) to E, red granite, 7 ft (2.1 m) h, re-erected 1955. In field wall. Exc 1857. Sherds and querns found near base. de Guèrin, 50; *Prehistoric Monuments of Guernsey*, 1976, 21–3; Johnston, 101; Bender, 229; Kinnes & Grant, 52.

JERSEY

*Trois Rocques, St Peter. (5). 571 516. 2 low blocks, WNW–ESE, 11 ft (3.4 m) apart. 3 cms on W st? In circular bank. Thin pillar well to E. 'White Menhir' 250 yds (230 m) to S. Excs 1913, 1933, no finds or packing-stones. Modern? Rybot, 343–4; Johnston, 89; Patton, 75; Kinnes & Hibbs, 73.

ENGLAND

CORNWALL

Boscawen-Ros. (1). SW 428 239. 2 st st 8 ft 6 and 7 ft 10 (2.6, 2.4 m) h. Adj st st 3 ft 11 (1.2 m) h. Michell, 68; Barnatt, 1982, 229.

Crousa Common. (3). SW 775 200. 1 st st 6 ft (1.8 m) h, 1 pros. *Meyn Mamvro 8*, 1989, 12.

De Lank quarry, Bodmin. (3). SX 100 753. 8 ft (2.4 m) h st st + adj broken by it. At RtLs. *Meyn Mamvro 9*, 1989, 2.

Faughan, Paul. (1). SW 452 282. 2 st st on E side of circ hillfort. 9 ft (2.7 m) apart and 5 ft 6 and 6 ft (1.7, 1.8 m) h. Re-used as gateposts at hillfort ent? Weatherhill, 49; Michell, 54–5.

Higher Drift. 'The Sisters'. (1). SW 437 283. Fine pair of st st 17 ft (5.2 m) apart, SE (taller)–NW. 8 ft 6 and 7 ft 6 (2.6, 2.3 m) h. Exc 1871. Just E of centre a pit 6 ft by 3 ft 3 (1.8 × 1 m) found. Empty. Borlase, W., 1769, 164, 187; Borlase, W.C., 1872, 23–4; Michell, 34–5; Weatherhill, 1981, 23; ibid, 1985, 102; Barnatt, 1982, 232; Williams, G., 1988, 73.

Pipers, Land's End. (1). SW 433 245. [S1/14]. st st. NE (taller)–SW. 15 ft and 13 ft 6 (4.6, 4.1 m) h. 317 ft (97 m) apart. NE st is tallest in Cornwall. Exc 1871, reputedly no finds. Lukis, 1885, 21. Before 1898 a 'potful of ashes' found at base. Lewis, A.L. *JRAI 35*, 1905, 429. Borlase, W., 1769, 194; Borlase, W.C., 1872, 106–7; Michell, 64; Weatherhill, 1981, 25; Barnatt, 1982, 226–8.

Legend. Two Pipers and a Blind Fiddler, the Trenuggo Stone at SW 425 282, petrified for profaning the Sabbath. Grinsell, 1976, 90; Weatherhill, 1981, 20. Early 19th century exc. at Blind Fiddler found 'bone chips and ashes' at its base. Borlase, W.C., 1872, 102.

Pipers, Bodmin Moor. (1). SX 257 713. [S1/1]. 3 StCs in NNE–SSW line, 'The Hurlers', SX 258 714. 363 ft (111 m) to WSW of central StC, 2 st st. WSW (taller)–ENE. 5 ft 5 and 4 ft 9 (1.7, 1.5 m) h. 7 ft (2.1 m) apart. Camden, 1695, 9; Borlase, W., 1769, 199, 206, pl. 17; *JBAA 35*, 1879, 304 (plan); *PPS 4*, 1938, 319; Thom,

1966, 40–1, figs. 27, 28; Barnatt, 1982, 185–6.

Legends, men turned to stone for playing at ball on the Sabbath. Stones cannot be counted. Grinsell, 1976, 88. Astr: February SS. Thom, 1967, 100.

Trewern. (4). SW 429 313. As late as 1871 2 st st here, WSW (taller)–ENE, 6 ft and 5 ft (1.8, 1.5 m) h, 10 ft (3 m) apart. Exc October 21, 1752. A central rect pit 6 ft 6 ft l, 2 ft 9 w, 4 ft 6 deep (2 × 0.8 × 1.4 m), empty. 'Near the bottom it was full of black greazy Earth, but no bone to be seen', Borlase, W., 1769, 187. Barnatt, 1982, 255–6; Weatherhill, 1981, 60; Williams, G., 1988, 101.

CUMBERLAND

*Giant's Grave. SD 135 810. [L1/11]. See 3St Gazetteer.

DEVON (EXMOOR)

Badgworthy Lees. (1). SS 784 446. 2 st st, SSW–NNE 8 ft 10 (2.7 m) l. Quinnell & Dunn, 11. SS74 SE 23.

Brayford NW. 'Bray Common'. (4). SS 725 397. NE–SW. 27 ft 3 (8.3 m) l. 2 ft 5 and 1 ft 11 (74, 59 cm) h. Chanter & Worth, 1905, 396, Pl X, l. SS 719 388. Quinnell & Dunn, 7. SS73 NW 16.

Long Stone. (5). SS 727 475. P? Re-erected, 1906, but moved and re-erected pre-1974. Quinnell & Dunn, 25. SS74 NW 17.

Rooshitchen. (1). SS 717 400. 2 st st, N–S. Both have Q veins. 27 ft (8.2 m) l. Quinnell & Dunn, 19. SS74 SW 91.

HUNTINGDONSHIRE

Robin Hood and Little John. (5). TL 139 983. [D3/1]. N bank, River Nene. 2 st st, each c. 3 ft (1 m) h, 33 ft (10 m) apart. NE–SW. 'Two large monoliths, believed to be of the Bronze Age'. A. Mee., *King's England. Bedfordshire & Huntingdonshire*, 1973, 289.

Legend, stones were thrown by Robin Hood and Little John from Alwalton church-yard, 1½ miles (2.4 km) away. Grinsell, 1976, 162.

SOMERSET (EXMOOR)

Bill Hill. (1). SS 723 408. 2 low st, SE–NW. 36 ft (11 m) l. 3 mounds just to E. Quinnell & Dunn, 52. SS74 SW 88.

Hoscombe NW. (1). SS 830 441. 2 st st, SW–NE. 16 ft (5 m) l. Quinnell & Dunn, 49. SS84 Sw 127.

Long Chains Coombe SW. (1). SS 743 420. 2 low st, SE–NW but across axis. 19 ft (5.8 m) l. Quinnell & Dunn, 42. SS74 SW 95.

Porlock Allotment NE. (4). SS 840 447. 2 st, both 2 ft (60 cm) h. Destr. pre-1973. Quinnell & Dunn, 61. SS73 NW 4.

Squallacombe NE. (1). SS 739 382. 2 st st, SE–NW, but set across the line. 23 ft (7 m) l. Quinnell & Dunn, 49. SS73 NW 33.

Whit Stones. (5). SS 853 462. 2 big st, both sandstone. NNE flat-topped block, c. 5 ft (1.5 m) h, leans 60° to E. SSW, triangular, same ht, leans 70° to E. 14 ft 3 (4.4 m) l. Outcrops on E slope? Grinsell, 1970, 48–9; Eardley-Wilmot, 40–1; Quinnell & Dunn, 64. SS84 NE 14.

Confused with Fifstanes a mile away. Legend, thrown by Devil at a giant. Grinsell, 1976, 103.

Yenworthy Common. (1). SS 798 483 2 st st, both 3 ft (1 m) h. SSE–NNW. 63 ft (19 m) l. Quinnell & Dunn, 58. SS74 NE 14.

SOMERSET (OUTSIDE EXMOOR)

Compton Bishop. (3). ST 409 548. 2 little st, 1 pros, 'thrown by the Devil'. Grinsell, 1976, 99.

Devil's Quoits. (4). c.ST 576 565. In Shrowl Field. 2 st st thrown by the Devil at the church. Gone before 1882. Grinsell, 1976, 138.

*Lower Tyning. (5). c. ST 591 633. 2 adj pros. st. SW–NE. 4 ft 11, 5 ft 9 (1.5, 1.8 m) l. Wood, J., 1765, 150; Dymond, 1896, 29, 34.

FRANCE (Brittany)

CÔTES-DU-NORD

Caillouan, Plésidy. St st 7.2 m (23 ft 7) h. 9.5 m (31 ft) to S, pros. st. N–S. Scouëzec & Masson, 76–7.

St-Jacut du Méné, Collinée. (3). Pointed-top granite pillar, 5.5 m (18 ft) h. 5 m (16 ft 6) to S pros st 3 m (10 ft) l. Gilbert, 1964, 170, no. 481.

FINISTÈRE

*Délivrande, Île-de-Seins. (3). 2 menhirs. du Chatellier, 158.

Feuillé, La, Huelgoat. (3). St st + orig, 1 pros. du Chatellier, 129.

Kéréléoc. No details. Pontois, 1929, 124.

Kergadiou, Porspoder. 2 st st. SSW 8.8 m (29 ft) h, NNE almost pros, 10.5 m (35 ft) l. Weighs c. 60 tons. 80 m (260 ft) l. Smoothed, granite pillars. Burl, 1985, 60–1, no. 63.

Kerguelvan, Plonéour-Lanvern. (3). 2 st st 5 m, 2.5 m (16 ft 5, 8 ft 2) h. Large flat stones between. Grave-slabs?, du Chatellier, 149.

Lesquivit, Plougastel-Daoulas. (1). 2 st st, 3 m, 3.8 m (9 ft 10, 12 ft 6) h. 3 m (10 ft) apart. In 'Parc-ar-Menhir' field. du Chatellier, 91.

Lézaouréguen, Poullan. (3). St st 3 m (10 ft) h. 50 m (55 yds) to S pros st, 4.5 m (14 ft 9) l. du Chatellier, 139.

Men Marz, Brigognon-Plage. 'Stone of Miracle'. (3). Tall tapering st st, 'christianised' with cross on top. 8 m (26 ft) h. 2.2 m (7 ft) to NE a huge pros st. Scouëzec, 158; Burl, 1985, 70, no. 81a.

Mezdoun, Porspoder. (1). 2 st st, WSW–ENE. Granite. 4.2, 3.7 m (13 ft 9, 12 ft 2) h. Pontois, 123, fig. 118; Scouëzec & Masson, 100.
    Astr: May SR, Lockyer, 1909, 485.

Palue, La. No details. Pontois, 1929, 120.

Traonigou, Porspoder. (1). 2 st st, red granite. WSW–ENE. 4.2, 3 m (13 ft 9, 10 ft) h. Scouëzec & Masson, 100–1.

ILLE-ET-VILAINE

Baillerie, La, Chelun. 'Pierre-Marie'. St st, 1.8 m (6 ft) h, Q. 10 m (33 ft) to E, pros st, 2 m (6 ft 6) l. Bézier, 129–30.

Bellevue, Janzé. Pierre des Fées, (3). 4.4 m (14 ft 5) h. 10 m (33 ft) to N a pros st 4.3 m (14 ft 1) l. 4St nearby. Bézier, 19.

Brignereault, Bazouges-sous-Hédé. (3). St st 2.1 m (6 ft 10) h. 9 m (30 ft) to N, pros st, 2.8 m (9 ft 2) l. Bézier, 13.

Mont Belleux, Luitré. (4). 2 st st. 1, 2.4 m (7 ft 10) l, broken for Laval road in 1828. Local Q.
    Legend, treasure underneath is guarded by a blackbird. Bézier, 76.

Rocher, St-Just. (3). St st 3.3 m (10 ft 10) h. 4 m (13 ft) away a pros st 3 m (10 ft) l. Bézier, 197.

Sel-de-Bretagne, Le, Janzé. (1). 2 st st. NW, taller, grey, pointed-SE, white, flat-topped, 3.3 m and 2.5 m (10 ft 10, 8 ft 2) h. 20 m (66 ft) apart. Gilbert, 1964, 109, no. 436.

MORBIHAN

Clos Pernal, Castellic. (2). 2 st st 2.2 m (7 ft 2) h. Re-erected by le Rouzic in 1927. Kergal, 1980a, 58.

*Crifol, Carnac. (4). St st 2.9 m (9 ft 6) h. Adj, pros. destr. 1900. Exc. Miln, 1879. No finds. Kergal, 1980a, 74; Burl, 1985, 132, no. 170.

Roches-Piquées, Les, La Gacilly. (3). Coarse granite st st 5 m (16 ft 4) h. 3 m (10 ft) to NW a pros st 2.5 m (8 ft 2) l. Burl, 1985, 123, no. 157.

NORTHERN IRELAND

ANTRIM

Tully N. (3). D 082 252. 2 st st, 1 ft 7 (0.5 m) h pointed, other 6 ft (1.8 m) away, pros. Chart, 18.

DOWN

Ballyloughlin. 'Slidderyford Bridge'. (1). J 392 342. 2 tall granite st st, 8 ft 9 and 4 ft 10 (2.7, 1.5 m) h. 4 ft (1.2 m) l. Chart, 126; Jope, 95, no. 289.

Castleward. J 569 499. (3). 1 st + 1 pros. 5 ft 11 (1.8 m) h, 7 ft 5 (2.3 m) l. 1 ft 4 (40 cm) apart. Jope, 95, no. 291.

Killybeg. (1). J 121 312. 3 × P. 2 st st, 3 ft 11 and 4 ft 6 (1.3, 1.5 m) h. Nearby 2 other P. (a) is small square stone, other is pointed stone with cms on west face. (b) see: Saval Mor below. Chart, 149.

Moneyslane. (3). J 254 399. 2 granite st st, 5 ft 2 and once 6 ft 5 (1.6, 2 m) h. 8 ft 9 (2.7 m) l. Chart, 114; Jope, 95, no. 293.

Portavo. (4). J 571 820. 1 st st at W, other gone. 3 ft (1 m) apart. By coast of Belfast Lough. Flint-knapping close by. *UJA* 39, 1976, 37–42; Williams, G., 1988, 87.

Saval Mor. (1). J 122 310. 2 granite st st. E–W. 7 ft 4 and 5 ft 10 (2.2, 1.8 m) h. 7 ft 9 (2.4 m) apart. Not quite alig. Chart, 131; Jope, 195, no. 295.

TYRONE

Creggandevesky. (1). H 636 740. StC + 2 st st 60 ft (18 m) to N of StC. Davies, 1939, 10; Chart, 238; McConkey, 65.

Crew Lower. (1). H 315 848. 5 ft 10 (1.8 m) l. E 5 ft 2 (1.6 m) h, pointed, W 5 ft 8 (1.7 m) h, flat-top. Chart, 220; Evans, 201.

Edentoit. (1). H 709 749. 2 st st, 30 ft (9 m) l. E = 6 ft (1.8 m) h, pointed; W, 4 ft (1.2 m) h, flat-top. 6 ft (1.8 m) to its S, pros st, probably unconnected. Chart, 238.

Grange. (1). H 830 752. 2 st st. 20 ft (6 m) l. c3 ft (1 m) h. E, is pointed, W, long, saddle-backed, slight groove across. Supported by large wedge-stone. Chart, 240.

Murnells. (1). H 662 757. Court-Cn, Cn alongside. To S 2 st st, 2 ft 6 (0.7 m) h, red granite, 12 ft (3.7 m) apart. E, squarish in section, pointed, W, long, flat-topped with groove. Chart, 238.

Sandville and Lisvidin. (1). C 388 048. 2 st in wall on either side of townland boundary fence. 2 ft 4 (0.7 m) l. E, pointed, 7 ft 2 (2.2 m) h. W, 6 ft (1.8 m) h, flat-topped, manmade groove across it. Chart, 214. Evans, 204. Killanin & Duignan, 1962, 427; *UJA 2*, 1939, 169.

Tulnacross. (1). H 705 801. 2 st st. 7 ft (2.1 m) l. E, square-sided, pointed, 5 ft (1.5 m) h. W, higher, flat-topped. Chart, 233.

REPUBLIC OF IRELAND

CORK

Annagannihy. (1). W 392 836. StC. 36 ft (11 m) to W, 2 st st 6 ft 8 (2 m) apart. NW (taller)–SW. 4 ft 6 (1.4 m) and 3 ft 6 (1.1 m) h. Conlon, 1916, 161–2, no. 167; O'Nuallain, 1984a, 47, no. 9; ibid, 1988, 242, no. 83, fig. 41.

Ardgroom Outward SW. (3). V 701 548. 1 st st + 1 pros. C 19 ft 8 (6 m) to W. O'Brien, 1970, 21, no. 132; Power *et al*, 38, no. 168.

Ardgroom Outward NE. (1). V 712 555. 2 st st. NE–SW (taller). 9 ft 10 (3 m) l. O'Brien, 1970, 21, no. 133; Power *et al*, 38, no 169.

Ballinvarrig. (1). W 648 789. 2 st st. NE (taller)–SW. 6 ft 6 (2 m) l. Conlon, 1916, 62, no. 12; O'Nuallain, 1988, 244, no. 101, fig. 39.

Ballycommane. (1). V 976 437. 2 st st. SSW–NNE. Each c. 2 ft 7 (0.8 m) h. 9 ft 6 (2.9 m) l. Adj boulder-burial to W. O'Nuallain, 1978, 93–4, no. 27; ibid, 1988, 248, no. 137, fig. 58.

Ballyhalwick. (1). W 252 521. 2 st st. NNE–SSW W (taller). 16 ft 9 (5.1 m) l. O'Nuallain, 1988, 246, no. 123, fig. 46; Power *et al*, 39, fig. 13.

Ballyhesty. (3). W 672 807. 1 st st, 1 pros E–W? W taller. 6 ft 3 (1.9 m) l. Conlon, 1916, 59–60, no. 5; O'Nuallain, 1988, 244, no. 100, fig. 39.

Ballynagree. (1). W 363 819. 2 st st. NE–SW (taller). 16 ft (4.9 m) l. *ABM*, 3; O'Nuallain, 1988, 243, no. 91, fig. 40.

Ballyvongane. (5). W 380 759. 2 st st. ENE–WSW 7 ft 10 (2.4 m) l. Adj 3rd st, pros. O'Nuallain, 1988, 243, no. 95, fig. 48.

Barryshall NE (a) & SW (b). W 462 425. (a). (1). 2 st st. NE–SW (taller). 15 ft 5 (4.7 m) l. 148 ft (45 m) to NE: (b). 2 st st. ENE (leans)–WNW (taller). 11 ft 2 (3.4 m) l. O'Nuallain, 1988, 248, no. 139, fig. 38.

Baurgaum. (3). W 023 469. 5st-StC. 18 ft (5.5 m) to S 1 st st + 1 pros. E–W? O'Nuallain, 1984a, 42–3, no. 85; ibid, 1988, 247, no. 126, fig. 57.

Bawnatemple. W1 405 710. 2 st st. NE (taller)–SW. 5 ft 3 (1.6 m) l. Conlon, 1917, 162, no. 189; O'Nuallain, 1988, 245, no. 105, fig. 39.

Bawnmore. (1). W 363 782. 2 st st. NNE–SSW (taller). 11 ft 1 (3.4 m) l. Conlon, 1916, 160, no. 165; O'Nuallain, 1988, 243, no. 93, fig. 41.

Behagullane. (1). W 275 567. 2 st st. NE–SW (taller). O'Nuallain, 1988, 246, no. 117, fig. 42.

Caherbaroul. 'Cooper's Rock'. (1). W 363 782. 2 st st. ENE–WSW (taller). 12 ft (3.7 m) l. Panoramic view. Near fine ring-fort. *ABM*, 3; O'Nuallain, 1988, 243, no. 94, fig. 39.

Cahermuckee. (3). W 083 572. 1 st st, 1 pros. ENE–WSW? O'Nuallain, 1988, 245, no. 113, fig. 40; Power *et al*, 40, no. 174.

*Candroma. (3). W 233 740. 1 pros, split. O'Nuallain, 1988, 252, no. 178, fig. 50.

Cappaboy Beg. (1). W 095 604. 330 ft (100 m) SW of 4-Poster are 2 st st. NE–SW, far taller and broader. 12 ft 1 (3.7 m) l. Adj radial-stone enclosure. Barber, 1972, I, 32, C12; O'Nuallain, 1984b, 69, no. 1; ibid, 1988, 245, no. 111, fig. 43.

Carrig. (3). W 422 450. 1 st st. In 1902, 'Two large stones . . . about 8 ft [2.4 m] long'. O'Nuallain, 1988, 247, no. 134, fig. 44.

Carrigadrohid. (4). W 418 726. 1 st st + 1 pros. NE–SW. Submerged in Lee Valley reservoir. Exc 1956. No finds. *JCHAS* 62, 1957, 65–76; O'Nuallain, 1988, 244, no. 103, no fig.

Caum. (4). W 387 716. 2 st st. NE (taller)–SW. 1 ft 7 (50 m) apart. Destr.1977–84. Conlon, 1917, 153, no. 169; O'Nuallain, 1988, 244, no. 104.

Ceancullig. (1). W 136 488. 2 st st. NE–SW (taller). 8 ft 6 (2.6 m) l. O'Nuallain, 1988, 247, no. 129, fig. 42.

Clashmaguire. (1). W 278 789. 2 st st. ENE–WSW (taller). 10 ft (3 m) l. O'Nuallain, 1988, 243, no. 90, fig. 41.

Clodagh SW. (1). W 152 499. 5st-StC. 10 ft 5 (3.2 m) to SW 2 st st. NE–SW (taller). 3 ft 4 (1.1 m) l. O'Nuallain, 1984a, 43–4, no. 88; ibid, 1988, 246, no. 131, fig. 57.

Clodagh NE. (1). W 153 502. 2 st st. O'Nuallain, 1988, 246, no. 121, fig. 42.

Clogagh. (3). W 453 470. 1 st st + 1 pros 16 ft (4.9 m) to W. O'Nuallain, 1988, 247, no. 135, fig. 46.

Coolcoulaghta. (1). W 932 393. Dunbeacon RSC 380 yds (350 m) to W of 2 st st. NE–SW, taller, at RtLs to axis. 5 ft 7 (1.7 m) l. O'Nuallain, 1988, 248, no. 136, fig. 40; Power *et al*, 40, no. 181.

Coolgarriff. (1). W 413 769. 2 st st. N (taller)–S. 10 ft (3 m) l. O'Nuallain, 1988, 243, no. 96, fig. 39.

Cools. (1). W 247 730. 2 st st. NE–SW. 13 ft 6 (4.1 m) l. Conlon, 1918a, 124–5, no. 205; O'Nuallain, 1988, 244, no. 192, fig. 39.

Coomleagh E. (3). W 100 537. 1 st + 1 pros. O'Nuallain, 1988, 246, no. 120, fig. 42.

Crumpane. (1). V 657 495. 2 st st. E (taller)–W. 10 ft (3 m) l. O'Nuallain, 1988, 247, no. 125, fig. 44.

Cullenagh. (3). W 160 526. 1 st st + 1 stump. ENE–WSW. 11 ft 4 (3.5 m) l. Inf. O'Nuallain, 1990; Power *et al*, 40, no. 184.

Curraghawaddra. (3). W 396 795. 1 st st + 1 pros. Boulder-burial 3 ft 3 (1 m) to SW. Conlon, 1917, 153, no. 170; O'Nuallain, 1988, 243, no. 92, fig. 58.

Cusloura. (1). W 313 807. 2 st st. ENE–WSW. 12 ft 9 (3.9 m) l. O'Nuallain, 1988, 243, no. 88, fig. 41.

Dromasta. (1). W 112 458. 2 st st. NE (taller)–SW. 12 ft 1 (3.7 m) l. O'Nuallain, 1988, 247, no. 130.

Foherlagh. (1). c. W 062 355. 2 st st. ENE–WSW (taller, leans). 15 ft (4.6 m) l. Commanding position. Roberts, J., 12; O'Nuallain, 1988, 248, no. 142, fig. 40.

Garrane. (1). W 477 908. 2 st st. NE (taller)–SW. 13 ft 1 (4 m) l. O'Nuallain, 1988, 241, no. 77, fig. 45.

Garraneleigh. (1). W 432 687. 2 st st. NE–SW. 13 ft 1 (4 m) l. O'Nuallain, 1988, 245, no. 108, fig. 43.

Garranenamuddagh. (3). W 442 650. 1 st st + 1 pros. O'Nuallain, 1988, 245, no. 110, fig. 45.

Glandine. 'Monkey's Bridge'. (4). W 481 888. 2 st st. NE

(taller)–SW. 17 ft (5.2 m) l. Prominent position. *ABM*, 3; O'Nuallain, 1988, 250, no. 161.

Glantane NE. (1). W 235 828. Ditched RSC is 330 yds (300 m) NE of 1 st st + 1 pros. NE–SW (taller). 16 ft 6 (5 m) l. O'Nuallain, 1984a, 11–12, no. 2; ibid, 1988, 242, no. 81, fig. 45.

Glenleigh. (1). W 323 903. 2 st st. NE (taller)–SW. 13 ft 2 (4 m) l. O'Nuallain, in litt, 1990.

Gortloughra. (1). W 112 593. 2 st st. NE–SW (taller). 7 ft 6 (2.3 m) l. O'Nuallain, 1988, 245, no. 112., fig. 43.

Gurteenaduige. (3). W 205 392. 1 st st + 1 pros. NW–SE. 165 yds (150 m) to E is st st, 6 ft (1.8 m) h. O'Nuallain, 1988, 253, no. 179, fig. 51.

Gurteenard. (1). R 397 023. 2 st st. WNW–ESE. 11 ft 10 (3.6 m) l. O'Nuallain, 1988, 241, no. 76, fig. 41.

Island. (3). W 604 908. 2 pros st. Wedge-tomb is 330 yds (300 m) to SW. Conlon, 1916, 66, no. 22; O'Nuallain, 1988, 242, no. 79, fig. 48.

Kealkil. (2). W 055 555. 5st-StC. 21 ft (6.4 m) to E are 2 st st. NE–SW taller). SW was 17 ft 4 (5.3 m) h. Fell and broke. Re-erected. Now 12 ft (3.7 m) h. NE = 8 ft 10 (2.7 m) h. Low Cn 7 ft (2.1 m) S of P. Exc. 1938. No finds. *JCHAS 44*, 1939, 46–9; Evans, 1966, 80; O'Nuallain, 1984a, 41–2, no. 81; ibid, 1988, 246, no. 119, fig. 55.

Keilnascarta N. (1). V 994 453. 2 st st. ENE–WSW. 13 ft 1 (4 m) l. 490 ft (150 m) N of 2nd P. Between is a 3St. O'Nuallain, 1988, 247, no. 127, fig. 44; Power *et al*, 41, no. 190.

Keilnascarta S. (1). V 994 451. 2 st st in fence. NE–SW. 10 ft 9 (3.3 m) l. O'Nuallain, 1988, 247, no. 128, fig. 44; Power *et al*, 41, no. 191.

Kilcrohan. (1). W 882 374. 2 st st. NNE–SSW. 8 ft 10 (2.7 m) l. O'Nuallain, 1988, 248, no. 140, fig. 40.

Kilcullen. (3). W 451 813. 1 st + 1 pros. O'Nuallain, 1988, 243–4, no. 97, fig. 45.

Kilmore. (1). W 125 436. 2 st st. ENE–WSW. 9 ft (2.7 m) l. O'Nuallain, 1988, 248, no. 138, fig. 45.

Kinneigh. (3). W 309 575. 1 st st + 1 pros. O'Nuallain, *in litt*, 1990; Power *et al*, 41, no. 194.

Knockane. (1). W 339 644. NE–SW (taller). 11 ft 10 (3.6 m) l. O'Nuallain, 1988, 245, no. 109, fig. 43.

Knockantota. (1). W 558 877. 2 st st. NE–WS. 9 ft 6 (2.9 m) l. Adj 5-StC, ruined. Conlon, 1916, 71–2, no. 35; O'Nuallain, 1984a, 242, no. 85; 1988, 242, no. 85, fig. 61.

Knockawaddra. (1). W 271 460. 2 st st. ENE–WSW (taller). 10 ft 2 (3.1 m) l. A 3St is 220 yds (200 m) to W. O'Nuallain, 1988, 247, no. 132, fig. 44.

Knockeennagrouagh. (1). W 806 830. 2 st st. ENE–WSW. 11 ft 9 (3.6 m) l. O'Nuallain, 1988, 252, no. 177, fig. 50.

Knocknakilla NW. (1). W 282 867. 2 st st. N–S. 8 ft 6 (2.6 m) l. O'Nuallain, 1988, 242, no. 80, fig. 45.

Knocknakilla SE. 'Muisire Beg'.(3). W 297 841. 5st-StC. 23 ft (7 m) to SW st st 12 ft 5 (3.8 m) h. Between it and StC a pros st 13 ft 9 (4.2 m) l. NE–SW. 25 ft (7.6 m) E of StC is radial-stone Cn. StC. Exc. 1931. No finds. Q frags strewn by ent. *JCHAS 36*, 1931, 9–19; O'Nuallain, 1984a, 32, no. 54; ibid, 1988, 242, no. 82, fig. 59.

Knockraheen NW. (3). W 300 812. 1 st st + 1 pros. O'Nuallain, 1988, 242, no. 87, fig. 41.

Knockraheen SE. (1). W 303 802. 5-StC. 74 ft (22.5 m) SW

are 2 st st. Both Q. ENE–WSW (taller). 3 ft 7 (1.1 m) gap between them. O'Nuallain, 1984a, 34, no. 62; ibid, 1988, 243, no. 89, fig. 57.

Knocks. (4). W 304 448. 2 st st? O'Nuallain, 1988, 247, no. 133; Power *et al*, 42, no. 196.

Lackabaun. (1). W 192 614. 2 st st. NE (taller)–SW. 10 ft (3 m) l. O'Nuallain, 1988, 245, no. 114, fig. 43; Power *et al*, 42, no. 197.

Loughane E. (3). W 570 781. 1 st only. 2nd, lower, at SW in 1934. Conlon, 1916, 137, no. 95; O'Nuallain, 1988, 244, no. 99, fig. 45.

Meenahony S. (1). W 469 835. 2 st st. NE (taller)–SW. 12 ft 1 (3.7 m) l. 144 ft (44 m) to ENE is st st 5 ft 6 (1.7 m) h. 110 yds (100 m) N of P is 2nd P. O'Nuallain, 1988, 242, no. 84, fig. 47.

Mill Little. (1). V 989 565. 5st-StC. 82 ft (25 m) to SW are 2 st st. NNE–SSW (taller). 2 ft 7 (80 cm) apart. 2 or 3 adj boulder-burials. O'Nuallain, 1978, 87, no. 11; ibid, 1984a, 40, no. 80; ibid, 1988, 246, no. 118, fig. 60.

Rathcool. (1). V 940 332. 2 st st. NE–SW. 11 ft 10 (3.6 m) l. O'Nuallain, 1988, 248, no. 141., fig. 40; Power *et al*, 42, no. 199.

Reavouler, Drinagh. (5). W 18. 44. 2 st st. So close, look like a single single split menhir. Roberts, J., 49. Sketch. Prob is a single st, 7 ft 3 (2.2 m) h. Power *et al*, 64, no. 468.

Rooves More. (3). W 456 701. 1 st st + 1 pros. Conlon, 1917, 159–60, no. 181; O'Nuallain, 1988, 245, no. 107, fig. 49.

Sarue. (3). W 284 429. 1 st st + 1 pros. NE–SW. Roberts, 1988, Ch. 6, no. 14.; Power *et al*, 42, no. 200.

Shandagan W. (5). W 408 694. 2 st st. E (taller)–W. 2 ft 7 (80 cm) apart. Loose Q block between. Conlon, 1917, 161, no. 188; O'Nuallain, 1988, 245, no. 106, fig. 43.

Shanlaragh. (1). W 258 595. 2 st st. NNE–SSW. 9 ft 6 (2.9 cm) l. O'Nuallain, 1988, 246, no. 116, fig. 42.

Shehy Beg. (3). W 145 591. 1 st st + 1 pros. O'Nuallain, 1988, 246, no. 115, fig. 46.

Slievereagh. (1). W 181 803. 2 st st. ENE (taller)–WSW. 13 ft 1 (4 m) l. O'Nuallain, 1988, 242, no. 86, fig. 48.

Teernahillane. (1). V 639 457. 2 st st. NNE (taller)–SSW. 6 ft 6 (2 m) l. Adj boulder-burial. O'Nuallain, 1978, 90, no. 16; ibid, 1988, 246, no. 124, fig. 55.

Toom. (1). W 284 555. 2 st st. NE–SW. 12 ft 1 (3.7 m) l. O'Nuallain, 1988, 246, no. 122, fig. 42; Power *et al*, 42, no. 204.

DONEGAL

Ballymagaraghy. (1). C 605 472. 2 st st. NE–SW (taller). In Cn 10 by 8 ft 10 (3 × 2.7 m). Lacy, 75, no. 350.

Ballymunterhiggin. (3). G 872 601. 1 st st. once 2 st st 36 ft (11 m) apart, E–W. Lacy, 77, no. 354.

Barnes Lower. (1). C 107 245. 2 st st. NW (taller)–SE. 10 ft (3 m) l. E face of SE st, at least 48 cms + arcs and gutters. Upper part, a forked design with 4 cms. NW st, W face, cross + 8 cms. E face, 7 cms. *JRSAI 18*, 1887–8, 432–6; Lacy, 77, no. 356, fig. 31; van Hoek, 24 fig. 3d, e, 27, DON 87.

Cloghfin. (3). C 355 111. Once 2 st st. Now 1 st st 3 ft (94 cm) h. 2nd, 10 ft (3 m) l, lies by it. Lacy, 79, no. 382.

Meenadoran. (1). C 392 437. 2 st st. N–S (taller). 14 ft 5

(4.4 m) to E is st st 4 ft 6 (1.4 m) h. Lacy, 84, no. 458.

Stroove. (1). C 673 430. 2 st st. E–W. 1 ft 6 (50 cm) apart. Lacy, 88, no. 489.

GALWAY

*Attigoddaun. (3). L 590 576. 1 st st + 1 pros (SSW). 4 ft (1.2 m) l. O'Nuallain, 1988, 197; Robinson, 1990, 43; Gosling, 1991, 25.

*Ballynew NW. (1). L 621 590. 2 st st, Q. NE–SW (taller). 4 ft and 4 ft 2 (1.2, 1.3 m) h. Gosling, 1991, 25.

Ballynew SE. (3). L 629 584. 1 st st + 1 pros (NW). NW–SE. 10 ft (3 m) l. 2 ft 10 l, 2 ft 10 h. (0.9, 0.9 m). Gosling, 1991, 26.

Barratrough, see: Streamstown.

*Cloonederown. (3). L 667 570. 1 st st + 1 pros. N–S. 6 ft 6 (2 m) l. N st broken, S 4 ft 7 (1.4 m) h. O'Nuallain, 1988, 197 (Cloonderavon). Gosling, 1991, 27.

Crocknaraw NE. (3). L 665 256. NW–SE (pros). 5 ft 10 (1.8 m) l. Both Q. N st 2 ft 7 (0.8 m) h. O'Nuallain, 1988, 195; Gosling, 1991, 28.

Crocknaraw SW. L 658 559. 2 Q st in cutaway bog. NE–SW (pros). 8 ft 10 (2.7 m) l. O'Nuallain, 1988, 197; Robinson, 1990, 30; Gosling, 1991, 27.

Knockaunbaun. (1). L 902 551. 2 Q st st. N–S (taller). 5 ft 7 (1.7 m) l. 1 ft 8 and 4 ft 7 (0.5, 1.4 m) h. O'Nuallain, 1988, 195; Robinson, 1990, 100; Gosling, 1991, 29.

Oorid. (3). L 924 245. 1 st st + 1 pros (N). N–S. 3 ft 9 (1.2 m) l. N = 3 ft 9 l, S = 3 ft 11 h (1.1, 1.2 m). Gosling, 1991, 30.

Rosleague. (1). L 687 574. NNW–SSE (taller). 8 ft 6 (2.6 m) l. 1 ft 7 and 4 ft 11 (0.5, 1.5 m) h. Gosling, 1991, 31.

*Sheeauns. (5). L 629 584. 1 st st + boulder. Both Q. (Inf. M. Gibbons).

*Streamstown. (3). L 647 535. 2 st st. NNE–SSW. 11 ft 6 (3.5 m) l. Outlier 30 ft (9.2 m) to E. O'Nuallain, 1988, 197; Robinson, 1990, 54; 2 pros st nearby, poss ruined 4-Poster. Gosling, 1991, 32.

KERRY

Ballineanig-Castlequarter. (3). Q 359 043. 2 st st. ENE–WSW. 21 ft 7 (6.6 m) l. Cuppage, 1986, 40, no. 55, fig. 28a; O'Nuallain, 1988, 249, no. 145, fig. 53.

Ballyrishteen. (3). Q 489 027. 1 st st + 1 pros. Cuppage, 1986, 40–1, no. 56, fig. 28b; O'Nuallain, 1988, 249, no. 150, fig. 49.

Bolus. (1). V 396 630. 2 st st. N–S. 7 ft 11 (2.4 m) l. O'Nuallain, in litt, 1990.

Caherpiece. (4). Q 682 017. Cuppage, 1986, 43, no. 67.

Canburrin. (3). V 504 773. 1 st leans + 1 pros. O'Nuallain, 1988, 253, no. 182, fig. 50.

Clogherane. (1). V 788 556. 2 st st. NNE (taller)2–SSW. 10 ft 2 (3.1 m) l. O'Nuallain, 1988, 250, no. 160, fig. 53.

Coomnahorna E. (1). V 555 607. 2 st st. NE–SW (taller). 17 ft 9 (5.4 m) l. Garrough 4St 380 yds (350 m) to NE. St st 110 yds (100 m) to SW. O'Nuallain, 1988, 250, no. 159, fig. 53.

Coumduff. (3). Q 581 043. 1 st st + 1 pros. Cuppage, 1986, 41, no. 57; O'Nuallain, 1988, 249, no. 152, fig. 52.

Derreenafoyle. (3). V 794 688. 1 st st + 1 pros. O'Nuallain, 1988, 250, no. 158, fig. 52.

Derrygorman. (3). Q 599 044. 2 st st. NE–SW (taller). 12 ft 9 (3.9 m) l. Cuppage, 1986, 41, no. 58, fig. 26; O'Nuallain, 1988, 249, no. 153, fig. 26.

Drom E. (5). Q 530 113. 2 st st. E (taller)–W. Was a 3rd st, pros. E, pointed, 9 ft 6 (2.9 m) h. W, rounded, 7 ft 6 (2.3 m) h. 12 ft (3.7 m) l. St st 220 yds (200 m) NE. Cuppage, 1986, 43, no. 66, fig. 28e; O'Nuallain, 1988, 248, no. 143, fig. 52.

Dromavally SE. (3). Q 593 053. 1 st st + 1 pros. Cuppage, 1986, 41, no. 59, O'Nuallain, 1988, 249, no. 151, fig. 55.

Dromod. (1). V 552 704. 2 st st. NE–SW (taller). 11 ft 9 (3.6 m) l. A st st 6 ft (2 m) from taller st. O'Nuallain, 1988, 250, no. 156, fig. 54.

Fahan. (4). V 351 975. 2 st st, 3 ft 1, 2 ft 4 (0.9, 0.7 m) h. 3 ft 2 (1 m) l. Cuppage, 1986, 43, no. 68.

Garrane. (3). Q 425 048. 1 st st + 1 pros. Cuppage, 1986, 41, no. 61; O'Nuallain, 1988, 249, no. 147, fig. 48.

Garrydine. (3). V 543 837. 2 st st. NE–SW. 16 ft 9 (5.1 m) l. O'Nuallain, 1988, 250, no. 155, fig. 49.

Gearha. (1). V 775 735. 2 st st. NE (taller)–SW. 10 ft (3 m) l. O'Nuallain, 1988, 250, no. 157, fig. 52.

Gowlaneard. (1). Q 530 021. 2 st st. NE (taller)–SW. 11 ft 2, 9 ft 2 (3.4, 2.8 m) h. 23 ft (7 m) l. Cuppage, 1986, 42, no. 62.

Kilnabrack Lower. (1). V 663 914. 2 st, NE (taller)–SW. 19 ft 9 (6 m) l. O'Nuallain, in litt, 1990.

Kimego. (3). V 450 808. 1 pros + 1 stump 5 ft (1.5 m) h. Orig 16 ft (4.9 m) h? 10 ft (3 m) l. O'Nuallain, 1988, 253, no. 181, fig. 51.

Knockavrogeen E. (3). Q 425 045. 1 st st + 1 pros. Cuppage, 1986, 42, no. 63, fig. 29; O'Nuallain, 1988, 249, no. 146, fig. 454.

Lissyviggeen. (1). V 997 906. CH. 38 ft (11.5 m) S of ent 2 st st. E (taller)–W. 7 ft 8, 6 ft 10 (2.3, 2.1 m) h. 7 ft 3 (2.2 m) l. O'Nuallain, 1984a, 25, no. 38; *ibid*, 1988, 250, no. 154, fig. 55.
    Astr: Equi SR, SS? *JRSAI 16*, 1883–4, 306.

Milltown N. 'Gates of Glory'. (3). Q 429 011. 2 st st. NE pros, SW broken, 2 ft 8 (0.8 m) h. 4 ft 7 (1.4 m) apart. Both have pointed ends. 165 ft (50 m) to S is Miltown South. Cuppage, 1986, 43, no. 64, fig. 28c; O'Nuallain, 1988, 249, no. 148, fig. 52.

Milltown S. (3). Q 429 010. 2 pros st. W 10 ft 10 (3.3 m) l. Plain. E 13 ft 9 × 4 ft 3 (4.2, 1.3 m), cms, crs, grooves. 230 ft (70 m) SW is Gallan na Cille Brice, 'the Milestone', a st st 9 ft 2 (2.8 m) h. 820 ft (250 m) SSW of the Milestone is 2nd st st 9 ft 6 (2.9 m) h. Macalister, 1898, 161–4; ibid, 1921, 305; Evans, 1966, 131; Cuppage, 1986, 64–5, no. 191 (2 st sts, nos. 131, 132); O'Nuallain, 1988, 249, no. 149, fig. 48.

Minard W. (1). V 536 991. 2 st st. ESE–WNW. 4 ft 11, 2 ft 3 (1.5, 0.7) h. 23 ft (7 m) l. Cuppage, 43, no. 65, fig. 30.

Reask. Q 367 046. 2 st st. NNW–SSE (taller). 9 ft 6 (2.9 m) l. Cuppage, 1986, 43, no. 66, fig. 28d; O'Nuallain, 1988, 248, no. 144, fig. 52.

Teeromoyle. (4). V 571 823. In 1845 2 st st. Larger destr. 1 st st 7 ft 4 (2.2 m) h. O'Nuallain, 1988, 253, no. 180, fig. 51.

LOUTH

Balregan. (4). J 027 000. 2 st st. Buckley, 1986, 19, no. 182.

Baltray. (4). O 144 851. 2 st st. N–S (taller). 5 ft 11 and

9 ft 6 (1.8, 2.9 m) h. 29 ft 6 (9 m) l. Buckley, 1986, 19, no. 183.

Millockstown. 'Garrett's Stone' and the 'Horse's Head'. (4). N 891 877. 1 pros + 1 destr. Buckley, 1986, 21, no. 203.

MAYO

Derryhillagh. (3). G 084 092. 1 st st + stump. NNW–SSE. 20 ft 4 (6.2 m) l. O'Nuallain, *in litt*, 1990.

MEATH

Ballinvally. (3). N 580 786. 1 st st 4 ft 6 (1.5 m) h + 1 pros. Moore, 1987, 42.

Farranaglogh. (3). N 534 827. 1 st st + 1 pros. 26 ft (8 m) apart. Moore, 1987, 43.

Grangegeeth. (3). N 964 792. 1 st st + 1 pros. Moore, 1987, 43.

WEXFORD

Robinstown Great. (3). S 811 291. 2 st. 13 ft 6 (4.2 m) l. 1 st leans, orig 2 ft 7 (80 m) h. Just E is pros block, Q, 5 ft 7 (1.7 m) l. Just SW of a 4-Poster. *JRSAI 42*, 1912, 15–16; O'Nuallain, 1984b, 17, no. 6; Burl, 1988, 89.

WICKLOW

Giant's Grave. (1). T 210 961. 2 st st. 5 ft 3 and 4 ft 3 (1.6, 1.3 m) h. 26 ft (7.9 m) l. 160 yds (150 m) from Cn. Price, 1934, 40.

SCOTLAND

ABERDEENSHIRE

Castle Fraser. (1). NJ 717 125. 2 st st. NNE–SSW. Each 7 ft (2.1 m) h. 48 ft (14.6 m) apart. Granite. 727 ft (220 m) E of RSC. The only Scottish RSC to have adj pair. *PSAS 35*, 1901, 197, no. 3.
  Astr: az = 32°–212°, h = 1.8°, decl. −29°.1. Maj S MS.

ANGUS

Auchterhouse. (1). NO 345 392. 2 st st. NE (taller)–SW, 5 ft and 3 ft 6 (1.5, 1.1 m) h. 3 ft 6 (1.1 m) apart. NE st has 15 cms. 160 yds (146 m) to E is possible 4-Poster. *JBAA 37*, 1881, 260–2; Burl, 1988, 103.

Corogle Burn. (3). NO 348 601. [P3/1. 'Glen Prosen']. A 4-Poster + 2 pros st to SSW. Each 8 ft (2.4 m) l. 6 ft (1.8 m) apart. 65 ft (20 m) to the NNE is the 4-Poster. Its NE st is missing. Thom, 1966, 34, fig. 20; Coutts, 1970, 19, no. 7; Burl, 1988, 108–9.
  Astr: Maj S MS. Thom, 1967, 100; Thom, Thom & Burl, 1990, II, 340.

Fletcherfield. (3). NO 401 525. 2 pros st. A boulder in railway embankment 42 ft (13 m) to N may be assoc. Coutts, 1970, 19.

ARGYLL

*Achnabreac. (3). NR 856 899 + NR 855 901. [A2/19]. St st 8 ft (2.4 m) h in wall. 820 ft (250 m) to NNW pros st 14 ft 9 (4.5 m) l. Exc. before 1872, human bones found at base. *PSAS 95*, 1961–2, 23, no. 155, 28, no. 191; Ruggles, 1984, 161, AR31.
  Astr: Maj S MS. Thom, 1967, 97; Thom, Thom & Burl, 1990, I, 119.

Balliemore. (1). NS 056 845. 2 st st 6 ft 6 (2 m) apart. N–S. 8 ft and 5 ft 7 (2.4 m, 1.7 m) h. *RCAHM-S, Argyll VI,*

1988, 126–7, no. 198.

Ballymeanoch. 'Farmstead of stones'. (1). NR 833 964. [2/8. Duncracaig. 'Fort of the red crag']. 4St + P + st st. P = NW–SE (taller). 9 ft 3 ft and 10 ft (2.8, 3 m) h. 6 ft (2.3 m) l. 4St 135 ft (41 m) to NE. A st st 65 ft (20 m) to SE. Allen, 1882, 114; *PSAS 95*, 1961–2, 24, no. 158; Thom, 1966, 21, fig. 6c; *ibid*, 1971, 2–3; *PSAS 109*, 1977–8, 104–11; Heggie, 1981, 121.
  Astr: (1) Az = 152°. hor = 1°.1. decl = −28°.6. Maj S MR. Az = 332°. hor = 3°.1. decl = 32°.1. Thom, 1971, 52; Thom, Thom & Burl, 1990, I, 109–11. (2) To SSE, decl limits = −25°.8 to −23°.7. MdW SR. To NW, decl limits = 28°.3 to 29°.3. Maj N MS. Ruggles, 1984, 149, 279, AR15, 'Duncraicraig'. (N.B. 'Dunchragaig' is a name more properly given to the Cn and 2 Cts at NR 853 968. See: Ritchie & Harman, 138).

Barbreck. (3). NM 831 064. 2 st st. NNE–SSW (taller). 5 ft 3 and 7 ft 10 (1.6, 2.4 m) h. 10 ft (3 m) l. 76 ft (23 m) to the ESE is a st st 8 ft 2 (2.5 m) h. *PSAS 95*, 1961–2, 24, no. 159; Patrick, 1979, S80–S85; Heggie, 1981, 185–6.
  (1) Astr: To S, decl limits = −30°.7 to −30°.5. Maj S MS. To N, decl limits = 38°.5 to 38°.6. Nothing. Ruggles, 1984, 279. (2) In the meridian? Thom, Thom & Burl, 1990, I, 100–1. 'Further up the glen ... there are two stones (NM 840 076)'. One is in the meridian.

Barcaldine. (3). NM 963 421. 1 st st + 1 leans against it. St st, NNW–SSE axis, 5 ft 7 (1.7 m) h. 2nd st, 5 ft 3 (1.6 m) l. *RCAHM-S, Argyll II*, 1975, 62, no. 111.

Carnasserie. (1). NM 834 008. [A2/6]. 2 st st. NNW–SSE (taller). 8 ft 7 and 8 ft 10 (2.6, 2.7 m) h. Lozenge and tapering. 7 ft 9 (2.4 m) apart. They face 'the Ford gap, which shows between them like a foresight of a rifle from higher up hill'. A large Cn is 490 ft (150 m) to SSW. *PSAS 65*, 1930–1; *ibid 95*, 1961–2, 12, no. 70, 25, no. 166; Ruggles, 1984, 148, AR12; Thom, Thom & Burl, 1990, I, 104–5.

Carse. (1). NR 742 615. [A3/6a, 'Loch Stornoway']. 2 st st. N–S. N flat top, 7 ft 10, S pointed, 10 ft 6 (2.4, 3.2 m) h. 8 ft 3 (2.5 m) apart. 360 ft (110 m) WNW a st st 7 ft 2 (2.2 m) h. Fragments of 'bronze plates' found at base of one. *PSAS 5*, 1862–4, 345; *PSAS 95*, 1961–2, 25, no. 168; *RCAHM-S, Argyll VI*, 1988, 131, no. 204.
  Astr: Az limits to S 177°.4–177°.8. Ruggles, 1984, 183, KT2; (2) 'Only 3° away from the meridian'. Thom, Thom & Burl, 1990, I, 129.

Cnoc Pollphail. (3). NR 931 683. 2 st st. NNW–SSE NNW, 9 ft 6, SSE 2 ft 3, broken (2.9, 0.7 m) h. 20 ft 6 (6.3 m) apart. *RCAHM-S, Argyll VI*, 1988, 131–2, no. 207.

Crinan Moss. (3). NR 808 941. S + 2 Ps + 3rd P? Robbed S. NE–SW. 56 ft (17 m) from:
  (a) (1). 2 st st 2 ft and 3 ft (0.6, 0.9 m) h. 7 ft 9 (2.4 m) apart. NE–SW.
  (b) (3). At SW end of S 2nd P, 1 st, 1 pros.
  (c) (5). 2 st of nearby gateway, each 6 ft (1.8 m) h, 'strongly suggesting re-used standing stones'. *PSAS 95*, 1961–2, 26, no. 173. Reminiscent of Kilmartin setting. See below.
  Astr: May SS? Thom, Thom & Burl, 1990, I, 124–5.

Dunamuck, Mid. (1). NR 848 924. [A2/14. 'Dunamuck II']. 2 st st. NNW–SSE (taller). 8 ft and 12 ft 6 (2.4, 3.8 m) h, one flat-topped, the other pointed. 20 ft (6.1 m) l. 60 yds (55 m) S of R. Add. SSE has cms. *PSAS 38*, 1903–4,

130; *ibid 95*, 1961–2, 27, no. 177; Ruggles, 1984, 161, AR29.

　　Astr: (1) 'Sun'. Thom, 1967, 97; Thom, Thom & Burl, 1990, I, 112–13. (2) To SE, Min S MR? Ruggles, 1984, 279.

Dunamuck S. Leacaichluaine, 'the dancing stones'. (3). NR 848 923. [A2/20. 'Dunamuck III']. 2 pros st. SE 13 ft 3 and NW 10 ft 2 (4, 3.1 m) l. 1 has cms. Cns and Cts nearby. *PSAS 38*, 1903–4, 127–9; *ibid 95*, 1961–2, 26, no. 176; Ruggles, 1984, 161, AR30; Thom, Thom & Burl, 1990, I, 113, 119.

*Kames. (3). NR 971 714. 2 st st. N–S. N 4 ft 10 and S 9 ft 2 (1.5, 2.8 m) h. 3 ft 3 (1 m) apart. Both embedded in bank. 128 ft (39 m) to S, a st st 5 ft (1.5 m) h. *RCAHM-S, Argyll VI*, 1988, 135, no. 219.

Kilmartin. (1). NR 827 979. [A2/8. 'Temple Wood', 'Slock-avullin']. 2 Ps of st st, NNE–SSW, 227 ft (69 m) apart, with a tall st st between. All local slate. Allen, 1882, 110–13; *PSAS 95*, 1961–2, 28, no. 187; *RCAHM-S Argyll VI*, 1988, 135–7, no. 222, 'Nether Largie'.

　　(a) NNE pair, 10 ft (3 m) l. NE–SW. NE (Thom, stone 2) 8 ft 10 (2.7 m) h (flat), 3 cms on SW face. SW (stone 3) 9 ft 4 (2.85 m) h, pointed.

　　(b) Central stone, 117 ft (35.7 m) to SSW. St (stone 1), 9 ft 2 (2.8 m) h, 40+ cms on SW face.

　　(c) 120 ft (37 m) to SSW pair. SW–NE. 11 ft (3.4 m) l. NE (st 4) 9 ft (2.7 m) h, pointed. SW (stone 5) 9 ft 2 (2.8 m) h, flat, 3 cms on NE face. Thom, 1966, 21, fig. 5b; *ibid*, 1971, 45–51.

　　Astr: (1) From NNE P to SSW P, St 3 to St 4. Az = 206°.1. hor = 0°.3. decl = −30°.3. Maj S MS. From SSW to NNE P. St 4 to St 3. Az = 26°.1. hor = 2°.6. decl = +32°.3. Capella rising, 1830 BC (c. 1500 bc). SSW P, St 5 to St 4. Az = 317°.9. hor = 4°.6. decl = +29°.04. Maj N MS. NNE P, St 3 to St 2. Az = 316°. hor = 4°.7. decl = +28°.6. For lunar extrapolation. Thom, 1967, 97; *ibid*, 1971, 47; Thom, Thom & Burl, 1990, I, 106–7, 'Slockavullin'. (2) To S, decl limits = −30°9 to −30°.7. Maj S MS; To N, decl limits = 29°.5 to 29°.3. Maj S MS. Ruggles, 1984, 148–9, AR13.

South Muasdale. 'Carragh Mualdale'. (3). NR 679 391. 1 st st + stump. ENE–WSW. St st 9 ft 6 (3 m) h. 39 ft (12 m) apart. *PSAS 64*, 1929–30, 306, no. 7; Ruggles, 1984, 183, KT19.

*Tarbert. (5). NR 606 823 to NR 608 822. [A6/5]. St st 8 ft 2 (2.5 m) h. 950 ft (290 m) to E, slab (prehistoric?) 5 ft 11 (1.8 m) h in churchyard. Christian crosses carved on faces. *PSAS 66*, 1931–2, 146–7; Moir, 1981, 231; Ruggles, 1984, 163, JU1.

Upper Fernoch. (1). NR 727 860. 2 st st 7 ft 6 and 5 ft (2.3, 1.5 m) h. N–S. 4 ft (1.2 m) apart. 3 pros st near them. 20 ft (6 m) to S a st st 3 ft (0.9 m) h. *PSAS 95*, 1961–2, 29, no. 195.

ARRAN

Auchenar. (3). NR 891 364. 1 st st 15 ft 9 (4.8 m) h + pros 5 ft 6 (1.7 m) to S. Bryce, T.H., 1910, 155.

BARRA

Borve. (3). NF 652 014. 1 st st + 1 pros, both gneiss. NE–SW. NE leans, 5 ft 5 (1.7 m) h. SW 9 ft 7 (2.9 m) l. 36 ft (11 m) apart. *RCHAM-S, Outer Hebrides*, 1928, 136, no. 461; Thom, Thom & Burl, 1990, I, 262.

Brevig. 'Druim a Charra'. 'the ridge of stones'. (3). NL 689 990. [H6/3]. On summit. 1 st st (NW), 9 ft 2 (2.8 m) h + 1 pros (SE, broken), 10 ft 7 (3.2 m) l. 14 ft 6 (4.4 m) l. Overthrown for a wager. Had narrower end in ground. Orig 24 ft 6 (7.5 m) l. *RCAHM-S, Outer Hebrides*, 1928, 136, no. 460. Ruggles, 1984, 120, UI59.

　　Astr: MdW SR. Thom, 1967, 99; Thom, Thom & Burl, 1990, I, 263.

BERWICK

Brothers' Stones. (1). NT 619 360. 2 st st. NW–SE (taller). 5 ft 3 and 8 ft 2 (1.6, 2.5 m) h. 43 ft (13 m) apart. 275 yds (250 m) down NE slope is bulkier st st, Cow Stone, 6 ft 6 (2 m) h. Baldwin, 1985, 164.

CAITHNESS

Loch of Yarrows. (1). ND 316 432. [N1/8]. 2 st st 8 ft 6 and 6 ft 6 (2.6, 2 m) h. 19 ft 10 (6 m) apart. NNW–SSE. Needle-like. On hill. 50 ft (15 m) to E was small Cn. Gunn, 1915, 349–50; Feachem, 73.

　　Astr: poss lunar to SSE. Thom, Thom & Burl, 1990, II, 293.

Watten. (3). ND 223 517. [N1/15]. St st 6 ft (1.8 m) h + 1 pros. Thom, 1967, 139, fig. 9.3.

COLL

Totronald. (1). NM 166 559. 2 granite st st. NNE–SSW. NNE, 5 ft 7 (1.7 m) h. SSW 6 ft 3 (1.9 m) h. 47 ft (14.3 m) l. *RCAHM-S, Argyll III*, 1980, 71, no. 120; Ruggles, 1984, 121, CT2. Boswell and Johnson visited the site in 1773. 'We came to two triangular flagstones placed, I imagine, about ten yards from each other. (I afterwards measured; fourteen of my paces). They have probable been a Druidical temple'. Boswell, J., *Journal of a Tour to the Hebrides with Samuel Johnson, LlD*, London, 1936, 262.

COLONSAY

Drumclash. 'Fingal's Limpet Hammers'. (5). NR 367 949. 2 st st. NNW–SSE. SSE 10 ft 1 (3.1 cm) h. 45 ft 3 (13.8 m) to NNW, 8 ft 6 (2.6 m) h. Both lean slightly. Shapes like tools used to detach limpets from rocks. *RCAHM-S, Argyll V*, 1984, 68, no. 96.

DUMFRIESS

*Skipknowe. (5). NY 11. 94. Massive whin boulder, 5 ft 7 (1.7 m) h, long axis EW. 18 ft (5.5 m) away is 2nd boulder in roadside bank. *RCAHM-S, East Lothian*, 1924, 212, no. 627.

FIFE

*Bandrum. (5). NT 036 915. Huge whin boulder, 7 ft 10 (2.4 m) h. 162 ft (49 m) W st 3 ft 10 (1.2 m) h. *RCAHM-S, Fife*, 1933, 267, no. 489.

North Glassmount. (1). NT 244 884. 2 st st. E–W (taller). 5 ft 7 and 6 ft 2 (1.7, 1.9 m) h. 19 ft 2 (5.9 m) l. *PSAS 40*, 1905, 291; *RCAHM-S, Fife...*, 1933, 346; Feachem, 1977, 77.

ISLAY

*Beinn Cham. (3). NR 349 679. 1 st st 3 ft 4 (1.1 m) h + adj pros slab. Ruggles, 1984, 165, IS6.

*Clachan Cean Ile. (5). NR 436 483. 2 st st . W–E. 5 ft 3 and 2 ft 8 (1.6, 0.8 m) h. 32 ft 9 (10 m) apart. Prehistoric?

Legend that they mark the grave of Yula, a daughter of a king of Denmark. *RCAHM-S. Argyll V*, 1984, 65, no. 85.

Finlaggan. NR 392 685. (5). A st st 6 ft 6 (2 m) h. No sign now of 2nd stone mentioned by Martin, 1716, 243. 'There are two Stones set up at the East-side of *Loch-Finlagan*, and they are six Foot high'. *RCAHM-S, Argyll V*, 1984, 68, no. 97.

*Kilbride. (3). NR 383 465. Slab 7 ft 7 (2.3 m) h. 10 ft (3 m) to SW sunken st 7 ft+ (2.1 m) l. Ruggles, 1984, 180, IS42.

*Knocklearoch. (1). NR 398 648. 2 st st. WNW–ESE. Local limestone. WSW 6 ft 6 (2 m) h. ENE, 5 ft 7 (1.7 m) h. 7 ft 10 (2.4 m) l. Both lean to S. *RCAHM-S, Argyll V*, 1984, 69, no. 108. Ruggles, 1984, 170. IS11.

Legend, 2 clerics were hanged here. Were once 3 st in triangle. A legal sanctuary. Grinsell, 1976, 229.

*Lagavullin. (3). NR 395 462. 1 st st 10 ft 8 (3.3 m) h + 1 pros. ENE–WSW. 7 ft (2 m) l. *PSAS 48*, 1913–14, 404–7, fig. 2; Ruggles, 1984, 180, IS 39. At NR 396 463 a st st 12 ft (3.7 m) h in drystone wall. *D & E*, 1964, 16.

JURA

Strone Farm. (3). NR 507 637. [A6/2]. 1 st st + 1 pros. SE–NW. St st 9 ft 6 (2.9 m) h. 6 ft 8 (2 m) to NW an embedded slab 8 ft 10 (2.7 m) l. *PSAS 66*, 1931–2, 148–9; *RCAHM-S, Argyll V*, 1984, 71, no. 120; Ruggles, 1984, 165, JU8.

Astr: Solar. Thom, 1966, 24, fig. 8g; Thom, 1967, 97; Thom, Thom & Burl, 1990, I, 153.

KINCARDINESHIRE

*Glassel House. (5). c. NO 649 997. 2 st st. NW–SE. 9 ft 9 (3 m) apart. *PSAS 39*, 1904–5, 205.

*Kempston Hill. (5). NO 876 894. [B3/5]. 2 st st 8 ft and 10 ft (2.4, 3 m) h. NE–SW (taller). 270 ft (82 m) l.

Astr: Min S MS. Thom, 1967, 98; Thom, Thom & Burl, 1990, I, 185.

KINROSS

Orwell. (2). NO 149 043. 2 st st. ESE (taller)–WNW. 12 ft 6 and 7 ft 5 (3.8, 2.3 m) h. 46 ft 10 (14.3 m) apart. 1972, WNW st fell. Re-erected. Exc. 1972. Crem in shallow hollow 1 ft 6 (50 cm) S of WNW st. In pit, SW side of ESE st double-storeyed crems, lower in crude Ct. On its slab, 2nd crem. 3rd crem at lip of s/h. Very like Easter Pitcorthie st st, NO 497 039 with crem in its socket. Walker & Ritchie, 1987, 175, no. 95. A stone pounder was found between the Orwell P. Adj Cts contained bones and charcoal. *PSAS 40*, 1905–6, 293–5, no. 2; *RCAHM-S, Fife*, 1933, 304, no. 577; *PSAS 105*, 1972–4, 187, 319; *D & E*, 1972, 55–6; *Arch J 131*, 1974, 8–9, 27–9; *PSAS 109*, 1977–8, 107.

KIRKCUDBRIGHTSHIRE

Bagbie. (1). NX 498 564. [G4/13. 'Kirkmabreck']. 27 ft (8.3 m) S of a 4-Poster are 2 st st. 4 ft (1.2 m) apart. N–S. 200 yds (180 m) to south is tall st st. *RCAHM-S, Galloway II*, 1914, 165, no. 297. Thom, 1967, 98; Burl, 1988, 135.

*Thieves. 'Blair Hill'. (5). NX 404 716 2 st st. [G4/2]. NE–SW (taller). 6 ft 8 and 7 ft 4 (2, 2.2 m) h. 14 ft 6 (4.4 m) apart. On inner edge of grassy elliptical ring. Low slab on edge, 3 ft 9 (1.1 m) l at RtLs between them at SE. May be survivors of StC. *RCAHM-S, Galloway II*, 1914,

no. 367; Feachem, 79; Ruggles & Whittle, 1981, 208.

Astr: Maj N MR. Thom, 1967, 98; Thom, Thom & Burl, 1990, I, 209.

LEWIS AND HARRIS

Cul a Chleit. 'Rocky hillock at the back of the moor'. (1). NB 247 303. [H1/6. 'Callanish VI']. 2 st st. NE (taller)–SW. 5 ft 6 and 3 ft (1.7, 1 m) h. 55 ft 9 (17 m) l apart. 2 tiny st st + 3 pros slabs to WNW. *RCAHM-S, Outer Hebrides*, 1928, 29, no. 95; *D & E*, 1976, 57; Ponting, G. & M., 1977, 29; Ruggles, 1984, 80–1, LH22.

*Druim nam Bidearan. (5). NB 233 297. 2 pros slabs, each c. 4 ft (1.3 m) l. Packing-stones at bases. *D & E*, 1976, 58.

Great Bernerna. 'Tursachan Barraglom'. 'Cleiter' (cliffs). (2). NB 164 342. [H1/7. 'Callanish VIII']. On steep, rocky slope, 12 ft (3.7 m) from cliff edge. 2 st st. NE (taller)–SW. 9 ft and 7 ft 6 (2.7, 2.3 m) h. 37 ft 3 (11.4 m) apart. A low st 10 ft (3 m) W of NE st. Row damaged by blasting. *RCAHM-S, Outer Hebrides*, 1928, 24, no. 86; *D & E*, 1976, 57; Ponting, G. & M., 1981, 81; Ruggles, 1984, 77, LH8. Exc. 1985. Fallen st wrongly re-erected, s/h found. Stone setting, paved area, retaining wall discovered. Worked Q, small polished axe, arrowhead; *ibid*, 1985, 64. St re-erected in correct stonehole, *ibid*, 1987, 61.

Astr: (1) Somerville, 1912. (2) Thom, 1967, 99, 'Sun'; equi, May SS, Thom, Thom & Burl, 1990, I, 232, 'Bernera Bridge'.

MORAY

East Port. (1). 2P? NJ 03. 27. 2 st st. E–W (taller). 4 ft 3 and 4 ft 8 (1.3, 1.4 m) h. 7 ft (2.1 m) apart. 351 ft (107 m) to N 2 st st 237 ft (72 m) apart. *PSAS 41*, 1906–7, 131–4.

MULL

*Ardalanish. (3). NM 378 188. 1 st st + 1 pros. Near shore. St st, rough schist, 6 ft 3 (1.9 m) h. NW–SE. Pros st, hard sandstone, 39 ft (12 m) to SE, 7 ft 10 (2.4 m) l. Unfinished quern. *RCAHM-S, Argyll III*, 1980, 65, no. 88. Ruggles, 1984, 139, ML33.

*Calgary. 'Franchadil'. (3). NM 384 523. 2 pros st, 9 ft 2 and 8 ft 6 (2.8, 2.6 m) l, close together. *RCAHM-S, Argyll III*, 1980, 68, no. 104; Ruggles, 1984, 127, ML 8.

Cladh Chatain, Branault. (3). NM 526 695. 2 basalt st st in hollow. SSE–NNW. SSE 7 ft 2 (2.2 m). h. 3 ft (0.9 m) to NNW, a stump 1 ft 6 (0.5 m) h. *RCAHM-S, Argyll III*, 1980, 66, no. 99; Ruggles, 1984, 121, NA1.

*Craigaid, Ulva. (3). NM 402 390. 2 st st, E–W. W 4 ft 3 (1.3 m) h. E 5 ft 7 (1.7 m) h. 13 ft 8 (4.2 m) l. *RCAHM-S, Argyll III*, 1980, 66, no. 100. Both broken? Ruggles, 1984, 128, ML18.

Dail na Carraigh. 'Rocky dale'. (1). NM 370 218. [M2/7]. 2 st st. E (taller)–W. 5 ft 9 and 3 ft 7 (1.7, 1.1 m) h. 4 ft (1.2 m) apart. E st is perforated. Just NNE of ruined ChT, 'Suie' (level shelf on a hillside). Henshall, 1972, 467. *RCAHM-S, Argyll III*, 1980, 88; Ruggles, 1984, 139, ML34; Thom, Thom & Burl, 1990, II, 275.

*Gruline. (5). NM 545 396 and 543 397. 2 impressive st st, SE 7 ft 6 (2.3 m) h. 886 ft (270 m) to NW, 8 ft 2 (2.5 m) h. *RCAHM-S, Argyll III*, 1980, 68, no. 106.

Lag. (3). NM 362 535. 1 st st + 1 pros. 5 ft 7 h and 4 ft 11 (1.7, 1.5 m) h. 3 ft (1 m) apart. *RCAHM-S, Argyll, III*, 1980, 68–9, no. 109; Ruggles, 1984, 127, ML6.

NORTH UIST

Boreray. (3). NF 85. 81. St st 4 ft 10 (1.5 m) h. 4 ft 5 (1.3 m) to N a pros st 6 ft 3 (1.9 m) l. *RCAHM-S, Outer Hebrides*, 1928, 85, no. 259.

Fir Bhreige. 'The False Men'. (1). NF 770 702. [H3/5]. 2 st st. WNW 3 ft 10 (1.2 m) h, ESE, broad, 2 ft 4 (0.7 m) h. 117 ft (36 m) apart. 3 ft (1 m) deep in peat. *RCAHM-S, Outer Hebrides*, 1928, 85, no. 255; Ruggles, 1984, 102, UI23.

Legend, men turned to stone for deserting their wives. Grinsell, 1976, 102.

Astr: Feb SS. Thom, 1967, 99; Thom, Thom & Burl, 1990, I, 241.

Leac nan Cailleacha Dubha. 'Stone slab of the black old women'. (1). NF 785 763. 2 st st 'where 2 old women milking other people's cows were killed and buried'. 'Black women' were nuns. *RCAHM-S, Outer Hebrides*, 1928, 85, no. 258. Grinsell, 1976, 194.

ORKNEY MAINLAND AND ISLANDS

Brodgar farm. (1). HY 300 129. 2 st st. N–S. 9 ft and 5 ft 6 (2.7, 1.7 m) h. 27 ft 3 (8.3 m) apart. *RCAHM-S, Orkney & Shetland, II*, 1946b, 304, no. 878.

Deepdale. (3). HY 271 116. 2 st st. Major axes, NW–SE. 6 ft and, SE, 7 ft 6 (1.8, 2.3 m) h. 120 ft (37 m) apart. *RCAHM-S, Orkney & Shetland II*, 1946b, 325, no. 922. 1978, larger removed for ploughing. Exc. 1978. Stump. Large packing-stones made boxlike socket for adj st st. *D & E*, 1978, 17.

Leafea. (1). H1Y 226 093. 2 st st 4 ft (1.2 m) apart. E–W. Major axes N & S. 4 ft and 3 ft 3 (1.2, 1 m) h. 'In strict alignment'. Exc. Farmer's dog unearthed bones from base. Human? *RCAHM-S, Orkney & Shetland, II*, 1946b, 325, no. 923.

Redland. (3). HY 38. 24. W side of Vishall Hill. St st 1 ft 4 (40 cm) h, orig 6 ft (1.8 m). Few ft away, stump of 2nd st. *RCAHM-S, Orkney & Shetland, II*, 1946b, 81, no. 273.

Spurdagove. (3). HY 255 246. 1 st st + 1 pros. NE, pros-SW. 3 ft 1 and 3 ft 6 h (0.9, 1.1 m). 12 ft 9 (3.9 m) apart. *RCAHM-S, Orkney & Shetland, II*, 1946b, 22, no. 33.

Stanerandy. (1). HY 268 277. On small damaged mound, 2 st st. NE–SW. 5 ft 4 and 5 ft 2 (1.6, 1.6 m) h. 6 ft (1.8 m) apart. *RCAHM-S, Orkney & Shetland, II*, 1946b, 22, no. 35.

PEEBLES

Menzion. (1). NT 094 238. 2 st st, NW–SE. NW 2 ft 6 (0.8 m) h. 75 ft (23 m) to SE, 2 ft (0.6 m) h. *RCAHM-S, Peebles*, 1967, 63, no. 105.

Sherriff Muir. (1). NT 200 400. 2 st st, N–S, 3 ft 9 and 4 ft 3 (1.1, 1.3 m) h. 7 ft (2.1 m) apart. *RCAHM-S, Peebles*, 1967, 63, no. 106.

PERTHSHIRE (TAYSIDE)

Balmuick. NN 784 251. Possible 4-Poster and outlying 2 st, now pros. *PSAS 45*, 1911, 51–4, no. 5; Burl, 1988a, 145.

Balnabroich. (3). NO 092 566. 2 st st, N–S, on gravelly mound 50 by 18 ft (15 × 5.5 m). N (taller) 4 ft 2 (1.3 m) h, leans, S 2 ft 6 (75 cm) h, almost pros. 10 ft 4 (3.1 m) apart. *PSAS 42*, 1907–8, 96–8; Stewart, 1966, 142–3, no. 1.

*Balnaguard. (5). NN 947 522. 2 pros st + st st. E–W. W 7 ft and E 7 ft 7 (2.3, 2.5 m) l. E st has cm on E side. St st 24 ft (7.3 m) from P. 7 cms at base. In line with P. Just to

S, ruined Cn with crem, charcoal and food-vessel? sherd. *D & E*, 1971, 34–5.

Bandirran. (3). NO 208 311. 1 st st + 1 pros. E–W. E st st 6 ft (1.8 m) h, W st 6 ft 6 (2 m) l. 5 ft 11 (1.8 m) apart. Stewart, 1966, 142–3, no. 2; Coutts, 1970, 18.

*Broadmoss. (3). NO 198 475. 2 pros blocks approx. E–W. W is 11 ft 2 (3.4 m) l, E is broken in 3, 8 ft 9 (2.7 m) l. *PSAS 45*, 1908–9, 106–7; Stewart, 1966, 142–3, no. 3.

*Broughdarg. (5). NO 138 671. 2 st st 5 ft 9 (1.8 m) h. NE–SW but not alig. Prob a ruined 4-Poster. *PSAS 29*, 1894–5, 99; Stewart, 1966, 142–3, no. 4; Burl, 1988a, 189.

*Cally. (3). NO 118 519. 2 st st. NW–SE (taller). 4 ft and 4 ft 8 (1.2, 1.4 m) h. 13 ft 3 (4 m) apart. Broad + narrow. Stewart, 1966, 142–3, no. 5.

*Clach an Tuirc. (1). NN 725 448. 2 st, 3 ft (90 cm) h + boulder. 3 ft (1 m) apart. Both have cms. *D & E*, 1968, 33.

Comrie Bridge. (1). NN 787 468. 1 st st + 1 pros 20 ft (6 m) E of 4-Poster. NNW–SSE. NNW 3 ft (90 m) h. *PSAS 34*, 1900, 327–8; *ibid 44*, 1910, 136–8, no. 11; Burl, 1988, 157.

Craggish. (4). NN 76. 21. 3-st row + P. Coles, F.R., 1911, 56, no. 8.

Craigmakerran. (1). NO 148 328. 2 st st. NNW–SSE (taller). 4 ft 6 and 5 ft (1.4, 1.5 m) h. 17 ft (5.2 m) apart. NNW playing-card, SSE at RtLs. Stewart, 1966, 142–3, no. 8.

*Cramrar. (3). NN 723 451. 2 pros. NNE–SSW. c. 10 ft (3 m) apart. NNE has cms. 110 yds (100 m) to N is a 4-Poster with cms on the SE st. Coles, F.R. 1910, 126; *D & E*, 1967, 40; Burl, 1988a, 160–1.

Croft Moraig. (1). NN 797 473. [P1/19]. StC. 15 ft (4.6 m) outside at ESE 2 large st st. NNE (taller)–SSW. 7 ft 6 and 7 ft 2 (2.3, 2.2 m) h. 7 ft 4 (2.2 m) apart. Base of NNE st has been keeled. Poss grave-pits at SE foot of each st. Exc. 1965. *PSAS 23*, 1888–9, 356–67; Coles, F.R., 1910, 139–47; Stewart, 1966, 142–3, no. 9; *PPS 37*, 1971, 1–15; Thom, Thom & Burl, 1980, 348–9.

Astr: April SR. Thom, 1967, 100; 'outliers' mark equi and Feb SRs. Thom, Thom & Burl, 1990, II, 333.

Dalchirla. (1). NN 824 159. [P1/1. Muthill]. 2 st st. WSW (taller)–ENE. 7 ft 6 and 4 ft 3 (2.3, 1.3 m) h. 8 ft (2.4 m) apart. Both st smoothed. 200 yds (180 m) N is tall st st. Coles, F.R., 1911, 72, no. 19; Stewart, 1966, 142–3, no. 10.

Astr: Min N MR. Thom, 1967, 100; Thom, Thom & Burl, 1990, II, 321.

Dowally. (1). NO 001 480. 2 st st. [P2/17]. WNW (taller)– ESE. 8 ft 4 and 7 ft 4 (2.5 m, 2.2 m) h. Unusually tall for Perthshire. 9 ft (2.7 m) apart. Typically 'broad and narrow'. Smooth sides to N. Coles, 1908, 144–5, no. 29; Feachem, 84; Stewart, 1966, 142–3, no. 11.

Astr: There has been disagreement about the alignment. Coles, F.R., 1908, 144, said about 3°–183° 'or, practically, nearly north and south'. Feachem, 84, followed this. Stewart, 1966, 142, recorded an E–W disposition. Thom, 1967, 100, said the alignment was WNW–ESE, 286°.4–106°.4. Later this was slightly revised to: 288°– 108°, suggesting intermediate calendar dates. Thom, Thom & Burl, 1990, II, 339.

East Cult. (5). NO 072 420 – 073 422. [P2/7] 2 st st, E–W (taller) + 1 pros. 6 ft 11 and 9 ft (2.1, 2.7 m) h. 35 ft

(10.7 m) apart. 39 ft (11.9 m) to E a large pros st, split. Flat-topped, with 158 cms, 2 with grooves. 6 ft (1.8 m) off line. *PSAS 15*, 1880–1, 83–5, figs. 1–3; Coles, 1908, 148–52; Stewart, 1966, 142–3, no. 12.

Astr: Equi SS. Thom, Thom & Burl, 1990, II, 334–5.

Ferntower. (3). NN 874 226. 1 st st + 1 pros. NW–SE. St st 7 ft 9 (2.4 m) h, pros st 6 ft (1.8 m) l. 27 ft (8 m) to W is a 4-Poster. Coles, F.R., 1911, 75–9; Stewart, 1966, 142–3, no. 13; Burl, 1988, 165.

Fincastle. (3). NN 872 628. 1 st st + 1 pros. NW–SE. St st 3 ft 4 (1 m) h. 9 ft (2.7 m) apart. 'Broad and narrow'. Between stones is low slab on edge 1 ft 8 (50 cm) l. Stewart, 1966, 142–3, no. 14.

Fowlis Wester NW. 'Crofthead'. (1). NN 920 241. [P1/11]. 2 st st. E–W. Each 6 ft 6 (2 m) h. 11 ft 6 (3.5 m) l. 'Broad and narrow'. Coles, F.R., 1911, 87–8, no. 32; Stewart, 1966, 144–5, no. 16, 'Fowlis Wester II'; Thom, Thom & Burl, 1990, I, 104; II, 326.

Fowlis Wester SE. (3). NN 921 240. 2 pros st. 8 ft 9 and 11 ft 8 (2.7, 3.6 m) l. WSW–ENE. E st 6 cms on W edge, 1 nr SE corner. Coles, F.R., 1911, 84–7, no. 31; Stewart, 1966, 144–5, no. 15, 'Fowlis Wester I'.

Gellybanks. (1). NO 082 313. [P1/12]. 2 st st. NNW (taller)–SSE. 3 ft 7 and 3 ft 3 (1.1, 1 m) h. 6 ins (15 cm) apart. Coles, F.R., 1911, 107, no. 41; Stewart, 1966, 144–5, no. 17; Thom, Thom & Burl, 1990, II, 327.

*Grantully Vale. (4). NN 90. 52. 1 st st 4 ft 6 (1.4 m) h. Tradition says once a 2nd st close to it. Coles, F.R., 1908, 138, no. 25; Stewart, 1966, 144, note 1.

Guildtown, see: Craigmakkeran.

Keppoch. (4). NN 879 252. 1 pros + 1 stump. E–W?. 7 ft 10 (2.4 m) l and 4 ft 4 (1.3 m) h. 21 ft 10 (6.7 m) apart. Coles, F.R., 1911, 79–81, no. 27; Stewart, 1966, 144–5, no. 18.

*Kindrogan. 'Giant's Grave'. (5). NO 056 632. Long grassy mound. 19 ft (5.8 m) l, NNW–SSE. NNW end st st 5 ft 4 (1.6 m) h. Low rounded boulder at SSE end. Coles, F.R., 1908, 99–100, no. 3.

Meikleour. (3). NO 158 384. 2 pros st, 1 very broken. W, larger, 7 ft (2.1 m) l, E 6 ft 5 (2 m) l before breakage. Coles, F.R., 1909, 121–3, no. 21; Stewart, 1966, 144–5, no. 20.

New Tyle. (1). NO 047 410. [P2/12. Dunkeld]. 2 st st. NNW (taller)–SSE, 311°–131°. 7 ft 2 and 4 ft 9 (2.2, 1.4 m) h. 9 ft (2.7 m) apart. 18 ft 3 (5.6 m) l. At S foot of steep, wooded slope. Both broad and narrow. Both lean. NNW has tapering top, SSE is flat-topped. Coles, 1908, 146–8, figs. 46, 47; Stewart, 1966, 144–5, no. 21.

Astr: MdS SS. Thom, 1967, 100; MdS SS, Maj S MR? Thom, Thom & Burl, 1990, II, 338.

Pitcastle. (3). NN 895 543. 1 st st + 1 pros. E–W. (pros, larger). 4 ft 9, 8 ft 9 l (1.5, 2.7 m). 14 ft 6 (4.4 m) apart. Stewart, 1966, 144–5, no. 22.

Stare Dam. (1). NO 050 383. 2 st st. ENE–WSW (taller). 4 ft 3 and 4 ft 6 (1.3, 1.4 m) h but WSW much bigger, flattish top. ENE pointed top. 13 ft (4 m) apart. ENE st has cross carved on coarser E face. Coles, F.R., 1908, 152–4, no. 34; Stewart, 1966, 144–5, no. 24.

*Taymouth. (1). NN 801 477. 2 st st. E–W. 4 ft 9 (1.5 m) h. 53 ft 3 (16.3 m) apart. Inner faces smooth. Stewart, 1966, 144–5, no. 25.

Ross

*Windhill. 'Clach-an-t-Seasaidh'. (5). NH 531 482. 2 st st. 300 ft (90 m) apart. Poss remains of StC or 2 Clava cairns. 'They look more like monolithic monuments raised for some brilliant event'.

Legend, for three successive days a raven will drink from the top of one stone, which is full of the blood of the MacKenzies. *PSAS 17*, 1882–3, 416; *ibid 88*, 1954–6, 85, no. 58.

Roxburgh

Dere Street. (3). NT 750 155. [G8/5]. 2 st st. NE–SW (taller). 2 ft and 2 ft 6 (60, 76 cm) h. 20 ft (6 m) l. 40 ft (12 m) to NE is ruined kerbed Cn, Black Knowe, and 80 ft (24 m) beyond Cn is a st st 3 ft (90 cm) h. *RCAHM-S, Roxburgh*, 1956, 384, no. 812. Thom, Thom & Burl, 1990, I, 223.

Shetland

Beorgs of Housetter. 'Giant's Grave'. (1). HU 361 854. 2 st st of red granite. N–S. 6 ft 6 and 8 ft 10 (2, 2.7 m) h. 19 ft (5.8 m) apart. White granite Cn between. 295 ft (90 m) to N is the Fairy Mound ChT. Ritchie, A., 1985, 154. *RCAHM-S Orkney & Shetland, III*, 1946c, 93–4, no. 1360.

Busta Brae. (5). HU 348 673. Huge granite st st 10 ft 6 (3.2 m) h, c. 22 tons. 26 ft (7.9 m) to NE is smaller triangular block, 3 ft 5 (1 m) h. On cliff-top. A 'useful sailing mark'.

Legend, the Devil threw the big stone. Grinsell, 1976, 182; Feachem, 1977, 85. Fojut, 1981, 57; Ritchie, A., 1985, 154; *RCAHM-S, Orkney & Shetland, III*, 1946c, 10, no. 117.

Gravlaba. (3). HU 325 558. St st + 1 pros. 7 ft (2.1 m) h and l. E–W. 14 ft 6 (4.4 m) apart. *RCAHM-S, Orkney & Shetland, III*, 1946c, 103, no. 1403.

Skye

*Boreraig. (3). NG 62. 162. St st 3 ft 9 (1.2 m) h. Pros st nearby 4 ft 4 (1.3 m) l. *PSAS 46*, 1911–12, 205–6, fig. 5. *RCAHM-S, Outer Hebrides*, 1928, 214, no. 665.

Crois Mhic Jamain. (5). NG 345 345. 2 small mounds. A st st on each, SW is rect slab, 3 ft (1 m) h, NE 1 ft 7 (52 cm) h. 18 ft 6 (5.6 m) apart. *RCAHM-S, Outer Hebrides*, 1928, 81, no. 243.

Stirling

*Craigmore Cottage. (1). NS 529 799. St st 3 ft 2 (1 m) h. Local lava. Nearby is similar, pros. *D & E*, 1957, 36.

Waterhead. (1). NS 657 839. 2 st st. N (taller)–S. 7 ft 6 (2.3 m) h, leans. S 5 ft (1.5 m) h. Feachem, 1977, 86.

West Lothian

Kaimes. (4). NT 130 665. 2 st st, N–S. Each 4 ft (1.2 m) h. 6 ft (1.8 m) apart. 150 ft (46 m) E of well of hillfort on N terrace of lower ward. *RCAHM-S. Midlothian and West Lothian*, 1929, 162, no. 216.

Wigtownshire

Gillespie. 'Officer's Stone'. (5). NX 245 528. Large, erect round boulder, 4 ft 10 (1.5 m) h. *RCHAM-S, Galloway I*, 1912, 126, no. 365. In 1898 reputedly there were 2 st st. but 'no notes made'. *PSAS 33*, 1898–9, 183.

*Laggangarn. (5). NX 222 717. [G3/3]. 2 st st 6 ft 3 and 5 ft 3 (1.9, 1.6 m) h. Both have Christian crosses carved on W face. Tradition says once 13 st. StC orig? An outlier of the 2 st is claimed to be grave of farmer who removed some stones. *TDGNHAS 52*, 1977, 41; Ruggles & Whittle, 1981, 208; Grinsell, 1976, 240.

Astr: MdS SS. Thom, Thom & Burl, 1990, I, 204.

Milton Hall. (1). NX 362 415. 2 st st. Both 6 ft 6 (2 m) h. 7 ft (2 m+) apart. *RCAHM-S Galloway I*, 1912, 12; *TDGNHAS 52*, 1977, 41.

Astr: MdW SS. Thom, 1967, 98. Misleadingly conflated with Wren's Egg: Thom, 1967, 137, G3/13.

Wren's Egg. (1). NX 361 420. [G3/13]. 2 granite boulders. ENE (taller)–WSW. 4 ft 7 and 4 ft 1 (1.4, tapering top, 1.3 m, flat-topped) h. 11 ft 6 (3.5 m) l. 56 ft (17 m) to W is the large erratic boulder known as the Wren's Egg. 440 yds (400 m) SSE is the Milton Hill P. *D & E*, 1975, 55; *TDGNHAS 52*, 1977, 28–43; Stell, 1986, 167.

Astr: Equi SS. Thom, Thom & Burl, 1980, 370–1.

WALES

CLWYD

Grey Stones. (3). SJ 27. 62. St st + 1 pros. St st = lozenge shaped, 6 ft (1.8 m) h. *RCAHM-W, Flintshire*, 1912, 59–60, no. 175; *Arch Camb III*, 5, 1859, 75.

Naid-y-March. 'The Horse's Leap'. (1). SJ 167 753. SE–NW. 2 st st. 4 ft and 2 ft 3 (1.2, 0.7 m) h. 24 ft 7 (7.5 m) apart. *RCAHM-W, Flintshire*, 1912, 5, no. 17; Dyer, 1981, 327.

Whitford. (4). SJ 152 766. 2 st st removed when Gorsedd church built in 1852. Used as gateposts. One 4 ft (1.2 m) h, on rt of road from Druid's Inn to Babell. Other, 5 ft 6 (1.7 m) h, behind Gorsedd vicarage. *RCAHM-W, Flintshire*, 1912, 94, no. 270.

DYFED

Abergwili. (1). SN 453 215. 450 ft (137 m) NE of Carreg Fyrddin (Merlin's Stone), a st st 5 ft (1.5 m) h, are 2 st st, each 4 ft (1.2 m) h. 50 ft (15 m) apart. 19th century treasure-seeker killed when st fell on him. *RCAHM-W, Carmarthen*, 1917, 7, no. 8; Barber & Williams, 107, no. 23.

Berribrook. 'Meini hirion'. (3). SN 71. 38. 2 st st, one 6 ft 6 (2 m) h. Now a gatepost. *RCAHM-W, Carmarthen*, 1917, 16, no. 77.

Cae garreg fawr. 'Field of the big stone'. (3). SN 413 084. St st, pointed top, 7 ft 2 (2.2 m) h. Once 2 st st here, both pointed. *RCAHM-W, Carmarthen*, 1917, 45, no. 146; Barber & Williams, 111, no. 51.

Carreg fawr nant jack. 'Great stone by the brook'. (1). SN 35. 10. St st, red sandstone, 5 ft 6 (1.7 m) h. 15 ft (4.6 m) to E a st st, grey grit, 1 ft (30 cm) h. Covered by high tide. *RCAHM-W, Carmarthen*, 1917, 192, no. 569.

Cilmaenllwyd. (1). SN 152 252. 2 st, each 6 ft (1.8 m) h. In Parc y maen. *Arch Camb*, 1974, 41; Barber & Williams, 108, no. 35.

Cwm Garw. (Carmarthen). 'The rough valley'. Cerrig Meibion Arthur, 'the stones of the sons of Arthur'. (1). SN 118 310. [W9/3]. 2 st st. WSW–ENE (taller). 7 ft and 8 ft 6 (2.1, 2.6 m) h. 25 ft (7.6 m) apart.

Legend, a monument to Arthur's sons killed by a wild boar. Grinsell, 1976, 249; Barber, C., 1982, 9.

Dolau Main. (Pembroke). 'Stone meadow'. (1). SN 158 313. [W9/8]. 2 st st each 7 ft 6 (2.3 m) h. 23 ft (7 m) apart.

NNE–SSW. On line of Glyn Saithmean, 'valley of seven stones', between Foel-drych and Carnmenyn. Thom, Thom & Burl 1989; Barber & Williams, 124, no. 124, 'Waun llwyd'.

Ffynnon Newydd. 'New well'. (1). SN 49. 21. 2 st st 6 ft and 4 ft 6 (1.8, 1.4 m) h. 9 ft (2.7 m) apart. *RCAHM-W, Carmarthen*, 1917, 116, no. 335.

Gors Fawr. 'The great marsh'. (1). SN 134 294. [W9/2]. StC + 2 st st. 440 ft (134 m) NE of StC pair of st st. NE–SW (taller). 5 ft 7 and 6 ft 2 (1.7, 1.9 m) h. 48 ft (14.6 m) apart. *RCAHM-W, Pembroke*, 1925, no. 731; Grimes, 1963, 145–6, no. 32; Thom, Thom & Burl, 1980. 286–7.

Astr: (1) Arcturus rising, 1420 BC (c. 1130 bc). *Arch Camb 11*, 1911, 318–20. (2) MdS SR. Thom, 1967, 101; From StC to between the st st, Nov and Jan SR, Thom, Thom & Burl, 1990, II, 358–9.

Gors, Llangynog, (Carmarthen). (4). SN 312 140. Pros st, once a pair. 5 ft 11 (1.8 m) l. Limestone. Exc. 1985. 39 ft (12 m) to SE were 17 clay-filled pits, rectangle of cobbles. p/hs? and stakeholes. Charcoal = C-14, 1340±70 bc (CAR-957). c. 1650 BC. *Archaeology in Wales 25*, 1985, 19; Williams, G., 1988, 72.

Parc y maen llyd. 'Field of the grey stone'. 'Quoit Stone'. (1). SN 385 163. 2 st st separated by a narrow lane. *RCAHM-W, Carmarthen*, 1917, 149, no. 441.

*Penparke. SN 091 358. (1). 2 st st, each 5 ft (1.5 m) h. 15 ft (4.6 m) apart. N–S. Barber & Williams, 125, no. 128.

Rhos-y-Clegyrn. (Pembroke). (4). SM 913 354. St st 9 ft (2.7 m) h. Stonehole of 2nd 35 ft (10.7 m) away. SW–NE (hole). Exc 1962, 1965–8. Between possible embanked StC to SW and a smaller ring to NE. On earlier settlement site. Assoc with the st st were pits, food-vessel sherds, stakeholes. Crem. Broken slate disc. Perforated pestle-shaped axe-hammer from ring. *Arch Camb 123*, 1974, 13–42; *ibid 125*, 1976, 162; Grimes, 1963, 150–1; Lewis, J.M., 1974; 1976; Williams, G., 1988, 89–91.

*Yr Allor. SN 142 336. See Three-Stone Gazetteer.

GLAMORGAN

Cae'r-hen-Eglwys, Laleston. 'The old church'. (1). SS 879 809. 2 st st, each 6 ft (1.8 m) h. 20 ft (6 m) apart. Barber & Williams, 161–2, no. 283.

GWYNEDD

Bryn seward meini hirion. 'Seward Hill standing stones', Llanbedr. (5). SH 583 270. [W5/3. 'Meini Hirion']. N–S. 2 st st, N, 'Maen hir', 7 ft 3, tapers, and S, 5 ft 4 (2.2 m, 1.6 m) h. Both probably moved to present position in iron railings. Perhaps a 3rd st, 3 ft (1 m) h. At beginning of mountain trackway. *RCAHM-W, Merioneth*, 1921, 90, no. 250; Bowen & Gresham, 62, 65, nos. 80, 81; Houlder, 101; Barber & Williams, 143, no. 202, 'Llanbedr'; Thom, Thom & Burl, II, 1990, 356.

Bryn-y-chain, Llanllyfni. (1). SH 468 494. 2 st st, N–S, 8 ft (2.4 m) h. 6 ft (1.8 m) apart. Re-used as gateposts, E side A487. Modern 3rd added as gatepost for adj field. Pers. obs.

Bwlch y ddeufaen. 'The pass of the two stones'. SH 715 717. 2 st st. 1 = 10 ft (3 m) h. 270 ft (82 m) to NW is 2nd, 6 ft (1.8 m) h. Near it are 2 low st st. *RCAHM-W, Caernarvon, I*, 1956, 36, no. 173.

Caerhun. SH 742 718. (1). 2 st st in line with Maen-y-Bard ChT. Taller is 4 ft (1.2 m) h. 54 ft (17 m) to W, in wall is 2nd st, 3 ft (0.9 m) h. *RCAHM-W, Caernarvon, I*, 1956, 36, no. 174; Houlder, 61.

Llyn Creigenen Issa Stones. (1). SH 601 103. 2 st st 6 ft 6 and 1 ft 6 (2, 0.5 m) h. *RCAHM-W, Merioneth*, 1921, 126, no. 408; Bowen & Gresham, 65, nos. 72–3.

Tir-gwyn. 'The white house'. (1). SH 344 390. 2 st st. N–S. S, 8 ft 6 (2.6 m) h. 190 yds (174 m) to N, 2nd st, 7 ft 3 (2.2 m) h. Exc. c. 1833. Prehistoric? Grave between. Bones of large man. *RCAHM-W, Caernarvon, II*, 1960, 83, nos. 1675, 1676.

POWYS

Cwm y Saeson Stones. 'Englishman's valley'. (3). SN 953 771. 1 st st + 1 pros. 5 ft 10 (1.8 m) h. 7 ft 1 (2.2 m) l. 1 mile (1.6 km) to E a huge st st, 8 ft 2 (2.5 m) h, reputedly the survivor of 5, 2 large, 2 small, 'arranged quadrangularly', a possible 4-Poster. *RCAHM-W, Radnor*, 1913, 142, no. 586; Burl, 1988, 203. Once an adj row of inscribed st st? Barber & Williams, 176, no. 346. 'St Harmons'.

Garreg wen. 'Y fuwch wen a'r llo', 'the white cow and calf'. (1). SN 82. 88. 2 white stones, 6 ft and 4 ft (1.8, 1.2 m) h. *RCAHM-W, Montgomery*, 1911, 115, no. 592.

Kinnerton. SO 246 627. (1). 2 st st, each 2 ft 6 (75 cm) h. 30 ft (9 m) apart. Barber & Williams, 168, no. 311.

Pennybont. SO 11. 54. (4). St st 6 ft (1.8 m) h + 1 pros c.

1818. 'A large stone, placed erect, seven feet broad, two foot thick. About two or three yards from this stone is another of nearby equal proportions, lying flat upon the ground'. *RCAHM-W, Radnor*, 1913, 49, no. 187.

Rhos dyrnog. 'Cae yr hen eglwys', 'old church field'. (4). SH 829 005. St st, mountain grit, 6 ft (1.8 m) h. Were once 2 st st here. Field was called 'cae meini llwydion', 'field of the grey stones'. St st is known as 'carreg noddfa', 'the sanctuary stone'. *Arch Camb III, 2*, 1856, 193; *RCAHM-W, Montgomery*, 1911, 31, no. 158.

YNYS MONA (ANGLESEY)

*Llanrhwydrys. (1). SH 334 906. 2 st st. Schist. N (taller)–S. 12 ft 3 and 8 ft 3 (3.7, 2.5 m) h. 380 yds (348 m) apart. Orig a huge equilateral triangle. E st, 11 ft (3.4 m) h, gone, Baynes, 66; *RCAHM-Anglesey*, 1937, 109a, nos. 3, 4; Lynch, F., 1991, 324.

*Maen y Gored. (3). SH 341 832. St st 8 ft 6 (2.6 m) h. Broken. In metal straps. Leans, 45°. 11 ft (3.4 m) away, st almost buried. P? Baynes, 73; RCAHM-Anglesey, 1937, 114b, no. 3.

Plas Meilw. 'Penrhos-feilw'. (1). SH 227 809. 2 st st. NNE–SSW, 28°–208°. Both, tall, thin, 10 ft (3 m) h. 10 ft 10 (3.3 m) apart. Reputedly, a Ct with bones, a spearhead and arrowheads once lay between stones. *RCAHM-W, Anglesey*, 1937, 23; Lynch, F., 1991, 152; *Arch J 24*, 1867, 238; *ibid 26*, 1869, 310; Anthony, 17; Dyer, 1981, 319; Williams, G., 1988, 84.

BIBLIOGRAPHICAL ABBREVIATIONS

Ant	*Antiquity*
Ant J	*Antiquaries Journal*
Arch	*Archaeologia*
Arch Camb	*Archaeologia Cambrensis*
Arch Ire	*Archaeology Ireland*
Arch J	*Archaeological Journal*
Arch Scot	*Archaeologia Scotica*
Archs Inst Hist Sci	*Archives Internationales d'Histoire des Sciences*
Caithness FC	*Caithness Field Club*
Curr Arch	*Current Archaeology*
D & E	*Discovery and Excavation, Scotland*
GAJ	*Glasgow Archaeological Journal*
Gents Mag	*Gentleman's Magazine*
J Anthr Inst	*Journal of the Anthropological Institute*
JBAA	*Journal of the British Archaeological Association*
J B Astr Ass	*Journal of the British Astronomical Association*
JCHAS	*Journal of the Cork Historical & Archaeological Society*
JGHAS	*Journal of the Galway Historical & Archaeological Society*
JHA	*Journal for the History of Astronomy*
JIA	*Journal of Irish Archaeology*
JKAS	*Journal of the Kerry Archaeological Society*
J Inst Navig	*Journal of the Institute of Navigation*
JRAI	*Journal of the Royal Archaeological Institute*
JRSAI	*Journal of the Royal Society of Antiquaries of Ireland*
JRSS	*Journal of the Royal Statistical Society*
Kergal	*Association Archaéologique Kergal, Fontenay-le-Fleury*
Meyn Mamvro	*Magazine of ancient stones and sacred sites in Cornwall, St Just*
Math Gaz	*Mathematical Gazette*
New Sci	*New Scientist*
PDAS	*Proceedings of the Devon Archaeological Society*
PDNHAS	*Proceedings of the Dorset Natural History & Archaeological Society*
PPS	*Proceedings of the Prehistoric Society*
PRIA	*Proceedings of the Royal Irish Academy*
PSAS	*Proceedings of the Society of Antiquaries of Scotland*
PSomANHS	*Proceedings of the Somerset Archaeological and Natural History Society*
Phil Trans Roy Soc	*Philosophical Transactions of the Royal Society*
RCAHM-E	*Royal Commission for Ancient and Historic Monuments, England*
RCAHM-S	*ibid, Scotland*
RCAHM-W	*ibid, Wales*
SAF	*Scottish Archaeological Forum*
SAR	*Scottish Archaeological Review*
TAMS	*Transactions of the Ancient Monuments Society*
TCWAAS	*Transactions of the Cumberland & Westmorland Antiquarian & Archaeological Society*
TDA	*Transactions of the Devonshire Association*
TDGNHAS	*Transactions of the Dumfriess & Galloway Natural History & Archaeological Society*
TGAS	*Transactions of the Glasgow Archaeological Society*
T Inv Sci Soc	*Transactions of the Inverness Scientific Society*
UBSS	*University of Bristol Spelaeological Society*
UJA	*Ulster Journal of Archaeology*
WAM	*Wiltshire Archaeological Magazine*
YAJ	*Yorkshire Archaeological Journal*

BIBLIOGRAPHY

ABM (n.d.). *Antiquities of the Boggeragh Mountains*. Cork.

ABRI (1990). *La Bretagne des Megalithes. Promenades en Morbihan*. Paris.

ALDRIDGE, MAJOR R.B. (1964–5). 'Some megalithic and other sites in Counties Mayo and Sligo', *JGAHS 31*, 11–15.

ALLCROFT, A.H. (1927). *The Circle and the Cross. I. The Circle*. London.

ALLEN, H.R. (1882). 'Notes on some undescribed stones with cup-markings in Scotland', *PSAS 16*, 1881–2, 79–143.

AMP (n.d.). *Antiquities of the Mizen Peninsula*. Cork.

ANDERSON, J. (1868). 'On the horned cairns of Caithness', *PSAS 7*, (1866–8), 480–512.

—— (1886). *Scotland in Pagan Times. The Bronze and Stone Ages*. Edinburgh.

ANTHONY, I. (1973). *Discovering Regional Archaeology. Wales*. Princes Risborough.

ATKINSON, R.J.C. (1979). *Stonehenge*. Revised ed. Harmondsworth.

AUBREY J. (1665–93). *Monumenta Britannica I. Parts I and II. 1–600*. Milborne Port, 1980.

—— *ibid II. Part III. 601–1143*. Milborne Port, 1982.

BALDWIN, J.R. (1985). *Exploring Scotland's Heritage. Lothian and the Borders*. Edinburgh.

BARBER, C. (1982). *Mysterious Wales*. London.

—— (1986). *More Mysterious Wales*. Newton Abbot.

—— and WILLIAMS, J.G. (1989). *The Ancient Stones of Wales*. Abergavenny.

BARBER, J. (1972). 'The stone circles of Counties Cork and Kerry, I, II'. Unpubl. MA thesis. University College, Cork.

BARING-GOULD, S. (1907). *A Book of Dartmoor*. 2nd ed. London.

BARNATT, J. (1982). *Prehistoric Cornwall. The Ceremonial Monuments*. Wellingborough.

—— (1989). *Stone Circles of Britain, I, II*. Oxford.

BATT, M., GIOT, P.-R., LECERF, Y., LECORNEC, J. and LE ROUX, C. (1980). *Mégalithes au Pays de Carnac*. Châteaulin.

BAYNES, E.N. (1912). 'The megalithic remains of Anglesey', *Trans Hon. Soc. Cymmrodorion*, 1910–11. 3–91.

BEAU, LE, B. (1894). *Catalogue du Musée J. Miln à Carnac (Morbihan)*. Vannes.

BECKINSALL, S. (1983). *Northumberland's Prehistoric Rock Carvings. A Mystery Explained*. Rothbury.

BÉNARD, C., see: Pontois, le. 'Usurpation de patronyme'.

BENDER, B. (1986). *The Archaeology of Brittany, Normandy and the Channel Islands*. London.

BERNET, D. (1984). *Guide de la France Avant la France*. Paris.

BEVERIDGE, E. (1911). *North Uist. Archaeology and Topography*. Edinburgh.

BÉZIER, P. (1883). *Inventaire des Monuments Mégalithiques du Département d'Ille-et-Vilaine*. Rennes.

Bodmin Survey. Cornwall Committee for Rescue Archaeology, Truro.

BORD, J. and C. (1974). *Mysterious Britain*. St Albans.

—— (1987). *Ancient Mysteries of Britain*. London.

BORLASE, W. (1769). *Antiquities, Historical and Monumental of the County of Cornwall*. London.

BORLASE, W.C. (1872). *Naenia Cornubiae*. Truro.

—— (1897). *The Dolmens of Ireland, I–III*. London.

BOWEN, E.G. and GRESHAM, C.A. (1967). *History of Merioneth, I*. Dolgellau.

BRADLEY, R. (1993). *Altering the Earth*. Society of Antiquaries of Scotland. Monograph Series No. 8.

BRAILSFORD, J.W. (1938). 'Bronze Age stone monuments of Dartmoor', *Ant 12*, 444–63.

BRIARD, J. (1987). *Mégalithes de Bretagne*. Rennes.

—— (1989). *Mégalithes de Haute Bretagne*, Paris.

—— (1990). *Dolmens et Menhirs*. Brittany.

BRYCE, T.H. (1910). 'The sepulchral remains', in: (ed. Balfour, J.A.). *The Book of Arran. Archaeology*. Glasgow. 33–155.

BUCKLEY, V.M. (1986). *Archaeological Inventory of Co. Louth*. Dublin.

BURGESS, C. (1980). *The Age of Stonehenge*. London.

BURL, A. (1976). *The Stone Circles of the British Isles*. New Haven and London.

—— (1979). *Prehistoric Avebury*. New Haven and London.

—— (1980). see: Thom, Thom and Burl.

—— (1981). *Rites of the Gods*. London.

—— (1983). *Prehistoric Astronomy and Ritual*. Princes Risborough.

—— (1985). *Megalithic Brittany: a Guide*. London.

—— (1987a). *The Stonehenge People*. London.

—— (1987b). 'The sun, the moon, and megaliths', *UJA 50*, 7–21.

—— (1988a). *Four-Posters. Bronze Age Stone Circles of Western Europe*. BAR British Series 195, Oxford.

—— (1988b). 'Without sharp north ... Alexander Thom and the great stone circles of Cumbria', in: (ed: Ruggles, C.L.N., 1988), 175–205.

—— (1988c). 'Coves: structural enigmas of the Neolithic', *WAM 82*, 1–18.

—— (1990). see: Thom, Thom and Burl.

—— (1991). 'The Devil's Arrows, Boroughbridge, North Yorkshire. The archaeology of a stone row', *YAJ 63*, 1–24.

—— (1992). 'Two early plans of Avebury', *WAM 85*, 163–72.

CAMDEN, W. (1610). *Britain. . . .* (trans. Holland, P.). London.

—— (1695). *Britannia*. (ed: Gibson, E.). London.

CHANTER, REV. J.F. and WORTH, R.H. (1905). 'The rude stone monuments of Exmoor and its borders. Part I', *TDA*

37, 375–97.

—— ibid, Part II, *TDA 38*, 1906, 538–52.

CHART, D.A., EVANS, E.E. and LAWLOR, H.C. (eds). (1940). *A Preliminary Survey of the Ancient Monuments of Northern Ireland.* London.

CHATELLIER, P. DU. (1889). *Les Époques Préhistoriques et Gauloises dans le Finistère. Inventaire des Monuments de ce Département.* Quimper.

CHÉNELIÈRE, G. DE LA. (1880). *Inventaire des Monuments Mégalithiques compris dans le Département des Côtes-du-Nord.* St-Brieuc.

CHILDE, V.G. (1935). *The Prehistory of Scotland.* London.

CHURCHER, I. (1985). 'A survey of stone circles in southern Leinster'. Unpubl. BA dissertation, University of Durham.

CLARE, T. (1978). 'Recent work on the Shap "Avenue"', *TCWAAS 78*, 5–15.

CLARKE, D. (1970). *The Beaker Pottery of Great Britain and Ireland, I, II.* Cambridge.

CLES-REDEN, S. VON. (1961). *The Realm of the Great Goddess.* London.

CLOSE-BROOKS, J. (1986). *Exploring Scotland's Heritage. The Highlands.* Edinburgh.

COLES, F.R. (1908). 'Report on stone circles surveyed in Perthshire – North-eastern Section', *PSAS 42*, 1907–8, 95–162.

—— (1909). 'Ibid. South-east district', *PSAS 43*, 1908–9, 93–130.

—— (1910). 'Ibid. Aberfeldy district', *PSAS 44*, 1909–10, 117–68.

—— (1911). 'Ibid. Principally Strathearn', *PSAS 45*, 1910–11, 46–116.

COLLINS, A.E.P. (1957). 'Excavations of two standing stones in Co. Down', *UJA 20*, 37–42.

CONLON, J.P. (1916). 'Rude stone monuments of the northern portion of Cork County', *JRSAI 46*, 58–76, 136–62.

—— (1917). 'ibid', *JRSAI 47*, 153–64.

—— (1918a). 'ibid', *JRSAI 48*, 121–39.

—— (1918b). 'Cape Clear island', *JCHAS 24*, 53–6.

CORNEY, W.J. (1967). 'A real stone row on Exmoor', *Exmoor Review 8*, 48–9.

COUTTS, H. (1970). *Ancient Monuments of Tayside.* Dundee.

CRONE, A. (1983). 'The Clochmabanestane, Gretna', *TDGNHAS 58*, 16–20.

CROSSING, W. (1912). *Guide to Dartmoor.* 1965 edition. Newton Abbot.

CUPPAGE, J. (1986). ed. *Archaeological Survey of the Dingle Peninsula.* Ballyferriter.

DANIEL, G. (1955). *Lascaux and Carnac.* London.

—— (1963). *The Hungry Archaeologist in France.* London.

DARVILL, T. (1987). *Prehistoric Britain* London.

DAVIES, O. (1939). 'Stone circles in Northern Ireland', *UJA 2 (1)*, 2–14.

DAVIS, A. (1986). 'The metrology of stone rows: a reassessment', *GAJ 13*, 44–53.

DE: see under full surname. e.g. LAET, DE.

DEVEREUX, P. and THOMSON, I. (1979). *The Ley Hunter's Companion.* London.

DEVOIR, A. (1911). 'Les grands ensembles mégalithiques de la presqu'île de Crozon et leur destination originelle', *Bull. de la Archéologique Finistère 38*, 3–38.

—— (1912). 'Témoins mégalithiques des variations des lignes des rivages armoricains', *Bull. Soc. Arch. Finistère 39*, 220–39.

DOBSON, D.P. (1931). *The Archaeology of Somerset.* London.

DRYDEN, SIR H. (1872). 'Letter to the editor of the "John o' Groat's Journal"', in: Fergusson (1872). 529–32.

DYER, J. (1981). *The Penguin Guide to Prehistoric England and Wales.* London.

DYMOND, C.W. (1880). 'A group of Cumberland megaliths', *TCWAAS 5 (O.S.)*, 1879–80, 39–57.

—— (1896). *The Ancient Remains at Stanton Drew in the County of Somerset.* Bristol.

EARDLEY-WILMOT, H. (1983). *Ancient Exmoor.* Dulverton.

ECROYD-SMITH, H. (1852). *Reliquae Isurianae. Remains of the Roman Isurium (now Aldborough near Boroughbridge, Yorkshire).* London.

EKWALL, E. (1959). *The Concise Oxford Dictionary of English Place-Names.* 4th edition. Oxford.

ELGEE, F. (1930). *Early Man in North-East Yorkshire.* Gloucester.

—— and H.W. (1933). *The Archaeology of Yorkshire.* London.

EMMETT, D.D. (1979). 'Stone rows: the traditional view reconsidered', in: Maxfield, V.A. (ed).

EOGAN, G. (1964). 'The excavation of a stone alignment and circle at Cholwichtown, Lee Moor, Devonshire, England', *PPS 30*, 25–38.

EUDES, O. (1981). *Dolmens et Menhirs de Bretagne.* Paris,

EVANS, E.E. (1966). *Prehistoric and Early Christian Ireland.* London.

FEACHEM, R. (1977). *Guide to Prehistoric Scotland.* 2nd edition. London.

FERGUSSON, J. (1872). *Rude Stone Monuments of All Countries.* London.

FLEMING, A. (1988). *The Dartmoor Reaves.* London.

FOJUT, N. (1981). *A Guide to Prehistoric Shetland.* Lerwick.

FORDE, C.D. (1927). 'The megalithic monuments of southern Finistère', *Ant J 7*, 6–37.

FOX, LADY A. (1973). *South-West England.* Revised edition. Newton Abbot.

FREER, R. and MYATT, L.J. (1982). 'The multiple stone rows of Caithness and Sutherland, 2. Their description, 1', *Caithness F.C. Bull. 3 (3)*, 58–63.

—— (1983). 'ibid. Their description, 2', *Caithness F.C. Bull. 3 (5)*, 120–6.

GAILLARD, F. (1892). *Inventaire des Monuments Mégalithiques du Morbihan.* Paris.

GENESTE, J.-M., SOTO, J.G. DE, JOUSSAUME, R., and RIGAUD, J.-P. (1989). *Les Hauts Lieux de la Préhistoire en France.* Paris.

GIBBONS, M. and HIGGINS, J. (1988). 'Connemara's emerging prehistory', *Arch Ire 2*, 63–6.

GILBERT, M. (1962). *Pierres Mégalithiques dans le Maine et Cromlechs en France.* Guernsey.

—— (1964). *Menhirs et Dolmens dans le Nord-Est de la Bretagne.* Guernsey.

GIOT, P.-R. (1960). *Brittany*. London.

—— (1983). *Les Alignements de Carnac*. Rennes.

—— (1988a). 'Stones in the landscape of Brittany', in: (ed. Ruggles, C.L.N. 1988a). 319–24.

—— (1988b). *Préhistoire en Bretagne*. Chateaulin.

—— l'HELGOUACH, J., and MONNIER, J. P. (1979). *Préhistoire de la Bretagne*. Rennes.

GOGAN, L.S. (1931). 'A small stone circle at Muisire Beag', *JCHAS 36*, 9–19.

GOSLING, P. (1991). ed. *Archaeological Inventory of County Galway: I*.

GRAVES, R. (1961). *The White Goddess*. London.

GRIFFITHS, W.E. (1960). 'The excavation of stone circles near Penmaenmawr, North Wales', *PPS 26*, 303–39.

GRIMES, W.F. (1963). 'The stone circles and related monuments of Wales', in: (eds. Foster, I. Ll. and Alcock, L.). *Culture and Environment. Essays in Honour of Sir Cyril Fox*, London. 93–152.

GRINSELL, L.V. (1970). *The Archaeology of Exmoor*. Newton Abbot.

—— (1976). *Folklore of Prehistoric Sites in Britain*. Newton Abbot.

—— (1978). 'Dartmoor Barrows', *PDAS 36*, 85–180.

GUÈRIN, DE, T.W.M. (1921). 'List of dolmens, menhirs and sacred rocks', *Report. Trans. Soc. Guernesiais*, 30–64.

GUNN, G. (1915). 'The standing stones of Caithness', *Trans. Inverness Sci Soc 7*, 337–60.

HAMOND, F.W. (1979). 'Settlement, economy and environment on prehistoric Dartmoor', in: Maxfield, V.A. (ed). 146–75.

HARBISON, P. (1970). *Guide to the National Monuments in the Republic of Ireland*. Dublin.

—— (1988). *Pre-Christian Ireland*. London.

—— (1992). *Guide to National and Historic Monuments of Ireland*, Dublin.

—— see also: Killanin and Duignan (1989).

HARDING, A. with Lee, G. (1987). *Henge Monuments and Related Sites of Great Britain*. Oxford.

HARRISON, R.J. (1980). *The Beaker Folk. Copper Age Archaeology in Western Europe*. London.

HAWKINS, G.S. (1966). *Stonehenge Decoded*. London.

—— (1977). *Beyond Stonehenge*. London.

—— (1989). see: Petrie and Hawkins, 1989.

HEGGIE, D.C. (1981). *Megalithic Science. Ancient Mathematics and Astronomy in Northwest Europe*. London.

—— (1982). (ed). *Archaeoastronomy in the Old World*. Cambridge.

HELGOUAC'H, J. L'. (1984). 'Les temps préhistoriques', in: (ed. Abbad F.). *La Loire-Atlantique. Des Origines à Nos Jours*. St-Jean-d'Angély, 25–60.

HENSHALL, A.S. (1963). *The Chambered Tombs of Scotland, I*. Edinburgh.

—— (1972). *ibid, II*. Edinburgh.

HERITY, M. and EOGAN, G. (1977). *Ireland in Prehistory*. London.

HIBBS, J. (1984). 'The Neolithic of Brittany and Normandy', in: (ed. Scarre, C.). *Ancient France*. Edinburgh. 271–323.

HODDER, I. (1990). *The Domestication of Europe*. London.

HOULDER, C. (1974). *Wales. An Archaeological Guide*. London.

—— and Manning, W.H. (1966). *South Wales*. London.

HUTCHINSON, W. (1794). *The History and Antiquities of Cumberland, I, II*. Carlisle.

HUTTON, R. (1991). *The Pagan Religions of the Ancient British Isles*. London.

JOHNSTON, D.E. (1981). *The Channel Islands. An Archaeological Guide*. Chichester.

JOPE, E.M. (1966). ed. *An Archaeological Survey of Co. Down*. Belfast.

JOYCE, P.W. (1984). *Pocket Guide to Irish Place Names*. Belfast.

KEILLER, A. and PIGGOTT, S. (1936). 'The West Kennet avenue: excavations, 1934–5', *Ant 10*, 417–27.

KENDRICK, T.D. (1928). *The Archaeology of the Channel Islands. I. The Bailiwick of Guernsey*. London.

KERGAL. (1978). *Essai Géographie Mégalithique, II*. Fontenay-le-Fleury.

—— (1979). *La Tradition Mégalithique en Armorique*. Fontenay-le-Fleury.

—— (1980a). *À Travers Carnac d'Avant l'Histoire*. Fontenay-le-Fleury.

—— (1980b). *Aspects du Mégalithisme Atlantique*. Fontenay-le-Fleury.

—— (1980c). *Les Mégalithes de la Presqu'Île de Quiberon*. Fontenay-le-Fleury.

—— (1981). *Locmariaquer: Aperçu de la Pensée Mégalithique dans le Golfe du Morbihan*. Fontenay-le-Fleury.

KERMODE, P.M.C. and HERDMAN, W.A. (1914). *Manks Antiquities*. Liverpool.

KILLANIN, LORD, and DUIGNAN, M.V. (1962). *Shell Guide to Ireland*. London.

—— (1989). *Ibid*. Revised and updated by P. Harbison. Dublin.

KINNES, I. and GRANT, J.A. (1983). *Les Fouillages and the Megalithic Monuments of Guernsey*. Alderney.

KINNES, I. and HIBBS, J. (1988). *The Dolmens of Jersey*. Jersey.

L', LA, LE: see under full surname. e.g HELGOUAC'H, J. L'.

LACY, B. (1983). *Archaeological Survey of Co. Donegal*. Lifford.

LAET, S.J. DE (1958). *The Low Countries*. London.

LAMBRICK, G. (1988). *The Rollright Stones. Megaliths, Monuments and Settlement in the Prehistoric Landscape*. London.

LEASK, H.G. (1937). 'The Long Stone, Punchestown, Co. Kildare', *JRSAI 67*, 250–2.

LELAND, J. (1553–6). *The Itinerary of John Leland, the Antiquary, I–IX*. (ed. Hearne, T.). 3rd edition. Oxford, 1770.

LEWIS, A.L. (1878). 'The "Devil's Arrows", Yorkshire', *J. Anthr. Inst. 8*, 180–3.

—— (1905). 'Prehistoric remains in Cornwall, II', *JRAI 35*, 427–34.

LEWIS, J.M. (1966). 'The standing stones of Pembrokeshire', *Pembrokeshire Historian 2*, 7–18.

—— (1974). 'Excavations at Rhos-y-Clegyrn prehistoric site, St Nicholas. Pembs', *Arch Camb 123*, 13–42.

—— (1976). 'A modern C-14 date from Rhos-y-Clegyrn',

Arch Camb 125, 162.

Livret-Guide de l'Excursion à 3. Bretagne. (1976). Union Internationale des Sciences Préhistoriques et Protohistoriques. Paris.

LOCKYER, SIR N. (1909). *Stonehenge and Other British Stone Monuments Astronomically Considered*. 2nd edition. London.

LONGWORTH, I.H. (1984). *Collared Urns of the Bronze Age in Great Britain and Ireland*. Cambridge.

LUKIS, REV. W.C. (1870). *The Stone Avenues of Carnac*. Salisbury. [see also: *WAM 13*, 1872, 78–91].

—— (1875). *Guide to the Chambered Barrows etc of South Brittany*. Ripon.

—— (1878). 'The Devil's Arrows', *PSAL 7*, 134–8.

—— (1882). *The Family Memoirs of the Rev. William Stukeley, MD, and the Antiquarian and Other Correspondence of William Stukeley, Roger and Samuel Gale etc. I*. Surtees Society 73, 1880. Durham, London and Edinburgh.

—— (1883). *ibid, II*, Surtees Society 76, 1881.

—— (1885). *The Prehistoric Stone Monuments of the British Isles. Cornwall*. London.

—— (1887). *The Family Memoirs of the Rev. William Stukeley, MD, etc. III*. Surtees Society 80, 1885. Durham, London and Edinburgh.

LYNCH, A. (1981a). *Man and Environment in S.W. Ireland*. Oxford.

—— (1981b). 'Astronomical alignment or megalithic muddle?', *Irish Antiquity*. Cork. 23–7.

—— (1982). 'Astronomy and stone alignments in S.W. Ireland', in: (ed.) Heggie, D.C. (1982). 205–14.

LYNCH, F. (1970). *Prehistoric Anglesey*. Llanfegni.

—— (1991). *Prehistoric Anglesey* (2nd ed). Llanfegni.

MACALISTER, R.A.S. (1908). 'The legendary kings of Ireland', *JRSAI 38*, 1–16.

—— (1921). *Ireland in Pre-Celtic Times*. Dublin.

—— (1928). *The Archaeology of Ireland*. London.

—— (1935). *Ancient Ireland*. London.

——, ARMSTRONG E.C.R. and PRAEGER, R. LL. (1913). 'A Bronze Age interment near Naas', *PRIA 30C*, 351–60.

MACKIE, E.W. (1975). *Scotland. An Archaeological Guide*. London.

—— (1977). *Science and Society in Prehistoric Britain*. London.

MACLEOD, F.T. (1912). 'Further notes on the antiquities of Skye, chiefly in the districts of Sleat and Strath', *PSAS 46*, 1911–12, 202–12.

MALLORY, J.P. and McNEILL, T.E. (1991). *The Archaeology of Ulster*. Belfast.

MANX MUSEUM (1981). *The Ancient and Historic Monuments of the Isle of Man*. Douglas.

MARTIN, M. (1716). *A Description of the Western Islands of Scotland*. 2nd edition. London.

MARWICK, E. (1976). 'The Stone of Odin', in: Ritchie, J.N.G. 'The Stones of Stenness, Orkney', *PSAS 107*, 1–60. 28–34.

MASTERS, L. (1977). 'Excavations at the Wren's Egg, Port William, Wigtown District', *TDGNHAS 52*, 28–43.

MAXFIELD, V.A. (ed) (1979). *Prehistoric Dartmoor in its Context*. Torquay.

MAY, A. McL. (1953). 'Neolithic habitation site, stone circles and alignments at Beaghmore, Co. Tyrone', *JRSAI 83*, 174–97.

McCONKEY, R. (1987). 'Stone circles of Ulster'. Unpubl. MA thesis, Queen's University of Belfast.

McLELLAN, R. (1977). *Ancient Monuments of Arran*. Edinburgh.

McNEILL, M. (1962). *The Festival of Lughnasa*. Oxford.

MEE, A. (1942). ed. *The King's England. Oxfordshire*. London.

MERCER, R.J. (1982–3). *Archaeological Field Survey in Northern Scotland, 3*. Department of Archaeology, Edinburgh University.

MERLET, M. (1974). ed. *Exposé du Système Solsticial Néolithique Reliant Entre Eux Certains Cromlechs et Menhirs Dans Le Golfe du Morbihan, par R. Merlet*. Rennes.

MERLET, R. (1929). 'Peut-on calculer, à l'aide de l'astronomie, la date approximative de certains monuments mégalithiques? *Soc. d'Histoire et d'Archéologie de Bretagne, 10*, 13–26.

—— (1935). 'Valeur métrique du pied . . .', *Soc. d'Histoire et d'Archéologie de Bretagne, 16*, 133–45.

MICHELL, J. (1974). *The Old Stones of Land's End*. London.

—— (1982). *Megalithomania. Artists, Antiquarians at the Old Stone Monuments*. London.

MILES, H. and T. (1971). 'Excavations at Longstone Downs, St Stephen-in-Brannel and St Mewan', *Cornish Archaeology 10*, 5–28.

MILN, J. (1881). *Excavations at Carnac (Brittany) . . . The Alignments of Kermario*. Edinburgh.

MINOT, R.S. (n.d. post-1961). *Les Monuments Mégalithiques du L'Île aux Moines*. Vannes.

MITCHELL, F. (1990). *The Shell Guide to Reading the Irish Landscape*. Dublin.

MITCHELL, G.F. (1940). 'The grooves on the Long Stone at Mullaghmast, Co. Kildare', *JRSAI 70*, 164–6.

M'LAUGHLAN, T. (1864). 'Notice of monoliths in the island of Mull', *PSAS 5*, 1862–4, 46–52.

MOHEN, J.-P. (1989). *The World of Megaliths*. London.

MOIR, G. (1981). 'Some archaeological and astronomical objections to scientific astronomy in British prehistory', in: (eds. Ruggles, C.L.N. and Whittle, A.W.R., 1981). 221–42.

MOORE, M.J. (1987). *Archaeological Inventory of Co. Meath*. Dublin.

MORRIS, R.W.B. (1977). *The Prehistoric Rock Art of Argyll*. Poole.

—— (1979). *The Prehistoric Rock Art of Galloway and the Isle of Man*. Poole.

—— (1981). *The Prehistoric Rock Art of South Scotland except Argyll and Galloway*. Oxford.

MYATT, L.J. See also: FREER and MYATT.

—— (1980). 'The multiple stone rows of Caithness and Sutherland, I. Their distribution'. *Caithness F.C. Bull. 2 (7)*, 191–5.

—— (1985). 'A Survey of the Tormsdale Stone Rows', *Bull. Caithness F.C. 4*, 4–9.

—— (1988). In: (ed. Ruggles, C.L.N. 1988a). 'The stone rows of northern Scotland', 277–318.

NIEL, F. (1976). *Connaissance des Mégalithes*. Paris.

O'BRIEN, D.M. (1970). 'A list of archaeological sites on the Berehaven peninsula', *JCHAS 75*, 12–24.

O'CONNELL, J. (1979). *The Meaning of Irish Place Names*. Belfast.

O'KELLY, M.J. (1989). *Early Ireland*. Cambridge.

—— and C. (1978). *Illustrated Guide to Lough Gur, Co. Limerick*. Cork.

O'NUALLAIN, S. (1975). 'The stone circle complex of Cork and Kerry', *JRSAI 105*, 83–131.

—— (1978). 'Boulder-burials', *PRIA 78C*, 75–114.

—— (1984a). 'A survey of stone circles in Cork and Kerry', *PRIA 84C*, 1–77.

—— (1984b). 'Grouped standing stones, radial-stone cairns, and enclosures in the south of Ireland', *JRSAI 114*, 63–79.

—— (1988). 'Stone rows in the south of Ireland', *PRIA 88C*, 179–256.

O'RIORDAIN, S.P. (1964). *Antiquities of the Irish Countryside*. 3rd edition. London.

O'TOOLE, E. and MITCHELL, G.F. (1939). 'A group of grooved standing stones in North Carlow', *JRSAI 69*, 99–111.

PATRICK, J. (1979). 'A reassessment of the lunar observatory hypothesis for the Kilmartin stones', *Archaeoastronomy 1*, S78–S85.

PATTON, M. (1987). *Jersey in Prehistory*. La Haule, Jersey.

—— (1992). 'Megalithic transport and territorial markers: evidence from the Channel Islands', *Ant 66*, 392–4.

PEARCE, S.M. (1981). *The Archaeology of South West Britain*. London.

PEARSON, G.W., PILCHER, J.R., BAILLIE, M.G.L., CORBETT, D.M. and QUA, F. (1986). 'High precision ^{14}C measurement of Irish oaks to show the natural ^{14}C variations from AD 1840 to 5210 BC', *Radiocarbon 28*, 911–34.

PEARSON, M. PARKER. (1993). *Bronze Age Britain*. London.

PENNANT, T. (1772). *A Tour in Scotland, and Voyages to the Hebrides, I*. London.

PETRIE, W.M.F. and HAWKINS, G.S. (1989). *Stonehenge: Plans, Descriptions and Theories*. Reprint of Petrie's 1880 volume. Appendix. Hawkins: 'Stonehenge astronomy – an update'. 41–80. London.

PETTIT, P. (1974). *Prehistoric Dartmoor*. Newton Abbot.

PILCHER, J.R. (1969). 'Archaeology, palaeoecology and C14 dating of the Beaghmore stone circle site', *UJA 32*, 73–91.

—— (1975). 'Finds at Beaghmore stone circles', *UJA 38*, 83–4.

PONTING, G. and M. (1977). *The Standing Stones of Callanish*. Stornoway.

—— 'Callanish. The documentary record'. Unpubl. MS. Callanish.

—— (1981). 'Decoding the Callanish complex – some initial results', in: (eds. Ruggles, C.L.N. and Whittle, A.W.R.). 63–110.

—— (1982). 'Decoding the Callanish complex – a progress report', in: (ed. Heggie, D.C.). 191–203.

—— (1984). *New Light on the Stones of Callanish*. Stornoway.

PONTING, M. (1988). 'Megalithic Callanish', in: (ed. Ruggles,

C.L.N., 1988a), 423–41.

PONTOIS, B. LE. (1929). *Le Finistère Préhistorique*. Paris.

POWER, D. with BYRNE, E., EGAN, U., LANE, S. and SLEEMAN, M. (1992). *Archaeological Inventory of Co. Cork. I. West Cork*. Dublin.

PRICE, L. (1934). 'The ages of Stone and Bronze in County Wicklow, *PRIA 42C*, 31–64.

PRIOR, DR. (1872). 'Archaic stone monuments', *Proc Beds. Arch. and Arch Soc*, 343–60.

PURDY, J.D. (1972). *The Church of All Saints and the Monolith, Rudston*. Bridlington.

QUINNELL, N.V. and DUNN, C.J. (1992). *Lithic Monuments within the Exmoor National Park. A New Survey for Management Purposes*. RCHM-England.

RAFTERY, J. (1951). *Prehistoric Ireland*. London.

RAY, K. and THOMAS, J. (1989). 'Banc Rhosgoch Fach. Trial excavations, 1989', interim report, Archaeology Unit, St David's University College, Lampeter.

RCAHM-E *Royal Commission for Ancient and Historical Monuments. England*. London.

—— (1936). *Westmorland*.

—— (1973). *Bedfordshire and Huntingdonshire*.

RCAHM-S *Ibid. Scotland*. Edinburgh.

—— (1911a). *Caithness*.

—— (1911b). *Sutherland*.

—— (1912). *Galloway, I. Wigtownshire*.

—— (1914). *Galloway, II. Kirkcudbrightshire*.

—— (1915). *Berwickshire*.

—— (1920). *Dumfriess-shire*.

—— (1924). *East Lothian*.

—— (1928). *Outer Hebrides*.

—— (1929). *Midlothian and West Lothian*.

—— (1933). *Fife, Kinross and Clackmannanshire*.

—— (1946a). *Orkney and Shetland, I. Introduction*.

—— (1946b). *ibid, II. Orkney*.

—— (1946c). *ibid, III. Shetland*.

—— (1956). *Roxburghshire, I, II*.

—— (1967). *Peebles-shire*.

—— (1971). *Argyll, I. Kintyre*.

—— (1975). *Argyll, II. Lorn*.

—— (1980). *Argyll, III. Mull, Tiree, Coll and North Argyll*.

—— (1984). *Argyll, V. Islay, Jura, Colonsay and Oronsay*.

—— (1988). *Argyll, VI. Mid Argyll and Cowal*.

RCAHM-W *Ibid. Wales*. London.

—— (1911). *Montgomeryshire*.

—— (1912). *Flintshire*.

—— (1913). *Radnorshire*.

—— (1914). *Denbighshire*.

—— (1917). *Carmarthenshire*.

—— (1921). *Merioneth*.

—— (1925). *Pembrokeshire*.

—— (1937). *Anglesey*.

—— (1956). *Caernarvonshire, I*.

—— (1960). *Caernarvonshire, II*.

—— (1964). *Caernarvonshire, III.*

REYNOLDS, K.M. (1984). *A History of the Christian Community in the Parish of Aldborough from 1330 AD to 1980 AD.* Harrogate.

RIGAUD, J.-P. (1989). See: Geneste *et al.*

RISKINE, A.-E. (1992). *Carnac. L'Armée de Pierres.* Paris.

RITCHIE, A. (1985). *Exploring Scotland's Heritage. Orkney and Shetland.* Edinburgh. 154.

RITCHIE, J.N.G. and A. (1972). *Regional Archaeologies. Edinburgh and South-East Scotland.* London.

RITCHIE, J.N.G. and HARMAN, M. (1985). *Exploring Scotland's Heritage. Argyll and the Western Isles.* Edinburgh.

ROBERTS, J. (n.d.). *Sketches of Ancient Carbery.* Dublin. (Unpaginated).

—— (1988). *Exploring West Cork.* Skibbereen.

ROBINSON, T. (1990). *Connemara.* Roundstone.

ROESE, H.E. (1980). 'Some aspects of topographical locations of Neolithic and Bronze Age monuments in southeast Wales. I. Menhirs', *Bulletin of the Board of Celtic Studies 28,* 645–55.

ROGERS, E.H. (1947). 'The raised beach, submerged forest and kitchen midden of Westward Ho and the submerged stone row of Yelland', *TDAES 3 (3),* 109–35. 114, 121–5.

ROUX, C.-T., LE. (1985). *Gavrinis et les Îles du Morbihan.* Paris.

ROUZIC, Z. LE. (1930). *Les Cromlechs de Er-Lannic.* Vannes.

—— (1935). *Les Monuments Mégalithiques de Carnac et de Locmariaquer: Leur Destination–Leur Âge.* Nantes. (7th ed.).

—— (1939). *Carnac. Légendes, Traditions, Coutumes et Contes de Pays.* Vannes.

—— and PÉQUART, M. and ST-J. (1927). *Corpus des Signes Gravés des Monuments Mégalithiques du Morbihan.* Paris.

RUGGLES, C.L.N. (1981). 'A critical examination of the megalithic lunar observatories', in: Ruggles and Whittle, 153–209.

—— (1984). *Megalithic Astronomy. A New Archaeological and Statistical Study of 300 Western Scottish Sites.* Oxford.

—— (1988a). (ed.) *Records in Stone. Papers in Memory of Alexander Thom.* Cambridge.

—— (1988b). 'The stone alignments of Argyll and Mull: a perspective on the statistical approach in archaeoastronomy', (in: ed. Ruggles, C.L.N. 1988a), 232–50.

—— (1992). 'The North Mull project (3): prominent hill summits and their astronomical potential', *JHA 23.*

—— (1993). 'The stone rows of south-west Ireland: a first reconnaissance', *Archaeoastronomy 18. (Supplement to JHA 24).* In press.

—— and MARTLEW, R.D. (1989). 'The North Mull project (1): excavations at Glengorm, 1987–8', *JHA 20,* S137–S149.

—— and HINGE, P.D. (1991). 'The North Mull project (2): the wider astronomical potential of the sites' *JHA 22,* S52–S75.

RUGGLES, C.L.N. and WHITTLE, A.W.R. eds. (1981). *Astronomy and Society in Britain during the Period 4000–1500 BC.* Oxford.

RYAN, M. ed. (1991). *The Illustrated Archaeology of Ireland.* Dublin.

RYBOT, N.V.L. (1934). 'The surviving menhirs of Jersey', *Ann. Bull. Soc. Jersiaise 12,* 336–46.

SCARRE, C. (1983). editor: *Ancient France.* Edinburgh.

SCARTH, H.M. (1857). 'On ancient earthworks in the neighbourhood of Bath', *JBAA 13,* 98–113.

SCOTT, J.G. (1964). 'The chambered tomb at Beacharra, Kintyre, Argyll', *PPS 30,* 134–58.

SCOUËZEC, G. LE. (1979). *Guide de la Bretagne Mystérieuse.* Paris.

—— and MASSON, J.-R. (1987). *Bretagne Mégalithique.* Paris.

SERVICE, A. and BRADBERY, J. (1979). *Megaliths and Their Mysteries. The Standing Stones of Old Europe.* London.

SHEE, E. and EVANS, E.E. (1965). 'A standing stone in the Townland of Newgrange, Co. Meath', *JCHAS 70,* 124–30.

SHEPHERD, I.A.G. and RALSTON, I.B.M. (1979). *Early Grampian: a Guide to the Archaeology.* Aberdeen.

SIMMONS, I.G. (1961). 'Stallmoor Down stone row', *TDA 93,* 65.

—— (1962). 'An outline of the vegetational history of Dartmoor', *TDA 94,* 555.

—— (1969). 'Environment and early man on Dartmoor', *PPS 35,* 203–19.

SIMPSON, SIR J.Y. (1867). *Archaic Sculpturings of Cups, Circles etc.* Edinburgh.

SITWELL, BRIG-GEN. W. (1930). *Stones of Northumberland and Other Lands.* Newcastle-upon-Tyne.

SMITH, C. (1750). *The Ancient and Present state of the County and City of Cork.* Dublin.

SMITH, I.F. (1965). *Windmill Hill and Avebury. Excavations by Alexander Keiller, 1929–35.* Oxford.

SODEN-SMITH, R.H. (1870). 'Notice of circles of stones in the parish of Crosby Ravensworth, Westmorland', *TCWAAS 27 (O.S.),* 200–3.

SOMERVILLE, H.B. (1912). 'Prehistoric monuments in the Outer Hebrides, and their astronomical significance', *JRAI 42,* 23–52.

—— (1913). 'Astronomical indications in the megalithic monument at Callanish', *J B Astr Ass 23,* 68–71.

—— (1923). 'Instances of orientation in prehistoric monuments of the British Isles', *Archaeologia 73,* 193–224.

—— (1928). 'Prehistorics', *JCHAS 33,* 57–68.

SPENCE, L. (1917). *Legends and Romances of Brittany.* London.

SPENCE, M. (1894). *Standing Stones and Maeshowe of Stenness.* Paisley.

SPOONER, G.M. and RUSSELL, F.S. eds. (1967). *Worth's Dartmoor.* Newton Abbot.

STELL, G. (1986). *Exploring Scotland's Heritage. Dumfriess and Galloway.* Edinburgh.

STEVENSON, J.B. (1985). *Exploring Scotland's Heritage. The Clyde Estuary and Central Region.* Edinburgh.

STEWART, M.E.C. (1966). 'The excavation of a setting of standing stones at Lundin Farm near Aberfeldy, Perthshire', *PSAS 98,* 1964–6, 126–49.

STOUT, G.T. (1984). *Archaeological Survey of the Barony of Ikerrin.* Roscrea.

STUKELEY, W. (1723). 'The history of the temples and religion of the antient Celts'. MS 4.253, Cardiff Public

Library.

—— (1740). *Stonehenge. A Temple Restor'd to the British Druids*. London.

—— (1743). *Abury, a Temple of the British Druids*. London.

—— (1776). *Itinerarium Curiosum, II*. London.

'T.H.' (1790). 'The Devil's Arrows near Burrowbridge', *Gent's Mag, II*, 1081.

TAYLOR, J. J. (1980). *Bronze Age Goldwork of the British Isles*. Cambridge.

TAYLOR, M.W. (1886). 'The prehistoric remains on Moor-divock, near Ullswater', *TCWAAS 8*, 323–47.

THOM, A. (1966). 'Megalithic astronomy: indications in standing stones', *Vistas in Astronomy 7*, 1–57.

—— (1967). *Megalithic Sites in Britain*. Oxford.

—— (1971). *Megalithic Lunar Observatories*. Oxford.

—— (1972a). 'The Carnac alignments', *JHA 3*, 11–26.

—— (1972b). 'The uses of the alignment at le Menec, Carnac', *JHA 3*, 151–64.

—— and A.S. (1971). 'The astronomical significance of the large Carnac menhirs', *JHA 2*, 147–60.

—— (1974). 'The Kermario alignments', *JHA 5*, 30–47.

—— (1976). 'Avebury (2): the West Kennet avenue', *JHA 7* 193–7.

—— and A.S. (1977). *La Géométrie des Alignements de Carnac. (Suivi de Plans Comparatifs)*. Rennes.

—— (1978). *Megalithic Remains in Britain and Brittany*. Oxford.

—— and BURL, A. (1980). *Megalithic Rings. Plans and Data for 229 Sites in Britain*. BAR British Series 81, Oxford.

—— (1990). *Stone Rows and Standing Stones. I, II*. BAR International Series 560, Oxford.

THOM, A., A.S. and GORRIE, J.M. (1976). 'The two megalithic lunar observatories at Carnac', *JHA 7*, 11–26.

THOM, A.S. (1980). 'The stone rings of Beaghmore: geometry and astronomy', *UJA 43*, 15–19.

THOMAS, N. (1976). *Guide to Prehistoric England*. London.

TOLAND, J. (c. 1726). *A Critical History of the Celtic Religion and Learning, containing an Account of the Druids*. 1814 edition. London.

TRATMAN, E.K. (1958). 'The lost stone circles of Somerset', *Univ. of Bristol Spel Soc 8*, 110–18.

UCKO, P.J., HUNTER, M., CLARK, A.J. and DAVID, A. *Avebury Reconsidered. From the 1660s to the 1990s*. London.

VALERA, R. DE, and O'NUALLAIN, S. (1964). *Survey of the Megalithic Tombs of Ireland, II. Co. Mayo*. Dublin.

—— (1982). *Ibid, IV. Counties Cork, Kerry, Limerick, Tipperary*. Dublin.

VAN HOEK, M.A.M. (1988). 'The prehistoric rock art of Co. Donegal, II', *UJA 51*, 21–47.

WADDELL, J. (1990). *The Bronze Age Burials of Ireland*. Galway.

WALKER, B. and RITCHIE, J.N.G. (1987). *Exploring Scotland's Heritage. Fife and Tayside*. Edinburgh.

WATERHOUSE, J. (1985). *The Stone Circles of Cumbria*. Chichester.

WATERMAN, D.M. (1964). 'The stone circle, cairn and alignment at Drumskinny, Co. Fermanagh', *UJA 27*, 23–30.

WATSON, K. (1965). *North Wales*. London.

WEATHERHILL, C. (1981). *Belerion. Ancient Sites of Land's End*. Penzance.

—— (1985). *Cornovia. Ancient Sites of Cornwall and Scilly*. Penzance.

WEIR, A. (1990). 'Potency and sin: Ireland and the phallic continuum', *Arch Ire 4 (2)*, 52–6.

WESTWOOD, J. (1987). *Albion. A Guide to Legendary Britain*. London.

WHYBROW, C. (1966). 'The discovery of an Exmoor stone row', *Exmoor Review 7*, 69–70.

—— (1970). *Antiquary's Exmoor*. Dulverton.

WILLIAMS, G. (1988). *The Standing Stones of Wales and South-West England*. Oxford.

WILSON, D. (1863). *Prehistoric Annals of Scotland, I*. London and Cambridge.

WOOD, E.H. (1947). 'The grooves on the Devil's Arrows, Boroughbridge, Yorks', *PPS 13*, 180–2.

WOOD, J. (1765). *A Description of Bath, I*. Oxford.

WOOD, J.E. (1978). *Sun, Moon and Standing Stones*. Oxford.

WORSFOLD, T.C. (1898). *The French Stonehenge, an Account of the Principal Megalithic Remains in the Morbihan Archipelago*. London.

WORTH, R.H. (1932). 'The prehistoric monuments of Scorhill, Buttern Hill, and Shuggledown (Shovel Down), *TDA 64*, 279–87.

—— (1941). 'Retaining-circles associated with stone rows, Dartmoor', *TDA 73*, 227–38.

—— (1946). 'The stone rows of Dartmoor, I', *TDA 78*, 285–315.

—— (1947). 'The stone rows of Dartmoor, II', *TDA 79*, 175–86.

—— (1967). *Worth's Dartmoor*. See: Spooner, G.M. and Russell, F.S.

WORTH, R.N. (1892). 'The stone rows of Dartmoor, I', *TDA 24*, 387–417.

—— (1893). Ibid, II, *TDA 25*, 541–6.

—— (1894). Ibid, III, *TDA 26*, 296–307.

—— (1895). Ibid, IV, *TDA 27*, 437–42.

—— (1896). Ibid, V, *TDA 28*, 712–13.

—— (1903). Ibid, VI, *TDA 35*, 426–61.

—— (1906). Ibid, VII, *TDA 38*, 535–7.

—— (1908). Ibid, VIII, *TDA 40*, 281–2.

—— (1911). Ibid, IX, *TDA 43*, 348–9.

—— (1918). Ibid, X, *TDA 50*, 402–4.

INDEX

Major references are in bold print, illustrations in italics. References in the Notes are shown by n. following the page number.